REVOLUTIONS IN INTERNATIONAL LAW

In 1917, the October Revolution and the adoption of the revolutionary Mexican Constitution shook the foundations of the international order in profound, unprecedented and lasting ways. These events posed fundamental challenges to international law, unsettling foundational concepts of property, statehood and non-intervention – and indeed the very nature of law itself. This collection asks what we might learn about international law from analysing how its various sub-fields have remembered, forgotten, rejected or sought to manage the revolutions of 1917. It shows that those revolutions had wide-ranging repercussions for the development of laws relating to the use of force, intervention, human rights, investment, alien protection and state responsibility, and for the global economy subsequently enabled by international law and overseen by international institutions. The varied legacies of 1917 play an ongoing role in shaping political struggle in the form of international law.

KATHRYN GREENMAN is a lecturer at the University of Technology Sydney (UTS). Prior to joining UTS, she was a PhD candidate and junior researcher at the Amsterdam Center for International Law at the University of Amsterdam, as well as a Kathleen Fitzpatrick Visiting Doctoral Fellow with the Laureate Program in International Law at Melbourne Law School. She also holds an LLM in Public International Law from the University of Kent and a BA in Jurisprudence from Oxford University. Her work has appeared in the *Leiden Journal of International Law*, the *International Journal of Refugee Law* and the *Nordic Journal of International Law*.

ANNE ORFORD is Redmond Barry Distinguished Professor and Michael D Kirby Chair of International Law at Melbourne Law School. Her publications include *Reading Humanitarian Intervention* (2003), *International Authority and the Responsibility to Protect* (2011), *The Oxford Handbook of the Theory of International Law* (2016) (as co-editor), and *Pensée Critique et Pratique du Droit International* (2020). Her latest book, *International Law and the Politics of History* will be published by Cambridge University Press in 2021.

ANNA SAUNDERS is LLM candidate and Frank Knox Memorial Fellow at Harvard Law School. She has been a Teaching Fellow at Melbourne Law School and holds a JD and MPhil from Melbourne Law School and a BA from the University of Adelaide.

NTINA TZOUVALA is a Senior Lecturer at the College of Law, Australian National University. Before taking up this position, she was an ARC Laureate Postdoctoral Fellow at Melbourne Law School. Her work focuses on the history, theory and political economy of international law. Her first monograph, *Capitalism as Civilisation: A History of International Law*, was published by Cambridge University Press in 2020.

REVOLUTIONS IN INTERNATIONAL LAW

The Legacies of 1917

Edited by

KATHRYN GREENMAN

ANNE ORFORD

ANNA SAUNDERS

NTINA TZOUVALA

CAMBRIDGE
UNIVERSITY PRESS

CAMBRIDGE
UNIVERSITY PRESS

University Printing House, Cambridge CB2 8BS, United Kingdom

One Liberty Plaza, 20th Floor, New York, NY 10006, USA

477 Williamstown Road, Port Melbourne, VIC 3207, Australia

314–321, 3rd Floor, Plot 3, Splendor Forum, Jasola District Centre, New Delhi – 110025, India

79 Anson Road, #06–04/06, Singapore 079906

Cambridge University Press is part of the University of Cambridge.

It furthers the University's mission by disseminating knowledge in the pursuit of education, learning, and research at the highest international levels of excellence.

www.cambridge.org
Information on this title: www.cambridge.org/9781108495035
DOI: 10.1017/9781108860727

First published 2021

A catalogue record for this publication is available from the British Library.

ISBN 978-1-108-49503-5 Hardback

CONTENTS

NOTES ON CONTRIBUTORS

AMANDA ALEXANDER is a Lecturer at the Thomas More Law School, Australian Catholic University.

DARIA DAVITTI is an Assistant Professor of Law at the University of Nottingham, UK and a Postdoctoral Fellow at the Department of Law, Lund University, Sweden.

ALISON DUXBURY is a Professor at Melbourne Law School, Australia.

KATHRYN GREENMAN is a Lecturer at the Faculty of Law, University of Technology Sydney, Australia.

ROBERT KNOX is a Senior Lecturer at the School of Law, University of Liverpool, UK; Laureate Program in International Law, Melbourne Law School, Australia.

DINO KRITSIOTIS is Chair of Public International Law at the University of Nottingham, UK.

ANDREA LEITER is an Assistant Professor at the Amsterdam Center for International Law.

KATE MILES is a Fellow and Lecturer in Law, Gonville and Caius College, University of Cambridge, UK.

SCOTT NEWTON is a Reader in Laws of Central Asia, SOAS, University of London, UK.

ANNE ORFORD is Redmond Barry Distinguished Professor and Michael D Kirby Chair of International Law at Melbourne Law School, Australia.

ANNA SAUNDERS is an LLM candidate and Frank Knox Memorial Fellow at Harvard Law School.

JUAN PABLO SCARFI is an Assistant Professor in the Humanities Department, Universidad de San Andrés, Argentina.

MAI TAHA a Lecturer at the Department of Law, Goldsmiths, University of London.

OWEN TAYLOR is a Postdoctoral Researcher at Aix-Marseille University, France.

NTINA TZOUVALA is a Senior Lecturer at the College of Law, Australian National University.

FABIA FERNANDES CARVALHO VEÇOSO is a Postdoctoral Fellow at the Laureate Program in International Law, Melbourne Law School, Australia.

JESSICA WHYTE is Scientia Fellow and Associate Professor in the School of Humanities and Languages (Philosophy) and the School of Law, University of New South Wales, Australia.

ACKNOWLEDGEMENTS

This collection came out of the conference '1917: Revolution, Intervention and International Law(s)' held at Melbourne Law School in August 2017. We would like to thank all of the speakers and participants at the conference, for their efforts in thinking through the concerns of the conference and this volume, and for the stimulating discussion and exchange that ensued. Our gratitude is due to the contributors to this volume for the brilliant and considered set of chapters they provided. It has been our pleasure to work with you all.

The conference was able to take place as a result of the generous support of the Australian Research Council through Anne Orford's Laureate Fellowship and Melbourne Law School's International Collaboration Fund. Our warm thanks go to Jack Stanovsek and Wendy Chen for their extremely capable and diligent efforts in making the event possible. Wendy Chen also provided editorial assistance for this book, for which we are grateful.

Our thanks are due to Finola O'Sullivan and Marianne Nield at Cambridge University Press, who have been supportive throughout the entire process. We would also like to thank the anonymous referees for their comments on the proposal. These helped greatly in improving and sharpening the contribution of the collection.

Finally, we would like to thank those who have supported us during the bringing together of this volume, with particular thanks to Justin from Anna.

1

International Law and Revolution

1917 and Beyond

KATHRYN GREENMAN, ANNE ORFORD, ANNA SAUNDERS AND NTINA TZOUVALA

In 1917, the October Revolution and the adoption of the revolutionary Mexican Constitution shook the foundations of the international order and international law in profound, unprecedented and lasting ways. The Mexican and Russian revolutions posed fundamental challenges to the still embryonic profession of international law, its practitioners then largely committed to various forms of liberalism and capitalism. In bringing the 'social question' to the forefront of international legal debates, the Mexican and Russian revolutions offered new ways of thinking about foundational concepts of property, statehood and non-intervention – and indeed about the very nature of law itself.[1] The Mexican Revolution, which began in 1910, is often described as the first social revolution.[2] The 1917 Mexican revolutionary Constitution, which predated its Russian/Soviet counterparts, was the most socially progressive the world had seen.[3] It recognised the eight-hour day, the minimum wage, maternity protections, the right to strike and free secular education.[4] Most famously, its Article 27 radically reformed the institution of private property in Mexico.[5] The Bolshevik revolution of October 1917 in Russia, seen by participants as the prelude to world revolution, led to the creation of the Soviet Union and inspired a wave of revolutionary

[1] See, further, Anne Orford, *International Law and the Social Question* (Asser Press, 2020).

[2] See, for example, William H Beezly and Michael C Meyer (eds), *The Oxford History of Mexico* (Oxford University Press, 2010) vii.

[3] For a detailed history of the 1917 Constitution, see Berta Ulloa, *Historia de la Revolución Mexicana*, vol 6: 1914–1917: La Constitución de 1917 (Colegio de Mexico, 1983).

[4] Arts 3 and 123. See, for example, N Andrew and N Cleven, 'Some Social Aspects of the Mexican Constitution of 1917' (1921) 4 *The Hispanic American Historical Review* 474; Fernando Yllanes Ramos, 'The Social Rights Enshrined in the Mexican Constitution of 1917' (1967) 96 *International Labour Review* 590.

[5] See John P Bullington, 'Problems of International Law in the Mexican Constitution of 1917' (1927) 21 *American Journal of International Law* 685.

movements in Europe and around the world that shaped the history of the twentieth century.[6] The two revolutions represented the possibility of radical social and economic change at the national level, created legal systems that survived for many decades, inspired transnational movements striving against imperialism and for social revolution, decisively changed international relations and motivated international legal innovators to create new forms, principles and institutions. With the liberal international order and global economy that were consolidated over the intervening century now facing serious challenges, this collection of essays revisits the revolutions of 1917 and their legacies for international law.

The aim of this book is not – or at least not only – to ask what we can learn about the revolutionary events of 1917 from studying international law but instead to explore what we might learn about international law from the way that different aspects of the field have remembered, forgotten, imagined, incorporated, rejected, or sought to manage the revolutions of 1917. Our starting point is that there is no one position taken by a monolithic 'international law' to revolution in general or to the Mexican and Russian revolutions in particular. International law is a set of techniques, doctrinal positions, concepts, processes, arguments and institutions, along with a way of placing those more routine legal practices within larger conceptual, normative or ideological frames. In order to get a sense of how international lawyers at the time and since have responded to the revolutions of 1917, this collection explores a range of responses across diverse sub-fields of international law. As the chapters in this collection show, the revolutions of 1917 had wide-ranging repercussions for the development of laws relating to the use of force, intervention, human rights, investment, alien protection and state responsibility, and for the global economy subsequently enabled by international law and overseen by international institutions.

The focus on responses to two revolutionary situations and across numerous sub-fields works to complicate any straightforward assumption that international law and international lawyers responded in a unified way to those revolutions. The collection explores when and how international law and international lawyers sought to incorporate new revolutionary polities within the general framework of existing laws and principles, in order to minimise the disruptive effect of revolutionary

[6] See, for example, China Miéville, *October: The Story of the Russian Revolution* (Verso, 2017).

ideologies and practices on existing rights, entitlements and relations. Equally, it explores when and how law or lawyers sought to treat these new states as exceptional entities that required different and special treatment. The collection seeks to show the stakes of the decisions to employ legal techniques and practices as responses to revolution, and the way that these decisions in turn enabled or justified particular forms of action on the part of elites in other states.

We take as a given that there is no neutral way to discuss the revolutions of 1917, or indeed any revolution, insurrection, civil war, rebellion or uprising. Revolutions represent rupture, and this has profound implications for the way that they are represented in scholarship. Writing about the October Revolution in particular has been, in the words of Eric Hobsbawm, 'drenched in polemics'.[7] In the Cold War context that dominated many histories of the communist revolutions over the twentieth century, the stylistic and substantive choices made in presenting such narratives were often overdetermined, leading to a 'deadening predictability' in the writing of both sides.[8] Something similar could be said of the writing about revolutions in international law. The sense of international law as a liberal and capitalist project that is firmly opposed to communist revolutionaries has a long history. In 1884, James Lorimer, one of the more conservative representatives of the first generation of professional international lawyers, stated in stringent tones: 'Agrarian or communistic outrages are not sources of law, even in cases in which they lead to more accurate definitions of the natural right of persons, or of the limits of private property'.[9] Written in the aftermath of the bloody repression of the Paris Commune, Lorimer's aphorism was put to the test by subsequent generations of international lawyers who were faced with new revolutionary states resulting from 'communistic outrages' and with deciding whether and when they would be recognised as subjects and sources of law. As the chapters in this book reveal, international law became a medium for fraught communications across the divide between communist and capitalist states for much of the twentieth century, as well as one site for playing out the ideological and material struggles over their incommensurable visions of world order.[10]

[7] Eric Hobsbawm, *The Age of Extremes 1914–1991* (Abacus, 1995).

[8] Sheila Fitzpatrick, 'A Spy in the Archives' (2010) 32(23) *London Review of Books*.

[9] James Lorimer, 'La Doctrine de la Reconnaissance, Fondement du Droit International' (1884) 16 *Revue de droit international et de législation comparée* 333, 335.

[10] For examples of attempts at different moments to reflect upon forms of communication between communist and capitalist states through international law, see 'Exchange of Communications between the President of the United States and the President of the All

The centenary of the Mexican and Russian revolutions has provoked new reflections from historians on the legacies of those events,[11] although they have rarely been considered in conjunction.[12] Some of that literature was very dubious about the legacies of communist revolution, reflecting a more widespread 'apologetic and deprecatory downgrading of the Russian Revolution [that] reflects the impact of the Soviet collapse on its status'.[13] International law scholars, too, used the anniversary as a moment to reassess the Soviet approach to international law and the legacy of the various doctrines and principles the Soviets developed.[14] For example, Anne Peters argued that the Russian Revolution offers a

Union Central Executive Committee' (1934) 28 *American Journal of International Law Supplement* 1; Grigory I Tunkin, 'Co-existence and International Law' (1958) 95 *Recueil des cours* 5; Earl A Snyder and Hans Werner Bracht, 'Coexistence and International Law' (1958) 7 *International and Comparative Law Quarterly* 54; Edward McWhinney, *'Peaceful Coexistence' and Soviet-Western International Law* (AW Sythoff, 1964); W E Butler (ed), *Perestroika and International Law* (Kluwer, 1990).

11 For centennial histories of the Russian revolution, see Miéville, n 6; S A Smith, *Russia in Revolution: An Empire in Crisis, 1890 to 1928* (Oxford University Press, 2017); Rex A Wade, *The Russian Revolution, 1917* (Cambridge University Press, 3rd ed, 2017); Sean McMeekin, *The Russian Revolution: A New History* (Basic Books, 2017); Tony Brenton (ed), *Historically Inevitable? Turning Points of the Russian Revolution* (Profile Books, 2017); Laura Engelstein, *Russia in Flames: War, Revolution, Civil War, 1914–1921* (Oxford University Press, 2017); Sheila Fitzpatrick, *The Russian Revolution* (Oxford University Press, 4th ed, 2017). For art historians and curators on the Russian revolution, see John Milner and Natasha Murray, *Revolution: Russian Art 1917–1932* (Royal Academy of Arts, 2017); Roxana Marcoci and Sarah Suzuki with Hillary Reder, 'A Revolutionary Impulse: The Rise of the Russian Avant-Garde' (MoMA, 2017) www.moma.org/calendar/exhibitions/1668; Harvard Art Museums, 'What about Revolution? Aesthetic Practices after 1917' www.harvardartmuseums.org/visit/exhibitions/5573/what-about-revolution-aesthetic-practices-after-1917; Sue Kramer and Lesley Harding, *Call of the Avant-Garde: Constructivism and Australian Art* (Heide Museum of Modern Art, 2017). For responses to the centenary of the Mexican Revolution, see Stuart Easterling, *The Mexican Revolution: A Short History 1910–1920* (Haymarket, 2013); Douglas W Richmond and Sam W Haynes (eds), *The Mexican Revolution: Conflict and Consolidation, 1910–1940* (Texas A&M University Press, 2013); Renata Keller, *Mexico's Cold War: Cuba, the United States, and the Legacy of the Mexican Revolution* (Cambridge University Press, 2015); Matthew Affron et al., *Paint the Revolution: Mexican Modernism, 1910–1950* (Philadelphia Museum of Art, 2016).

12 For an exploration of the 'tangled' Mexico–Russia relationship following their revolutions, see Daniela Spenser, *The Impossible Triangle: Mexico, Soviet Russia, and the United States in the 1920s* (Duke University Press, 1999).

13 Sheila Fitzpatrick, 'What's Left?' (2017) 39(7) *London Review of Books.*

14 See the three special journal issues published as: '100th Anniversary of the Russian 1917 Revolution' (2017) 5(4) *Russian Law Journal*; 'On the Centenary of the Russian Revolutions' (2017) 2(2) *Jus Gentium*; 'A Century after Russian Revolution: Its Legacy in International Law, 2017' (2017) 19(2) *Journal of the History of International Law.*

'negative blueprint'; it only teaches us that 'the radically other, revolutionary, alternative to incremental social reform should not be repeated'.[15] For Peters, 'real existing socialism' had 'thoroughly discredited itself', teaching that the 'shockingly uneven distribution of wealth' that 'leads to massive social unrest needs to be tackled with different instruments than those derived from socialism'.[16]

In contrast, this collection does not treat the version of neoliberal international law that triumphed at the end of the twentieth century as a neutral arbiter between states or as offering a set of technocratic tools or best practices for managing poverty and inequality. Rather, we take seriously the idea that both law and history are forms through which political responses to revolutionary events are expressed and transmitted. There is no one neutral method for thinking about the past and no innocent way of representing the revolutions of 1917. Rather, international law is one site of an ongoing struggle over what the revolutions of 1917 meant and may still yet mean for the future, and neoliberal internationalists are just one party in that struggle. For this collection, the events of 1917 reverberate into the 1930s and even beyond: the economic, political, legal and social struggles that marked the Second World War, the Cold War, the decolonisation era and even the twenty-first century cannot be comprehended, nor can the significance of what was foreclosed be grasped, without an understanding of 1917. This has implications for understanding the Mexican and Russian revolutions since, as Sheila Fitzpatrick argues, 'the end points people choose for their histories of revolution reveal a lot about their assumptions of what it was "really about"'.[17] By not ending its accounts of the Mexican and Russian Revolutions in 1917, the volume understands their legacy for international law as multivalent and ongoing.

One of the most significant ways in which that legacy persisted was in relation to decolonisation. A number of the chapters touch on the relationship between the Mexican and Russian revolutions and the end of formal empire. Decolonisation was itself an important revolutionary process that put forward not only a demand for statehood but also a

[15] Anne Peters, 'The "Great October Socialist Revolution": What Remains in and for International Law?' (MPIL Research Paper Series No. 2017-09) 12.

[16] Anne Peters, 'Introduction. A Century after the Russian Revolution: Its Legacy in International Law' (2017) 19 *Journal of the History of International Law* 133, 145.

[17] Fitzpatrick, 'What's Left?', n 13.

novel, yet ultimately unsuccessful, vision of the 'international'.[18] It was one that, as this volume explores, was inspired and supported by the Soviet Union and Bolshevik ideology and Latin American resistance to intervention. However, it was also constrained by some of the international legal techniques that had been developed and deployed in response to the impact of the Mexican and Russian Revolutions, particularly in regard to economic ordering.[19] The fear of sudden change and uncontrollable revolutionary violence was, for example, omnipresent in the proceedings of the *South-West Africa* saga in the International Court of Justice.[20] The lawyers for South Africa constantly emphasised the fear of communist contamination and the unleashing of revolutionary violence that the end of their white-minority rule would bring about in Namibia.[21] This was, indeed, the red 'elephant in the room' that heavily influenced the thinking of the Court's judges and led to the infamous *volte-face* of 1966.[22]

In the post–Cold War years, following the dissolution of the Soviet state, this type of argument was again deployed to minimise the legal effects of the political independence produced by decolonisation. The idea that decolonisation proceeded too quickly and radically, thereby producing states unworthy of full sovereignty, permeated debates over the possibility of military or economic interventions in order to save and to remake 'failed states'.[23] In this vision of international law, rapid,

[18] Regarding decolonisation as a revolutionary moment, see, for example, the comments of B S Chimni in Anne Orford, Philip Allott, Nathaniel Berman, Ruth Buchanan, B S Chimni, China Miéville, and Vasuki Nesiah, 'War, Force and Revolution' (2006) 100 *American Society of International Law Proceedings* 261, 265.

[19] On international law as a restraint on decolonisation, see Antony Anghie, *Imperialism, Sovereignty and the Making of International Law* (Cambridge University Press, 2005); Anne Orford, *International Authority and the Responsibility to Protect* (Cambridge University Press, 2011).

[20] See further, Ntina Tzouvala, *Capitalism as Civilisation: A History of International Law* (Cambridge University Press, 2020).

[21] 'Disintegration of the traditional systems of control can give rise to destructive emotional patterns ... The gap tends to be filled by revolutionary politics'. 'Counter-Memorial of the Republic of South Africa', *South West Africa (Ethiopia v South Africa; Liberia v South Africa)* [1966] 2 ICJ Pleadings 1, 413.

[22] Victor Kattan, '"There Was an Elephant in the Court Room": Reflections on the Role of Judge Sir Percy Spender (1897–1985) in the *South West Africa Cases* (1960–1966) After Half a Century' (2018) 31 *Leiden Journal of International Law* 147.

[23] 'Rapid decolonization during the 1950s and 1960s, and again in the 1990s in the wake of the collapse of the Soviet Union, produced a large number of new states that had little history or experience with self-governance': John Yoo, 'Fixing Failed States' (2011) 99 *California Law Review* 95, 98.

unauthorised change, especially of the sort that challenges the discipline's core values, needs to be contained, if not undone. Upon closer examination, however, the significance of this line of argument lies not in any inherent aversion toward radical change. Rather, it lies in an unarticulated but powerful theory about the actors who are authorised to enact radical change and its acceptable parameters. That theory proposes that 'in the 21st century, only the "international community" – rather than the people, or the State, or the proletariat, or the party – may legitimately stage a revolution in the decolonized world'.[24] As Anne Orford has observed, such a theory 'would seem to have significant implications for the unfinished project of decolonization'.[25]

Finally, the collection offers a contribution to the still somewhat undertheorised question of the connection between international law and revolution. The profession and discipline of international law has a complicated relationship to revolution. On the one hand, international lawyers have a secret – or perhaps not so secret – romance with revolution, indicated by the place of self-determination as a central legal principle or the enthusiasm for regime change in some international law quarters.[26] International law, as many scholars have recognised, is a discipline organised around incidents, events, interventions and crises.[27] Situations of revolutionary upheaval, and the foreign interventions carried out in response, have often provided the material for the development or transformation of international law. The liberal variant of international law that dominated during the latter half of the twentieth century can itself be understood as part of a revolutionary tradition and as 'one site for the unfolding of this revolutionary tradition in the modern world'.[28] On the other hand, as the examples given above

[24] Anne Orford, 'International Territorial Administration and the Management of Decolonisation' (2010) 59 *International and Comparative Law Quarterly* 227, 249.

[25] Ibid.

[26] Orford et al., n 18.

[27] See, for example, W Michael Reisman and Andrew R Willard (eds), *International Incidents: The Law That Counts in World Politics* (Princeton University Press, 1988); Anne Orford, 'Locating the International: Military and Monetary Interventions after the Cold War' (1997) 38 *Harvard International Law Journal* 443; Anne Orford, 'Muscular Humanitarianism: Reading the Narratives of the New Interventionism' (1999) 10 *European Journal of International Law* 679; Hilary Charlesworth, 'International Law: A Discipline of Crisis' (2002) 65 *Modern Law Review* 377; Fleur Johns, Richard Joyce and Sundhya Pahuja, 'Introduction' in Fleur Johns, Richard Joyce and Sundhya Pahuja (eds), *Events: The Force of International Law* (Routledge, 2010).

[28] Anne Orford, 'International Law and the Populist Moment' (2020) 35 *American University International Law Review* 427.

illustrate, international lawyers are also ready to dismiss those they see as the wrong kind of revolutionary, and to develop legal arguments justifying non-recognition, military intervention, targeted killing, economic sanctions or the more routine but no less effective weapon of investment arbitration to contain the capacity of revolutionary forces or non-state actors to destabilise economic relations. In that sense, as Nathaniel Berman has argued, 'the international law of the twentieth century, in its institutionalised form, might be said to arise as a response to some perceived revolutionary challenge'.[29]

Yet despite that intimate and ongoing practical relation between international law and revolution, the theoretical or conceptual relationship between international law and revolution has not been widely discussed in the century following the seismic events of 1917.[30] Revolution remains largely in the subconscious or unconscious of international law.[31] There exist studies of particular revolutions, such as the series of uprisings known as the Arab Spring,[32] and considerations of revolution in respect of particular sub-fields of international law.[33] Perhaps unsurprisingly, both Soviet international lawyers and scholars

[29] Orford et al., n 18, 262.

[30] Vidya Kumar, 'Revolutionaries' in Jean d'Aspremont and Sahib Singh (eds), *Concepts for International Law: Contributions to Disciplinary Thought* (Edward Elgar, 2019) 773. For examples of international legal scholarship that reflect upon that relation directly, see Edward McWhinney, *International Law and World Revolution* (A W Sijthoff, 1967); Philip Allott, *International Law and International Revolution: Reconceiving the World* (University of Hull Press, 1989); Orford et al., n 18; Vidya Kumar, 'International Law, Kelsen and the Aberrant Revolution: Excavating the Politics and Practices of Revolutionary Legality in Rhodesia and Beyond' in Nikolas M Rajkovic, Tanja Aalberts and Thomas Gammeltoft-Hansen (eds), *The Power of Legality: Practices of International Law and Their Politics* (Cambridge University Press, 2016) 157; Owen Taylor, *Revolution and International Law* (Routledge, 2019); Deborah Whitehall, 'The International Prospects of the *Soixante-Huitard*' (2019) 29 *European Journal of International Law* 1337.

[31] Kumar, 'International Law', n 30, 159.

[32] See, for example, Carlo Panara and Gary Wilson, *The Arab Spring: New Patterns for Democracy and International Law* (Martinus Nijhoff, 2013); Rosa Brooks, 'Lessons for International Law from the Arab Spring' (2013) 28 *American University International Law Review* 713.

[33] See, for example, Guy Fiti Sinclair, *To Reform the World: International Organizations and the Making of Modern States* (Oxford University Press, 2017); Kate Miles, *The Origins of International Investment Law: Empire, Environment and the Safeguarding of Capital* (Cambridge University Press, 2013); Alison Duxbury, *The Participation of States in International Organisations: The Role of Human Rights and Democracy* (Cambridge University Press, 2011).

of Soviet law were concerned with foundational questions about the nature, function and even the possibility of international law after revolution.[34] However, international lawyers on the whole have not engaged in a more sustained exploration of the relationship between international law and revolution. The chapters in this volume reveal in detailed ways how revolution has shaped international law, as the latter developed both to contain but also to incorporate revolutionary ideas and practices.[35] The focus on the response of international law and international lawyers to the events of 1917 provides a means of inquiring into how international law conceptualises, juridifies and manages revolution.

This volume does not purport to be comprehensive in terms of covering all revolutions or even types of 'revolution'. Nevertheless, we consider that the study of the first social revolutions fundamentally to challenge the idea of a liberal international legal order enables important reflections about the techniques, processes, fantasies and narratives developed by international law in response. As these chapters reveal, from early on international law was interested in order *within* states just as much as in order *between* them.[36] The collection explores the different mechanisms that international lawyers employed in response to the various challenges posed by revolution to particular interests, regimes or paradigms. In so doing, it raises the question of whether international law may itself be a revolutionary force for change in the world, counter-revolutionary in its nature or operation, or both.[37] On balance, the essays collected here suggest that it is containment that has dominated the relationship between international law and revolution. While international law is able to incorporate and legitimate revolutionary changes

[34] See, for example, EA Korovin, *Meždunarodnoe Pravo Perekhodnogo Vremeni [International Law of the Transition Period]* (Moskva Gosudarstvennoe, 1924); John N Hazard, 'The Soviet Union and International Law' (1950) 1 *Soviet Studies* 189; Grigory I Tunkin, *Co-existence and International Law* (1958) 95 *Recueil des cours* 5 (commenting that 'the event of primary historic significance in the 20th century was the Great October Socialist revolution in Russia', at 6); William E Butler, Peter B Maggs and John B Quigley Jr (eds), *Law after Revolution: Essays in Socialist Law in Honour of Harold J Berman* (Oceana Publications, 1988); W E Butler (ed), *Perestroika and International Law* (Kluwer, 1990); John Quigley, *Soviet Legal Innovation and the Law of the Western World* (Cambridge University Press, 2007); Scott Newton, *Law and the Making of the Soviet World: The Red Demiurge* (Routledge, 2015).

[35] For containment and incorporation, in contrast to elevation, as modes through which international law responds to disruptive events, see Johns et al., n 27, 2–3.

[36] Anne Orford, 'Food Security, Free Trade and the Battle for the State' (2015) 11(2) *Journal of International Law and International Relations* 1, 23.

[37] For a reflection on these questions, see Orford et al., n 18.

of government, the status quo – especially in terms of international economic governance – has been insulated against the impact of such changes through international institutions and legal regimes, restraining the possibility of radical reformulation of economic relations.

As well as understanding the Mexican and Russian revolutions as 'raw material' for the development of international law, this volume is a contribution to the remembering, narrativising and interpreting of revolutions as events in international law.[38] In this sense, international law can be 'viewed as a project of exclusion and inclusion of events and ideas into its narrative'.[39] This collection reflects upon such acts of memory and memorialisation. Vasuki Nesiah suggests that there are two forms of remembering revolution: the nostalgic and the utopian (or 'retro-futurist'). While the former focuses on the possibilities lost, Nesiah prefers the latter, which looks to the paths not taken in search of 'alternative political imaginaries' for the present.[40] Many of the chapters in this collection take a similar approach to remembering past events, in order to explore the 'unrealized potential' of the past or keep alive the experience of forms of internationalism or solidarity.[41] The focus is on 'normative surplus' rather than nostalgia for what could have been.[42] Revolution exceeds its containment in this way. The attempts to found new international orders have not succeeded yet, but they might do so in the future,[43] inspired by the return to the alternative visions, choices and legal regimes that were fought for in the past. As Vidya Kumar has argued, 'international legal history plays an important role in understanding developments that continue to shape the legal imaginary on the nature and possibilities of revolutionary change'.[44] By exploring how international law has played a role in the elevation and containment of revolution and revolutionary ideas and practices at various times and places, we can see 'what might be undone or done differently to achieve other goals'.[45]

[38] Johns et al., n 27, 3 (discussing the tension between events as 'raw material' and events as 'discursive phenomena').

[39] Innokenty Karandashov and Ksenia Shestakova, 'The Principle of Equality of States in the Wake of the Russian Revolution' (2017) 5(4) *Russian Law Journal* 8.

[40] Orford et al., n 18, 264–5.

[41] Ingo Venzke, 'Possibilities of the Past: Histories of the NIEO and the Travails of Critique' (2018) 20 *Journal of the History of International Law* 263, 265.

[42] Ibid., 267.

[43] Orford et al., n 18, 28–9.

[44] Kumar, 'International Law, Kelsen and the Aberrant Revolution', n 30, 187.

[45] Orford et al., n 18, 26, 28.

This collection is organised in five parts: imperialism, institutions and orders, intervention, investment and rights. These represent some of the issues in respect of which the Russian Revolution and the Mexican Revolution posed particularly fundamental challenges, had the most significant impact or provoked the strongest reaction. That imperialism, institutions, intervention, investment and rights have also represented five central pillars of the liberal international legal order during the past century and a half is of course not a coincidence. The Mexican and Russian revolutions struck at the heart of that order and so the chapters in this volume gravitate towards its core aspects, as well as considering the extent to which the events of 1917 led to the construction of alternative orders.

1.1 Part I: Imperialism

The chapters in Part I consider the legacy of the Bolshevik theory of imperialism for international law, challenging liberal narratives about self-determination and humanitarianism. This is one of the areas where the Russian Revolution has had the most significant, wide-ranging and lasting impact. These chapters show how the Bolshevik understanding of, and opposition to, imperialism reverberated not only through the Cold War and the decolonisation era but also in more unexpected places, such as contemporary anti-racism struggles and international criminal law.

In Chapter 2, Robert Knox and Ntina Tzouvala explore the significance of the October Revolution in terms of the impact the Bolshevik theory of imperialism had on the 'international legal strategies and tactics' of people fighting for decolonisation in the non-European world and racial equality in the advanced capitalist states.[46] They argue that this impact stemmed, first, from the crucial role that the Bolshevik theory of imperialism granted to the oppressed and racialised peoples of the colonised world in the coming world revolution, since it understood defeating colonialism as essential to defeating capitalism. At the same time, the Bolshevik theory of imperialism shaped Bolshevik engagement with international law in a way that was profoundly influential on later Third World and anti-racist movements. On the one hand, it was the foundation for pioneering arguments that international law should recognise such political subjectivity through the formal equality of all

[46] Robert Knox and Ntina Tzouvala, 'Looking Eastwards: The Bolshevik Theory of Imperialism and International Law' in this volume.

nations and the right to self-determination, challenging the international legal order's prevailing hierarchies between the civilised and non-civilised world. On the other hand, it was clearly understood that international legal liberalism could only do so much in light of prevailing economic and social realities; international law could be useful only as part of a wider struggle against imperialism and capitalism. As a case study of how this legacy played out, Knox and Tzouvala look at the *We Charge Genocide* petition to the United Nations authored by US civil rights communist-affiliated organisation the Civil Rights Congress (CRC) and how the CRC's use of international legal argument was buttressed by the Bolshevik theory of imperialism. Ultimately, the authors conclude that, despite the contradictions of the Soviet State, especially in regard to its neighbouring states and ethnic minorities, the legacy of the Bolshevik theory of imperialism 'fundamentally informed the development and deployment of international law' during the Cold War and to this day.

In Chapter 3, Amanda Alexander also examines the legacy of the Bolshevik theory of imperialism, this time for international criminal law. Alexander argues that the way in which crimes against humanity were codified and then narrativised at the Nuremberg trials was underpinned by an understanding of war as 'the result and the expression' of the evils of imperialism that reflected Marxist theory and the tenets of the Bolshevik revolution.[47] On this account, imperialism was an economic institution, and it was aggressive imperialist war that was the crime of crimes rather than genocide or crimes against humanity; it was this crime that enabled and led to all the others. Only the influence of this understanding of war and imperialism in 'shap[ing] the laws and the history produced at Nuremberg', explains Alexander, can make sense of why crimes against humanity were only criminalised to the extent that they could be linked to crimes against peace and why the history of the persecution of Jews was distorted as part of the preparation for war. According to Alexander, the Nuremberg trials did not only reflect the liberal narrative of universal humanity. Despite the recent emphasis of Nuremberg's universalist humanism,[48] the texts of the judgments also 'spoke about imperialism and economic exploitation in terms that recall Marxist thought and the Bolshevik Revolution'. It was this latter aspect

[47] Amanda Alexander, 'Lenin at Nuremberg: Anti-Imperialism and the Juridification of Crimes against Humanity' in this volume.

[48] Notably, Philippe Sands, *East West Street: On the Origins of 'Genocide' and 'Crimes against Humanity'* (Alfred A Knopf, 2016).

that enabled crimes against humanity to come into international law, with enduring ramifications for the field.

1.2 Part II: Institutions and Orders

The chapters in Part II explore the relationship between international institutions and international order, and revolution and revolutionary states. On the one hand, international institutions seek to contain or provide an alternative to revolution. While they can have a troubled relationship with revolutionary states, caught between accommodation and exclusion of states that often undermine their founding aims, international institutions are also profoundly shaped by their engagement with the challenge that revolution and revolutionary states pose. On the other hand, whether revolutionary states offered another possible vision of international governance and order remains a live question.

In Chapter 4, Alison Duxbury tells the story of Mexico and Russia's participation in the League of Nations, and thus the story of the League's relationship with revolutionary states. Mexico and Russia were excluded from initial membership, in part due to their revolutionary status – for some at least, such as British Prime Minister David Lloyd George, the League was an alternative to Bolshevism. This is not to say that either revolutionary state would necessarily then have chosen to join had they been asked, although each was subsequently admitted by invitation during the 1930s. Duxbury argues that there is 'a certain distrust and wariness in the interactions between international organisations and revolutionary states which continues to this day'.[49] She identifies three problems for the relationship between international organisations and revolutionary states: first, the question of whether the ideology and aims of revolutionary states are 'compatible with the rationale for the existence of the international organisations in which they seek membership'; second, the question of the implications of the practice of international organisations for the recognition of revolutionary states; and third, the tension between an institution's desire for universal or full regional membership and its formal membership conditions. Duxbury concludes that long after the dissolution of the League, and indeed of the Soviet Union, 'the differential treatment of revolutionary governments

[49] Alison Duxbury, 'Excluding Revolutionary States: Mexico, Russia and the League of Nations' in this volume.

in membership decisions has continued in the practice of contemporary organisations'.

In Chapter 5, Mai Taha considers the 'reformist, yet counterrevolutionary' law and politics of the International Labour Organization (ILO).[50] Established two years after the October Revolution, its founding was a recognition of the need to give an increasingly militant working class a voice in the post–World War I peace settlement, with the aim of deterring the Bolshevik threat. The ILO was novel in the representation that it gave to labour in international law, but, as Taha argues, this was designed as a means of taming workers, ensuring they did not revolt or become communists. This was especially so in colonised states, where workers organising, not just as workers but also as racialised subjects, was deemed dangerous to the stability of empire. Just as with the League, there was tension between the universal aims of the ILO and its membership criteria, which required 'complete independence of governments, employers' and workers' organisations' – at odds with the realities of socialist and colonised countries. The ILO's 'tripartism' was based on a vision of 'peaceful deliberations between workers, bosses and governments', which 'would lay down the foundation of a new and reformed capitalism'. The goal was class harmony – class struggle was denounced. Taha concludes that 'while the contributions of the ILO were significant, or even radical, for a conservative discipline like international law, its vision of social justice was only to maintain the status quo – a sustainable and reformed class society under capitalism'.

In contrast, in Chapter 6, Scott Newton analyses the Soviet Union as a model, or microcosm, of 'a nascent rival international legal order', parallel and antagonistic to that of the League and ILO constituted at Versailles, which 'shared broad cultural presuppositions with the Versailles order and its developmental, custodial colonialism while marking a radical break with its economic and political premises'.[51] Following the Bolshevik Revolution, Russia was the setting for 'a new mode of socialist governance internationality'. In 1917, the Bolsheviks inherited an empire. In response to the challenge of how to deimperialise it without breaking up its territory, the 'governance scheme they devised … transformed an imperial expanse into an arena for an extended constitutional experiment in internal self-determination'. Newton understands Soviet internationality 'in the context of other

[50] Mai Taha, 'Law, Class Struggle and Nervous Breakdowns' in this volume.
[51] Scott Newton, 'Microcosm: Soviet Constitutional Internationality' in this volume.

efforts to accommodate national-ethnic pluralism, culturally and politically, under the broader League of Nations' regime for nationalism'. The Soviet system was, however, 'radically innovative'. Soviet internationality 'contemplated territorially premised political-institutional autonomy . . . [and] introduced an unprecedented level of structural complexity to the organisation of the state itself'. While the Versailles order conceived of self-determination in purely external terms, Soviet internality represented, concludes Newton, 'the first application of self-determination law in an internal rather than a purely external context, presaging by almost seventy years the development of modern conceptions of internal self-determination as applying to pluralist structures of governance'.

In Chapter 7, Owen Taylor challenges the 'image of the Soviet state as representing "socialist" international law, in contrast to the existing norms and practices of law that guided the behaviour of contemporary states'.[52] In fact, Taylor argues, Soviet practice was relatively orthodox, demonstrating significant continuity with standard practice. Although the Soviets were willing to use the international legal system in the defence or pursuit of revolutionary goals where possible, this disjuncture reveals the difficulty in 'articulating revolutionary principles in legal form', despite law's relative indeterminacy. Taylor explores how Soviet legal theorists understood the international legal system as fundamentally 'opposed to the goals of socialist revolution, in that this legal system underpinned international capitalism and the imperial domination of much of the world's population'. Taylor argues that the widespread perception of Soviet deviance when it came to international law reflects 'a deep and symbiotic relationship between certain legal norms and the smooth functioning of international capitalism'. For Taylor, 'it is possible to imagine an unravelling of the logic of the international legal system if certain revolutionary claims for compensation, redistribution or debt alleviation were made into principles of international law'. This move, however, would put legal principle and powerful interest at odds, 'an impossibility that reveals a great deal about the limits of legal struggle'. In light of his conclusions, Taylor counsels those seeking to use international law to achieve revolutionary change today to adopt an approach combining 'principled opportunism' with 'a rigorous process of delegitimation of the law, in the form of sustained critical reflection'.

52 Owen Taylor, 'Law and Socialist Revolution: Early Soviet Legal Theory and Practice' in this volume.

1.3 Part III: Intervention

The chapters in Part III take account of practices of intervention in revolutionary states, and the principle of non-intervention and its development or denigration in response, both at the centre and the periphery of the international legal order. The question of intervention is central to international law's relationship with revolution. The extent to which international law enables foreign states to intervene in situations of revolution to protect the status quo is fundamental to international law's revolutionary or counter-revolutionary potential. As these chapters show, however, resistance to intervention by revolutionary states has also shaped international law, even if scholars have often overlooked this influence.

In Chapter 8, Dino Kritsiotis asks how public international law regulated the behaviour of states in responding to the Russian and Mexican revolutions.[53] In particular, his chapter traces the relevance of the principle of non-intervention before the prohibition on the use of force in the UN Charter. Considering the work of Lassa Oppenheim, Kritsiotis notes how, in general, a change of government was an internal matter not giving rise to a right to interfere on the part of other states, either by withholding recognition or by intervening militarily. However, Kritsiotis argues that the experience of the Mexican and Russian revolutions shows that 'the granting and withholding of recognition do not always conform to [this], and recourse to the discourse of intervention is not necessarily misplaced or without appropriate cue'. In response to revolution, states 'explored various levers of power other than the recourse to direct armed intervention'. This raises questions about the 'range and modalities' of interference, and even the meaning of intervention – 'whether an intervention can be constituted by the mere act of recognition by one State of another State's government, or the withdrawal of diplomatic representation, or by the emplacement of arms or other embargoes or even by the revocation of said embargo, or by the very decision taken not to intervene in the very moment of major upheaval'. The implications are significant, since if the international legal order's foundation on the premise that states can choose their own political and economic system is to mean anything, argues Kritsiotis, 'that "choice" must include the choice of

[53] Dino Kritsiotis, 'Intervention: Sketches from the Scenes of the Mexican and Russian Revolutions' in this volume.

radical change as well as the various means by which that "freedom" is exercised'.

In Chapter 9, Juan Pablo Scarfi looks at how the Mexican Revolution and 1917 Constitution transformed international law in Mexico and Latin America, with particular implications for regional debates about intervention. Focusing on the international legal thought of Isidro Fabela, foreign minister to President Venustiano Carranza whose administration was responsible for the 1917 Constitution, Scarfi investigates 'the germination of new international legal doctrines concerning intervention and US unilateralism in the face of US armed intervention in Veracruz, Mexico, in 1914'.[54] While the revolution in international law produced by the Mexican Revolution 'remained for a long time in the margins of the discipline, because the main revisionist figures of this legal revolution ... remained outside the dominant canon of international law scholarship', Scarfi seeks to recover the legacy of Fabela's international legal thought for Latin American and Third World understandings of international law. At the same time, the revolutionary process also exposes the limits of international law. Following the US intervention, as Fabela and Carranza sought to institutionalise the revolution and seek international recognition, Scarfi argues that 'the process of legal and political innovation and revision declined, and adapted itself to the international legal status quo'. For Scarfi, 'the language of international law and constitutional order, and the need to legitimise the transformations introduced by the revolution both in the domestic constitution and under international law, contributed to placating the radical revision of legal and political norms, inaugurated by the revolutionary process'.

In Chapter 10, Fabia Veçoso examines the legal campaign that revolutionary Mexico undertook at the League of Nations in the context of intervention in the Spanish Civil War.[55] Veçoso concentrates on the innovations of Mexican diplomats – again with a focus on Isidro Fabela, this time in a later phase of his career – in legally justifying Mexico's support to the Spanish Republic in terms that were consistent with Mexico's strong and principled commitment to non-intervention. The chapter probes Mexico's engagement with international law in light

[54] Juan Pablo Scarfi, 'Mexican Revolutionary Constituencies and the Latin American Critique of US Intervention' in this volume.

[55] Fabia Fernandes Carvalho Veçoso, 'Mexican Post-Revolutionary Foreign Policy and the Spanish Civil War: Legal Struggles over Intervention in the League of Nations' in this volume.

of President Lázaro Cárdenas' broader project of revolutionary nation building and 'the ways in which the ideals of the Mexican revolution were extrapolated to the international sphere'. It also argues that Fabela's complex and innovative interpretations of non-intervention, neutrality law and the League Covenant rules on collective security played an important role in the development of international law at the time. Although the British and French interpretations eventually became authoritative, for Veçoso this was by no means predetermined – the British and French interpretations were also experimental. Veçoso concludes that recalling the history of Mexico's position on intervention in the Spanish Civil War at the League 'brings to the surface the many legal interpretations and political possibilities that are still available to us in respect of intervention, civil war and international law today'. Although the Mexican arguments in defence of the Spanish Republic were not taken up at the time, their unrealised potential is still relevant for thinking about non-intervention today.

1.4 Part IV: Investment

The chapters in Part IV locate the origins of modern international investment law in the revolutionary period of which 1917 was a part. They trace the legacy of the international legal strategies of containment that were adopted in response to the radical challenge to the international economic order that the Russian and Mexican revolutions represented. Touching on different aspects of the doctrines and mechanisms used to try and insulate this order from revolution, such as alien protection, the law of expropriation, restitution and arbitration, these chapters explore how international law has been used to restrain revolution within states. Despite ongoing contestation, they suggest that international law continues to be counter-revolutionary in this respect.

In Chapter 11, Kate Miles analyses the October Revolution and the 1917 Mexican Constitution as challenges to an international legal order that has the protection of property as one of its ongoing central commitments. She considers how these events rejected the prevailing conceptualisation of private property in the international legal order in the form of the law of expropriation and alien protection. They sought to constitute a right of nationalisation without compensation in the event of 'widespread reform programmes for the public good'.[56] This was a social justice

[56] Kate Miles, '1917: Property, Revolution and Rejection in International Law' in this volume.

exemption from the rule requiring compensation for expropriation. Yet this alternative vision of international law and property was in its turn rejected – a rejection which, Miles argues, 'reverberated so significantly into the shaping of international investment law in the second half of the twentieth century'. This practice of nationalisation by revolutionary states like Russia and Mexico, and later by decolonising states, failed to create new international law. The capital-exporting states successfully continued to reassert their traditional conception of the rules – which required compensation for expropriation and an international minimum standard of treatment for foreign nationals, despite ongoing contestation. Ultimately, Miles concludes, international law favours stability and seeks to contain revolution and its effects on private property. For Miles, at least when it comes to property, international law 'neutralises the rupture of revolution'.

In Chapter 12, Daria Davitti examines how the law of expropriation developed in response to Article 27 of the 1917 Mexican Constitution and the 1917 Bolshevik Decree of Land as a means to contain these revolutionary events. To do so, the chapter considers three specific legal interventions arising as a result of the events of 1917: the 1927 decision on the expropriation of the factory at Chorzów, the 1930 Lena Goldfields arbitration and the United States' pronouncement of the Hull formula in 1938. Davitti argues that studying these legal interventions in their particular revolutionary contexts reveals the contested and contingent nature of the doctrines and principles they generated that have played, and continue to play, a significant role in the development of modern international investment arbitration. This outcome undermines investment arbitration's claims to neutrality and to depoliticise investment disputes. At the same time, it calls into question the continued authority of these events as applicable to contemporary investment disputes. As a result, 'their importance in establishing clear standards of compensation is largely overestimated, not least because these standards remain highly contested' and continue to reflect the long-standing and ongoing 'political tensions over the meaning of property at the heart of the revolutionary events of 1917'.

Chapter 13, by Andrea Leiter, looks in greater depth at the story of the gold mines concession granted to Lena Goldfields by the USSR and the resulting arbitration. Leiter frames the concession agreement as a pragmatic solution to the tension between international law's commitment to sovereign equality and the state's right to choose its own political economic system on one hand and the obligation to accept sovereign debts and private restitution claims on the other. For Leiter, the 'creation of a legal framework regulating concession agreements became one of the most important means of implementing an international legal order shielding parts of the economy from sovereign decision-making' in the revolutionary context.[57] For the Soviets, concession agreements were a functional tool on the way to a classless society, subordinate to the goals of the revolution and opposed to liberal prioritising of the sanctity of contract or acquired rights. This view played out in the subsequent arbitration, which ultimately upheld the liberal order by establishing jurisdiction outside the national sphere. This was done through the assertion of the principle of *Kompetenz-Kompetenz*, which 'allowed the tribunal to escape review by a national court, and the introduction of general principles enabled the dislocation of Soviet law as applicable law'. Although now an established feature of modern international investment law, the Lena Goldfields arbitration was innovative in this respect. 'Viewed in this light', Leiter concludes, 'international investment law emerges as an international legal regime aimed at containing the potential of redistribution, as proclaimed by the Soviet revolution, through an assertion of international legal principles'.

In Chapter 14, Kathryn Greenman studies the establishment of the mixed claims commissions that adjudicated the numerous alien protection claims made against Mexico in respect of injuries caused to foreign nationals as a result of the Mexican Revolution. The establishment of those commissions was part of a wider practice of intervention in Mexico to protect the property, investments and lives of foreign nationals during the revolutionary period. Greenman argues that international law played a significant role in 'mediating the threat posed to the international economic order by revolution in Mexico'. When the revolution disrupted Mexico's integration into the North Atlantic economy, 'the question of alien protection was one important means through which the contest over the shape of Mexico's economic and political relations with the North Atlantic system played out'. Greenman places the story of the Mexican mixed claims commissions within a larger struggle over attempts to use international law as a vehicle for prioritising the protection of foreign investment against revolution in the decolonised world, as well as of resistance to this. At stake in this struggle, she argues, 'is the space for radical economic and political change at the domestic level and

[57] Andrea Leiter, 'Contestations over Legal Authority: The Lena Goldfields Arbitration 1930' in this volume.

the post-colonial state's right to require foreign capital to bear the risk of revolutionary violence'. Greenman concludes that this struggle has shaped the trajectory of modern international investment law, which continues to provide a high standard of protection to foreign investors in times of revolution and civil war, yet also faces ongoing resistance.

1.5 Part V: Rights

The two chapters in Part V offer perspectives on the legacy of the Russian Revolution and Soviet communism for the European Convention on Human Rights (ECHR) and the Universal Declaration of Human Rights (UDHR) respectively. Those chapters contribute to the wave of revisionist histories of human rights that have emerged to challenge conventional liberal narratives about the origin and revolutionary potential of human rights. They consider different ways in which the legacies of the October Revolution shaped human rights treaty-making, both as a counter-revolutionary response to Soviet communism in the European setting, and as a product of Soviet engagement with the drafting of international instruments. Those chapters pose questions about the role of the human rights movement in ongoing struggles for a different future.

In Chapter 15, Anna Saunders argues that European human rights, while seeming to be politically open in principle, can be understood as a counter-revolutionary reaction to Soviet communism.[58] On Saunders' account, the European human rights' project developed as a means of internationalising the protection of the liberal-capitalist model of the state. At stake was ensuring that political freedoms could be expressed and enabled in law while also ensuring that those freedoms were not available to support revolutionary politics. The chapter traces the thought of André Mandelstam during the interwar period and his efforts in designing an international human rights instrument responsive to the revolutionary politics of the Mexican and Soviet states. Saunders suggests that Mandelstam's argument for limiting political rights through procedural restrictions was also the choice made by the drafters of the ECHR. That choice was realised through the mechanism of Article 17 of the ECHR, designed and interpreted as a means of excluding communist politics from the European regional order. Saunders argues that the first application of Article 17 in *Kommunistiche Partei Deutschlands v*

[58] Anna Saunders, 'Animated by the European Spirit': European Human Rights as Counterrevolutionary Legality' in this volume.

Germany, in which the European Commission of Human Rights held that the German communist party could not rely on the freedoms of the ECHR, reveals that 'the revolutionary Soviet state loomed large in the workings of rights', and provides one means of attending to the ways that law acts to limit or circumscribe rights' political potential.

In Chapter 16, Jessica Whyte explores the Soviet influence on the UDHR and the relationship between human rights and revolutionary politics. She traces the contest over a proposed 'right to a good social and international order' during the drafting of the UDHR.[59] Soviet diplomats objected to such a right, arguing that 'a good society would be achieved by workers' revolutions, not rights declarations'. Although it is often assumed that the inclusion of economic, social and cultural rights in the UDHR was a result of Soviet influence, Whyte argues that, on the contrary, the Soviets did not believe such rights would lead to economic and social equality or could be achieved in capitalist society. In fact, the Soviets' key concerns during the drafting of the UDHR were the resurgence of fascism and racial discrimination. Their primary contribution to human rights was in this area of formal equality. The Soviets, Whyte argues, agreed that 'the most we can hope for from human rights is that they bolt the gates of hell'. However, Whyte concludes, 'in refusing to accept that a society of human rights would necessarily be a "good society" the Soviet Bloc delegates also held open a gap between formal equality and a communist horizon ... even as the Soviet Union betrayed such hopes at home'. The Soviet commitment to formal equality inspired the revolution that was decolonisation and continues to remind us that the good society remains to be fought for.

Together, these chapters reveal the wide-ranging and ongoing impact of the Russian and Mexican revolutions for international law. Tackling the subject from a range of perspectives, they also offer a comprehensive reflection on the complicated relationship between revolution and international law. By taking the two revolutions of 1917 as a focal point and reaching beyond them to theorise this relationship more broadly, this collection analyses the legacy for international law of these two specific revolutionary events, and of revolutionary thought, politics and laws more broadly. It does so without assuming one unified theory of international law, instead taking a pluralist approach to what international law is and where to find it. The chapters in this volume reflect an

[59] Jessica Whyte, 'Human Rights, Revolution and the 'Good Society': The Soviet Union and the Universal Declaration of Human Rights' in this volume.

understanding of international law as 'encompass[ing] a very wide body of practices, concepts, ideas, processes, and techniques, and claimed by an equally wide range of actors, experts, and institutions'.[60] Nevertheless, editors and contributors alike share an intuition that international law is not a neutral force that simply registers the events of the 'real world'. Rather, we are curious about the productive, restraining and enabling functions of our discipline, especially as they become visible in liminal moments of generalised political upheaval.

By proposing that the Mexican and Russian revolutions, as complex and multivalent events, should be understood as posing an ongoing challenge to the existing liberal and capitalist international order, this volume seeks to make those revolutions available for new analyses, without ignoring or effacing their violence or seeing them through rose-tinted glasses. Moments of revolutionary change raise the question of the relationship between violence and legality in ways that cannot be diffused or ignored. If the international legal order rests upon a constant denial of its violent origins, the treatment of both violence and law in these chapters creates a space of thinking that does not draw a sharp line between the two. Rather, it acknowledges the problems and opportunities that arise from normative efforts to create authority out of the chaotic events of condensed and accelerated political activity. Even as the hopes of those revolutionary events were betrayed, they continued to inspire hopes that another world is possible. Focusing both on the interconnectedness of historical events and on the ways that lawyers make certain kinds of meaning move across moments of rupture, our volume explores the legacies of 1917 and their ongoing role in shaping political struggle in the form of international law.

[60] See Orford et al., 'War, Force and Revolution', n 18, 20.

PART I

Imperialism

2

Looking Eastwards

The Bolshevik Theory of Imperialism and International Law

ROBERT KNOX* AND NTINA TZOUVALA†

2.1 Introduction

Turning to Woodrow Wilson's Fourteen Points as the starting point for self-determination in international law has become part of the received wisdom of the field. In a 2017 article, Lauri Mälksoo examined the relationship between the liberal-Wilsonian and the socialist-Bolshevik conceptualisations of self-determination, rejecting the idea that the Bolsheviks contributed at all to the international right of self-determination. In his account, the right is an intrinsically liberal one, concerned with the 'extension of human freedom from individuals to peoples'.[1] By contrast, the Bolshevik tradition mobilised self-determination purely 'for tactical and propaganda purposes'.[2] In Mälksoo's telling, therefore, the Bolshevik advocacy of self-determination was ultimately hollow, since it was subordinated to the 'higher goal' of achieving a communist society. Mälksoo's particular reading dovetails neatly with a common international legal analysis of the Russian Revolution and the Soviet Union. In these accounts, the overarching concern of the Bolsheviks was the defence of the socialist revolution – as embodied in the Soviet state – with support for self-determination and anti-colonialism as well as their advocacy for other causes, notably racial equality – a purely tactical decision to gain them legitimacy. At first sight, such readings have a superficial validity. It is certainly true that the

* School of Law and Social Justice, University of Liverpool.

† College of Law, Australian National University.

1 Lauri Mälksoo, 'The Soviet Approach to the Right of Peoples to Self-Determination: Russia's Farewell to *jus publicum europaeum*' (2017) 19 *Journal of the History of International Law / Revue de l'histoire du droit international* 200, 203.

2 Ibid., 204.

socialist and communist movements had historically been focused on achieving revolution within industrially advanced capitalist states. This tended to mean a focus on Europe as a site of revolutionary action, with anti-colonial movements at best ignored and at worst condemned in the name of the 'advances' that capitalist industrial society would bring.[3]

However, such arguments about the liberal character of self-determination and Bolshevik instrumentalisation of the concept miss a crucial set of facts. First, the accusation of insincerity ignores the Bolshevik analysis of imperialism. As we will show in this chapter, the Bolsheviks understood imperialism as one of the key elements supporting capitalism's reproduction. As such, there was no tension between fighting for socialism and fighting for national liberation, since the latter was a precondition of the former. Second, anchoring self-determination to Wilson's liberal vision ignores the fact that he was at best suspicious of the capacity of racialised people to govern themselves or to live in equality with whites both at home and abroad. Wilson had staunchly opposed the participation of emancipated slaves in the political life of the American South since he saw them as 'unpracticed in liberty, unschooled in self-control, never sobered by the discipline of self-support, never established in any habit of prudence; excited by a freedom they did not understand'.[4] Furthermore, as Adom Getachew has recently argued, Wilson's vision of international order oscillated between the promise of independence for colonies provided that their 'schooling' by their colonial masters turned out to be successful, and a conviction that independent statehood was 'a specific inheritance of the Anglo-Saxon race'.[5] By contrast, an understanding of the (radical) political agency of racialised

[3] The literature on this subject is vast – and contested – but for a thorough account see J M Blaut, 'Marxism and Eurocentric Diffusionism' in R M Chilcote (ed). *The Political Economy of Imperialism* (Springer, 1999) 127. For a compelling account of how Marx's own views changed on the subject – and provided material for the Bolshevik theory and practice of anti-imperialism – see Kevin Anderson, *Marx at the Margins: On Nationalism, Ethnicity, and Non-Western Societies* (University of Chicago Press, 2010); Pranav Jani, 'Karl Marx, Eurocentrism, and the 1857 Revolt in British India' in Crystal Bartolovich and Neil Lazarus (eds), *Marxism, Modernity and Postcolonial Studies* (Cambridge University Press, 2002) 81.

[4] Woodrow Wilson, 'The Reconstruction of the Southern States' in M Dinunzio (ed), *Woodrow Wilson: Essential Writings and Speeches of the Scholar-President* (New York University Press, 2006) 206.

[5] Adom Getachew, *Worldmaking after Empire: The Rise and Fall of Self-Determination* (Princeton University Press, 2019) 47.

and colonial peoples was a key conclusion of the Bolshevik theory of imperialism. It was for this reason that anti-colonial struggles were profoundly influenced by that theory. Therefore, if we understand self-determination as a liberal right, we would have to concede that it was mostly irrelevant to the actual processes of decolonisation.

Taking on these aporias, this chapter argues that the Bolshevik analysis of imperialism was one of the key determinants of the way in which the Bolsheviks engaged with international law, and that the formulations first crafted by the Bolsheviks came to inform international legal strategies and tactics adopted by peoples in the non-European world and racialised groups within the advanced capitalist states. The first part of the chapter reconstructs the Marxist theory of imperialism as elaborated and concretised by the Bolsheviks. It goes on to emphasise the practical consequences of this theory, particularly in respect of acknowledging – and nurturing – the political agency of non-European peoples. It then tracks how the legal arguments pioneered by the Bolsheviks became a contested political legacy. The second part examines how these techniques played out at the micro-level, examining the way in which the African-American Civil Rights Congress' use of international legal argument was undergirded by a Marxist theory of imperialism. In doing so, we will recover the importance of the October Revolution for the struggles for decolonisation and racial equality, while interrogating the role assigned to international law in this context.

2.2 What's in a Theory?

2.2.1 Imperialism and Capitalism

The term 'imperialism' is a distinctly modern one. While 'empire' (or *imperium*) has existed since the days of ancient Rome, 'imperialism' only appeared on the global political scene in the 1840s. The term first emerged as an insult directed at Louis Napoleon Bonaparte following his establishment of the 'Second French Empire' in 1852, as famously chronicled by Marx in *The Eighteenth Brumaire of Louis Napoleon* and *The Civil War in France*. The term 'imperialist' was applied to Louis' regime and its supporters, and essentially denoted the autocratic rule of an Emperor.[6] However, a key feature of the Second French Empire was

6 Richard Koebner and Helmut Dan Schmidt, *Imperialism: The Story and Significance of a Political Word, 1840–1960* (Cambridge University Press, 1964) 20.

its rivalry with other European powers, which culminated in the Franco–Prussian War. When used to denounce these acts, the term imperialism began to take on a more international hue, referring specifically to empires based on militarism.[7] Over the course of the 1880s and 1890s, direct and violent European expansion into the non-European world intensified. The 'Scramble for Africa', clashes over spheres of influence in China (following its 1895 defeat by Japan) and the Boer War of 1899 led a number of radicals to posit that a new, aggressive phase of international expansion was beginning.[8] These critics sought to link these changes in foreign policy to transformations in European capitalism. It was in this context that the modern understanding of 'imperialism' was born.

The most important of these critics was John A Hobson, a radical English liberal. In his 1902 work, *Imperialism: A Study*, Hobson argued that imperialism came about as a result of the development of *financial* interests in the advanced capitalist world. These financial capitalists did not invest their profits in productive capitalism but saved them, leading to a crisis of underconsumption and overproduction. To offset this, it was necessary for capital to go abroad, since underdeveloped countries, without large finance sectors, would be a better source of profitable investment. Accordingly, for Hobson, the period was characterised by attempts to annex and transform non-European territories through force, and competition between European powers for this investment space.[9]

While Hobson was not a Marxist, his analysis, which rooted imperialism in the crisis tendencies of European capitalism, was influential on the Marxist tradition, especially the thought of Rudolf Hilferding, a German Social Democrat. In *Finance Capital*, Hilferding argued that European capitalism had become *monopoly capitalism*. Crucial to this theory was the fusion of industrial and financial capital into cartels. These cartels, he argued, pushed for tariff walls around their economic territory so as to ensure their own profits; yet as these profits fell, finance capital pushed to *expand* tariff walls through the acquisition of colonial territory and the direct export of capital.[10] Both of these solutions required a continuous policy of state expansion to acquire and protect territory for investment.

[7] Ibid., 147.

[8] P J Cain, *Hobson and Imperialism: Radicalism, New Liberalism, and Finance 1887–1938* (Oxford University Press, 2002) 67.

[9] J A Hobson, *Imperialism: A Study* (Gordon Press, 1975).

[10] Rudolf Hilferding, *Finance Capital: A Study of the Latest Phase of Capitalist Development* (Routledge & Kegan Paul, 1981) 322.

Under imperialism 'the idea now is to secure for one's own nation the domination of the world, an aspiration as unbounded as the capitalist lust for profit from which it springs'.[11]

2.3 The Bolsheviks and Imperialism

Hilferding's diagnosis of imperialism exerted a direct influence on the Bolsheviks, particularly Nikolai Bukharin and Vladimir Lenin. Although they had their differences, their mutually reinforcing formulations were of crucial theoretical and political importance for the Bolsheviks. While Hilferding was primarily concerned with charting the transformations of monopoly capitalism internal to Europe, Lenin and Bukharin argued that imperialism had become an international system. The starting point of the Bolsheviks' understanding of imperialism was therefore a blurring of the lines between the 'domestic' and the 'international'. As Bukharin put it, 'the struggle between "national" states ... is nothing but the struggle between the respective groups of the bourgeoisie'.[12] This struggle 'is not suspended in the air' but is instead 'the struggle of various parts of the world economy'.[13] At the same time, following Hilferding, Bukharin and Lenin argued that the monopoly tendencies of advanced capitalism had resulted in the emergence of a number of trusts and cartels directed by financial capital. These tendencies also produced pressures on the profit rates of capitalism: accordingly, finance capital – acting through the state – expanded outwards, seeking new sources of higher profit rates. If finance capitalists exported capital – as opposed to commodities – to less-advanced states and societies, they could attract greater profits because 'capital is scarce, the price of land is relatively low, wages are low, raw materials are cheap'.[14] Accordingly, capitalist states used their political, economic and military power to secure these territories so as to initiate and protect projects of capitalist accumulation, earning higher profits and sending them back to the advanced capitalist countries. It was this drive that gave rise to an international division of labour, which consisted of 'a few consolidated, organised economic bodies ("the great civilised powers") ... and a periphery of undeveloped countries with a

[11] Ibid., 335.
[12] N I Bukharin, *Imperialism and World Economy* (Merlin Press, 1972) 17.
[13] Ibid., 18.
[14] Vladimir Il'ich Lenin, *Imperialism, the Highest Stage of Capitalism: A Popular Outline* (Foreign Languages Press, first published 1917, 1970 ed) 73.

semi-agrarian or agrarian system'.[15] As such, imperialist capitalism was a 'world system of colonial oppression and ... the financial strangulation of the ... majority ... of the world by a handful of "advanced" countries'.[16]

In the epoch of imperialism this could only lead to increased competition *between* imperialist states, since:

> As there are no unoccupied territories – that is, territories that do not belong to any state – in Asia and America, it is necessary to ... say that the characteristic feature of the period under review is the final partition of the globe ... .For the first time the world is completely divided up, so that in the future only redivision is possible, ie, territories can only pass from one 'owner' to another, instead of passing as ownerless territory to an 'owner'.[17]

In the context of imperialist capitalism this could not be 'peaceful' economic competition but would necessarily involve war.[18] As such, imperialism was marked by the intensification of the tendencies towards violence and war inherent in capitalism. Accordingly, for the Bolsheviks imperialism was not 'an accidental entity caused by nothing'.[19] Rather, in Lenin's words it was 'a special stage in the development of capitalism'.[20] While relationships of inequality have 'always existed between big and little states', under imperialism 'they become a general system, they form part of the sum total of "divide the world" relations, become links in the chain of operations of world finance capital'.[21] Far from being a mere prelude to the 'real' political battles, the fight against imperialism *was* the fight against capitalism.

The Bolsheviks' advocacy of self-determination, therefore, stemmed from their analysis of the nature of contemporary capitalism and how to fight it. In this respect there were, indeed, fundamental differences between their position and that of Wilson. First, for Wilson, self-determination was intended for the peoples of the 'civilised' world.[22]

[15] Bukharin, n 12, 74.
[16] Lenin, *Imperialism, the Highest Stage of Capitalism*, n 14, 5.
[17] Ibid., 90.
[18] Bukharin, n 12, 54.
[19] Ibid., 131.
[20] Lenin, *Imperialism, the Highest Stage of Capitalism*, n 14, 103–8.
[21] Ibid., 103.
[22] For the 'standard of civilisation' in international law, see Ntina Tzouvala, 'Civilisation' in Jean d'Aspremont and Sahib Singh (eds), *Concepts for International Law: Contributions to Disciplinary Thought* (Edward Elgar, 2019) 83.

His Fourteen Points explicitly mentioned sovereignty or independence only with regard to Belgium, the 'Turkish part of the Ottoman Empire' and Poland, while the peoples of Austria–Hungary were promised the 'freest opportunity to autonomous development'.[23] Notably, Point V envisioned the future of colonialism as follows:

> A free, open-minded, and absolutely impartial adjustment of all colonial claims, based upon a strict observance of the principle that in determining all such questions of sovereignty the interests of the populations concerned must have equal weight with the equitable claims of the government whose title is to be determined.[24]

Here sovereignty was exclusively reserved for the colonisers, and not the colonised. The reference to the interests, but not to the political agency, of the colonised peoples was indicative of a paternalist approach towards colonial peoples, since their interests were to be determined by others, preferably by the United States, who positioned itself as the independent arbiter of these processes of colonial readjustment. Consequently, self-determination, which was not even explicitly mentioned in the Fourteen Points, was not something to be struggled for and supported; rather, it was to be bestowed 'from above' by powerful states and international organisations. By contrast, the Bolsheviks envisaged self-determination as primarily referring to the rights of colonised, non-European peoples, precisely because these societies were the bulwarks of imperialism. Their argument was that the struggles of these peoples against imperialism were to be given support. Such a conception was a radical break from Wilson's vision – and European political traditions more generally – because it granted non-white, non-European peoples a sense of their own political agency. Alone among European political parties the Bolsheviks saw oppressed peoples as a force for radical political change in their own right.

In this respect, the 'Wilsonian moment' was, as Erez Manela has pointed out, a brief, yet decisive one.[25] By 1919 it was made clear to anti-imperialist movements and leaders in places such as China, Korea, Vietnam or Egypt that self-determination was not for them. There is an

[23] See points VII, X and XII of Woodrow Wilson, 'The Fourteen Points' in Lewis Copeland, Lawrence W Lamm and Stephen J McKenna (eds), *The World's Great Speeches* (Dover Publications, 1999) 360.

[24] Ibid., point V.

[25] Erez Manela, *The Wilsonian Moment: Self-Determination and the International Origins of Anticolonial Nationalism* (Oxford University Press, 2009).

infamous anecdote that summarises this political moment of the rise and fall of liberal internationalism in the colonised world: a young Vietnamese leader tried to meet Wilson and advocate for the case of his people against French colonialism, but he was shown the door. The man, Ho Chi Minh, was bitterly disappointed and turned to the Leninist account of imperialism for inspiration instead.[26] This was by no means a unique incident. Rather, the popularity of the Bolshevik theory of imperialism in the colonised world was, as we will argue shortly, not only an indisputable fact but also a direct outcome of the rejection of the colonised peoples' aspirations and agency both by liberal internationalism conceptually and by Wilson personally.

2.4 Looking Eastwards

2.4.1 War and Social Democracy

Perhaps the most direct consequences of the Bolshevik theory of imperialism were the heated debates and political effects that it generated within European social democracy. Most famously, Lenin engaged in an extended polemic with Kautsky, his former political mentor,[27] over the implications of imperialism for global capitalism and military conflict. The political conclusion that Lenin drew from the theoretical position sketched above was clear. In the context of the First World War, the Bolsheviks did not simply advocate peace, they adopted the slogan 'convert the imperialist war into civil war'.[28] This meant that one should not 'defend the fatherland' but rather attack one's own ruling class in order to bring the war to an end.[29] This position was in stark contrast to that of social democracy. In August 1914, the Social Democratic Party of Germany (*Sozialdemokratische Partei Deutschlands* or SPD) had voted to authorise 'war credits' in the German Reichstag, thus supporting Germany's entry into the First World War. The SPD claimed the war was a defensive one, conducted against an aggressive and reactionary Tsarist Russia.[30] The SPD's position split the left internationally, with

26 Ibid., 3–4.

27 Lars T Lih, *Lenin Rediscovered: 'What Is to Be Done?' in Context* (Haymarket Books, 2008).

28 V I Lenin, *Socialism and War* (Foreign Languages Press, first published 1915, 1970 ed) 21.

29 Ibid., 14.

30 Harold Kent Schellenger, *The SPD in the Bonn Republic: A Socialist Party Modernizes* (Springer, 2012) 18–21.

anti-war and anti-imperialist social democrats (the Bolsheviks among them) going on to conduct a series of conferences outside the ambit of the Second International.[31]

In the traditional Marxist scheme, the working class of the advanced capitalist countries was to be the leading element in the struggle against capitalism. But on the eve of the First World War the most politically advanced wing of the European working class – as represented by the SPD – had sided with their own imperialist bourgeoisie. For the Bolsheviks this could only be explained by the material structure of imperialism. Bukharin pointed out that since the bourgeoisie controls the means of production under capitalism, there is a limited sense in which the working class *needs* them to be successful to survive. As such, it is possible for there to be a momentary 'solidarity of interests' between the two, particularly when a section of the working class is able to receive higher wages.[32]

Accordingly: 'European workers, considered from the point of view of the moment, are the winners, because they receive increments to their wages due to "industrial prosperity"'.[33] The super-profits generated by imperialist monopolies could be used by capitalists to 'bribe their own workers, to create something like an alliance . . . between the workers of the given nation and their capitalists against the other countries'.[34] The net effect of this was the creation of a 'labour aristocracy' whereby to 'a certain degree the workers of the oppressor nations are partners of their own bourgeoisie in the plundering . . . of the oppressed nations'. These workers occupy 'a privileged position in many spheres of political life' and 'ideologically . . . are taught . . . disdain and contempt for the workers of the oppressed nations'.[35]

The Bolshevik theory of imperialism, then, involved a double transformation of the 'traditional' theory of political agency. On the one hand, the centrality of imperialism to capital accumulation granted the non-European world a hugely important role in political transformation. On the other hand, the European working class was understood as a politically divided and compromised subject. The logical – and practical –

[31] R Craig Nation, *War on War: Lenin, the Zimmerwald Left, and the Origins of Communist Internationalism* (Duke University Press, 1989).

[32] Bukharin, n 12, 161–2.

[33] Ibid., 165.

[34] V I Lenin, 'Imperialism and the Split in Socialism' in V I Lenin, *Collected Works* (M S Levin ed, MS Levin et al. trans, Progress Publishers, 1964) vol 23, 105, 114.

[35] V I Lenin, 'A Caricature of Marxism and Imperialist Economism' in ibid., vol 23, 28, 56.

conclusion of this was the articulation of a political alliance between the revolutionary European working class and the oppressed peoples in the colonies.

2.4.2 An Anti-Imperialist Front

All of this analysis was articulated in the context of the First World War. This was, of course, of immediate practical relevance, with the Bolsheviks refusing to side with the Russian state, and instead using the discontent generated by the war to make political inroads and eventually seize power during the October Revolution. After a great deal of debate about whether or not to continue the war effort as a 'revolutionary war', the Bolsheviks declared peace with Germany in the Brest–Litovsk Treaty, and hoped for further European revolutionary uprisings. While the end of the war did prompt a wave of working-class unrest – most famously with the uprising of the Spartacus League in 1918 but also through the 1920s across the rest of Europe – these uprisings were unsuccessful. Hopes for a world revolution to save the embattled Soviet state could not be invested in Europe. This failure, combined with increasing unrest in the colonial world, appeared to vindicate the Bolshevik thesis that the key to the revolution was an anti-imperialist alliance between the advanced European working class and the non-European oppressed peoples.

This analysis had concrete and immediate practical and political implications. In the Annual Congresses of the Communist International, the 'colonial question' began to assume a greater and greater role. The Second Congress, held in 1920, adopted a set of 'theses on the national and colonial question' that stated that 'the entire policy of the Communist International on the national and colonial question must be based primarily on bringing together the proletariat and working classes of all nations and countries for the common revolutionary struggle for the overthrow of the landlords and of the bourgeoisie'.[36] The task was 'to bring into being a close alliance of all national and colonial liberation movements with Soviet Russia'.[37] Accordingly: 'All Communist Parties must support by action the revolutionary liberation

[36] 'Theses on the National and Colonial Question Adopted by the Second Comintern Congress [28 July 1920]' in Jane Degras (ed), *The Communist International 1919–1943: Documents* (Frank Cass, 1956) vol 1, 113, 121.

[37] Ibid., 141.

movements in these countries'.[38] It was in the context of the Second Congress that explicit links began to be made between the 'Negro question' and the colonial question.[39]

As a direct consequence of the Second Congress, in September 1920 the Congress of the Peoples of the East was held in Baku. The Congress brought together revolutionaries across Asia with figures from the Communist International to discuss strategic and tactical questions. The conference comprised delegates from 'the Muslim countries of central Asia, including many from Turkey and Iran ... as well from ... the North Caucasus, Azerbaijan and Khiva. There were in addition Indian, Afghani, Chinese and Arab delegates'.[40] The Congress culminated in the 'Manifesto of the Peoples of the East', which called for a 'holy war under the red banner of the Communist international' against imperialism and capitalism.[41] The Baku Congress was to provide a model for future organising within the International. At the Fourth Congress of the International, it was resolved that the Communist Parties in colonial countries 'have a double task: both to fight for the most radical possible resolution of the tasks of the bourgeois-democratic revolution, aimed at winning political independence, and also to organise the worker and peasant masses in struggle for their particular class interests'.[42] For their part, 'every Communist party in countries that possess [ed] colonies' had the task of 'organising systematic ideological and material assistance for the proletarian and revolutionary movements in the colonies'.[43]

In its 'Theses on the Black Question', the Fourth Congress linked the fate of Africans with those of oppressed black people in the United States. The Congress resolved that 'the blood, and the tears of the "emancipated" Blacks formed part of the material from which American capitalism was constructed' and noted the continuing suffering of the black populations.[44] It further resolved that it was vital to demonstrate that capitalism and imperialism were the cause of black oppression and that it was 'duty-bound to support and promote the international organisation of Blacks

[38] Ibid., 143.

[39] 'Fourth Session July 25' in *Second Congress of the Communist International: Minutes of the Proceedings* (Bob Archer trans, New Park Publications, 1977).

[40] Robert J C Young, *Postcolonialism: An Historical Introduction* (Blackwell, 2001) 135.

[41] John Riddell, *To See the Dawn: Baku, 1920: First Congress of the Peoples of the East* (Pathfinder, 1993) 261.

[42] John Riddell, *Toward the United Front: Proceedings of the Fourth Congress of the Communist International, 1922* (Haymarket Books, 2012) 1186.

[43] Ibid., 1190.

[44] Ibid., 948.

in their struggle against the common enemy'.[45] The Congress declared its intention to fight for 'the equality of the white and Black races, and for equal wages and equal political and social rights' and to compel trade unions to work with black workers.[46]

The Congresses of the International – as well as the Baku Congress – had immediate and wide-ranging effects. First, as a direct result, a number of institutional bodies were set up in order to monitor and intervene in the colonial situation. Particularly important in this respect, was the Communist University of the Toilers of the East, an educational institute under the auspices of the Comintern whose alumni included Ho Chi Minh, Deng Xiao Ping, Liu Shaqui and Harry Haywood.[47] Second, the various members of the Comintern provided material and political support to the anti-colonial movements.[48] As the result of these two factors, the period saw a flourishing of communist and Marxist tendencies within the nascent national liberation movements.[49] Similarly, communists played an active and important role in the civil rights movement and the organisation of black workers.[50] A less obvious, but no less important, result of this was the deepening of non-European political agency. Although not perfect, the various Comintern Congresses, organisations and fronts were unique spaces in which Europeans and non-Europeans engaged as political equals. This was to have a wider political and social impact. As Neil Lazarus puts it, the Third International:

> altered European agendas and tastes by situating the European in a global relationship that was previously unimaginable. [It] brought emissaries from throughout the colonies, who now formed a single, unified front meeting European intellectuals on a formally equal footing. This was unique in European history.[51]

[45] Ibid., 950.
[46] Ibid.
[47] Jonathan W Daly and Leonid Trofimov, *The Russian Revolution and Its Global Impact: A Short History with Documents* (Hackett, 2017) 44.
[48] Sobhanlal Datta Gupta, 'Communism and the Crisis of the Colonial System' in Silvio Pons and Stephen A Smith (eds), *The Cambridge History of Communism* (Cambridge University Press, 2017) 189.
[49] Young, n 40, 139–334.
[50] See Paul M Heideman, *Class Struggle and the Color Line: American Socialism and the Race Question 1900–1930* (Haymarket Books, 2018); Robin D G Kelley, *Hammer and Hoe: Alabama Communists during the Great Depression* (University of North Carolina Press, first published 1990, 2006 ed).
[51] Timothy Brennan, 'Postcolonial Studies between the European Wars: An Intellectual History' in Crystal Bartolovich and Neil Lazarus (eds), *Marxism, Modernity and Postcolonial Studies* (Cambridge University Press, 2002) 185, 193.

2.5 Imperialism and International Law

The Bolshevik understanding of imperialism – and its attendant politics – rested on three key pillars. First, that imperialism was a *special stage* of capitalism that resulted from the crisis-prone nature of the global capitalist economy. Second, that the economic logic of this system gave rise to an international division of labour, in which a small number of advanced capitalist countries vied to exploit the rest of the world. Third, that this structure enabled a section of the working class in the advanced capitalist countries to gain levels of wages which wedded them materially to their own imperialist capitalism. The logical corollary of these three pillars was that fighting colonialism was not simply an 'added extra' to the European revolutionary movement: rather, it was the only way to overcome global capitalism. Accordingly, oppressed non-European peoples were assigned a high level of political agency and importance. Aside from having practical political consequences, this understanding of imperialism also fundamentally conditioned the Bolshevik approach to international law, both in terms of the substance of their legal arguments *and* the overall importance assigned to international law. First and foremost, the Bolsheviks insisted that the non-European world could not be treated as legally inferior to the European world owing to its 'backwardness' or supposed lack of civilisation. This was particularly important in respect of treaties of capitulation, of which Tsarist Russia had been a beneficiary. The Soviet government denounced capitulations 'as a violation of the rights of those countries where the major powers maintained such regimes'.[52] Accordingly, the Soviet government unilaterally surrendered its extraterritorial rights in 1919[53] and concluded a series of treaties with Persia (1921), Turkey (1921) and China (1924) that formalised the surrender.[54] This was coupled with a more general commitment to the equal rights of nations, and an opposition to formally entrenching great-power status. Consequently, Soviet international legal practice emphasised the equality of states and non-intervention in the internal affairs of states throughout the 1920s.[55]

[52] John B Quigley, *Soviet Legal Innovation and the Law of the Western World* (Cambridge University Press, 2007) 136.

[53] Lauri Mälksoo, 'Russia–Europe' in Bardo Fassbender and Anne Peters (eds), *The Oxford Handbook of the History of International Law* (Oxford University Press, 2012) 764, 783.

[54] Quigley, n 52, 136.

[55] Innokenty Karandashov and Ksenia Shestakova, 'The Principle of the Equality of States in the Wake of the Russian Revolution' (2017) 5(4) *Russian Law Journal* 8.

The most crucial manifestation of the Bolsheviks' sense of the political agency of colonised peoples was in their approach to the right of self-determination. In their debates within the Russian revolutionary movement, but also with figures like Rosa Luxemburg and the Jewish Bund socialists, the Bolsheviks argued that the right of self-determination had to include an immediate right to form an independent nation: that is, secession.[56] It was for this reason that in the 1917 'Declaration of the Rights of the People of Russia' the Congress of Soviets argued for 'the right of the peoples of Russia to free self-determination, even to the point of separation and the formation of an independent state'.[57] The relationship of the Soviet state to its own nationalities was profoundly contradictory, with the federative form of revolutionary Russia often hiding the reality of political centralisation and coercion. No such compromises were to be found in relation to the European colonies, however. In contrast to Wilson, who – at best – envisaged a slow, managed transition for Europe's colonies, the Bolsheviks called for immediate colonial independence. Lenin denounced the League of Nations as an 'an alliance of robbers, each trying to snatch something from the others'.[58] He noted of the Treaty of Versailles:

> It is an unparalleled and predatory peace, which has made slaves of tens of millions of people, including the most civilised . . . A situation has arisen wherein seven-tenths of the world's population are in a condition of servitude. These slaves are to be found throughout the world and are at the mercy of a handful of countries – Britain, France and Japan. That is why this international system in its entirety, the order based on the Treaty of Versailles, stands on the brink of a volcano, for the enslaved seven-tenths of the world's population are waiting impatiently for someone to give them a lead in a struggle which will shake all these countries.[59]

As Mälksoo himself puts it: 'Soviet Russia was perhaps the main power that made possible the demise of the international law of the era of European colonialism'.[60] During the interwar period, unequal treaties

[56] V I Lenin, 'The Right of Nations to Self-Determination' in V I Lenin, *Collected Works* (Julius Katzer, ed, Bernard Isaacs and Joe Fineberg, trans) vol 20, 393.

[57] 'Declaration of the Rights of the People of Russia' (2 November 1917) www.marxists.org/history/ussr/government/1917/11/02.htm.

[58] V I Lenin, 'Speech Delivered at a Conference of Chairmen of Uyezd Volost and Village Executive Committees of Moscow Gubernia October 15, 1920' in V I Lenin, *Collected Works* (Julius Katzer ed, Progress Publishers, 1966) vol 31, 318, 323.

[59] Ibid., 326.

[60] Mälksoo, 'Russia–Europe', n 53, 781.

became an increased source of anger for nationalist movements, particularly in China.[61] In this context, the Soviet insistence on the equality of nations, combined with their outreach to the nationalist movements, made the European position increasingly untenable.

By insisting that non-European peoples had political subjectivity that ought to be recognised by international law, the Soviet government fundamentally repudiated the premises of the old international law. However, such a stance was ultimately compatible with a liberal capitalist international order. This was explicitly recognised by the international Communist movement. The 'Theses on the National and Colonial Question' passed at the Second Congress noted that an 'abstract or formal conception of the question of equality in general, and of national equality in particular, is characteristic of . . . bourgeois democracy'.[62] Accordingly, the Communist International 'cannot confine itself to the bare and formal recognition of the equality of nations'.[63] It was a logical consequence of the Bolshevik theory of imperialism that legal recognition would not end imperialism. 'Laws are political measures' and 'no political measure can prohibit economic phenomena'. Consequently, even if a state has formal legal independence 'there is no prohibiting or repealing her dependence on the finance capital of the imperialist powers'.[64] Precisely because the Bolshevik theory of imperialism was rooted in a systematic economic logic, there was little faith in the idea that international law – or international institutions – would be able to abolish imperialism by fiat.[65] Indeed, international law and institutions were, in this sense, understood as a field of struggle, within which the different interests of imperialism struggled for domination.[66] Therefore, the Bolsheviks' understanding of imperialism meant that they pushed international legal liberalism to its limits – arguing for formal equality and

[61] Dong Wang, *China's Unequal Treaties: Narrating National History* (Lexington Books, 2005).

[62] 'Theses on the National and Colonial Question Adopted by the Second Comintern Congress [28 July 1920]' n 36, 139.

[63] Ibid., 142.

[64] Lenin, 'A Caricature of Marxism', n 35, 48.

[65] V I Lenin, 'Terms of Admission into the Communist International' in V I Lenin, *Collected Works*, n 58, vol 31, 206, 208.

[66] This approach was reflected in the legal theory of the Marxists associated with the Bolsheviks, particularly Evgeny Pashukanis: see Evgeny Bronislavovich Pashukanis, *Pashukanis: Selected Writings on Marxism and Law* (Academic Press, 1980). For a contemporary application of Pashukanis' theory, see China Miéville, *Between Equal Rights: A Marxist Theory of International Law* (Brill, 2005).

immediate independence. However, this commitment was underpinned by a deeper understanding of imperialism and not a liberal commitment to international law on its own terms. Thus, a second logical consequence of the Bolshevik theory of imperialism was a certain *irreverence* for international law, and an explicit sense that it needed to be subordinated to the wider anti-imperialist project.

This positioning was perhaps most prominent in the Bolshevik approach to the question of war. Lenin argued that 'the philistine does not realise that war is the "continuation of policy", and consequently limits himself to the formula that "the enemy has attacked us"'. Such a position was unable to ask '*what issues* are at stake in the war, *which* classes are waging it, and with *what* political objects'.[67] Against this, Lenin argued that the 'substance' of a war could only be determined by examining the 'policy pursued prior to the war, the policy that led to and brought about the war'.[68] As he boldly put it, 'if tomorrow, Morocco were to declare war on France, India on England, Persia or China on Russia, and so forth, those would be "just", "defensive" wars, *irrespective* of who attacked first'.[69] Such an approach cut against both an older colonial international law, in which only the civilised European powers had a recognised legal right to make war, and the emerging liberal international legal order that prioritised the abstract equality of states. Instead, for the Bolsheviks, international law was one particular weapon to be wielded against the wider *material* relations of imperialism – which meant differentiating between the national liberation movements and imperialist states.

2.6 Revolutionary Legacies?

As is well known, the earlier radicalism of the Russian Revolution was tempered as time went on. After Lenin's death, the political struggle within Russia itself was eventually won by Stalin's line, which proclaimed that socialism could be built *within* the Russian state. The regime also pushed for normalisation of relations with the capitalist states. Indeed, the Soviet Union joined the League of Nations in 1934 despite the theoretical and political objections to this move occasioned by the theory of imperialism. This was of course complicated by the rise of fascism

[67] Lenin, 'A Caricature of Marxism', n 35, 33 (emphasis in original).
[68] Ibid.
[69] Lenin, *Socialism and War*, n 28, 6 (emphasis in original).

during the interwar period. While the Soviet government had initially opposed fascism, geopolitical considerations led to the Soviet government concluding a treaty of non-aggression with Germany in 1938.

Despite these complexities, the legacy of the Marxist theory of imperialism was hugely important throughout the Cold War period, and fundamentally informed the development and deployment of international law. First, despite their 'normalisation' of status, the Soviet Union continued to be heavily invested in the anti-colonial and anti-imperialist movements, promoting itself as the 'sponsor' of the anti-colonial movements as against the capitalist powers during the Cold War. It provided material and political support to national liberation movements and Third World governments.[70] At the same time, the Soviet Union continued to practice a much more contradictory relationship with its own nationalities, minorities and other states in the socialist bloc. This was in part framed through the fact that imperialism was understood as a *capitalist* phenomenon, meaning that self-determination need not apply within the socialist bloc itself. Indeed, in the 1970s, Brezhnev began to speak of the idea of a 'Soviet people' over and above the constituent nationalities of the Soviet Union.[71] The ultimate realisation of this view was to be found in the 'Brezhnev doctrine', according to which, military intervention within the socialist bloc by 'fraternal' socialist states could be justified in the name of preserving socialism, and socialism – as a non-exploitative social system – could not be imperialist.[72]

All of this had crucial and direct implications for the development of international law: it was at Soviet insistence that the UN Charter included a reference to 'self-determination' in its preamble, and the Soviet Union that introduced the 'Declaration on the Granting of Independence to Colonial Countries and Peoples' to the General Assembly.[73] The language of that declaration – with its insistence on the political subjectivity of the non-European world irrespective of its supposed backwardness –

[70] See, for example, Galia Golan, 'Moscow and Third World Liberation Movements: The Soviet Role' (1987) 40 *Journal of International Affairs* 303; G Guan-Fu, 'Soviet Aid to the Third World: An Analysis of Its Strategy' (1983) 35 *Soviet Studies* 71.

[71] Boris Meissner, 'The Soviet Concept of Nation and the Right of National Self-Determination' (1976) 32 *International Journal* 56.

[72] Stephen G Glazer, 'The Brezhnev Doctrine' (1971) 5 *International Lawyer (ABA)* 169, 170–2.

[73] Bill Bowring, *The Degradation of the International Legal Order: The Rehabilitation of Law and the Possibility of Politics* (Routledge-Cavendish, 2008) 32.

owed a direct debt to the Marxist theory of imperialism. The connection between Marxism and the anti-colonial movement was deepened in the 1940s and 1950s by the Chinese and Cuban revolutions. Even where the anti-colonial revolutions did not directly result in avowed communists coming to power, Marxists – and communist parties – were often directly supported by the Soviet Union, China or Cuba. Some famous examples of this include Algeria, Egypt, Iraq, Syria and Sudan.[74] These anti-imperialist movements generated their own distinctive brands of Marxism that foregrounded the question of imperialism and racism in the critique of capitalism, producing prominent figures such as Aimé Césaire, Frantz Fanon, Amílcar Cabral and Walter Rodney.

Crucially, even the less radical anti-imperialist movements were greatly influenced by the Marxist theory of imperialism. As Koebner and Schmidt put it, 'an international *communis opinio*' had formed for which 'economic imperialism had become an accepted fact'.[75] In this way, some variant of the Marxist understanding of imperialism – that it was rooted in the economic logic of capitalism – informed the majority of the new governments in the non-European world. The less radical of these governments – such as those in Singapore and India – argued that capitalism might be reformed in such a way as to level the playing field. The more radical governments argued that only a fundamental transformation in international capitalism would do. These governments – including Algeria, Cuba and Tanzania – argued for military solidarity against neo-colonial regimes, and advocated various indigenous forms of socialism.[76]

This division between the radical and conservative wings of the Third World movement is perhaps most important when it comes to the abstract character of international law. As previously noted, a key contribution of the Marxist theory of imperialism to the political and legal practice of the Bolsheviks was the understanding that the abstract

[74] Vijay Prashad, *The Darker Nations: A People's History of the Third World* (New Press, 2007).

[75] Koebner and Schmidt, n 6, 272. See also Amanda Alexander, 'Lenin at Nuremberg: Anti-Imperialism and the Juridification of Crimes Against Humanity' in this volume.

[76] See, for example, Piero Gleijeses, *Conflicting Missions: Havana, Washington, and Africa, 1959–1976* (University of North Carolina Press, 2003); Jeffrey James Byrne, *Mecca of Revolution: Algeria, Decolonization, and the Third World Order* (Oxford University Press, 2016); Marina Ottaway and David Ottaway, *Algeria: The Politics of a Socialist Revolution* (University of California Press, 1970); Priya Lal, *African Socialism in Postcolonial Tanzania* (Cambridge University Press, 2015).

equality of international law tended to obscure the real social relations of imperialism. This insight formed a central part of the Third World movement's understanding of international law. Throughout the period of decolonisation Third World states insisted that the military violence needed to secure independence from colonial domination could not be understood as 'aggression' or a breach of article 2(4) of the UN Charter. Perhaps the high point of this was the Indian invasion of the Portuguese colonial enclave of Goa, which India justified by arguing that article 2(4) could not be understood to protect colonialism.[77]

What differentiated the more radical elements of the Third World movement from the more conservative was the mode in which they embraced the law. Although all governments drew – to varying degrees – on the Bolshevik experience, for many the ultimate goal was integration into the formal equality of the law. In contrast, the more radical elements continued with the Bolshevik practice of *instrumentalising* the law as but one weapon in the fight against imperialism.

2.7 Charging Genocide: Bringing a Theory of Imperialism to a Legal Fight

These examples of tactical deployment of international law in order to serve broader purposes of radical social transformation concerned not only interstate relationships but also domestic relations of racial oppression and exploitation. In fact, as we will see later on in this section, socialists and communists in the United States drew heavily from the Bolshevik theory of imperialism in order to theorise and to challenge the position of African Americans, while also enriching, revising and advancing this theory in crucial ways. To elucidate these synergies, we turn our attention to a largely forgotten moment in the intersection of international law and Bolshevik conceptions of imperialism: the controversial *We Charge Genocide* petition to the UN in 1951 by the radical US civil rights group, the Civil Rights Congress (CRC).[78] As is clear from the title, the petition alleged that all three branches of the US government were guilty of the crime of genocide as defined in the 1951 Genocide

[77] Nathaniel Berman, 'Legitimacy through Defiance: From Goa to Iraq' (2005) 23 *Wisconsin International Law Journal* 93.

[78] Civil Rights Congress, *We Charge Genocide: The Crime of Government against the Negro People* (International Publishers, 1970).

Convention[79] (the 'Convention') with regard to black Americans. Offering a broad interpretation of the Convention, the petition not only argued that the 'partial destruction' of black Americans through lynching, police killings and the detrimental effects of Jim Crow amounted to genocide, it also linked racial oppression at home with American imperialism abroad in multiple ways. It is because of this structural understanding of genocide and imperialism that we are particularly interested in this initiative.

Incorporating a distinctly Marxist conceptualisation of racial oppression and imperialism, *We Charge Genocide* offered a radically different approach to the legal concept of genocide. Moreover, locating genocide at the heart of the West, as it did to the dismay of most observers, poses a challenge to both past and present conceptualisations of the crime as something that happens 'over there', whether in the Soviet Union or, more recently, in Africa.[80] The second reason for turning to the document is methodological. If we understand twentieth-century anti-imperialism and anti-colonialism as mass, transnational, revolutionary movements seeking fundamental change, then understanding the relationship between (anti)imperialism and international law requires us to look beyond conventional sources of international law that recognise the modern, capitalist state as its sole author.[81] This is an exercise in rendering 'immediate and visible all communities which continue to find themselves on the receiving end of the discipline's historical violence'.[82] This exercise in 'international law from below'[83] also registers our scepticism toward efforts to reduce the history of international law, particularly in the aftermath of the Second World War, to the will and idiosyncrasies of 'great men'.[84] This tendency ignores the impact of the

[79] *Convention on the Prevention and Punishment of the Crime of Genocide*, opened for signature 9 December 1948, 78 UNTS 277 (entered into force 12 January 1951) ('*Genocide Convention*').

[80] For the implications of naming as genocide the material suffering of the Indigenous populations of settler colonies, see Asad Kiyani, John Reynolds and Sujith Xavier, 'Third World Approaches to International Criminal Law: Forward' (2016) 14 *Journal of International Criminal Justice* 915; Anne Orford, 'Ritual, Mediation, and the International Laws of the South' (2007) 16 *Griffith Law Review* 353.

[81] For a concise elaboration of this point, see Rose Parfitt, 'The Spectre of Sources' (2014) 25 *European Journal of International Law* 297.

[82] Ibid., 306.

[83] We borrow the expression from Balakrishnan Rajagopal, *International Law from Below: Development, Social Movements and Third World Resistance* (Cambridge University Press, 2003).

[84] We are mainly thinking here of the popular Philippe Sands, *East West Street: On the Origins of 'Genocide' and 'Crimes against Humanity'* (Penguin, 2016). Koskenniemi's *The*

rise of mass politics in the form of anti-colonial and anti-racist struggles, workers' militancy or feminism on international law; it ends up offering a methodologically impoverished and politically partisan picture of the discipline while posing as neutral. Resisting this tendency, we shed light on how the Bolshevik conception of imperialism underpinned attempts by oppressed people to use international law as a tactic.[85]

In 1946, three radical left-wing groups, the National Federation for Constitutional Liberties, International Labor Defense and the National Negro Congress merged to form the CRC. The group existed for merely a decade, and by 1956 the impact of McCarthyism, combined with grave financial issues, forced them to disband.[86] In 1951 the CRC decided to submit a petition to the UN with the Genocide Convention as its legal basis. The idea was that international public opinion had to be made aware of racial oppression, and domestic authorities had to be pushed into decisive action, especially since the return of black soldiers from the Second World War marked a spike in lynchings and police brutality. Only the charge of genocide would both alert the world to the oppression of black Americans and also offer black Americans a glimpse of the ample opportunities to advance their cause that the UN purported to offer.[87]

Even though this specific legal basis was new, hopes that the UN could be a useful forum for early civil rights advocacy were not. In 1946, the National Negro Congress (NNC), which was later to merge with the CRC, addressed a petition 'on behalf of 13 million oppressed Negro citizens' to the UN Secretary-General, urging him to place it for consideration in front of the Economic and Social Council.[88] The NNC argued that the Council had jurisdiction to examine the petition, invoking the Preamble of the Charter, as well as article 1(3) designating the promotion and protection of human rights 'without distinction as to race' as one of

Gentle Civilizer of Nations, which stands as the single most authoritative history of the discipline to date, is also not free from this methodological tendency: Martti Koskenniemi, *The Gentle Civilizer of Nations: The Rise and Fall of International Law, 1870–1960* (Cambridge University Press, 2002).

85 Robert Knox, 'Marxism, International Law and Political Strategy' (2009) 22 *Leiden Journal of International Law* 413.

86 For a comprehensive (yet implausibly positive) account, see Gerald Horne, *Communist Front? The Civil Rights Congress, 1946–1956* (Associated University Presses, 1988).

87 William L Patterson, *The Man Who Cried Genocide: An Autobiography* (International Publishers, 1971) 175.

88 National Negro Congress, *A Petition to the United Nations on Behalf of 13 Million Oppressed Negro Citizens of the United States of America* (New York, 6 June 1946).

the purposes of the UN.[89] The short petition was accompanied by a report on the living conditions of black Americans, focusing on a diverse range of issues including income, health, housing, education and civil rights.[90] Authored by the Marxist historian and expert on the history of black Americans Herbert Aptheker, the report placed economic deprivation and exploitation at the centre of its account. Nevertheless, fierce resistance from the United States meant that the petition was largely ignored. Notably, the FBI speculated that the petition was merely an attempt to distract attention from the Greek Civil War and the difficulties the Greek communists (and therefore, the Soviet Union) had run into.[91]

Taking note of the NNC's initiative, and believing that its failure was due to its brevity, the renowned black intellectual, leftist activist and prominent member of the National Association for the Advancement of Colored People (NAACP), W E B Du Bois, took it upon himself to coordinate the authoring of an extensive report that would meticulously document the oppression of black Americans as a violation of the UN Charter.[92] The fact that Eleanor Roosevelt had joined the board of directors of the NAACP a few years earlier inspired hopes within the organisation that they could find a powerful liberal ally at the UN to support their cause.[93] Their optimism turned out to be misplaced. The final report, known as 'An Appeal to the World',[94] was received by the ECOSOC's Commission for Human Rights, but besides vague reassurances that the report would inform the drafting of an International Bill of Rights no specific action was taken.[95]

This inaction was despite the fact that Rayford Logan, the author of the report's section on the relevant UN law, went to great lengths to counter the 'domestic jurisdiction' argument. This argument, drawing from article 2 paragraph 7 of the Charter, was increasingly being used as a legal shield against attempts to subject racist regimes to international

[89] Ibid., 4–5.

[90] Ibid., 8–14.

[91] Carol Anderson, *Eyes Off the Prize: The United Nations and the African American Struggle for Human Rights, 1944–1955* (Cambridge University Press, 2003) 85.

[92] Ibid., 94.

[93] Ibid., 93.

[94] W E B Du Bois (ed), *An Appeal to the World: A Statement of Denial of Human Rights to Minorities in the Case of Citizens of Negro Descent in the United States of America and an Appeal to the United Nations for Redress Prepared for the National Association for the Advancement of Colored People* (National Association for the Advancement of Colored People, 1947).

[95] Anderson, n 91, 105.

scrutiny.[96] This was the case not only regarding Jim Crow but also South Africa. Indeed, the political and legal battle against the emerging apartheid and the role of the United States is essential in order to understand the context of *We Charge Genocide*. India's decision to bring the issue of discriminatory legislation to the UN General Assembly, the international outcry when South Africa attempted to annex South West Africa and the lukewarm reaction of the United States to both indicated a number of trends. First, the potential of the UN General Assembly to serve as a forum for counter-hegemonic legal action regarding decolonisation, despite the fundamentally ambiguous position of the Charter on the issue,[97] might not have been in full swing in 1951, but signs of it were nonetheless emerging.[98] Second, the willingness of the United States indirectly to finance the continuation of colonialism through the Marshall Plan that revitalised the economies of European colonial powers and enabled them to channel funds to the repression of rebellions abroad, combined with the gradual softening of the administration's position toward South Africa, made it obvious that anti-communism was to trump decolonisation and racial equality whenever the dilemma arose.[99]

For the Marxists of the CRC, including the lawyer William L Patterson, this evolution of US foreign and domestic policy only confirmed their conviction that racial oppression at home, imperialism and capitalism were impossible to disentangle. The CRC did not limit its allegations of complicity in genocide, per article 3(e) of the Convention, to the Ku Klux Klan, prominent Dixiecrats or Southern segregationists. Rather, all three branches of government, including the President himself, were argued to be complicit in the crime due to their sustained inaction and political and institutional accommodation of the most explicitly racist political actors.[100] The argument went as follows:

[96] Rayford W Logan, 'The Charter of the United Nations and Its Provisions for Human Rights and the Rights of Minorities and Decisions Already Taken under the Charter' in Du Bois, *An Appeal to the World*, n 94, 147–51.

[97] See Sundhya Pahuja, *Decolonizing International Law: Development, Economic Growth and the Politics of Universality* (Cambridge University Press, 2011) 49–53.

[98] See Mark Mazower, *No Enchanted Palace: The End of Empire and the Ideological Origins of the United Nations* (Princeton University Press, 2009) ch 4, 'Jawaharlal Nehru and the Emergence of the Global United Nations'.

[99] For an account of the USA's gradual tactical alignment with the Apartheid regime, see Thomas Borstelmann, *Apartheid's Reluctant Uncle: The United States and Southern Africa in the Early Cold War* (Oxford University Press, 1993).

[100] Ibid., 191–2.

> The policy of non-enforcement of basic American constitutional laws written and passed to protect the Negro people, has become a legal authorization of genocide. It is the enabling act for genocide. It is the foundation for segregation and other discriminatory practices in law and by the courts. Non-enforcement of the Fourteenth Amendment of the Constitution of the United States, which guarantees the Negro people 'due process of law' and 'equal treatment before the laws', obviously incites genocide.[101]

Even though Raphael Lemkin was dismissive of the initiative and argued that it constituted an effort to distract attention from what he understood to be the only ongoing genocide, that of the Baltic peoples by the Soviet Union,[102] the staunchest advocates of segregation were less confident that they were on the right side of the law. Numerous senators and the American Bar Association successfully campaigned against the ratification of the Convention, taking issue with the fact that intention to destroy a group 'in part' sufficed for the crime to be committed:[103]

> If, for example, in a town in the United States of America, where a crime has allegedly been committed by some unidentified Chinaman, I should decide to get rid of all or most of all the Chinamen in the town by force, and should in the process kill or maim one Chinaman, I would be guilty of genocide, in that with intent to destroy part of the racial group, I had killed or maimed one individual. The Chinaman could well be a colored person, or a member of any other minority group.[104]

The editor of the *American Journal of International Law*, G A Finch, also opined against the ratification of the Convention in a 1949 editorial for similar reasons, raising the issue of the Convention's reallocation of criminal jurisdiction away from (Southern) states to the federal government.[105]

[101] Ibid., 44.

[102] On Lemkin's sustained hostility towards the petition that led him to contradict his own earlier work on, for example, cultural genocide, and some speculation on his motives, see John Docker, 'Raphaël Lemkin: Creator of the Concept of Genocide: A World History Perspective' (2010) 16(2) *Humanities Research* 49, 59–63; Anton Weiss-Wendt, *The Soviet Union and the Gutting of the UN Genocide Convention* (University of Wisconsin Press, 2017) 243–4.

[103] Article 2 of the *Genocide Convention* defines the crime as follows: 'In the present Convention, genocide means any of the following acts committed with intent to destroy, in whole or in part, a national, ethnical, racial or religious group, as such'.

[104] Alfred J Schweppe, 'Statement' in *The Genocide Convention: Hearings before a Subcommittee of the Committee on Foreign Relations of the United States Senate* (81st Congress, Second Session) (US Government Printing Office, 1950) 154, 199.

[105] George A Finch, 'Editorial Comment: The Genocide Convention' (1949) 43 *American Journal of International Law* 732.

Our main point here, however, is not that this was a legally plausible argument but rather that it was a highly original one, offering a distinctly Marxist interpretation of genocide that demonstrated the intrinsic link between the imperialist oppression of racialised peoples abroad and black Americans at home. It did so in a number of ways. The first was in arguing that American imperialism was the projection of domestic white supremacy. In the petitioners' words: 'The lyncher and the atom bomber are related'.[106] In this view, the oppression of black Americans at home was inseparable from US aggression, war and disregard for the lives of racialised peoples abroad. Going back to the nineteenth century, the petitioners argued that: 'The genocide that was American slavery, the killing of part of the group so that the remainder could more readily be exploited for profit, resulted in two wars. The first was the aggression against Mexico in 1846 seeking more territory for the expansion of slavery. The second was the Nineteenth Century's deadliest war, the Civil War of the states'.[107] Concomitantly, the intensification of US imperial adventures abroad was seen as fuelling racist oppression at home. The 1898 Spanish–American War and the conquest of the Philippines featured prominently in the report as the points where the gains of Reconstruction were reversed,[108] since between 1898 and 1910 disenfranchisement laws proliferated rapidly, formalising the political and economic marginalisation of black Americans.[109]

Crucially, at different points of the petition, Jim Crow and imperialism were argued to stem from the same causes, even if their legal and political modalities were different. The authors of the petition put in motion the Bolshevik theory of imperialism, as articulated above, in order to explain black oppression in the United States. They argued, epigrammatically, that 'the foundation of this genocide of which we complain is economic. It is genocide for profit. The intricate superstructure of "law and order"

[106] Civil Rights Congress, n 78, 7.

[107] Ibid., 24.

[108] The Reconstruction Era (1863–1877) followed the US Civil War and was marked by the effort to address the deep inequities of the slavery era through promoting economic redistribution and the genuine participation of black Americans in the political structures of the South, as well as by efforts to form a political alliance between former slaves and poor whites. With the Compromise of 1877, federal troops were pulled out of the South, leaving black Americans vulnerable to a counter-revolution of immense proportions. For a canonical work see: W E B Du Bois, *Black Reconstruction in America: 1860–1880* (Free Press, first published 1935, 1999 ed).

[109] Civil Rights Congress, n 78, 24–5.

and extra-legal terror enforces an oppression that guarantees profit'.[110] The steps of this argument were as follows: American capitalism had entered a stage of monopoly and financial capital was the hegemonic faction of capital. In this context, the maintenance of the rate of profit depended on the over-exploitation of, and the extraction of super-profits from, black labour at home and abroad. In this context, the Deep South of the United States was not qualitatively exceptional, an embarrassing anomaly within an otherwise unobjectionable system. It was rather a quantitative intensification of the objective processes of capitalist reproduction that in its monopoly stage was imperialist by necessity: 'The super-exploitation, and the conspiracy which gains from it, continue today on a larger and more profitable scale than ever before. As American monopoly gains in strength, reaching out for control of the world, the exploitation of the Negro people in the United States increases in scope and severity'.[111]

The petitioners further argued that the purportedly genocidal violence black Americans faced was not due to a natural racial order, nor was it due to malice or irrationality. Rather, the objective social function of lynchings, police brutality and disenfranchisement was to ensure that black Americans would not challenge these conditions of super-exploitation and would accept working for suppressed wages or renting substandard housing at high prices:

> We have proved that monopoly profits from it to the sum of four billions of dollars yearly; that through killing part of the Negro people on the basis of race, monopoly exploits the remainder; that through the genocide practiced against the Negro people, monopoly secures political and economic control of the entire American people, that this genocide in short is the decisive link in the chain that binds Americans to the plans and profits of Wall Street.[112]

In a direct application and extension of the Leninist theory of imperialism, racism at home and imperialism abroad were understood as two different, yet equally violent and destructive methods of extracting super-profits, that, therefore, constituted the lifeline of monopoly capitalism.

The analysis of racial oppression that informed the petition has since been characterised as one of 'crude Marxism'.[113] This accusation

110 Ibid., 23.
111 Ibid., 136.
112 Ibid., 186.
113 Charles H Martin 'Internationalizing "The American Dilemma": The Civil Rights Congress and the 1951 Genocide Petition to the United Nations' (1997) 16(4) *Journal of American Ethnic History* 35, 45.

contains more than a seed of truth. *We Charge Genocide* repeatedly drifted toward an openly conspiratorial idea of history and exploitation in which racist violence was not an objective precondition for the reproduction of racial capitalism but a conscious strategy on behalf of monopoly capital, which was heavily anthropomorphised and imagined to be in total control of the US state apparatus.[114] Nonetheless, one needs to appreciate the intellectual and political rupture involved in grounding racial oppression on the specific modalities of capitalist exploitation in the era of monopolies. The racial order emerges as a historically concrete situation and not as the outcome of biology, God's will or some supposedly eternal, naturalised 'will to power': 'The Negro is oppressed in the United States not because of God but because of monopoly capital. . . . Profits, not the spurious rationale of "race" and "God", are the reasons for "deliberately inflicting on the group conditions of life calculated to bring about its physical destruction in whole or in part"'.[115]

It is in this sense that we can directly observe the influence of the Bolshevik theory of imperialism on *We Charge Genocide*. The petition rests on the idea that the logic of racism and imperialism are rooted in the systematic economic logic of capitalism. Accordingly, the petition conceived of non-white and non-European peoples as active political subjects who were able to challenge their own condition, in this case through the law. Precisely in attempting to bring their own case before the UN, the CRC was demonstrating that they were subjects and not objects of history. Following on from the Bolshevik theory, this subjectivity was necessarily internationalist – a subjectivity of those in the common condition of oppression by imperialism. Perhaps most importantly, the petition was not undergirded by a sense that the law would be able to 'fix' the problem. Rather, it was invoked tactically to strengthen those forces who were opposing racism and imperialism.

The petition was an abject failure within the UN. Although its immediate political impact might not have been negligible, it failed to attract the open support of the states of the Global South – much to Patterson's disapproval.[116] Nonetheless, its main propositions kept resurfacing for

[114] Civil Rights Congress, n 78, 134.

[115] Ibid., 132.

[116] 'Every effort to get the Human Rights Commission of the UN to discuss the genocide charge had been blocked by the influence of American imperialism. The Latin American delegates were wholly in the US grab bag', Patterson, n 87, 212. On the unwillingness of India, Egypt and the black republics of the Caribbean and Africa to promote the petition, owing to their efforts to secure US aid and military support, see ibid., 196–7.

decades inside the civil rights movement. The anxiety that the United States would eliminate its black population was present in the thought of black Americans who never subscribed to the CRC's Marxism, such as Martin Luther King Jr or the novelist James Baldwin.[117] Moreover, both the idea of the economic roots of black oppression and the intuition that imperialism and racism at home were somehow related gained popularity outside the Marxist left during the next two decades. Dr King enraged many of his liberal allies when he spoke out against the Vietnam War, insisting that 'genuine equality' involved not simply legal desegregation but also economic equality and refused to join mainstream US anti-communism.[118]

Arguably, the legacy of the petition was predominantly carried by those sections of the movement that rejected the pacifist commitments of Martin Luther King Jr, especially the Black Panther Party for Self-Defense (BPP). Their analysis drew both from the interwar position of the US Communist Party (CPUSA) that black people in the South were a colonised people who were entitled to self-determination and the establishment of their own state (the so-called Black Belt thesis)[119] and from the thought of 'Third Worldist' Marxists, such as Frantz Fanon, who emphasised the importance of racial oppression for the workings of global capitalism and attempted to 'stretch' Marxism so that it would properly theorise the role of race.[120] Thus, the Black Panthers argued that despite the socially upward mobility of some, black Americans as a whole

[117] 'They needed us to pick the cotton and now they don't need us anymore. Now they're going to kill us all off', Michelle Amor, interview with Raoul Peck, 'Raoul Peck Brings to Life James Baldwin's Unfinished Manuscript', *Los Angeles Review of Books* (4 February 2017). See also: 'In the final analysis, racism is evil because its ultimate logic is genocide . . . if one says that I am not good enough to eat at a lunch counter, or to have a good, decent job, or to go to school with him merely because of my race, he is saying consciously or unconsciously that I do not deserve to exist', Martin Luther King Jr, 'The Other America' (speech delivered at Stanford University, Palo Alto, CA, 14 April 1967).

[118] Martin Luther King Jr, 'Beyond Vietnam – A Time to Break Silence' (speech delivered at Riverside Church, New York City, 4 April 1967); King, 'The Other America', n 117; Martin Luther King Jr, 'Honoring Dr Du Bois' (speech delivered at Carnegie Hall, New York City, 23 February 1968).

[119] The CPUSA held this position between 1928 and 1944. For the transnational origins of this position as the result of the osmosis between black communists and Irish radicals, see David Featherstone, 'Black Internationalism, International Communism and Anti-Fascist Political Trajectories: African American Volunteers in the Spanish Civil War' (2014) 7 *Twentieth-Century Communism: A Journal of International History* 9, 10.

[120] For a summary of this argument and its relevance for the critique of international law, see Robert Knox, 'Valuing Race? Stretched Marxism and the Logic of Imperialism' (2016) 4 *London Review of International Law* 81.

were a colonised people and they, therefore, occupied class positions distinct to poor whites. In this context, the BPP argued that the US state was conducting genocide against its colonised peoples through a variety of means, including direct violence, deprivation and inadequate living conditions, war, as well as family planning and abortion.[121] As they moved away from Black Nationalism and towards revolutionary socialism, the BPP came to see the links between oppression of black Americans and other ethnic minorities, including Native Americans. Hence, in their 1973 petition to the UN the BPP asserted that genocidal racist oppression extended to 'black, brown, red and yellow citizens of the United States' and that the situation was not unlike that in South Africa, urging the UN to implement sanctions against the United States.[122]

Such sanctions were, of course, never implemented. The next decade witnessed the rapid decline of black radicalism at home and the rise and fall of the efforts of the Global South to reform the international legal order. For three decades, the radical ideas of the petition seemed totally forgotten, but things turned out to be more complicated. In September 2014, while the Black Lives Matter movement was unfolding, a group of black radicals in Chicago submitted a shadow report to the UN Committee Against Torture.[123] The name of the group was 'We Charge Genocide'.

[121] Franziska Meister, *Racism and Resistance: How the Black Panthers Challenged White Supremacy* (Transcript Verlag, 2017) 85. Black radical feminists, such as Angela Davis, criticised the linking of abortion rights with genocide, treating them as signs of the macho culture within the black power movement: Angela Davis, *Women, Race, and Class* (Random House Digital, first published 1981, 2011 ed) 203.

[122] Black Panther Party, 'Black Panther Party Petition to the United Nations 1973' in Michael T Martin and Marilyn Yaquinto (eds), *Redress for Historical Injustices in the United States: On Reparations for Slavery, Jim Crow, and Their Legacies* (Duke University Press, 2007) 606.

[123] We Charge Genocide, *Police Violence against Chicago's Youth of Color: A Report Prepared for the United Nations Committee against Torture on the Occasion of Its Review of the United States of America's Third Periodic Report to the Committee Against Torture* (September 2014).

3

Lenin at Nuremberg

Anti-Imperialism and the Juridification of Crimes against Humanity

AMANDA ALEXANDER*

3.1 Introduction

The Nuremberg trials stand as a pivotal moment in any history of international law, international humanitarian law, international criminal law and international human rights.[1] As Teitel writes, 'the trials at Nuremberg represented a unique historical crossroads for the three legal orders that form the humanity law framework'.[2] By introducing crimes against humanity into international law, the trials are said to have contributed to the creation of a new normative order, aimed at protecting vulnerable humanity.[3] For prosecuting individuals for these and other war crimes, they are presented as an example of the rationality and calm procedure of international law overcoming violence, power and the baser instincts of revenge.[4]

* Lecturer at the Thomas More Law School, Australian Catholic University.

1 See, for example, Dominic McGoldrick, 'Criminal Trials before International Tribunals: Legality and Legitimacy' in Dominic McGoldrick, Peter Rowe, and Eric Donnelly (eds), *The Permanent International Criminal Court: Legal and Policy Issues* (Hart Publishing, 2004) 9, 19.

2 Ruti Teitel, *Humanity's Law* (Oxford University Press, 2011) 76.

3 See, for example, Raymond M Brown, 'The American Perspective on Nuremberg: A Case of Cascading Ironies' in Herbert R Reginbogin and Christoph Safferling (eds), *The Nuremberg Trials: International Criminal Law since 1945* (De Gruyter, 2006) 21; Norman Geras, *Crimes against Humanity: Birth of a Concept* (Manchester University Press, 2011) 16; Theodor Meron, 'Reflections on the Prosecution of War Crimes by International Tribunals' (2006) 100 *American Journal of International Law* 551, 577.

4 See, for example, Jonathan Turley, 'Transformative Justice and the Ethos of Nuremberg' (2000) 33 *Loyola of Los Angeles Law Review* 655, 662–3; Meron, n 3, 552, 577; M Cherif Bassiouni, *Crimes against Humanity: Historical Evolution and Contemporary Applications* (Cambridge University Press, 2011) 114.

These accounts of international criminal or international humanitarian law relate what could be described as a liberal or Enlightenment narrative of international law. International law, in these narratives, embodies the enlightened values of rationality, legality and humanity – and the Nuremberg trials represent an important moment in the (slow) movement towards the advancement and realisation of these values. This account is supported by Robert Jackson's well remembered opening at Nuremberg:

> That four great nations, flushed with victory and stung with injury stay the hand of vengeance and voluntarily submit their captive enemies to the judgment of the law is one of the most significant tributes that Power has ever paid to Reason.[5]

This approach to the Nuremberg trials not only places the International Military Tribunal (IMT) in an Enlightenment narrative about international law, it also looks to the trials to *tell* this narrative. The pedagogical role of the Nuremberg trials, and other war crimes trials, has been noted by a number of observers.[6] Such trials are expected to relate an accurate, impartial history while demonstrating enlightened values through the 'civilised institutional drama of a trial at law'.[7] Mark Osiel termed such trials 'liberal show trials'.[8]

The Nuremberg trials therefore have an important place in any account of the advancement of humanitarian, liberal values in international law. Yet, when held up against these expectations, the Nuremberg trials often seem to fall short – both as a legal institution and as an historical account. The Nuremberg trials bear the stain of victors' justice and they stir doubts about retrospective law.[9] The trials were uninspiring;[10] they relied too much on documentary evidence and

[5] Mr Justice Jackson, opening statement, in *Trial of the Major War Criminals before the International Military Tribunal* (International Military Tribunal, 1947) vol II, 99 ('*Trial of the Major War Criminals*').

[6] See, for example, Turley, n 4, 672; Mark J Osiel, 'Ever Again: Legal Remembrance of Administrative Massacre' (1995) 144 *University of Pennsylvania Law Review* 463, 511; Judith Shklar, *Legalism, Law, Morals and Political Trials* (Harvard University Press, 1964) 154, 169.

[7] See, for example, McGoldrick, n 1, 20. See also Turley, n 4, 662–3.

[8] Osiel, n 6, 511.

[9] Matthew Lippman, 'Nuremberg' (1988) 6 *Law in Context* 20, 20.

[10] David Cesarani, 'The International Military Tribunal at Nuremberg: British Perspectives' in Herbert R Reginbogin and Christoph Safferling (eds), *The Nuremberg Trials: International Criminal Law Since 1945* (De Gruyter, 2006) 36.

listened too little to the voices of victims.[11] Most importantly, crimes against humanity, observers note, were oddly limited.[12] Under the Charter, they had to be linked to crimes against peace or war crimes.[13] As a result, the IMT told a distorted history.[14]

In this chapter, I suggest that the IMT falls short when assessed according to these measures because it did not just tell the expected Enlightenment narrative and it did not intend to prosecute crimes against humanity in the way we understand them now. Rather, I will argue that the way the crimes were codified and then described at the trials shows that another narrative was also at work. This was an anti-imperial narrative that drew on Marxist theory and was given a practical impetus by the Bolshevik Revolution. It spread, in a diluted form, to 'advanced opinion' throughout the West.[15] The Marxist approach described war, even European wars, as the result and expression of imperialism. Imperialism was an economic institution, and its depredations were depicted primarily in economic terms. Aggressive, imperialist war was, in this narrative, the worst crime – the crime that led to all the other horrors of war. An international legal regime that condoned imperialist war was, therefore, so ethically misguided that it should be changed.

It was the strength of this belief that enabled the delegates at the London Conference of 1945 to introduce the new crimes against peace, and to drag crimes against humanity into law alongside them as a secondary offence. If we neither acknowledge this belief nor take note of the Marxist narrative underlying it, then some of the choices made at Nuremberg *do* now seem peculiar or incomprehensible. Once, however, we trace the presence of this narrative in the trials, we can see how it shaped the laws and the history produced at Nuremberg. As such, this account shows the extent to which narratives and theories influence the development of international law. In particular, this account shows that these narratives do not always come from the liberal theories that are often considered contiguous with international law. In this case, the Marxist narrative was highly critical of liberal values, yet it still facilitated

[11] Lawrence Douglas, *The Memory of Judgment: Making Law and History in the Trials of the Holocaust* (Yale University Press, 2001) 16–17, 78.

[12] Matthew Lippman, 'Crimes against Humanity' (1997) 17 *Boston College Third World Law Journal* 171, 201.

[13] Geras, n 3, 14.

[14] Douglas, *The Memory of Judgment*, n 11, 77.

[15] E H Carr, *The Bolshevik Revolution 1917–1923* (Penguin Books, 1953) 234.

the introduction of one of the central concepts of contemporary international law.

3.2 The History of International Law and the Nuremberg Trials

The history of the institutionalisation of humanitarian principles is currently one of the central stories of international law – whether told in a positive or critical register. In orthodox histories of international law, which celebrate the progress of humanitarianism and the realisation of liberal values, the Nuremberg trials are a crucial milestone. At Nuremberg, international law represented civilisation standing against 'dictatorship and oppression, malevolence and passion, militarism and lawlessness'.[16] The trials were intended to showcase 'forensic fairness' and human decency.[17] Their Charter introduced crimes against humanity into positive international law,[18] thereby establishing a new ethic of humanitarianism in the development of international law.[19] Moreover, the trials set out to create an 'authentic record of Nazi crimes and criminality'[20] that would establish historical truth through credible evidence.[21]

Yet, even while histories of international law place Nuremberg in this Enlightenment account of the development of international law and look to the IMT for a liberal historical narrative, they see the Nuremberg trials as flawed according to these liberal standards.[22] The trials fall short of the

[16] Mr Justice Jackson, opening statement, in *Trial of the Major War Criminals*, n 5, vol II, 154.

[17] Stephen Breyer, 'Crimes against Humanity: Nuremberg, 1946' (1996) 71 *New York University Law Review* 1161.

[18] Bassiouni, n 4, 95.

[19] Leslie Mansfield, 'Crimes against Humanity: Reflections on the Fiftieth Anniversary of Nuremberg and a Forgotten Legacy' (1995) 64 *Nordic Journal of International Law* 293.

[20] See, for example, R H Minear, *Victor's Justice: The Tokyo War Crimes Trial* (Princeton University Press, 1972) 10; Mark Osiel, *Mass Atrocity, Collective Memory and the Law* (Transaction Publishers, 1997) 81; Nicola Henry, *War and Rape: Law, Memory and Justice* (Routledge, 2011) 22; Luc Reydams and Jed Odermatt, 'Mandates' in Luc Reydams, Jan Wouters and Cedric Ryngaert (eds), *International Prosecutors* (Oxford University Press, 2012) 81, 85.

[21] Breyer, n 17, 1162.

[22] See, for example, Turley, n 4, 675; Shklar, n 6, 171. In Gerry Simpson, *Law, War and Crime: War Crimes, Trials and the Reinvention of International Law* (Polity Press, 2007), these perceived flaws are described as the constant negotiation between liberal cosmopolitanism and illiberal nationalism.

liberal expectation for impartiality; they are described as victors' justice because they ignored Allied crimes.[23] For Osiel, this is an example of Power, rather than Reason.[24] There are lingering doubts about the legality of the new crimes that the IMT introduced – crimes against peace and crimes against humanity.[25] Both lacked a clear pedigree in international law, and both were subject to the complaint of *nullum crimen sine lege*.[26] And even when it is accepted that the obvious importance of crimes against humanity warranted their inclusion in the Charter,[27] modern observers consider the way they were included to be 'odd'.[28] Under s 6(c) of the Charter, crimes against humanity were a secondary crime that had to be connected to the principal crimes of aggressive war or war crimes to fall within the ambit of the Tribunal. This is described as an unfortunate limitation to the category and to the trial's vindication of humanity.[29]

These perceived flaws in the legal aspects of the trial also had an impact on its ability to produce the proper historical narrative desired by liberal observers.[30] The exclusion of Allied crimes meant a partial historical account.[31] The 'peculiarity'[32] of the decision to link crimes against humanity to crimes against peace, and the odd focus on aggressive war,[33] meant that the prosecution had to distort the history of the persecution of the German Jews before the war, making it appear as part

23 See, for example, Lippman, n 9, 6; Osiel, n 6, 653.

24 Osiel, n 6, 653.

25 See, for example, Lippman, n 9, 6; M Cherif Bassiouni, Richard A Falk and Yasuaki Onuma, 'Nuremberg: Forty Years After' (1986) 80 *American Society of International Law Proceedings* 59, 61–2.

26 See, for example, Ellis Washington, 'The Nuremberg Trials: The Death of the Rule of Law (in International Law)' (2003) 49 *Loyola Law Review* 471, 501.

27 Shklar, n 6, 170.

28 Douglas, n 11, 52.

29 See, for example, Lippman, n 12, 201; Douglas, *The Memory of Judgment*, n 11, 52.

30 Herbert R Reginbogin and Christoph J M Safferling, 'Introduction: Lessons of Nuremberg' in Herbert R Reginbogin and Christoph J M Safferling (eds), *The Nuremberg Trials: International Criminal Law Since 1945* (De Gruyter, 2006) 11, 12.

31 Osiel, n 6, 653, William Schabas, *Unimaginable Atrocities: Justice, Politics, and Rights at the War Crimes Tribunals* (Oxford University Press, 2012) 73; Simpson, n 22, 102.

32 Reydams and Odermatt, n 20, 83; Simpson, n 22, 50.

33 See, for example, Sam Garkawe, 'The Role and Rights of Victims at the Nuremberg International Military Tribunal' in Herbert R Reginbogin and Christoph J M Safferling (eds), *The Nuremberg Trials: International Criminal Law since 1945* (De Gruyter, 2006) 86; Douglas, *The Memory of Judgment*, n 11, 78.

of the preparations for aggressive war.[34] Indeed, as scholars have pointed out, the IMT did not relate the history of crimes that we now associate with the Second World War.[35] It was not, in the main, a history of the Jewish Holocaust nor a record of the victims of the war. Victims' voices were seldom heard in a trial that prioritised the probative value of documentary evidence.[36] These choices undermined the ability of the IMT to write a history that emphasised the value of humanity. They also made for a 'boring' trial[37] that failed to produce the 'compelling' liberal narrative that Osiel expects war crimes trials to strive for.[38]

Thus, in these orthodox histories of international law, the Nuremberg trials are presumed to be part of the liberal history of law, because this is presumed to be *the* story of international law, and they are expected to contribute to and retell this narrative. When they fall short of the liberal expectations of law or they fail to tell the narrative that we expect, it is seen as an oddity – an error that will have to be corrected by later legal developments.

There are other, more critical, approaches to the history of international law and war crimes trials. Yet even these more critical accounts agree with the depiction of international law as a Western, liberal project.[39] The main difference is that they see these 'civilised' values and Enlightenment narratives as oppressive and exclusionary. Nielsen has depicted war crimes trials as part of this imperialist project. The practice of war crimes trials, she states, is 'animated by exclusions, notions of civilization, and imperialism'.[40] Nielsen suggests that the association between crimes against humanity and crimes against peace was intended to exclude colonial violence from international criminal law.[41] In these

34 See, for example, Richard Wilson, *Writing History in International Criminal Trials* (Cambridge University Press, 2011) 9; Douglas, *The Memory of Judgment*, n 11, 52.

35 See, for example, Samuel Moyn, *The Last Utopia: Human Rights in History* (Harvard University Press, 2012) 82.

36 Erich Haberer, 'History and Justice: Paradigms of the Prosecution of Nazi Crimes' (2005) 19 *Holocaust and Genocide Studies* 487, 492.

37 Cesarani, n 10, 36.

38 Osiel, n 6, 520.

39 See, for example, Frédéric Mégret, 'From "Savages" to "Unlawful Combatants": A Postcolonial Look at International Humanitarian Law's "Other"' in Anne Orford (ed), *International Law and Its Others* (Cambridge University Press, 2006); Antony Anghie, *Imperialism, Sovereignty and the Making of International Law* (Cambridge University Press, 2005) 312.

40 Claire Nielsen, 'From Nuremberg to The Hague: The Civilizing Mission of International Criminal Law' (2008) 14 *Auckland University Law Review* 81, 83.

41 Ibid., 93. The same point is made in William Schabas, *Unimaginable Atrocities: Justice, Politics, and Rights at the War Crimes Tribunals* (Oxford University Press, 2012) 74.

accounts the limitations of Nuremberg are perhaps less surprising, and its flaws are easier to explain, but they are still measured against a Western Enlightenment narrative. Nuremberg is still expected to tell a (problematic) liberal story because the law is still presumed to be liberal and Western.

3.3 The Leninist Critique of Imperialism

Thus, the perception of international law and the Nuremberg trials as part of a Western, Enlightenment story is widely shared. There have, however, been a few attempts to dent the image of international law as a monolithic imperial project. Some international lawyers have begun to trace the influence of 'peripheral' states, lawyers and movements on the development of international law.[42] Others have observed ambivalence towards imperialism in Western political and legal thought. Koskenniemi, although concluding that international lawyers were apologists for empire,[43] nevertheless reports some criticism of imperialism.[44] Fitzmaurice and Young have further emphasised this discomfort, arguing that there has been a tradition of opposition to conquest and colonisation in the West from the earliest days of European expansion.[45]

These descriptions of peripheral nations struggling to reinterpret international law to serve their interests might not seem like a serious challenge to the orthodox framework of international law. And the examples of some critiques of colonialism from the intellectual quarters of an imperial power might not seem like enough to dent the post-colonial critique of international law. I will argue, however, that the particular form that this critique took in the first half of the twentieth

[42] See, for example, Arnulf Becker Lorca, *Mestizo International Law: A Global Intellectual History 1842–1933* (Cambridge University Press, 2014) 7; Balakrishnan Rajagopal, *International Law from Below: Development, Social Movements and Third World Resistance* (Cambridge University Press, 2003); Matthew Craven, *The Decolonization of International Law: State Succession and the Law of Treaties* (Oxford University Press, 2007); M Sornarajah, 'Power and Justice: Third World Resistance in International Law' (2006) 10 *Singapore Year Book of International Law* 19.

[43] Martti Koskenniemi, *The Gentle Civilizer of Nations: The Rise and Fall of International Law 1870–1960* (Cambridge University Press, 2001) 166.

[44] Ibid., 99.

[45] Andrew Fitzmaurice, 'Anticolonialism in Western Political Thought: The Colonial Origins of the Concept of Genocide' in A Dirk Moses (ed), *Empire, Colony, Genocide: Conquest, Occupation, and Subaltern Resistance in World History* (Berghahn, 2008) 55, 72; Robert Young, *Empire, Colony, Postcolony* (Wiley, 2015) 88.

century *did* influence the introduction of one of the central provisions of contemporary international law – the idea of crimes against humanity.

The dominant critique of imperialism, at this time, was shaped by Marxist theory.[46] In 1916, Lenin had written *Imperialism: The Highest Form of Capitalism,* in response to the work of other socialists on imperialism.[47] According to Lenin, imperialism was an economic institution; it embodied the monopoly stage of capitalism.[48] Capitalist states had sought colonies to gain a monopoly on resources. And now, when the world was almost completely divided into colonial empires, all that was left was the possibility of redivision and repartition. The Great War, with its 'tens of millions dead or left maimed'[49] was the manifestation of this aspect of monopoly capitalism. It was, as Lenin put it: 'imperialist (that is, an annexationist, predatory, war of plunder) on the part of both sides; it was a war for the division of the world, for the partition and repartition of colonies, and spheres of influence of finance capital, etc'.[50]

Although Lenin does describe imperialism as 'a world system of colonial oppression and of the financial strangulation of the overwhelming majority of the population of the world by a handful of "advanced" countries',[51] this is a critique that focuses more on the effects of imperialism on the Western proletariat than on the colonial oppressed. For example, one of the main problems of imperialism, according to Lenin, is that it allows the capitalist state to realise 'superprofits'.[52] The existence of superprofits means that part of the working class will benefit a little from the wealth generated from imperialism. In this way, the more capable elements of the working class – those who would have become socialist campaigners – become politically neutralised.[53] This pacification of the worker was a concern for those seeking widespread revolution. Therefore, it was useful for socialists to encourage the dissolution of imperial empires by promoting self-determination – even when it meant supporting bourgeois national claims.[54]

[46] Young, n 45, 92.
[47] Ibid., 92; Carr, n 15, 232.
[48] V I Lenin, *Imperialism: The Highest Stage of Capitalism* (Resistance Books, 1999) 91.
[49] Ibid., 29.
[50] Ibid., 27.
[51] Ibid., 28.
[52] Ibid., 131.
[53] Ibid., 121.
[54] Vladimir Ilyich Lenin, *The Right of Nations to Self-Determination*, www.marxists.org/archive/lenin/works/1914/self-det/ch04.htm; Carr, n 15, 234.

The Russian Revolution of 1917 meant practical support and publicity for these principles.[55] First the Provisional government and then the Bolshevik government declared their support for self-determination.[56] The Bolsheviks issued the 'Declaration of the Rights of the Peoples of Russia' in November 1917, which granted a right of self-determination,[57] and 'The Declaration of the Rights of the Toiling and Exploited People' in January 1918, which repudiated the 'barbarous policy of bourgeois civilisation, which built up the prosperity of the exploiters in a few privileged nations on the enslavement of hundreds of millions of the toiling masses in Asia, in the colonies in general, and in the small countries'.[58] In 1920, the Bolsheviks' Congress of the Peoples of the East called for anti-colonial struggles.[59]

The Bolshevik approach to self-determination, as indicated by Lenin, applied to all people; it rejected the traditional nineteenth-century division between civilised and uncivilised regimes.[60] The Bolsheviks were also, because of their theoretical understanding of national emancipation as a bourgeois movement,[61] willing to allow for the self-determination of non-socialist regimes.[62] As such, the Bolshevik Revolution provided something of an inspiration for oppressed people, socialist or not.[63]

The Marxist narrative of anti-imperialism and self-determination had echoes outside the Soviet Union, even among thinkers who did not necessarily subscribe to Marxism. In the United States, President Wilson, although concerned by Bolshevik action, shared some of the Bolshevik distaste for imperialism.[64] He, too, considered that imperialism, understood as a struggle for overseas markets and raw materials, was one of the causes of the Great War.[65] In response to the Bolshevik

[55] See Bill Bowring, 'Positivism versus Self-Determination: The Contradictions of Soviet International Law' in Susan Marks (ed), *International Law on the Left: Re-Examining Marxist Legacies* (Cambridge University Press, 2008) 133, 144.

[56] Eric D Weitz, 'Self-Determination: How a German Enlightenment Idea Became the Slogan of National Liberation and a Human Right' (2015) 120 *American Historical Review* 462, 484.

[57] Ibid., 486.

[58] Carr, n 15, 236.

[59] Weitz, n 56, 486.

[60] Bowring, n 55, 144.

[61] Carr, n 15, 234.

[62] Bowring, n 55, 145.

[63] Carr, n 15, 265.

[64] William Roger Louis, *Imperialism at Bay, 1941–1945: The United States and the Decolonization of the British Empire* (Clarendon Press, 1977) 2.

[65] Ibid., 3.

support for self-determination, and arguably as an attempt to 'forestall Bolshevik influence',[66] he proposed a fair adjustment of colonial claims, taking into account the interests of the governed populations in his Fourteen Points. A short while later he referred to self-determination in a speech to Congress as the principle that 'people may now be dominated and governed only by their own consent'.[67]

Wilson's understanding of self-determination was more limited than that of the Bolsheviks; his expectation was of a slow process of civilisation and preparation for self-governance.[68] Yet there was a degree of congruence between Wilson's hopes and the Bolshevik willingness to support bourgeois national emancipation. Carr argues that this allowed the message of anti-imperialism and self-determination to appeal not only to the colonised but to 'advanced opinion throughout the bourgeois world'.[69]

Indeed, similar critiques of imperialism in economic terms and the same connection between war and imperialism were made in a number of works. In a 1915 article, written a year before Lenin's *Imperialism,* Du Bois argued that the Great War was caused by the jealousies inspired by imperialism.[70] Du Bois also described imperialism as an economic institution, stating that the 'primary reality of imperialism in Africa today is economic':[71]

> Immense sums have been derived from raw material and labor whose price has been depressed to a minimum while the resulting goods processed in the mother country are sold at monopoly prices. The profits have not been evenly distributed at home; but the net return to the white races for their investment in colored labor and raw material in Africa has been immense.[72]

Leonard Woolf gave a similar account of imperialism in *Empire and Commerce in Africa*[73] and *Economic Imperialism.*[74] Woolf also described

[66] Weitz, n 56, 464.

[67] Erez Manela, *The Wilsonian Moment: Self-Determination and the International Origins of Anticolonial Nationalism* (Oxford University Press, 2007) 67.

[68] Louis, n 64, 4.

[69] Carr, n 15, 234.

[70] W E B Du Bois, 'The African Roots of War' in Bonnie Kime Scott (ed), *Gender in Modernism: New Geographies, Complex Intersections* (University of Illinois Press, 2007) 438, 441.

[71] W E Burghardt Du Bois, 'The Realities in Africa: European Profit or Negro Development' (1943) 21 *Foreign Affairs* 721.

[72] Ibid.

[73] Leonard Woolf, *Empire and Commerce in Africa: A Study in Economic Imperialism* (Labour Research Department and Allen & Unwin, 1919).

[74] Leonard Woolf, *Economic Imperialism* (Swarthmore Press, 1920).

imperialism as stemming from economic motives, and other justifications for imperialism as a façade.[75] Woolf, too, argues that the 'chief cause' of the Great War was economic imperialism:

> There is no statesman or writer in any European country to-day who would contest the political axiom that the power of the State can be and should be used upon the world outside the State for the economic purposes of the world within the State. It is almost impossible to visualize the total effect which the acceptance of this axiom in the last sixty years has had upon the world. It has turned whole nations into armies, and industry and commerce into weapons of economic war. It has caused more bloodshed than ever religion or dynasties caused in an equal number of years, when gods and kings, rather than commerce, were the 'greatest of political interests'.[76]

The effects of imperialism on Europe are addressed by Woolf first. Only after this does he look at the effect of economic imperialism on Africans. Taking East Africa as his example – because Britons, born to Empire, have the most favourable form of imperialism[77] – he looks at the effect on the colonised. Here too, Woolf's understanding of the depredations of colonialism are essentially economic. He recounts the seizure of land, and the mechanisms, such as threat of starvation and higher taxes, used to force Africans to work for the colonisers for meagre wages.[78]

Some international lawyers expressed the same opinion of imperialism. Quincy Wright described the establishment of colonies in his text on the mandate system:

> As for policy, colonies were considered tributary to the parent state supplying its raw materials and taking its manufactures .... In brief, the principles governing the relations of European and non-European peoples at the beginning of the modern period was that described by Seeley: 'Everywhere the country fell into the hands of the immigrating race and was disposed of as so much plunder', thus furnishing 'one of the most terrible pages to the annals of the world'.[79]

As imperialism progressed, Wright explained, natives were sometimes viewed (and occasionally more kindly treated) as 'important economic

[75] Ibid., 15.
[76] Woolf, n 73, 10.
[77] Ibid., 337.
[78] Ibid., 343–50.
[79] Quincy Wright, *Mandates under the League of Nations* (University of Chicago Press, 1930) 8.

assets'.[80] Yet even though humanitarian principles were formulated, the economic and military exploitation of natives continued through the World War.[81] Wright was later to advise Jackson at the Nuremberg trials.[82] Lauterpacht, who was also to give advice on the Nuremberg trials, described imperialism as 'the most ruthless economic exploitation of native peoples, maintained by the despotic rule of military administration'.[83]

During the Second World War, Lemkin, in *Axis Rule in Occupied Europe*, described the German police as colonisers, carrying out a program of deporting native populations in order to facilitate German colonisation of the occupied regions.[84] It was in the context of this description of German colonisation, or Germanization, that he introduced the term genocide. Indeed, Lemkin seems to use the terms 'colonisation' and 'genocide' to discuss the same process – the imposition of a German national pattern on the colonised areas.[85] Historians who have traced Lemkin's intellectual lineage have argued that colonialism was central to his conception of genocide,[86] and they have described it as the culmination of a long tradition of European anti-colonial writing, stretching back to Vitoria and Las Casas.[87]

As such, by the end of the Second World War there was an established and widespread critique of imperialism, in both the East and West, that took as its givens the tenets that imperialism was driven by economic motives, that its aim was to increase the wealth of the metropole and that it led to war and aggression in Europe as well as the colonised world.

[80] Ibid., 10.
[81] Ibid.
[82] A W B Simpson, *Human Rights and the End of Empire: Britain and the Genesis of the European Convention* (Oxford University Press, 2004) 191.
[83] Described in Martti Koskenniemi, 'The Victorian Tradition in International Law' (1997) 8 *European Journal of International Law* 2, 130.
[84] Raphaël Lemkin, *Axis Rule in Occupied Europe: Laws of Occupation, Analysis of Government, Proposals for Redress* (Carnegie Endowment for International Peace, 1944) 21.
[85] Ibid., 83.
[86] Michael A McDonnell and Dirk Moses, 'Raphael Lemkin as Historian of Genocide in the Americas' (2005) 7 *Journal of Genocide Research* (2005) 501.
[87] A Dirk Moses, 'Empire, Colony, Genocide: Keywords and the Philosophy of History' in A Dirk Moses (ed), *Empire, Colony, Genocide: Conquest, Occupation, and Subaltern Resistance in World History* (Berghahn, 2008) 1, 9; Thomas Kühne, Colonialism and the Holocaust: Continuities, Causations, and Complexities (2013) 15 *Journal of Genocide Research* 339, 344; Fitzmaurice, n 45, 80.

Within this critique, there was an understanding that imperialism led to suffering among the colonised, but this suffering was not clearly articulated.

3.4 Crimes against Humanity and Crimes against Peace

The influence of this particular understanding of war and imperialism can be seen in the way that the London Charter was drafted. The delegates to the London Conference inscribed two new categories of crimes into international law: crimes against humanity and crimes against peace. Although much work can be, and has been, done sourcing prehistories for these crimes,[88] it is hard to deny that both crimes were new to positive international law. As Egon Schwelb said, at the time, of crimes against humanity:

> The provision of sub-paragraph (c), referring to crimes against humanity, has, from the very beginning, caught the imagination of international lawyers as laying down, prima facie, a set of novel principles of law. The provisions relating to crimes against humanity have been acclaimed as 'a revolution in international criminal law'. Others have described it as an innovation inconsistent with international law.[89]

Crimes against peace were equally problematic. The UK[90] and French[91] delegations at the London Conference stated clearly that they did not consider aggression or crimes against peace to be part of international law. Professor Gros, speaking for France, warned that 'we do not want criticism in later years of punishing something that was not actually criminal, such as launching a war of aggression'.[92]

Even Robert Jackson recognised that this was new. He made an argument for the criminalisation of aggression based on the series of

[88] See, for example, Geras, n 3, 3–10; Bassiouni, n 4, 83.

[89] Egon Schwelb, 'Crimes against Humanity' (1946) 23 *British Yearbook of International Law* 178, 178.

[90] See, for example, 'Aide-Mémoire from the United Kingdom, April 23 1945' in *Report of Robert H Jackson United States Representative to the International Conference on Military Trials* (Division of Publications, Office of Public Affairs, 1945) 19 ('*Report of Robert H Jackson*'). This states that 'under the procedure suggested this would be a matter for the tribunal, and would at any rate give the accused the opportunity of basing arguments on what has happened in the past and what has been done by various countries in declaring war which resulted in acquiring new territory, which certainly were not regarded at the time as crimes against international law'.

[91] See 'Minutes of Conference Session of July 19, 1945' in ibid., 295–6.

[92] Ibid.

treaties and declarations made between the wars, but he acknowledged that this crime was novel.[93] Nevertheless, he argued that 'unless we are prepared to abandon every principle of growth for International Law, we cannot deny that our own day has its right to institute customs and to conclude agreements that will themselves become sources of a newer and strengthened International Law'.[94]

Yet, despite the dubious provenance of both these new laws, the drafters were, ultimately, more confident about introducing crimes against peace into international law than crimes against humanity. Crimes against peace were a principal crime, in fact *the* principal crime, as will be discussed below. Crimes against humanity, meanwhile, were codified as a secondary crime that had to be linked to crimes against peace or war crimes.

Later commentators have been puzzled and dismayed by this decision, this failure to provide a 'principled distinction' between war crimes and crimes against humanity.[95] Going back to the records, they regret that they can find little documentation or record of discussion to explain the introduction or the limitation of crimes against humanity.[96] It has been suggested that the connection was not properly thought through, or that it may have been the unfortunate result of a change to the punctuation of the clause[97] – although Schwelb, at the time, thought this change very deliberate.[98] Bassiouni writes that while it was understandable that crimes against humanity were linked to war crimes, as an established international crime, he considers the link to crimes against peace to be 'incomprehensible' since the initiation of a war was not deemed an international crime at the time.[99]

Yet an examination of those reports that do exist suggests that the delegates saw the link as obvious. In discussing a Soviet draft of the crimes to be prosecuted, Sir David Maxwell Fyfe spoke of his hope that the word 'preparation' covered 'the terrorization and murder of their own Jewish population in order to prepare for war'.[100] He explained:

[93] 'Report to the President by Mr Justice Jackson, June 6, 1945' in ibid., 51–2.
[94] Ibid., 51–2.
[95] Lippman, n 12, 201.
[96] Bassiouni, n 4, 86, 126.
[97] Ibid., 122–5.
[98] Schwelb, n 89, 194.
[99] Bassiouni, n 4, 112.
[100] 'Minutes of Conference Session of July 23, 1945' in n 90, 329.

> I just wanted to make it clear that we had this in mind because I have been approached by various Jewish organizations and should like to satisfy them if possible. I have in mind only such general treatment of the Jews as showed itself as a part of the general plan of aggression.[101]

Jackson responded:

> It has been a general principle of foreign policy of our Government from time immemorial that the internal affairs of another government are not ordinarily our business; that is to say, the way Germany treats its inhabitants, or any other country treats its inhabitants, is not our affair any more than it is the affair of some other government to interpose itself in our problems. The reason that this program of extermination of Jews and destruction of the rights of minorities becomes an international concern is this: it was a part of a plan for making an illegal war. Unless we have a war connection as a basis for reaching them, I would think we have no basis for dealing with atrocities.[102]

Thus, despite the connection between crimes against German Jews and crimes against peace being 'incomprehensible' to Bassiouni, it was a very obvious and important connection to the delegates at the London Conference. Changing international law to prosecute crimes against people, however horrific, without a connection to the war, was not something they felt they could do.

The delegates did, however, despite the concerns of the English and the French, ultimately feel they could change the law concerning aggression – even though it was just as radical a change. Although this readiness is often attributed to the peculiar *idée fixe* of Jackson,[103] historical work has pointed to a range of proponents for the idea that aggressive war should be illegal. Some of this research has been aimed at salvaging the work of unknown Americans,[104] and some at recovering the influence of Soviet[105] or European[106] jurists from a triumphalist American

[101] Ibid., 329.

[102] Ibid., 331.

[103] Samuel Moyn, discussing Judith Shklar's *Legalism*, in Samuel Moyn, 'Judith Shklar on the Philosophy of International Criminal Law' (2014) 14 *International Criminal Law Review* 717, 730.

[104] Jonathan A Bush, '"The Supreme . . . Crime" and Its Origins: The Lost Legislative History of the Crime of Aggressive War' (2002) 102 *Columbia Law Review* 2324.

[105] Francine Hirsch, 'The Soviets at Nuremberg: International Law, Propaganda, and the Making of the Postwar Order' (2008) 113 *American Historical Review* 701.

[106] See, for example, Kirsten Sellars, *'Crimes against Peace' and International Law* (Cambridge University Press, 2013) 50. Sellars points to a memorandum written by

account.[107] This chapter cannot assess which of these sources was most influential, but what is clear is that this was a fairly widespread concern and that both the Soviet and American sources base their arguments about the criminalisation of aggressive war on similar beliefs about war and imperialism – beliefs that echo the narrative outlined above.

The Soviet argument for the criminalisation of aggressive war was made most clearly and most publicly in the 1944 tract by the Soviet jurist A N Trainin, *The Criminal Responsibility of the Hitlerites.*[108] In this work, Trainin argued that international law had not developed as 'a system of rules protecting the liberty, independence and sovereignty of nations'[109] because of 'the policy of aggressive imperialistic supremacy, a constant threat to peace, a policy systematically giving ample scope for the use of force in the sphere of international relations'.[110] Now, however, the Soviet Union, as protector of the sovereignty and rights of small (and great) nations, was in a position to develop international relations for 'liberty-loving nations' on the bases defended by the Soviet Union.[111]

This work would include the development of new international crimes. And, according to Trainin, aggression was the most dangerous international crime.[112] Aggression undermined the peaceful relations between nations – which are a basic foundation of international association. The exception to this statement, Trainin points out in a footnote, is 'obviously' a just war of liberation.[113]

When describing the Nazi liability for crimes against peace, Trainin emphasised that the Nazis were 'rapacious and piratic imperialists', determined to seize foreign territories.[114] He points to a German Memorandum that stated: 'The conquered Eastern provinces must be considered as German economic territory. The land, all the livestock and equipment must be considered as the property of the German Reich'.[115]

Lauterpacht that shows that the idea of a crime of aggression emerged in Europe, rather than just being born in Washington.

107 Hirsh, n 105, 701.

108 A N Trainin, *The Criminal Responsibility of the Hitlerites* (Legal Publishing House NKU, 1944). See also Sellars, n 106, 55; Hirsh, n 105, 706–8.

109 Trainin, n 108, 7.

110 Ibid.

111 Ibid., 8–9.

112 Ibid., 48.

113 Ibid., 47.

114 Ibid., 56.

115 Ibid., 61.

In this way, Trainin highlighted the imperialist and economic aspects of German aggression.

Trainin's description of international crimes was innovative and normative;[116] he recognised that these crimes were not yet prohibited by international conventions and that the law was only in the stage of formulation and development.[117] Indeed, Sellars suggests Trainin's work was part of a pointed Soviet attempt to change the international legal order after the war and she states that the work was translated into English, French and German as a deliberate promotional strategy.[118]

As a strategy this clearly had some effect and the tract gained influence in the West.[119] Hirsh states that it was discussed at a meeting of the United Nations War Crimes Commission in October 1944.[120] She writes that it was described by Maxwell Fyfe as 'a godsend' for clarifying important issues of the day.[121] Trainin was present at the London Conference and his work was referred to by the French delegate, Professor Gros,[122] and Robert Jackson.[123] The Lord Chancellor of the United Kingdom, Sir William Jowitt, also stated his preference for following Trainin's terminology of 'crimes against peace', rather than the 'crime of war' when naming the new crime.[124]

Hirsh considers that the United States' understanding of the crime of aggression was shaped by Trainin's influence.[125] She argues that Murray Bernays, who was instrumental in planning the US case, used Trainin's definition of crimes against peace and that Jackson was given his work and approved of his definition of aggressive war.[126] This argument is shared by other commentators; George Finch made this point in 1947.[127] He argued that crimes against peace were not envisaged before the end of

116 Hirsh, n 105, 706–7.
117 Trainin, n 108, 54.
118 Sellars, n 106, 49.
119 Hirsh, n 105, 708; Sellars, n 106, 57.
120 Hirsh, n 105, 708.
121 Ibid.
122 See 'Minutes of Conference Session of July 19, 1945' in n 90, 295–6.
123 Ibid., 299.
124 See 'Minutes of Conference Session of August 2, 1945' in ibid., 416–7.
125 Hirsh, n 105, 708.
126 Ibid. Interestingly, Murray Bernays is considered responsible for the emphasis on conspiracy at Nuremberg, which Simpson describes as a 'curiously Marxist idea': Simpson, n 22, 91.
127 Ibid.

the war and can be attributed to Professor Trainin's book.[128] Finch went on to point out the similarity of Trainin's and Jackson's words when they both ascribed the limitations of pre-existing international law to an epoch of imperialism that sought to make war respectable.[129]

Sellars makes reference to the same words and argues that the only theorists to whom Jackson acknowledged any debt were Trainin and Lauterpacht.[130] Sellars also, however, points to the influence of William C Chanler, following Bush's account of how a little known lawyer was able to use his private networks to get Roosevelt to support a prosecution for aggression.[131] Bush, in contrast, refuses to acknowledge any Russian influence on the development of this doctrine. He describes only Russian scepticism,[132] and insists that Trainin's 'simply confusing' work had little impact.[133] Instead, Bush argues that Chanler developed a crime of aggressive war and convinced Sheldon Glueck, the leading American authority on war crimes law,[134] of the plausibility of prosecuting Germans for this crime.

Whether or not Bush is correct in rejecting Trainin's influence, what is significant for the purposes of this chapter is that Chanler's correspondence repeats the same anti-imperial sentiments found in the Soviet doctrine and in Jackson's comments. Chanler also states that the period of colonial expansion had destroyed the distinction between just and unjust wars and had, therefore, facilitated all war. What was needed, Chanler wrote, was for this distinction to be reintroduced and war itself to be prosecuted:

> You will recall that prior to the 'age of imperialism', international lawyers were struggling to draw a distinction between the 'just' and the 'unjust' war. Then, with the urge for colonial expansion, it became apparent that any such theory would be extremely embarrassing to heads of the state seeking to build their empires through military conquest.[135]

Thus, for Trainin, Jackson and Chanler, the idea that aggressive war was criminal, that there could be unjust, unlawful wars, did entail a significant

[128] George A Finch, 'The Nuremberg Trial and International Law' (1947) 41 *American Journal of International Law* 20, 28–9.

[129] Ibid., 28. Sellars also makes this point: Sellars, n 106, 109.

[130] Sellars, n 106, 109–10.

[131] Ibid., 72.

[132] Bush, n 104, 2369.

[133] Ibid., 2349.

[134] Ibid., 2345.

[135] Ibid., 2410, reproducing Letter from W M C Chandler to Sheldon Glueck, 9 May 1945.

change to international law. It was, however, a justified change; it meant leaving behind an imperial era where colonisation was acceptable and acknowledging the injustice of colonial wars. This would change the international order from an unethical order to a better one. The similarity of these sentiments in US thought and Soviet literature shows that the idea of a crime against peace was not just a bizarre obsession urged by Robert Jackson. Rather it was a widespread sensibility, found in Marxist and Western anti-imperial literature, that informed the way war could be described, understood and condemned.

3.5 The International Military Tribunal's History of Imperialist War

This was the story, the story of aggressive, imperialist war, that was presented at the Nuremberg trials. Once the trial began, the Soviet, English and US prosecution stifled any of their doubts about crimes against peace. Together, they agreed on the legal provenance of aggression. The prosecution pointed to a series of acts and treaties that had recognised aggression as an international crime,[136] starting with the Kellogg–Briand pact.[137] Any insistence that aggressive war was not prohibited was, according to Jackson, part of the antedated and amoral theory of imperialism:

> The age of imperialistic expansion during the eighteenth and nineteenth centuries added the foul doctrine, contrary to the teachings of early Christian and international law scholars such as Grotius, that all wars are to be regarded as legitimate wars.[138]

Aggressive war was, the Soviets, British and Americans insisted, the central and principal crime from which the other crimes stemmed. General Rudenko, making the opening speech for the Soviet prosecution, stated that nations in the pursuit of peace had advocated 'the idea that aggression constitutes the gravest encroachment on the peaceful relations between nations, a most serious international crime'.[139] Shawcross, in his

[136] See, for example, General R A Rudenko, opening statement, in *Trial of the Major War Criminals*, n 5, vol VII, 148; Sir Hartley Shawcross, opening statement, at vol III, 96–7; Jackson, opening statement, at vol II, 145.

[137] See, for example, Jackson, opening statement, in ibid., vol II, 145; Shawcross, opening statement, at vol III, 103.

[138] Jackson, opening statement, in ibid., vol II, 145.

[139] Rudenko, opening statement, in ibid., vol VII, 148.

closing statement for the United Kingdom, described the crime of war as the object and parent of the other crimes.[140] In the US volumes on *Nazi Aggression and Conspiracy*, which summarise and expand on the account which the US prosecution sought to put forward at Nuremberg,[141] it is stated:

> The aggressive war phase of the case against the Nazi conspirators is, in the view of the American prosecution, the heart of the case. Everything else in this case, however dramatic, however sordid, however shocking and revolting to the common instinct of civilized peoples, is incidental or subordinate to, the fact of aggressive war.
>
> All the dramatic story of what went on in Germany in the early phases of the conspiracy – the ideologies used, the techniques of terror used, the suppressions of human freedom employed in the seizure of power, and even the concentration camps and the crimes against humanity, the persecutions, tortures and murders committed – all these things would have had little international juridical significance except for the fact that they were the preparation for the commission of aggressions against peaceful neighboring peoples.[142]

Thus, crimes against peace were, according to the prosecution, the source of the war crimes and the crimes against humanity. This was seen as self-explanatory in terms of the war itself. As Jackson put it, 'could men of their practical intelligence expect to get neighboring lands free from the claims of their tenants without committing crimes against humanity?'[143] Or as Shawcross pointed out, 'these things occur when men embark on total war as an instrument of policy for aggressive ends'.[144]

When, however, it came to the persecution of the Jews in Germany, it was harder for the prosecution to connect the crimes against humanity with aggressive war. Nevertheless, the prosecution insisted that the link did exist. 'Let no one be misled by the metaphysical explanations which are put forward for this most frightful crime'.[145] said Shawcross: the persecution of the Jews was part of the preparation for aggressive war. The Nazis, the prosecution explained, believed that the Germans had lost the First World War because of the collapse of the home front. They

140 Ibid., vol XIX, 448.

141 Office of United States Chief of Counsel for the Prosecution of Axis Criminality, *Nazi Conspiracy and Aggression* (United States Government Printing Office, 1946) vol 1.

142 Ibid., vol 1, 370.

143 Jackson, closing statement, in *Trial of the Major War Criminals*, n 5, vol XIX, 425.

144 Shawcross, closing statement, in ibid., vol XIX, 448.

145 Shawcross, closing statement, in ibid., vol XIX, 443.

hoped to avoid this in their war by removing the groups they believed to be responsible for the collapse: the Jews and the labour movement.[146] Thus, Major Walsh stated that 'the treatment of the Jews within Germany was therefore as much of a plan for aggressive war as was the building of armaments and the conscription of manpower'.[147]

The judges found this connection as unconvincing as future commentators,[148] but this was the way that these crimes against humanity were introduced into court. As a result of these difficult legal maneuvers some victims' accounts were able to be heard in court and documents about crimes against humanity were assembled, which later formed the basis of historical work on the Holocaust.[149] But the IMT was not attempting to describe these crimes in the way they are now understood.

Instead, it was unwavering in its efforts to fit the events of the Nazi period into an overarching story of aggressive war. Nor was this just any aggressive war that the court described – it was an aggressive *colonial* war, and the crimes it produced were shown to be the consequences of imperialism. I should acknowledge that historians and genocide scholars have shown some interest in the relationship between colonialism and Nazi expansion. They have pointed out that European colonialism and Nazism deployed 'fundamentally similar' concepts of space and race,[150] that they practiced warfare in the same ruthless manner[151] and they treated subjugated people in a similar way.[152] These historians have also pointed out that the Nazis perceived their war as a colonial war within Europe,[153] a war which they explicitly compared to the European conquest of the Americas.[154]

146 Major William F Walsh, speaking, in ibid., vol III, 519.

147 Ibid., vol III, 520; Jackson, closing statement, in ibid., vol XIX, 419.

148 Douglas, *The Memory of Judgment*, n 11, 49.

149 Lawrence Douglas, 'History, Memory and Crimes against Humanity: A Response to Todorov' (2000–2001) 128/129 *Salmagundi* 320, 322; Simpson, n 22, 91.

150 Jürgen Zimmerer, 'Colonialism and the Holocaust: Towards an Archaeology of Genocide' (2008) 50 *Development Dialogue* 95, 99.

151 Enzo Traverso, *The Origins of Nazi Violence* (Janet Lloyd trans, New Press, 2003) 19.

152 Shelley Baranowski, *Nazi Empire: German Colonialism and Imperialism from Bismarck to Hitler* (Cambridge University Press, 2011) 237.

153 David Furber and Wendy Lower, 'Colonialism and Genocide in Nazi-Occupied Poland and Ukraine' in A Dirk Moses (ed), *Empire, Colony, Genocide: Conquest, Occupation, and Subaltern Resistance in World History* (Berghahn Books, 2008) 373.

154 Traverso, n 151, 19.

These arguments have generated some objections,[155] which I cannot engage with here. It is interesting, however, to note that this recent historiography does cause some disquiet[156] – as do the older statements of Césaire[157] and Fanon[158] – about the relationship between Nazism and colonialism. Yet, at the same time, there exists at the IMT – a forum which has been posited as a centre of Western law – an unproblematised account of the Nazi war and occupation as a colonial war.

The language of imperialism and the critique of colonialism is a constant through the trial. It is constantly reiterated by the prosecution and evidenced by German documents. Rudenko, for example, described the war as predatory German imperialism against freedom-loving nations.[159] And it was not just the Soviets who used this language – the French also described themselves as the victims of wars launched by German imperialism.[160] The prosecution and judges referred repeatedly to a Nazi document that they declared was essential evidence of Nazi imperial aims.[161] This document describes the need to form a German empire:

> We live in a period of economic empires, in which the tendency to colonies, again approaches the condition which originally motivated colonization; in Japan and Italy economic motives are the basis of their will to expand, and economic need will also drive Germany to it.
>
> The history of all times – Roman Empire, British Empire – has proved that every space expansion can only be effected by breaking resistance and taking risks. Even set-backs are unavoidable; neither formerly nor today has space been found without an owner; the attacker always comes up against the proprietor.[162]

The prosecution described the imperial ambitions of the Nazi regime and the colonising nature of their occupation in all the invaded countries. The French prosecution described German measures in Alsace Lorraine which were aimed at Germanization (the destruction of the national

155 See Thomas Kühne, 'Colonialism and the Holocaust: Continuities, Causations, and Complexities' (2013) 15 *Journal of Genocide Research* 339, 342.

156 See Zimmerer, n 150, 97, for a discussion of the discomfort this debate causes.

157 Aimé Césaire, *Discourse on Colonialism* (Joan Pinkham trans, Monthly Review Press, 1972) 36.

158 Frantz Fanon, *The Wretched of the Earth* (Richard Philcox trans, Grove Press, 1963) 236.

159 Rudenko, opening statement, in *Trial of the Major War Criminals*, n 5, vol VII, 158.

160 Ibid., vol V, 368.

161 Ibid., vol II, 266.

162 See, for example, ibid., vol II, 266; repeated again at vol III, 201; repeated in *Judgment of the International Military Tribunal at Nuremberg* (30 September 1946) at vol XXII, 431.

character) and, as a separate matter, measures of agricultural and industrial colonisation.[163]

In other areas, the prosecution stated that the Nazis planned to transform the Baltic states into part of the Greater German Reich through colonisation by Germans and removal of undesirables,[164] and it described the conversion of the Crimea, an area north of the Crimea, the Volga territory, and the district around Baku into German colonies.[165]

The prosecution and judges described an even more extreme plan of colonisation in the East: the destruction of native populations for the purpose of German colonisation and spoliation. As Shawcross put it:

> Their aims went beyond mere Germanization, the imposition of the German cultural pattern upon other peoples. Hitler was resolved to expel non-Germans from the soil he required but that they owned, and colonize it by Germans.[166]

In Poland, the prosecution explained, the Nazis planned to create German settlements to engulf the native Polish population and accelerate Germanization.[167] It quoted a German document stating: 'Poland shall be treated as a colony; the Poles shall be the slaves of the Greater German World Empire'.[168] In the Soviet Union, the prosecution showed, the plan was to destroy the Russian population altogether to ensure that only Germans should inhabit the East.[169] The judgment summarises this account:

> The foregoing crimes against the civilian population are sufficiently appalling, and yet the evidence shows that at any rate in the East, the mass murders and cruelties were not committed solely for the purpose of stamping out opposition or resistance to the German occupying forces. In Poland and the Soviet Union these crimes were part of a plan to get rid of whole native populations by expulsion and annihilation, in order that their territory could be used for colonization by Germans.[170]

Thus, the war crimes described were not just a normal part of aggressive war – they were also a crucial part of the colonial undertaking. The

[163] See, for example, ibid., vol VI, 438, 473.
[164] Ibid., vol III, 357.
[165] Ibid., vol IV, 549.
[166] Ibid., vol XIX, 495.
[167] Ibid., vol III, 575.
[168] Office of United States Chief of Counsel for the Prosecution of Axis Criminality, n 141, vol 1,1025.
[169] *Trial of the Major War Criminals*, n 5, vol VII, 338; *Judgment of the International Military Tribunal at Nuremberg* (30 September 1946) at vol XXII, 480.
[170] *Judgment of the International Military Tribunal at Nuremberg* (30 September 1946) in ibid., vol XXII, 480.

prosecution, the judges and the Nazi documents they cited showed that this undertaking was partly motivated by the desire to obtain space for German settlement, but they also stated that it was motivated by the desire to achieve the additional economic benefits that were understood to flow from colonisation. This combination of aims is shown in the trial through a variety of German documents:

> In the East, Germany is carrying on a three-fold war: a war for the destruction of Bolshevism, a war for the destruction of the greater Russian Empire, and finally a war for the acquisition of colonial territory for colonizing purposes and economic exploitation.[171]

The much-cited document mentioned above, discussing German colonial aims, also stressed that this was a war for an *economic* empire, encouraged by economic motives and economic needs.[172]

The trials represent these economic motives in terms which reflect the economic critique of imperialism that was current between the wars. The prosecution describes the German aims of 'economic spoliation' – by which it means the plans to plunder public and private property and, in general, exploit the people and natural resources of occupied countries.[173] The prosecutors also frequently refer to the acquisition of raw materials[174] and resources.[175] The attack on the Soviet Union, in particular, was described as having a 'materialistic' basis – the compulsion to steal food and raw material:[176]

> This war is not a war for a throne nor an altar; this is a war for grain and bread, a war for a well-laden breakfast, dinner, and supper table ... a war for raw materials, for rubber, iron, and ore.[177]

Another cited German document outlines the Nazi plans:

> Seen from a long range point of view the newly-occupied eastern areas will be exploited economically from the point of view of colonial administration and by colonial methods.[178]

171 Office of United States Chief of Counsel for the Prosecution of Axis Criminality, n 141, vol 1, 1051.
172 *Trial of the Major War Criminals*, n 55, vol II, 265.
173 Office of United States Chief of Counsel for the Prosecution of Axis Criminality, n 141, vol 1, 1023–4.
174 *Trial of the Major War Criminals*, n 5, vol II, 264.
175 Ibid., vol III, 345, 366, 574.
176 Ibid., vol III, 366; vol VII, 246.
177 Ibid., vol VII, 168.
178 Office of United States Chief of Counsel for the Prosecution of Axis Criminality, n 141, vol 1, 1049.

Other documents were submitted to show German plans to treat Poland as a colony and to administer it through 'ruthless exploitation'.[179]

The Tribunal described this decision to carry out the economic spoliation of newly won territory, along colonial lines, as underpinning some of the Nazi crimes that it considered most abhorrent: the planned starvation in the Soviet Union and the programme of slave labour. The prosecution and the judges outlined the Nazi plan to take all the food and raw material from 'the south and southeast of the Soviet Union, over and above the needs of the Nazi invading forces and leaving the absolute minimum necessary to supply the bare needs of the people in these particular regions'.[180] They did this, the prosecution and judges pointed out, knowing clearly that the result would be the starving to death of millions of people.[181] This plan, aimed at plundering the economic resources of the region and leaving it empty for German settlement, is described in *Nazi Aggression and Conspiracy* as a 'program of premeditated murder on a scale so vast as to stagger human imagination'.[182]

The use of slave labour from occupied countries is also represented as a colonial and an economic project. The prosecution and judges describe it as a terrible crime:

> And is the world to overlook the revival of slavery in Europe, slavery on a scale which involved 7 million men, women, and children taken from their homes, treated as beasts, starved, beaten, and murdered?[183]

This crime served the regime's colonial aims by helping it to destroy or weaken other peoples.[184] It is also, however, described throughout the trials and judgment as an extreme example of the economic benefits of colonialism and economic spoliation. It was, the judges said, conceived by the German government as an integral part of the war economy.[185]

In this way, the IMT told, as it had intended to tell, a history about the dangers of aggressive, imperialist war. The history it told understood and presented the dangers of imperialism in a certain way – as an economic

179 Ibid., vol 1, 1025.

180 Ibid., vol 1, 1041.

181 *Trial of the Major War Criminals*, n 5, vol III, 366.

182 Office of United States Chief of Counsel for the Prosecution of Axis Criminality, n 141, vol 1, 1046.

183 See, for example, Shawcross, closing statement, in *Trial of the Major War Criminals*, n 5, vol XIX, 434.

184 See, for example, Mr Dodd, speaking, in ibid., vol III, 404. See also at vol IV, 391.

185 *Judgment of the International Military Tribunal at Nuremberg* (30 September 1946) in ibid., vol XXII, 490.

regime that led to war and war crimes. As such, the narrative related at Nuremberg echoes the narratives found in the contemporary literature about imperialism – even to the point of highlighting the economic effects of imperialism over the suffering of victims. It is not a story that satisfies the sensibility or fulfils the expectations of later observers, but it did fit into the narratives and ethical framework of the time.

3.6 Conclusion

The history told by the IMT is criticised today for failing to present crimes against humanity properly, for failing to hear the voices of victims, for failing to properly represent the Holocaust and the Second World War. Most of all, perhaps, it is criticised for not being the exemplar of enlightened law and truth that we presume it was intended to be. These failures are either seen as incomprehensible or they are attributed to the legal constraints of the IMT and the political interests of its members.

I would suggest that the legal and historiographical 'failures' of the IMT are not due to these factors but rather due to the prevalence of a particular narrative about the evils of imperialism as an economic institution that led to war and suffering. This narrative was spoken by Marxists, and strengthened by the Bolshevik revolution, but it was also related by influential thinkers and lawyers who did not subscribe to Marxism. The influence of this narrative can be seen most clearly in the stories, decisions and conclusions of the IMT that seem most peculiar today. Indeed, the IMT could actually be described as being extremely successful in translating this narrative and this sensibility into law and history.

The importance of the anti-imperialist narrative at Nuremberg shows that even at the heart of international law not all narratives tell the Enlightenment history we expect to find, and not all ethics come from the liberal sources we anticipate. Nuremberg might have told a story about civilisation and the liberal values of legality and reason, but it also spoke about imperialism and economic exploitation in terms that recall Marxist thought and the Bolshevik Revolution.

It was this account of imperialism that was powerful enough to indirectly bring crimes against humanity into law. It did so by presenting crimes against peace as so ethically and politically wrong that it was possible to change international law to prohibit them. This meant that crimes against humanity were not introduced into international law with the prominence contemporary lawyers think they should be owed, nor in the form they now have. Nevertheless, they were introduced, and once the term was in positive law it was available to be changed later to suit a new theory and a new ethical environment, and ultimately shift the nature of international law.

PART II

Institutions and Orders

4

Excluding Revolutionary States

Mexico, Russia and the League of Nations

ALISON DUXBURY*

4.1 Introduction

In his opening address at the Paris Peace Conference, the president of France welcomed the assembled nations and introduced the idea of the League of Nations with these stirring words:

> You do not intend this International Association to be directed against anybody in future; it will not of set purpose shut out anybody; but, having been organized by the nations that have sacrificed themselves in defense of right ... it will lay down conditions to which its present or future adherents will submit ...
>
> By establishing this new order of things, you will meet the aspirations of humanity, which, after the frightful convulsions of these bloodstained years, ardently wishes to feel itself protected by a union of free peoples against the ever-possible revivals of primitive savagery.[1]

With these phrases the president spoke of the Allied Powers' plan to establish a new organisation – one based on the principles of universality and freedom. Nevertheless, while this association would not 'shut out anybody', it was clear that the terms of its creation would be dictated by a limited group – the delegates of the states who would constitute the Commission on the League of Nations. Of course, the leaders who heard this address on 18 January 1919 were by no means representative of the international community. The most notable absences were the former enemy powers, but there were others not present at the meeting in Paris, including Russia and Mexico. While the absence of the former was keenly

* Professor at Melbourne Law School.

[1] *Foreign Relations of the United States*, The Paris Peace Conference, 1919, vol III (Government Printing Office, 1943) Document 3, Preliminary Peace Conference: Protocol No 1, Session of January 18, 1919.

felt by the Allied Powers, and the 'Russian question' was the subject of much discussion, the lack of an invitation to Mexico, as a neutral power, did not excite the same interest, at least in the formal discussions.[2]

Neither Mexico nor Russia were officially represented at the Peace Conference[3] – one because of its policy of neutrality during the war, the other because it had concluded a peace treaty with Germany in March 1918.[4] In that context it is not surprising that both were omitted from the list of original members of the League. In the case of Russia, the reason was clear – Lord Robert Cecil, a representative of the British Empire on the Commission, proposed that 'definitely untrustworthy and hostile States should be excluded' from the League.[5] This phrasing was originally directed at Russia 'should the Bolshevik Government remain in power'.[6] These sentiments were shared by other leaders, including President Woodrow Wilson and Prime Minister Lloyd George – the latter was concerned about the 'spirit of revolution' in Europe and viewed the League as an alternative to 'Bolshevism'.[7] Mexico's omission from the list of original members has been attributed to a number of factors, including the non-recognition of the Carranza government by Britain and France at the time of the Peace Conference.[8] However, the exclusion of Mexico and Russia from original membership did not prevent their subsequent admission by invitation – a process that was outside the organisation's usual practice. Consequently, there were many similarities in the position of these two revolutionary states vis-à-vis the League:

[2] The impact of Russia on the Peace Conference is examined in John M Thompson, *Russia, Bolshevism, and the Versailles Peace* (Princeton University Press, 1967).

[3] Mexico was unofficially represented in Paris by Alberto J Pani. Members of a Russian delegation led by Prince L'vov were invited to appear before some commissions at the Conference. For a discussion of the various claims to Russian representation in Paris and the Allied Powers' approach to these claims, see ibid., 62–81.

[4] The Treaty of Brest–Litovsk (1918). This treaty was subsequently abrogated by Article 116 of the Treaty of Versailles (1919): *Treaty of Peace between the Allied and Associated Powers and Germany*, signed 28 June 1919, 225 ConTS 188 (entered into force 10 January 1920).

[5] 'The Cecil Plan, January 14, 1919' in David Hunter Miller, *The Drafting of the Covenant* (G P Putnam's Sons, 1928) vol II, 61.

[6] The version of the Cecil Plan included in Miller's collection of drafts of the Covenant notes that an earlier draft specifically included the quoted words: ibid.

[7] See H W V Temperley (ed), *A History of the Peace Conference of Paris* (Frowde, Hodder & Stoughton, 1924) vol VI, 579–80.

[8] Georg Schwarzenberger, *The League of Nations and World Order: A Treatise on the Principle of Universality in the Theory and Practice of the League of Nations* (Constable & Co, 1936) 37.

neither was represented at the Commission on the League of Nations, the membership of both states was originally opposed by others in Paris, both were admitted by the extra-legal process of invitation and, once admitted, each had a seat on the Council – one permanent, the other non-permanent.

The story of the participation of Mexico and Russia in the League of Nations is one of exclusion, inclusion and, in the case of Russia (by then, the USSR), exclusion again. It is also the story of the relationship between revolutionary states and the League – the first international organisation with broad aspirations to 'achieve international peace and security' and universal membership.[9] Consequently, the League was the first international organisation that had to grapple with the question of admission in the context of an article in its constituent instrument providing that if a member resorted to war in breach of the Covenant, 'it shall ipso facto be deemed to have committed an act of war against all other Members of the League'.[10] On that basis, membership could have the (somewhat frightening) 'practical consequence that members may be called on to defend a State which they had refused to recognise'.[11] Finally, it is the story of a certain distrust and wariness in the interactions between international organisations and revolutionary states which continues to this day. Such treatment has included separate and exceptional practices in decisions concerning participation. This chapter will recount these stories and situate the membership of Mexico and Russia in the League in an account of the practice of other international organisations in excluding states with revolutionary governments. The second section examines the process of constituting the League: what factors did the Commission on the League of Nations take into consideration when debating the admission criteria? Why were Mexico and Russia excluded? The third section analyses the interpretation of the membership criteria by the First Assembly, before turning to the admission of Mexico and the USSR. The final section will consider whether this episode (or episodes) in League history represents a forerunner to the way in which the membership of revolutionary states has been treated in other international organisations.

[9] *Treaty of Versailles* pt I, *Covenant of the League of Nations*, preamble.

[10] Ibid., Article 16.

[11] 'First Assembly, Meetings of the Committees, Minutes of the Fifth Committee', *League of Nations Records*, 161 (Viviani, France).

A few points to note at the outset. This discussion takes as its starting point the principle that criteria for admission to an international organisation are important as they not only inform us about the extent of membership but also the aspirations of the organisation.[12] If we accept this proposition, then the when and why of the exclusion and subsequent inclusion of Mexico and Russia in the League are important for determining the future composition and direction of an international peace organisation. Second, the basic premise of this chapter is that the revolutionary status of these two states was important to their treatment with respect to membership in the League. This raises the question of how we should define a 'revolutionary' state.[13] It is not the intention of this chapter to adopt a particular definition of a 'revolution', since on any description the events in Mexico and Russia would suffice. There are other forms of governmental instability, including unconstitutional changes of government such as military coups d'état, that do not meet the profound break signified by a revolution and so are not discussed here. International organisations have certainly punished such types of democratic failure through membership sanctions.[14] Finally, the term 'revolutionary state', rather than 'revolutionary government', is used to describe Mexico and Russia, as states are admitted to membership of international organisations, not governments. The significance of the distinction between a revolutionary state and other governmental change is relevant when analysing the subsequent practice of other international organisations where issues have arisen as to the seating of governments that have assumed power following a revolution.

[12] Clive Archer, *International Organizations* (Routledge, 4th ed, 2015) 41. Archer made this comment when distinguishing between membership criteria in universal and regional organisations.

[13] A note in the *Yale Law Journal* highlights that the concept of revolution is 'not well-defined in international law': see 'Revolutions, Treaties, and State Succession' (1967) 76 *Yale Law Journal*, 1669, 1682. This note identifies the characteristics of a revolution as including: 'a radical change in national policies and identities, and the lack of "legal continuity" between the old and the revolutionary regimes ... usually manifested in fundamental changes in social, economic, or political institutions'. On international law's lack of engagement with the concept of revolution, see Vidya Kumar, 'International Law, Kelsen and the Aberrant Revolution: Excavating the Politics and Practices of Revolutionary Legality in Rhodesia and Beyond' in Nikolas M Rajkovic, Tanja Aalberts and Thomas Gammeltoft-Hansen (eds), *The Power of Legality: Practices of International Law and Their Politics* (Cambridge University Press, 2018) 157, 158–60.

[14] See Alison Duxbury, *The Participation of States in International Organisations: The Role of Human Rights and Democracy* (Cambridge University Press, 2011) 172–214, 255–63.

4.2 Constituting the League of Nations

4.2.1 The Question of Membership in the Establishment of the League

The question of the composition of a future organisation devoted to international peace and security was debated by a number of societies during the First World War. Proposals for a post-War League were drafted by groups such as the British League of Nations Society and the Fabian Society in the United Kingdom, the Association française pour la Société des Nations in France and the League to Enforce Peace in the United States. Two major concerns regarding the future membership of the League were evidenced in these early proposals: first, the relationship between the Great Powers and smaller states, and second, the involvement of the Central Powers.[15] Despite statements advocating a broad membership in a few of these plans, exclusionary policies were written into the early drafts. Participants in these non-governmental groups used terms such as 'civilised'[16] and 'settled conditions'[17] to describe the character of potential members, with both Russia and Mexico featuring in these discussions. For example, Oppenheim's observations on the plan of the United States' League to Enforce Peace included his belief that states with a 'stable Government' should be invited to join and this would exclude states 'like Mexico' which are 'in the throes of a Civil War'.[18] The Association française pour la Société des Nations described a Society of Nations founded by the Allies with membership being conditioned on the possession of democratic institutions.[19] Russia was not explicitly mentioned in this plan. However, on the other side of the Channel, Woolf rejected democracy as a membership condition on the basis that it would lead to the exclusion of Russia, which the Fabians regarded as having the status of a Great Power.[20]

[15] For a discussion of these early proposals see ibid., 63–6.

[16] British League of Nations Society, *Project of the League of Nations* (1917), reproduced in Florence Wilson, *The Origins of the League Covenant: Documentary History of Its Drafting* (Leonard and Virginia Woolf, 1928) 144–5.

[17] 'Resumé of Discussions at a Private Dinner' in Theodore Marburg, *Development of the League of Nations Idea* (Macmillan, 1932) vol II, 725.

[18] 'Notes by Professor L Oppenheim on the Tentative Plan for the Organisation of the League to Enforce Peace as Submitted by Theodore Marburg' in ibid., 806.

[19] Association française pour la Société des Nations, 'Appel du comité d'initiative' (Georges Cadet, 1918) 7.

[20] Leonard S Woolf, *International Government* (Brentano's, 1916) 108. See also discussion of Article 7 of the Fabian Committee's draft at 383–4.

Prior to the Commission on the League of Nations meeting in Paris, several other proposals were discussed on both sides of the Atlantic. The Phillimore Committee, appointed by Arthur Balfour, Foreign Secretary of the United Kingdom, produced a draft in March 1918 envisaging that only 'Allied States' would be parties to a convention to establish the League.[21] This draft suggested that other states could join in the future but that 'terms' might be imposed.[22] General Jan Smuts' 'practical suggestion' for a League, dated December 1918, took a more universal approach – his position was that 'the league will include a few great Powers, a larger number of medium or intermediate states and a very large number of small states'.[23] Russia featured in Smuts' plan for a League, but as a past empire whose former 'peoples and territories' would be subject to the League's 'right of ultimate disposal'.[24] Central Russia would be a non-permanent member in Smuts' council as an 'important intermediary Power' but was not entitled to a permanent seat as one of the Great Powers.[25]

By the time the Commission on the League of Nations was convened in Paris in February 1919 there were several governmental proposals on the table, including from Britain, France, Italy and the United States.[26] The Italian draft enabled 'any state' whose constitution conformed to certain principles to join the organisation.[27] The French believed that the scope of the League should be 'universal', but that only states with representative institutions that were responsible for the acts of their governments could be admitted.[28] The most advanced proposals were

[21] 'The Phillimore Plan, March 20, 1918', in Miller, n 5, vol II, 3–6.

[22] 'The Phillimore Plan', Article 17, in ibid., 6. Such terms included 'reparations for past outrages' or 'partial disarmament' – clear references to conditions that could be imposed on the (former) enemy states. The Phillimore Committee's interim report is reproduced in Miller, n 5, vol I, 4–8 at 8.

[23] 'The Smuts Plan: The League of Nations: A Practical Suggestion by Lieut-Gen the Rt Hon J C Smuts, P C', in Miller, n 5, vol II, 23, 39.

[24] Ibid., 27.

[25] Ibid., 41.

[26] The Commission on the League of Nations at the Paris Peace Conference included representatives from the British Empire, Belgium, Brazil, China, France, Italy, Japan, Portugal, Serbia and the United States.

[27] 'Draft Scheme for the Constitution of the Society of Nations Submitted by the Italian Delegation' (translation), Annex 3 to the Minutes of First Meeting, Minutes (English) of the Commission on the League of Nations, in Miller, n 5, vol II, 254.

[28] 'Draft Adopted by the French Ministerial Commission for the League of Nations – Statement of the Principles to be taken as Basis of the League of Nations' (translation),

those produced by the British and the Americans – by the time the Commission met, the two plans were combined into one document (the Hurst–Miller draft).[29] Both states recommended limits on membership, with President Wilson's proposal that membership should be restricted to states with 'popular self-government'[30] being the most well known. Terms such as 'independence', 'responsible government', '*pays libres*' and 'democracy' were used by various representatives on the Commission to describe the character of future League members.[31] But Wilson's view that the recognition of democracy was crucial ('if we are ready to fight for this, we should be ready to write it into the covenant') was not necessarily shared by all.[32] Prior to the Paris Conference, in July 1918 Cecil wrote to Colonel House (Wilson's advisor) emphatically rejecting France's attempt to link membership of the League to democracy, arguing that any attempt 'to impose on all the nations of the world a form of government which has been indeed admirably successful in America [and Britain] . . . shall plant the seeds of very serious international trouble'.[33] At the Commission, Cecil was concerned that the inclusion of self-government as an admission criterion would exclude India, which he described as both 'autocratically governed' ('willingly') and 'democratically administered'.[34]

4.2.2 *The Position of Mexico and Russia*

While terms such as 'self-government' and 'democracy' were used by representatives on the Commission, the question of whether

June 1918, Annex 2 to the Minutes of First Meeting, Minutes (English) of the Commission on the League of Nations, in Miller, n 5, vol II, 239.

29 See Miller, n 5, vol I, 130–2. Hurst and Miller were the legal advisers to the British and US delegations, respectively, at the Paris Peace Conference.

30 See 'Wilson's Second Draft or First Paris Draft, January 10, 1919', Article XII, in Miller, *Drafting of the Covenant*, n 5, vol II, 85; 'Third Meeting (5 February 1919), Minutes of the Commission on the League of Nations' in Miller, n 5, vol II, 260–1.

31 See 'Third Meeting (5 February 1919), Minutes of the Commission on the League of Nations' in Miller, *Drafting of the Covenant*, n 5, vol II, 261; 'Ninth Meeting (13 February 1919), Minutes of the Commission on the League of Nations' in Miller, n 5, vol II, 303; Miller, n 5, vol I, 164–5.

32 Miller, n 5, vol I, 165.

33 'Lord Robert Cecil to Colonel House, London, July 22, 1918' in Charles Seymour, *The Intimate Papers of Colonel House: The Ending of the War* (Houghton Mifflin, 1928) 41.

34 Miller, n 5, vol I, 164.

revolutionary states could satisfy the membership conditions was not explicitly discussed in the abstract. Nevertheless, both Mexico and Russia featured in the drafters' minds at various points, giving us a hint as to where these states would fit (or not) in the new peace organisation. Cecil was in favour of openness to a degree (unlike the French, he was against excluding Germany)[35] but balked at the membership of Bolshevik Russia.[36] British opposition to Soviet Russia was noted in their original draft convention, which concluded with the rather oblique sentence that 'Russia cannot probably be invited to adhere, but it may be advisable to state in a protocol the reasons for this omission'.[37] In private conversations, members of the US delegation expressed their doubts about Russia's willingness to adhere to international agreements.[38] Although the exclusion of Soviet Russia from the League was taken for granted, membership of a different (democratic) Russia was considered desirable.[39] For example, Miller concurred with Cecil's view on Russia's membership and believed that it would 'undoubtedly be welcomed to the League as soon as she has an anti-Bolshevic democratic Government'.[40] In 1919 it was hoped that a democratic Russia led by Admiral Kolchak could join the League, but when his forces were defeated there was no question of membership.[41]

The Commission's distrust of Russia was matched by Soviet suspicion of the League, a view not helped by Allied military interventions in Russia following the revolution.[42] It is reported that the Soviet Foreign Commissar, Chicherin, informed Wilson in October 1918 that Russia would not participate in the League unless the other powers were prepared to adopt 'the expropriation of the capitalists of all countries . . . as

[35] Robert Cecil, *A Great Experiment* (Jonathan Cape, 1941) 85; David Hunter Miller, *My Diary at the Conference of Paris: With Documents* (printed for the author, 1924) vol I, 176–7.

[36] See n 6 and accompanying text.

[37] 'British Draft Convention, 20 January 1919' in Miller, n 5, vol II, 116.

[38] Miller, *My Diary*, n 35, vol I, 206 (conversation between Colonel House and Miller).

[39] Donald I Buzinkai, 'The Bolsheviks, the League of Nations and the Paris Peace Conference, 1919' (1967) 19 *Soviet Studies* 257, 260.

[40] David Hunter Miller, 'Voting in the Assembly of the League of Nations' (9 October 1919) in Miller, *My Diary*, n 35, vol XX, 566.

[41] Kathryn Davis, *The Soviets at Geneva: The USSR and the League of Nations, 1919–1933* (Hyperion Press, 1977) 18.

[42] Ingeborg Plettenberg, 'The Soviet Union and the League of Nations' in *The League of Nations in Retrospect: Proceedings of the Symposium* (Walter de Gruyter, 1982) 144, 147.

another of the basic principles of the League of Nations'.[43] The 1919 May Day Manifesto of the Communist International proclaimed the basic incompatibility between the League and the 'proletarian revolution':

> In Paris the imperialist extortioners are trying to create their own black 'international', the so-called League of Nations. Conscious workers throughout the world know perfectly well that the so-called League of Nations is in fact a league of bourgeois robbers for the oppression of nations, for the division of the world, for the enslavement of the workers, for strangling the proletarian revolution.[44]

Notwithstanding such sentiments, the prospect of Russia with a different government joining in the future was encouraged by members of the Commission. For example, proposed amendments to the draft Covenant included a provision acknowledging the possibility of increasing the membership in the Executive Council to include Russia (and Germany).[45] Thus, while Bolshevik Russia was not considered suitable for membership in 1919 (and in any event, had no intention of joining), the representatives on the Commission still recognised Russia's standing as a Great Power.[46] Despite the mutual antipathy, the Peace Conference did not formally recognise any of the rival representatives for Russia – distaste for the revolutionary regime did not extend to seating any other contender for this position in Paris.[47]

Mexico's status, and the place of Latin America in the Covenant as a whole, was also considered in discussions in Paris. An invitation to the Conference was originally sent to Brazil (it having declared war against the Central Powers in 1917) and then extended to other states in South America.[48] While six Central American states were invited,

[43] Davis, n 41, 16. Davis writes that 'if Wilson ... was favourably impressed with Chicherin's argument he left no answering note or memorandum to that effect'. See further Schwarzenberger, n 8, 81. For Lenin's view of the League, see Temperley, *A History of the Peace Conference*, n 7, 579.

[44] 'Extracts from an ECCI May Day Manifesto' (20 April 1919) in Jane Degras (ed), *The Communist International 1919–1943 Documents* (Oxford University Press, 1956) vol I, 51.

[45] Miller, n 5, vol I, 296; Miller, *My Diary*, n 35, vol XX, 567. See also 'Meetings with the Neutral Powers March 20 and March 21, 1919' in Miller, n 5, vol II, 624.

[46] See also Buzinkai, 'The Bolsheviks', n 39, 22.

[47] See at n 3.

[48] Alan McPherson, 'Anti-Imperialism and the Failure of the League of Nations' in Alan McPherson and Yannick Wehrli (eds), *Beyond Geopolitics: New Histories of Latin America at the League of Nations* (University of New Mexico Press, 2015) 21, 22.

this did not include Mexico.[49] No Latin American states were represented on the Commission, although a number were present at the meeting with the neutral powers in March 1919 where a draft of the Covenant was debated.[50] The discussion surrounding Latin American states and the League was complicated by the insistence of the United States that some form of the Monroe Doctrine should be included in the Covenant. Wilson not only perceived the Monroe Doctrine – originally designed to guard against future European colonisation on the American continent – to be compatible with the Covenant but considered the Covenant as a logical extension of the Doctrine.[51] At the Fourteenth Meeting of the Commission, Wilson sidestepped a push from Larnaude (France) to define the Monroe Doctrine and instead spoke of the need to reject 'any understanding which infringed upon the territorial integrity or political independence of any State' as inconsistent with the Covenant.[52] Larnaude was opposed to explicit reference to the Doctrine, labelling it as 'unnecessary' and therefore 'dangerous'.[53] Alberto Pani, Mexico's unofficial observer at the Paris Conference, also viewed the Doctrine's inclusion as problematic, potentially signalling US hegemony in the region.[54] Both Carranza and Mexico's foreign minister expressed their disapproval, stating that the Doctrine was not recognised by the Mexican government.[55] Although the Monroe Doctrine was hotly debated at the Commission,[56] a direct link between Mexico's omission and Wilson's desire to include a version of the Monroe Doctrine in the Covenant is difficult to draw. For example, Miller's notes from the Eleventh

[49] Ibid.

[50] See 'Meetings with the Neutral Powers March 20 and March 21, 1919' in Miller, n 5, vol II, 592–4.

[51] The Monroe Doctrine was discussed at the 'Fourteenth Meeting (April 10, 1919), Minutes of the Commission on the League of Nations' in Miller, n 5, vol II, 369–74. For discussion of the evolution of the Monroe Doctrine see Mark T Gilderhus, 'Wilson, Carranza, and the Monroe Doctrine: A Question in Regional Organization' (1983) 7 *Diplomatic History* 103.

[52] 'Fourteenth Meeting (April 10, 1919), Minutes of the Commission on the League of Nations' in Miller, n 5, vol II, 371.

[53] Ibid., 372.

[54] Gilderhus, n 51, 114.

[55] Ibid., 115; Philip Marshall Brown, 'Mexico and the Monroe Doctrine' (1932) 26 *American Journal of International Law* 117, 117.

[56] See Miller, *My Diary*, n 35, vol I, 242–4.

Meeting, when the membership provision was discussed, refer to both Mexico's exclusion and the Monroe Doctrine:

Cecil proposes amendments – as in text.
Portuguese suggests amendment which Cecil sits on.
Larnaude explains to Bourgeois.
Orlando overcome with laughter.
Cecil excepts Mexico.
Violent discussion by Hymans, W.W. and Cecil.
. . .
I handed Colonel House a copy of my Monroe Doctrine (amendment) marked M.D.[57]

When matching Miller's notes with the Commission's Minutes, it is not clear why Orlando was overcome with laughter, although we know that the 'violent' discussions between Belgium, the United States and Britain were concerned with whether any of the neutrals should be 'deemed "original" members'.[58] Despite the final reference in Miller's notes to the Monroe Doctrine, the minutes to this meeting do not indicate that it was a topic of discussion or that its inclusion in the Covenant would prevent Mexico's membership.

Britain and the United States' views of Mexico were not as strongly expressed as their opposition towards Soviet Russia. Nevertheless, they both considered that Mexico could not be a founding member. In this respect Cecil displayed the greatest obstinacy towards Mexico.[59] The British Draft Convention provided that invitations to join the League should be issued to Latin American states not represented at the Peace Conference 'except Mexico, Hayti, Santo Domingo, and any other State which, in the opinion of the United States, may be considered unready for membership'.[60] The possibility that Mexico and the other two Latin American states might join in the future was, however, conceded in this draft.[61] When representatives on the Commission debated the possibility

[57] Miller, n 5, vol I, 318–19 (footnote omitted).

[58] Ibid., 317. Hymans (Belgium) 'thought that the honour of having been the founders of the League of Nations should be reserved for those States which had participated in the War'. Wilson believed that 'it was best to avoid giving the League the appearance of an alliance between victorious belligerents': see 'Eleventh Meeting (March 22, 1919), Minutes of the Commission on the League of Nations' in Miller, n 5, vol II, 341.

[59] Malbone W Graham, *The League of Nations and the Recognition of States* (University of California Press, 1933) 50.

[60] 'British Draft Convention, January 20, 1919, with Notes' in Miller, n 5, vol II, 116.

[61] The draft convention noted the possibility of applying for membership at a later stage.

of admitting the neutral powers there was no explicit mention of Mexico.[62] Miller wrote a memorandum for President Wilson in April 1919 highlighting that Cecil was 'quite opposed to the inclusion of Mexico', whereas Robert Lansing (a member of the US delegation) was in favour.[63] Miller suggested to Wilson that an invitation to the present government of Mexico would constitute recognition of the government of Venustiano Carranza by France and Britain.[64] When the matter was taken to Wilson, he replied: 'I think on the whole it would be wise not to include any one of these three states in the invitation'.[65] Thus, the non-recognition of the government of Mexico by Britain and France has been described 'as an excuse' for excluding them from the list.[66]

At the time of the League's establishment, the practice of non-recognition of revolutionary governments was certainly not new.[67] What was new in the context of the League was the relationship between non-recognition and membership of an international organisation. Neither the Carranza nor the Soviet governments were recognised by some (or all) members of the Commission – and in both cases, the failure to recognise was linked to the character of the two governments.[68] Britain's non-recognition of Carranza was motivated by its revolutionary status and its attitude to foreign investments – as described by León, the 'ominous nationalist politics' contained in the 1917 Mexican

[62] See 'Ninth Meeting, February 13, 1919' in Miller, n 5, vol II, 303–4. Miller notes that 'no allusion' was made to Mexico or Costa Rica at the meeting and the fact that they did not have diplomatic relations with some of the Powers: see at vol I, 227.

[63] Miller, *My Diary*, n 35, vol VIII, 308. See also at vol I, 241. Lansing's support is not surprising – as Secretary of State he played a crucial role in brokering US recognition of Carranza in 1915: Louis G Kahle, 'Robert Lansing and the Recognition of Venustiano Carranza' (1958) 38 *Hispanic American Historical Review* 353.

[64] Miller, *My Diary*, n 35, vol VIII, 308.

[65] Ibid., 309.

[66] Schwarzenberger, *The League of Nations*, n 8, 37. Brown states that the British government was 'holding out for guarantees' with respect to the rights of foreigners before recognising Carranza and was 'startled' by US recognition in 1915. See Jonathan C Brown, *Oil and Revolution in Mexico* (University of California Press, 1993) 246.

[67] Frederick Arnold Middlebush, 'Non-recognition as a Sanction of International Law' (1933) 27 *Proceedings of the American Society of International Law* 40.

[68] Anderson notes that the reason for President Wilson's failure to recognise the Soviet government was on the basis that 'it did not have the sanction of the Russian people' and 'refused to respect its international obligations': Chandler P Anderson, 'Recognition of Russia' (1934) 28 *American Journal of International Law* 90.

Constitution.[69] But, as León notes, there were other relevant factors, not least Mexico's 'questionable neutrality' during the war.[70] As a result, two revolutionary states – Russia and Mexico – were excluded from original membership of the League. Their revolutionary status was an important factor in their exclusion, but it is difficult to disentangle their governmental status from their absence at Paris as a result of their war experience – one as a neutral, the other due to its decision to sign a peace treaty with the enemy.[71]

4.3 Interpreting Article 1 of the Covenant

4.3.1 The Relevance of Stability and Recognition

The thorny questions surrounding the admission of individual entities to the League were finally resolved by the adoption of Article 1 of the Covenant. The text drew a distinction between original members (not subject to any conditions), who were included in a list annexed to the Covenant, and future applicants, who had to satisfy the Assembly that they were 'fully self-governing'.[72] The Commission did not explicitly deal with the relationship between recognition and membership, nor the

[69] Fabián Herrera León, 'Latin America and the League of Nations' in *Oxford Research Encyclopaedia of Latin American History* (Oxford University Press, 2016) 2. See also Fabián Herrera León, 'La Sociedad de Naciones y el Problema del Distanciamiento Mexicano: la Misón Internacional de Julián Nogueira en Mexico, Agosto-Septiembre de 1923' (2013) 57 *Revista de Estudios Historicos* 125, 128–35.

[70] León, 'Latin America and the League of Nations', n 69, 2. Mexico remained formally neutral during the First World War but did approach Germany during the conflict. In January 1917, the German foreign minister, Arthur Zimmerman, sent a telegram proposing an alliance between Germany and Mexico. The 'Zimmerman telegram', as it is known, was intercepted and deciphered by the British, who sent it to the United States: see John Womack Jr, 'The Mexican Revolution, 1910–1920' in Leslie Bethall (ed), *The Cambridge History of Latin America* (Cambridge University Press, 1986) vol V, 79, 126–30.

[71] Clemenceau was bitter about Russia's signing of the Treaty of Brest-Litovsk as he believed the decision imposed additional burdens on France: see Thompson, n 2, 80.

[72] *Covenant of the League of Nations* Article 1 provided that:

> A fully self-governing State, Dominion or Colony ... may become a member of the League on a two-thirds vote of the Assembly, provided that it shall give effective guarantees of its sincere intention to observe its international obligations, and shall accept such regulations as may be prescribed by the League in regard to its military, naval and air forces and armaments.

status of revolutionary states. Implicitly, however, such states were perceived to be outside the organisation, although the reasons for exclusion were many. When it came to the interpretation of the new admission conditions at the First Assembly, two issues could have consequences for the future membership of revolutionary states: the need for a stable government, and recognition. When deliberating on the membership applications in the Fifth Committee of the First Assembly, there was no general discussion of the meaning of 'self-governing' in the Covenant, or of the question whether recognition (or non-recognition) was determinative of admission.[73] Instead, each application was examined on a case-by-case basis. A questionnaire devised for the sub-committees charged with considering each applicant required them to investigate whether a government was recognised de jure or de facto by other states, whether the applicant had a 'stable government' and whether it was 'fully self-governing'.[74] Although the relationship between recognition and membership was debated at the Fifth Committee with a variety of views being expressed,[75] when the plenary meeting of the First Assembly deliberated on the membership applications, Huneeus (Chile) affirmed the Committee's decision to leave to one side the question of recognition, emphasising that 'we did not allow legal considerations to hamper us'.[76]

In interpreting the admission conditions the Fifth Committee used a number of terms to describe the attributes of prospective members, including a 'stable' government (Austria and Bulgaria),[77] the inhabitants' 'desire to live under a democratic regime' (Austria)[78] and a 'freely governed' state (Luxembourg).[79] Discussions surrounding two applications for admission at the First Assembly potentially had implications for

[73] Such an approach was rejected by Cecil (South Africa) in the Fifth Committee: see 'First Assembly, Meetings of the Committees, Minutes of the Fifth Committee', *League of Nations Records*, 157, 161.

[74] Ibid., 159.

[75] Cecil believed that admission did not affect 'the liberty of action of individual states', whereas Politis (Greece) suggested that 'admission might imply *de jure* recognition by all Members of the League': ibid., 157.

[76] 'First Assembly, Plenary Meetings', *League of Nations Records*, 561. Friedlander noted that the political atmosphere in the First Assembly 'tended to blur subtle juristic arguments': Lilian M Friedlander, 'The Admission of States to the League of Nations' (1928) 9 *British Yearbook of International Law* 84, 87.

[77] 'First Assembly, Meetings of the Committees, Minutes of the Fifth Committee', *League of Nations Records*, 163, 169.

[78] Ibid., 167.

[79] Ibid., 184.

the admission of revolutionary states in the future (although neither would have met that description): Costa Rica and the Ukraine. The report on Costa Rica alluded to the fact that in 1919 'certain States' had not recognised a government they regarded as based on military force.[80] In contrast, by the date of the First Assembly, the election of a new president was noted with approval.[81] There was no opposition to Costa Rica's admission at the Plenary Meeting, but Restrepo (Colombia) used the debates to remind the Assembly that although Costa Rica was 'ostracised' in Paris because the government was not recognised by the United States following a coup d'état, such events 'were not rare in South America and in Africa; it also, sometimes, happens in Europe'.[82] He contrasted the former situation of Costa Rica, under General Tinoco, with the current 'orderly and civilised Government'.[83] Thus, although coups were not rare, stability was a legal and a moral imperative when it came to admission to the League. Ukraine's application for admission was treated less favourably. The application was brought by the (unrecognised) London Diplomatic Mission of the Ukrainian National Republic (UNR), led by Simon Petlyoura, who was in exile in Poland at the time.[84] Previously, the Ukrainian Republic had unsuccessfully attempted to gain representation at the Paris Peace Conference and membership of the League – this attempt suggested a desire for both individual recognition from states at the Conference as well as collective recognition from the future organisation.[85] Despite the members' opposition to Russia, and the fact that the UNR was the rival to a Bolshevist government in the Ukraine, the subcommittee tasked with considering the application at the First Assembly could not 'conscientiously affirm ... that the Government of Petlyoura is a stable Government'.[86] Notwithstanding their dislike of revolutionary regimes,

[80] 'Report of Sub-Committee Vc on the Admission of Armenia, Azerbaijan, Costa Rica, Georgia and the Ukraine', ibid., 218, 220.

[81] Ibid.

[82] 'First Assembly, Plenary Meetings', *League of Nations Records*, 583.

[83] Ibid.

[84] The Mission's pleas for recognition can be found in its weekly bulletin, *The Ukraine*, issue 1 (5 July 1919) 1–2. British policy towards the UNR and its desire for an independent Ukraine was complicated by British support for the White Russian General Deniken who was unlikely to approve of Ukrainian independence: see David Saunders, 'Britain and the Ukrainian Question (1912–1920)' (1988) 103 *English Historical Review* 40, 65–7.

[85] Graham, *The League of Nations*, n 59, 8–9.

[86] 'Annex 3: Report of Sub-Committee Vc on the Admission of Armenia, Azerbaijan, Costa Rica, Georgia and the Ukraine' in 'First Assembly, Meetings of the Committees, Minutes of the Fifth Committee', *League of Nations Records*, 222.

there was simply no appetite for admitting an entity that was not stable, was recognised by few and did not have control of its territory.[87]

4.3.2 *The Admission of Mexico and Russia*

Whether Mexico would become a member of the League in the future was not raised at the First Assembly. Nevertheless, when discussing Costa Rica's application, Huneeus took the opportunity to affirm his desire to see all Latin American states included in the League.[88] In any event, while the First Assembly was debating the membership applications in November 1920, Carranza declared that Mexico would not enter the League as the organisation was not based on principles of equality.[89] Although Russia was not an applicant in the First Assembly, its spectre was still felt by the representatives. When discussing membership, Motta (Switzerland) took the opportunity to describe Russia as a nation 'in a state of ferment' with leaders who 'hate us', although at the same time he called for the League to attain a 'universal character'.[90] Similarly, Viviani (France) decried the Bolshevist's 'mockery' of the League and the lack of democracy and universal suffrage in Russia.[91] These passionate statements were not articulated in terms of the criteria in Article 1 and demonstrated that distrust of the regime had not abated. Russia again made an appearance (at least in the minds of the representatives) at the Second Assembly, when Balfour (British Empire) doubted whether members 'would regard the addition of Bolshevik Russia as an improvement to the League of Nations'.[92]

Despite the presence of the admission criteria in the Covenant, over the years the League moved away from the practice of 'homogenous universality', whereby the League only comprised 'communities of a certain constitutional structure', to one of 'heterogenous universality' as more states were admitted to the organisation.[93] The admission of Mexico and Russia in the 1930s further evidenced this push towards a

[87] See 'First Assembly, Meetings of the Committees, Minutes of the Fifth Committee', *League of Nations Records*, 174.

[88] 'First Assembly, Plenary Meetings', *League of Nations Records*, 583.

[89] See León, 'La Sociedad de Naciones', n 69, 134.

[90] 'First Assembly, Plenary Meetings', *League of Nations Records*, 572–3.

[91] Ibid., 575.

[92] 'Second Assembly, Meetings of the Committees, First Committee', *League of Nations Records*, 6.

[93] See Schwarzenberger, *The League of Nations*, n 8, 175–6.

truly universal organisation. Both states were admitted by invitation – a procedure which sidestepped the prospect of the Committee examining and debating their respective abilities to fulfil the Article 1 requirements.[94] A 1931 resolution proposed that 'Mexico be invited to accede . . . as though it had been invited from the outset'.[95] The resolution referred to Mexico's 'omission' from the Annex of original members to the Covenant as something 'wholly contrary to its true spirit'.[96] This choice of wording almost suggests an oversight in the original Annex which needed to be rectified, but of course, as discussions in Paris in 1919 demonstrate, Mexico's omission was not an oversight. The use of the invitation was a departure from previous precedents[97] and was far removed from Motta's conviction, expressed in the First Assembly, that the League 'does not solicit anybody'.[98]

In the Assembly debate on the invitation, no member spoke out against the admission of Mexico, with numerous delegates attesting to the importance of universality as a means of enabling the League to fulfil its objectives.[99] Indeed, Cecil showed the greatest conversion to Mexico's membership, describing it as 'one of the most ancient and one of the most influential of the States of the American continent'.[100] Cecil spoke of the need to correct the omission in Paris for which he acknowledged he was, in part ('I suppose') responsible.[101] While most representatives diplomatically skated over the reasons for Mexico's omission from the original list, not so Restrepo. As at the First Assembly, he claimed that Latin American countries were sometimes criticised for 'always having

94 Duxbury, *The Participation of States,* n 14, 80.

95 'Records of the Twelfth Ordinary Session of the Assembly, Second Plenary Meeting' (1931) *League of Nations Official Journal,* Special Supplement 93, 35. García references an earlier invitation to join the League from the Latin American members. This was refused by Alberto J Pani (as foreign minister) who viewed the failure to include Mexico with the other neutral powers at Paris as a matter of national dignity: see Itzel Toledo García, 'The Dilemma of Revolution and Stabilisation: Mexico and the European Powers in the Obregón–Calles Era, 1920–28' (PhD dissertation, University of Essex, 2016) 79.

96 'Records of the Twelfth Ordinary Session of the Assembly, Second Plenary Meeting' (1931) *League of Nations Official Journal,* Special Supplement 93, 35.

97 Manley O Hudson, 'Mexico's Admission to Membership of the League of Nations' (1932) *American Journal of International Law,* 114, 116.

98 'First Assembly, Plenary Meetings', *League of Nations Records,* 572.

99 'Records of the Twelfth Ordinary Session of the Assembly, Second Plenary Meeting' (1931) *League of Nations Official Journal,* Special Supplement 93, 35–6.

100 Ibid., 35.

101 Ibid.

revolutions'.[102] He blamed Wilson's adherence to the Monroe Doctrine for Mexico's exclusion, and attributed to Wilson the view that 'in the interests of pacification in South America, we should refuse to recognise Governments which were the outcome of revolutionary movements, coup d'état … or military plots'.[103] In Restrepo's words, now that a stable government had been established and 'calm reigns' in Mexico (for 'the present time'), it should be admitted.[104] In accepting the invitation to join the League, Mexico again highlighted its opposition to the Monroe Doctrine stating that it had 'never recognized the regional understanding mentioned in Article 21 of the Covenant'.[105] As stated previously, it is difficult to find support for Restrepo's claim that the inclusion of the Monroe Doctrine in the Covenant led directly to the exclusion of Mexico, at least in discussions surrounding the Commission on the League of Nations. While the impact of the Monroe Doctrine on Mexico's omission from the Annex can be debated, the Colombian representative's comments in 1931 confirm the reasons for the 'oversight' – Mexico's exclusion may have been a mistake, but it was a mistake with a message to revolutionary states.

In 1933 Graham viewed the admission of Mexico at the Twelfth Assembly as potentially marking a turning point whereby admission would become a juridical rather than a political process, governed by the criteria in the Covenant, instead of 'the political grounds which [originally] kept Mexico out of the League'.[106] In this respect, Graham's language mimics the question submitted to the International Court of Justice fifteen years later in the *First Admissions Case*, when the General Assembly of the United Nations requested an advisory opinion on whether a UN member was juridically entitled to make its consent to admission dependent on conditions not provided in the membership provision in Article 4(1) of the Charter of the United Nations.[107] Graham would no doubt have supported the International Court of Justice's

[102] 'Records of the Twelfth Ordinary Session of the Assembly, Second Plenary Meeting' (1931) *League of Nations Official Journal*, Special Supplement 93, 37.

[103] Ibid.

[104] Ibid.

[105] Despite this statement, the League's Council noted that Mexico had agreed 'without reservation to enter the League on the terms announced'. See Brown, n 55, 117.

[106] Graham, n 59, 36.

[107] *Conditions of Admission of a State to Membership in the United Nations (Article 4 of the Charter) (Advisory Opinion)* [1948] ICJ Rep 57, 58.

reasoning that the Charter's provisions must be regarded both as the 'necessary conditions' and as 'the conditions which suffice'.[108] Nevertheless, it is difficult to view Mexico's admission to the League in 1931 as demonstrating a move to greater legality in the adjudication of membership – for example, there was no substantive debate on the Article 1 criteria and the procedure adopted was outside the usual practice of the Assembly.

Whereas no representative spoke against Mexico's admission in 1931, the same could not be said when the invitation to admit the USSR was presented for approval in 1934. It was France, concerned about Germany (now withdrawn from the League), that pursued hints from the Soviets that they were ready to join the League.[109] And it was France who spoke at the greatest length in favour of admission at the Sixth Committee of the Assembly.[110] The invitation to the USSR came from thirty members and, as is noted by Walters, once the device of an invitation had been used in relation to Mexico and Turkey, 'no great power could be expected to submit an application in the old way'.[111] Despite the invitation, the debates in the Assembly demonstrate that the USSR's membership was still controversial. In the Sixth Committee, Caeiro Da Mata (Portugal) spoke of the 'manifest opposition' ('I may even say incompatibility') between the principles of the League and the principles of Soviet Russia.[112] Motta referred to the Soviet government's 'expansive and militant Communism' and included in the list of the characteristics of communism its 'ambition [of] world revolution'.[113] Both Caeiro Da Mata and Motta highlighted the problem of recognition, with the Portuguese representative asking: 'Are we to have recognition at Geneva and non-recognition elsewhere?'[114] Motta was concerned that if the USSR was admitted to the League then it would lead to 'the resumption of regular diplomatic relations', even if it did not amount to recognition in law.[115] Barthou (France), in support of admission,

[108] Ibid., 62.

[109] F P Walters, *A History of the League of Nations* (Oxford University Press, 1960) 580–1.

[110] 'Records of the Fifteenth Ordinary Session of the Assembly, Sixth Committee' (1934) *League of Nations Official Journal*, Special Supplement 130, 21–4.

[111] Walters, n 109, 581.

[112] 'Records of the Fifteenth Ordinary Session of the Assembly, Sixth Committee' (1934) *League of Nations Official Journal*, Special Supplement 130, 17.

[113] Ibid., 19.

[114] Ibid., 18.

[115] Ibid.

spoke against weighing one system and doctrine against another and urged members to 'endeavour to ascertain the real interests of the League and of peace'.[116] The opposition expressed in the Plenary Meeting of the Fifteenth Assembly was less virulent than in the Sixth Committee and, with thirty-nine votes in favour, the USSR gained membership.[117] Once admitted, a permanent seat for the USSR on the Council was a foregone conclusion.[118] Following the vote, the Soviet representative emphasised that the Soviet state was 'new' – in terms of its 'external aspects, its internal political and social structure, and its aspirations and ideals'.[119] For the Soviets, admission to the League demonstrated an acceptance of this new state, without the need to renounce 'any of its special features'[120] – that is, its revolutionary aims. If a fear of instability and revolution, in particular communist revolution, had previously prevented Russia's membership, by 1934 it held little sway over the majority of members in an organisation that was already beginning to shed members.[121]

Despite notifying the Secretary-General of its intention to withdraw from the League in 1932 due to the economic depression (a notification that was later withdrawn), Mexico remained a member of the organisation until it was dissolved.[122] However, with respect to the USSR, the League had one final message. In 1939, after the invasion of Finland, the USSR was expelled.[123] The Assembly resolution recommending expulsion stated that the USSR had 'not merely violated a covenant of the

[116] Ibid., 22.

[117] 'Fifteenth Ordinary Session of the Assembly, Ninth Plenary Meeting', *League of Nations Records*, 4.

[118] Ibid. For the brief discussion in the Council of the Soviets' seat see 'Eighty-First Session of the Council' (1934) 15 *League of Nations Official Journal*, 1392–6.

[119] 'Fifteenth Ordinary Session of the Assembly, Ninth Plenary Meeting', *League of Nations Records*, 6.

[120] Ibid., 7.

[121] By 1934, Costa Rica (1924), Brazil (1926), Japan (1933) and Germany (1933) had given notice of their withdrawal from the League.

[122] See 'Letter from the Minister of Foreign Affairs of the United States of Mexico to the Secretary-General' (3 December 1932) (1933) 14 *League of Nations Official Journal* 395; 'Cancellation by the Mexican Government of its Note of December 3rd, 1932, Notifying its Intention to Withdraw from the League of Nations' (1934) 15 *League of Nations Official Journal*, 428.

[123] The question whether the Soviet Union was truly expelled as a matter of law is discussed in Leo Gross, 'Was the Soviet Union Expelled from the League of Nations?' (1945) 39 *American Journal of International Law* 35.

League', it had 'placed itself outside the Covenant'.[124] Following a Council resolution expelling the USSR, the Soviets railed against the League's 'stupid decision' and declared that it would 'henceforth have its hands free'.[125] Despite statements in the Assembly that the League's action was not a response to the Soviet form of government but to its aggressive policies,[126] the lack of League action in response to events in the Rhineland demonstrates that there were certainly other motivating factors. As Walters writes: 'All those States whose policy had been affected by fear and hatred of Communism denounced the perfidy of Stalin in language which none of them used about Hitler'.[127]

4.4 Beyond the League: Revolutionary Governments in Contemporary International Organisations

The exclusion and method of inclusion of Mexico and Russia in the League, and the later expulsion of the USSR, demonstrates a distrust of these states motivated in part by their revolutionary aims. Mexico's outsider status ceased once the 'mistake' of its exclusion was rectified in 1931. However, the USSR's Great Power status did not prevent it remaining an 'outlaw' in the eyes of many League members.[128] While the League of Nations may have been formally dissolved at the end of the Second World War, the differential treatment of revolutionary regimes by international organisations has continued, albeit in different forums and expressed in different forms. Two examples of practice are illustrative of this contemporary treatment of revolutionary regimes: first, the denial of representation and the use of the credentials process in the United Nations to deprive effective governments from representation in the organisation, and second, the practice of regional organisations in excluding governments following revolutionary change.

[124] 'Records of the Twentieth Ordinary Session of the Assembly, Plenary Meetings, Resolutions Adopted by the Assembly', *League of Nations Records*, 53.

[125] 'Statement on the Expulsion of the USSR from the League of Nations' (16 December 1939) reproduced in Jane Degras (ed), *Soviet Documents on Foreign Policy* (Oxford University Press, 1953) vol III, 412–14.

[126] 'Assemblies 1937–9, Twentieth Session of the Assembly, Third Plenary Meeting, 15 December 1939', *League of Nations Records*, 14; 'Assemblies 1937–9, Twentieth Session of the Assembly, Fourth Plenary Meeting', *League of Nations Records*, 27.

[127] Walters, *A History of the League of Nations*, n 109, 805.

[128] Simpson has used the term 'outlaw' to describe Bolshevik Russia's status vis-à-vis the League: see Gerry Simpson, *Great Powers and Outlaw States: Unequal Sovereigns in the International Legal Order* (Cambridge University Press, 2004) 261–3.

The denial of representation and the use of the credentials process have been used at various points in the history of the United Nations as methods of demonstrating disapproval of a government's policies. While denial of the right of representation is not as severe a sanction as suspension or expulsion under the Charter, it can lead to the effective exclusion of a state if the regime in effective control is not seated. The seating of Nationalist China rather than the People's Republic of China (PRC) in the United Nations between 1949 and 1971 is perhaps the clearest example of the denial of representation to indicate disapproval of a revolutionary government at the UN.[129] Unlike the situation of Mexico and Russia in the League, 'China' remained a member of the UN and thus the state was not suspended from the organisation. But the PRC, as the government in control of the mainland territory, was not represented. During this period, a number of proposals were submitted on the question of determining representation at the UN. For example, the UN Secretary-General believed that recognition by individual states and credentials at the United Nations were separate issues and supported an approach whereby the government with effective authority over a territory would be seated in the event of a contest between two rival claimants.[130] Thus, for the Secretary-General, 'effective control' was determinative of the question of representation, rather than recognition or the character of a regime.

The PRC's exclusion was largely the result of the policy of non-recognition by the United States and its allies, driven by the character of the communist government. But as stated by Singh in 1957: 'to penalise China for her new Communist Government established by a revolution while permitting other Governments installed in a similar way some decades ago to continue in the United Nations is, to say the least, discriminatory in the extreme'.[131] In October 1971 the General Assembly finally passed a resolution declaring that the PRC was the 'only lawful

[129] Lyman M Tondel (ed), *The International Position of Communist China: Background Papers and Proceedings of the Fifth Hammarskjöld Forum* (Oceana Publications, 1965) 50–1.

[130] *Letter Dated 8 March 1950 from the Secretary-General to the President of the Security Council Transmitting a Memorandum on the Legal Aspects of the Problem of Representation in the United Nations*, UN SCOR, 5th session, UN Doc S/1466 (9 March 1950).

[131] Nagendra Singh, *Termination of Membership of International Organisations* (Stevens & Sons, 1957) 163.

representative of China in the United Nations'.[132] As the League of Nations discovered many decades earlier, an international organisation with universal aspirations may exclude a revolutionary state (or government, in the case of the UN) to show initial disapproval, but at some point it will have to recognise an effective representative if it has aspirations of universality.

Regional organisations are more likely to be concerned about the 'like-mindedness'[133] of their members than universal organisations and frequently have constitutional provisions setting out criteria for admission and exclusion.[134] They have also demonstrated their distaste for revolutionary governments based on communist ideologies through exclusionary policies. An example of such an action is the 1962 decision of the Organization of American States (OAS), to exclude Cuba from participation on the basis that the Marxist–Leninist government of Fidel Castro was 'incompatible with the Inter-American system'.[135] The OAS did not actually expel Cuba from the organisation: rather the resolution stated that 'as a consequence of repeated acts, the present Government of Cuba has voluntarily placed itself outside the inter-American system'.[136] The resolution did not detail the precise infringements of the OAS Charter committed by Cuba, but the request from the Colombian government to convene the meeting at which the matter was debated referenced concern at the 'intervention of extracontinental powers' (that is, the USSR) in the Americas.[137] Although this was a decision concerning the representation of a revolutionary government, rather than the expulsion of the state of Cuba from the OAS, that does not obscure the fact that the rejection of the revolutionary government – the only potential representative of Cuba – led to the effective removal of the state from the organisation.

[132] *Restoration of the Lawful Rights of the People's Republic of China in the United Nations*, GA Res 2758, UN GAOR, 26th session, 1976th plenary meeting, UN Doc A/RES/2758 (XXVI) (25 October 1971).

[133] Louis B Sohn, 'Expulsion or Forced Withdrawal from an International Organisation' (1964) 77 *Harvard Law Review* 1381, 1461.

[134] See generally, Duxbury, *The Participation of States*, n 14, chs 3 and 4.

[135] 'Resolution VI: Exclusion of the Present Government of Cuba from Participation in the Inter-American System' in *Final Act of the Eighth Meeting of Consultation of Ministers of Foreign Affairs*, Doc No OEA/Ser.C/II.8 (22–31 January 1962).

[136] Ibid.

[137] Note of Colombian Government, 13 November 1961, as cited in 'OAS Council Resolution of 4 December 1961' in Inter-American Institute of International Legal Studies, *The Inter-American System: Its Development and Strengthening* (Oceana Publications, 1966) 158.

As was the case with the decision to expel the USSR from the League, the legality of the resolution excluding Cuba from the OAS has been doubted.[138] Following this decision, Cuba was still described as a member of the OAS but was unable to participate in the organisation's activities due to the perceived incompatibility between Castro's government and the aims of the OAS.[139] Once more, as was the case when the League invited Mexico and Russia to join, the attitude of the OAS towards Cuba has thawed over the years and in 2009 a resolution was adopted stating that the 1962 resolution 'ceases to have effect'.[140] Despite this thaw, the offer from the OAS to start a dialogue on Cuba's return has so far been rebuffed by the Cuban government.[141]

4.5 Conclusion

The story of the exclusion of Mexico and Russia from the League of Nations illustrates several problems with continued relevance to the relationship between international organisations and revolutionary states. The first is a problem of ideology: are the ideologies of revolutionary states, with their calls for radical social and political upheaval, compatible with the rationale for the existence of the international organisations in which they seek membership? The second is a problem of law: states may have moved away from the practice of formally recognising governments, but there are still circumstances where states grant or withhold recognition to demonstrate approval or disapproval of a regime. Are we closer to a practice of collective recognition (or non-recognition) through the decisions of international organisations on participation?[142] The third is a problem of aims: should the objective of an international organisation be to attain and retain universal membership (or full membership in a region), or should it be rigorously to

[138] See discussion in Duxbury, *The Participation of States*, n 14, 175–6.

[139] 'Resolution VI – Exclusion of the Present Government of Cuba from Participation in the Inter-American System' in *Final Act of the Eighth Meeting of Consultation of Ministers of Foreign Affairs*, OAS Doc OEA/Ser.C/II.8 (22–31 January 1962).

[140] *Resolution on Cuba*, OAS AG, 39th session, 3rd plenary meeting, Resolution No. AG/RES.2438 (XXXIX-0/09) (3 June 2009) para 1.

[141] In 2016 President Raul Castro called the OAS 'an instrument of imperialist domination': see 'Cuba Will Never Rejoin OAS over Venezuela Row, Says Castro', *BBC News* (5 June 2016).

[142] See Brad Roth, *Governmental Illegitimacy in International Law* (Clarendon Press, 1999) 413. See n 151 and accompanying text for discussion of the action by the OAS against President Maduro in Venezuela.

uphold the membership conditions in a founding instrument? In the atmosphere of the Paris Peace Conference these problems were complicated by numerous other factors, including the intervention of the Allies against the Bolsheviks, the presence of more than one possible representative for Russia at the Peace Conference, the non-recognition of Mexico by some members of the Commission on the League of Nations, the insistence by the United States that the Monroe Doctrine be mentioned in the Covenant and the actions of the two states during the war. In this respect, the story of Mexico and Russia's membership in the League could be told in a number of ways. This chapter has framed the story as one concerning the treatment of revolutionary states by an international organisation.

More recent examples of the practice of international organisations demonstrate that while the League may have been dissolved over seventy years ago, the differential treatment of revolutionary governments in membership decisions has continued in the practice of contemporary organisations. While the exclusion of the PRC from the UN, and of Castro's government from the OAS, demonstrates the marginalisation of revolutionary regimes through participation sanctions, it is important to recognise that not all revolutionary change has been sidelined by regional organisations in this way. In a rare example, the League of Arab States implicitly lent its support to a revolutionary movement when it suspended the participation rights of Libya in February 2011 following the violent suppression of the supporters of the popular uprising that formed part of the Arab Spring, or the Arab revolution, depending on the terminology employed.[143] Rather than condemning those joining the uprising in Libya, the regional organisation later recognised one aspect of the outcome, that is, the Libyan Transitional Council, rather than the former regime of Colonel Gaddafi.[144] As such, the League of Arab States viewed the revolutionary movement positively, or, at the very least, as an improvement on its predecessor.[145] Whether this example demonstrates a more nuanced approach by international organisations to revolutionary

143 League of Arab States, *Statement of the Council in Its Extraordinary Session No 136 on 22 February 2011*, as discussed in Mervat Rishmawi, 'The League of Arab States in the Wake of the "Arab Spring"' in *Delivering Democracy: Repercussions of the 'Arab Spring' on Human Rights: Human Rights in the Arab Region, Annual Report 2012* (Cairo Institute for Human Rights Studies, 2012) 49, 56.

144 *Council Resolution 7370*, League of Arab States, Extraordinary Session (27 August 2011) as discussed in Rishmawi, n 143, 56.

145 Ibid.

change in the future, or merely that members of the League of Arab States had run out of patience with Gaddafi, remains to be seen.[146]

The use of a participation sanction to condemn the suppression of the uprising in Libya as part of the Arab Spring brings us back to a problem touched on at the beginning of this chapter: the definitional question.[147] This story has concentrated on revolutionary change, but, as is noted in the introduction, there are other circumstances where international organisations have shown disapproval of governmental instability, mainly military coups, through membership sanctions. What constitutes revolutionary change, as distinct from another form of upheaval, may be in the eyes of the beholder, and the beholder in these situations is the organ that determines continuing participation in the organisation. Two examples demonstrate the impact of conflicting interpretations of the nature of governmental change. In 2013, the African Union's Peace and Security Council described the overthrow of the elected president in Egypt and the suspension of the constitution as 'an unconstitutional change of government' and an 'illegal seizure of power', resulting in the decision to suspend Egypt's participation.[148] The interim authorities in Egypt rejected this interpretation of events, instead describing the change in power as the result of a 'popular revolution, which unfolded in Egypt'.[149] In 2017 the Southern Common Market (MERCOSUR) suspended Venezuela from participation for violations of the organisation's principles of democracy.[150] The Permanent Council of the OAS also resolved to 'not recognize the legitimacy' of Maduro's' new presidential term.[151] President Maduro claims that he is continuing the 'Bolivarian revolution' begun by his predecessor, Hugo Chávez – a claim that is

[146] Ibid. Rishmawi notes that Gaddafi had 'made an enemy out of almost every Arab regime' and that the Arab League's approach to the uprisings across the Arab world was by no means consistent.

[147] See n 13 and accompanying text.

[148] *Communiqué*, African Union Peace and Security Council, 384th Meeting, Doc No PSC/PR/COMM.(CCCLXXXIV) (5 July 2013) paras 5–6.

[149] *Progress Report of the African Union High-Level Panel for Egypt*, African Union Peace and Security Council, 416th meeting, Doc No PSC/AHG/4(CDXVI) (29 January 2014) para 7.

[150] *Decisión Sobre la Suspención de la República Bolivariana de Venezuela en el Mercosur en Aplicación del Protocolo de Ushuaia Sobre Compromiso Democrático en el Mercosur*, MERCOSUR (5 August 2017).

[151] *Resolution on the Situation in Venezuela*, OAS PC, Special Meeting, Resolution No CP/RES 1117 (2200/19) (10 January 2019).

doubted by his opponents.[152] Whether both these states experienced, or are experiencing, revolutionary change in these circumstances may be doubtful, but clearly the characterisation of the action is important for both the government, which is using the concept of a revolution as shorthand for the popular will, and the international organisation, which is concerned with unconstitutional changes and democratic failure. While not all governmental change can be described as revolutionary in the sense of the events in Mexico and Russia, the decision to remove participation rights in such cases demonstrates that international organisations continue to use the carrot of membership and the stick of exclusion to demonstrate distrust and disapproval of some forms of governmental instability. The line back to 1919 may be a little wobbly, but this practice began with the story of the exclusion of Mexico and Russia from the League of Nations over one hundred years ago.

[152] See discussion in Pedro E Carillo, 'How Today's Crisis in Venezuela Was Created by Hugo Chávez's "Revolutionary" Plan', *The Conversation* (6 July 2016); Ryan Bradling, 'How Venezuela's Revolutionary Dream Descended into Chaos', *The Conversation* (24 April 2016).

5

Law, Class Struggle and Nervous Breakdowns

MAI TAHA*

5.1 Introduction

> And so you get in the Treaty of Versailles, for the first time in the long history of great international treaties, the word 'Labour'. You get the word 'Labour' and a whole chapter devoted to what was to be done on behalf of labour, which opens with a very remarkable preamble, a preamble so remarkable that in the mass of those extremely dry and technical documents which are called treaties it appears almost as incongruously as a passage from 'Alice in Wonderland'.[1]

This was part of a speech delivered by E Phelan, a British civil servant in the Ministry of Labour and later the director of the International Labour Organization (ILO) (1941–1948), in support of the creation of the ILO. For Mr Phelan, inserting 'labour' in the Treaty of Versailles was a success so wonderful that it could only be fathomed through the realm of the mystical and the fantastic. For the first time, and through the ILO, workers would be represented as voting members of an international institution through the innovation of tripartism. Almost like the anthropomorphic characters of *Alice in Wonderland*, the working class, at least theoretically, came to have a voice in the machineries of international labour policy.

Some argued that the institution's name 'belies its nature', for it would have been more accurate to call it an 'International Organization for Social Justice'.[2] J T Shotwell, the historian member of the American delegation to the Paris Peace Conference and author of the provisions establishing the ILO, saw that working internationally on social justice

* Lecturer at the Department of Law, Goldsmiths, University of London.

1 E J Phelan, 'The Necessity for International Labour Organization: An Address Delivered to the League of Nations Union Summer School, Geneva' (League of Nations Union, 1923) 7.

2 James T Shotwell, 'Forward' in Bernard Béguin, *ILO and the Tripartite System* (Carnegie Endowment for International Peace, 1959) 2.

was essential, especially in the wake of the 1917 Bolshevik Revolution.[3] The ILO's record number of ratified conventions in a short period of time, and in an entirely new field, bore witness to the urgent need for such an organisation.[4] For many, the ILO had a remarkable impact across the ideological spectrum with its increased focus on technical assistance to newly industrialising countries, and its shift away from the strict legal-standard-setting system that was commonly associated with international institutions.[5] For Shotwell, it was in the world's best interests that 'capital as well as labor . . . continue to strive for the success of this *non-revolutionary* institution in its efforts to achieve social justice'.[6]

The years leading up to the Paris Peace Conference witnessed a rise in labour protests, including general strikes and different forms of work stoppages. At the same time, the International Federation of Trade Unions and the Socialist International started calling for international labour legislation.[7] Léon Jouhaux, a famous syndicalist and secretary of the Confédération Générale du Travail (CGT) in France,[8] who later collaborated with the ILO, also saw the importance of international labour legislation as a means of spreading socialism to countries where workers had not yet organised themselves.[9] Many trade unionists understood that 'labour, like capital, internationalises itself more and more'.[10] And it was only natural that international labour legislation would become part of this process. As world leaders were passing through the famous hall of mirrors at Versailles, workers were rising up against working conditions and increasing unemployment. In France alone, the national frequency of strikes was four times higher than usual in the year

3 Lisa Anderson, 'James T Shotwell: A Life Devoted to Organizing Peace' (Winter 2005) *Living Legacies Columbia Magazine* www.columbia.edu/cu/alumni/Magazine/Winter2005/llshotwell.

4 Shotwell, n 2.

5 Ibid.

6 Ibid., 3 (emphasis added).

7 Bernard Béguin, *ILO and the Tripartite System* (International Conciliation, Carnegie Endowment for International Peace, 1959) 5. The International Federation of Trade Unions (IFTU) was an international organization of trade unions that officially existed from 1919 to 1945. See Dimitris Stevis and Terry Boswell, *Globalization and Labor: Democratizing Global Governance* (Rowman & Littlefield, 2008) 49.

8 The CGT was dominated by anarcho-syndicalists until 1919 when the union experienced internal divisions under the leadership of Jouhaux, who collaborated with the government in anti-war efforts.

9 Béguin, n 7.

10 Ibid., 6.

1919–20.[11] The rates from 1919 show that every other member of metal smelting walked out, and every other chemical worker and miner, as well as every fourth metalworker, went on strike. The industrial action of this year was so significant, it was even viewed as forming the genesis of the French Communist Party.[12] Labour action in Europe was intense to the extent that some argued that the working classes across the continent believed 'the years, if not the weeks, of capitalism were numbered'.[13]

The ILO attracted many anti-capitalists, including the ILO's celebrated first director, Albert Thomas, a self-declared socialist,[14] whose appointment was secured by the efforts of European trade union leaders.[15] More radically, Léon Jouhaux thought that the ILO should devote itself to the 'emancipation of the working class'.[16] Through the ILO, and for the first time, class subjectivity became part of international legal thought and practice. The working class, at least theoretically, became a direct agent in international labour policy through the tripartite system of representation within a largely state-centric international law. In other words, the ILO was somehow different. It was celebrated (with caution) by many working-class activists across the European continent. At the same time, it was used by the Allies to demonstrate to the increasingly agitated working classes that they were accounted for in the post-war settlement. In fact, the final Constitution of the ILO became part of all the former peace treaties.[17]

More significantly, the ILO presented an alternate vision of class society under capitalism. It was explicitly anti-communist, yet it sought a regulated version of capitalism. In this chapter, I interrogate this alternate vision of class society that saw social reform as essential to the post-war global order. First, the ILO saw class society not as inherently antagonistic but as potentially harmonious. This was reflected in its two

11 Edward Shorter and Charles Tilly, *Strikes in France 1830–1968* (Cambridge University Press, 1974) 124.

12 Ibid.

13 Béguin, n 7, 5.

14 Interview with M Remo Becci, the head of the ILO Archives (ILO headquarters, Geneva, June 2012).

15 Robert W Cox, 'ILO: Limited Monarchy' in Robert W Cox et al. (eds), *The Anatomy of Influence: Decision Making in International Organization* (Yale University Press, 1973) 102, 103.

16 Béguin, n 7, 7.

17 The exception was the 1923 Lausanne Treaty, which stipulated the terms of the peace between the Allied Powers and Turkey and determined the Mandate framework for the former Arab provinces of the Ottoman Empire: Wilfred Jenks, 'The International Labour Organization as a Subject of Study for International Lawyers' (1940) 22(1) *Journal of Comparative Legislation and International Law* 36.

most central principles: tripartism and universality. Tripartism represented a belief in peaceful deliberations between workers, bosses and governments. These deliberations would lay down the foundation of a new and reformed capitalism. At the same time, this alternate vision of class society would have universal application. In other words, class harmony through deliberation and representation would embody the ideological basis of membership in the organisation. Theoretically, the principle of universality meant that all countries could become members of the ILO. However, complete independence of governments, employers' and workers' organisations was a prerequisite for membership that immediately posed a contradiction, since this requirement effectively excluded socialist and colonised countries from the arrangement. Organised labour had not yet formed strongholds of representative labour unions in the colonies. And in socialist countries, there was almost no separation between government, employers' and workers' organisations.

Second, the ILO, especially its early leadership, had formulated a particular conception of alienation under capitalism. The ILO's alternate vision of class society was driven by a specific critique of workers' alienation. Although perhaps not in the Marxist sense of the term, Harold Butler, the second director of the ILO, had argued that the alienation of workers in modern society was one of the driving forces behind the ILO's main functions. Alienation, at least on the philosophical level, was never part of the international legal agenda. Through the ILO, states were forced to probe the pitfalls of modern industry and technology, and its effect on workers in society. Still, the ILO's position, albeit significant, was fundamentally at odds with a serious critique of industrial capitalism. In fact, the very existence of the ILO was (and still is) dependent on class society.

Created only two years after the Bolshevik Revolution, the ILO promoted its version of class society through its own institutional design and underlying principles, as well as its professed critique of modern technology and its 'nervous' effects on workers. Essentially, this vision constituted the material and ideological basis for reformist, yet counter-revolutionary, labour law and politics that deemed any radical workers' movement as either mad or illegal.

5.2 Tripartism, Universality and the Fantasy of the Enlightened Employer

A more durable and reformed class society entailed a particular conception of 'class', premised on harmony rather than struggle. Through the concept of the 'enlightened employer', labour relations were framed as potentially synchronous.[18] From the early nineteenth century, reform in working conditions was predicated on the notion of class harmony. To avoid an angry labour movement, class harmony required both an enlightened employer and a state that was ready for social legislation. This became the genesis of the ILO's tripartism – tamed workers, enlightened employers and a socially conscious state.[19]

Tripartism was undoubtedly a novel idea. It was born out of the Allies' fears of an angry working class that was increasingly becoming more militant, if not potentially communist, after the war. It became quickly very clear to the Allies that the League of Nations was simply not equipped to address all post-war problems. Both Lloyd George, who had to attend to Glasgow's 40-hour strike of 70,000 workers that erupted during the Paris Peace conference,[20] and Georges Clemenceau, who had mobilised 30,000 workers to the conference,[21] knew very well that workers needed their share in the peace treaty. A labour organisation was deemed necessary to deal with conditions of labour 'involving such injustice, hardship and privation ... [causing] unrest so great that the peace and harmony of the world are imperilled'.[22]

This was an important decision: an international institution would have representation from non-state entities with voting powers. To prevent an outvoting of government delegates by non-governmental delegates, each government would have two votes, and the employers' associations and workers' trade unions would each have one vote.[23] At the same time, this tripartite representative system was certainly a cause of concern for positivist international lawyers who characteristically believed that international law was 'a law between states only and exclusively'.[24] In one sense, this was a radical move for international law.

The inclusion of labour as part of the post-war settlement grew from a frustration of workers in many countries who made it clear to the Allies

[18] Béguin, n 7, 4.
[19] Ibid.
[20] Ian McLean, 'The Labour Movement in Clydeside Politics, 1914–1922' (DPhil dissertation, University of Oxford, 1971) 183.
[21] Béguin, n 7, 5.
[22] *Constitution of the International Labour Organization*, signed 28 June 1919 (entered into force 4 June 1934).
[23] Antony Alcock, *History of the International Labour Organization* (Macmillan Press, 1971) 22.
[24] Jenks, n 17, 51 (citing Oppenheim).

that social justice and workers' rights needed to be part of the Peace Treaties, but the ILO could not simply represent workers. To ensure that there was 'a *just* equilibrium', employers would also be represented, exerting their influence and securing their interests in international labour policy.[25] For this tripartite system to work, trade unions and employers' associations needed to be completely independent from their respective governments.[26] And, accordingly, they would be able to voice their concerns or demands without fear of governmental control. The logic was simple: guided by a spirit of collaboration rather than confrontation, independent parties would together frame international labour policy. Social classes would not stand in contradiction or in opposition to each other. This was a good solution. The Allies would deter the Bolshevik threat by including labour without unsettling the forces of capital, while having control over the process. In this narrative, the ILO aimed to create an equilibrium in an otherwise uneven and antagonistic relationship. The state was elevated outside or above class antagonisms.[27] Conflicts would be mediated by an impartial justice system regardless of class, race or gender,[28] where formal equality would simply collapse material inequalities. And, most significantly, trade unions would be the only possible form of labour organisation, even in the colonies where workers had not yet organised themselves or were organised along more radical lines.[29]

In this version of an immaculate class society, class struggle, as Harold Butler had argued, would become irrelevant because the employers' class would make 'concessions with good grace', the working class would not protest too much and the state would mediate employer–labour relations

[25] *Report of the Governing Body Committee on Freedom of Association* (1956) Official Bulletin of the International Labour Office, vol XXXIX, no. 1, ILO Archives, 478 (emphasis added).

[26] Ibid.

[27] Georg Lukács, *History and Class Consciousness: Studies in Marxist Dialectics* (MIT Press, 1971) 66.

[28] Ibid.

[29] For an excellent account of different forms of labour organising from the nineteenth century to the mid-twentieth century, see John T Chalcraft, *The Striking Cabbies of Cairo and Other Stories: Crafts and Guilds in Egypt, 1863–1914* (State University of New York, 2004) 200. Chalcraft emphasises popular agency in workers' movements despite the structural limitations imposed by the mercantilist expansion and the colonial presence in Egypt. See also Ilham Makdisi, *The Eastern Mediterranean and the Making of Global Radicalism, 1860–1914* (University of California Press, 2010) 130. Makdisi identifies different spaces for workers' organising, such as workers' night schools where they were exposed to revolutionary ideas in the early twentieth century.

through social legislation.[30] It followed that all deviations from a well-ordered and a non-political workers' movement would either be deemed mad or illegal, as I discuss in the next section. The push towards trade union laws in the colonies, for example, was only to the extent that those unions did not contest racialised property relations of colonial capitalism. The complete negation of class struggle came to define the ILO's very existence. In what follows, I examine how this negation was manifested in the application of the principles of tripartism and universality in the colonies and in socialist countries.

5.2.1 Labour in the Colonies

The ILO had a non-conflictual conception of class that not only flattened the tensions within class society, including its intersections with race and gender, but also universalised the European working-class experience. This became clear in the ILO's legal interventions in the colonies that aimed at tempering workers' political organisation while maintaining a reformed colonial relationship. When the ILO intervened in Egypt in the 1930s, for example, it helped draft a new labour code that explicitly aimed at limiting labour organising to strictly industrial and non-political demands.[31] Political organisation for workers in the colony was deemed dangerous, otherwise workers would organise against their mostly European bosses. The ILO's intervention in class relations was intended to separate the politics of work from the politics of race and gender. Through universality, it ignored the specificities of class relations in the colonies that were also constitutive of race relations. And through class harmony, it denied the fundamental tension in the history of capitalist society – class struggle.

Using Hegelian dialectics, political theorist David McNally explains the basis of class struggle through dualities in opposition. Value entails use of value/exchange value; concrete labour/abstract labor; commodity/money; wage-labour/capital. Its dual forms cannot simply be harmonised with its social framework.[32] As a result, one 'moment' of the process must drive to suppress another. This is what it means for the use-value of

[30] Harold Butler, *The Lost Peace: A Personal Impression* (Harcourt, Brace & Co, 1942) 66.

[31] Mai Taha, 'Reading "Class" in International Law' (2016) 25 *Social & Legal Studies* 567.

[32] David McNally, 'The Dialectics of Unity and Difference in the Constitution of Wage-Labour: On Internal Relations and Working-Class Formation' (2015) 39 *Capital and Class* 131, 138.

a commodity (or the 'usefulness of a thing')[33] to be reduced to the role of a mere bearer of exchange-value (or the 'mode of expression'),[34] for instance; or for living labour to be dominated by dead labour in the form of capital. In circumstances of estrangement, one side of a doubled phenomenon dominates the other, even though the dominant element is in fact dependent on the dominated (as in Hegel's dialectic of lordship and bondage). It follows that alienated doubles are unstable insofar as the two moments are at odds with each other (which is the basis of class struggle).[35] Dead labour, in the form of capital, extracts surplus-value from living labour. It is the struggle by capitalists to increase the length of the working day and the workload without raising wages and, accordingly, appropriating all the benefits reaped from increased labour productivity.[36] The other side of this struggle is that of workers against capitalist exploitation. It is the struggle to reduce the workload and reduce the length of the working day without a decrease in wages.[37]

While class is a relation to the means of production, it is also fundamentally a social relation among different actors.[38] As Marx had put it: 'He discovered that capital is not a thing, but a social relation between persons, established by the instrumentality of things'.[39] In their awareness of the systemic nature of these relations, the actors become 'class agents in the fullest sense'.[40] At the same time, 'class is not a "structure" nor even a "category", but . . . something which in fact happens (and can be shown to have happened) in human relationships', as E P Thompson has argued.[41] The historian's task is thus to understand class through its lived reality in historical time.[42] The problem with the ILO's version of class is that it is immaterial and ahistorical. It posits class relations as harmonious, without dualities, contradictions and dynamism.

If class is not an undifferentiated structure but a complex and dynamic social relation, it follows that it cannot be fully understood without its

[33] Karl Marx, *Capital: A Critique of Political Economy, Volume I* (Ben Fowkes trans, Vintage Books, 1976) 35. For Marx, every commodity has a use-value and an exchange-value.
[34] Ibid.
[35] McNally, n 32, 138.
[36] Marx, *Capital*, n 33, 35.
[37] Ibid.
[38] McNally, n 32, 140.
[39] Marx, *Capital*, n 33, 932.
[40] McNally, n 32, 138.
[41] E P Thompson, quoted in ibid., 141.
[42] Ibid.

co-constitutive divisions – race, gender, sexuality, nationality, among others. Here, different elements of the dominated class can find avenues for expressing their specific experiences of oppression.[43] Only through these possibilities of self-expression can the working class truly constitute itself as a 'class' – a *totality* in the dialectical sense of the term that unifies without suppressing the other totalities that constituted it.[44] Himani Bannerji imagines social relations, not as discrete and autonomous categories that intersect with one another but as coming into being 'in and through each other'.[45] Class cannot be articulated independently from race or gender; otherwise it becomes radically incomplete. 'It is absurd', Bannerji argues, to view identity and difference as unconnected to class formation and capital accumulation.[46] In fact, this view leads to an understanding of class solely as an abstraction.[47]

This analysis moves the conversation outside of the narrow compass of 'culture or class' and 'the politics of identity or class struggle'.[48] Here, class is constituted in and through difference, and class struggle embodies dualities and antagonisms. In this sense, a class analysis of labour in the colonies, for example, shows the complexity of class as a social relation – a *totality* of other *totalities* of race, nationality and gender. It also shows class as a social relation of opposition and struggle – indigenous workers against foreign bosses – hence centring the specificities of class struggle in the colonies.

Such an analysis targets the ILO's two main defining principles: tripartism and universality. And universality, at least formally, meant that the ILO would be open to all states regardless of their economic system or the nature of labour relations in their respective countries.[49] This also meant that the ILO would welcome countries that had not yet reached complete independence – which it did. While universality here represented a nominal commitment to universal membership in the ILO, it also implicitly represented a belief in the universality of capitalism and the European working class experience as simply translatable to other contexts – *sans* race. In fact, in 1920, the ILO created the Native Labour

[43] Ibid., 142.
[44] Ibid.
[45] Ibid., 143.
[46] Himani Bannerji, *Thinking Through: Essays on Feminism, Marxism and Anti-Racism* (Women's Press, 1995) 30.
[47] Ibid.
[48] Ibid., 19.
[49] *Report of the Governing Body Committee on Freedom of Association*, n 25, 474.

Section to deal with colonial labour. The Section had only one to three employees throughout the entire interwar period and was responsible for collecting information and giving recommendations on labour conditions in the colonies.[50] Through this Section, the ILO collaborated with the colonial and security apparatuses in non-self-governing territories and in the process formulated a distinct colonial labour policy. The Native Labour Code (NLC) was later added to the International Labour Code (comprising all the conventions of the ILO) and was to be applied selectively by European powers, giving effect to the 'colonial clause' in the ILO Constitution.[51] Article 19 (or the 'colonial clause' of the ILO Constitution) stated that in countries where 'climatic conditions, the imperfect development of industrial organization, or other special circumstances make the industrial conditions substantially different', state parties could modify labour standards to address the specificities of labour conditions in the colonies.[52] In fact, the ILO's interventions in countries like Egypt and Iraq stemmed from the belief that these interventions were necessary for the maintenance of a stable empire.[53] It was therefore unsurprising that the interwar period saw a significant increase in policing colonial workplaces, a policy adopted by both the ILO and the colonial administrations in the periphery.[54]

By 1944, the ILO had affirmed the universality of its principles in the Philadelphia Conference. More importantly, it recognised that the application of international labour standards would be determined according to 'the stage of social and economic development reached by each people, their progressive application to peoples who are still dependent, as well as to those who have already achieved self-government'.[55] This was basically a crude form of recognition of colonial labour, but articulated with the logic of tutelage reminiscent of the notorious Article 22 of the Covenant of the League of Nations that established the mandate system. Irrespective of this small change, the philosophy of tripartism remained intact.

[50] Daniel R Maul, *Human Rights, Development and Decolonization: The International Labour Organization, 1940–70* (International Labour Organization, 2012) 20.

[51] Ibid., 23.

[52] *Constitution of the International Labour Organization*, n 22.

[53] Martin Thomas, *Violence and Colonial Order: Police, Workers and Protest in the European Colonial Empires 1918–1940* (Cambridge University Press, 2012) 22.

[54] Ibid., 23.

[55] Béguin, n 7, 19.

Additionally, class relations as imagined in the ILO's Constitution assumed that labour was organised in trade unions, that the state was not a major employer and that the private sector and trade unions were completely independent from government. Basically, the ILO either had no grasp of the nature of labour in the colonies (and in socialist countries) or, more likely, it had effectively excluded colonial labour from genuine participation in the organisation, and socialist labour from formal participation. Taken on its own terms, tripartism was essentially inconsistent with universality.

5.2.2 Labour in Socialist Countries

Initially, the possibility of the Soviet Union joining the ILO and forcing the organisation to confront these contradictions seemed remote. The Soviet Commissariat for Labour had demanded that 'all attempts at collaboration with the International Labour Office must be stopped once and for all . . . any form of collaboration, even in the scientific sphere, between Soviet institutions and international institutions [entailed] divorcing science from politics and separating the study of facts from analysis in the light of Marxist doctrines . . . the only true science'.[56] But this did not last long. The Soviet Union joined the League of Nations in 1934 and the ILO in 1935.[57] Harold Butler, the pragmatic civil servant that he was, defended the ILO's universality:

> [The permanent nature of the ILO] shows that its activities are required to adapt themselves to all possible forms of life of the nations and cannot be hedged round with rigid and abstract formulae. The fact that the particular social organisation of a State brings a new element into the working of the Conference does not in itself run counter to any principle of the Constitution.[58]

He adopted a value-free definition of employer and worker, where it did not matter whether the state was the employer or whether it was a private entity. 'According to the dictionary', Butler noted, 'the term employer means someone who employs people'.[59] If the state was the employer, then it should be the party appointing the employer's representative. This

56 International Labour Office, *The International Labour Organization: The First Decade* (Allen & Unwin, 1931) 46.
57 Béguin, n 7, 17.
58 Ibid., 18.
59 Ibid., 17.

position was radically rejected by the employers' group to the extent that by 1937 they demanded an advisory opinion from the Permanent Court of International Justice (PCIJ). The last thing the employers wanted was socialist delegates among their ranks, posing as fellow employers and property owners.

> The Employers' Group ... is of the unanimous opinion that in point of fact the Constitution of the Union of Soviet Socialist Republics does not recognize private property, and does not recognize the status of employer within the meaning [of,] and in the spirit in which this term may have been adopted to the exclusion of any other concept in the Peace Treaty, Article 389 ... was the nomination of Mr. Nicolas Andreev, non-Government Delegate, as Employers' representative at the Twenty-third Session made in conformity with the provisions laid down in Article 389 of the Peace Treaty?[60]

This quickly became a moot point as the Soviet Union was expelled from the League of Nations and the ILO as a result of its invasion of Finland.[61] Still it showed the extent to which the two logics – socialism and tripartism – were completely at odds with each other. One was premised on abolishing private property, the other relied on it.

The philosophy of tripartism was challenged by leftist governments across the world. For example, the Latin American workers' delegates argued that:

> the State in various ways and by different methods has become a producer or director of undertakings ... the number of nationalized undertakings ... is multiplying ... Finally, the world of today is not based, as in 1918, on a universal economic system; a Union of Socialist Republics now exists, covering one-sixth of the world, which has abolished the system of private property and has given new characteristics and a new content to the State, and new forms to the relations between workers, undertakings, and the Government.[62]

By 1954 this contradiction became difficult to ignore. The Governing Body of the ILO requested the formation of a committee that would investigate the problems of application of the principle of tripartism, 'a unique feature of the ILO [and] essential to the effective functioning of the Organization'.[63] The committee would address the question of the

60 Ibid., 20.
61 Ibid., 19.
62 Ibid., 20.
63 *Report of the Governing Body Committee on Freedom of Association*, n 25, 474.

independence of employers' and workers' organisations from governments in different countries with different economic systems.[64] The committee was headed by Lord Arnold McNair, the influential British legal academic, who was the teacher of Hersch Lauterpacht and others; a former president of the International Court of Justice; and a former member of the ILO Committee of Experts on the Application of Conventions and Recommendations.[65] McNair, along with Pedro de Alba of Mexico and Justice A R Cornelius of Pakistan, formed the committee, focusing on the operation of the principles of universality and the freedom of independence of workers' and employers' representatives.

> Throughout the history of the Organisation the principle of universality is found in operation ... It was in this spirit that the doors of the Organisation were opened to States which were not yet Members of the League of Nations, both the States which had been enemies to the Allied Powers primarily responsible for the establishment of the Organisation and the neutral States which had not participated in the Peace Treaties and the establishment of the Organisation.[66]

The committee claimed that the principle of universality had also received renewed support from the United Nations, notably through the 1955 General Assembly resolution in favour of encouraging the widest possible membership in the organisation.[67] What the committee failed to mention was that this General Assembly resolution, adopted only a few months after the Bandung Conference, came out of increased pressures by Afro-Asian nations on the UN to take a firm stance on colonialism.[68] A moment of fundamental global friction on the future of empire was repackaged by the committee as a question of universality and diversity, not conflict and exploitation.

Another problem that emerged with the membership of socialist countries as the ILO was struggling to abide by its own principles was the independence of parties. Article 4(1) of the ILO Constitution reads: 'Every delegate shall be entitled to vote individually on all matters which

[64] Ibid.

[65] R Y Jennings, 'Arnold Duncan McNair' (1965) 23 *Cambridge Law Journal* 1, 1–2. See also ibid.

[66] *Report of the Governing Body Committee on Freedom of Association*, n 25, 477.

[67] Ibid.

[68] *Declaration on the Granting of Independence to Colonial Countries and Peoples*, GA Res 1514 (XV), UN GAOR, 15th session, 947th plenary meeting, UN Doc A/RES/1514 (XV) (14 December 1960).

are taken into consideration by the Conference'.[69] The logic behind this provision was articulated in the report to the 1919 Peace Conference of its Commission upon International Labour Legislation: 'if the Conference was really to be representative of all those concerned with industry and to command their confidence the employers and work-people must be allowed to express their views with complete frankness and freedom, and . . . a departure from the traditional procedure of voting by national units was therefore necessary'.[70] In practice, the tripartite structure could only work if complete frankness and freedom were guaranteed.[71] In fact, at the 1954 session of the International Labour Conference, delegates of thirty-two countries submitted objections to the credentials of the employers' delegates of the USSR, Bulgaria, the Byelorussian SSR, Czechoslovakia, Hungary, Poland and the Ukrainian SSR precisely because they did not represent 'genuine' employers.[72] The same objections to the credentials of the workers' delegates from socialist countries were also lodged by international trade union organisations on the grounds that trade unions were subservient to the state.[73] It is true that Soviet socialism in the 1930s–1950s under Joseph Stalin's iron fist took a decidedly oppressive turn, moving far from the ideas formed in the Bolshevik Revolution. Still, the ILO was effectively unfit to deal with any country that had abolished private property and socialised the labour process, regardless of their substantive merit and accuracy in relation to the Soviet Union during that period.

Interestingly, challenges to the credentials of workers' delegates on the grounds that they did not enjoy freedom of association and independence from the state were consistently raised at every single session of the International Labour Conference from 1923 to 1938.[74] To put it more clearly, the tripartite structure was also inconsistent with European fascism. Objections against the Italian delegation, for example, were based on the fact that there were no trade union rights in the country because of the monopoly of fascist corporations.[75] Similarly, in 1933, the objections to the credentials of the German delegation were because the

[69] *Constitution of the International Labour Organization*, n 22.

[70] *Report of the Governing Body Committee on Freedom of Association*, n 25, 478, citing the report to the Paris Peace Conference 1919.

[71] Ibid., 477.

[72] Ibid., 481.

[73] Ibid.

[74] Ibid., 483.

[75] Ibid.

state directly appointed the workers' delegates.[76] Neither the communists nor the fascists were denied admission by the Conference.

The ILO's Committee on Freedom of Association was of the opinion that political ideology was almost irrelevant to the functioning of the organisation. The ILO was the melting pot for political ideology – a place where fascists, liberals and communists assembled. Following the same logic, the Committee found that the expansion of the public sector in many countries was 'not inspired by any particular political or economic philosophy but ha[d] come about empirically and due to pressure of circumstances'.[77] It simply happened. None of the contradictions in the structure of the ILO seemed to have been relevant to the functioning of the organisation. The drive toward an empty universality superseded the organisation's coherence to the extent that fascism was inconsequential as long as formal membership was secured.

5.3 Speed, Alienation and the Nervous Diseases

> I should prefer to be considered a disciple of Locke, Hume, and other empiricists rather than a disciple of Kant and Hegel, but a pragmatic approach to the economic problems of the present day means looking at things as they are, and trying to understand them as they are, without spending too much time in lamenting that they are not different.[78]

Harold Butler, the ILO's second director and the self-declared disciple of Locke and Hume, understood the functioning of government bureaucracies and was known to be 'more impartial and less dogmatic' than his socialist predecessor, Albert Thomas.[79] Butler was a pragmatist. Like the empiricists, he saw the world as it was, without the agonies of thought

[76] Ibid.

[77] Ibid., 491.

[78] Director's Reply (Mr Harold Butler), International Labour Conference, 23rd Session (3–23 June 1937) 17.

[79] Francis Graham Wilson, *Labor in the League System: A Study of the International Labor Organization in Relation to International Administration* (Stanford University Press, 1934) 335. Harold Butler was a British civil servant and a central figure in the preparatory work that led to the creation of the ILO in 1919. He became the Organization's first deputy director under the leadership of Albert Thomas, and its second director after the death of Thomas in 1932: *Harold Butler: Director of the International Labour Organization, 1932–1938*, International Labour Organization, www.ilo.org/global/about-the-ilo/who-we-are/ilo-director-general/former-directors-general/WCMS_192737/lang–en/index.htm.

and ideology. For Butler, class struggle was not a serious issue in Britain because the wealthy had made 'great concessions with good grace' and the labour and liberal factions were not too forceful.[80] At the same time, he rejected the hypothesis, popular among employers, that a reduction of working hours would have catastrophic effects on prices and production, and disrupt the balance between industry and agriculture.[81] The truth of the matter was that the reduction of working hours had not caused such calamities in countries that instituted the change. 'A *prima facie* case in favour of the shorter working-week has therefore been made out by the *actual* experience of a number of countries. It is no longer a battle of words and ideas, but a confrontation of facts'.[82] For 'the battle of words and ideas' was essentially irrelevant to the conditions of life and labour. The modern worker, or in Butler's words, the 'human machine', had not yet been adapted to the new age of the technological revolution that was slowly snatching time from the labourer.[83] In fact, the main driver for change was the need for greater leisure time.

> In all spheres of life we are only subconsciously aware of the increasing pressure on our nervous system. We hardly yet realize the immense physiological and psychological implications of the technical revolution of the last forty years. . . . The introduction of speed, both in locomotion and in the transmission of ideas, has transformed the conditions of urban life. . . . The careful, self-regulated work of the handicraftsman is now performed by machines moving at ever-increasing speeds, exacting ever greater attention from the workman, imposing the most arbitrary limits on the pace of his work, while at the same time depriving him of any personal feeling of satisfaction in the product to which he makes an infinitesimal contribution.[84]

In other words, the affective relationship of the worker to their labour is pilfered by deprivation and alienation. Each worker makes an 'infinitesimal contribution' against which their self-worth is measured. To put it simply, workers experience alienation under modern capitalism. Not only are workers estranged from the products of their labour, but, as Marx famously argued, they are estranged from the act of production

[80] Butler, *The Lost Peace*, n 30, 66.
[81] Director's Reply (Mr Harold Butler), International Labour Conference, 23rd Session (3–23 June 1937) 18.
[82] Ibid. (emphasis added).
[83] Ibid.
[84] Ibid., 19.

itself.[85] Unlike Marx, Butler's conception of alienation was a frustration that is due to the vagaries of mechanisation and technology. For Marx, alienation also entailed the fact that labour is not intrinsic to the worker's nature. In labour, the worker 'denies' themselves. Work 'mortifies' a worker's body and damages the mind.[86]

> He feels at home when he is not working, and when he is working he does not feel at home. His labor is therefore not voluntary, but coerced; it is forced labor. . . . Its alien character emerges clearly in the fact that as soon as no physical or other compulsion exists, labor is shunned like the plague.[87]

Like the Black Death traveling along the silk road, labour takes the form of an epidemic under capitalism; it travels and permeates. Butler's alienation was something else. It was a call for reform through labour legislation. It did not strike at the very essence of the capitalist system, demystifying its 'divine or diabolical activity', as Marx had put it.[88] In Butler's alienation, workers did not lose themselves: they simply needed to be organised on the basis of strictly industrial and non-political lines.[89]

Still, Butler repeatedly emphasised the physiological and psychological effects of technology on the production process. While the burdens of physical labour had been significantly reduced, it was replaced by 'an increased strain on the nervous system, which the human body is less prepared to resist'.[90] For Butler, technology under capitalism was basically driving people mad, or driving them to what he called 'nervous diseases' – the new diseases.

Labour and physical toil had been intrinsic to human activity for thousands of years, but mental or nervous exertion was a new phenomenon, or so Butler claimed. If Butler was not reading Freud, his version of alienation was still tied to some crude form of psychoanalysis:

> We hear of 'nervous breakdown' in all walks of life, not only among hard-driven intellectual and professional workers, but also among the least skilled workers exposed to the noise, the speed, the inexorable rhythm and discipline of the modern factory.[91]

[85] Karl Marx, 'Estranged Labour' in *Economic & Philosophic Manuscripts of 1844* (Martin Mulligan trans, first published 1932, Progress Publishers, 1959 ed).
[86] Ibid.
[87] Ibid.
[88] Ibid.
[89] Taha, n 31, 567.
[90] Director's Reply (Mr Harold Butler), International Labour Conference, 23rd Session (3–23 June 1937) 19.
[91] Ibid.

Here workers and intellectuals alike fall into a nervous breakdown in the wake of the modern factory. This connection was not particularly new. In fact, early neurologists in the second half of the nineteenth century argued that neurasthenia (or what is commonly known as a nervous breakdown) was caused by the stress and strain of modernity.[92] 'There exist[ed] no reasonable doubt that modern life, with its hurry, its tensions' had an impact on the increased cases of nervous breakdowns.[93] Neurologists cited increased urbanisation and the introduction of 'so-called time-saving, ie distance-annihilating instruments, such as the telephone, telegraph, [and] railroad' as reasons for the increased number of cases.[94] For Butler, it was the combination of those 'time-saving' and 'distance-annihilating' technological devices with industrial labour that led to nervous breakdowns. Butler was making a significant claim: modern technology under industrial capitalism spurred mental and nervous breakdowns, or what psychologists today call depression.

The strain was particularly severe for 'Eastern people', who had been introduced to mechanical industry many years after its introduction in the West – a concern that Butler had worked on throughout his tenure as director of the ILO.[95] Today, neurasthenia is an 'anachronistic illness . . . an exotic "culture-bound syndrome"' that has a clear colonial genealogy.[96] Butler, first and foremost a British civil servant who had organised as well as engaged in many adventures in Latin America, Asia and the Middle East through the ILO's technical assistance program, was certainly not making a critique of empire. In fact, his missions to many non-Western countries to study and give recommendations on the labour conditions made no reference to colonialism and its impact on labour relations.[97] Still, it was clear to him that workers outside of the West were

92 Megan Barke, Rebecca Fribush and Peter N Stearns, 'Nervous Breakdown in 20th-Century American Culture' (2000) 33 *Journal of Social History* 565, 567, citing George Beard, *American Nervousness: Its Causes and Consequences* (G P Putnam's Sons, 1881) 96–133.

93 Frantz Fanon, *Alienation and Freedom* (Jean Khalfa and Robert Young ed, Bloomsbury Academic, 2015) 567.

94 Ibid.

95 Director's Reply (Mr Harold Butler), International Labour Conference 23rd Session (3–23 June 1937) 19.

96 Laurence Monnais, 'Colonised and Neurasthenic: From the Appropriation of a Word to the Reality of a Malaise de Civilisation in Urban French Vietnam' (2012) 14 *Health and History* 121, 121–2.

97 Taha, n 31. As Fanon argued, 'colonized people cannot conceive any struggle except by foregrounding the radical contestation of the domination of his country by another

more susceptible to those new nervous diseases, not because of the specificities and intensity of racial capitalism but because technology and capitalism came later in those countries.

More leisure was necessary for sanity in the metropole and in the colony. Therefore, the question for Butler returned to the length of the working day. Before the industrial revolution, people worked twelve hours a day, but at their own pace.[98] Since 1848 workers struggled for the eight-hour working day as a result of the rigidity, surveillance and control of the modern factory.[99] This was a significant intervention. In fact, any serious critique of labour conditions needs to address time and temporality. Fanon put it seamlessly:

> The time clock has its nicknames, the 'bargainer', the 'grand-father'. The boss calls it the 'antitheft device' . . . The time clock prevents and limits the endemic guilt of the worker. . . . It represents the overall apparatus that employs the worker. Before the time clock, the worker had the possibility to apologize; from now on, the worker is constantly rejected in the solitude with the impossibility of persuading the employer about his good faith.[100]

These are the ways in which capital eats time and leisure. For Butler, however, this was a resolvable problem: give workers more leisure time – regulate the clock. Otherwise, the pathological symptoms appear: 'nervous tensions, explosive angers, dreams of these workers/nightmares: a train that departs and leaves me, a gate that shuts, a door that does not open, a game that I am not allowed to play, the boss has vanished, leaving the time clock in his place'.[101] For a regulated and depoliticised workforce, give them a good night's sleep free from demons and nightmares. Through the ILO, law would put an end to this insanity, suppressing the workers' violent desires.[102]

country'. Colonised workers cannot struggle on the same plane as miners in the North of France: Fanon, n 93, 528. On race and capitalism, see Robert Knox, 'Valuing Race? Stretched Marxism and the Logic of Imperialism' (2016) 4 *London Review of International Law* 81.

98 Director's Reply (Mr Harold Butler), International Labour Conference, 23rd Session (3–23 June 1937) 19. The year 1848 saw a revolutionary wave across Europe, famously known as the 'Spring of Nations.' See Karl Marx, *The Revolutions of 1848: Political Writings* (David Fernbach ed, Verso, 2010).

99 Ibid.

100 Fanon, n 93, 522.

101 Ibid.

102 This is borrowed from Freud's famous argument that the maintenance of human civilisation that distinguishes us from animals is dependent on the disavowal of violent and sexual instincts. See generally Sigmund Freud, *Civilization and Its Discontents* (W W Norton & Company, 2010). For an analysis of the role of law in regulating

The ILO, through Butler, was making an important critique. It highlighted the significance of the struggle for the forty-hour working week through a critique of modernity, and not through the common lethargic and essentialist account of the nature of workers as lazy and ungrateful. On the contrary, Butler argued that man is an 'irrationally industrious animal. He really likes work as long as it is within his compass'.[103] And to give workers more leisure time is to avoid the eruption of violent tendencies, such as strikes and protests, *and* nervous breakdowns. More significantly, Butler argued, the improvement of living standards was no longer inconsistent with sound economy, and it was possible to advance civilised living without relying on force.[104]

The logic was as follows: diminished leisure time led to nervous breakdowns among workers, which in turn led to labour strikes. As such, *normal* workers did not go on strike. And, to complicate matters further, *normal* women workers did not work after 8 pm and they did not work in professions deemed unbecoming. The work of women during the night became one of the central areas of intervention and laid the groundwork for the first labour codes drafted through the ILO's missions to the colonies. In this view, the factory, for women, becomes a place of promiscuity that would corrupt their moral character.[105] Furthermore, the regulation of women's night work also meant that the sanctity of the family institution would be protected. This way, their labour would not interfere with their unpaid reproductive labour at home.

Fanon, responding to a similar sentiment, explains it succinctly and with sharp irony: if a 'normal' person is 'someone who does not make a fuss ... then, the trade unionists who protest and make demands, are they not normal?'[106] For many, the criterion of normality is uninterrupted work – free from agitation and wildcats.[107] 'But a prostitute works! Well, she can nonetheless be neurotic'[108] – a common claim in mainstream psychiatry that was also manifested, albeit indirectly, in the

madness and human desires, see Martha Merrill Umphrey, Austin Sarat and Lawrence Douglas, 'Madness and Law: An Introduction' in Martha Merrill Umphrey, Austin Sarat and Lawrence Douglas (eds), *Law's Madness* (University of Michigan Press, 2003) 11.

103 Director's Reply (Mr Harold Butler), International Labour Conference, 23rd Session (3–23 June 1937) 19.

104 Ibid., 15.

105 Silvia Federici, 'Marx and Feminism' (2018) 16 *TripleC* 468, 469.

106 Fanon, n 93, 518.

107 Ibid.

108 Ibid.

ILO's and Butler's own policies on labour legislation regulating sex work and night work for women in Europe and the colonies.[109] Women needed to be protected from night work, while the family and the factory needed to be protected from their promiscuity. The duality of victimisation and demonisation of women workers, especially as they boisterously protested their conditions, fed into the ILO's constructed notions of the 'normal worker'.[110] The ILO was fearful of that 'abnormal' or 'mad' worker with nervous diseases – the *political*, *rowdy* and *sexual* worker – for madness was outside of the law.[111]

Workers' alienation, depression and reduced leisure time became part of the international legal agenda. While Butler was simply adjusting to an increasingly militant working class across the industrialised world, his intervention was still significant and should be acknowledged. Nevertheless, Butler's theory of alienation and his solutions to its pitfalls were theoretically at odds with emancipatory labour politics. The ILO was to ensure that workers were satisfied only to the extent that they did not rebel or, worse, become communists.[112] The need for greater leisure time was precisely an outcome of speed that was brought about by the advancement in transportation and communication technologies. Butler's critique was essentially a critique of technology, not capitalism. England – the first country to see the impact of urban industrialism – became the first country to have organised sports, he claimed.[113] It wasn't because the English had a special gift for sports, but because they needed it as a substitute for the physical exercise formerly exerted in manual labour, or in riding a donkey as a means of transport.[114] As the donkey was ditched for the railroad, law was needed to regulate the madness that was to ensue within the labour movement as time was slowly being chipped away by capital. Law would reduce the working day but certainly not socialise the production process or intervene in property relations.

The ILO declared itself the organisation for social justice, but its vision of social justice was only to sustain the status quo as the 'red threat' was quickly becoming a reality. For the ILO, class society was inevitable and

[109] Taha, n 31.
[110] Federici, n 105, 469.
[111] Umphrey, Sarat and Douglas, n 102.
[112] See Taha, n 31.
[113] Director's Reply (Mr Harold Butler), International Labour Conference, 23rd Session (3–23 June 1937) 19.
[114] Ibid.

unstoppable – natural.[115] It was not even desirable to disrupt it, let alone revolt against it. Its policies were intended only to make it more sustainable – a durable and reformed class society under capitalism.

5.4 Conclusion

The establishment of the ILO with its dual principles of universality and tripartism was celebrated as a momentous if not magical development in international legal history. The ILO made it possible for workers to participate for the first time in international labour policy in a way that challenged the very fabric of traditional state representation. It centred workers through a social justice framework that made it possible to engage with workers' alienation and mental health (or 'nervous breakdowns') in the context of industrial capitalism. This was a significant contribution. However, as the Belgian delegate at Versailles, Emile Vandervelde, put it: 'there are two methods of making the revolution we feel is happening throughout the world, the Russian and the British method', and it was clearly the British method that had won in the Labour Commission.[116] Through 'the British method of making the revolution', the working classes would receive their due gratitude when the Europeans were about to make peace. The creation of the ILO would allow the Allied Powers to involve organised labour in the crafting of social and industrial reform within the accepted framework under capitalism.[117]

While the contributions of the ILO were significant, or even radical for a discipline like international law, its vision of social justice was only to maintain the status quo – a sustainable and reformed class society under capitalism. It 'remains a disgrace to American intelligence', as J T Shotwell argued, that the Congress of the United States had characterised the ILO as 'a dangerous and revolutionary body'.[118] If the American Congress was correct, then the ILO would have been something else altogether, something other than simply 'an alternative to violent revolution'.[119]

[115] In contrast, for example, in the '1844 Manuscripts' and 'Excerpts from James Mill's *Elements of Political Economy*', Marx had consistently discussed alienation from an historical perspective, not a natural one. See Marcello Musto, 'Revisiting Marx's Concept of Alienation' (2010) 24(3) *Socialism and Democracy* 79, 82.

[116] Alcock, n 23, 37.

[117] Robert W Cox, 'Labor and Hegemony' (1977) 31 *International Organization* 385, 387.

[118] James T Shotwell, 'The International Labor Organization as an Alternative to Violent Revolution' (1933) 166 *Annals of the American Academy of Political and Social Science* 18, 25.

[119] Ibid.

6

Microcosm

Soviet Constitutional Internationality

SCOTT NEWTON*

6.1 Soviet Internationalism and Soviet Internationality

The adoption of the *Internationale* as the anthem of the newborn Russian Soviet Republic in 1917, and then for the Soviet Federation, the union of republics it would soon become, announced to the world that the revolution was only accidentally national but essentially international. It was launched from the ruins of one international movement (the Second Socialist International) and immediately established another (the Third Socialist International, the Comintern). The Comintern gave the movement and the project a national home for the first time, as well as national leadership and control, but the project remained international in its scope and programme. The Bolshevik project was world-historical, international in its very self-imagining, and it embraced and embodied the international in its subsequent self-fashioning. It sprang from an internationalist commitment and aspired to realise an internationalist vision in its constitutional architecture. In 1917 Russia became the capital of socialist internationa*lism* and over the next several years set the stage for a new mode of socialist governance internationa*lity* corresponding to it.

Over the five years of civil war and the Bolshevik struggle to produce an affirmative response to Lenin's famous question – can the Bolsheviks retain state power? – the Soviet socialist experiment underwent a fundamental and fateful transformation. Conceived as a national redoubt from which to propagate and foment world revolution – a hope that was quickly dashed by revolutionary misfires and failures in Germany, Poland, Hungary and elsewhere – the Soviet Republic proceeded to reinvent itself as an entirely novel state form, a model and a demonstration of a radically original form of domestic internationality, a proto-world-state.

* Reader in Laws of Central Asia, SOAS University of London.

Over the life of the USSR, Soviet socialist internationalism would continue to animate its foreign policy and set it apart from other sovereigns (at least until it was joined by fellow socialist states after 1945). The force and effects of Soviet internationalism on the development of international law, before and during the Cold War, are well appreciated and analysed.[1] Consistent Soviet solidarity with working-class movements and communist parties and Soviet moral and material support for socialist revolutions (with some exceptions, notably Yugoslavia and Greece) was a staple of Soviet international relations. So, too, was its urgent demand for the end of colonial empires and its championship of anticolonial liberation and self-determination struggles.[2] But Soviet internationality and its challenge to international law are by contrast neglected and undertheorised.[3]

The Treaty of the Formation of the Union of Soviet Socialist Republics was regarded as a treaty of dubious status under international law, since the international legal subjectivity of the signatories was generally unrecognised (notwithstanding that that of the resulting Union *was* recognised, at least eventually). The signatories were the Russian Socialist Federative Soviet Republic, also known as Soviet Russia, the Ukrainian Socialist Soviet Republic, the Belarussian Socialist Soviet Republic and the Transcaucasian Socialist Federative Soviet Republic. The last itself comprised the Georgian-Abkhaz Soviet Socialist Republic (SSR) – the Bolshevik Republic having replaced the Menshevik predecessor – the Azerbaijan SSR and the Armenian SSR. These entities had each been stitched together from constituent imperial Russian governorates following their secure Bolshevisation over the course of the Civil War. That is, they were differentially reconfigured and reaggregated

[1] See, for example, Boris N Mamlyuk, 'Russian International Law and Indeterminacy: Cold War and Post-Soviet Dynamics' in Tatiana Borisova and William Simons (eds), *The Legal Dimension in Cold War Interactions: Some Notes from the Field* (Brill-Nijhoff, 2012) 81. Early (revolutionary) Soviet international legal theory, exemplified by Pashukanis, was political (insisting on the categorical difference between the socialist and bourgeois international law), whereas later (Cold War) Soviet international legal theory was ostensibly positivist.

[2] Bill Bowring, *The Degradation of the International Legal Order? The Rehabilitation of Law and the Possibility of Politics* (Routledge-Cavendish, 2008) ch 1.

[3] By internationalism, I mean an ideology asserting the objective pre-eminence of class over nation state, rejecting nationalism as false consciousness and embracing the norm of class (or popular) solidarity across national borders. By internationality, I mean incorporating and fostering multinationalism and intercultural respect in the architecture, practice and imaginary of a state itself, modelling a microcosm.

component jurisdictions of an empire itself disaggregated in the tumult of revolution and war. International lawyers at the time and now might be tempted to smirk at this exercise in 'quasi-' if not 'pseudo-internationality', but it reveals something essential in the Bolshevik project.

For the Bolsheviks found themselves accidental federalists and constitutionalists upon inheriting from the freshly overthrown Romanov dynasty an overland empire of greater territorial extent than many overseas empires, an altogether singular Eurasian *Großraum*. This was a geographic space unlike any in the world, assembled by inexorable eastwards and southwards Muscovite settlement and conquest over four hundred years. This migration had placed a vast, heterogeneous array of non-European peoples – from small-scale non-literate Siberian societies to the longstanding Islamic (Turco-Persian) civilisations of Central Asia, as well as European nations of variable historical consistency and integrity (Transcaucasian, Eastern Slavic, Baltic) – in geographic proximity and political subordination to a dominant European nation and polity. Fervent and dedicated anti-imperialists had broken with their Western socialist comrades on that very point at the Zimmerwald Conference. This meeting, in which the Bolsheviks took the hardest left position, was convened in September by the anti-war factions of the Socialist International in the teeth of fierce opposition from pro-war factions and their belligerent governments. Lenin and his fellow revolutionaries now confronted the problem of de-imperialising an empire while maintaining its territorial extent (apart from its Western fringes, forfeited in the Brest–Litovsk Treaty).

The governance scheme they devised for this unexampled space, of complex, multi-tiered ethno-territorial federalism, transformed an imperial expanse into an arena for an extended constitutional experiment in internal self-determination, a parallel Versailles order on a national scale. If 'Socialism in One Country' was the fallback the October Revolution had to adopt in the face of capitalist encirclement, 'Self-Determination in One Country' was its defiant innovation and provocation: if the socialist future now had a homeland (and a beachhead), the world's future must necessarily share it, in the same space. The USSR would become a great socialist homeland of sundry national homelands. This multinational and multicultural federation of peoples great and small, major and minor, developed ('advanced') and undeveloped ('backward') would stand as a microcosm, a modest-scale model and an adumbration of the destined global socialist macrocosm. The scope and audacity of this particular constituent project can hardly be overstated: neither the French Jacobins nor the American Framers essayed anything nearly as radical, not merely a new political order but a new social and (multi)cultural order – a radical *novus ordo saeculorum* together with a *novus ordo gentium*, a socialised and multinational dispensation for the future not the ages.

This Eurasian *Großraum* exhibited features of both overland (settler) and overseas empires. Continental settler colonial states such as those in North America and Australasia marginalised or eliminated native populations, but metropolitan overseas empires generally left colonial peoples physically and culturally intact (at least outside of islands), contenting themselves with political dominion and economic exploitation (or organisation). Imperial Russia had succeeded in politically incorporating and (patchily) Russifying or Europeanising geographically and culturally adjacent swathes of its acquired territories (the Steppes, Western Siberia, the Trans-Caucasus) but leaving much of the imperial peripheries (Central Asia, Siberia, Caucasus) for the most part culturally and to some extent politically intact.[4]

Lenin had long been obsessed with the national question.[5] Paralleling and provoking the rise of socialism, it became a conjunctural 'Question' (like the 'Jewish Question') of the greatest possible urgency and exigency, leading to the outbreak of hostilities in August 1914 that threatened to torpedo the entire socialist project. National identity and solidarity had always posed the most serious challenge to Marxist theory and praxis and competed for its core class constituency. It was, however, a damnably complex question in an age which was imperialist in the same degree as it was nationalist, a question which could not be solved by a simplistic stance of staunch anti-nationalism. For nationalism – in Lenin's eyes a particularly vicious false consciousness since it diabolically exercised a militant and successful rival appeal for working-class sympathies, sapping internationalist revolutionary

[4] Thus, for example, the Bokharan emirate and the Khivan khanate of Turkestan survived the Russian annexation of Central Asia, but the Khanate of Kokand was dissolved.

[5] Selected writings demonstrating the evolution of Lenin's complex views include: 'The National Question in Our Programme' in V I Lenin, *Lenin Collected Works* (Progress Publishers, 1960–1970) vol 6, 454–63; 'Theses on the National Question': at vol 19, 243–51; 'On the Question of National Policy': at vol 20, 217–25; 'The Revolutionary Proletariat and the Right of Nations to Self-Determination': at vol 21, 407–14; 'Draft Theses on National and Colonial Questions': at vol 31, 144–51.

energies – had also acquired a paradoxically virtuous character in the anti-imperialist struggles of 'small nations'.[6]

Second, and precisely in the context of the Leninist distinction between revolutionary defensive nationalism (legitimate, anti-imperial, socialist) and counterrevolutionary (illegitimate, imperialist, capitalist) great power nationalism (or chauvinism), for Lenin the national question could not have been closer to the Russian home. Alone among the imperialist belligerents, Russia's imperial structure, as its geographic empire, was indivisible from its status as European polity and Great Power: it was a State-Empire. It was not self-governing at home and imperialist abroad, it was imperial through and through – it governed *itself* as empire, not merely its imperial possessions and territories. This distinctive imperial governance uniformity, though not unqualified, is evident even in the Russian Empire's late, abortive gestures towards limited democratic rule. In the elections to the first 1906 imperial state Duma, the entirety of the empire was to return deputies, even 'indigenous nomadic peoples' (albeit by special electoral legislation).[7] Ironically, Moscow did not serve as an imperial metropole in the same sense as London or Paris did: the 'internal' Romanov empire could not be said to have possessed a hemispherically remote nerve centre in a 'mother country'.

6.2 International Legal Subjectivity and International Legal Order

The Bolsheviks understood themselves as having just overturned a national order in a first step towards a socialist international order to replace the existing Westphalian one. For Lenin the latter order – and particularly in the age of Finance Capital – was just the Committee of Committees, an international executive committee of the various executive committees of national bourgeoisies,[8] the World Club of national Capitals, lately riven by an inter-imperialist clash.[9] The assumption of international legal subjectivity in this context was problematic and

[6] 'Theses on the National Question', n 5.

[7] *Statute on Elections to the State Duma* (6 August 1905) Article 1.

[8] 'The executive of the modern state is but a committee for managing the common affairs of the whole bourgeoisie': Karl Marx and Frederick Engels, *Manifesto of the Communist Party* (1848) ch 1.

[9] 'Imperialism, the Highest Stage of Capitalism' in V I Lenin, *Lenin Selected Works* (Progress Publishers, 1963–1964) vol 1, 667–766.

fraught, from the Brest–Litovsk Treaty (hardly an auspicious commencement) onwards. Even after figuratively paying the price of the renunciation of its world-revolutionary aims (and less figuratively the price of the acknowledgement of contractual commercial obligations) for admission to and recognition by civilised interstate society, the Bolshevik insistence on socialist exceptionalism impeded the normalisation of Soviet interstate relations.[10]

Initially, the advent of a socialist sovereign produced shock and dismay among other sovereigns, prompting the Allied intervention in the Russian Civil War to strangle the monster in its cradle.[11] Bolshevik success was a call to arms for discontented proletarians everywhere, and it was subversion that struck terror into their governments, rather than any military threat posed by a weakened and war-exhausted Russia, however ardently and militantly revolutionary. Churchill feared the Glaswegian dockworkers, not the Red Army. The menace from the East was to the civil order and the international order in equal measure. The case for the essential ineligibility of Soviet Russia for international recognition was memorably put by US Secretary of State Colby:

> It is not possible for the Government of the United States to recognize the present rulers of Russia as a government with which the relations common to friendly governments can be maintained. ... the existing regime in Russia is based upon the negation of every principle of honor and good faith, and every usage and convention, underlying the whole structure of international law; the negation, in short, of every principle upon which it is possible to base harmonious and trustful relations. ... We cannot recognize, hold official relations with, or give friendly reception to the agents of a government which is determined and bound to conspire against our institutions.[12]

Recognition was bestowed only grudgingly and conditionally, a foretaste of the earned sovereignty idea after the collapse of the socialist bloc seven

[10] Andrea Leiter, 'Contestations over Legal Authority: The Lena Goldfields Arbitration 1930', Chapter 13 in this volume.

[11] Matthew Hughes and William J Philpott, 'Allied Intervention in the Russian Civil War' in Matthew Hughes and William J Philpott (eds), *The Palgrave Concise Historical Atlas of the First World War* (Palgrave Macmillan, 2005) 98.

[12] Colby to Avezzana (9 August 1920) in *The Papers of Woodrow Wilson* (Princeton University Press, 1992) vol 66, 22–4, cited in David W McFadden, 'After the Colby Note: The Wilson Administration and the Bolsheviks, 1920–21' (1995) 25 *Presidential Studies Quarterly* 741, 742.

decades later.[13] Only once the new Soviet authorities were willing to accept at least some of the liabilities of succession to the Romanov state, and to behave responsibly as a commercial and economic power, were fellow sovereigns willing to overlook its eccentricities and its lurking menace.

The recognition dilemma was mutual, although on balance it was the new regime that had to make the most significant accommodations, tempering its rhetoric and its posturing. The Soviet rupture defined itself as a rupture with the old public international and capitalist normal; the Soviet state embodied and adumbrated a new normal – a progressive and enlightened normal that was defined socially and economically before all else. Nonetheless, whatever its initial difficulties when faced with the prospect of an upstart sovereign with revolutionary designs on the others, an international society long accustomed to indifference regarding the internal governance and social arrangements of its membership had less difficulty digesting the new Soviet state than the other way around: *cuius regio, eius ideologia* was no novelty, and no biggie, for the international legal order.

With time, however, the Soviets learned not merely to make the necessary adjustments that assertion of international legal subjectivity required but to embrace that subjectivity ardently and exploit its capacities both strategically and ideologically, with ingenuity, elan and native Russian legal nous. The long and vivid history of accomplished and assured Soviet international *lawyering* is perhaps the definitive manifestation of the USSR's engagement with international law.[14] The novelty of Soviet international legal subjectivity however pales beside the novelty of the USSR as a *quasi-international legal order*, an internal international order, a rival international order to the one valorised and renewed after the Versailles treaties. Soviet internationality was a specifically

[13] For a lucid critique of the emergence of the concept of earned sovereignty in the 1990s, see Rose Parfitt, *The Process of International Legal Reproduction: Inequality, Historiography, Resistance* (Cambridge University Press, 2019) 403–8.

[14] For native accounts of Soviet international law, see especially E B Pashukanis, *Ocherki po mezhdunarodnomu pravu* [Essays in International Law] (Sovetskoe zakonodatel'stvo, 1935); G I Tunkin, 'The Contemporary Soviet Theory of International Law' (1978) 31 *Current Legal Problems* 177. Perhaps ironically, perhaps unsurprisingly, Soviet international lawyers established a reputation as hard-nosed positivists, skilled in the deployment of international legal argumentation to advance the state interests of their client, but not otherwise invested in it: Mamlyuk, n 1. Bowring maintains that Soviet international legal positivism was mitigated by Soviet ideological commitment to self-determination: n 2.

constitutional internationality that had a long and complex genealogy and was finally assembled across a set of contingencies – political contingencies, contingencies of circumstance, cultural contingencies and the contingencies of personality.

6.3 Soviets, Republics, Soviet Republics

The difficulty in reckoning fairly with Soviet governance begins with the mystification of its half-translated, half-transliterated name, 'Soviet Union'. Soviet means simply council or conciliar. The novelty in conciliar governance was its capacity to be replicated at any and all levels of authority, from the village to the Union, making for a kind of fractal governance geometry – as though Parliament were to be structured in precisely the same fashion as a local council; the only difference was one of scale. This scalar isomorphism was the hallmark of Soviet soviet (conciliar) democracy. Councils – soviets – at whatever level were elected by direct universal suffrage.[15] The conciliar principle eventually took precedence over the self-determination principle. At an early point, 'National Soviets', that is, ethnic councils, were set up for smaller (for example, Siberian) nationalities, but these were phased out and the principle of territorial rather than ethnic suffrage was universalised.[16]

At the base of this extraordinary constitutional framework, one of the few examples in history of sweeping constitutional innovation and experimentation rather than variations on established themes, lay the 'Soviet Republic'. The Soviet Republic (something of a contradiction

[15] The 1936 'Stalin Constitution' provided as follows:

> Article 134. Members of all Soviets of Working People's Deputies – of the Supreme Soviet of the USSR, the Supreme Soviets of the Union Republics, the Soviets of Working People's Deputies of the Territories and Regions, the Supreme Soviets of the Autonomous Republics, and Soviets of Working People's Deputies of Autonomous Regions, area, district, city and rural (station, village, hamlet, kishlak, aul) Soviets of Working People's Deputies – are chosen by the electors on the basis of universal, direct and equal suffrage by secret ballot. [Articles 84–91 provided for direct election on the ground of universal suffrage on the basis of electoral districts.]
>
> Article 139. Elections of deputies are direct: all Soviets of Working People's Deputies, from rural and city Soviets of Working People's Deputies to the Supreme Soviet of the USSR, inclusive, are elected by the citizens by direct vote.

[16] Terry Martin, *The Affirmative Action Empire, Nations and Nationalism in the Soviet Union, 1923–1939* (Cornell University Press, 2001).

given the anti-statist thrust of classic Marxist doctrine) originated as an expedient to ensure Bolshevik political control but in the context of an at least formally or nominally radically democratic, workerist (proletarian) form of representative public authority. Lenin's slogan, 'All Power to the Soviets', committed the revolutionary state to a conciliar governance structure, enabling the Bolsheviks to claim for their own the legitimacy of the (defensibly) organic, authentic workers' councils while reliably domesticating them and sparing themselves the labour of having to contrive something novel and significantly less spontaneous and credible. The councils were preferred precisely because they did not originate as Party instrumentalities (although they rapidly became such). Once the template for the Soviet Republic had been elaborated for the Russian heartland, it could be replicated, as it rapidly was across tsarist space under Bolshevik control, Soviet authority, *Sovietsakaia vlast'* (*советская власть*).

The Soviet Republic was established immediately for European Russia and the Romanov lands over which the Bolsheviks at least could pretend to exercise authority in the circumstances of 1917–18. Lenin built federalism into the scheme from the inception: this very first in the line of anticipated Soviet republics was a *federal* republic, the 1918 Russian Socialist Federated Soviet Republic,[17] or RSFSR (an acronym it retained once incorporated as the plinth of the new Union, although 'Socialist' and 'Soviet' soon changed places in the official name). Article 11 of the new constitution provided:

> The Soviets of those regions which differentiate themselves by a special form of existence and national character may unite in autonomous regional unions, ruled by the local Congress of the Soviets and their executive organs. These autonomous regional unions participate in the Russian Socialist Federated Soviet Republic upon the basis of a federation.

In its very first year, Lenin contrived the establishment of the first autonomy, the Turkestan Autonomous Socialist Republic, for tsarist Central Asia, with its own constitution.[18] The Bashkir Autonomous

[17] *Constitution (Fundamental Law)*, Russian Socialist Federative Soviet Republic, Resolution of the 5th All-Russian Congress of Soviets, adopted 10 July 1918.

[18] *Constitution of the Turkestan (Autonomous) Soviet Republic*, 15 October 1918, in *Soviet constitutions: Chrestomathy in 4 parts* (D V Kuznetsov compiler, Blagoveshchenskii State Pedagogical University, 2015) pt 1, First Soviet Constitutions 1918–1922 [Д В Кузнецов, *Советские конституции. Хрестоматия. В 4 частях.* Часть 1 Первые советские

Soviet Socialist Republic was established in 1919[19] and a century later itself remains (as the Republic of Bashkortostan), like many of the autonomies set up within the RSFSR, a Subject of the Russian Federation.

As the Civil War drew to its conclusion, Soviet Republics under firm Bolshevik control were rapidly established in the non-Russian areas of the empire, once Bolshevik authority and military control were secured by the Red Army . The Trans-Caucasus, for example, saw the national democratic republics[20] (in Georgia uniquely a Menshevik government)[21] established following the 1917 revolution each replaced with Soviet Socialist Republics in 1920–1. This pattern of effective conquest- (or putsch-) cum-constitution was followed generally for the Romanov peripheries (for example, the Bokharan Soviet People's Republic), but also beyond them (for example by Béla Kun in Hungary in 1919 or by Stalin in Galicia in 1920). Thus, the Soviet Republic was a jurisdictional and constitutional template, a genus, which could be replicated and rolled out. It came to form the fundamental constituent unit of the mature Soviet constitutional scheme, the chosen building block of Soviet internationality. The commitment both to constitutionalism and federalism was characteristic of the Bolshevik approach to governance and led to realised Soviet internationality in the mature Union scheme.

6.4 Realised Soviet Internationality

The ethno-territorial federalist conception worked out by Lenin and Stalin, endlessly tweaked over the protracted course of 'national delimitation', and subject to perennial readjustment and revision thereafter, ultimately yielded an entire parallel multinational universe, a Soviet microcosm of internationality that in its scalar, specular fashion reflected like a funhouse mirror the macrocosm of the international order outside. The compound federalism of the mature USSR recalls in its nested, graduated series of autonomies a Russian matryoshka doll.[22] Soviet constitutional law created four tiers of autonomy.

Республики 1918–1922, гг.,Благовещенский государственный педагогический университет: Благовещенск 2015].

[19] Richard E Pipes, 'The First Experiment in Soviet National Policy: The Bashkir Republic, 1917–1920' (1950) 9 *The Russian Review* 303.

[20] Azerbaijan Democratic Republic, Republic of Armenia, Democratic Republic of Georgia.

[21] Eric Lee, *The Experiment: Georgia's Forgotten Revolution 1918–1921* (Verso, 2017).

[22] The scheme was not perfectly nested. Sub-Union-Republican autonomies of all levels shared the same Union Republican space side-by-side, so that autonomous areas were not

First, at the top, the Union Republic,[23] endowed with sovereignty and a right of secession, established pursuant to its own constitution, vested with an entire institutional armature of government (separate legislature, judiciary and executive), granted a sphere of exclusive and shared legislative competencies, and provided with an entire complement of social, cultural, educational and economic institutions (universities, academies of science, conservatories, scientific institutes and so on). Second, just beneath it was the Autonomous Soviet Socialist Republic (ASSR),[24] similarly endowed with sovereignty but without a right of secession, established pursuant to its own constitution, jointly subordinate to the central Union and the Union Republic, vested with a legislature and judiciary, and provided with some social, cultural, educational institutions, authorised to chart its own economic policies. Third came the Autonomous Oblast [Province] (AO),[25] not endowed with sovereignty but equipped with a legislature, and organised pursuant to a law adopted for it by the Supreme Soviet of its superior Union Republic. Finally, at the lowest tier was the Autonomous *Okrug* [area],[26] with its own administrative authority (centrally appointed).[27]

Lenin and Stalin shared the authorship of the distinctive constitutional mode of Soviet internationality in a tense but immensely productive architectural partnership, and the governance scheme of tiered federalism was particularly their joint effort. Only Lenin at this period conceived of a multinational state organised on the principle of self-determination for its component nations: self-determination in one country. Imperial geographic and demographic complexity confronted the Bolsheviks with a task of the political and administrative organisation of culture on an unexampled scale. In particular, the simultaneous presence among the former Imperial subject peoples of so many different degrees of perceived

located inside autonomous provinces, nor autonomous provinces inside autonomous republics.

[23] *1977 USSR Constitution*, Articles 76–80. There were ultimately fifteen Union Republics after the annexation of the Baltic States in 1939 and the demotion of the Finno-Karelian SSR to an ASSR.

[24] Ibid., Articles 82–3.

[25] Ibid., Article 86.

[26] Ibid., Article 88.

[27] In earlier iterations of the Soviet Constitution, even smaller autonomies were contemplated, down to the Kolkhoz National Soviet, perhaps the tiniest of the matryoshka dolls at the very centre. See discussion on 'national councils' at nn 15–16 and accompanying text; Martin, n 16.

cultural proximity to a putative European standard posed the 'civilisational' question in a uniquely radical form.

In shepherding the Soviet internationality project, Lenin and Stalin were forced to grapple creatively with this 'civilisational question' and all the formidable culturalist anxiety it provoked. Lenin, in devising the formula of ethno-territorial partition to resolve the 'civilisational' question, and Stalin, in subsequently refining and operationalising it, had to shoulder the task of designing and assigning *suitable forms of autonomy* to ethno-territorial jurisdictional units – that is, of establishing a hierarchy of institutional forms of autonomy corresponding to a posited hierarchy and trajectory of cultural development from 'backward' to 'advanced'.[28] For in Lenin's view, self-determination was a means to socialist development and modernisation, not an end in itself.[29] Differentiation and autonomous development of peoples was but a waystation, an interim stage, on the path to amalgamation [*слияние, sliianie*]. In this distinctive context of an industrialisation drive, an overarching integrationist Marxist-Leninist ideology and concentrated political authority possessing unmatched dispersed (social) penetration, the self-determination of Soviet internationality was a programme, not merely a constitutional principle. It was a set of governance arrangements designed not merely to enable but to foster and encourage the political, social and cultural development of its constituent ethnic collectives in the common pursuit of a single, goal-orientated ideology. As a result, the self-determination of the constituent nations of the USSR was, ironically, very much a canalised and directed affair: other-determined self-determination.

For if the ideology and constitutional premise of Soviet internationality lay in self-determination, its purpose and rationale were ultimately grounded in Soviet directive 'socialist developmentalism'. The system of

[28] According to a resolution of the 10th Party Congress (1922), Soviet autonomy was called upon 'to develop and strengthen Soviet statehood in *the forms corresponding to the national-living conditions* of these peoples' (emphasis added): *Konstitutsionnye osnovy narodovlastiya v SSSR* (Leningrad University, 1980).

[29] Indeed, Lenin only reluctantly and belatedly embraced self-determination as a necessary, albeit tainted, anti-imperial instrument; the nationalities problem was an especially knotty one for a Marxist-universalist position. Nationalism was defanged for Bolshevik purposes by being entirely subordinated to the requirements of socialism, rather than as enjoying any intrinsic value. Only in this way could it be sharply demarcated from bourgeois nationalism, which was ideologically construed as a rival (and polar) principle of social and economic organisation.

autonomies was fundamentally an aspect of the comprehensive Soviet development regime that Lenin envisaged for the uniquely complex challenge of 'uneven geographical development'[30] confronting Soviet power – a regime that once in place in the 1920s produced the first 'affirmative action Empire'.[31] The USSR did not pioneer internal self-determination alone but internal developmentalism, or centre-periphery development assistance, as well. Soviet internationality was a complex constitutional and policy response (or a constitutional policy response) to the extraordinary 'uneven geographical development' of Eurasian space, a consequence of the spatial and temporal unevenness of tsarist-mediated industrialisation and modernisation (and the institutional and psycho-cultural penetration underlying them) across the vast miles and down the several centuries. The Soviet 'Second World' contained its own inner European or Europeanised 'First World' on the near side of the Urals and its peripheral 'Third World' beyond and below, in the Far North, Siberia, Central Asia and the Caucasus.

Lenin famously was a splitter and Stalin a lumper when it came to fixing and calibrating the jurisdictional units of this anomalous post-imperial and anti-imperialist empire.[32] The level of autonomy was, however, not straightforwardly a function of 'civilisational status'. Other demographic, historical, political and geographic factors such as territorial concentration, numbers, historical coherence as a polity and political reliability (subordination to Soviet power) necessarily also furnished criteria for fixing the level of autonomy as well as delimiting its territory. Ukrainians and Georgians, Kazakhs and Uzbeks all merited Union Republics; Chechens and Tatars, Buryat and Jews qualified for lesser degrees of autonomy.[33] Apart from the Slavic states of Belarus and

[30] The phrase is David Harvey's: David Harvey, *Spaces of Global Capitalism: Towards a Theory of Uneven Geographical Development* (Verso, 2006) 70–5.

[31] Martin, n 16.

[32] Lenin favoured more less-inclusive autonomies, a mosaic; Stalin (Commissar of Nationalities) favoured fewer more-inclusive autonomies, a patchwork. See ibid. At the largest of scales, Stalin was opposed to the Union concept of notionally equivalent constituent republics, preferring to enlarge the Russian republic, the RSFSR, to incorporate all other autonomies.

[33] The Soviet version of the Jewish Question centred around the status of the Jews as a nationality, but a floating, cosmopolitan one without a homeland – a tension eventually resolved by the 1934 creation of Birobidzhan, a Jewish AO in Siberia. The status of Birobidzhan as an Autonomous Oblast (which has been maintained through the present day), that is, the highest *non-sovereign* form of an autonomy, furnishes provocative matter for analysis and interpretation.

Ukraine, no peoples within imperial territory prior to the conquest of Central Asia and the Caucasus in the nineteenth century were accorded the status of a Union Republic.[34] The Russian republic was itself federated (as the RSFSR) rather than fragmented into Union Republics.[35] Behind this complex and asymmetric, quadruple-tiered hierarchy of autonomy lay an elaborate cultural calculus, exceeding in its baroque architecture any scheme concocted for the colonial empires.

This cultural calculus relied on two principal criteria: autochthony (the historical association of a collectivity with a territory) and backwardness, a term carried over directly from the tsarist political vocabulary.[36] 'Advanced' meant Western; 'backward' meant Eastern, so a familiar orientalist/colonialist terminology was adopted by the Bolsheviks, albeit for avowedly anti-imperialist ends. The cultural status of the population was not a necessary determinant of the institutional level of autonomy: the titular population of an SSR could be backward (Azerbaijan, the Central Asian republics); the titular population of an ASSR or AO could be advanced (Armenians in Nagorno-Karabakh). Nonetheless, as a general rule (at least outside Central Asia, which was regarded as a backward region altogether), ethnic groups regarded as more advanced merited higher levels of autonomy.

[34] These were also the only two SSRs to be accorded membership of the UN and seats (and votes) at the General Assembly (as a result of a deal struck between the United States and the USSR), suggesting that even within the fictional sovereignty of the SSRs, there were degrees and a hierarchy.

[35] With the exception of Kazakhstan and the Central Asian republics, which alone among SSRs were carved out of the territory of the RSFSR. It is an interesting subject for analysis why the Central Asian republics were treated in this fashion. On the one hand, they were accorded the dignity of Union Republics, on the basis of such factors as the historical significance of the region, its recent conquest and differential incorporation into the Russian polity (that is, its status as contiguous colonies). On the other hand, they were the only Union Republics which did not participate in the Union Treaty of 1922, not enjoying even a notional Bolshevik independent political existence in the manner of Georgia, Armenia, Ukraine etc., only subsequently having such an existence effectively conferred upon them by Union authority. Moreover, they could even be said to have been conjured into existence, since none of the 'stans' corresponded to any historical polity (or, for that matter, to any historical ethnicity) and their boundaries were arbitrarily fixed by Stalin. All of this suggests that the culturalist hierarchy ran within categories of autonomy, and not merely between them. Not all SSRs were created equal, and there seem to have been at least four de facto tiers: the RSFSR, followed by the Slavic republics, then the Transcaucasian republics and last the Central Asian republics, in descending order of 'Europeanness' ('Russianness').

[36] Martin, n 16.

Soviet constitutional internationality brooked no competition from outside when it came to the self-determination of Soviet nations. Thus, although Soviet internationalism strongly promoted and endorsed liberation/national movements in colonies abroad and among subaltern peoples generally (under the banner of 'defensive nationalism'), it strictly quarantined and guided the nationalism of Soviet subaltern nations. When the Congress of Peoples of the East was convened in Baku in 1920, the Russian (Bolshevik) delegates spoke out against separate, uncoordinated, nationalist action in favour of (Bolshevik-) guided and coordinated action. The Peoples of the East were required to be reframed as the Peoples of the Soviet East, a shift that was accomplished with the Sovietisation of the formerly imperial East (Central Asia, Siberia) but that rendered problematic those Peoples of the East not thereby enfranchised. The problem posed by rival, extra-Soviet self-determination became acute with the rise of pan-Turkism and Kemalism, from which Soviet Eastern nations needed to be quarantined politically, culturally and linguistically – hence the shift toward Cyrillicisation of scripts across the Soviet East in the 1930s.[37] The microcosm of Soviet internationality had to be shielded from the macrocosm if it were to preserve its integrity and distinctiveness – and its political tractability.

6.5 Self-Determination and Soviet Internationality

Soviet constitutional internationality can now be profiled against its broader epistemic and generational context. The legal and political ideas behind Soviet ethno-federalism, adapted as they might have been to the needs of the Bolshevik leadership to centralise a multinational polity without a classically imperial framework of domination, were not unique to it. Rather, they partook of a wider set of values, ideas, concepts and projects circulating around the turn of the twentieth century under the umbrella of nationalism and self-determination and set aflow in international law by the Versailles agreement following the breakup of all the Central and Eastern European empires (German, Hapsburg and Ottoman) save the Romanov. That is, Leninist and then Stalinist approaches to Soviet internal internationality represent an instantiation of the general or common set of ideas revolving around self-determination.

[37] Ibid., 182–207.

Self-determination is anything but a determinate concept: it runs an extraordinarily shifting and serpentine course as international legal doctrine. It is very much a moveable feast, so much so that it has been characterised as a 'historically contingent array of doctrinal and policy deployment by a contingent embodiment of international authority on nationalist conflicts whose protagonists are designated by a contingent set of legal categories'.[38] Indeed, international law provides the basis for the identification of 'general roles . . . for protagonists in its accounts of specific nationalist dramas; they may, accordingly, be referred to as "protagonist-positions" ready to be filled by particular groups, states, or institutions in particular contexts'.[39]

The 'original' self-determination regime emerging from the Versailles agreement was itself complex and overdetermined, reflecting an inconsistent-where-not-downright-contradictory welter of Enlightenment and post- and anti-Enlightenment ideas. The Versailles order was predicated on the core Enlightenment beliefs in the inevitable historical tendency from arbitrary political domination (heteronomy) towards liberation and self-government (emancipation) and the popular basis for the legitimacy of any system of rule and of any ruling authority (democracy, Rousseau). However, it also enshrined the singularity, coherence, duration and immutability of cultures (essentialism, Herder); the vindication of recognition rights through struggle (Hegel); the appropriate basis for modern statehood and membership in the community of states (nation-state form as standard, Hegel again); the proper gauging of territory to demography (nationalism); and the geographic and temporal hierarchy of cultures as civilisations (imperialism).

The resultant regime translated these ideas into a series of legal norms and categories (rules and institutions) governing self-determination, beginning with the nature and scope of the right (or its realisation). Self-determination in its ideal or limit variant was predicated on the ideal-type of a nation state and signified the right of a nation to a state. It included as lesser variants forms of political and/or cultural autonomy for minorities within states. Thus self-determination was glossed as fundamentally and generally a *national* right, exercisable by nations in an external context, and only secondarily and exceptionally as a

[38] Nathaniel Berman, 'The International Law of Nationalism: Group Identity and Legal History' in David Wippman (ed), *International Law and Ethnic Conflict* (Cornell University Press, 1998) 25.

[39] Ibid.

subnational right, exercisable by minorities in an internal context. The right thus established was made subject to conditions on its exercise: self-determination was granted to (some, though by no means all) ethnically plural states on the condition that they undertake to protect the cultural rights of ethnic minorities (post-imperial European states), in a manner analogous to earned sovereignty; to others it was granted only prospectively and contingently, provided they developed the requisite civilizational capacity under authorised tutelage (the Mandates system). These conditions in turn implied standing to assert the self-determination right (or capacity to realise it): only bona fide and politically mature or capable 'nations' were entitled to the full external political right. Finally, the Versailles self-determination scheme was made subject to the competence of an international authority to regulate assertion and recognition of the right (the League of Nations).

Self-determination law, the international regulatory regime emerging from Versailles that Berman has felicitously termed the 'international law of nationalism', thus encompassed a hierarchy of autonomy with statehood at the apex. Within this hierarchy, the first category was national independence for sufficiently large and cohesive constituent European peoples of the defeated empires, either (a) unconditional, for example, Czechoslovakia or (b) conditional on the protection of national minorities, for example, Poland or the Serb-Croat-Slovene State (Yugoslavia). The second was deferred self-government (and eventual statehood) for non-European territories and colonies of the former empires (Mandates system), further subdivided into graded categories by a criterion of civilisational maturity.[40] The third comprised limited instances of special political autonomy regimes for minorities in Europe, for example, the Aaland islands. Fourth came cultural autonomy regimes for minorities in the states under category 1(b) listed earlier.

Albeit reminiscent of the Soviet autonomies scheme, notably absent from the regime, however, is a corresponding normative structure for regional political autonomy within states, that is, territorial federalism. Self-determination was conceived in exclusively external terms, and not as touching the internal political architecture of the polity. Federal states had of course existed in Europe (notably, Switzerland, Belgium, the United Provinces of the Netherlands) but as exceptional cases, and did

[40] Antony Anghie, 'Colonialism and the Birth of International Institutions: Sovereignty, Economy, and the Mandate System of the League of Nations' (2002) 34 *International Law and Politics* 513.

not seem to come under the field of application of self-determination law as such. Indeed, the two most obvious candidates for federalism (and the two eventual federations) among the Habsburg successor states, Czechoslovakia and the Kingdom of the Serbs, Croats and Slovenes, were constituted as centralised, unitary states. That is, the international law of nationalism did not purport to regulate, therefore effectively excluding from its purview, the political rights of subnational communities. Indeed, it could be argued that to the extent that the minorities treaties required governments to undertake categorical protection obligations, they required strong unitary authority and militated *in favour* of centralisation and *against* decentralisation and federalism. Thus federalism, where it developed in this period, most notably in the USSR, did so *apart* from the international law of nationalism, as isolated national experiments, in accordance with an emerging and parallel *national* (constitutional) law of nationalism.[41] This constitutional law of nationalism found its most elaborate and baroque elaboration in the production of Soviet constitutional internationality.

Soviet constitutional internationality as the Bolshevik solution to the national question is overdetermined by ideology, episteme, strategy and contingency and is not reducible to a cynical ruse of cultural or political domination. It is drawn from a contemporaneous (post-Versailles) repertoire of embodiments of self-determination principles but in this one instance within a single polity, a deployment of self-determination along federalist rather than nationally independent lines. Soviet internationality borrowed principles articulated for nation states and applied them to autonomies within a single multinational state.[42] In this way a model of the imperial organisation of cultural pluralism, premised on domination

[41] The experience of federal states organised on a principle of pure territorial federalism, absent any ethnic or national component, is not especially relevant to self-determination law as such. Thus US constitutional law, the primary tradition of federalist jurisprudence at the time of Versailles, would appear to be largely tangential. However, inasmuch as US federalism is tripartite and not bipartite, including as it does the Indian tribes as well as the states, it does in fact include a (historically neglected) component of ethno-territorial federalism. Nonetheless, the 'constitutional law of nationalism' remained for the most part a Soviet monopoly, at least until the advent of post-colonial ethno-territorial federalism (India, Nigeria).

[42] Brubaker has described this phenomenon as 'the official, objectified codification and institutionalisation of nationhood and nationality exclusively on a sub-state rather than state-wide level': Rogers Brubaker, 'Nationhood and the National Question in the Soviet Union and Post-Soviet Eurasia: An Institutionalist Account' (1994) 23 *Theory and Society* 47, 50.

(core/periphery), would yield to a model of the federal organisation of cultural pluralism, premised on self-determination.

Soviet internationality, either in its initial Leninist (maximally differentiated and anti-imperial, or 'splitting') or Stalinist (hierarchical and 'Soviet-imperial', or 'lumping') form should be seen in the context of other efforts to accommodate national-ethnic pluralism, culturally and politically, under the broader League of Nations' regime for nationalism. This programme included everything from the self-determination of post-imperial states, the minorities protection regime to which some were supposed to be subordinated and the Mandates system for colonial territories. Purely as a legal-institutional device, it is but one species of a genus. What is more, again purely as a legal-institutional device, the Leninist/Stalinist system was radically innovative as against the other contemporary species, since it contemplated territorially premised political-institutional autonomy (however notional and subordinate to the directions of the centre) rather than just cultural autonomy (as in the League minorities regime), and it introduced an unprecedented level of structural complexity to the organisation of the state itself (unlike the self-determination regime for post-Imperial states, premised on unitary state structure).

Soviet constitutional internationality was an extension of the principles of Wilsonian territorial self-determination to the case of the constituent nations of a multinational state rather than the 'state-nation' (*Staatsvolk*) of a predominantly homogeneous state. It was thus the first application of self-determination law in an internal rather than a purely external context, presaging by almost seventy years the development of modern conceptions of internal self-determination as applying to pluralist structures of governance.[43] It was in many ways an adumbration of such complex internal self-determination schemes characteristic of the resolution of contemporary ethno-nationalist autonomy claims as Bosnia-Herzegovina or Northern Ireland, rather than the 'simple' external determination scheme (independence of a sovereign nation state) characteristic of the post-imperial European order (leavened by minorities regimes) or the post-colonial non-European order.

Just as the League regime entailed a hierarchy of categories that tracked culturalist prejudices, so the Bolshevik nationalities regime also

[43] Patrick Thornberry, 'The Democratic or Internal Aspect of Self Determination with Some Remarks on Federalism' in Christian Tomuschat (ed), *Modern Law of Self-Determination* (Martinus Nijhoff, 1993) 101.

encoded culturalist premises and ideas. The hierarchisation of cultures was an integral aspect of the ethno-federalist project of Soviet internationality.[44] The overt reliance on categories of backward and advanced (or Western and Eastern) in Soviet nationalities policy[45] and ideology recalls the categories A, B and C of the Mandates system (introducing a hierarchy among Mandatory territories of West Asian (Arab), African and primitive/indigenous). Unlike the Mandates system, autonomous republics, provinces and *okrugs* were never on a 'track' to greater self-governance the way Mandatory territories were (an autonomous province was never understood to be moving along a path to elevated status within the system). Nonetheless, they merited special developmental attention from the centre and were the beneficiaries of numerous subsidies and development interventions. The elaborate system of internal development assistance, established on an ethnic basis and gauged to perceived ethnic needs on a scale of 'backwardness' is analysed by Terry Martin as the 'affirmative action empire'.[46] Two criteria were employed for entitlements to preferential treatment: backwardness and autochthony. The system was primarily orientated toward social and cultural, rather than economic, equalisation per se. That is, investment in the underdeveloped regions was never comprehensively institutionalised and did not give rise to specific ethno-territorial economic entitlements but was carried out contingently and arbitrarily. The lesser autonomies were not political apprentices, but they were social, cultural and economic wards.[47]

6.6 Conclusion: The Fate of Soviet Internationality

Soviet constitutional internationality – Soviet federalism, the legislative, judicial and executive appurtenances of autonomy, the delineated competencies, the sovereignty of the SSRs and the ASSRs, together with the legislation regulating nationalities generally for the purposes of ensuring equality of participation and outcome (if not power-sharing) – might, all of it, be dismissed as an elaborate legal-institutional fiction masking the comprehensive domination of all aspects of public life at all levels of the

44 Laurence Broers, 'Containing the Nation, Building the State: Coping with Nationalism, Minorities and Conflict in Post-Soviet Georgia' (PhD dissertation, SOAS, 2004).

45 See generally Martin, n 16.

46 Ibid.

47 Ibid., 14.

Union by the Communist Party of the Soviet Union. But however remote from a robust substantive concept of autonomy, Soviet internationality is still more than an empty form of words, insofar as (a) its particular institutionalisation may have equated to a relative autonomy in the Soviet system environment and (b) its logic always residually escaped the limitations of any particular institutionalisation. The forms of autonomy were precisely legal-institutional forms and not 'mere forms', and the formalism of the Soviet constitutional law of nationalism was always potentially of real (that is, substantive) consequence. Institutionalists like Roeder have decisively overcome the objection of autonomy-as-nullity-in-fact by pointing to the elaborate complex of titular institutions, the control over material and financial resources, the administrative authority over cadres, the scope for law- and policy-making (however constrained by Party control), all as indisputably real and tangible consequences of constitutionalised Soviet federalism, which structured collective life and individual lifeworlds.[48] Soviet internationality predicated on the constitutional law of nationalism fashioned multiple, parallel ethnic worlds, using a standard set of institutional building blocks.

Inevitably all such ethnic worlds closely resembled one another, and there was little practical difference in laws, policies, administrative and political culture, incentives, career trajectories, and so on. The autonomy (sovereignty in the case of SSRs and ASSRs) ostensibly lying at the base of all of these worlds, and supplying the rationale for their creation in the first place, was both qualified (*qua* substance) and confirmed (*qua* form) by their sameness or standardisation. Even where indigenisation had progressed and those worlds were staffed and administered by indigenous personnel rather than Russians, they remained all stamped with the Soviet die. Nothing is more illustrative of this essential sameness than the former exhibits at the Exhibition of the Accomplishments of the People's Economy (*VDNKh*, *ВДНХ*), the permanent Soviet World's Fair in Moscow, where many autonomies would maintain pavilions in which were showcased ethnic arts and crafts, agricultural and industrial

[48] Philip Roeder, 'Soviet Ethnic Federalism' (1991) 43 *World Politics* 196. Nationalities law alongside federalism constituted identities and organised the social world objectively and subjectively. Brubaker tabulates the dimensions: 'a pervasive system of social classification, an organising principle of "vision and division" of the social world, a standardised scheme of social accounting, an interpretative grid for public discussion, a set of boundary-markers, a legitimate form for public and private identities, and when political space expanded under Gorbachev, a template for claims to sovereignty': Brubaker, n 42, 48.

production, costumes and folkways, and so on. They all were variations on a standard design theme (even down to the national flag and emblem).

Yet Soviet internationality, however odd and hermetic a universe it spawned – so evocatively represented in the pavilions of the *VDNKh* – had repercussions well beyond the parochialities of Soviet lifeworlds. The Soviet microcosm was both a standing challenge to the international macrocosm outside and a powerful influence upon it. The Soviet experiment in the elaboration of the constitutional law of nationalism was a model for post-colonial multi-ethnic federations like India and Nigeria, which borrowed its devices and its linguistic/ethnic logic of territorial division, as well as for the People's Republic of China, which retains the Soviet ethno-territorial autonomy scheme in largely unreconstructed form.[49] It modelled an entirely distinct form for normatively structuring the relations among distinct ethnic traditions and collectivities: a new kind of large nation/small nation, European/non-European dynamic (ostensibly) predicated on non-exploitation and equality and driven by a specifically socialist developmentalism. It manifested on the part of the USSR a socialist internationalism grounded in a praxis and a structure of socialist internationality. It enabled the USSR, emphatically unlike any of its Western adversaries – former colonial powers like the United Kingdom or France or former colonial jurisdictions like the United States or Australia, alike in their subjugation of native populations – to preach only what it practiced, to instruct by example and precept, simultaneously to promote and to model or instantiate self-determination. Soviet internationality, blazoned in the name of the polity, aspired to serve as a general principle of world governance: the Union of Soviet Socialist Republics was always only the prelude to the eventual 'Federation of Mankind', the microcosm anticipating the macrocosm, a World Union of Soviet Socialist Republics.

[49] Haiting Zhang, 'The Laws on the Ethnic Minority Autonomous Regions in China: Legal Norms and Practices' (2012) 9 *Loyola University Chicago International Law Review* 249.

7

Law and Socialist Revolution

Early Soviet Legal Theory and Practice

OWEN TAYLOR*

7.1 Introduction

There are few events in modern history that evoke as much controversy, and possess as much political salience, as the Bolshevik Revolution. The events of 1917 continue to animate a variety of political projects, as was evident with the various symposiums on the centenary of the revolution, and the different ways in which narratives about the events inform contemporary politics. The field of international law is no different. For a long time, scholars of international law looked to the revolutionary Soviet state for an example of how a radical political orientation clashed with the principles of international law and challenged its claim to universal representation. Numerous scholars on both sides of the political divide presented an image of the Soviet state as representing 'socialist' international law, in contrast to the existing norms and practices of law that guided the behaviour of contemporary states.

This chapter sets out to challenge this view, drawing attention to the fact that even comprehensive studies of Soviet international legal practice from the time did not present substantive evidence of contrary practice, and acknowledged that, in many areas, the Soviet Union mirrored its contemporaries. The Soviet state justified its position using conventional legal arguments, and its political opponents were as selective in their adherence to supposedly firm principles of international behaviour as the Soviet state was accused of being. Support for this position is found in secondary sources that discuss general Soviet deviancy, in addition to the writings of leading Soviet legal theorists from the 1920s, like Evgeny Pashukanis.

* Postdoctoral Researcher at Aix-Marseille University.

However, the fact that so much scholarship stressed Soviet deviancy from international norms in the face of contrary evidence provokes the question of why this was the case, especially those accounts where the scholars themselves noted consistency of practice with standard norms yet asserted Soviet deviancy irrespectively. In such cases, the argument was made that it was this common practice that was in fact inconsistent with the general deviation of the Soviet state from established norms, despite the lack of evidence for that general deviation. It is also noteworthy that, in a period in which many states, in their practice as imperial powers, were making extremely liberal use of international law, the supposed deviancy of the early Soviet state failed to prompt any introspection as to the 'binding' nature of these legal norms and principles on those states seen as progenitors of the entire international system. In other words, when surrounded by copious examples of hard-nosed *realpolitik*, it was the Soviet state that attracted opprobrium for threatening established international norms.[1]

There are a variety of possible reasons why some mainstream and Soviet scholarship tended to come to the same conclusions of Soviet deviancy, despite the evidence before them. Most likely, the notion of a revolutionary break came with both conceptual and political baggage: conceptual baggage in the form of preconceptions held about the nature of revolution – such that the observer is convinced behaviour must have changed because there has been a 'revolution'– and political baggage in the need for both revolutionaries and counter-revolutionaries to point to evidence of change to support the legitimacy of their own positions.[2] This view is evident in some of the claims both within and without the Soviet Union about the interaction of the Soviet state with the international

[1] There are numerous potential examples, embodied in the mandate system and broader colonialism. On the US occupation of Haiti, a burden shouldered under the 'oblig[ation] of circumstances', see Mary A Renda, *Taking Haiti: Military Occupation and the Culture of US Imperialism, 1915–1940* (University of North Carolina Press, 2001) 100. On the British administration in Iraq, where British officials looked for 'Arab institutions we can safely leave while pulling the strings ourselves; something that won't cost very much . . . but under which our economic and political interests will be secure', see Peter Sluglett, *Britain in Iraq 1914–1932* (Ithaca Press, 1976) 37. For an excellent history of the relationship between international law and empire, see Antony Anghie, *Imperialism, Sovereignty and the Making of International Law* (Cambridge University Press, 2005).

[2] See discussion in Owen Taylor, 'Reclaiming Revolution' (2011) 22 *Finnish Yearbook of International Law* 259.

legal system. Soviet jurists like Eugene Korovin[3] went so far as to describe the birth of an entirely new, opposing system of international law, created by the existence of the revolutionary state.[4]

However, more than the politics of revolution, this chapter argues that the depiction of a particular Soviet approach to international law is rooted in the absence of a rigorous theory of law. Without this, it is possible to ascribe an innate lawlessness to the Soviet state, and imagine that law governs the activity of other states in an unproblematic manner. Thus, although scholars were able to examine early Soviet legal practice and note its high level of continuity with standard international practice, the idea that communist states would not adhere to standard international legal principles came to overdetermine their subsequent analysis. A more rigorous engagement with legal theory would have had to make explicit why law was only a natural extension of Western states. Critical legal theory that examines the openness of international law to a wide variety of differing positions also suggests that there would be no need for the Soviet state to reject existing international law. For the indeterminacy thesis, it is the language, forms and procedures by which a position is articulated, and disagreement mediated, that defines law as law.[5] From this perspective, one would expect the Soviet Union to find ample space to express its positions within legal language.

Alongside examining this misrecognition of early Soviet international legal practice by its political opponents, this chapter also draws attention to those areas of Soviet practice that did offer a partial break with existing norms. This chapter argues that early Soviet legal theory provides a more apposite theoretical lens for interrogating the spaces between legal argument and a deeper 'legal form' than that presented by the indeterminacy thesis. There were, in fact, many forums in which Soviet scholars made theoretical observations about the relationship between revolutionary ideals and the nature of law, particularly in relation to domestic law. Although early Soviet legal theory was lambasted as an ex post facto

[3] His name is alternately spelled Korovine and Korovin in his publications in English. The English 'Eugene' is adopted here in place of Yevgeni in line with those same publications.

[4] E A Korovin, *Mezhdunarodnoe Pravo Perekhodnogo Vremeni* (Gosudarstvennoe Izd-vo, 1924) 25–6. For discussion, see Jan F Triska and Robert M Slusser, 'Treaties and Other Sources of Order in International Relations: The Soviet View' (1958) 52 *American Journal of International Law* 699, 703.

[5] For two variants of this position, see David Kennedy, *International Legal Structures* (Nomos, 1987); Martti Koskenniemi, *From Apology to Utopia: The Structure of International Legal Argument* (Cambridge University Press, 2005).

justification of Soviet policy, closer observation of the claims made by Soviet legal theorists, particularly in the lesser known commodity form school, demonstrates a deep and rigorous engagement with the meaning of law in the process of revolution.

On the international stage, Soviet legal theorists were quick to point out that the international legal system was one opposed to the goals of socialist revolution, in that this legal system underpinned international capitalism and the imperial domination of much of the world's population, and that the system of international loans in particular stood at stark odds with the interests of the working population of the world. However, the observation that the international legal system was generally opposed to the goals of socialist revolution did not preclude the use of that legal system in the defence or pursuit of those same revolutionary goals where possible – this use being the basis of Lenin's 'principled opportunism' when it came to law.[6]

On the other hand, the vitriolic response of some commentators to Soviet claims regarding Soviet liabilities pointed to a deep and symbiotic relationship between certain legal norms and the smooth functioning of international capitalism. In this vein, it is possible to imagine an unravelling of the logic of the international legal system if certain revolutionary claims for compensation, redistribution or debt alleviation were made into principles of international law. This would present a system in which the legal consolidation of capital was undone and the international economic system would cease to function in its current form. However, without such redistributive claims as a general principle, it is clear that any isolated legal victory would only effect a minor redistribution of resources between actors – an exception to the general rule that property (particularly financial property) and contract are sacrosanct. Imagining general principles of this kind, we would also be presented with a world where legal principle and powerful interest were in direct and generalised opposition, an impossibility that reveals a great deal about the limits of legal struggle.

This chapter concludes with the lessons that might be drawn from such observations. First, the combination of a fervently (at least in the early years) revolutionary state and conservative international legal practice implies the rather unsurprising conclusion that it is difficult to articulate revolutionary principles in legal form. Second, it became painfully obvious throughout the 1920s that whatever the legal arguments

[6] For a broader discussion of this principled legal opportunism, see discussion in Robert Knox, 'Strategy and Tactics' (2010) 21 *Finnish Yearbook of International Law* 193.

made by the Soviet state, international law followed the facts of power (a power that was also legally constituted). The Soviet state was outnumbered and outgunned – and legal protestations aside, there were no consequences either for the international intervention it was subjected to, or for its pariah status in international forums. Crucially, Russian revolutionary theorists never approached law, international or domestic, as a vehicle to help carry the revolution or build its principles. Indeed, the domestic debates on law in the Soviet state reveal a deep-rooted scepticism about the capacity of law, and particularly lawyers, to do this kind of work. Their perspective encourages a generalised caution against investing the form of law with revolutionary potential.

7.2 The Early Soviet Union in International Law

The standard narrative of early Soviet international legal practice paints a mixed and contradictory picture of the early Soviet divergence from standard practice: as either a disregard for international law altogether, an extreme positivism or the subordination of international law to the policy purposes of the Soviet state.[7] The positivism of the Soviet state is traced to the early Soviet focus on treaties and its claimed rejection of customary international law as applicable to the Soviet state. The disregard of the law, or on the other hand, the subordination of law to policy, was seen as self-evident, and repeated by a variety of observers, swiftly extending to interpretations of the role of legal theory in the Soviet state. Robert Slusser and Jan Triska, authors of the most comprehensive collection of Soviet treaty material in the English language in the early 1950s, noted the 'absolute dependence of Soviet theory on the practice of the Soviet state [as] a well-known fact'.[8] Continuing this trend into the second half of the twentieth century, Kazimierz Grzybowski summarised his own work as '[examining] the actions of the Soviet Government . . . in order to give meaning to rules and institutions of international law as they were used to legitimate Soviet conduct in international relations'.[9]

[7] A perspective that now informs textbook discussions of international legal theory: see Iain Scobbie, 'Wicked Heresies or Legitimate Perspectives? Theory and International Law' in Malcolm D Evans (ed), *International Law* (Oxford University Press, 3rd ed, 2010).

[8] Triska and Slusser, n 4, 721.

[9] Kazimierz Grzybowski, *Soviet Public International Law: Doctrines and Diplomatic Practice* (A W Sijthoff, 1970) 507.

The result of these perspectives was that Soviet legal theorists were interpreted as operating primarily in a pragmatic manner, inconsistently and in reaction to state practice. John Hazard detected a 'confusion' in that some Soviet legal theorists held an 'attitude' that law was bourgeois, and therefore had to be rejected, but then these same theorists came up against the crucial difficulty that 'it was necessary to live in a world with other states'.[10] Others also noted the supposedly beleaguered position of Soviet legal scholars: 'lagging behind Soviet practice in time, theorists . . . had certain governmental practices to follow, to systematize, to analyze in terms of official ideology, and to justify and defend'.[11]

The kinds of opening statements Western scholars felt the need to make when discussing the Soviet Union and international law are highly revealing in this regard. When introducing the Soviet Union, Hazard opened with the observation that:

> it is clear that the Soviet Government places itself among those who recognize the existence of international law and espouse its principles. At the same time, the literature indicates that the Soviet government considers international law, like all law, to be an instrumentality of the state, to be utilized in pursuit of the politics of the state. It expects other states to call upon international law to further interests which they believe to be their own, and it will do the same.[12]

This perspective on Soviet practice is predicated on an implicit or explicit contrast with the idea of generalised faithful compliance with international law – one in which other states looked to the principles of international law to guide their behaviour rather than further their interests, and in which, presumably, international legal theorists held great power to affect state policy simply through their intellectual labours. For illustrative purposes, it is very difficult to imagine similar scholars opening discussion of North American or European governments by pointing out that they recognise international law and espouse its principles.[13] In a manner consonant with the practice of Orientalism, the Soviet state was depicted as the dark shadow of Western states; an aberration in the international order, one whose engagement with

[10] John N Hazard, 'The Soviet Union and International Law' (1950) 1 *Europe-Asia Studies* 189, 190.

[11] Triska and Slusser, n 4, 722.

[12] Hazard, n 10, 198.

[13] Barring a certain glib anti-legalism articulated in recent times by US officials, arguments which sit alongside simultaneous support for a robust international trade regime.

international law had to be highly circumspect because of the nature of the actor itself.

For scholars like Hazard, this depiction extended to the claim that 'Soviet leaders [were] not always . . . interested in international law'.[14] The idea behind this was that the immediately hostile international environment in which the Soviet state found itself was justified through international legal arguments and that, therefore, international law was the 'weapon of the enemy',[15] demonstrated through the various doctrines of succession, recognition, liability for debts, the expected compensation for expropriated property and justifications for armed intervention against the Soviet state. The implication was that the Soviet leaders were so at ease in their hostile environment that they would take no interest in the various weapons the enemy deployed against them.

In addition to such logical holes and lack of comparative objectivity regarding the use of international law by the dominant capitalist powers, even early advocates of this 'Soviet approach' to international law struggled to find actual evidence to support the position they wished to take. T A Taracouzio's *The Soviet Union and International Law*, published in 1935, is exemplary in this regard.[16] Lauded as 'the only comprehensive treatment in this field' for over three decades,[17] the book set out to explore the radical difference posed by the Soviet state. However, throughout the volume, Taracouzio notes with surprise that the Soviet Union closely followed traditional practices, offered limited innovation and operated in a rather conservative manner in regard to all major areas of international law.

Addressing territory, Taracouzio observes that the 'international practice of the Soviet Union' shows a very close following of 'generally adopted international practice'.[18] Soviet approaches to diplomacy were summed up as consisting of no real outstanding contribution or change, other than the abolition of ranks (in practice circumvented at a later

[14] Hazard, n 10, 189.

[15] Ibid.

[16] T A Taracouzio, *The Soviet Union and International Law: A Study Based on the Legislation, Treaties and Foreign Relations of the Union of Socialist Soviet Republics* (Macmillan, 1935).

[17] Grzybowski, n 9, xvii. Grzybowski was wrong; for a list of the other comprehensive treatments in the intervening periods, see Ivo Lapenna, '*Soviet Public International Law: Doctrines and Diplomatic Practice* by Kazimierz Grzybowski' (1973) 21 *American Journal of Comparative Law* 600.

[18] Taracouzio, n 16, 56.

date) and the special status of trade representatives,[19] blurring the traditional boundaries in international law between persons with diplomatic status (and immunity) and those engaged in trade.[20] Interestingly, 'in most of these [trade-related] treaties the principle of reciprocity is followed, the same privileges being granted to the foreign trade agencies in the USSR when such agencies are established therein'.[21] In conclusion, 'innovations are not outstanding'.[22] With regard to nationality and international personality, 'Soviets lay primary emphasis . . . upon political allegiance'[23] (thus adopting a standard position in relation to nationality) and 'the Soviet law and practice in regard to natural persons in international law are not much different from those of non-communist states'.[24] Taracouzio noted that 'the Soviet law on diplomatic and consular service may well be called conservative',[25] and in treaty-making Soviets 'follow in almost every detail general international practice'.[26]

One of the primary driving forces for this continuing search for, or assertion of, difference in the face of continuity is revealed by Taracouzio when he notes that Soviet treaties concluded with Western states 'do not correctly reflect communist ideas'.[27] The self-fulfilling nature of this logic is evident. Western scholars and politicians alike understood the Soviet state to be a revolutionary communist state, meaning that it was expected to denigrate, or deviate from, international legal principles. When the Soviet state adhered to or espoused those principles, it could only be doing so out of cynical necessity, only further proving its difference.[28] Although Taracouzio was one of the most egregious examples, this

19 Ibid., 194.

20 Which is by no means to endorse the idea that these two roles did not, in actual fact, have intimate informal relations for all states.

21 Taracouzio, n 16, 195.

22 Ibid., 206.

23 Ibid., 122.

24 Ibid., 163.

25 Ibid., 234.

26 Ibid., 290.

27 Ibid., 289.

28 There were some notable exceptions, particularly Phillip Jessup, who in his review of Taracouzio's book noted that Taracouzio's recurrent and 'rather obvious' observations of Soviet adherence to international law in the face of a strawman communism were interesting not because they revealed some revolutionary 'communist theory' but because they demonstrated the *consistency* evident in Soviet state practice with 'traditional' international law: Phillip C Jessup, '*The Soviet Union and International Law* by T A Taracouzio' (1936) 9 *Pacific Affairs* 127, 128.

direction of thought dominated research on the Soviet Union well into the 1950s and 1960s, particularly in the United States.[29]

In the face of this, the Soviet government also repeatedly stressed its adherence to general legal obligations,[30] as well as decrying the disregard of legal norms and diplomatic courtesy conducted by its political opponents. Western powers intervened on behalf of military opponents of the revolution during the civil war period of 1919–21, and openly excluded the Soviet government from the Washington Conference of Pacific Powers in 1921, claiming they would represent Russia's interests in their absence and that a new Russian government would be invited to accept the agreements reached during the conference. Not only did the Soviet government see this as explicit 'favouring [of a] Russian counter-revolution' but as the further 'demonstration of the system of intervention'.[31] This diplomatic maltreatment was continued in the Paris Pact of 1928,[32] where the Soviet Union was invited to join the pact after the fact of its creation, conducted on a restrictive membership basis in the interests of 'expediency'.[33] Taracouzio's work included copies of these communiqués by the Soviet government, and, coupled with his own observations about the conservative practice of the early Soviet Union, it is remarkable that the interpretive lens of dissonance continued to dominate both his own and other studies on the subject.

The serious problems of such scholarship were acknowledged in US academic circles during the slight thaw in Cold War relations that marked the late 1960s and early 1970s. At the time, William Butler observed that:

> in identifying the manipulative, opportunistic side of Soviet international law we tend to overlook larger, more important issues: how, if at all, does the Soviet use of international law differ from that of non-socialist states? Are there certain types of situations where the style of Soviet use of

29 William E Butler, 'American Research on Soviet Approaches to Public International Law' (1970) 70 *Columbia Law Review* 218.

30 For example, the Soviet memorandum to the Genoa Conference of 1922 noted that the 'Soviet Government ... has always fulfilled and intends always to fulfil all obligations undertaken by itself, and that, therefore, all its public and legal guarantees are no less solid than those of any other sovereign power': Rex A Wade (ed), *Documents of Soviet History: Volume 2, Triumph and Retreat, 1920–1922* (Academic International Press, 1993) 364.

31 Taracouzio, n 16, 411–12.

32 Alternatively named the Kellogg–Briand Pact; the official title is 'General Treaty for the Renunciation of War'.

33 Included in Taracouzio, n 16, 417.

> international law varies from ours and certain types where it is basically the same? In what situations does the Soviet use of international law appear to have been effective? Where not? How is effectiveness to be measured? How has Soviet use of international law changed over time, if at all? How does the USSR value and balance the normative, stabilizing aspects of international law with its dynamic policy dimensions?[34]

Butler's admirable aspirations for future scholarship came as part of a more general shift in how the Soviet Union was understood in relation to international law, in which Soviet revolutionary radicalism faded, and the supposed clarity of early twentieth-century international law was subsumed by the growing complexity of international politics. Slusser and Triska observed that by the mid-twentieth century, the previous primacy of custom in Soviet legal policy now played a subordinate role, due to what Charles de Visscher called the 'acceleration of history, and above all [the] diminishing homogeneity in the moral and legal ideas that have long governed the formation of [international] law'.[35]

There are problems with this account (addressed below) that also stymie the promise of Butler's intervention.[36] In part, these problems are deeply embedded in the same conditions that enabled the early depictions of Soviet engagement with international law as radically different, in which the political environment had a powerful effect upon scholarly production. As is evident in work like Taracouzio's, scholars' preconceptions about communism overdetermined their analytical engagement, which was coupled with a remarkable lacuna towards the contradictions or self-serving elements of the practice of international law by its more 'long-standing adherents' – namely, Western European states and their extensive empires and settler colonies (including those that subsequently became empires in their own right).

However, the argument here is that there exists a more important, enabling factor: namely, the absence of any sustained theorising of the law itself. For example, the 'manipulative, opportunistic side of Soviet international law' that Butler refers to above has to be opposed to a more formal, rigorous aspect of law. But recognising that this 'side' of law was common to both the Soviet Union and its opponents would imply a different understanding of law itself – one in which it was seen to have a

[34] Butler, n 29, 228.

[35] Charles de Visscher, *Theory and Reality in Public International Law* (P E Corbett trans, Princeton University Press, 1957) 156, cited in Triska and Slusser, n 4, 726.

[36] See text accompanying nn 48–50.

much closer relationship to these political 'sides' than is otherwise implied.

The lack of a rigorous theory of law supports the contrasting of some states that abuse the principle of law or use it opportunistically against those states for which the legality of their practice is a given aspect of state identity. Again, any deviation from this basic frame can always be explained within the existing logic. When an aberrant state like the Soviet Union engages with international law in a 'traditional' manner, it is doing so deviously and with the aim of manipulating the system, whereas when a Western power demonstrates an apparent disregard for international law, or stretches the limits of legal plausibility in pursuit of its own interests, this is an exception that proves the rule of general adherence.

A more rigorous understanding of law would see that both of these 'sides' are aspects of the standard functioning of the legal form. After all, one of the most commonly recognised aspects of law is its use as a tool to negotiate disagreement without recourse to arms,[37] in which it is necessary that an actor brings their own particular interest to the legal forum and utilises the best means possible to achieve a favourable outcome. With this understanding of law, it would be far harder to maintain the opposition sketched above based on the nature of the parties involved, or to hold on to the idea that the law somehow adhered better to a particular European cultural type.[38]

One way of theorising the law in this instance would be as a discursive instrument. Here, the grammar of law, to use Martti Koskenniemi's structuralist language, is not determinative of any particular outcome.[39] This theory is a necessary characteristic of law if it is to serve its function as an arena for dispute resolution that is characterised by the trappings of law: its language, formalism and appeal to an objective and rational balancing of interests, obligations, legitimate expectations and so on. Koskenniemi's analysis of the grammar of international law, known as the indeterminacy thesis, postulates at a very basic level this intuitive fact

[37] See Kennedy, n 5, 50. See further Philip Allott's description of a treaty as a disagreement in writing: Philip Allott, 'The Concept of International Law' (1999) 10 *European Journal of International Law* 31, 43. However, such observations subsume the presence of a force to the law that is arguably always present.

[38] For critical discussion, see Robert Knox, 'Valuing Race? Stretched Marxism and the Logic of Imperialism' (2016) 4 *London Review of International Law* 81–6; Makau Mutua, 'Savages, Victims, and Saviors: The Metaphor of Human Rights' (2001) 42 *Harvard International Law Journal* 201.

[39] Koskenniemi, n 5.

about law: that every potential legal argument comes with its opposite counter-position, equally valid in terms of the grammar of law. The indeterminacy thesis does not state that international law has become indeterminate as a result of some contemporary development – say, for example, the fragmentation of international law. Rather it states that international legal argument is fundamentally indeterminate.[40] One small consequence of such a theoretical position applied to the study of early Soviet international law would be the expectation that valid legal arguments were available to the Soviet state to express its interests.

However, while offering powerful insights into the nature of legal argument, the indeterminacy thesis has explanatory limits when it comes to understanding the depiction of the Soviet approach to international law, and to understanding the nature of law more generally. With law reduced to legal argument, it is difficult to analyse the distinctions made between Soviet engagements with international law – which provoked angry Western responses – and legally acceptable Western practice. It is also harder to distinguish between legal arguments made by radical Soviet jurists, and their broader understanding of the law itself as something separate and intimately related to the functioning of the capitalist system and therefore fundamentally hostile to the goals of revolutionary socialism.[41] Theory in this tradition has attempted to formulate an idea of the distinctive essence, or form, of law, rooted in its material functions within the social environment – alongside and embedded within the broader capitalist political economy.[42]

Adopting such a perspective provides a means of challenging the dominant understanding of the early Soviet Union's relationship to international law and how this changed over time. For example, the standard narrative of the Soviet Union and international law describes a gradual convergence between the Soviet position and general

40 For Koskenniemi, this interpretation creates the need to examine 'institutional biases' in order to understand the concrete nature of international law in practice: n 5, 60–9. For an alternative understanding of indeterminacy as a particular legal argument, rather than a characteristic of the legal form, see Susan Marks, 'International Judicial Activism and the Commodity-Form Theory of International Law' (2007) 18 *European Journal of International Law* 199.

41 See, for example, Evgeny Pashukanis, *Law and Marxism: A General Theory* (Ink Links, 1978).

42 For a comprehensive exposition of this argument relating to international law, see China Miéville, 'The Commodity-Form Theory of International Law' in Susan Marks (ed), *International Law on the Left: Re-Examining Marxist Legacies* (Cambridge University Press, 2008) 92.

international law.[43] In this perspective, the Soviet Union shifts from its early radicalism to a more standard engagement with international law, while at the same time the general principles of international law themselves shift towards that same postulated middle ground, as the international legal system adjusts to the upheaval of a radical expansion in legal personalities.

This narrative confuses shifting legal arguments with the nature of law itself. Furthermore, such conflation occurs without any explicit theory of law within which this transformation can be explained. Without engaging in such theoretical work, it is not possible to maintain the distinction between legal argument and the law more broadly conceived (the legal form). The result is that a narrative of convergence is enabled and not sufficiently interrogated, and there is very little insight into the relationship between the legal form and the international environment, particularly the revolutionary aspirations of the early Soviets.

The narrative of convergence itself is also highly problematic. If the theory of law that this rests on were made explicit, it would run like this: international law is defined by the actions of a specific group of Western European states and North American settler colonies. Their shifting practice over the course of the twentieth century, and the decolonisation and formal independence won by ex-colonial states, transformed international law, making it less homogenous and therefore bringing it in line with the Soviet Union's own shifting international legal practice. Note that this does not present a theory of what is specifically *law-like* about international law. In this narrative, international law is simply some reflection of the political configuration of the international system, without any particular need to interrogate how that system is constituted. It also rests on the implicit notion that some shared civilisational attributes unite Western Europe in the face of the most catastrophic conflicts between them.

In that same narrative, the early Soviet Union was incapable of using international law, because of its radical alterity. Alongside other categories of 'barbarous and uncivilised' peoples, such actors were precluded from legal practice as a consequence of their social position.[44] However, as this chapter has argued, the supposed early radicalism of the Soviet Union when it came to international law was largely projected onto it by observers and political opponents. As noted by scholars like Taracouzio,

[43] See Slusser and Triska, n 4, 726; and the introduction to Grzybowski, n 9.
[44] For a critique of which, see Mutua, n 38.

the legal practice of the Soviet Union was actually very consonant with the general practice of the time. In this light, the narrative of convergence looks increasingly tenuous.[45]

There are further consequences to this theoretical lacuna. First, the claim of international law as the cultural product of Western civilisation, implicit in the narrative of convergence and early Soviet deviance, has led to a distinct academic endeavour to discover and define other cultural 'contributions' to the formation of international law.[46] It is possible to see this as stemming from a resistance to the implicit (and often explicit) racism in the law-and-civilisation blend of cultural imperialism, and therefore producing an important corrective to a skewed historical narrative based on those racist ideas. However, it also holds the potential to produce a dubious narrative of international law as a grand multicultural project, similar to the utopian self-image of the United Nations, which fails to hold weight against the historical record. In an attempt to resist the racism of colonising powers and their legal justifications, looking for precolonial traditions of international law in order to rewrite international legal history as the gradual discovery of a rich multicultural legal heritage reinforces the idea of law as a neutral cultural good – a marker of civilisation and cultural worth. Perhaps some notions of law might fulfil this rosy vision of cultural achievement, but that is not the law that exists. Noting that international law was (and continues to be) a

[45] The narrative of convergence also subsumes the struggle over the general orientation of legal norms that do bring about shifts in the general content of international law – for example, the support of the USSR in helping newly decolonised states turn international law against colonialism. For discussion of that support, see Bill Bowring, *The Degradation of the International Legal Order? The Rehabilitation of Law and the Possibility of Politics* (Routledge, 2008).

[46] For the Russian tradition, see Lauri Mälksoo, 'The History of International Legal Theory in Russia: A Civilizational Dialogue with Europe' (2008) 19 *European Journal of International Law* 211. For Canadian perspectives in a similar vein (if somewhat internal to the European dynamic), see discussion in Ronald St John MacDonald, 'Maxwell Cohen at Eighty: International Lawyer, Educator, and Judge' (1989) 27 *Canadian Yearbook of International Law* 3; Ronald St John MacDonald, 'Leadership in Law: John P Humphrey and the Development of the International Law of Human Rights' (1991) 29 *Canadian Yearbook of International Law* 3; Ivan L Head and Pierre Elliott Trudeau, *The Canadian Way: Shaping Canada's Foreign Policy 1968–1984* (McClelland & Stewart, 1995). For a contemporary setting of this, see Onuma Yasuaki, 'A Transcivilizational Perspective on Global Legal Order in the Twenty-First Century: A Way to Overcome West-Centric and Judiciary-Centric Deficits in International Legal Thoughts' in Ronald St John MacDonald and Douglas M Johnston (eds), *Towards World Constitutionalism: Issues in the Legal Ordering of the World Community* (Brill, 2005).

tool of European dispossession and exploitation should not deny those on the receiving end of this practice access to any of the cultural 'good' we might associate with the concept of law.

The problems of this comparative 'contributions to international law' approach are evident in reformative scholarship on the Soviet Union and international law of the late 1960s. Butler's intervention, discussed earlier,[47] attempted to redress the problems in the standard accounts of Soviet international law in scholarship in the United States, caused by the 'conviction' that studying Soviet approaches involved 'investigating how the Soviets violate[d] international law' in the face of innumerable examples 'which suggest[ed] that the relationship between international law and foreign policy in the USSR may be as dynamic and complex as it [was] in the foreign offices of the other large powers'.[48] As much as this represented a tentative (given the qualifying 'may be') step in the right direction, Butler's recommendations for future research failed to address the reasons for the early narrative of Soviet deviance. Instead, Butler suggested an attempt to (re)discover the 'Russian Heritage' and a call to cease 'ignor[ing] the Russian contribution to international law'.[49] The method suggested was one of comparative research, addressed through the development of regional expertise,[50] as opposed to addressing the theoretical reasons for the original failings and any broader understanding of what a common practice across actors might tell us about the nature of law.

By turning to comparative legal studies with the objective of uncovering the multicultural heritage of international law, it is possible to continue to avoid a critical examination of the law itself. Doing so as part of a project to redeem international law from its colonial and racist origins will almost certainly fall foul of this avoidance. Similarly, trying to overturn the historical narrative of the Soviet approach to international law by looking to uncover their contribution to a universal project avoids looking closely at why it was possible to paint the original picture of Soviet deviancy in relation to the law, what politics this served and what law might have had to do with the whole process. It enables a simplistic narrative of convergence, rather than prompting examination of how different states use law when attempting to achieve different goals with

[47] See n 34 and accompanying text.
[48] Butler, n 29, 229–30.
[49] Ibid., 224.
[50] Ibid., 222, 232–3.

different relative strengths within the international system. Adopting a comparative law approach also does not force the question as to why it did not help the early Soviet position to have legal arguments in its defence. Similarly, more generalised study of how different cultures have contributed to the history of international law will not address the reasons for why having their own traditions of law did not aid those communities on the receiving end of the so-called civilising mission. These are questions that would benefit from close examination, and would shed some light on what might be specific to law; something that has little to do with ideas of culture and civilisation but everything to do with more concrete social relations.

7.3 Revolution and the Legal Form

In the terms of this volume, this chapter argues that it is this essence, or form, of law that renders it a hostile environment to certain kinds of aspiration or expression – most particularly the ideals embodied in the October Revolution. This is revealed in two ways: first through the use and discussion of law in the Soviet Union during the 1920s, and second in some early responses by scholars to Soviet rhetoric around international law. It is also in these areas that we come closest to uncovering any kind of revolution of the law itself, but as will be evident in the analysis, this falls far short of constituting recognisable law-with-revolutionary-content. However, the reaction to this revolutionary engagement with law, dovetailing with the characterisation of Soviet deviancy just discussed here, does insinuate something about the nature of law more broadly.

The revolutionary legality that stoked the fires of legal indignation in the opponents of the Soviet Union did not come in the form of new laws or unusual legal practice. Rather it came in the form of radical diplomatic statements, calls to international revolution and an uncompromising critical light shed on the theory of law. It meant recognising law and lawyering for being that in which it was made manifest: a logical system of mediation, couched in the language of objectivity that privileged the already wealthy, naturalised existing inequality of ownership and, on the international stage, underpinned the vast system of colonial oppression and the exploitation of both humans and natural resources.[51] It was a

[51] This range of critical vision can be seen in the class and commodity form theories of law espoused by leading legal scholars in the early years following the revolution. See P I

tool in which subjective interests were articulated through the language of law, to the symbiotic benefit of those trained in law, arbitrated by people similarly trained, conducted under the rubric of objectivity, and to the benefit of those richest in material and cultural capital.[52] For critical, revolutionary eyes, the international legal system was based on an awareness of how the law in practice fell short of its liberal dream – requiring, for example, the balancing of judges' nationalities in cases, revealing the expectation that political affiliations would feed into judgments – but under a sort of gentlemen's agreement that one did not discuss this openly. To have the Soviets point this out, and lay claim to a right to use the system (where possible) as it was used against them, was untenable (just as it was untenable to have the oppressed lay claim to their own *realpolitik*).[53]

We can see evidence of this in some of the positions taken by legal theorists in the early Soviet Union. Although there were plenty of firebrands describing law in ways that would undoubtedly rile their liberal opponents,[54] there were others noting that to attribute to the Soviet Union a rejection of custom was to assign to it a 'doctrine it [had] nowhere expressed', and represented an attempt to deprive it of 'those rights which require no treaty formulation and derive from the fact that normal diplomatic relations exist'.[55] As this chapter has argued, the legal practice of the Soviet Union supports this assessment of its legal position, as does the theory that the structure of international law is sufficiently open and indeterminate to accommodate Soviet positions even if they had taken on a particularly radical character. However, such

Stučka, *Selected Writings on Soviet Law and Marxism* (Piers Beirne, Peter Maggs and Robert Sharlet trans, M E Sharpe, 1988).

52 In this way there is a complementary connection between early Soviet scholarship and later sociological critiques of law. See, for example, Pierre Bourdieu, 'The Force of Law: Toward a Sociology of the Juridical Field' (1987) 38 *Hastings Law Journal* 814.

53 See comments by China Miéville in Anne Orford et al., 'Roundtable: War, Force and Revolution' (2006) 100 *American Society of International Law Proceedings* 261.

54 See, for example, Tumanov at the 1930 Georgian Conference on law, arguing that 'Marxists assert that law is carried out in practice by means of coercion and violence, because all law is class law, and the law of a class without coercion is not a law'. Added to this was the following cautionary note against academicism: 'Understand that in our country of proletarian dictatorship, in the epoch of an intensified class struggle . . . a calm academic presentation of the view of our enemies is unsuitable': cited in Dennis Lloyd, *Introduction to Jurisprudence* (Stevens, 1972) 670. See also Richard Kinsey, 'Marxism and the Law: Preliminary Analyses' (1978) 5 *British Journal of Law and Society* 202, 207.

55 Evgeny Pashukanis, *Essays on International Law* (Moscow, 1935) ch 2, quoted in Triska and Slusser, n 4, 705.

traditional legal defences were accompanied by theories of law articulated in a manner that rendered explicit the opposition of the Soviets to the liberal idealism of international law. This challenged the law's projected self-image of objectivity and rationality but also laid bare discomforting fundamental principles that unsettled the image of international law as the flagbearer of some universal justice.

Evgeny Pashukanis, a leading Soviet jurist in the late 1920s and early 1930s, noted that 'modern international law is the legal form of the struggle of the capitalist states among themselves for domination over the rest of the world'.[56] However, Pashukanis also observed that:

> The bourgeois jurists are not entirely mistaken ... in considering international law as a function of some ideal cultural community which mutually connects individual states. But they do not see, or do not want to see, that this community reflects (conditionally and relatively, of course) the common interests of the commanding and ruling classes of different states which have identical class structures ... The victory of the bourgeoisie, in all the European countries, had to lead to the establishment of new rules and new institutions of international law which protected the general and basic interests of the bourgeoisie, ie bourgeois property.[57]

Despite this unrelentingly harsh vision of international law, and law more generally, Soviet theorists understood the necessity of using legal means to defend themselves against their opponents, and saw no contradiction in recognising the law for what it was and at the same time using it where possible. Although, as mentioned, outside observers claimed that legal theorists in the Soviet Union were only seeking to justify Soviet policy after the fact, the traditional use of the law by the Soviet state was entirely consistent with the legal theory of early Soviet revolutionaries.

When it came to the more immediate relationship between existing law and the aims of the revolution, Pashukanis relied heavily on the pragmatism of Lenin, demanding both the support of the law when it aided the revolutionary cause and the defensive use of the law against counter-revolutionary forces. Pashukanis noted that 'Lenin brilliantly took into consideration the fact that the legality which our enemy

[56] Evgeny Pashukanis, 'Selections from the Encyclopaedia of State and Law' in Piers Beirne and Robert S Sharlet (eds), *Selected Writings on Marxism and Law* (P B Maggs trans, Academic Press, 1980) 165, 169 (emphasis removed).

[57] Ibid., 172.

imposes upon us is re-imposed on him by the logic of events'.[58] Legal positions could also merge perfectly with victories forced by political and economic circumstance, as Pashukanis went on to note: 'the German imperialists, whatever their subjective dislike of the Soviet revolution, were compelled by the force of the general international situation to conclude a treaty with the Soviet government'.[59] The logic of this position stressed that there would be nothing to gain from denying the legal implications of the treaty, or the recognition of the Soviet Union, through a fundamental moral distaste for law.

This approach to the law is both opportunistic, in terms of its usage of existing legal forms when available, and principled, in terms of being guided by the overall objective of advancing the revolution. Although it is clear that political opposition motivated the narrative of Soviet deviancy when it came to the law, it is also evident that such an open claim to legal and political *realpolitik* provided not only a political challenge to be overcome but threatened the functioning of legal argument itself. After all, the logic of law is not such that one can acknowledge the process as a sham while engaging in it – at least not if you intend to continue to profit from lucrative international legal work. Even though the legal form is designed to accommodate opposing, and infinitely varied, positions, it also requests a minimal ritual participation – the rites must be performed authentically, even if the priesthood has no faith.[60]

There is yet more that emerges from this confluence of revolutionary criticism, legal opportunism and liberal reaction. Pashukanis' nod to 'some ideal cultural community' in the quotation above draws attention to the crux of international law (and all law) in private property. Thus, although the general picture of the early Soviet Union is one of a conservative use of international law, with some revolutionary aspirations behind it, this chapter argues that the vociferous liberal opposition outside the Russian state stems not only from politics but from what can be thought of as a hostility of the legal form to certain kinds of assertion.

The most revealing example of this is given by Alexander Sack in his discussion of diplomatic claims against the Soviet state.[61] In the early

58 Ibid., 139.

59 Ibid.

60 The metaphor comes from Roberto Mangabeira Unger, *The Critical Legal Theory Movement: Another Time, A Greater Task* (Verso, 2015) 210.

61 Alexander N Sack, 'Diplomatic Claims against the Soviets (1918–1938): Part I' (1937) 15 *New York University Quarterly Review* 507; Alexander N Sack, 'Diplomatic Claims against the Soviets (1918–1938): Part II' (1938) 16 *New York University Quarterly Review* 253.

years following the revolution, the Soviet government had refused liability for the debts of tsarist Russia, as well as claims for compensation made for property lost during the revolution. It is worth noting that, in line with the general argument of this chapter, the potential radicalism of this position was tempered by the fact that the Soviet state deployed a series of traditional legal arguments to defend its claim, among which were a series of counterclaims for damages during the civil war (and substantial foreign intervention) and subsequent acceptance of some portion of the debt under treaty negotiation.[62] However, Sack made notable observations about the fundamental nature of the international system, sovereign debt and international law.

First, echoing the arguments made by Francisco De Vitoria to justify Spanish military intervention in the Americas,[63] Sack stated that:

> Modern States are organic parts of the world's social and economic system which is based on the principle of free (even if regulated) and continuous international circulation and interchange of capital and goods, services and men. All states are intercommunicating and interconnected parts of a world-wide economy, and, being interdependent, live together as members of a world polity. Modern States, therefore, necessarily have mutual 'obligations of intercourse'.[64]

Under this formulation it is clear that Sack's vision of a principled international order with its mutual obligations is actually a very particular social and economic system that is, by necessity, global in scope. Within such a system, the Soviet arguments for debt repudiation and refusal to compensate for expropriated property are more than legal arguments to be defeated. They represent positions hostile to the social and economic system in which they are articulated. Sack goes on to note that:

[62] For example, at Brest–Litovsk, the Soviets agreed, admittedly under significant duress, to six billion marks of compensation to Germany for the confiscation and nationalisation of the property of German citizens – under which the German state agreed to meet the claims of its nationals. Although this treaty was later annulled by both sides, the substantial initial Soviet payment in gold remained in German hands, and subsequently was taken by the Allies upon the defeat of Germany at the end of the war – justified as being in lieu of part-payment towards Soviet liabilities. See Sack, 'Diplomatic Claims against the Soviets (1918–1938): Part II', n 61.

[63] China Miéville, *Between Equal Rights: A Marxist Theory of International Law* (Brill, 2005) 173. Drawing on a critical history of international law from the sixteenth century to 2006, Miéville argues that international law is fundamentally constituted by the violence of imperialism.

[64] Sack, 'Diplomatic Claims against the Soviets (1918–1938): Part I', n 61, 509.

> if such expropriation would, by International Law, be permissible at the free discretion of the sovereign, the foundation of the modern system of international intercourse, which guarantees to foreigners and their property due process of law on the part of any sovereignty under whose dominion they may be found, would be destroyed.[65]

Allowing for a certain hyperbole, Sack's intention regarding the destructive potential of the Soviet position is clarified in the following manner. Sack states that 'the public debt of Russia was "annulled", not because it was impossible to continue the full and timely payment of current obligations, but in order to deal a "first blow to international financial capital"'.[66] The meaning here is clear. Even though there are conditions in which debt repayments might be altered, or even written off, doing so in order to challenge the capitalist foundations of the world's social and economic system is unacceptable.

This relationship between international law and a specifically *capitalist* economic and social system can be rendered more explicit by noting the double standards involved. Specifically regarding expropriations, Sack noted that Soviet actions were:

> doubly violative . . . first, because they deprived foreign nationals of their property without due process of law; and second, because, taken partly with a view to undermine the foundations of the social and economic regime of foreign countries, they constituted an interference in the domestic affairs of those States.[67]

That is, they were an offence in terms of legal due process, but also because they threatened the social and economic system of which the law was a component. However, when the Soviet state complained about foreign intervention and the fomenting of civil war and counter-revolution, these claims fell on deaf ears. Of course we could read this as politically biased, and this bias is very clearly in evidence (on both sides), but to do so shields the law from further critical analysis. It shies away from attempting to theorise the legal form with sufficient rigour to understand its role in revolutionary times, and also enables problematic narratives like those discussed in this chapter: that the Soviet state was deviant despite the lack of evidence, and that the Soviet position and general international law somehow converged at a later date.

[65] Ibid., 509–10.

[66] Ibid., 510. Sack is quoting the words of the decree on annulment of the public debt of 21 January 1918.

[67] Ibid., 514.

Undoubtedly the two moved into a more harmonious relationship, if by 'general international law' we mean the practice of other states. The Soviet state abandoned its early revolutionary principles, and the legal arguments of dominant powers could arguably be said to have altered under the pressure of their own inter-imperial competition and the liberation struggles of colonised peoples. However, this narrative reveals something about the shifting power dynamics of international politics, not something about the nature of the legal form. To claim the latter would be to over-determine the nature of law by the type of arguments made within it – which is clearly unsatisfactory.

This chapter suggests instead that the relative indeterminacy of the legal form – that is, its receptivity to a wide variety of arguments – has limits. Those limits are posed by the economic and social system of which the law is both a fundamental constitutive part and an expression. The history of the early Soviet relationship to international law reveals this in stark contrast. By turning attention to the nature of the legal form, it is possible to recognise early Soviet legal practice for what it was – conservative legal practice, used opportunistically to advance and defend the revolution, and a tool used with full knowledge of the fact that the law was an integral part of a *capitalist* social and economic system. It would also be possible to see the ways in which the validity of those legal arguments, on a formal level, could not penetrate the minds of most contemporary legal observers outside of the Soviet sphere. Rather than seeing any change in international law as the early radicalism of the Soviet Union faded, it would be possible to see the continuity of a legal system as the actors within it shifted positions.

It is also possible to theorise the relationship between law and power at a deeper level. Observers noted that:

> the initial period of doctrinal fervor [in the Soviet Union] which spawned most of the radical theorems on the nature of international politics and law coincided with the low point in Russia's exercise of global power and authority, so that the dreams could not be tested for lack of adequate physical strength to sustain them.[68]

The discussion in this chapter implies that we would learn more about the nature of law and its relationship to revolutionary upheavals by paying closer attention to the interconnections between law, power and

[68] George Ginsburgs, 'The View from Without' (1968) 62 *American Society of International Law Proceedings* 196, 202.

dominant socio-economic systems rather than maintaining their separation. In other words, we should understand the nature of the legal form as presenting a particular facet of capitalist social relations – relations of commodity production, exchange and formal equivalence, built on dispossession, subjugation and vast material inequality.

7.4 Conclusion

The discussion in this chapter tells us one of many things about the nature of the relationship between international law and revolution. In general, the Soviet Revolution found the structures of international law extremely hostile to revolutionary aspirations, despite the law being relatively indeterminate. Although the Soviets made numerous legal arguments and appealed to the principles of international law for defence, this did not offer the revolution any salvation. There is a message here that, in an age of unbridled legal idealism, is important to emphasise. Being legally 'right' gives no guarantee of safety in the international order (or domestic legal orders, for that matter).

For progressively minded scholars and activists on the political Left, public international law is often depicted as a vital arena in which to struggle. There are numerous examples of political or environmental struggles where it seems that achieving a legal victory is feasible and will offer some protection or restitution – from environmental pollution, access to land, water, or housing in the form of economic and social rights, to the use of biological and chemical weapons, war and other forms of systematic violence. The struggle of the Palestinians against Israeli occupation, annexation and settlement building has long been presented as one in which the law is on the side of the oppressed. The invasion of Iraq in 2003 offered another example of international law offering clear opposition to the actions of the United States and its allies. Perhaps the law offers the illusion of an easier victory against the inexorable destruction present in these examples. However, the history of the early Soviet relationship to international law should give some pause to the investment of excessive energy in the struggle over legal ground.

Legal victories are just one manifestation of social struggle, and one that occurs in an environment that can be incredibly hostile to left-wing politics. Hard-won legal victories will also be meaningless without continuing social struggle to push for broader transformation and a social environment in which violations are prohibited by other means than mechanisms associated with law – those requiring monitoring, enforcement and systems of punishment. The law is a double-edged sword in this regard, as fighting for specifically legal victories strengthens all the apparatuses of the state and the legal system: lawyers, courts, judges, police and the prison system. This is not to say that none of these things can ever serve progressive purposes (under radically different social conditions) but to demand an awareness that the means may very well undermine the ends in these cases.

There are further insights to be taken from the discussion at hand. Sack's observations are revealing about the sanctity of private property in international law. Although it may be possible to expropriate without compensation or to refuse to honour nefarious investments, and thereby effect a redistribution of power and resources, legal orders are incredibly hostile to the principle behind such action – to any radically transformative redistribution of resources. In the best case, it may be possible to win temporary legal victories and have no effect on the legal order, while at the same time reinforcing and legitimising that order via participation in its rituals. It is more likely, however, that legal argument will favour the principle of ownership, despite the fact that at some point those rights had their origin in some form of violent dispossession. With sufficiently dogged determination and resources, these rights can be pursued over vast periods of time and effect a rebalancing in the interests of the wealthy.[69]

From the legacy of the early Soviet Union, there are clear lessons for legal struggle and revolutionary aspirations. The revolutionary legality of the early Soviets did not take the form of new laws or surprising and innovative legal arguments but took the form of ruthlessly subjecting the law to critical analysis, and towards using the law where opportune to pursue the aims of the revolution. This form of principled opportunism has offered at least one methodology for approaching the law from a radical standpoint.[70] When accompanied by a rigorous process of delegitimation of the law, in the form of sustained critical reflection, there is perhaps some limited hope for efficacy.

However, it would be naive to hold on to such an aspiration against the weight of the role played by law historically. Although further work could

[69] Two egregious examples that spring to mind would be the émigrés' billion following the French Revolution, and the compensation of French collectors by the Russian state in 1994 for losses incurred during the Revolution in 1917.

[70] Knox, 'Strategy and Tactics', n 6.

undoubtedly be done to try and find examples of legal progressivity that redeem something of law's liberal promise, there is substantial reason to be wary of such endeavours. Recalling a debate from the 1970s, Isaac Balbus offered this insightful response to scholarship in Critical Legal Studies in the United States:

> Those who would argue that delegitimation can result from the failure of law to live up to its 'promises' (ie, from the gap between its promises and its performance) fail to understand that the legitimation of the legal order is not primarily a function of its ability to live up to its claims or 'redeem its pledges' but rather of the fact that its claims or pledges are valued in the first place. As long as 'formality', 'generality', and 'equality before the law' are seen as genuine human values, even gross and systematic departures from these norms in practice will not serve to delegitimate the legal order as a whole, but will at most tend to delegitimate specific laws and specific incumbents of political office who are responsible for these laws.[71]

It is worth seriously reflecting on at what point scholars of international law might consider international law to have failed to live up to its promises. This is not just a case of the most obvious failings of public international law to limit war and conflict under the auspices of the United Nations Security Council but more deeply to effect a transformation of the international order towards something remotely more egalitarian, less exploitative and compatible with a life-sustaining ecosystem. This is not to claim that international law does not promise a better future as the law progressively develops – this is its allure. If, however, revolutionary struggle becomes sublimated by legal dreams, then when law's limits are reached, the only ideals that remain will be those of an abstract, formal, balancing of rights, and the grey wasteland will be endless.

[71] Isaac D Balbus, 'Commodity Form and Legal Form: An Essay on the "Relative Autonomy" of Law' (1977) 11 *Law and Society Review* 571, 581.

PART III

Intervention

8

Intervention: Sketches from the Scenes of the Mexican and Russian Revolutions*

DINO KRITSIOTIS†

8.1 Introduction

We have been invited to consider the memory and significance of the October Revolution on this, its centennial, anniversary, and have been asked to do so alongside the surprise, colour and ineffable promise of Konstantin Yuon's resplendent *New Planet*, which can be read 'either as a will for change or as a fear of what is to come'.[1] The year 1917 also saw the adoption of the Mexican Constitution, which had 'legitimate pride in showing the world that it is the first to consign in a constitution the sacred rights of the workers',[2] and that had occurred in February of that tumultuous year,[3] well before the Constitution of the Russian Soviet Federated Socialist Republic of July 1918 delivered its 'declaration of rights of the labouring and exploited people'.[4]

* Adapted from the keynote presentation delivered at the University of Melbourne on 24 August 2017.

† Chair of Public International Law at the University of Nottingham.

1 As put by Zelfira Tregulova and Faia Balakhovskaya, 'Constructors of the Future in Search of the New' in Royal Academy of the Arts, *Revolution: Russian Art 1917–1932* (Royal Academy of the Arts, 2017) 101 (describing the work as 'apocalyptic'). Yuon was awarded the Stalin Prize in 1943 and membership of the Communist Party in 1951.

2 *Diario de los debates del congreso constituyente de 1916–1917* (1960) vol 1, 1028 (Cravioto).

3 H N Branch and L S Rowe, 'The Mexican Constitution of 1917 Compared with the Constitution of 1857' (1917) 71 *Annals of the American Academy of Political Science* 1.

4 As per its preamble. It is worth recalling in this context that the penultimate preambular recital of the Constitution of the International Labour Organization recognised that 'the failure of any nation to adopt humane conditions of labour is an obstacle in the way of other nations which desire to improve the conditions in their own countries': *Constitution of the International Labour Organization*, signed 28 June 1919, 203 CTS 12 (entered into force 4 June 1934).

Of course, the Mexican Constitution had itself been a good while in coming: it succeeded the revolution kindled by the Plan de San Luis de Potosí of October 1910 that had called for the nullification of the presidential election of June 1910.[5] That development had precipitated the end of the 'one-man's government' of President Porfirio Díaz, who had ruled the country since 1884,[6] and President Francisco Madero was duly sworn into office following the landslide at a further election held in October 1911.[7] This, then, was a revolution of an altogether different order to that of its Russian counterpart several years hence, but what China Miéville had said for the later event can surely be ventured for both:

> the revolution resonates now not only for the analytical insights it offers but as a horizon, the sheer fact, both bathetic and momentous, that things were other, it could be so again. That's what connects to today's indignities and violence and inequality and oppression and to what they bring forth, as in very different circumstances they did a century ago: an ache for a radical reconfiguration.[8]

If the world had been set alight by these moments of great social upheaval and their ensuing constitutional enactments and legacies, one question for public international law is how, if at all, it purported to deal with change – specifically with revolutionary change. Was there a law – was there any law – governing how states should react in such circumstances? Did the law make any expectations or demands of states in the event of revolution? And what principles or policies had steered this law into being? Granted, this was a period well before the world had condemned 'recourse to war for the solution of international controversies' and renounced it 'as an instrument of national policy in their relations with one another'.[9] These

[5] The plan had been written by Francisco Madero while in prison in San Luis de Potosí but was issued in San Antonio, Texas, after he had been smuggled across the border into the United States by sympathisers: Enrique Krauze, *Mexico: Biography of a Power: A History of Modern Mexico, 1810–1996* (HarperCollins, 1997) 255.

[6] As it was so frankly put in Editorial Comment, 'Mexico' (1912) 6 *American Journal of International Law* 475, 475 (the editorial advising, at 476, that 'those that draw the sword perish by the sword, and that a presidency won by revolution is apt to be lost by revolution'.)

[7] Madero had been the author of the Plan de San Luis de Potosí where, 'in the echo of the national will', he declared 'the late election illegal and, the Republic being accordingly without rules, provisionally assume the Presidency of the Republic until the people designate their rulers pursuant to the law'. The Plan is reproduced at https://archivos.juridicas.unam.mx/www/bjv/libros/6/2884/26.pdf.

[8] China Miéville, 'Why Does the Russian Revolution Matter?', *The Guardian* (6 May 2017).

[9] As it had been put in Article I of the 1928 Kellogg–Briand Pact: *General Treaty for Renunciation of War as an Instrument of National Policy*, signed 27 August 1928, 94 LNTS 57 (entered into force 25 July 1929).

events occurred on the eve of the procedural innovations for the recourse to war set forth in the Covenant of the League of Nations of June 1919.[10] However, and perhaps most notably in respect of Russia, US President Woodrow Wilson had articulated as the sixth of his Fourteen Points of January 1918, 'an unhampered and unembarrassed opportunity for the independent determination of her own political development and national policy'.[11] On that very occasion, he had also assured Russia 'of a sincere welcome to the society of free nations under institutions of her own choosing; and, more than a welcome, assistance also of every kind that she may need and may herself desire'.[12] And all of this coming barely two months after the October Revolution, with President Wilson maintaining that 'the treatment accorded to Russia by her sister nations in the months to come will be the acid test of their good will, of their comprehension of her needs as distinguished from their own interests, and of their intelligent and unselfish sympathy'.[13]

With his Fourteen Points, President Wilson might well be taken to have 'emphatically decreed the death of Machiavellian power politics and all its essential components',[14] but where did public international law stand beyond such matters of 'intelligent and unselfish sympathy' when confronted by revolution and radical change? For this chapter, and with this question in mind, I would like to make a deliberate return to the principle of non-intervention. My interest is to single out that principle and put it front-and-centre of the analysis that follows, for it is a principle that remains with us to this day but, somehow, has come to be eclipsed by many of the other laws appearing in the heady firmament of the 1945 Charter of the United Nations.[15] And, yet, this principle was one of seven identified for solemn proclamation by the General Assembly in its

[10] (1919) 13 *American Journal of International Law Supplement* 128.

[11] Ibid.

[12] Ibid.

[13] Ibid. On this sixth point more generally, consider the note of Soviet Commissar of Foreign Affairs Chicherin to President Woodrow Wilson, transmitted through the Norwegian Attaché in Moscow, 24 October 1918, and reproduced in *Fourth International* (1942) vol III, no 4, 119.

[14] Francis A Boyle, 'American Foreign Policy toward International Law and Organizations: 1898–1917' (1983) 6 *Loyola of Los Angeles International and Comparative Law Journal* 185, 188 (that is, the balance of power, secret diplomacy, trade barriers, armament races and the denial of self-determination).

[15] See Antonio Cassese on the principle of non-intervention and 'the old pattern of the world community': *International Law in A Divided World* (Clarendon Press, 1986) 143 (§85).

Declaration on Principles of International Law Concerning Friendly Relations and Co-operation among States in accordance with the Charter of the United Nations of October 1970.[16] There, the sheer force and unmistakable bluntness of the expression of that principle – that 'no State or group of States has the right to intervene, directly or indirectly, for any reason whatever, in the internal or external affairs of any other State'[17] – cannot leave anyone in doubt about its status as a matter of modern international law.[18] Yet, that realisation quickly provokes the question of its relevance at earlier points in the history of public international law,[19] especially when set against some of the other principles also articulated by the General Assembly in Resolution 2625 (XXV).[20]

The chapter shall proceed as follows. The next section returns us to the principle of non-intervention as it stood before the Mexican Revolution. As we shall see, at least on one interpretation of its scope and meaning, the law on non-intervention was not really amenable to crude or categorical postulation. Instead, taking our cue from Lassa Oppenheim's classic treatise on public international law from the first decade of the twentieth century, we observe that the law presented a series of discrete twists and turns that attempted to capture the dynamics of sovereignty

[16] GA Res 2625, 25 UN GAOR, Supp (No 28), UN Doc A/5217 (24 October 1970) Annex.

[17] Itself a repetition of the formulation contained in General Assembly Resolution 2131 (XX); and a principle 'stated in remarkably absolute terms': Anthony Carty, *The Decay of International Law? A Reappraisal of the Limits of Legal Imagination in International Affairs* (Manchester University Press, 1986) 87.

[18] For Cassese, 'one of the fundamental standards of behaviour of international subjects': n 15, 143 (§85).

[19] Although it is interesting that the abbreviated section title for the principle appearing earlier in the Resolution – namely 'the duty not to intervene in matters within the domestic jurisdiction of any State, in accordance with the Charter' – does seem to set a different tone, and is more closely affiliated with Article 2(7) of the Charter of the United Nations ('Nothing contained in the present Charter shall authorize the United Nations to intervene in matters which are essentially within the domestic jurisdiction of any state or shall require the Members to submit such matters to settlement under the present Charter, but this principle shall not prejudice the application of enforcement measures under Chapter VII'). The provision is indeed addressed to the United Nations but, for the record, the *chapeau* of Article 2 of the Charter does specify that 'the Organization and its Members, in pursuit of the Purposes stated in Article 1, shall act in accordance with the following Principles'.

[20] I am thinking in particular of the principle that states shall refrain in their international relations from the threat or use of force against the territorial integrity or political independence of any state, or in any other manner inconsistent with the purposes of the United Nations and the principle of equal rights and self-determination of peoples (from Articles 2(4) and 1(2) of the Charter: ibid.).

(or independence) and the prevailing power politics at one and the same time. It was thus a law of non-intervention but also, as it turned out, one of permissible intervention. This exercise serves as a necessary preface to the third section of the chapter where we shall learn more of the detail of the unfolding of the Mexican Revolution itself. That section will also relate how various practices of states in responding to revolution – as in the recognition of governments or the proffering of good offices or even the stance of neutrality – put demands on the understanding or appreciation of 'intervention'. We then turn, in the fourth section, to the experience of the Russian Revolution of October 1917 itself. Throughout, the focal point is on the very idea and invocation of intervention – its core meaning, its possibilities, its limitations – including (as we shall see in the final section of the chapter) the values and interests that it was organised to uphold.

8.2 Non-Intervention and Intervention

Five years before the Mexican Revolution began in earnest, the first edition of Lassa Oppenheim's two-volume treatise on public international law appeared. The year was 1905. In the first volume devoted to the laws of peace, a chapter concerning the position of the states within the family of nations dealt with the questions of international personality; equality, rank and title; dignity; independence and territorial and personal supremacy; self-preservation; intercourse and jurisdiction.[21] It is among this inventory that we find 'intervention' itemised and then analysed, with Oppenheim observing 'that intervention is as a rule forbidden by the Law of Nations which protects the International Personality of the States, there is no doubt'. Equally, he went on, 'there is just as little doubt that this rule has exceptions, for there are interventions which take place by right, and there are others which, although they do not take place by right, are nevertheless admitted by the Law of Nations and are excused in spite of the violation of the Personality of the respective States they involve'.[22]

This almost seemed to speak to the inevitability of intervention as a practice within international relations, an entire taxonomical structure

[21] Appearing in the first part on the subjects of the law of nations: L Oppenheim, *International Law: A Treatise* (Longmans, Green, and Co, 1905) vol I, 158–97. The second volume of the treatise deals with war and neutrality.

[22] Ibid., vol I, 182 (§134).

devised in order to compute interventions in all of their evident plurality. And this structure proceeded from the definition awarded to 'intervention' that famously, according to Oppenheim, involved 'dictatorial interference by a State in the affairs of another State for the purpose of maintaining or altering the actual condition of things'.[23] What was therefore essential to the meaning of this doctrine was the dictatorial nature of a given interference. 'It always concerns', Oppenheim wrote, 'the external independence or the territorial or personal supremacy of the respective State, and the whole matter is therefore of great importance for the position of the States within the Family of Nations'.[24] That aspect thus served as a threshold factor for any assessment,[25] but what is striking from this exposition is how it related *intervention* back to qualities identified earlier in the analysis: the idea of 'independence' (for 'sovereignty is independence')[26] as well as 'the territorial or personal supremacy' ('the power of a State to exercise supreme authority over all persons and things within its territory').[27]

[23] Ibid., vol I, 181 (§134).

[24] Ibid., vol I, 181–2 (§134).

[25] Ibid., vol I, 182 (§134) ('it must be emphasised that intervention proper is always *dictatorial* interference, not intervention pure and simple') (emphasis in original). Hence, good offices, meditation, intercession and co-operation were to be disqualified for consideration as *intervention* 'because none of these imply a *dictatorial* interference' (again, emphasis in original). Importantly, co-operation was 'the appellation of such interference as consists in help and assistance lent by one State to another at the latter's request for the purpose of suppressing an internal revolution': at 183 (§134).

[26] Ibid., vol I, 170 (§123) (emphasis in original) ('sovereignty as supreme authority . . . is independent of any other earthly authority'). See, too, Carty, n 17, 89 (on non-intervention as 'the converse of independence'). However, in this designation of intervention, it will be observed that Oppenheim confined it to *external* independence ('the liberty of action outside its borders in the intercourse with other States which a State enjoys'), which, for Oppenheim, involved a State's management of 'its international affairs according to discretion': at 171 (§124). Examples given included the forming of alliances, the conclusion of treaties, the sending and receiving of diplomatic envoys, the acquisition and cession of territory and the making of war and peace. As for *internal* independence ('the liberty of action of a State inside its borders'), this was not mentioned in the context of intervention: at 170–1 (§123). The latter involved the adoption of 'any Constitution it likes', the arrangement of its administration 'in any way it thinks fit', the making use of the legislature 'as it pleases' and the organisation of its forces on land and sea, the building and pulling down of fortresses, the adoption of any commercial policy it likes and so on: at 171–2 (§124). That said, while Oppenheim regularly emphasised the 'external' independence, he also admitted that 'intervention can take place in the external as well as in the internal affairs of a State': at 182 (§134).

[27] Ibid., vol I, 171 (§123).

So, when we come to understand what intervention is as a practice, it is important to appreciate its essential relation with these apparent qualities of sovereignty, if not with sovereignty itself. 'These three qualities', Oppenheim maintained for independence and territorial and personal supremacy, 'are nothing else than three aspects of the very same sovereignty of a State',[28] but, central as they were to the design or anatomy of the sovereign, they were not to be regarded as 'rights' or as potential claims of action for states.

> Independence and territorial as well as personal supremacy are not rights, but recognized and therefore protected qualities of States as International Persons. The protection granted to these qualities by the Law of Nations finds its expression in the right of every State to demand that other States abstain themselves, and prevent their organs and subjects, from committing any act which contains a violation of independence and its territorial as well as personal supremacy.[29]

There is therefore some correlation here with the so-called dignity of states, which also features in Oppenheim's analysis,[30] since a state possesses dignity by virtue of its existence as an international person: dignity is a 'quality' that is 'recognized by other States, and it adheres to a State from the moment of its recognition till the moment of its extinction, whatever behaviour it displays',[31] although Oppenheim was quick to dismiss its status as a 'right'[32] since 'no duty corresponding to it can be traced within the Law of Nations'.[33] There is a similar disqualification of the purported 'right' of self-preservation,[34] since 'if every State really had a *right* of self-preservation, all the States would have the duty to admit, suffer, and endure every violation done to one another in self-preservation. But such duty does not exist'.[35]

28 Ibid.

29 Ibid.

30 Ibid., vol I, 167–70 (§§120–2).

31 Ibid., vol I, 168 (§120).

32 As had been proclaimed for it by 'the majority of text-book writers': ibid., vol I, 167 (§120) (where it is understood as 'a fundamental right of reputation and of good name on the part of every State': at 167 (§120)).

33 Ibid., vol I, 167 (§120).

34 See, further, Alejandro Alvarez, 'The State's Right of Self-Preservation' (1919) 3 *St Louis Law Review* 113, 118 ('All publicists are unanimous in recognizing that States have the right, indeed the duty, to take such steps as are deemed necessary for self-preservation and defense'.)

35 Oppenheim, n 21, vol I, 177–8 (§129) (emphasis in original).

The situation is different with respect to intervention, and if one is not able to obtain an assured sense of what this entailed from Oppenheim's definition, then it is sure to emerge from those practices that came to be labelled as 'exceptions' in his rubric:

> It is apparent that such interventions as take place by right must be distinguished from others. Where there is no right to intervention, although it may be admissible and excused, an intervention violates either the external independence or the territorial or the personal supremacy. But if an intervention takes place by right, it never contains such a violation, because the right of intervention is always based on a legal restriction upon the independence or territorial or personal supremacy of the State concerned, and because the latter is in duty bound to submit to the intervention.[36]

It transpires that it is this schematics of intervention – the distinction between an intervention occurring by right and an intervention that is merely admitted or excused – that informs the determination of the lawfulness of a specified action, but, crucially, it also governed the legal position of the state that was targeted for intervention.[37] Much therefore turned on the identification of a recognised 'right' for intervention as a matter of law,[38] or on the circumstances for 'interventions in default of right' that are admitted or excused,[39] for, in the former case, the intervention 'never contains such a violation'[40] – that is, a violation of public international law.[41] A close association is then developed between the

[36] Ibid., vol I, 183 (§135).

[37] Since, with admissible/excusable interventions, the targeted state 'has by no means any legal duty to submit patiently and suffer the intervention': ibid., vol I, 185 (§136).

[38] And Oppenheim admits 'several grounds': the intervention of the suzerain state in 'many affairs of the vassal'; the right of protection over citizens abroad; non-compliance with treaty terms and the effect on other treaty partners; the unilateral handling of an 'external affair' is 'at the same time by right an affair of another State' and, finally, any delinquency in respect of the universally recognised principles of the Law of Nations: ibid., vol I, 183–4 (§135).

[39] Ibid., vol I, 185 (§136). Oppenheim identified 'two kinds' – interventions for the purpose of self-preservation and those in the interest of the balance of power. A third kind of intervention was considered – interventions 'exercised in the interest of humanity for the purpose of stopping religious persecution and endless cruelties in time of peace and war' – but 'whether there is really a rule of the Law of Nations which admits such interventions may well be doubted', even though some had contended it existed on the basis of right: at 186 (§137).

[40] Ibid., vol I, 183 (§135).

[41] *Quaere* how this sits with the idea of an 'exception' employed at the outset of his analysis: ibid., vol I, 182 (§134).

permissibility of intervention and the confines or extent of independence and territorial and personal supremacy,[42] such that permissible interventions emerge as correctives to the behavioural excesses of states.

Before we close this section, a word should be said on the Monroe Doctrine, which resulted from the seventh State of the Union address of President James Monroe to the United States Congress in December 1823: 'Our policy in regard to Europe, which was adopted at an early stage of the wars which have so long agitated that quarter of the globe', the president declared, 'remains the same, which is not to interfere in the internal concerns of any of its powers; to consider the government *de facto* as the legitimate government for us; to cultivate friendly relations with it, and to preserve those relations by a frank, firm, and manly policy, meeting in all instances the just claims of every power, submitting to injuries from none'.[43] And so resulted the central claim for which the doctrine was to become so well known: 'It is impossible that the allied powers should extend their political system to any portion of either continent without endangering our peace and happiness; nor can anyone believe that our southern brethren, if left to themselves, would adopt it of their own accord. It is equally impossible, therefore, that we should behold such interposition in any form with indifference'.[44] Coming as this did from a former colony of the British Empire, the signalling of the idea of non-intervention carried even greater symbolic significance – but so, too, did the undertones for what was to happen in the event of transgression: 'it is equally impossible . . . that we should behold such interposition in any form with indifference'.[45] A statement of sorts, then, on the importance of non-intervention, accompanied as it was by the suggestion of the possibility of intervention as conceived and as undertaken by the United States.[46]

[42] Where independence 'is not a boundless liberty of a State to do what it likes without any restriction whatever': ibid., vol I, 173 (§126).

[43] The relevant portion of this address is reproduced by The Avalon Project at Yale Law School: 'Monroe Doctrine' (2 December 1823) http://avalon.law.yale.edu/19th_century/monroe.asp.

[44] Ibid. A doctrine that thus 'synthesized the administration's concerns with Latin America, the Pacific Northwest, and Anglo-American relations': Daniel Walker Howe, *What Hath God Wrought: The Transformation of America, 1815–1848* (Oxford University Press, 2007) 111 (and describing the doctrine as 'a fundamental statement of American foreign policy'). For further discussion, see Juan Pablo Scarfi, *The Hidden History of International Law in the Americas: Empire and Legal Networks* (Oxford University Press, 2017) 63–9.

[45] Howe, n 44, 115.

[46] Carty, n 17, 99 ('recognising no limits other than its own making'). See also Margaret Macmillan, *Paris 1919: Six Months that Changed the World* (Random House, 2002) 9.

For Oppenheim, though, the importance of the Monroe Doctrine 'is of a political, not of a legal character',[47] and, indeed, came to affirm 'the *de facto* political character of the whole matter of intervention'.[48] This may well have been so; it was only with the Covenant of the League of Nations that it was given something of a normative imprimatur, since it was there provided that 'nothing in this Covenant shall be deemed to affect the validity of international agreements, such as treaties of arbitration or regional understandings like the Monroe doctrine, for securing the maintenance of peace'.[49] Still, the ambiguity of this formulation aside, the counterposition of 'understandings' as against international agreements cannot go unnoticed, although it is telling that the Covenant chose to spell out the supposed virtue of the Monroe Doctrine ('securing the maintenance of peace') – and this has echoes of Oppenheim's endeavour to chart its 'merits', whatever might be said of its status.[50] Be this as it may, the truth of things is that the Monroe Doctrine came much closer to the form of a declaration,[51] an uninhibited projection of both the evolving interests and power of the United States,[52] and putting at its heart the prospect of intervention as remedy – at least as and when deemed necessary by the United States.[53]

[47] Oppenheim, n 21, vol I, 190 (§140). See also Carty, n 17, 99.

[48] Oppenheim, n 21, vol I, 188 (§139). See also at 191 (§140).

[49] *Covenant of the League of Nations*, Article 21. Note Howe's assessment, however: that 'the doctrine always remained purely a unilateral policy statement, never recognized in international law', n 44, 116. Consider, too, the relation of the Monroe Doctrine to the idea of collective self-defence under the Charter of the United Nations: Anne Orford, 'NATO, Regionalism, and the Responsibility to Protect' in Ian Shapiro and Adam Tooze (eds), *Charter of the North Atlantic Treaty Organization Together with Scholarly Commentaries and Essential Historical Documents* (Yale University Press, 2018) 302.

[50] Oppenheim, n 21, vol I, 190 (§140). 'In the interest of balance of power in the world, the United States considers it a necessity that European Powers should not acquire more territory on the American continent than they actually possess. She considers, further, her own welfare so intimately connected with that of the other American States that she thinks it necessary, in the interest of self-preservation, to watch closely the relations of these States with Europe and also the relations between these very States, and eventually to intervene in conflicts': at 190–1 (§140).

[51] Carty, n 17, 99.

[52] See Herbert Ingram Priestly, 'Mexican Literature on the Recent Revolution' (1919) 2 *Hispanic American Historical Review* 286, 300, and, also, Susan Pedersen's reference to 'hemispheric hegemony': *The League of Nations and the Crisis of Empire* (Oxford University Press, 2015) 285.

[53] See R J Vincent, *Nonintervention and International Order* (Princeton University Press, 1974) 130 (on the significance of counter-intervention) and, also, Editorial Comment,

8.3 Scenes from the Mexican Revolution

Let us now return to the Mexican Revolution, which did not come to a close with President Madero's ascension to power; opposition to his regime grew quickly, exposing deep divisions within society that led to the famous 'ten tragic days' that shook Mexico City in February 1913.[54] The unrest culminated in the eventual resignation of President Madero and the installation of General Victoriano Huerta and his successor,[55] with the pages of the *American Journal of International Law* reporting that ever since Porfirio Díaz's flight for exile, 'the country has been a continuous scene of revolution and counter-revolution, in which thousands of lives have been sacrificed and inestimable damage done to the property and business interests of the country'.[56] Mexico's experience was a fulsome demonstration, if it were needed, that the change wrought by revolution is infinitely uncertain as it is complex. Indeed, writing of the Mexican Revolution in the *Socialist Appeal* as late as June 1938, Leon Trotsky – a living embodiment, if you will, of both the Mexican and Russian Revolutions[57] – would observe how 'semi-colonial Mexico' was

'The Monroe Doctrine Again' (1911) 5 *American Journal of International Law* 729, 730, 732.

54 Editorial Comment, 'Mexico' (1913) 7 *American Journal of International Law* 832, 833 ('uprising in different parts of Mexico, each headed by its own separate leader, soon broke out, and the embers of revolution and brigandage burst into flame over a large part of the country').

55 On 20 February 1913; on the following day, Madero and his vice president (José María Pino Suárez) were assassinated. Not to be forgotten is the implication of Henry Lane Wilson, US Ambassador to Mexico, in the downfall of President Madero: Lowell L Blaisdell, 'Henry Lane Wilson and the Overthrow of Madero' (1962) 43 *Southwestern Social Science Quarterly* 126.

56 'Mexico', n 54, 832–3.

57 Trotsky is not alone here. John Reed, of *Ten Days that Shook the World* fame, authored *Insurgent Mexico* (D Appleton & Co, 1914), which related his experiences accompanying Pancho Villa – and which 'served as a precursor to his *Ten Days that Shook the World* . . . documenting the triumph of the Bolshevik Revolution'; 'together [these] suggest additional dimensions of the relationship between the Mexican and Russian Revolutions and historically and politically related phenomena'. See Camilo Pérez-Bustillo, 'Mexican Revolution and Anti-Imperialism' in Immanuel Ness and Zak Cope (eds), *The Palgrave Encyclopedia of Imperialism and Anti-imperialism* (Palgrave Macmillan, 2016) vol I, 367, 373. See also at 368 ('[Emma] Goldman and [John] Reed were among those at various stages between 1905 and 1917 who helped connect contemporaneous and ultimately convergent revolutionary processes underway under analogous conditions in Mexico and Russia; these potential convergences were also explicitly present in the writings of Zapata'). Emma Goldman (1869–1940) was an anarchist activist and writer.

still 'fighting for its national independence, political and economic. This is the basic meaning of the Mexican revolution at *this* stage'.[58]

Although the administration of General Huerta was recognised by several powers,[59] the United States was not among them: it refused to do so.[60] This approach was initially spearheaded by President William H Taft since President Wilson only took office in the first week of March 1913,[61] and, just after a week of doing so, President Wilson enunciated the US policy of recognition: 'just government', he declared, 'also rests on the consent of the governed [since] disorder, personal intrigue, and defiance of constitutional rights weaken and discredit and … injure … the people. We can have no sympathy with those who seek to seize the power of government to advance their own personal interests or ambitions'.[62] This statement sets out in clear terms the position of the United States, but it may also go some way in explaining the various labours that had been taken by the United States to reverse the act of recognition of the government of General Huerta. No doubt these developments came in sufficient time to influence the later doctrine on recognition advanced by Genaro Estrada, Secretary of Foreign Affairs in Mexico between 1930 and 1932,[63] but, more immediately, they had provoked John

[58] Leon Trotsky, 'Mexico and British Imperialism', *Socialist Appeal* (25 June 1938).

[59] Led by Great Britain; Great Britain was followed by Germany, Spain, France, Norway, Japan, Italy, Portugal, Belgium and China: see, further, Peter V N Henderson, 'Woodrow Wilson, Victoriano Huerta, and the Recognition Issue in Mexico' (1984) 41 *The Americas* 151, 170–1.

[60] And recalled its ambassador in the process: ibid., 160.

[61] Serving as sole arbitrator in the *Tinoco* Arbitration, Arbitrator Taft observed that 'the merits of the policy of the United States in this non-recognition it is not for the arbitrator to discuss, for the reason that in his consideration of this case, he is necessarily controlled by principles of international law, and however justified as a national policy non-recognition on such a ground may be, it certainly has not been acquiesced in by all the nations of the world, which is a condition precedent to considering it as a postulate of international law'. See *Aguilar-Amory and Royal Bank of Canada Claims* (*Great Britain v Costa Rica*) I RIAA 369, 381.

[62] Arthur S Link, David W Hirst, John E Little, Edith James, Sylvia Elvin and Phyllis Marchand (eds), *The Papers of Woodrow Wilson* (Princeton University Press, 1978) vol 27: 1913, 172–3. As Henderson maintains, 'revolutions against constitutional governments were, in the Wilsonian scheme, intolerable evils', n 59, 163.

[63] According to the Estrada Doctrine:

> After a very careful study of the subject, the Government of Mexico has transmitted instructions to its Ministers or Chargés d'Affaires in the countries affected by the recent political crises, informing them that the Mexican Government is issuing no declarations in the sense of grants of recognition, since that nation considers that such a course is an insulting

Bassett Moore, then the legal adviser to the Department of State, to remind his own government of a few home truths:

> The government of the United States having originally set itself up by revolution has always acted on the *de facto* principle. We regard governments as existing or not existing .... Our depreciation of the political methods which may prevail in certain countries cannot relieve us of the necessity of delaying with the government of those countries. We cannot become the censors of the morals or conduct of other nations and make our approval or disapproval of their methods the test of our recognition of their governments without intervening in their affairs.[64]

History was therefore especially resonant in these circumstances, since the practice of the United States had itself been forged in the white heat of its own revolution, with Thomas Jefferson, the first Secretary of State of the United States, adopting 'a great catholic policy of recognition'.[65] He had done so by his instruction to Gouverneur Morris, the American Minister at Paris, during the fallout from the French Revolution, that 'it accords with our principles to acknowledge any Government to be rightful which is formed by the will of the nation, substantially declared'.[66] The provision of 'the will of the nation, substantially declared' did seem to intimate a filtering function of some sort, but, almost invariably, it was in the application of the principle rather than its abstract framing that things seemed to matter most.[67] Even so, this did become the foundation of the so-called de facto principle of the United

> practice and one which, in addition to the fact that it offends the sovereignty of other nations, implies the judgment of some sort may be passed upon the internal affairs of those nations by other governments, inasmuch as the latter assume, in effect, an attitude of criticism, when they decide, favorably or unfavorably, as to the legal qualifications of foreign régimes.

'Declaration of Señor Don Genaro Estrada, Secretary of Foreign Relations of Mexico, Published in the Press on September 27, 1930, Relating to the Express Recognition of Governments' (1931) 25 *American Journal of International Law Supplement* 203.

64 Link et al., n 62, vol 27: 1913, 437. See also Henderson, n 59, 159 (on the technical correctness of the Huerta succession).

65 Green H Hackworth, 'The Policy of the United States in Recognizing New Governments during the Past Twenty-Five Years' (1931) 25 *Proceedings of the American Society of International Law* 120, 131.

66 John Bassett Moore, *A Digest of International Law* (Government Printing Office, 1906) vol I, 120.

67 'A formula permitting of some elasticity', according to H Lauterpacht, *Recognition in International Law* (Cambridge University Press, 1947) 126.

States for many subsequent generations;[68] at least on its face, it tended to guard against 'censors of the morals or conduct of other nations',[69] with all the connotations of intervention there entailed. The slightest hint that revolution, or that revolutionary change, could be choreographed by the strings of the recognition of governments seemed problematic to its very core,[70] and impossible to reconcile with any notion of sovereign choice or destiny.[71]

[68] Or 'guiding principle': ibid., 146 (that informed the practice of the United States for the next 130 years). See also Henderson, n 59, 154–5.

[69] Link et al., n 62, vol 27: 1913, 437.

[70] Hackworth, n 65, 121 (on 'a greater degree of caution in the recognition of governments born of revolution'). Lauterpacht frames this question in terms of 'a fundamental rule of international law that every independent State is entitled to be represented in the international sphere by a government which is habitually obeyed by the bulk of the population of the State and which exercises effective authority within its territory' – and that 'to deny that right to a State is to question its independence': n 67, 87 (§35). These are heady words, but they are very much qualified by the apparent objectivity of the indicators of a government that is 'habitually obeyed' and 'exercises effective authority' over territory; just under a page later, Lauterpacht formulates it thus: 'When that government enjoys, with a reasonable prospect of permanency, the habitual and – though this is controversial – willing obedience of the bulk of the population, outside States are under a legal duty to recognize it in that capacity'.

[71] Especially in the context of claims of an obligation of recognition: see, further, Herbert W Briggs, 'Recognition of States: Some Reflections on United States Doctrine and Practice' (1949) 43 *American Journal of International Law* 261. It is very interesting that immediately before the events in Mexico as examined here, the 5 October 1910 Revolution in Portugal – which witnessed its conversion from a monarchy to a republic – elicited the following forthright statement in the *American Journal of International Law*:

> It is a fundamental principle of international law that changes in the internal government or constitution of a state, as from a monarchy to a republic or a change of dynasty, do not affect its identity or continuity as an international person or member of the international community. This principle is now so universally accepted and so firmly established that it really requires no citation for its support.

See Editorial Comment, 'The Revolution in Portugal – The Recognition of New Governments' (1909) 5 *American Journal of International Law* 178, 178. Shortly thereafter, the overthrow of the Qing Dynasty in China – the Xinhai Revolution of 1911 – prompted the following observation in the same journal: 'the executive act of recognition of the Republic of China . . . will doubtless take place in due time in accordance with the usual standards established by international law. Meanwhile, the United States has along with the other Powers entered automatically into informal relations with the *de facto* provisional government pending the establishment of such ultimate government as may be adopted'. See Editorial Comment, 'Recent Political Developments in China' (1912) 6 *American Journal of International Law* 467, 472–3. The former revolution (Portugal) resulted in the collective recognition of numerous European countries; the latter revolution (Republic of China) involved consultation with a view to common action at the insistence of the United States: Lauterpacht, n 67, 167.

That said, historically, a special place does appear to have been reserved for recognition by the United States, at least in respect of its relations with the other countries of the Americas.[72]

Quite apart from the matter of recognition,[73] we also need to consider President Wilson's plan for good offices offered to the various factions of the Mexican Revolution – that is, his announcement in August 1913 'to offer to assist, if we might, in effecting some arrangement which would bring relief and peace and set up a universally acknowledged political authority'.[74] We will recall that good offices specifically did not come within the confines of Oppenheim's definition of intervention,[75] and, in the same vein, it must be said that President Wilson was keen to emphasise that 'we cannot thrust our good offices' on Mexico.[76] This may well have been the position in theory, but Mexico made a point of 'abstain[ing] from replying to the allusion that it is the purpose of the United States of America to show the greatest respect for the sovereignty and independence of Mexico, because ... there are matters which not even from the standpoint of the idea itself could be given an answer in

[72] US State Department to United States Minister in Nicaragua: 'It is more imperatively necessary to apply this rule to the Spanish-American republics, in consideration of the frequent and not seldom anomalous changes of organization or administration which they undergo, and the revolutionary nature of most of the changes': Moore, n 66, vol I, 142.

[73] It should be said, however, that there is one strand of thinking on the recognition of governments that does not associate itself with the idea of intervention: and that is that some official indication did need to be provided for relationships that arose on a day-to-day basis that affect the legal capacity of an entity to sue or be sued in domestic courts. See Edwin M Borchard, 'The Unrecognized Government in American Courts' (1932) 26 *American Journal of International Law* 261, and, also, Henderson, n 59, 151, 174.

[74] 'Address of the President of the United States on Mexican Affairs: August 27, 1913', reproduced in (1913) 7 *American Journal of International Law Supplement* 279, 281. He did so by dispatching his personal representative John Lind, former governor of Minnesota, with the following instruction for conditions of any satisfactory settlement (at 282):

(a) An immediate cessation of fighting throughout Mexico, a definite armistice solemnly entered into and scrupulously observed;
(b) Security given for an early and free election in which all will agree to take part;
(c) The consent of Gen. Huerta to bind himself not to be a candidate for election as President of the Republic at this election; and
(d) The agreement of all parties to abide by the results of the election and co-operate in the most loyal way in organizing and supporting the new administration.

[75] See Oppenheim, n 21, vol I, 181 (§134). See, further, Tyler Dennett, 'American "Good Offices" in Asia' (1922) 16 *American Journal of International Law* 1.

[76] 'Address of the President of the United States' n 74, 282.

writing'.[77] As one might have expected, it did not react kindly to President Wilson's imperative of 'honest constitutional government',[78] where, he had claimed: 'The territory in some sort controlled by the provisional authorities at Mexico City has grown smaller, not larger'.[79]

Additionally, great concern was expressed by Mexico at the conditions specified for a satisfactory settlement proposed as part of the good offices of the United States: 'Were we to agree with [rebels] to the armistice suggested, they would, *ipso facto*, recognize their belligerency, and this is something which can not be done for many reasons which can not escape the perspicacity of the Government of the United States of America, which to this day, and publicly, at least, has classed them as rebels just the same as we have'.[80] Moreover, it was maintained that the stay on General Huerta's participation in the election 'can only be decided by Mexican public opinion when it may be expressed at the polls'.[81] There was some sense that the United States had in fact contradicted its own position: 'The assurance asked of [the Mexican] Government that it should promptly convene to free elections is the most evident proof and the most unequivocal concession that the Government of the United States considers it legally and solidly constituted and that it is exercising, like all those of its class, acts of such importance as to indicate the perfect civil operation of a sovereign nation'.[82]

There is a final factor to consider here, and that is the question of neutrality, or 'the attitude of impartiality towards belligerents adopted by third States and recognized by belligerents, such attitude creating rights and duties between the impartial States and belligerents'.[83] More specifically, it related to those 'statutory provisions' forming part of the law of

[77] 'Reply of the Secretary for Foreign Affairs of Mexico to Proposals of the American Government Conveyed through Hon John Lind: Mexico, August 16, 1913' (1913) 7 *American Journal of International Law Supplement* 284, 287. President Wilson has even claimed that 'we shall yet prove to the Mexican people that we know how to serve them without first thinking how we shall serve ourselves': 'Address of the President of the United States', n 74, 280.

[78] 'Address of the President of the United States', n 74, 280.

[79] Ibid., 281.

[80] 'Reply of the Secretary for Foreign Affairs of Mexico', n 77, 289.

[81] Ibid.

[82] Ibid.

[83] As defined by Oppenheim, n 21, vol II, 316 (§293). Importantly, this related to war between states – hence the reference to third states. As far as civil war was concerned: 'As civil war becomes real war through recognition of the insurgent as a belligerent Power, neutrality during a civil war begins for every foreign State from the moment recognition is granted. That recognition might be granted or refused by foreign States independently of the attitude of the legitimate Government': at vol II, 329 (§309).

the United States in its relation with other countries.[84] Originally devised during the administration of President George Washington in respect of the French Revolutionary Wars involving France and Great Britain,[85] they have been described as 'an instance of the enforcement of international law by the municipal law of the United States'.[86] These laws were also relevant for situations beyond inter-state violence to be sure,[87] although it was clear from the rebellion – or 'civil war', as President Martin Van Buren termed it in the Proclamation he issued on 5 January 1838 – in Upper Canada in December 1837 that the mere promulgation of neutrality laws could prove insufficient in and of themselves.[88] Indeed, even the insistence on that occasion from the governors of New York and

[84] Edward Dumbauld, 'Neutrality Laws of the United States' (1937) 31 *American Journal of International Law* 253. Dumbauld concluded that 'the real purpose of the neutrality laws is to prohibit the commission of unauthorized acts of war by individuals within the United States': at 260. It was therefore as much a projection of the exclusivity of sovereignty as a statement of impartiality by any one country: Jules Lobel, 'The Rise and Decline of the Neutrality Act: Sovereignty and Congressional War Powers in United States Foreign Policy' (1983) 24 *Harvard International Law Journal* 1, 4, 24–6.

[85] Following President Washington's Neutrality Proclamation on 22 April 1793. This was followed by the enactment of the *Neutrality Act of 1794*, ch 50, 1 Stat 381, 383–4 (1794), which required not only impartiality 'but non-involvement in foreign conflicts': Lobel, n 84, 17.

[86] Dumbauld, n 84, 253. Indeed, to be distinguished from 'the obligations imposed upon the United States by international law'. See, especially, at 262 ('While the law of nations prescribes the duties which neutrals are bound to observe, it leaves to the discretion of the individual state the determination of what particular statutory authority or administrative machinery may be necessary to secure compliance with those duties'.) See, further, Oppenheim, n 21, vol II, 330 (§310). As for the overt acts coming within the compass of the Neutrality Act of 1794, these included training; the enlistment of men; the contribution of money, clothing or provisions; the furnishing of transportation as well as the provision of arms: Lobel, n 84, 37–8.

[87] Note the following observation from the United States Supreme Court in *The Three Friends* (1897) 166 US 1, 52:

> Neutrality, strictly speaking, consists in abstinence from any participation in a public, private or civil war, and in impartiality of conduct toward both parties, but the maintenance of unbroken of peaceful relations between two powers when the domestic peace of one of them is disturbed is not neutrality in the sense in which the word is used when the disturbance has acquired such head as to have demanded the recognition of belligerency. And, as a mere matter of municipal administration, no nation can permit unauthorized acts of war within its territory in infraction of its sovereignty, while good faith towards friendly nations requires their prevention.

[88] The 'selective disregard' of the Act – and, more precisely, its enforcement – is a recurring theme even through to the modern period: see, further, Lobel, n 84, 4, 43.

Vermont that 'their citizens . . . refrain from any unlawful acts within the territory of the United States' had come to naught.[89] President Van Buren found it fitting to issue his own exhortation even so (to 'all citizens of the United States who have thus violated their duties to return peaceably to their respective homes'),[90] with the Proclamation, for the most part, given to necessary warning ('any persons who shall compromit the neutrality of this Government by interfering in an unlawful manner with the affairs of the neighbouring British Provinces will render themselves liable to arrest and punishment under the laws of the United States, which will be rigidly enforced').[91]

As far as developments unfolding in Mexico were concerned, the United States Congress adopted a Joint Resolution in March 1912, providing that 'whenever the President shall find that in any American country conditions of domestic violence are promoted by the use of arms or munitions of war procured from the United States, and shall make proclamation thereof, it shall be unlawful to export except under such limitations and exceptions as the President shall prescribe any arms or munitions of war from any place in the United States to such country until otherwise ordered by the President or by Congress'.[92] This was very much in keeping with earlier iterations of the neutrality laws of the United States,[93] and President Taft duly made such a finding.[94] So, too, did President Wilson, in August of that same year, when he declared:

[89] The transcript of the Proclamation is reproduced at https://millercenter.org/the-presidency/presidential-speeches/january-5-1838-proclamation. Notably, President Van Buren spoke of 'any unlawful interference on the part of our citizens in the contest unfortunately commenced in the British Provinces'.

[90] The Proclamation gave a flavour of the 'scenes of commotion' on the northern frontier of the United States: 'the excitement, instead of being appeased, is every day increasing in degree; that arms and munitions of war and other supplies have been procured by the insurgents in the United States; that a military force, consisting in part, at least, of citizens of the United States, had actually been organized, and congregated at Navy Island, and were still in arms under the command of a citizen of the United States, and that they were constantly receiving accessions and aid': ibid.

[91] Ibid.

[92] 37 Stat 1733 (14 March 1912).

[93] An earlier Joint Resolution of Congress, dated 22 April 1898, enacted during the Spanish–American War, for example, authorised the president 'in his discretion, and with such limitations and exceptions as shall seem to him expedient, to prohibit the export of coal or other material used in war from any seaport of the United States until otherwise ordered by the President or by Congress': 30 Stat 739.

[94] On the very day of the enactment of the Joint Resolution – in a Proclamation announcing that 'there exist in Mexico such conditions of domestic violence promoted by the use of arms or munitions of war procured from the United States as contemplated by the said

> I deem it my duty to exercise the authority conferred upon me by the law of March 14, 1912, to see to it that neither side to the struggle now going on in Mexico receive any assistance from this side of the border. I shall follow the best practice of nations in the matter of neutrality by forbidding the exportation of arms or munitions of war of any kind from the United States to any part of the Republic of Mexico – a policy suggested by several interesting precedents and certainly dictated by many manifest considerations of practical expediency. We can not in the circumstances be the partisans of either party to the contest that now distracts Mexico, or constitute ourselves the virtual umpire between them.[95]

Rarely do the course of revolutions run smooth, and, within Mexico, General Huerta's authority had not gone unchallenged. In fact, it had been repudiated in the Plan of Guadalupe of March 1913, issued by General Venustiano Carranza under the banner of 'the Constitutionalists' (who had taken a stand against the 'illegal and unpatriotic procedures' of his régime).[96] President Wilson's sympathies for this movement were already a matter of record, most possibly because the Constitutionalists had made a public commitment to the protection of American property and interests.[97] He issued a Proclamation in February 1914 announcing that the conditions of his earlier Proclamation of March 1912 'have essentially changed', and went on to revoke his earlier arms embargo. This was regarded, as least in one of the newspapers of that time, as 'placing the contending elements on a basis of equality with respect to the purchase of arms and supplies' in the United States,[98] although there was surely no doubt that this development was designed

Joint Resolution'. See, further, Charles G Fenwick, *The Neutrality Laws of the United States* (Carnegie Endowment for International Peace, 1913) 105 ('owing to the fact that Mexico had not declared the existence of a state of war, it devolved upon the United States, as being at peace with Mexico, to forbid a commerce in contraband which directly tended to further revolt in that country').

95 'Address of the President of the United States', n 74, 283–4.

96 As announced in the preamble of the Plan of Guadalupe ('Considering that the Legislative and Judicial Powers in spite of the laws and constitutional rules have recognized and protected General Victoriano Huerta and his illegal and unpatriotic procedures, and considering, finally, that some Governments of the States of the Union have recognized the illegitimate Government imposed by that part of the Army that carried out the treason, headed by the same General Huerta, in spite of having violated the sovereignty of those States, whose Governors should have been the first not to recognize him').

97 Indeed, the first volume of the *American Journal of International Law* advised its readers that 'in no other foreign country has American capital invested so much money as in Mexico': Editorial Comment, 'Secretary Root's Visit to Mexico' (1907) 1 *American Journal of International Law* 964, 965.

98 'Wilson Lifts Arms Embargo', *The Walsenburg World* (5 February 1914).

to edge fortunes in favour of the Constitutionalists.[99] As it happened, the advantage took a while to materialise for the Constitutionalists, in part because of the deepening division within their own ranks in respect of Carranza and Pancho Villa, but the Constitutionalists also had to contend with the growing prestige and power of Huerta.[100] It was only in October 1915 that President Wilson made his decision to recognise – and that was the government of General Carranza.[101]

Our discussion thus far has catalogued a series of differing interactions between the United States and Mexico that occurred during the first years of the Mexican Revolution. Whether these episodes, either each or *ensemble*, amounted to 'intervention' in the legal sense as discussed earlier in this chapter is a matter propitious for investigation, but the closest the conduct of the United States came to deserving this appellation was in respect of the Tampico Affair of April 1914. This had come at a time when relations were severely strained between the United States and General Huerta and his administration. In his State of the Union Address some months earlier, in December 1913, for example, President Wilson had spoken of 'but one cloud upon our horizon'.[102] This

[99] Arthur S Link, *Wilson* (Princeton University Press, 1956) vol II, 391. Although the Proclamation was apparently preceded by the smuggling of arms across the border: Friedrich Katz, *The Life and Times of Pancho Villa* (Stanford University Press, 1998) 355.

[100] A disaffected General Francisco Villa, the commander of the northern division of the Constitutionalist Army, led a force of some 1,500 men into Columbus, New Mexico, on 9 March 1916, with numerous Americans killed including some soldiers: James Brown Scott, 'The American Punitive Expedition in Mexico' (1916) 10 *American Journal of International Law* 337. Brown Scott regarded the reaction of the United States – 'an adequate force will be sent at once in pursuit of Villa with the single object of capturing him and putting a stop to his forays', as pledged by President Wilson in a statement on the following day – as an example of 'abating a nuisance in adjoining jurisdiction', akin to the action of Great Britain in the *Caroline* incident: at 339. Importantly, in his statement, President Wilson claimed that the action 'can and will be done in entirely friendly aid of the constitutional authorities of Mexico and with scrupulous respect for the sovereignty of that Republic'.

[101] As reported in George A Finch, 'The Recognition of the De Facto Government of Mexico' (1916) 10 *American Journal of International Law* 357. This was despite the fact that 'the General is not in the saddle in all parts of his distracted country': ibid., 380. See, further, George A Finch, 'Mexico and the United States' (1917) 11 *American Journal of International Law* 399. The apparent delays in recognizing the Huerta régime seemed to have stemmed in part from the difficulties associated with the Chamizal Arbitration and from the failure of Mexico to address claims that had impacted on the United States' citizens and interests: Henderson, n 59, 166–9.

[102] This has been reproduced in www.let.rug.nl/usa/presidents/woodrow-wilson/state-of-the-union-1913.php.

happened to be the cloud that 'hangs over Mexico'. 'There can be no certain prospect of peace in America until General Huerta has surrendered his usurped authority in Mexico; until it is understood on all hands, indeed, that such pretended governments will not be countenanced or dealt with by the Government of the United States'.[103] Political temperatures were then undoubtedly at an appreciable high.[104]

At Tampico, three members of the *USS Dolphin* had been apprehended at the port in the Gulf of Mexico by forces of General Huerta on 9 April when they stopped to fill with regular supplies. While engaged in the loading of the vessel, the paymaster of the *USS Dolphin* was arrested, as were two men who were on board at that time. None were armed; all were taken into custody, 'notwithstanding the fact that the boat carried, both at her bow and at her stern, the flag of the United States'.[105] Within an hour and a half of the incident, the order was received to release the paymaster and his men; this was followed by an apology from the relevant commander on the ground and an expression of regret was made by General Huerta himself for what had occurred. However, Admiral Mayo of the US Navy regarded the arrests 'as so serious an affront'[106] that he thought something more should be forthcoming from the other side. He demanded that the flag of the United States be saluted in a special ceremony by the military commander of the port. In the words of President Wilson:

> The incident cannot be regarded as a trivial one, especially as two of the men arrested were taken from the boat itself – that is to say, from the territory of the United States – but had it stood by itself it might have been attributed to the ignorance of a single officer. Unfortunately, it was not an isolated case. A series of incidents have recently occurred which cannot but create the impression that the representatives of General Huerta were willing to go out of their way to show disregard for the dignity and rights

[103] Ibid. See, further, Kendrick A Clements, 'Woodrow Wilson's Mexican Policy, 1913–15' (1980) 4 *Diplomatic History* 113.

[104] Although President Wilson did not believe that the United States would be 'obliged to alter our policy of watchful waiting', he had considered in private the prospect of blockading Mexican ports and the sending of troops into northern Mexico at the end of October 1913: John Milton Cooper, Jr, *Woodrow Wilson: A Biography* (Alfred A Knopf, 2009) 242 ('such sentiments disclosed an interventionist streak in him, and these remarks eerily predicted much of what he would eventually do').

[105] As it was put by President Wilson in his 'Message Regarding Tampico Incident' (20 April 1914), reproduced at https://millercenter.org/the-presidency/presidential-speeches/april-20-1914-message-regarding-tampico-incident.

[106] In the words of President Wilson, ibid.

> of this Government and felt perfectly safe in doing what they pleased, making free to show in many ways their irritation and contempt.[107]

President Wilson felt that 'such wrongs and annoyances' have 'been suffered to occur only against representatives of the United States', for he had heard of 'no complaints from other Governments of similar treatment'.[108] He then endorsed the position that had been taken by Admiral Mayo,[109] but admitted that he hoped not to be forced into war with Mexico or its people. Why the expression of this point was found at all necessary in circumstances as delicate as these is difficult to say,[110] other than to put General Huerta on notice of the ultimate intentions of the United States: 'If armed conflict should unhappily come as a result of [General Huerta's] attitude of personal resentment toward this Government, we should be fighting only General Huerta and those who adhere to him and give him their support, and our object would be only to restore to the people of the distracted Republic the opportunity to set up again their own laws and their own government'.[111] Still, this salvo did not seem to sit at all well with what President Wilson maintained was the operating paradigm of relations with Mexico. 'I believe that I speak for the American people when I say that we do not desire to control in any degree the affairs of our sister Republic.. . . The people of Mexico are entitled to settle their own domestic affairs in their own way,

[107] Ibid.

[108] Ibid. He recounted how, a few days after the incident at Tampico, an orderly from the *USS Minnesota* was arrested at Vera Cruz 'while ashore in uniform to obtain the ship's mail, and was for a time thrown in jail'. An official dispatch from the US government to its embassy in Mexico City was withheld by the authorities of the telegraphic service until it was demanded by the *chargé d'affaires* in person. It is interesting that these further incidents were characterised as 'acts of aggression' in Editorial Comment, 'Mediation in Mexico' (1914) 8 *American Journal of International Law* 579, 581.

[109] 'Message Regarding Tampico Incident', n 105 ('It was necessary that the apologies of General Huerta and his representatives should go much further, that they should be such as to attract the attention of the whole population to their significance, and such as to impress upon General Huerta himself the necessity of seeing to it that no further occasion for explanations and professed regrets should arise'.)

[110] Earning the admonishment of Ian Brownlie, *International Law and the Use of Force by States* (Clarendon Press, 1963) 37. For his part, Oppenheim felt that the remedy for infractions of a state's dignity should occur through 'the Municipal Laws of all the States' that must 'provide punishment for those who commit offences against the dignity of foreign States, and, if the Criminal Law of the land does not contain such provisions, it is no excuse for failure by the respective States to punish offenders'. Oppenheim, n 21, vol I, 169 (§121). No mention was made of any recourse to intervention.

[111] 'Message Regarding Tampico Incident', n 105.

and we sincerely desire to respect their right. The present situation need have not of the grave implications of interference if we deal with it promptly, firmly, and wisely'.[112]

Nor did his subsequent request to Congress for approval to 'use the armed forces of the United States in such ways and to such an extent as may be necessary to obtain from General Huerta and his adherents the fullest recognition of the rights and dignity of the United States, even amidst the distressing conditions now unhappily obtaining in Mexico',[113] which a joint resolution of Congress duly provided on 22 April.[114] However, moments before President Wilson had addressed Congress on 20 April, he had met with four members of Congress – two representatives from each political party – in the Executive Offices of the White House. He did so in order to advise them that word had been received from William W Canada, the US consul in Veracruz, that a large shipment of arms for General Huerta was soon to arrive at that port on the German freighter *Ypiranga* and that it was his intention to intercept those arms.[115] He explained that this was the reason for his haste, but, also, that he was not keen to disclose this fact to Congress.[116] We can presume that to have done so would have fatally jeopardised President Wilson's public narration of events, especially his rhetoric concerning the 'desire' he proclaimed *not* 'to control in any degree the affairs of our sister Republic'.[117] And that haste was borne out by the arrival of 6,500

[112] Ibid.

[113] Ibid.

[114] 38 Stat 770 ('the President is justified in the employment of armed forces of the United States to enforce his demand for unequivocal amends for certain affronts and indignities committed against the United States'). See, further, 'Mediation in Mexico', n 108, 582.

[115] These details are adapted from John S D Eisenhower, *Intervention! The United States and the Mexican Revolution, 1913–1917* (W W Norton & Co, 1995) 104. See, further, John N Petrie, *American Neutrality in the 20th Century: The Impossible Dream* (National Defence University, McNair Paper 33, 1995) 48.

[116] See, further, Eisenhower, n 115, 104 (President Wilson 'wanted congressional authorization for intervention, but he wanted it granted without revealing his secret reason for the haste. And Wilson considered "protection of Americans" as too broad a basis for requesting authority to act. Such a proclaimed objective, he said, would widen the issue and possibly lead to war'.) Senator Henry Cabot Lodge was one of the four, and he argued that any action of the sort proposed for Vera Cruz would constitute an act of war and that, under international law, the interception of a foreign ship could not occur in the absence of war between the United States and Mexico: as reported by Eisenhower, 104–5.

[117] See 'Message Regarding Tampico Incident', n 105. And the fact of this secrecy is now accepted: Michael Lind, *The American Way of Strategy: US Foreign Policy and the American Way of Life* (Oxford University Press, 2006) 90.

Marines and soldiers under the command of Vice Admiral Frank F Fletcher at Vera Cruz on 21 April,[118] the day before President Wilson obtained the aforementioned congressional approval,[119] in an episode that by all accounts came to mark the demise of General Huerta.[120]

8.4 Scenes from the Russian Revolution

From the experiences and reactions to the Mexican Revolution, we have been able to see in rather intimate and telling ways how states explored various levers of power other than the recourse to direct armed intervention,[121] the most obvious manifestation one can say of the 'dictatorial interference' that was contemplated by Oppenheim. As we have done so, the question about the range and modalities of 'dictatorial' interference have come scrambling to the fore, especially in view of the fragility – the essential negotiability – of change wrought by revolution and, indeed, by counter-revolution. This, in turn, has come to probe the meaning of 'intervention' itself, whether an intervention can be constituted by the mere act of recognition by one state of another state's government, or the withdrawal of diplomatic representation, or by the emplacement of arms or other embargoes, or even by the revocation of said embargo, or, indeed, by the decision taken *not* to intervene at all at the very moment of major upheaval.[122] This chapter's focus has been not only on

[118] Michael C Meyer, 'The Arms of Ypiranga' (1970) 50 *Hispanic American Historical Review* 543. See also Thomas Baecker, 'The Arms of the Ypiranga: The German Side' (1973) 30 *Americas* 1, and Diana Preston, *Wilful Murder: The Sinking of the Lusitania* (Transworld Publishers, 2002) 40–1.

[119] Where they were met with popular hostility: Enrique Krauze, 'The April Invasion of Veracruz' *International New York Times* (21 April 2014) ('the Veracruzans reacted with rage .... It was the people of Veracruz – masons, police officers, carpenters, street sweepers, shopkeepers, students of the Naval Academy, even prisoners').

[120] See, further, Michael Beschloss, *Presidents of War: The Epic Story, From 1807 to Modern Times* (Crown Publishing, 2018) 311.

[121] Note the observation of his Secretary of State, William Jennings Bryan: 'The President feels it his duty to force Huerta's retirement, peaceably if possible but forcibly if necessary[.] The steps which he has in mind are (A) withdrawing of diplomatic representatives (B) raising of embargo on arms shipped to Constitutionalists (C) blockading of powers (D) use of army'. See Link et al., n 62, vol 28, 566. It is worth recalling that as early as August 1913, the War and Navy Departments had made plans to raise and transport 40,000 troops for an expedition into Mexico: Clements, n 103, 123.

[122] Note that Lauterpacht regards non-recognition as 'much more serious than the refusal to entertain normal diplomatic relations': n 67, 90 (§36).

revolutions themselves but on revolutions that were immediately succeeded by civil wars, and if we are to endeavour to get a proper handle on the extent or impact of any interference as well as its essential character, we should be more fully apprised of the context in which these actions came to have their consequences.

To set the scene for our discussion of the reception of the outcome of the October 1917 Revolution in Russia, it is befitting to recall the speed with which the administration of President Wilson recognised the government of the February Revolution earlier that same year – an event that had witnessed the abdication of the Romanov dynasty and the installation of the Provisional Government under Prince Georgy Lvov. A brief notice appearing in the *American Journal of International Law* at the time stated: ‘It is a source of congratulation to the Americans that the United States should have been the first nation to recognize the new government of Russia based upon the consent of the governed’, reporting that the United States Ambassador to Petrograd, David R Francis, had formally recognised the new government on 22 March.[123] In his communication to the Department of State, Ambassador Francis had advised: ‘Our recognition will have a stupendous moral effect especially if given first’, and he wrote of the revolution as ‘the practical realization of that principle of government which we have championed and advocated, I mean consent by the governed’.[124]

Within weeks of the October Revolution, President Wilson delivered his fifth State of the Union Address in December 1917, where he spoke of the Russian people and ‘the very moment of their revolution’ as well as, more cryptically, of ‘the sad reverses which have recently marked the

[123] James Brown Scott, ‘Democratic Russia’ (1917) 11 *American Journal of International Law* 416, 419.

[124] File No 861.00/284 (18 March 1917) in *Foreign Relations of the United States*, 1918, Russia, vol I (Government Printing Office, 1931) 6. According to the same communication, ‘The six days between last Sunday and this have witnessed the most amazing revolution. A nation of two hundred million people who have lived under absolute monarchy for more than one thousand years and who are now engaged in the greatest war ever waged have forced their Emperor to abdicate for himself and his heir and have induced his brother to whom he transferred the Imperial authority to accept it on condition that a constituent assembly of the people so request and when so accepted to exercise its functions under authority of the government framed by that assembly’. See, further, Green H Hackworth (ed), *Digest of International Law* (Government Printing Office, 1940) vol I, 298, and, also, ‘The Special Diplomatic Mission of the United States to the Provisional Government of Russia’ (1917) 11 *American Journal of International Law* 757.

progress of their affairs towards an ordered and stable government of free men'.[125] In fact, the Wilson administration had taken the decision to suspend financial credits and contracts for military supplies to Russia in the immediate wake of the October Revolution, for it was unsure if the new régime in Petrograd would be able to meet its existing obligations to the United States.[126] And, a matter of days after President Wilson's address, Ambassador Francis informed the Department of State: 'Think impossible for Soviet government to [last] long. Even extreme socialist and peace champions are disgusted with sailor and Red Guard excesses such as Dukhonin murder and other outrages'.[127] For his part, President Wilson desired that 'American representatives withhold all direct communication with [the] Bolshevik Government',[128] suggesting that recognition was much farther afield than anyone could have anticipated – although it is not likely that anyone could have anticipated that recognition would finally occur during the first term of President Franklin D Roosevelt, some sixteen years after the Bolsheviks had trodden their path to power![129]

For President Wilson, there remained the crucial question of whether the Bolshevik government could be regarded as the real representative of

[125] Reproduced at www.let.rug.nl/usa/presidents/woodrow-wilson/state-of-the-union-1917.php. President Wilson's position apparently oscillated between antipathy and tolerance toward the Bolsheviks: David S Foglesong, *America's Secret War against Bolshevism: US Intervention in the Russian Civil War, 1917–1920* (University of North Carolina Press, 1995) 37–8 (and distinguished between the 'true Russian people and the radicals in Petrograd': at 57).

[126] As reported by the *New York Times* (10 November 1917).

[127] File No 861.00/792 (7 December 1917) in *Foreign Relations of the United States*, 1918, Russia, vol I (Government Printing Office, 1931) 291. This is notwithstanding the fact that the British government considered changing its (original) position in order to recommend recognition of the Bolshevik government, but on condition that they were compelled to negotiate peace with Germany: Ambassador Francis to the US Secretary of State: File No 861.00/748 (29 November 1917) in *Foreign Relations of the United States*, 1918, Russia, vol I (Government Printing Office, 1931) 272. The British ambassador expected the new government to be in power 'some time': File No. 861.00/743½ (30 November 1917) in *Foreign Relations of the United States*, 1918, Russia, vol I (Government Printing Office, 1931) 274. See, further, George A B Dewar, 'Britain's Recognition of the Soviet Government' (1924–5) 3 *Foreign Affairs* 313.

[128] As instructed by Secretary of State Robert Lansing to Ambassador Francis: File No. 861.00/796a (6 December 1917) in *Foreign Relations of the United States*, 1918, Russia, vol I (Government Printing Office, 1931) 289.

[129] Chandler P Anderson, 'Recognition of Russia' (1934) 28 *American Journal of International Law* 90 (though making the adroit observation that this was *twice* the length of time that Tsar Nicholas I had taken to recognise 'the new American Republic' – which he had apparently done in 1809: at 90).

the Russian people. This factor does urge further consideration of the statement he had made as part of his Fourteen Points in January 1918 that the 'treatment accorded to Russia by her sister nations' – a formulation that no doubt included the United States – would be 'the acid test of their good will, of their comprehension of her needs as distinguished from their own interests'.[130] Given the response of the United States to the October Revolution, President Wilson's expressed commitment to 'the independent determination of [Russia's] own political development and national policy' as the sixth of his Fourteen Points has now been regarded as 'ambiguous': 'instead of embracing the Soviet regime, Wilson was assuming the position of a trustee of Russia's independence and territorial integrity while trying to help Russia emerge from the deep waters of her revolutionary turmoil'.[131] It is indeed instructive to return to the original political and diplomatic exchanges of that time, for they tended to make clear the operationality of a principle of non-intervention but, also, of a conceivably broad berth for it, as in the major declaration made by Secretary of State Bainbridge Colby in August 1920 that came to define relations between these two states for over a decade:

> Without any desire to interfere in the internal affairs of the Russian people or to suggest what kind of government they should have, the Government of the United States does express the hope that they will soon find a way to setting up a government representing their free will and purpose. When that time comes, the United States will consider the measures of practical assistance which can be taken to promote the restoration of Russia . . .. The existing regime is based upon the negation of every principle of honor and good faith and every usage and convention underlying the whole structure of international law – the negation, in short, of every principle upon which it is possible to base harmonious and trustful relations, whether of nations or individuals . . . the Bolshevist government is itself subject to the control of a political faction with extensive international ramifications through the Third International, and this body, which is heavily subsidized by the Bolshevist government from the public revenues of Russia, has for its openly avowed aim the promotion of Bolshevist revolutions throughout the world . . .. In the view

[130] Point VI: see (1919) 13 *American Journal of International Law Supplement* 128. For some sense of perspective on how other states dealt with the matter of recognition, see the list furnished by the Department of State reproduced in 'Recognition of Soviet Union' (1934) 28 *American Journal of International Law* 97. See also Betty Miller Unterberger, 'Woodrow Wilson and the Bolsheviks: The "Acid Test" of Soviet–American Relations' (1987) 11 *Diplomatic History* 71.

[131] Foglesong, n 125, 65.

> of this Government, there cannot be any common ground upon which it can stand with a power whose conceptions of international relations are so entirely alien to its own, so utterly repugnant to its moral sense.[132]

For all of the abundant rhetoric concerning non-intervention and the kindred philosophy of self-determination,[133] President Wilson authorised the provision of financial aid to anti-Bolshevik forces in the Don and Caucus regions of Russia in December 1917. This was, however, an initiative to be undertaken by the United States on a covert basis since it did not wish to revise its policy of the recognition of the provisional government; it had also not made any commitment regarding the recognition of belligerency in the civil war then unfolding in the country.[134] Hence the observation made that same month by Secretary of State Robert Lansing:

> It would seem unwise for this Government to support openly [Alexey] Kaledin [of the White movement] and his party because of the attitude which it seems advisable to take with the Petrograd authorities .... Without actually recognizing his group as a *de facto* government, which is at present impossible because it has not taken form, this Government cannot under law loan money to him to carry forward his movement. The only practicable course seems to be for the British and French Governments to finance the Kaledine enterprise in so far as it is necessary, and for this Government to loan them the money to do so.[135]

[132] Benson Grayson, *The American Image of Russia: 1917–1977* (Frederick Publishing, 1978) 57–9.

[133] See John W Long, 'American Intervention in Russia: The North Russian Expedition, 1918–19' (1982) 6 *Diplomatic History* 45, 48–9.

[134] Foglesong, n 125, 76. Again, see Foglesong, at 144 (Wilson 'showed a consistent interest in indirect methods of assisting Russia'). Presumably, in the view of the United States, the applicable law was that specified by the Institut de Droit International in its Resolution II of Neuchâtel (1900): 'Droits et devoirs des Puissances étrangères, au cas de movement insurrectionel, envers les gouvernements établis et reconnus qui sont aux prises avec l'insurrection' www.idi-iil.org/app/uploads/2017/06/1900_neu_02_fr.pdf. According to Article 1 of that Resolution, public international law imposes on third Powers 'in case of insurrection or civil war, certain obligations towards established and recognized governments, which are struggling with an insurrection'. One of these obligations was that 'every third Power, at peace with an independent nation, is bound not to interfere with the measures which this nation takes for re-establishing of internal peace' (Article 2(1)), where every third Power 'is bound not to furnish to the insurgents either arms, munitions, military goods, or financial aid' (Article 2(2)). The key to understanding this resolution is that 'established and recognized governments' (Article 1) were awarded the commanding hand, but the difficulty in this context is the calibration of *who* constitutes such governments as a formal matter of ascertainment.

[135] In correspondence with the US embassy in London: Link et al., n 62, vol 45, 274–5. Along these lines, see Foglesong, n 125, 77 (remarking that 'although American historians have often suggested that the liberal Wilson administration only grudgingly went along with Allied schemes for intervention in Russia, the United States was not dragged

This appeared in correspondence that emphasised the 'importance of avoiding it being known that the United States is considering showing sympathy for the Kaledin movement, much less of providing financial assistance'.[136]

Aside from these financial facilities and interpositions,[137] and among much procrastination, President Wilson elected to dispatch armed forces to north Russia and Siberia in July 1918.[138] He did so following the persistent urging of Allied Powers and the Supreme War Council to adopt this course of action,[139] although, at heart, he appeared to remain profoundly sceptical – no doubt because of the experiences that had been sustained during the course of the Mexican Revolution – of the extent to which intervention could and would be able to shift the direction of events.[140] It is clear that various imperatives were at work calling out for intervention as far as the Allied Powers were concerned,[141] and these were stirred by the Bolshevik decision to exit their participation in the

by its anti-Bolshevik allies into bankrolling a covert financial intervention in south Russia. American leaders took the initiative in suggesting covert methods to the British and offering to repay them for any aid they gave'). See, further, William Philipps, *Ventures in Diplomacy* (Beacon Press, 1953) 88–9.

136 Link et al., n 62, vol 45, 274–5. It is interesting that in the (private) diplomatic correspondence between Secretary of State Lansing and Ambassador Francis many months later, the former remarked that 'the United States is unable to extend direct aid to the people of Russia at this time'. File No. 861.00/1322 (23 March 1918) in *Foreign Relations of the United States*, 1918, Russia, vol I (Government Printing Office, 1931) 487.

137 See, especially, Oleh S Pidhainy, Loventrice A Scales and Alexander S Pidhainy, 'Silver and Billions: American Finances and the Bolshevik Revolution' (1974) 1 *New Review: A Journal of East European History* 1.

138 Eugene P Trani, 'Woodrow Wilson and the Decision to Intervene in Russia: A Reconsideration' (1976) 48 *Journal of Modern History* 71.

139 Trani writes that between November 1917 and July 1918, pressure from Great Britain 'was massive, continual, and in the long run decisive': ibid., 445. See, further, Betty Miller Unterberger, 'President Wilson and the Decision to Send American Troops to Siberia' (1955) 24 *Pacific Historical Review* 63, 66 (writing of President Wilson being 'overwhelmed with appeals for intervention from his Allies'). And, ultimately, the position of Great Britain was dictated by the desire to intervene in the civil war: at 455.

140 See, further, Arthur S Link, *Wilson: Campaigns for Progressivism and Peace, 1916–1917* (Princeton University Press, 1965). See also Trani, n 138, 444. Trani dates this change of heart to April and May 1918, when 'Wilson realized [that] he would have to give in somewhat on Russia': at 454.

141 Among which, and of chief concern to Japan, was the protection of the Amur and Trans-Siberian railways and the stores and munitions located at Vladivostok. Japan's battleships were the first to reach Vladivostok, followed by *HMS Suffolk* from Great Britain: see, further, Leonard A Humphreys, *The Way of the Heavenly Sword: The Japanese Army in the 1920s* (Stanford University Press, 1996). The possibility of the imperial ambitions

Great War courtesy of the Treaty of Brest–Litovsk of March 1918.[142] Yet, despite the apparent pervasive appeal of intervention in Russia, there is abundant evidence of the continuing hold of the principle of *non-intervention*, certainly as far as President Wilson and the United States were concerned (for President Wilson, 'Russia's misfortune' at that time imposed 'the obligation of unswerving fidelity to the principle of Russian territorial integrity and political independence'.)[143] Again, this was a time well before the enactment of any general prohibition of force in public international law,[144] so it was the prohibition of intervention that assumed the constitutional significance of ordering the relations between states at that time.[145]

Whether this rhetoric is indicative of the convenient summoning of principle to ward off or stay the hand of the Allies, or whether it exhibits the influence of public international law on the decision(s) of the United States is, of course, impossible to say,[146] but matters do seem to have taken a decisive turn in May 1918 with the 'fortuitous appearance' or fate of the Czech Legion in Siberia.[147] A large cohort of Czechoslovak forces had become stranded on Russian soil following the signing of the Treaty of Brest–Litovsk, and they wanted to continue their fight against the Austro-Hungarian Empire from France. Rather than running enemy lines, they sought to reach Europe by travelling east along the Trans-Siberian railway via Vladivostok.[148] When their advance along this route came to be impeded by the Red Army, President Wilson proved amenable to sending an expeditionary force to secure their rescue. Additionally, reinforcements were required in northern Russia in support

of Japan itself became a spur for other interventions: See also Long, n 133, 47, and, also, Cooper, n 104 431.

142 Apparently, Great Britain attempted to persuade the Soviet authorities to participate in the war with Germany with Allied military assistance: Unterberger, 'Wilson and the Decision to Send American Troops to Siberia', n 139, 68.

143 According to General Peyton C March, Chief of Staff, in a communication with Tasker H Bliss, Chief of Staff of the United States Army, dated 28 May 1918.

144 Although consider the 1907 Hague Convention (II) on the Limitation of Employment of Force for Recovery of Contract Debts: 36 Stat 2241.

145 As posited by P H Winfield, 'The History of Intervention in International Law' (1922–3) 3 *British Yearbook of International Law* 130.

146 Long is of the view that during the 'long interval' between January and May 1918, 'American opposition to intervention was founded primarily on principle': n 133, 51.

147 Foglesong, n 125, 164. See, however, Long, n 133, 52–4, and, further, Carl J Richard, '"The Shadow of a Plan": The Rationale behind Wilson's 1918 Siberian Intervention' (1986) 49 *Historian* 64.

148 Orlando Figes, *Revolutionary Russia, 1891–1991* (Pelican, 2014) 147.

of Great Britain's operation in Murmansk following the landing of its forces there in May 1918.[149] This overall change in conditions facilitated something of a change of heart on the part of the Wilson administration, who, through Secretary of State Lansing, issued a now famous *aide-mémoire* on 17 July expressing its intent on:

> assuring the people of Russia in the most public and solemn manner that none of the governments uniting in action either in Siberia or in northern Russia contemplates any interference of any kind with the political sovereignty of Russia, any intervention in her internal affairs, or any impairment of her territorial integrity either now or hereafter, but that each of the associated powers has the single object of affording such aid as shall be acceptable, and only such aid as shall be acceptable to the Russian people in their endeavour to regain control of their own affairs, their own territory, and their own destiny.[150]

This is truly an extraordinary statement for the Wilson administration to have made for, in the very same breath of declaring the importance of upholding the principle of non-intervention, the groundwork *for* an intervention of some sort was being set. Note the vehement respect professed here for 'the political sovereignty of Russia', for the firm stand taken against 'any intervention in her internal affairs' or 'any impairment of her territorial integrity either now or hereafter'. Yet, somehow, it was felt entirely possible to square the envisaged actions in *both* Siberia *and* northern Russia with the principle of non-intervention,[151] presumably

[149] That expanded to Archangel: see Michael Jabara Carley, 'Allied Intervention and the Russian Civil War, 1917–1922' (1989) 11 *International History Review* 689.

[150] *Foreign Relations of the United States*, 1918, Russia, vol II (Government Printing Office, 1931) 289–90, reproduced in George F Kennan, *The Decision to Intervene* (Princeton University Press, 1958) 482–5. Indeed, President Wilson was keen that the expedition occur *without* the involvement of Great Britain or France for, as his Secretary of State Lansing was to point out, 'the participation of these two Governments will give the enterprise the character of interference with the domestic affairs of Russia and create the impression that the underlying purpose is to set up a new pro-Ally Government in Siberia, if not in Russia'. See Lansing to Polk (3 August 1918). Indeed, in March 1918, Great Britain had already endeavoured the occupation of Murmansk in north Russia by a small contingent of Royal Marines. Long acknowledges President Wilson's 'strong attachment' to the tenets of non-intervention and self-determination: n 133, 49.

[151] And, to this end, a detailed *apologia* was delivered by Secretary of State Lansing in his *aide-mémoire* of July 1918, in which it was maintained that:

> Military action is admissible in Russia, as the Government of the United States sees the circumstances, only to help the Czecho-Slovaks consolidate their forces and get into successful cooperation with their Slavic kinsmen and to steady any efforts at self government or self defense in which the

for so long as they were confined by 'affording such aid' as 'shall be acceptable to the Russian people in their endeavour to regain control of their own affairs, their own territory, and their own destiny'. There is a grand feel of irony to what is being posited with these eloquent, even poetic, words, but, very quickly, this sensation is overtaken by one of profound obscurity and dislocation,[152] for it remains unclear how assistance of the kind intended could not affect the outcome – and, indeed, the destiny – of Russia's brutal civil war.[153]

8.5 Concluding Remarks

In its landmark judgment in *Case Concerning Military and Paramilitary Activities in and Against Nicaragua* in June 1986, the International Court of Justice concluded that it 'cannot contemplate the creation of a new

> Russians themselves may be willing to accept assistance. Whether from Vladivostok or from Murmansk and Archangel, the only legitimate object for which American or allied troops can be employed, it submits, is to guard military stores which may subsequently be needed by Russian forces and to render such aid as may be acceptable to the Russians in the organization of their own self-defense. For helping the Czecho-Slovaks there is immediate necessity and sufficient justification. Recent developments have made it evident that that it is in the interest of what the Russian people themselves desire, and the Government of the United States is glad to contribute the small force at its disposal for that purpose. It yields, also, to the judgment of the Supreme Command in the matter of establishing a small force at Murmansk, to guard the military stores at Kola and to make it safe for Russian forces to come together in organized bodies in the north. But it owes it to frank counsel to say that it can go no further than these modest and experimental plans. It is not in a position and has no expectation of being in a position, to take part in organized intervention in adequate force from either Vladivostok or Murmask and Archangel. It feels that it ought to add, also, that it will feel at liberty to use the few troops it can spare only for the purposes here stated and shall feel obliged to withdraw these forces, in order to add them to the forces at the western front, if the plans in whose execution it is now intended that they should develop into others inconsistent with the policy to which the Government of the United States feels constrained to restrict itself.

152 Hence the 'highly ambiguous aide-mémoire of 17 July 1918', according to Long, n 133, 55.

153 Especially since the landing of American forces in northern Russia in early September resulted in 'numerous small-scale combats' with Bolshevik forces: at Murmansk: ibid., 58. At Archangel, see at 59–60.

rule opening up a right of intervention by one State against another on the ground that the latter has opted for some particular ideology or political system'.[154] Admittedly, this statement came many, many decades after the events – the revolutions, the civil wars – that have been recounted in these pages. It came in the midst of the Cold War in circumstances that are wholly different from those that ushered in and defined the revolutions of Mexico and Russia. Yet, what was revelatory about the Court's statement was the manner of its expression rather than the content of any rule it had identified. To be clear, the Court was saying that it 'cannot contemplate' a rule positing a right of intervention 'by one State against another on the ground that the latter has opted for some particular ideology or political system'.[155] In this very moment, the Court was therefore not simply exhibiting a methodological fidelity to empiricism, a bare commitment to positivistic enquiry. It was saying that it 'cannot contemplate' – it could not imagine – the instantiation of such a rule within the international legal system. The implication was that the rule in question was not only law at the time of the decision in June 1986, but that the Court could not imagine that rule ever becoming law. And for good reason, for, moments earlier in its judgment, the Court had said that 'to hold otherwise would make [a] nonsense of the fundamental principle of State sovereignty, on which the whole of international law rests, and the freedom of choice of the political, social, economic and cultural system of a State'.[156]

In other words, in the Court's view, the law on intervention not only has to reconcile itself with the normative ebbs and flows of state practice, but it also, ultimately, has to contend with the apparent fundamentals of this system.[157] One of these fundamentals, maintained the Court, was the 'principle' – the fundamental organising principle of state sovereignty no less, 'on which the whole of international law rests' – addressed in its judgment, which entails 'the freedom of choice of the political, social, economic and cultural system of a State'. Freedom of choice. Political, social, economic and cultural system of a State. These are powerful ideas invoked in order to define and furnish meaning to sovereignty, and if

[154] [1986] ICJ Rep 14, 133 (§263).
[155] Ibid.
[156] Ibid.
[157] Note in this respect the positioning of the importance of legal doctrine as against the 'legal analysis' commonly adopted by international lawyers in Carty, n 17, ix.

they are to mean anything, that 'choice' must include the choice of radical change as well as the various means by which that 'freedom' is exercised. Indeed, the preamble of the 1948 Universal Declaration of Human Rights regards it as 'essential, if man is not to be compelled to have recourse, as a last resort, to rebellion against tyranny and oppression, that human rights should be protected by the rule of law',[158] and, to wit, it has been said that 'international law does not prohibit revolution as a means of constitutional or purely governmental change within the State'.[159]

Writing in his classic text on *Recognition in International Law* in 1947, Hersch Lauterpacht observed: 'It is of the essence of the notion of independence of States that changes in the structure or in the composition of their governments are, in international law as at present constituted, an internal question of the States concerned and that foreign States are not, in general, entitled to interfere in the matter by raising the question of recognition or by refusing to grant it'.[160] These words anticipate the judgment of the International Court of Justice delivered some four decades later. Lauterpacht entered his brief qualification in respect of change that was of 'revolutionary character and accompanied by violence', because, he argued, 'the question often arises whether the new government, based as it is on force in the first instance, is an effective government with a reasonable prospect of permanency'.[161] We can perhaps appreciate the need for some latitude in the context of revolution and revolutionary change, but, for Lauterpacht, in such moments of epic uncertainty, it is essentially public international law that has provided continuity in the form of the legal continuity of the affected state.[162] However, as the relation of the Mexican and Russian revolutions in this chapter has hopefully shown, the granting and withholding of recognition do not always conform to the niceties of these preordained metrics or intentions, and recourse to the discourse of intervention is not necessarily misplaced or without

158 GA Res 217A (III), UN Doc A/810 (1948) 71.

159 Lauterpacht, n 67, 92 (§37).

160 Ibid., 91 (§37).

161 Ibid., 92 (§37).

162 Where 'within the State the revolution destroys irrevocably the continuity of the system; the former law subsists only in so far as it is adopted by the new, revolutionary order': ibid., 92 (§37).

appropriate cue.[163] We have also seen how, more frequently than not, recognition has assumed its place alongside other tropes of behaviour that states have adopted in dealing with revolution and revolutionary change, and as we have done so, it should have become apparent how the discourse of intervention has proved less and less possible to avoid.

[163] Note, again, Lauterpacht: 'So long as the lawful government offers resistance which is not ostensibly hopeless or purely nominal, the *de jure* recognition of the revolutionary party as a government constitutes premature recognition which the lawful government is entitled to regard as an act of intervention contrary to international law': ibid., 94 (§38).

9

Mexican Revolutionary Constituencies and the Latin American Critique of US Intervention

JUAN PABLO SCARFI*

9.1 Introduction

The Mexican Revolution and the new Constitution of 1917 produced transformations in the field of international law both in Mexico and across the Americas. The impact of these transformations, and particularly their implications for continental and regional debates over armed and unilateral interventionism, have tended to be overlooked by scholarship on international relations and the Mexican Revolution.[1] Although revolutions have not tended to be assimilated and conceptualised as such within the language of international law but rather as civil wars, the Mexican Revolution has had an important and enduring impact on how international law and diplomacy

* Email: jpscarfi@gmail.com (Departamento de Humanidades, Universidad de San Andrés - CONICET). A first version was presented at the conference '1917: Revolution, Intervention and International Law(s)', held at the University of Melbourne, Australia, on 24–5 August 2017. A second version was later presented at the V Jornadas de Relaciones Internacionales de FLACSO, 'América Latina en la Disciplina Global de las Relaciones Internacionales', held on November 2017 in Buenos Aires. I am grateful to Anne Orford, Fabia Veçoso, Vidya Kumar and Carsten Schultz for their comments on these two previous versions of this paper, as well as the editors of the volume for their comments and feedback. Translations are the author's own.

1 The existing scholarship devoted to the international dimensions of the Mexican Revolution has tended to be dominated by studies of diplomatic history and bilateral relations between the United States and Mexico, the oil industry and the impact of the agrarian reform in Mexico and the Pan-American projects that emerged in the context of the US–Mexican conflict, among other topics. See, for example, W Dirk Raat and Michael M Brescia, *Mexico and the United States: Ambivalent Vistas* (University of Georgia Press, 4th ed, 2010); P Edward Haley, *Revolution and Intervention: The Diplomacy of Taft and Wilson with Mexico* (MIT Press, 1970); Mark T Gilderhus, *Diplomacy and Revolution: US-Mexican Relations under Wilson and Carranza* (University of Arizona Press, 1977); Mark T Gilderhus, *Pan American Visions: Woodrow Wilson in the Western Hemisphere, 1913–1921* (University of Arizona Press, 1986); Jonathan C Brown and Alan Knight (eds), *The Mexican Petroleum Industry in the Twentieth Century* (University of Texas Press, 1992).

were envisioned in Mexico and in Latin America more broadly.[2] As such, it created the grounds and scope for redefining notions of absolute non-intervention in the critical context of the potential isolation of Mexico from the international legal order and international institutions. This chapter examines the redefinition of Mexican and Latin American conceptions of the international legal order, and the germination of new international legal doctrines concerning intervention and US unilateralism in the face of US armed intervention in Veracruz, Mexico, in 1914.

The chapter focuses on the international legal thought of Isidro Fabela in the context of the Mexican Revolution and the rise of the so-called Carranza Doctrine. Fabela was Minister of Foreign Affairs under Venustiano Carranza (1913–15), also serving as Mexican representative at the League of Nations (1937–41) under the government of Lázaro Cárdenas and as a judge of the International Court of Justice (1946–51). It argues that the transformations produced by the revolution and the 1917 Constitution and the international legal doctrines developed by Fabela led to a reconstruction of the Latin American doctrine of absolute non-intervention. This reconstruction also created the grounds for a robust legal critique of both US armed and unilateral interventions in the region and the foundations and unilateral enforcement of the Monroe Doctrine by the United States. More generally, this created scope for a new legal and political 'constituent power', opening grounds for a revisionist approach to international law. 'Constituent power' has in itself a revolutionary dynamic in contrast with and, indeed, in opposition to the static and closed nature of constituted power.[3] Therefore, revolutions, and in this case the revolutionary constituencies forged by the Mexican Revolution, contributed to generating a constituent power and thus the formulation of a new set of legal and political frameworks – in particular a legal critique of the Monroe Doctrine and, more importantly, a robust approach to the principle of absolute non-intervention, as advanced by Fabela and Carranza. This approach was to inform the new Mexican Constitution as well as Mexican approaches to international law and diplomacy. The Mexican revolutionary experience produced a revolution

[2] As addressed in this volume, particularly in chapters by Alison Duxbury, Dino Kritsiotis, Fabia Fernandes Carvalho Veçoso, Kathryn Greenman, Kate Miles and Daria Davitti.

[3] On the concept of constituent power, as opposed to constituted power, see Antonio Negri, *Insurgencies: Constituent Power and the Modern State* (University of Minnesota Press, 1999). For a brief and synthetic definition, see also Antonio Negri, 'Constituent Republic' in Michael Hard and Paolo Virno (eds), *Radical Thought in Italy: A Potential Politics* (University of Minnesota Press, 1996) 213.

in international law that remained for a long time in the margins of the discipline because the main revisionist figures of this legal revolution, such as Fabela and Carranza, remained outside the dominant canon of international law scholarship and thus were overlooked or even forgotten. This chapter seeks to show why this was so with the Mexican Revolution and to make a case for exploring the specific and broader implications of such a revolution for international law and international relations.

At the same time as the new constitution of 1917 was consolidated, an attempt was made by the new Mexican republican government to gain international recognition under international law. The progressive institutionalisation of the revolutionary process showed the limits of the language of international law and the constitutional status quo for adopting and internationally recognising the new norms and the transformations introduced by the Mexican experience, especially in matters of non-intervention. In other words, following US intervention in Veracruz, a process of radical revision of legal and political norms expanded across Mexico, resulting in a quest for the construction of a new constituent power. However, as soon as Fabela, Carranza and Cárdenas began to institutionalise these transformations, seeking international legal recognition and making use of European-led international organisations, the process of legal and political innovation and revision declined, adapting itself to the international legal status quo. As such, the chapter will argue that the language of international law and constitutional order and the need to legitimise the transformations introduced by the revolution – both in the domestic constitution and under international law – contributed to placating the constituent power, and the radical revision of legal and political norms inaugurated by the revolutionary process. The Mexican Revolution and the revision of international legal norms that emerged with it can be seen as a laboratory for exploring a much broader and important issue: namely, the limits of international law as a tool for creating power balances and safeguarding weak nations from unilateral and armed interventions.

Stepping back from the dominant Pan-American approach to international law promoted in the region by Alejandro Álvarez, Fabela – within the margins of international law – adopted an anti-imperialist legal sensibility and solidarity for safeguarding the sovereignty of 'weak nations' from interventionist policies and power politics.[4] He had a sense

[4] Fabela used the term 'nations' and 'weak republics' alternatively throughout his work on international law when referring to Latin American nations. See, for instance, 'La Casa Blanca, fábrica de doctrinas imperialistas' in Isidro Fabela, *Los Estados Unidos y la*

of the weakness of small Latin-American states, anticipating the doctrines of absolute non-intervention long before the Montevideo Conference of 1933 and promoting the right of asylum. Fabela can be seen as one of the most eloquent opponents of Álvarez, the most celebrated Latin-American jurist of the twentieth century. While Álvarez epitomised a solidarist, Pan-American and US-led monist approach to international law, advocating the redefinition of the Monroe Doctrine as a Pan-American and continental foundational principle for an American hemispheric international law, Fabela advocated a pluralist and Latin American regional and defensive understanding of international law. This understanding combined a political understanding of the logic of power politics and great power diplomacy, and a strong legalist notion and attachment to the principle of non-intervention and international legal norms.

Before the idea of the Third World was invented, Latin America occupied a strange and unsettled place. It was not clear whether it was part of the West or the non-West.[5] In the critical conjuncture of the revolutionary process and when seeking to internationally legitimise the new regime, it was vital for Fabela and Carranza to create new legal and political 'constituencies' in favour of sovereignty and non-intervention. This was done to safeguard Mexico from foreign and especially US unilateral interventions, as well as to gain Western recognition in Europe and Latin America, thereby assimilating Latin American states to a European-led international society.[6] It was risky to isolate Mexico from Europe and European-led institutions, so the anxiety to build new revolutionary constituencies for Mexico and Latin America went hand in hand with another, contradictory impulse: to legitimise those constituencies in the European-led international legal order. A later stage of Fabela's career, which is not the subject of this chapter, shows the extent to which Mexico sought to give shape to some of the normative concerns of the League of Nations and

América Latina (1921–1929) (Cuadernos Americanos, 1955) 23; 'La defensa de las naciones débiles' in Isidro Fabela, *Buena y mala vecindad* (Editorial América Nueva, 1958) 64. For an important and influential example of an analysis of Third World perspectives and understandings of the historical and cultural dimensions of sovereignty, see Antony Anghie, *Imperialism, Sovereignty and the Making of International Law* (Cambridge University Press, 2005) 1–12.

5 On the unsettled place of Latin American international thought, see Louise Fawcett, 'Between West and Non-West: Latin American Contributions to International Thought' (2012) 34 *International History Review* 679; Juan Pablo Scarfi, 'Globalizing the Latin American Legal Field: Continental and Regional Approaches to the International Legal Order in Latin America' (2018) 61 *Revista Brasileira de Política Internacional* 1.

6 See again Negri, 'Constituent Republic', n 3.

adapt the goals of the Mexican Revolution to an existing European-led framework.[7] This is not to say that the Mexican Revolution lost its revisionist and 'constituent power' and meaning, but rather that it adapted itself somehow to the existing international legal and political framework.

The international legal thought and trajectory of Fabela merits examination not only because he played a crucial role in the context of the Mexican Revolution, but also because he adopted a revisionist Latin American approach to international law, sovereignty and the principle of non-intervention. Fabela's approach projected a modern legal sensibility especially concerned to safeguard the sovereignty of weaker Latin American states and nations in the international legal order, and conscious of the need to deploy international law and international institutions and norms for the protection of 'weak nations', especially Latin American ones. The chapter focuses on two stages of this important process and Fabela's contribution and trajectory. First, it examines the formulation of revolutionary constituencies and Fabela's articulation of the Carranza Doctrine, and his role as Carranza's Minister of Foreign Affairs in the context of US intervention in Veracruz (1914). Second, it explores the legitimisation of the Carranza Doctrine and the revolutionary constituencies of the new Mexican Constitution in the region and Fabela's diplomatic mission in both the 'ABC' countries (Argentina, Brazil and Chile) and in Europe to disseminate the ideals of the Mexican Revolution and the Carranza Doctrine and gain international recognition under international law. The conclusion offers some reflections on the legacy of the transformations introduced by the Mexican Revolution for the doctrines of non-intervention and sovereignty in the history of international law in Latin America, and for Latin American and Third World understandings of international law and international institutions.

9.2 The Carranza Doctrine and the Redefinition of International Law

The internal conflicts that eventually led to the revolutionary period that began in 1910 in Mexico can be traced back to the authoritarian regime

[7] In this later stage, as a Mexican delegate at the League of Nations, Fabela played an important role in institutionalising the right of asylum, but given space constraints, this chapter will focus on Fabela's contribution to forging a new approach to the principle of non-intervention. On Fabela's role at the League of Nations, see Fabia Fernandes Carvalho Veçoso, Chapter 10 in this volume.

of Porfirio Díaz. In this context, the close ties of the Mexican economy to the United States contributed to the rise of the nationalist reaction against the United States and in favour of the revolution. In other words, US capital and commercial influence in Mexico created the conditions for an export-orientated economy 'modernized from without',[8] the commercialisation of agriculture and the politicisation and radicalisation of the peasantry and poor rural sectors in reaction to the US-oriented economic and political structure during the so-called Porfiriato. The special relationship that Mexico maintained with the United States is important for understanding both the origins of the revolution, and the cultural and intellectual milieu that created the conditions for the new internal policies of the revolutionary regime in the domestic and international arenas. Fabela's legal and diplomatic ideas germinated in, and were a product of, this conjuncture. Although the revolution created a great deal of anxiety in the United States, and had repercussions in US politics, media and public opinion, it was not until the United States intervened in Veracruz in 1914 that the transformations introduced internally by the revolutionary process had a broader impact on the international arena.

US intervention in Veracruz in 1914 sought to depose Victoriano Huerta, who was seen by Fabela – and many other intellectual and political figures in Mexico belonging to the Carranza-centred coalition in favour of creating a new constitutional regime – as a traitor to the original spirit of the revolution.[9] In the context of an internal conflict between different coalitions in Mexico, especially between Huerta and the Constitutionalists grouped around Carranza, the US administration maintained an arms embargo and refused to recognise the government of Huerta.[10] By contrast, the British Foreign Office did not put any pressure on Huerta, and Britain's friendly relations with Huerta, and its influence over the oil and railway industries in Mexico, created a great deal of anxiety in the United States, particularly for the president, Woodrow Wilson.[11] Although Wilson sought to build an alliance with Carranza

8 The expression 'modernization from without' was coined by John Coatsworth. See John H Coatsworth, *Growth against Development: The Economic Impact of Railroads in Porfirian Mexico* (Northern Illinois University Press, 1981), cited in Raat and Brescia, n 1, 117.

9 Haley, n 1, 77–140. See also 'La Doctrina Carranza' in Fernando Serrano Migallón, *Isidro Fabela y la diplomacia mexicana* (Fondo de Cultura Económica, 1981) 183–98.

10 Gilderhus, *Diplomacy and Revolution*, n 1, 7–12; Gilderhus, *Pan American Visions*, n 1, 30–5.

11 Gilderhus, *Diplomacy and Revolution*, n 1, 7–9.

and the Constitutionalists to protect the rights of US companies and foreigners located in Mexico, Carranza did not accept such an arrangement and interpreted this proposal as an interference in Mexican internal affairs and its right to self-determination.[12] The incident that eventually led to US intervention took place in Tampico, one of the richest areas of Mexico, where most oil fields were located and US and British investments in oil industries were concentrated. On 9 April 1914, Mexican soldiers arrested a small group of US sailors from the *USS Dolphin* for violating a restricted zone. The US sailors were then released and the Mexican army apologised for the incident, but these verbal apologies were not enough to satisfy the US commander. This crisis was interpreted by Wilson as an affair of honour and he became convinced that it was imperative to intervene in Mexico in order to establish a legitimate government in replacement of Huerta. However, the situation was aggravated when rumours circulated that the German steamer *Ypiranga* was about to land in Veracruz with a shipment of arms for Huerta. This final incident led to the landing of a US navy force and marines in the port of Veracruz on 20 April 1914 and the so-called US intervention in Veracruz. While Wilson intervened in turn for the paternalistic objective of safeguarding Mexican sovereignty, the intervention was resented in Mexico and was indeed interpreted by Carranza and Fabela as a violation of the territorial rights and dignity of a free, sovereign and independent nation.[13] In the aftermath of US intervention in Veracruz, the quest for creating a new 'constituent' legal and political power to enforce the principle of absolute non-intervention became a central component of the agenda of the Mexican Revolution, especially for the Constitutionalist coalition grouped around Carranza and thus for Fabela himself.[14] The so-called Carranza Doctrine can thus be seen as a legal and defensive response to this controversial and highly resented US intervention in Mexico.

The impact of US intervention in Veracruz was particularly felt in the 'ABC countries'. Indeed, the US armed and unilateral intervention in Veracruz, by 1914, had created opposing reactions in Mexico and the ABC countries. The reaction of the ABC countries was orientated towards the promotion of mediation between Mexico and the United

[12] Ibid., 9–14.

[13] For a detailed analysis of US intervention in Veracruz and the ABC mediation, see Gilderhus, *Diplomacy and Revolution,* n 1, 7–14; Haley, n 1, 29–40.

[14] On the notion of constituent power, see again Negri, 'Constituent Republic', n 3.

States, leading later to the Niagara Falls Conference in Canada, and initiatives, advocated mainly by President Woodrow Wilson, for a Pan-American Pact between the United States and the ABC countries. In this context there was an important liberal internationalist optimism about the progress of Pan-Americanism, as well as great hopes for the construction of a specific continental American international law, the American Institute of International Law (AIIL) and the consolidation of peace in the Americas. The Chilean jurist Alejandro Álvarez epitomised this Pan-American approach to American international law.[15] From the time of its proposal, the ABC mediation itself had been enthusiastically supported in the United States, and the Argentine ambassador to the United States, Rómulo Naón, a fervent supporter of Pan-Americanism, was one of its main promoters.[16] On the other hand, Mexican reactions were radically defensive and especially distrustful of the ABC mediation. Indeed, according to Fabela 'the ABC assumed the role of intervening in the internal affairs of our republic'.[17] The official response of the Mexican Foreign Office, formulated by Fabela, was to reject the ABC mediation and the armistice thereby proposed, arguing that Mexico should act according to its sovereign interests.[18] These US and ABC interventions in the internal affairs of Mexico led in turn to the germination of the so-called Carranza Doctrine, which, according to Fernando Serrano Migallón, was formulated by Fabela himself.[19]

US intervention in Veracruz and even the ABC mediation were regarded by Fabela and Carranza as an interference in the internal affairs of Mexico. Neither Fabela nor Carranza advocated a radical anti-interventionist approach before the 1914 intervention. Indeed, in the United States, Venustiano Carranza, who was to become a force behind

15 See Gilderhus, *Pan American Visions*, n 1, 37–45; Juan Pablo Scarfi, *The Hidden History of International Law in the Americas: Empire and Legal Networks* (Oxford University Press, 2017) 31–85.

16 See Pablo Yankelevich, *Miradas australes: Propaganda, cabildeo y proyección de las Revolución Mexicana en el Río de la Plata, 1910–1930* (Secretaría de Relaciones Internacionales, 1997) 73–9; Gilderhus, *Pan American Visions*, n 1, 30–5; 'El primer embajador argentino' in Gustavo Ferrari, *Esquema de la política exterior argentina* (Editorial Universitaria de Buenos Aires, 1981) 115–32.

17 *La Vanguardia*, Buenos Aires (6 July 1915) cited in Yankelevich, *Miradas australes*, n 16, 97.

18 See Serrano Migallón, *Isidro Fabela y la diplomacia mexicana*, n 9, 49.

19 Ibid., 161–2. See also Fernando Serrano Migallón, 'Estudio preliminar', in Fernando Serrano Migallón (ed), *Con certera visión: Isidro Fabela y su tiempo* (Fondo de Cultura Económica, 2000) 17, 61.

the Constitution of 1917, was not seen initially as a threat to US economic interests in Mexico.[20]

The Carranza Doctrine was to be defined in opposition to the Monroe Doctrine as a unilateral US principle. Originally, the Monroe Doctrine had been formulated by US President James Monroe in 1823 as a US foreign policy principle requiring non-intervention by Europe in the continental affairs of the Western Hemisphere and as a unilateral statement of US supremacy in the Americas. In the late nineteenth and early twentieth centuries, it began to be redefined in relation to the interventionist and expansionist policies of the United States in Central America and the Caribbean as an interventionist principle, especially through its reformulation as the Roosevelt Corollary (1904) of the doctrine. In this very same context, Latin American and US jurists, diplomats and politicians, such as Luis María Drago (Argentina), Baltasar Brum (Uruguay) and Alejandro Álvarez (Chile), but also Woodrow Wilson (United States) and John Barrett (United States) sought to reformulate the doctrine along the lines of the emerging continental policy of Pan-Americanism as a multilateral and continental principle of non-intervention based on liberal international ideas, traditions and norms of mutual understanding and cooperation between the United States and Latin America.[21] Therefore, when Fabela and Carranza began to put forward a revisionist legal and political critique of the Monroe Doctrine as a flexible and elastic principle with no legal and international legitimacy as a proper principle of international law, there were competing visions of the place of Latin America in the international legal order. These visions were rooted in contending understandings of the Monroe Doctrine as both a US unilateral interventionist and multilateral non-interventionist continental principle.

In an article originally written in 1913, before the United States intervened in Veracruz, Fabela explicitly condemned the regime of Porfirio Díaz as a tyranny, contrasting the past with Carranza's constitutional project of creating a new government based on the rule of law and republican institutions. He affirmed that 'Porfirio Díaz was a tyrant;

[20] See Gilderhus, *Diplomacy and Revolution*, n 1, 7–14.

[21] On the competing interventionist and non-interventionist understandings of the Monroe Doctrine in the early twentieth century, see Juan Pablo Scarfi, 'In the Name of the Americas: The Pan-American Redefinition of the Monroe Doctrine and the Emerging Language of American International Law in the Western Hemisphere, 1898–1933' (2016) 40 *Diplomatic History* 189.

a tyrant who governed in Mexico for thirty years. Tyrannies cannot last forever. We were rich, but slaves'.[22] However, he continued, 'Carranza has raised the Constitution', so 'with guns, justice and law, we will win soon'.[23] Fabela went as far as to invoke a continental Americanist vision of liberty and self-determination, based on the US Monroe Doctrine and a liberal internationalist Wilsonian approach, affirming that the Monroeist ideal of 'America for the Americans', defined as a broader continental principle, could be redefined in the revolutionary context of inaugurating a new constitutional regime as 'America for Liberty'.[24] But his understanding of US interventionism became more radical in subsequent years, especially following US intervention in Veracruz in 1914, and even more so when Fabela sought to disseminate the goals of the Mexican Revolution in South America, as will be shown in more detail in the following section.

Not only did Fabela play a central role as Carranza's foreign minister in the context of US intervention, he also reconstructed these events in a series of writings devoted to the diplomatic history of the Mexican Revolution.[25] His performance and writings contributed in turn to reshaping his legal and diplomatic understanding of US interventionism in Veracruz and US interventionist policies in Latin America more broadly. As a member of *Ateneo de la Juventud* (*Ateneo*)[26] and advocate of the consolidation of a constitutional regime for Mexico in support of Carranza, Fabela combined, like other Latin America international

[22] 'Al Congreso Yanky' (10 August 1913) in Isidro Fabela, *Arengas revolucionarias: discursos y artículos políticos* (Tipografía Artística, 1916) 88, 90.

[23] Ibid.

[24] Ibid., 91.

[25] Fabela reconstructed these events in a series of different registers and writings, including impressions from his experiences as minister of foreign affairs under Carranza, as well as extensive studies. See for instance, Fabela, *Arengas revolucionarias*, n 22; Serrano Migallón, *Isidro Fabela y la diplomacia mexicana*, n 9; Isidro Fabela, *Historia diplomática de la Revolución Mexicana* (Fondo de Cultura Económica, 1958).

[26] The *Ateneo de la Juventud* was founded in 1909 and grouped together a number of figures who played a central role in challenging the dominant and orthodox positivist trend in the context of the authoritarian regime of Porfirio Díaz that predated the Mexican Revolution. They did so by promoting an intense cultural campaign in the field of education through recreating a popular university in order to disseminate alternative forms of knowledge and the study of the humanities. More importantly, some prominent members of the *Ateneo*, such as Fabela himself, José Vasconcelos, Alberto J Pani and Luis Guzmán, played a central role in the revolutionary process. See Javier Garciadiego, 'Los intelectuales y la Revolución Mexicana' in Carlos Altamirano (ed.), *Historia de los intelectuales en América Latina* (Katz, 2010) vol 2, 31, 32.

lawyers and diplomats in Argentina and Cuba, a legalist discourse in support of a new constitutional regime founded on the rule of law and republican and democratic legitimacy with the humanist, modernist and cultural anti-imperialist critique of US culture and idiosyncrasy that characterised the generation of Mexican intellectuals and politicians grouped around the *Ateneo*.[27] This combination of a critique of US culture, constitutional discourse and a legal anti-interventionist approach against US hegemonic policies took on a special cast in Mexico. The cultural and political milieu of the revolution stimulated this combination, and Fabela epitomised this tendency. Fabela's testimony of his experience as foreign minister under Carranza in the context of the US occupation of Veracruz from April to November 1914 is a symptomatic example of this combination. Fabela emphasised the extent to which Carranza was committed 'to sustain the cause of legality by all means', in an attempt to show why the intervention could potentially threaten, as Fabela was to affirm, 'the independence – and autonomy – that every country has the right to maintain within its frontiers' and therefore 'could be justified neither under the law of nations nor under the utilitarian convenience of any party or nation'.[28] Equally, it was 'a tragic act' causing general disgust across the region, so Fabela also invoked a Latin American cultural sensibility to denounce the intervention in the name of Martí's 'Our America', in the almost-literary form of an exclamation.[29] He thus stated: 'our America protested with indignation against the Saxon invasion on Latin soil!'[30] Carranza and Fabela regarded US intervention as a turning point: it was from that point on that they began to interpret the Monroe Doctrine as an interventionist doctrine, rather than a continental principle, and the United States as an aggressive and imperialist neighbour intervening in the internal affairs and acting against Mexican sovereign autonomy, rather than part of the land of liberty of the Americas.

[27] This combination of a cultural critique of US political culture with a legalist anti-imperialist discourse can be found in other Argentine and Cuban jurists. See Juan Pablo Scarfi, 'La emergencia de un imaginario latinoamericanista y antiestadounidense del orden hemisférico: de la Unión Panamericana a la Unión Latinoamericana (1880–1913)' (2013) 39 *Revista Complutense de Historia de América* 81; and Scarfi, 'Globalizing the Latin American', n 5.

[28] Fabela, *Arengas revolucionarias*, n 22, 99, 105.

[29] José Martí, *Nuestra América* (Editorial Losada, 1980).

[30] Fabela, *Arengas revolucionarias*, n 22, 105.

Although the Carranza Doctrine was recognised at the time in the diplomatic arena, it is not well known outside Mexico and Mexican foreign relations.[31] The Carranza Doctrine affirmed the principles of equality among nations, sovereignty and absolute non-intervention in the internal affairs of another state as fundamental and universal interconnected principles; equality between foreigners and nationals and thus state legislation leaving no room for national distinctions; and diplomacy based on the establishment of universal confraternity, avoiding the pressure of powerful states over 'weak nations'. It also rejected the Monroe Doctrine and any redefinition of it. Although some of these ideas were formulated by Calvo and Drago and were to be institutionalised later in 1933 at the 7th Pan-American Conference held in Montevideo, the Carranza Doctrine was a pioneering one. It was incorporated into Article 27 of the Mexican Constitution.[32] It was crucial for the political and legal agenda of the Mexican Revolution, advanced by Carranza and Fabela, to consolidate domestic legitimacy as a constitutional regime and gain recognition of the new government that emerged from the revolution in the international arena under the norms of international law. The Carranza Doctrine can be seen as an initial attempt to create a new legal and political 'constituent power' for legitimising the Mexican Revolution under international law on the basis of domestic constitutional

[31] Serrano Migallón, *Isidro Fabela y la diplomacia mexicana*, n 9, 154–63.

[32] Fabela regarded Article 27 of the 1917 Constitution as a confirmation and consolidation of the Carranza Doctrine, in that it stated the principle of non-intervention and non-interference of foreign capital or commercial interests for any exploitation of land and properties included in the national jurisdiction of the Mexican state and nation. More importantly, it also affirmed the equal status of foreigners and nationals for the acquisition of properties or land in Mexico. Article 27 famously declared that:

> 'the domain of the nation is inalienable and imprescriptible' and that 'only Mexicans by birth or naturalisation, and Mexican companies, have the right to acquire ownership of lands, waters, and their appurtenances, or to obtain concessions for the exploitation of mines, waters or minerals in the Mexican Republic. The State may concede the same right to foreigners as long as they agree to be considered by the Ministry of Foreign Affairs as nationals with respect to these goods and not to invoke, for this purpose, the protection of their own governments with regard to them'.

See *Texto original de la Constitución de 1917 y de las reformas publicadas en el Diario Oficial de la Federación del 5 de febrero de 1917 al 1o. de junio de 2009*, Biblioteca Jurídica Virtual del Instituto de Investigaciones Jurídicas de la UNAM, 138–9. See also 'La Doctrina Carranza' in Serrano Migallón, *Isidro Fabela y la diplomacia mexicana*, n 9, 195; 'La Constitución de 17 y la Doctrina Carranza' (Speech given by Isidro Fabela, governor of the state of Mexico, at the banquet offered to the constitutional deputies, 5 February 1943) in Fernando Serrano Migallón (ed), *Con certera vision: Isidro Fabela y su tiempo* (Fondo de Cultura Economica, 2000) 343–6.

legitimacy.[33] The fragile conditions of the revolutionary constitutional coalition grouped around Carranza, however, made this project difficult. The original spirit of the Carranza Doctrine sought to trace a connection between constitutional and international legal rules. In order to avoid unilateral interventions, such as US intervention in Veracruz, it was crucial to create solid constitutional rules internally and rules of absolute non-intervention internationally. Therefore, according to Fabela, constitutionalism and non-intervention were interconnected. Carranza incarnated this combination, bridging the gap between the domestic and international promotion of the rule of law under a constitutional regime. Fabela himself sought to provide legal and political foundations for the leadership of Carranza, who became a constitutional president only in 1917 but, as has been already noted, had advocated the constitutional cause since at least 1913. Tracing this connection proved to be a useful strategy for Fabela in legitimising both the constitutional coalition grouped around Carranza and, eventually, the emerging constitution of 1917, as well as the principle of absolute non-intervention as a consistent legal norm supported by the constitution and the law of nations at the very same time. In the context of the US occupation of Veracruz, Fabela made two important and interconnected declarations, offering a common legal basis for a new emerging domestic constitutional and international legal order in Mexico and contributing in turn to delineating the foundations of the so-called Carranza Doctrine. He thus stated:

> First, in conformity with the law of nations, the landing and remaining of foreign troops in an independent country is an intervention and there cannot be a right to intervention, since there cannot be a right against the right to territorial inviolability.
>
> Second, a political party that for the success of its cause tolerates a foreign invasion, even if it is a partial one, is not committed to fulfilling its duties towards the state.[34]

According to Fabela, the Carranza Doctrine was rooted in previous Latin-American doctrines of absolute non-intervention and the resolution of disputes over the collection of public debts between foreigners and nationals in national courts, as formulated by Argentine jurists

[33] On the notion of constituent power, see again Negri, 'Constituent Republic', n 3.

[34] Isidro Fabela (ed), *Documentos históricos de la Revolución mexicana: Revolución y régimen constitucionalista* (Fondo de Cultura Economica, 1960) vol 2, 33–4, cited in Serrano Migallón, *Isidro Fabela y la diplomacia mexicana*, n 9, 47–8.

Carlos Calvo and Luis María Drago.[35] At the same time, it implied a rejection of the Monroe Doctrine, which was interpreted by Carranza and Fabela as producing an arbitrary protectorate with no juridical legitimacy and no reciprocity, and as creating the conditions for validating US unilateral interventions. Carranza himself defined the Monroe Doctrine as follows:

> The Monroe Doctrine constitutes an arbitrary protectorate, imposed over countries that have not solicited it and nor do they need it. The Monroe Doctrine is not reciprocal and therefore is unfair .... We are in an analogous case to where someone has been offered a favour and rejects it, but in spite of this the acceptance of the favour, which he did not need, is imposed upon him.[36]

Fabela's critical understanding of the Monroe Doctrine was also founded on the idea that it was a US unilateral imposition. These sceptical ideas about the threat posed by the Monroe Doctrine deeply informed the formulation of the Carranza Doctrine to the extent that it could be seen as an attempt to contest and demolish the US Monroe Doctrine. In this regard, Fabela's complete rejection of the Monroe Doctrine implied a radical departure from some of the legal and political approaches advanced by other Latin American jurists in the early twentieth century, such as Alejandro Álvarez and even Luis María Drago, who were fervent supporters of the continental redefinition of the Monroe Doctrine as a multilateral principle of non-intervention.

Although Fabela was Carranza's speechwriter, and himself delineated the basic principles that were to be associated with the so-called Carranza Doctrine, the doctrine became publicly known through two famous speeches by Carranza in 1915 and 1918, following the US intervention in Veracruz. The Carranza Doctrine was based on five premises.[37] The first premise was its express rejection of the Monroe Doctrine as an

35 See Isidro Fabela, *Intervención* (Universidad Nacional Autónoma de México, 1959) 138, as well as Isidro Fabela, 'México en la posguerra' (1944) in Fernando Serrano Migallón (ed), *Con certera vision: Isidro Fabela y su tiempo* (Fondo de Cultura Economica, 2000) 208, 215–16.

36 Interview with Venustiano Carranza, *El Mundo* (La Habana, 11 May 1919) cited in Serrano Migallón, *Isidro Fabela y la diplomacia mexicana*, n 9, 185.

37 On the basis of Fabela's formulation of the Carranza Doctrine and two important speeches delivered by Carranza, Fernando Serrano Migallón summarised the doctrine in four premises, adding that it also implied a rejection of the Monroe Doctrine. See 'La Doctrina Carranza' in Serrano Migallón, *Isidro Fabela y la diplomacia mexicana*, n 9, 183–98; Fabela, 'La Constitución de 17 y la Doctrina Carranza', n 32, 343.

arbitrary and hegemonic principle imposed by the United States over Latin American nations without their request or need, violating their sovereignty. The second premise affirmed that 'all nations are equal before the law. Therefore, they should mutually and strictly respect their institutions, laws and sovereignty, safeguarding and attaching themselves strictly and with no exceptions to the universal principle of non-intervention'.[38] Fabela's approach to non-intervention was particularly assertive to the extent that, in his later work devoted to the question of intervention, he went as far as to condemn collective interventions, explicitly criticising Alejandro Álvarez for accepting such interventions, which he viewed as creating exceptions to absolute non-intervention and grounds for legitimising interventions.[39] The third premise, drawing on the Calvo clause, stated: 'Nationals and foreigners should be equal against the sovereign state in which they reside; thus no individual should pretend to have a better situation than that of the citizens of the country where he or she is established, neither make of his condition of foreigner a title for protection or privilege'.[40] The fourth premise stated that 'state legislation should be uniform and similar as far as possible, without establishing distinctions based on nationality, except regarding the exercise of sovereignty'.[41] Finally, the fifth premise affirmed that 'diplomacy should be based on the general interests of civilisation and the establishment of universal confraternity; it should not serve the protection of particular interests, nor for putting at its service the resort to the force and power of nations. Neither should it serve to exert pressure over the governments of weak nations, with the aim of obtaining modifications of the laws that are not convenient for the subjects of powerful nations'.[42]

After the formulation of the Carranza Doctrine, Fabela contrasted the Monroe and Drago doctrines. While the former was enounced as a unilateral political principle, the Drago Doctrine (1902), originally formulated by Argentine Minister of Foreign Affairs Luis María Drago, was consistent with the principles of international law in that it drew on the Calvo Doctrine (1868), formulated by Argentine jurist Carlos Calvo. The

[38] 'La Doctrina Carranza' in Serrano Migallón, *Isidro Fabela y la diplomacia mexicana*, n 9, 192. See also 'El principio de no intervención' in Isidro Fabela, *Buena y mala vecindad* (Editorial Nueva América, 1958) 233.

[39] See Fabela, *Intervención*, n 35, 161.

[40] 'La Doctrina Carranza' in Serrano Migallón, *Isidro Fabela y la diplomacia mexicana*, n 9, 192–3.

[41] Ibid., 193.

[42] Ibid.

so-called Drago Doctrine stated that no intervention should be enforced or permitted for the collection of public debts. It drew on the Monroe Doctrine, but it emerged instead as a defensive Latin-American reaction to the joint intervention of European powers (Germany, the United Kingdom and Italy) in Venezuela for the collection of public debts in 1902.[43] Fabela's attempt to contrast the Drago with the Monroe Doctrine proved to be an effective strategy for legitimising a series of Latin American legal doctrines in opposition to the Monroe Doctrine, tracing a binary opposition between Latin Americanism and Pan-Americanism, anti-interventionism and interventionism, and anti-imperialism and imperialism. As Fabela was to affirm later, Drago was 'one of the champions of the principle of non-intervention', as well as an inspirational figure for the Carranza Doctrine and the Mexican Constitution of 1917.[44] By opposing the Drago Doctrine to the Monroe Doctrine, Fabela redefined the former in radical contrast to the latter: that is, as an authentic Latin American legal principle of absolute non-intervention.

Interestingly, the Carranza Doctrine was formulated at the same time as Álvarez was defending the Monroe Doctrine as a multilateral Pan-American legal principle with continental legitimacy and as the basis of what he termed 'American international law'.[45] This should not be seen as coincidence, since Fabela's radical anti-interventionist approach and the international legal ideas that emerged in the context of the Mexican Revolution could be seen not only as a rejection of Pan-American approaches to international law, as advanced by Álvarez, but also as a much broader and ambitious attempt to create the grounds for a Latin American approach to international law, excluding US influence. This approach would be founded on some of the goals advanced by the Mexican Revolution, in opposition to the US-led Pan-American movement and other liberal internationalist Wilsonian projects that had informed and inspired the ABC mediation and even Wilson's intervention in Veracruz.

[43] 'La Casa Blanca, fábrica de doctrinas imperialistas', *El Universal* (1921) in Isidro Fabela, 'Los Estados Unidos y la América Latina (1921–1929)' (1955) 14 *Cuadernos Americanos* 7, 24. See also Isidro Fabela, *Las doctrinas Monroe y Drago* (Universidad Nacional Autónoma de México, 1957) 11–12; Isidro Fabela, *La doctrina Drago* (Secretariá de Educación Pública, 1946).

[44] Fabela, *Intervención*, n 35, 154.

[45] On American international law and Álvarez, see Scarfi, *The Hidden History*, n 15. For a more detailed comparison and contrast between the international legal thought of Álvarez and Fabela, see Scarfi, 'Globalizing the Latin American Legal Field', n 5.

9.3 Disseminating the Carranza Doctrine and the Goals of the Mexican Revolution in South America

Creating revolutionary constituencies and a 'constituent power' entailed not only generating the grounds for international regional legal approaches and validating them in the new Constitution but also disseminating and legitimising these legal innovations across Latin American nations and even in Europe. In other words, this meant disseminating the Carranza Doctrine, advancing a more consistent and robust critique of the Monroe Doctrine and aspiring to put international law at the service of weak nations. It was during this international experience that Fabela began to delineate a more specific concern for Latin-American weak nations, as well as a more sophisticated legal critique of US unilateral and armed interventions, not only in Mexico but also across the whole region. US politicians and diplomats disseminated a critical overview of Mexican affairs and the transformations introduced by the Mexican Revolution; and Carranza and Fabela were perceived as advocates of Pan-Hispanism and anti-Americanism.[46] The US press presented the revolution as a threat for the continent, lowering the image of the revolution in the international arena and condemning Mexico to isolation.[47] This was aggravated by the fact that Article 27 of the new Constitution placed restrictions on private companies investing or doing business in Mexico.[48]

In 1916, Fabela was sent to Europe and then to the ABC countries to undo these prejudices and images of the Mexican Revolution, as promulgated by the US press and many other important political figures.[49] He was to do this through providing alternative news and reports to these countries, disseminating the Carranza Doctrine in South America and legitimising the revolution under international law in a series of European countries. In most of the European capital cities he visited in the United Kingdom, France, Italy, the Netherlands, Belgium, Sweden,

[46] See John A Britton, 'Redefining Intervention: Mexico's Contribution to Anti-Americanism' in Alan McPherson (ed), *Anti-Americanism in Latin America and the Caribbean* (Berghahn Books, 2006) 39.

[47] See Pablo Yankelevich, 'América Latina en la agenda diplomática de la revolución mexicana' in Jorge A Schiavon, Daniela Spenser and Mario Vázquez Olivera (eds), *En busca de una nación soberana: Relaciones internacionales de México, siglo XIX y XX* (Secretaría de Relaciones Exteriores de México/CIDE, 2006) 277.

[48] On the tensions between Mexico and the United States in this period, see, for example, Gilderhus, *Diplomacy and Revolution*, n 1.

[49] Yankelevich, *Miradas australes*, n 16, 96–103.

Norway and Russia, Fabela had limited success in his mission. For instance, in Rome the Carranza government was recognised only for a few days following Fabela's visit.[50]

It is no coincidence that Fabela's main Latin American targets were the ABC countries that had offered to mediate in the conflict between Mexico and the United States in the context of the intervention in Veracruz, promoting a Pan-American alliance with the United States. Visiting these South American nations could be seen as part of a deliberate project of Carranza's government to disseminate the goals and achievements of the Mexican Revolution in South America as a defensive Latin American diplomatic reaction to US-led Pan-Americanism. As part of Carranza's dissemination project, along with other Mexican diplomats and politicians, Fabela encouraged the publication of a book devoted to disseminating the Carranza Doctrine in South America, *The Carranza Doctrine and the Indo-Latin Rapprochement* (*La Doctrina Carranza y el acercamiento Indolatino*) by Hermila Galindo.[51] Like those who supported Pan-Americanism, Fabela sought to promote cultural cooperation but restricted this to the notion of Latin Americanism. This was a defensive reaction to US interventionism in the region and its hemispheric supremacy within the Pan-American movement, as well as the pejorative image that the US press promoted and presented of the Mexican Revolution. As articulated by Fabela in an interview following his arrival in Buenos Aires, 'the Revolution was not only distorted but also slandered by the US press and government, which sees this context as more opportune than ever for enforcing an armed intervention in my country'.[52]

Before Fabela was sent to the ABC countries, the modernist Argentine writer and anti-imperialist intellectual Manuel Ugarte had created a committee of solidarity with the Mexican Revolution in Argentina. Ugarte's campaign contributed to an internal atmosphere of solidarity, albeit restricted to a limited group of intellectuals and political activists linked to Ugarte.[53] This solidarity was not shared by the official authorities in Argentina. For this reason, when Fabela visited Argentina, he was not a recipient of receptions by the official authorities and legal and

[50] See 'Su actuación en el servicio exterior' in Serrano Migallón, *Isidro Fabela y la diplomacia mexicana*, n 9, 58–68.

[51] Yankelevich, *Miradas australes*, n 16, 135.

[52] *La Prensa* (Buenos Aires, 27 July 1915) cited in ibid., 97.

[53] Yankelevich, *Miradas australes*, n 16, 155–72.

diplomatic circles but was instead welcomed by anti-imperialist intellectuals and writers who had been promoting solidarity networks and campaigns in support of Mexico in the context of the Mexican Revolution. Local authorities in Argentina, Brazil and Chile were reluctant to accept and welcome a diplomat like Fabela who sought to legitimise a regime that did not yet have constitutional legitimacy. Fabela spoke in the name of the constitutional enterprise of Carranza, but the constitutional reform was not yet implemented. It does not come as a surprise that Fabela's dissemination project and his international legal ideas found greater echo among anti-imperialist Latin American intellectuals and political activists than among the international law and diplomatic community and official authorities in South America.

One of his more famous works, *The United States against Liberty* (*Los Estados Unidos contra la libertad*), written in the course of his journey across Europe and South America and published a few years later in 1920, should be read as a result of this international experience of dissemination in an attempt to gain international legal recognition.[54] Published in Barcelona in the aftermath of the creation of the League of Nations and written with a sense of the weakness of small nations and the aspiration of warning South Americans and Europeans about US interventions in the Caribbean, Central America and Mexico, it had potential appeal for both Latin American and even European local readers. Interestingly, an explicit reference was made in the first paragraph of the book to US intervention in Veracruz.[55] At the same time, it was a critical study of the US invocation of the Monroe Doctrine to legitimise interventions across the region. Fabela sought to make clear that there was a sharp contradiction between US formal advocacy for Pan-Americanism and hemispheric solidarity, its promotion of the rule of law, justice and liberty, and its verbal defence of weak nations, as opposed to the systematic practice of regular interventions and hegemony over Latin America. This work was, according to Modesto Seara Vázquez, a 'fervent repudiation of intervention' and a warning of what Fabela considered to be a systematic and constant violation of international law on the part of the United States.[56] In this ambitious study

[54] See Isidro Fabela, *Estados Unidos contra la libertad: Estudios de historia diplomática americana* (Talleres Gráficos Lux, 1920).

[55] Ibid., 9.

[56] Modesto Seara Vázquez, 'El pensamiento y la contribución de Don Isidro Fabela al derecho internacional' (1961) 5 *Cuadernos Americanos* 71, 84.

devoted to examining US interventions in Cuba, the Philippines, Panama, Nicaragua and the Dominican Republic, and considered a foundational text in the field of international relations in Latin American scholarship, Fabela concluded with an analysis of the Treaty of Versailles, where the Monroe Doctrine was formally incorporated into the League Covenant as Article 21 and thus implicitly accepted.[57] Fabela affirmed that the Monroe Doctrine was elastic and flexible and this was a 'danger' for Latin America and a 'brilliant instrument' for US intervention in the region. Thus, as long as the United States did not define it accurately and it continued to be a flexible principle and a 'malleable entity', it had to be rejected by both Europe and Latin America as a principle of international law.[58]

As Fabela maintained a deep sense of the weakness of Mexico's isolated situation, he emphasised the importance of deploying international law for safeguarding weak Latin American nations from US interventionism, categorically rejecting the Monroe Doctrine as a principle of international law. He concluded this important work by making his concern for the sense of isolation and weakness experienced by Mexico in the international legal arena explicit:

> The Mexican President, Venustiano Carranza, is the only statesman who did not accept the doctrine, rejecting it politically and officially, since it implies a tutelage for Hispanic America that his country has not solicited and does not need. But President Carranza is alone. The United States, arbiters of the world, in a recent moment of our history, has imposed their ideas and will on many nations. An effect of this powerful influence has been the acceptance of the Monroe Doctrine.[59]

The demolition of both the Monroe Doctrine, as a legal principle, and the broader Pan-American movement were central objectives of both Fabela and Carranza, but this ambitious mission was pursued at a moment of extreme isolation for Mexico. Fabela sought to maintain a strong attachment to international law in order to denaturalise the legitimacy of the Monroe Doctrine as a proper international legal principle. At the same time, he was perfectly conscious of the isolation

[57] Luis Ochoa Bilbao, 'Radiografía del imperio: Los Estados Unidos contra la libertad, de Isidro Fabela' in Alexandra Pita González and Carlos Marichal (eds), *Pensar el antiimperialismo: ensayos de historia intelectual latinoamericana, 1900–1930* (El Colegio de Mexico, 2012) 99, 103.

[58] Fabela, *Estados Unidos contra la libertad*, n 54, 309–10.

[59] Ibid., 310–11.

and weakness of Mexico in his quest for the regional dissemination of the goals of the Mexican Revolution. Part of Fabela's mission was to construct networks of cultural and intellectual cooperation with the South American nations and invite intellectuals and writers from the region to come to Mexico. One of the direct products of his mission in the ABC countries was the official invitation, in 1916, for Ugarte to visit and deliver some lectures in Mexico in 1917.[60]

Fabela's writings and his mission in South America had some direct impact on intellectuals and political activists in Argentina and Cuba. This was particularly true, as has already been noted, of Ugarte, but also of Emilio Roig de Leuchsenring, who was originally an international lawyer by background but transformed himself into an anti-imperialist historian, denouncing the US diplomatic and economic tutelage and protectorate over Cuba. Fabela not only invited Ugarte to Mexico but also cited him in his important work *United States against Liberty* as a prominent defender of the Latin American race: 'This book has been written precisely with the intention that those who are mistaken open their eyes and contemplate the sad spectacle of a Spanish America that deserves well the title of The Suicidal Continent (*El continente suicida*), an expression that was coined by the noble defender of our race, Manuel Ugarte'.[61] Therefore, while Fabela was influenced by Ugarte, his book *United States against Liberty* had a significant influence on Roig de Leuchsenring, who devoted two essays to Fabela's important book, in an edited volume paying homage to Fabela and focusing on his exploration of the Cuban case and Cuban relations with the United States.[62]

While the international legal thought of Fabela had a greater impact on anti-imperialist intellectuals and political activists, the constitutional legacy of the Mexican Revolution – that is, the new Constitution of 1917 – had a much broader and more significant impact than the transformations it advanced in international legal norms. Recovering the implications of these revolutionary constituencies for international legal norms and the international legal thought of Fabela should not be seen simply as a historical reconstruction of doctrines and precedents. Rather, it can also

[60] Yankelevich, *Miradas australes*, n 16, 165.

[61] Fabela, *Estados Unidos contra la libertad*, n 54, 119.

[62] See Emilio Roig de Leuchsenring, 'Cuba en la obra antimperialista de Isidro Fabela', as well as Roig de Leuchsenring, 'Estudio histórico sobre las relaciones internacionales de Cuba con los Estados Unidos' in Isidro Fabela and Baldomero Segura García (eds), *Homenaje a Isidro Fabela* (Universidad Nacional Autónoma de México, 1959) 571, 739.

contribute to understanding the important legal and political dilemmas and powerful limitations that have to be faced in consolidating these Latin American aspirations and approaches to sovereignty and non-intervention within the language of international law. In other words, it illuminates the legal and political limitations that have long been faced by Latin American and later by Third World countries more broadly to assert and legitimise new constituencies in the international community. Exploring these past dilemmas could shed new light on our current legal and political limitations for reconstructing and redefining the language of international law from Latin America, and, at the same time, on the long-standing relevance and creativity of this weak Latin-American perspective that emerged from the margins of the discipline of international law.[63]

9.4 Conclusion

The Mexican Revolution created a foundation for a process of revising international law in Latin America. This process had an important political impact in Mexico but also in the ABC countries, where Fabela and other Mexican diplomats disseminated the goals of the revolutionary process, adopting a Latin-American posture. A promoter of international legal innovation in defence of Latin American weak nations, Fabela sought to redefine international law in a direction that, at the time, was not dominant among the jurists and diplomats of the region. Unlike Álvarez, who defended the Monroe Doctrine and sought to redefine it as a continental and beneficial legal principle for the continent, adopting a solidarist and monist approach, Fabela rejected the Monroe Doctrine altogether and placed Latin American legal traditions – and weak nations – at the centre of his concerns. Indeed, Fabela sought to create the grounds for a robust regional approach to non-intervention, promoting a pluralist conception of international law in which regionalism was

[63] For this line of argument in the study of the history of international law for understanding the past as law and the normative implications of historical and contextual arguments that advance a contemporary critical legal research agenda in international law and international legal and political theory, see Anne Orford, 'The Past as Law or History? The Relevance of Imperialism for Modern International Law' (Legal Studies Research Paper No 600, University of Melbourne, 9 September 2011). See also Juan Pablo Scarfi, 'Del giro ético al historicista: El potencial y los límites de la perspectiva histórica en los derechos humanos y el derecho internacional' (2017) 6 *Revista Latinoamericana de Derecho Internacional* 1.

combined with universalism; reformism with an attachment to formal multilateral principles; and law with an awareness for the threats posed by power politics and great power diplomacy.[64] Fabela also sought to integrate Mexico into the League of Nations, that is, into a European-based international organisation. The revolutionary context in Mexico created the conditions for, and saw instances of, the advancement of new legal 'constituent power' that led to forging more robust approaches to the principle of absolute non-intervention in the new Mexican Constitution of 1917 and in the diplomatic and international legal and political orientation of the revolutionary government.

Fabela was neither a legal formalist nor sceptical of the value of international law as a tool for political transformation. He might be regarded instead as an advocate of a legal pluralist approach based on an understanding of formal legal norms and principles as rooted in an attachment to legal codes and international institutions, as well as the logic of power politics in which weak countries are often exposed to hierarchical and hegemonic relations in the face of imperial and great power diplomacy. At the same time, Fabela combined revisionist and critical interpretations of the Monroe Doctrine and non-intervention with a more conventional adherence to, and formal respect for, the international rule of law and international organisations. Indeed, in the 1920s and 1930s Fabela sought to adapt the new revolutionary constituencies and the principle of absolute non-intervention to the existing legal framework of the League of Nations in order to gain international recognition and adapt the transformations introduced by the revolutionary process in Mexico to the international legal status quo in an attempt to avoid the isolation of Mexico from the emerging international legal order of the interwar period.[65]

However, these pioneering legal approaches advocated by Fabela, especially in relation to the principle of absolute non-intervention, remained marginal in the field of international law, at least until 1933. The Carranza Doctrine and the political and legal achievements of the Mexican Revolution generated more enthusiasm among intellectuals and advocates of anti-imperialist movements and circuits linked to the Latin American University Reform, such as Manuel Ugarte and Emilio Roig de

[64] On Alejandro Álvarez and his conception of the Monroe Doctrine, see Scarfi, 'In the Name of the Americas', n 21.

[65] For a detailed overview of Fabela's role in the League of Nations in the context of the Spanish Civil War in the 1930s, see again Chapter 10 in this volume.

Leuchsenring, than among jurists and diplomats within the Pan-American movement and inter-American institutions.

These Mexican revolutionary constituencies and pioneering legal approaches seem prescient. Fabela was ambivalent towards the status quo and the dominant legal approaches. There was a tension between this innovative attitude and one of caution that aimed to adapt to the dominant international legal order, avoiding the potential risk of isolating Mexico from the international legal and political arena. The quest for the construction of new revolutionary constituencies and the redefinition of international law from a Latin American perspective was a radical impulse that could potentially isolate Mexico. Therefore, new doctrines, such as the Carranza Doctrine, had to be disseminated and legitimised within the Latin American legal community in the face of an emerging Pan-American movement and in the context of Eurocentric international organisations, such as the League of Nations. There was an explicit attempt by Fabela to incorporate Mexico into international society, particularly the League of Nations, and thus make use of international organisations to promote the achievements of the Mexican Revolution. However, the tension between revisionism and adaptation to a Eurocentric legal framework was never resolved by Fabela. In this sense, we might regard him as a precursor to Third World international legal sensibilities.

10

Mexican Post-Revolutionary Foreign Policy and the Spanish Civil War

Legal Struggles over Intervention at the League of Nations

FABIA FERNANDES CARVALHO VEÇOSO*

10.1 Introduction

From October 1936, Mexico waged a growing legal campaign at the League of Nations ('the League') in favour of the Spanish Republic in the context of the Spanish civil war. The Mexican delegate at the League, Narciso Bassols, repeatedly denounced the intervention of Italy and Germany in the armed conflict, challenging the view that the war in Spain should be described solely as an internal issue.[1] In March 1937, the new Mexican delegate at the League, Isidro Fabela, presented a note to the Secretary-General on the Mexican position on intervention and the conflict in Spain stating that:

> My government considers it a duty to provide all means at its disposal in favor of world peace, and especially to try to bring to an end the armed conflict that has been afflicting the Spanish Republic for eight months. Accordingly, my country is allowed to appeal to the sentiments of humanity of the States brought together in the League of Nations. The way in which the so-called policy of non-intervention has been put into practice has only had the consequence of denying Spain the aid which, under International Law, the legitimate government of that country could logically expect from those who cultivate with it normal diplomatic relations.[2]

* Postdoctoral Fellow at the Laureate Program in International Law, Melbourne Law School.
I would like to thank Anne Orford, Kathryn Greenman, Anna Saunders and Ntina Tzouvala for their detailed and valuable comments on earlier drafts of this chapter. My gratitude to Juan Pablo Scarfi for all our exchanges about Isidro Fabela. All English translations are the author's own except where otherwise noted.

[1] Fabián Herrera León and Agustín Sánchez Andrés, *Contra todo y contra todos: la diplomacia mexicana y la cuestión española en la Sociedad de Naciones 1936–1939* (Ediciones Idea, 2011) 189–90.

[2] Ibid., 361–2.

The Mexican note presented legal justifications for the country's support to the Spanish Republic. Its main objective was to demonstrate that the Mexican aid was in accordance with the principle of non-intervention.[3] In September 1937, Fabela offered a comprehensive presentation on the legal foundations of the Mexican position to the Assembly of the League of Nations.[4] Both Bassols and Fabela were diplomats and lawyers committed to the revolutionary nationalist project of the Mexican president Lázaro Cárdenas (1934–40). Under his presidency, the principle of non-intervention was an important part of Mexican policy, and Mexican foreign relations played a fundamental role in a broader project of nation building.[5]

This chapter explores the position taken by Mexico at the League on the legal treatment of the Spanish civil war. Mexican diplomats worked to articulate a legal interpretation of how the League should engage with the war in Spain in contrast to the British and French positions advocating non-intervention. Through the establishment of a scheme of inter-state commitments and institutions outside the League that included the creation of the London Non-Intervention Committee in 1936, the British and French initiative aimed to prevent any kind of sovereign engagement with the warring parties in the conflict.[6] On the other hand, Narciso Bassols and Isidro Fabela argued in Geneva that refusing assistance to the Spanish government would constitute a form of intervention in the conflict. Consequently, Mexican support to the Spanish Republic should not be considered intervention but a legal obligation under the League Covenant, and under international law more broadly.

This contribution aims to assess in detail the legal interpretation constructed by Mexican diplomats, especially Isidro Fabela, to accommodate Mexico's principled commitment to non-intervention and the political context related to the country's aid to the Spanish Republic, and

[3] Ibid., 271–94.

[4] Ibid., 190–1.

[5] Abdiel Oñate, 'Nonintervention through Intervention: Mexican diplomacy in the League of Nations during the Spanish Civil War' in Alan McPherson and Yannick Wehrli (eds), *Beyond Geopolitics: New Histories of Latin America at the League of Nations* (University of New Mexico Press, 2015) 63–82; Fabián Herrera León, *México en la Sociedad de Naciones, 1931–1940* (México DF Secretaría de Relaciones Exteriores, Dirección General del Acervo Histórico Diplomático, 2014) 89.

[6] Nathaniel Berman, 'Between Alliance and Localization: Nationalism and the New Oscillationism' (1993) 26 *New York University Journal of International Law and Politics* 449, 456.

the ways in which the ideals of the Mexican revolution were extrapolated to the international sphere. The League and the London Non-Intervention Committee acted as venues for these legal struggles over the meaning of intervention during the Spanish civil war. Here, Mexican diplomacy played an important role in contesting the British and French positions on non-intervention through the articulation of an alternative legal interpretation of the armed conflict in Spain.

The argument unfolds as follows. The first section of this chapter contextualises the Mexican position on non-intervention in light of the revolutionary nature of its government. The next section assesses the legal stakes of the Mexican position, and the role of Isidro Fabela in using international law to crystallise the claim that Italy and Germany were fighting an international war in Spain. The chapter then interrogates the Mexican engagement with international law in light of Cárdenas' broader project of nation building. Beyond naive cosmopolitanism, Mexico had strategic reasons to present its own legal views on non-intervention to the international community, and the League proved to be an important venue to this end.

Recalling the history of the Mexican position at the League with respect to the Spanish civil war is not a novelty in itself. Although scholars in the fields of history and international politics have already explored Mexico's stance, there has been less attention paid to the innovative contribution that Mexico made to the development of international law during this period.[7] This chapter considers the Mexican campaign at the League in light of the international law issues at stake in this context, through a deeper exploration of the ways in which non-intervention, neutrality law, and the League Covenant rules on collective security were interpreted. Previous studies in the fields of history and international politics have not fully grasped the complexity of the interplay between these concepts in Fabela's legal interpretation, sometimes

[7] See especially León and Andrés, n 1; León, n 5. See also Mario Ojeda Revah, *Mexico and the Spanish Civil War: Political Repercussions for the Republican Cause* (Sussex Academic Press, 2015); Manuel Ortuño Martínez (ed), *Diplomáticos de Cárdenas: Una trinchera mexicana en la Guerra Civil (1936–1940)* (Trama Editorial, 2007). An earlier publication is T G Powell, *Mexico and the Spanish Civil War* (University of New Mexico Press, 1981). The study by Powell has been criticised for its lack of comprehension of both the Spanish and Mexican contexts, and for his stereotypical descriptions of key Mexican figures. On these critiques, see Javier Malagón Barceló, '*Mexico and the Spanish Civil War*' (1982) 39 *The Americas* 145; Robert H Whealey, 'T G Powell, *Mexico and the Spanish Civil War*' (1982) 87 *American Historical Review* 293.

presenting a simplistic opposition between intervention and neutrality law.[8] A deeper exploration of the Mexican legal position shows us that it was possible to have it both ways: support one warring party in a civil war and simultaneously justify this position as a lawful action in accordance with the principle of non-intervention.

Accordingly, redescribing the history of the Mexican engagement with international law in the context of the Spanish civil war sheds light on the diverse legal interpretations that were available at that time to cope with the conflict in Spain.[9] Importantly, the dominance of the British and French positions on non-intervention, and the failure of the League's legal scheme of collective security, were not predetermined outcomes. Examining the novel articulations that all parties put forward shows us that the legal treatment of the conflict in Spain was the subject of substantive struggles over how to regulate armed conflicts, and illustrates the possibilities open to international law to assert its authority in the context of civil war.[10] Despite their opposite outcomes in terms of sovereign involvement in the Spanish civil war, the Mexican and the British and French rearticulations of neutrality law in light of the League Covenant rules on collective security can be seen as legal experiments in a broader context of a modernist remaking of international law.[11]

Exploring the Mexican position at the League in the context of the war in Spain helps us to understand the conditions that allowed the British and the French positions on non-intervention to become the authoritative legal view on the conflict. In other words, there were diverse legal interpretations available regarding how to frame and regulate the Spanish civil war. Non-intervention in a civil war, as sustained by the British and the French, was only one of several possible legal responses that were circulating at that time to address the conflict. Redescribing the Mexican legal campaign at the League enables a deeper understanding of the ways in which legal concepts, ideas, doctrines and practices crystallise a 'complex set of political choices'.[12] The exploration of the political choices and related legal interpretations that were left to one side in the context of the Spanish civil war, such as the Mexican position, is politically productive

[8] See, for example, Oñate, n 5, 64.

[9] On redescription as a strategy, see Anne Orford, 'In Praise of Description' (2012) 25 *Leiden Journal of International Law* 609.

[10] C G Fenwick, 'Can Civil Wars Be Brought under the Control of International Law?' (1938) 32 *American Journal of International Law* 538.

[11] Berman, n 6, 452–68.

[12] Anne Orford, 'Food Security, Free Trade, and the Battle for the State' (2015) 11(2) *Journal of International Law & International Relations* 1, 25.

as it brings to the surface the many legal interpretations and political possibilities that are still available to us in respect of intervention, civil war and international law today.[13]

This contribution intends to move beyond a 'common sense' that might see us automatically dismiss the Mexican legal position because of asymmetrical power relations in the League – more specifically because of the powerful positions of the United Kingdom and France on legally addressing the conflict. The reproduction of this pattern of causal explanation – that is, thinking through the legal treatment of the Spanish civil war as a direct function of the interests of powerful states – ends up being a missed opportunity to explore innovative and strategic engagements with international law.[14] Moreover, with the benefit of hindsight, although the Mexican position may not have been successful at the time of the conflict in Spain, the Mexican defence of the de jure government would later became an important argument in the legal discussions on intervention and civil wars.[15]

10.2 Non-intervention and Revolution: The 'Mexican Question' at the League of Nations

Mexico became a member of the League in September 1931, after around a decade of isolation from the international organisation based in Geneva.[16] The invitation to join the League came in a resolution proposed by Spain, Germany, the United Kingdom, France, Italy and Japan, and was unanimously adopted by the Assembly in early September 1931. The invitation included an apology for the omission of Mexico from the annex of the League Covenant that listed all countries invited to join the international organisation, as though Mexico had been invited when the League was originally established.[17]

[13] Orford, 'In Praise of Description', n 9, 621.

[14] Ibid., 622–3.

[15] 'It could be said that the Mexican point of view was a harbinger of a new, substantive approach towards the law of internal armed conflicts and the law of consensual intervention in particular': Eliav Lieblich, *International Law and Civil Wars: Intervention and Consent* (Routledge, 2013) 116. I would like to thank Marnie Lloydd for the exchanges on this argument.

[16] See Chapter 4 in this volume, which also explores the issue of the late participation of Mexico in the League of Nations. The present contribution deals with this issue with special attention to the Mexican context.

[17] *League of Nations Official Journal*, Special Supplement no 93 (1931), cited in Manuel Tello, 'Algunos aspectos de la participación de México en la Sociedad de las Naciones' (1965) 6 *Foro Internacional* 358, 359. At the time Isidro Fabela was a permanent delegate

This section contextualises the Mexican effort to reconcile the provision of support to the Spanish Republic with the strong Mexican commitment to the principle of non-intervention in view of the revolutionary nature of its government. The particularities of the Mexican post-revolutionary position regarding property and the limitations imposed on foreigners owning land in the country, as well as the express rejection of the Monroe Doctrine and the resulting Mexican challenges to intervention in Latin America, became issues in Mexico's relationship with the League. When Mexico eventually became a member of the League in the 1930s, its views on non-intervention were extrapolated to the international sphere, contesting acts of aggression, which included its fierce criticism of the British and French stance on non-intervention in the Spanish civil war.

In other words, the way in which Mexico legally justified its provision of support to the Spanish Republic in accordance with the principle of non-intervention has to be understood in light of the policies adopted for the new revolutionary state in Mexico in relation to property and the Mexican stance against intervention in Latin America. The history of the 'Mexican question' at the League of Nations, as redescribed in this section, helps us to understand the ways in which the immediate post-revolutionary context created the conditions for Mexico to work out a way to maintain its commitment to the principle of non-intervention and, at the same time, justify providing support to Spain.

During the negotiations of the Treaty of Versailles in 1919, Venustiano Carranza was the president of Mexico (1917–20). After three years of civil war, which included different revolutionary factions fighting against each other,[18] Carranza's constitutionalist party triumphed.[19] On

to the League, Manuel Tello was the secretary of the Mexican delegation in Geneva. Manuel Tello was also Secretary of Foreign Affairs in Mexico both in the late 1940s and in the late 1950s. See Manuel Tello, 'Isidro Fabela en la Sociedad de las Naciones' in Comite de Amigos de Isidro Fabela (ed), *Homenaje a Isidro Fabela* (Universidad Nacional Autónoma de México, 1959) vol 2, 673.

18 On the violent years of the Mexican revolution, see Berta Ulloa, *La revolución escindida: Historia de la revolución mexicana* (El Colegio de México, 1979) pt 2, vol 4. On the popular movements that emerged during the Mexican revolution under the leadership of Emiliano Zapata and Francisco (Pancho) Villa, see Adolfo Gilly, *The Mexican Revolution* (The New Press, revised ed., 2005).

19 'Nearly a year of regular warfare among the revolutionaries had ended in Carrancista victory. And on 9 October [1915] the Pan-Americans concluded that "the Carranza party is the only party possessing the essentials for recognition as the de facto government of Mexico" . . . reducing the Villistas and Zapatistas to mere rebels': John Womack Jr, 'The

19 October 1915, Carranza's government was recognised as the de facto government of Mexico by the United States, which was then followed by Latin American countries, Great Britain, France, Italy, Russia, Japan and Germany, among others.[20] It is beyond the scope of this chapter to explore the complexities of the Mexican revolution. Nevertheless, Carranza's efforts to construct a new state in Mexico, which included the promulgation of the revolutionary constitution in February 1917 (1917 Constitution), and his (army-supervised) election as the first president of the new Mexican state in March 1917, help to understand the troubled relationship between Mexico and the League during the 1920s.

Carranza's policies for the new revolutionary state in Mexico were mixed with conservative aspects. They included the rejection of the Monroe Doctrine, higher taxes on foreign companies and the creation of a Mexican central bank. However, they also included the return of confiscated property to old property owners, the mediation of conflicts between workers and companies and the elimination of insubordinate workers and peasants.[21] Carranza's nationalism did not encompass land reform, as other revolutionary factions did, nor did it include expropriation of foreign-owned land – something that would be accomplished later, under the presidency of Lázaro Cárdenas.

Nevertheless, the 1917 Constitution expressly restricted the right of foreigners to own land in the country. Article 27 determined that expropriations were authorised in the interests of public utility and by means of indemnification. Accordingly, the state had the right to impose public-interest constraints on private property, and the exploitation of natural resources was to be regulated by the state based on social benefits and the equal distribution of wealth. Moreover, the 1917 Constitution determined that all subsoil mineral resources were the property of the nation. Their private exploitation could only be carried out through concessions to Mexicans by birth or naturalisation, or to Mexican companies.[22] The new constitutional provision on property paved the way for the transformation of the idea of individual property rights, which from that

Mexican Revolution, 1910–1920' in Leslie Bethell (ed), *The Cambridge History of Latin America* (Cambridge University Press, 1986) vol 5, 79, 119.

20 George A Finch, 'The Recognition of the De Facto Government in Mexico' (1916) 10 *American Journal of International Law* 357, 366.

21 Womack, n 19, 119.

22 *Mexican Constitution of 1917.*

moment on were subjected to 'social distribution and sustainable use of land'.[23] Importantly, the protection of property rights of foreign nationals was excluded from the new Mexican constitutional order.

Even taking account of the above-mentioned limits of Carranza's nationalism, his presidency under the 1917 Constitution raised concerns for the United States and European powers. Foreign capital had maintained a strong presence in Mexico since the government of Porfirio Díaz (1876–1911), and this was one of the main causes of general discontent in pre-revolutionary Mexico.[24] The new constitutional restrictions on foreign property were not well received among those with strong foreign influence in Mexico: the Americans, the British, the Germans and the French.[25]

Notwithstanding the possibility that Mexico would have rejected the invitation to join the League because of the formal recognition of the Monroe Doctrine in the League Covenant,[26] scholars have presented the view that Mexico 'had been excluded from the list of original Members by agreement between the British and American delegations in Paris'.[27] Beyond the general claim that the unstable internal conditions of revolutionary Mexico prevented its admission to the League,[28] the specific

[23] Judith Schacherreiter and Guilherme Leite Gonçalves, 'The Zapatista Struggle for the Right to Land: Background, Context and Strategies' in Andreas Fischer-Lescano and Kolja Möeller (eds), *Transnationalisation of Social Rights* (Intersentia, 2016) 265, 279.

[24] 'First, Americans as well as other foreign investors and promoters were granted concessions of every kind on extremely generous terms. Secondly, the Mexican government [of Porfirio Díaz] also attempted to do everything in its power to renew and then to strengthen its links to Europe to balance American influence. Thirdly, political stability was to be maintained at any price. Until about 1900–1910 they laid the basis for one of the most profound social upheavals to take place in twentieth-century Latin America: the Mexican revolution': Friedrich Katz 'Mexico: Restored Republic and Porfiriato, 1867–1910' in Leslie Bethell (ed), *The Cambridge History of Latin America*, (Cambridge University Press, 1986) vol 5, no 1, 23–4.

[25] 'Efforts of the *Científicos* [Mexico's ruling elite during Díaz government] to create a European counterweight to US influence had centered on three countries: Great Britain, France, and Germany. On the eve of the revolution, Great Britain was by far the dominant European power in Mexico, the only that constituted a serious challenge to US economic domination. Germany's economic and political influence in Mexico was far more limited': Friedrich Katz, *The Secret War in Mexico: Europe, the United States, and the Mexican Revolution* (University of Chicago Press, 1981) 50.

[26] Womack, n 19, 141.

[27] F P Walters, *A History of the League of Nations* (Oxford University Press, 1952) vol 1, 462; León, n 5, 92.

[28] Tello, 'Algunos aspectos de la participación de México en la Sociedad de las Naciones', n 17, 358; Manley O Hudson, 'Membership in the League of Nations' (1924) 18 *American*

issues of constitutional constraints on foreign property and higher taxes on foreign investment were also important elements in the agreement between the United Kingdom and the United States to exclude Mexico from participation in the League as an original member.[29]

Scholars narrate different reactions from the United States and the United Kingdom with regard to the new Mexican revolutionary policies towards foreign capital and property. The United States objected to the new constitutional provisions on property delaying de jure recognition to Carranza's government, which was eventually granted in September 1917.[30] Moreover, in light of the closer Mexican–German relations in the context of World War I (especially after 1915),[31] despite Mexico's neutrality in the conflict,[32] the United States asked itself how to 'safeguard American-owned property in Mexico without driving Venustiano Carranza into German arms'.[33] After the United States entered World War I in April 1917, the Mexican issue was left to be solved after the end of the war.[34] The American efforts against Article 27 did not result in its modification, nor in effective Mexican guarantees regarding the non-retroactivity of the revolutionary constitutional provisions on property, and the legal status of American property in Mexico remained uncertain at the end of World War I.[35]

The British position differed from that of the United States, with stronger political and military resistance to Carranza's government, including plans for a coup in Mexico at the beginning of his rule, and later an offensive orientation to further destabilise Mexico's internal struggles that would result in the overthrow of Carranza's government. Importantly, there were divergent orientations among the British. After the failed attempt at a coup, private actors started to defend the establishment of a better relationship with Carranza, in order to secure their acquired positions in Mexico.[36] Historically, the United Kingdom had maintained

Journal of International Law 436, 449; Luis Sánchez Pontón, 'México y la Sociedad de las Naciones' (1931) 4 *Revista de la Universidad de México* 284, 287.

29 León, n 5, 92.

30 Mark T Gilderhus, 'The United States and Carranza, 1917: The Question of De Jure Recognition' (1972) 29 *The Americas* 214.

31 Katz, *The Secret War in Mexico*, n 25, 345.

32 Ibid., 387.

33 Gilderhus, n 30, 214.

34 Katz, *The Secret War in Mexico*, n 25, 493.

35 Gilderhus, n 30, 231.

36 Katz, *The Secret War in Mexico*, n 25, 460. There were divergent positions on Mexico among the Americans too, but with reversed roles. 'Whereas American companies aimed

close relations with Mexican counterrevolutionary forces, giving its support to the previous government of Victoriano Huerta (1913–14).[37]

With the end of World War I, the United States became 'the most important investor and trading partner of most Latin American countries'.[38] At the beginning of 1919, in view of the resilient campaigns for the protection of foreign interests and rights in Mexico, American and European bankers suggested an agreement to Carranza. This agreement 'would in effect have neutralized the 1917 Constitution, allowed US interests unrestricted access to Mexico's natural resources, settled the Mexican debt on conditions favourable to foreign interests, and restricted Mexico's sovereignty'.[39] Carranza rejected the agreement, and demands for military intervention in favour of foreign interests in Mexico grew in the United States. In this context, a delegation of the Association of Foreign Oil Producers in Mexico, an organisation based in the United States directed 'to coordinate the resistance of all foreign companies toward the Mexicans',[40] was sent to the peace negotiations in Paris.[41] Even considering the statement by the US Secretary of State Robert Lansing that 'the peace conference did not deal with this question at all',[42] the Mexican admission would involve the acceptance, by the international community, of the Mexican revolutionary policies toward foreign investment and property, policies strongly opposed to the American and British interests in the country.

Carranza's reaction to the exclusion of Mexico came in the form of a strong critique of the Monroe Doctrine, which was formally recognised by Article 21 of the League Covenant.[43] According to Carranza, Mexico would not recognise the Monroe Doctrine, as it:

at the violent overthrow of the government, the Wilson administration was resigned to the fact that Carranza would remain in power until the end of the war': at 493.

37 Ibid., 156–83.

38 Ibid., 527.

39 Ibid., 529.

40 Jonathan C Brown, *Oil and Revolution in Mexico* (University of California Press, 1993) 239.

41 Katz, *The Secret War in Mexico*, n 25, 529; Brown, n 40, 242.

42 As cited in Katz, *The Secret War in Mexico*, n 25, 530. In a similar vein, Manley O Hudson, when commenting on the Mexican status as a non-member state at the League, mentioned that 'Secretary Lansing stated to the Senate Committee on Foreign Relations, on August 6, 1919, that the United States was not responsible for Mexico's not having been invited': Hudson, n 28, 449, n 91.

43 'Nothing in this Covenant shall be deemed to affect the validity of international engagements, such as treaties of arbitration or regional understandings like the Monroe doctrine, for securing the maintenance of peace': Treaty of Peace between the Allied and

> constitutes an arbitrary protectorate, imposed on peoples who have not requested it and do not need it. The Monroe Doctrine is not reciprocal and is therefore unjust. If it were thought necessary to apply it to the Spanish-American republics, it could equally be applied to the whole world. It is a kind of tutelage over Spanish America that should not exist for any reason.[44]

Carranza affirmed that Mexico 'will not entertain any action to enter that International Society [the League of Nations], since the bases that support it do not establish in its operation a perfect equality for all nations and all races'.[45]

According to Isidro Fabela, Carranza's rejection of the Monroe Doctrine had precedents in Mexican foreign policy. Fabela mentioned the presidential message by Porfirio Díaz to the Mexican congress in April 1896 on the boundary dispute between Venezuela and the United Kingdom and the April 1896 note by Ignacio Mariscal, Mexican Secretary of Foreign Affairs, on an invitation to participate in a conference about the Monroe Doctrine. On both occasions, it was stated that any attack, by any alien power, aimed at undermining the territory or the independence of the American republics, or aimed at changing their domestic institutions, should be regarded as an offence by the attacked nation, without the need for the Monroe Doctrine to protect the American republics.[46]

Since Carranza's government, Mexican foreign policy had expressly rejected the Monroe Doctrine. On the occasion of the invitation to join the League in September 1931, Mexican Secretary of Foreign Affairs Genaro Estrada sent a note to the president of the Assembly. It stated that 'Mexico considers it necessary to make it clear that in its acceptance [to join the League], it has never admitted the regional rationale mentioned in Article 21 of the Covenant'.[47] With the 'Mexican question' eventually overcome through an express apology and an offer of membership in 1931,[48] Mexico started a new stage in its foreign policy.

Associated Powers and Germany, signed 28 June 1919, 225 ConTS 188 (entered into force 10 January 1920) pt 1, Covenant of the League of Nations, Article 21.

44 As cited in Isidro Fabela, *Las doctrinas Monroe y Drago* (Universidad Nacional Autónoma de México, 1957) 189.

45 Ibid., 190.

46 Ibid., 186–8.

47 Ibid., 191.

48 For the view that the apology was a Mexican condition for accepting the invitation, see ibid., 118.

10.3 Between Non-intervention and Support to the De Jure Government: Isidro Fabela and the Mexican Campaign at the League

Isidro Fabela (1882–1964) had an active role in the Mexican revolution as a member of the constitutionalist party. Fabela is also recognised as one of the most important Mexican jurists of the twentieth century. He was Carranza's advisor on foreign policy (1913–15), and Mexican diplomatic representative in many countries in Europe and Latin America (1915–20). He was subsequently appointed as the Mexican commissioner at the Italian-Mexican Claims Commission (1929–33), and as the permanent Mexican delegate at the League and at the International Labour Organization (1937–40). He was also a judge at the International Court of Justice (1946–52).[49] As a scholar, Fabela published on the Mexican revolution,[50] on diplomatic history[51] and quite extensively on international law topics such as intervention, neutrality law and the Monroe and Drago Doctrines. His decisions as the Mexican commissioner at the Italian-Mexican Claims Commission were published in 1946,[52] among other publications.[53]

This section analyses his scholarly production in international law, and the ways in which Fabela theorised his own experience as the Mexican delegate at the League. Apart from Fabela's 1937 speeches at the League Assembly and at the Assembly's Sixth Committee (Political Questions), I will explore Mexico's legal treatment of the Spanish civil war, considering Fabela's own systematisation of the topic, especially the ideas presented in his book on neutrality law.[54]

[49] 'Síntesis Biográfica del Doctor Don Isidro Fabela' in Comite de Amigos de Isidro Fabela (ed), *Homenaje a Isidro Fabela* (Universidad Nacional Autónoma de México, 1959) vol 1, 703.

[50] Isidro Fabela, *Documentos Históricos de la Revolución Mexicana* (Fondo de Cultura Económica, 1960–4); Isidro Fabela, *História diplomática de la Revolución Mexicana (1912-1917)* (Fondo de Cultura Económica, 1958–9). These publications reflect Fabela's views on the revolution from the perspective of a constitutionalist.

[51] Isidro Fabela, *Los Estados Unidos contra la libertad: Estudios de historia diplomática Americana* (Talleres Gráficos Lux, 1918); Isidro Fabela, *Los precursores de la diplomacia mexicana* (Secretaría de Relaciones Exteriores, 1929).

[52] Isidro Fabela, *Votos Internacionales* (Editorial Orión, 1946).

[53] For a complete list of his publications, see www.isidrofabela.org.mx.

[54] To this end, I will consider the 1940 Spanish edition, and not the 1949 French edition, as only the former included a chapter focused on Mexico and the League. Isidro Fabela, *Neutralidad: estudio histórico, jurídico y político; la Sociedad de las naciones y el continente americano ante la guerra de 1939–1940* (Biblioteca de Estudios Internacionales, 1940); Isidro Fabela, *Neutralité* (Pedone, 1949).

As will be explained in more detail in the next section of this chapter, the Mexican role at the League in the 1930s helped to strengthen an autonomous Mexican position in the international sphere, transforming the negative image of a chaotic revolutionary country in international isolation. Having been able to keep control of internal struggles during the 1920s,[55] Mexico took advantage of its participation in the League to convey the image of a stable country in full economic development – features of a successful revolutionary process. Mexico had already developed the legal principles of foreign policy employed at the League, such as the so-called Carranza and Estrada doctrines – the former asserting the principle of non-intervention in the domestic affairs of a country, and the latter opposing conditional recognition of governments. In the 1930s, Mexico enjoyed the material conditions to be able to defend, in Geneva, the peaceful settlement of international disputes, the principle of non-intervention and the right to self-determination, adding to this 'Mexican doctrine of international law' the collective security scheme of the League Covenant.[56] In this setting, Mexican foreign policy strongly opposed acts of aggression by powerful states, not just in the context of the Spanish civil war, but also in all conflicts that were brought to deliberation in Geneva – such as the Japanese invasion of Manchuria in 1931, the Italian-Ethiopian war, the German annexation of Austria and the Soviet invasion of Finland, among others.[57]

Fabela's legal treatment of neutrality was consonant with broader interrogations of the relevance of neutrality law in the context of the emergence of international schemes of collective security in the first

[55] 'After a decade of civil war (1910–20) there emerged in Mexico, between 1920 and 1930, a new capitalist state. In this respect, conflict with foreign oil companies and the church, as well as negotiations with organized labour, in particular the CROM (Confederation Regional Obrera Mexicana/Regional Confederation of Mexican Labour), were more significant than the traditional military insurrections of 1923, 1927 and 1929 or the election crises of 1928–9. Innovation was more economic than political, and it was in particular institutional and administrative. It is impossible to separate the main political innovation, the creation of the National Revolutionary Party (PNR) in 1929, from the formation of a powerful state': Jean Meyer, 'Mexico: Revolution and Reconstruction in the 1920s' in Leslie Bethell (ed), *The Cambridge History of Latin America* (Cambridge University Press, 1986) vol 5, 155, 156. The PNR is the precursor of the Institutional Revolutionary Party (PRI), which ruled the country throughout the twentieth century.

[56] León and Andrés, n 1, 74–7.

[57] Ibid., 78. See also ibid., 87–133. For Fabela's explanations of the Mexican legal position on the many cases of aggression discussed at the League, see Fabela, *Neutralidad*, n 54, 255–76.

decades of the twentieth century.[58] For example, when debating the establishment of neutral groups in the context of the League, he asserted that

> the spirit of impartiality cannot, should not exist within the Member States of the League of Nations when one country attacks another. There is no path left for the member of the League other than to join the aggrieved, lending the aggrieved its help, if not military, at least moral and economic, never within an impartial spirit, but within an absolutely partial spirit. The opposite is to depart from the basic ideas and directives of the Covenant.[59]

Fabela asserted the total incompatibility between the Covenant and neutral groups formed among the League member states. For example, when assessing the legal measures the League should have adopted in light of the creation of the Oslo Group in 1930,[60] and its later declaration of neutral tendencies in 1937, Fabela stated that the League should have highlighted the obligations of the members of the Oslo Group under the Covenant. If they insisted on neutrality, Fabela supported their withdrawal from the League. Nevertheless, he conceded that in view of the many cases in which the Covenant had been violated, such as the Japanese invasion of Manchuria and the Italian-Ethiopian war, it would not have been possible for the League to rigorously apply the Covenant provisions to the Oslo Group.[61]

Fabela added a vision of an interconnected world to the League's scheme of collective security. When he discussed US policy towards neutrality, he asserted that an 'absolute neutrality, the perfect, the classic, cannot be practised by the great powers in modern times'.[62] In a modern world, in which the 'economic and technical progress of industry and modern communications have been perfected so much that they have established more or less narrow links between all countries ... none can live isolated from others'.[63] In this setting, not just the United States but

[58] Marnie Lloydd, 'Retrieving Neutrality Law to Consider "Other" Foreign Fighters Under International Law' (2017) (Paper presented at the European Society of International Law (ESIL) 2017 Research Forum, Granada, 29 September 2017) 2, https://ssrn.com/abstract=3045274.

[59] Fabela, *Neutralidad*, n 54, 68–9.

[60] In December 1930, Sweden, Norway, Denmark, Belgium, Luxemburg and the Netherlands signed the Convention of Economic Rapprochement, aiming to establish closer commercial cooperation in accordance with the principles of the League. This initiative became known as the Oslo Group. Finland joined it in 1933: ibid., 69–70.

[61] Ibid., 67–70.

[62] Ibid., 242.

[63] Ibid.

all countries in the world would suffer the consequences of a conflict like World War II, and strict neutrality would be untenable in such a context.[64]

These comments on a modern conception of neutrality, which relate to the League's scheme of collective security and to a vision of the world as interdependent, are important to understand Fabela's main legal thesis on how to regulate acts of aggression under the legal framework of the interwar period. To Fabela, 'the League Covenant substantively modifies the concept of neutrality'.[65] When an armed conflict breaks out between one or more members of the League and another member state (or a non-member state), all League members must break their commercial relations with the aggressor – although importantly, the League Covenant did not establish a declaration of war as mandatory.[66] League members should also apply the Council's recommendations towards the aggressor. Following the Covenant's provisions, in such conflicts, a member state could be either a non-belligerent or a pre-belligerent, but not a neutral state.[67]

For those member states declaring war against the aggressor, the rules of belligerency applied. A status of pre-belligerency would apply for those member states that did not declare war but broke their commercial and diplomatic relations with the aggressor. Finally, a non-belligerent status would apply to the League member that, while not declaring war, broke commercial but not diplomatic relations with the aggressor, strictly following the provisions of Article 16 of the League Covenant.[68]

Rather than trying to assert the correctness of Fabela's new categories of partial neutrality, the important legal issue here is the way in which he

[64] 'The interdependence of modern states has reached such a point that no one can be enclosed within its borders, subject to an autarchic, selfish and passive domestic policy. The life of each country depends to a greater or lesser degree on international life, so when a war breaks out, neutrality does not have, cannot have the same characteristics of yesteryear': ibid.

[65] Ibid., 250.

[66] Ibid., 248.

[67] Ibid, 253.

[68] 'Should any Member of the League resort to war in disregard of its covenants under Articles 12, 13 or 15, it shall ipso facto be deemed to have committed an act of war against all other Members of the League, which hereby undertake immediately to subject it to the severance of all trade or financial relations, the prohibition of all intercourse between their nationals and the nationals of the covenant-breaking State, and the prevention of all financial, commercial or personal intercourse between the nationals of the covenant-breaking State and the nationals of any other State, whether a Member of the League or not': *Covenant of the League of Nations*, Article 16.

connects non-intervention to this new perspective on neutrality under the legal framework of the League Covenant. Accordingly, Fabela sees non-intervention as one of the legal consequences of neutrality, and not the other way around.[69] In other words, non-intervention should be understood as connected to neutrality law in cases of armed conflict involving one or more members of the League. Non-intervention could not be used as a legal proxy to assure a neutral status precisely because total neutrality was not available to the League members under the Covenant. As he asserted, 'the alleged non-intervention that is said to apply in Spain would be admissible only if neutrality could be decreed previously, but it is the case that the members of the League should not be neutral to the aggression of which Spain is victim'.[70] Importantly, Fabela's rearticulation of neutrality law was not the only new legal interpretation proposed at the League in the context of the war in Spain. The United Kingdom and France proposed their own alternative view of neutrality law.

In August 1936, a non-intervention scheme was set up outside the League based on an exchange of notes between the United Kingdom and France. These notes established a common approach to the conflict in Spain through three policy declarations.[71] Accordingly, it was declared that the governments 'had decided to abstain rigorously from all interference [*de toute ingérence*], direct or indirect, in the internal affairs of Spain, on the basis of the desire to avoid complications prejudicial to the good relations between their "Peoples"'.[72] The three policy declarations related to: (1) the prohibition of direct or indirect exportation of arms, munitions and all war materials from the governments' territories to Spain; (2) the application of such prohibition to contracts being executed at that moment; and (3) the intention of the United Kingdom and France to inform other governments participating in the scheme of the measures undertaken to implement the referred prohibitions. Importantly, 'the declaration was made contingent upon the adherence of the other government, plus the governments of Germany, Italy, the Soviet Union, and Portugal'.[73]

[69] Jorge Castañeda, 'La aportación de Isidro Fabela a la seguridad colectiva internacional', in Comite de Amigos de Isidro Fabela (ed), *Homenaje a Isidro Fabela* (Universidad Nacional Autónoma de México, 1959) vol 2, 141, 146–7.

[70] Fabela, *Neutralidad*, n 54, 263–4.

[71] N J Padelford, 'The International Non-Intervention Agreement and the Spanish Civil War' (1937) 31 *American Journal of International Law* 578, 579–80.

[72] Ibid., 580.

[73] Ibid.

The non-intervention scheme was not based on an international agreement or treaty; it was a concert of policy settled among the participant states.[74] Nevertheless, a Non-Intervention Committee was created in London to assess complaints of violations of the non-intervention policy received from the participating governments. In September 1936, a subcommittee was created 'to aid the president in facilitating procedure and to consider and make recommendations to the full committee'.[75] By November 1936, the functions of the Non-Intervention Committee had already 'turned away from violations to the consideration of new schemes for observing and watching events at close range so that the Committee might have first-hand information at its disposal'.[76]

It is beyond the scope of this contribution to assess in detail the work of the Non-Intervention Committee. I focus on the Mexican legal position at the League, a much less studied issue in international legal scholarship. In general terms, it became clear that the non-intervention scheme set up outside the League was not succeeding in stopping the influx of fighters and war materials to Spain. Some international lawyers did concede that despite these problems, the scheme had successfully averted the conflict spreading beyond Spain,[77] even taking account of the Italian and German violations of the non-intervention policy.[78]

The Mexican way of dealing with non-intervention as subsumed to a broader status of neutrality makes a substantive difference in Fabela's legal interpretation of the Spanish civil war. Importantly, the British and French stance on non-intervention had a similar legal basis. Accordingly, at stake here are alternative reconstructions of neutrality law. On the one hand, there is the British and French stance on a new form of neutrality that leads to non-intervention. On the other hand, there is the Mexican stance and its own views on neutrality law, which justifies the support to the Spanish Republic.[79] As explained above, for Fabela, under the League

[74] Ibid.

[75] Ibid., 586.

[76] Ibid., 588.

[77] See, for example, Erik J S Castrén, *Civil War* (Suomalainen Tiedeakatemia, 1966) 65; Padelford, 'The International Non-Intervention Agreement and the Spanish Civil War', n 71, 578.

[78] Castrén, n 77, 64.

[79] To illustrate, Norman J Padelford developed a similar argument when he debated the legal consequences of the Italian and German recognition of the Franco regime as the lawful Spanish government. He too could not envisage intervention as a legal principle existent in a vacuum or disconnected from neutrality law, despite his support for the non-intervention stance. 'Even if it be argued that the Fascist states committed an act of

Covenant, member states cannot maintain an absolute neutral status in light of an act of aggression against one or more members of the League. Fabela legally justified his position using Article 10 of the League Covenant,[80] which establishes that:

> The Members of the League undertake to respect and preserve as against external aggression the territorial integrity and existing political independence of all Members of the League. In case of any such aggression or in case of any threat or danger of such aggression the Council shall advise upon the means by which this obligation shall be fulfilled.[81]

Fabela also relied on Article 11 of the League Covenant, and the notion of an armed conflict that matters to the League as a whole: 'Any war or threat of war, whether immediately affecting any of the Members of the League or not, is hereby declared a matter of concern to the whole League, and the League shall take any action that may be deemed wise and effectual to safeguard the peace of nations'.[82]

In an international press declaration given in April 1937, Fabela made it clear that the rules of neutrality and their derivatives, such as non-intervention, could perhaps be invoked as the international law foundation for denying help to the Spanish government by those few states that did not belong to the League. However, the League members could not rely on it, as Spain had the legal right to receive support through its government, the only representative of the Spanish state legally recognised by the League.[83]

This press declaration revealed the additional legal basis articulated by Fabela to justify the Mexican material support to the Spanish Republic during the Spanish civil war.[84] In other words, Fabela's efforts were to accommodate both the Mexican support to the Spanish Republic and the strong Mexican commitment to the principle of non-intervention. Fabela argued that the Convention on Duties and Rights of States in the Event of

intervention by their recognition and by their subsequent movements after November 19 [1936], *intervention does not in itself operate in such a manner as automatically to extend belligerent rights to the conflicting factions*': N J Padelford, 'International Law and the Spanish Civil War' (1937) 31 *The American Journal of International Law* 226, 236 (emphasis added). On the British and French stance as encompassing a new form of neutrality, see Berman, n 6, 462–4.

80 Fabela, *Neutralidad*, n 54, 263.

81 *Covenant of the League of Nations*, Article 10.

82 Ibid., Article 11.

83 Fabela, *Neutralidad*, n 54, 264.

84 León and Andrés, n 1, 288.

Civil Strife (1928 Convention), adopted during the Sixth International Conference of American States held in Havana in 1928, provided clear legal guidance on how states should proceed in the context of civil wars. Accordingly, Article 1(3) forbade 'the traffic in arms and war material, except when intended for the Government, while the belligerency of the rebels has not been recognized, in which latter case the rules of neutrality shall be applied'.[85] As Mexico had not recognised the belligerency of the rebels in the context of the Spanish civil war, Fabela asserted that Mexican material support to the Spanish Republic was legally justified under international law, as the Spanish Republic constituted the de jure government of Spain, with no violation of the principle of non-intervention.[86]

Fabela was aware that using a Pan-American convention in the context of the legal debates over the war in Spain could open space for critique of the Mexican position at the League, especially because Spain was not a member of the 1928 Convention. Nevertheless, Fabela defended the use of this document as a legal justification before the Mexican Secretariat of Foreign Affairs. To Fabela, the use of the 1928 Convention would show the international community the consistency of the Mexican foreign policy.[87] As pointed out by Mexican historians, another issue with the use of the 1928 Convention as a legal justification by Mexico was its focus on civil war, as the Mexican position so far had insisted on the international character of the war fought in Spain, in view of the Italian and German aggressions. These questions did not prevent the broad circulation of the Mexican press declaration, which had far more impact than the Mexican note sent to the Secretary-General of the League of Nations in March 1937.[88]

[85] *Convention on Duties and Rights of States in the Event of Civil Strife*, opened for signature 20 February 1928, 134 LNTS 45 (entered into force 21 May 1929).

[86] Fabela, *Neutralidad*, n 54, 264.

[87] León and Andrés, n 1, 286–7. See also Martínez, n 7, 32.

[88] León and Andrés, n 1, 288–9. To illustrate, the *Journal des Nations*, a League of Nations' newspaper with weekly circulation in Geneva, published the following on 20 April 1937: 'Tout ce qu'il fallait dire en tant que membre fidèle de la Société à l'égard de l'aspect international et des problèmes de droit que soulève la guerre d'Espagne est désormais énoncé par le Mexique. Ce dernier serait-il vraiment en train de devenir l'unique Etat-Membre respectueux des dispositions du Pacte et des stipulations de conventions signées? Le désarroi, au milieu duquel se développe cette véritable crise du droit international que nous vivons depuis quelques années, est tel que l'on serait tenté d'établir l'axiome: le Mexique unique Etat-Membre fidèle au Pacte et respectueux de la chose signée'. Cited by Fabela in his letter to president Cárdenas dated 17 May 1937: Martínez, n 7, 32.

In a nutshell, the Mexican position was based on the view that the war in Spain was not just a civil war but also an international war, with acts of aggression from both Germany and Italy.[89] The majority of the member states of the League did not share this view, seeing the war in Spain as a civil war, and therefore, a domestic issue in which they and the League should not intervene. Mexico sustained its position throughout the conflict in Spain in almost total isolation from the other League members.[90]

The Mexican position on the war in Spain proposed an alternative view to address the conflict. During the eighteenth ordinary session of the Assembly of the League, held in September 1937, Fabela defended the need to cope with the war in Spain under the framework of the League Covenant, strongly criticising the outsourcing of the conflict to the Committee of Non-Intervention.[91] Accordingly, Fabela argued that excluding fundamental problems of peace from the League's jurisdiction was a dangerous move. Importantly, he expressly stated that supporting the Spanish Republic was not merely a moral duty owed to a friendly government but a legal duty under the principle of non-intervention, as the principle 'allows the provision of material support to the legally constituted government, while forbidding such support to the rebels'.[92] Fabela denounced the lack of involvement of the League in the conflict as a de facto intervention, which would be contrary to the Mexican policy of non-intervention.

During the same session but before the Sixth Committee of the Assembly, which focused on political questions, Fabela added that an

[89] 'In the case of Spain, the majority of nations did not fulfil its duties either. The League never recognized the undeniable truth of the external aggression suffered by Spain by Germany and Italy. It always considered that the conflict in the Peninsula was a civil war, and not both, civil and international, as it really was. The Assembly and the Council, instead of recognizing that Spain had been the victim of an external aggression – for whose recognition it had an abundance of confessional, documentary, testimonial and public evidence – allowed the creation, outside the League, of the absurd "Committee of Non-Intervention", which contrary to the two Spanish parties in conflict, practically favored the rebels with irreparable damage to the constitutional party represented before the League by the Spanish State': Fabela, *Neutralidad*, n 54, 254–5.

[90] For a contrasting Latin American role at the League, see the analysis on the Chilean position on the war in Spain in David Jorge Penado, 'México y Chile ante la guerra civil española: dos polos opuestos de actuación latinoamericana en la Sociedad de Naciones' in *Congreso Internacional America Latina: La autonomía de una región* (Trama editorial/ CEEIB, 2013) 1449.

[91] Fabela, *Neutralidad*, n 54, 265–6.

[92] Cited in León and Andrés, n 1, 370–1.

external aggression was fully proven before the League as there was in Spain 'a foreign army fully staffed with senior officers of the same nationality'.[93] He discussed the reach of Article 10 of the Covenant, asserting that 'a country's territorial integrity is violated not only when the aggression is conducted with a view to conquest, but also when it violates national sovereignty, and as stated in the same article, "the political independence of States"'.[94] Fabela expressly criticised the setting-up of the Non-Intervention Committee as a scheme that, despite its good intentions, was not in accordance with neutrality law. To Fabela, even if one could admit that neutrality rules apply in cases of unjustifiable rebellion, these rules cannot 'be applied when a Member of the League of Nations is the victim of external aggression, as Spain was when the Non-Intervention Committee was established'.[95]

The vehement position of Mexico at the League illustrates the diverse possibilities of engagement with the vocabulary of international law that are open to skilled lawyers, even when facing powerful international actors. The Mexican engagement with international law was articulated using a familiar legal technique: the redescription of the situation at stake using different legal conceptualisations – in the case of Fabela's legal interpretation, subsuming non-intervention to neutrality law under the legal framework of the Covenant to justify a substantive engagement with a warring party in a civil war. It is worth noting that, beyond the League, international law scholars commenting on the war in Spain at that time did echo the Mexican position at the League.[96] In other words, the Mexican legal position on the Spanish civil war was not an isolated or an odd interpretation of international law. Nevertheless, the Mexican

[93] 'Records of the Eighteenth Ordinary Session of the Assembly: Meeting of the Committees' *League of Nations Official Journal,* Special Supplement no 175 (1937) 61–2.

[94] Ibid.

[95] Ibid.

[96] To illustrate: 'The practical failure of collective non-intervention is paralleled by its inherently immoral evasion of community responsibility': Fenwick, n 10, 540; 'If international law is to continue to predicate its existence and strength upon an orderly system of sovereign states, each independent of the other and sovereign over its internal affairs, distinction must be preserved between the rights and duties of foreign states in times of civil and of international war. Neutrality and non-intervention in time of unrecognized insurgency and in time of international warfare involve very different propositions. To apply to unrecognized and irresponsible rebels the same principles that are applicable to sovereign states and established governments is to encourage rebellion and disorder and to weaken public law and authority. The law cannot long afford to do this': Padelford, 'The International Non-Intervention Agreement and the Spanish Civil War', n 71, 586.

view was unable to change the course of events at the League. The next section further explores Mexican internationalism in view of the revolutionary nationalist project of Lázaro Cárdenas.

10.4 Mexico, Intervention and Nation-Building

Post-revolutionary Mexican society was still marked by local and regional violence, political struggles and disagreements among the ruling elites on how to consolidate revolutionary ends through political and economic reconstruction.[97] At the end of the 1920s, even with the end of widespread armed upheaval, 'the outcome of the Revolution remained unclear. Its course was still being run, and there were very different views as to where that course should lead'.[98] Notwithstanding that 'Mexico's economy had not been revolutionized by the Revolution',[99] new forms of institutional mobilisation emerged, such as new political parties founded on diverse political orientations, peasant leagues and trade unions, demonstrating the deep political and social changes brought by the revolution.[100] In such an open-ended context, the 1930s were marked by the rise of *Cardenismo*, a nationalist and radical project that deeply affected Mexican society, and was also the revolution's last great effort at reform.[101]

This section aims to elucidate the domestic conditions in Mexico that were implicated in the construction of Mexican internationalism at the League of Nations. In this setting, the brief analysis that follows of Cárdenas' nationalism will not be depicted as the 'true cause' behind Fabela's active role in the legal struggles over the war in Spain. My objective is to shed light on important facets of domestic politics that help us to understand the Mexican position at the League – an understanding that might go unnoticed in an exclusive focus on the technicalities of neutrality law, non-intervention and the rules of the League scheme of collective security. Equally, the exploration of these domestic conditions is not an historical undertaking per se. The context of the presidency of Lázaro Cárdenas is explored in this section to the extent

[97] Alan Knight, 'Mexico, c. 1930–46' in Leslie Bethell (ed), *The Cambridge History of Latin America* (Cambridge University Press, 1990) vol 7, 1, 3.

[98] Ibid., 6.

[99] Ibid., 3.

[100] Ibid.

[101] Ibid., 7.

that it helps to understand the Mexican legal position at the League. Therefore, I do not intend to produce a comprehensive historical analysis of Mexico and *Cardenismo*. Importantly, the same rationale applies to the ways in which I have been engaging with the Mexican Revolution in this contribution.

In general terms, Cárdenas started his presidency with a foreign policy that was based on the nationalism of the Mexican Revolution, 'a blend of classical liberalism, socialism, and native communalism'.[102] Importantly, according to the 1917 Constitution, the president had the faculty to determine the terms of Mexican foreign policy,[103] which also explains the close exchanges between Fabela and Cárdenas on the substance of the Mexican legal position on the war in Spain at the League. Cárdenas' foreign policy has to be seen as integrating a broader project of nation-building in Mexico – as mentioned above, an effort that was still ongoing in the country.

In short, Cárdenas 'aimed at eliminating foreign control of the country's natural resources, which had produced not only foreign debt but also economic dependency'.[104] As explored in the first section of this chapter, the issues of foreign capital and property were at the core of the Mexican Revolution. During the 1920s, the project of state-building and capitalist development did not allow foreign capital and property to be fully transformed according to revolutionary ideals. To illustrate: 'US direct investment in Mexico was higher in 1929 than it had been in 1910'.[105] Cárdenas' political orientation was clearly progressive, aiming at addressing the agrarian question in Mexico and the internal divisions in the Mexican labour movement, as well as integrating the popular support of the masses into his government.[106]

We can explore Cárdenas' material and moral support to the Spanish Republic in at least two ways. A more generic one has to do with the risks posed by a Franco victory to *Cardenismo* in Mexico, as 'a conservative victory in Spain risked encouraging Mexican conservatives to undertake hostile actions against the Cárdenas administration'.[107] Despite the progressive turn brought about by the Cárdenas administration, Mexico had

[102] Oñate, n 5, 66.
[103] Revah, n 7, 4.
[104] Oñate, n 5, 66.
[105] Knight, n 97, 3.
[106] Revah, n 7, 66.
[107] Oñate, n 5, 66.

its own internal polarisation, with social organisations like unions and politicians supporting Cárdenas, and the Mexican conservatives being composed of the Mexican middle class and most of the Spaniards living in the country.[108] To the conservatives, the discourse of *hispanidad*, 'a community of Spanish-speaking nations led by a Spanish Catholic monarchy',[109] was an important sensibility.

A second way to explore the Mexican support to the Spanish Republic has to do with the issue of oil nationalisation. In March 1938, Cárdenas nationalised Mexican oil. The legal basis was the previously mentioned Article 27 of the 1917 Constitution, which established that all subsoil mineral resources are property of the nation, and that their private exploitation may only be carried out through concessions to Mexicans by birth or naturalisation, or to Mexican companies. The nationalisation of oil in Mexico was strongly connected to the role of trade unions in the matter. In 1936, different trade unions from the oil sector created the *Sindicato de Trabajadores Petroleros de la República Mexicana*, an organisation that gathered workers from all different foreign oil companies operating in the country. The new organisation proposed a collective labour agreement, which was not accepted by the oil companies, even after strikes and attempts to settle the issue through arbitration and judicial means. The presidential decision to nationalise oil in Mexico was closely related to this deadlock: that is, this context of union struggles paved the way for the decision to expropriate, and a presidential decree of expropriation was issued on 18 March 1938. A constitutional amendment followed in Mexico in 1939, forbidding the concession of oil exploitation to private actors.[110]

In this setting, the legal justifications presented by Fabela at the League of Nations for the legality of Mexican aid to the Spanish Republic, and his critical stance towards the Non-Intervention Committee, can be seen as a clear message to the international community. Non-intervention should be understood under the international legal framework of the interwar period, that is, strictly under the rules of international law. This legalistic commitment would pave the way for Mexico's active role in confronting possible attempts at intervention in light of the nationalisation of oil in the country. In other words, the Mexican defence of the Spanish Republic

[108] León and Andrés, n 1, 73–80.
[109] Oñate n 5, 65.
[110] José Ovalle Favela, 'La nacionalización de las industrias petrolera y eléctrica' (2007) 40 *Boletín Mexicano de derecho comparado* 169, 178–84.

at the League would open space for the use of the (now) widely diffused understanding on non-intervention for Mexico's own benefit.[111]

The League proved to be an important venue for the diffusion of the Mexican legal view on non-intervention. This strategic engagement with the vocabulary of international law becomes visible when interrogating Mexican domestic politics. Going local here has less to do with 'revealing the truth' about the Mexican defence of the Spanish Republic, and more to do with fully grasping the ways in which Mexico used international law as a relevant vocabulary to put forward certain political projects.

10.5 Conclusion

This contribution has aimed to redescribe Mexico's position at the League on the legal treatment of the Spanish civil war. It has aimed to show in detail how the ideals of the Mexican Revolution and the 1917 Constitution were extrapolated to the international sphere through an innovative engagement with international law. The legal interpretation articulated by the Mexican international lawyer Isidro Fabela was a key feature in this process.

Using a very familiar legal technique, Fabela proposed a different legal description of the war in Spain, subsuming non-intervention to neutrality law under the framework of the League Covenant. In doing so, he was able to challenge the dominant legal view of the Non-Intervention Committee, as put forward by the British and the French. Notwithstanding the alleged appeasement policy of these two countries towards the conflict in Spain, Fabela denounced their hypocrisy to the international community: the outsourcing of the conflict to an organ alien to the League of Nations did not prevent the Italian and German support to the rebels and, what was worse, itself constituted a 'de facto' intervention.

Beyond mere historical curiosity, the study of the Mexican position at the League opens up space for broader interrogations of the principle of non-intervention in international law. At stake here is an idea of impartiality that, when connected to the principle of non-intervention in a conflict with unequal sides, can actually become a means of taking sides in such a conflict.[112] Fabela's legal interpretation of the war in Spain

[111] León and Andrés, n 1, 302–3.

[112] Anne Orford, *International Authority and the Responsibility to Protect* (Cambridge University Press, 2011) 8.

sheds light on the acute problem of the lack of a coherent articulation of the political choices involved in treating nationalists and republicans equally in the case of the Spanish civil war. In other words, one is led to wonder how France and the United Kingdom conceptualised 'their political and legal role' in the conflict.[113]

Even with all the evidence brought before the League regarding Italian and German support for Franco, no further robust justification was presented to keep the problem outside the reach of the scheme of collective security of the League. Mexico, however, attempted to challenge this idea of impartiality, presenting the view that until belligerency is declared, in a civil war the de jure government should be given precedence in terms of material support. Importantly, this was done not to weaken the principle of non-intervention, but as a way to foster its application in the future.

It is hard to say whether had the Mexican legal interpretation on non-intervention been adopted, the conflict in Spain would have had a different outcome. This is not my main conclusion here. My point instead is that the Mexican position at the League of denouncing a 'de facto' intervention is a familiar story in international law. It is a story related to the ways in which the exercise of power is legally conceptualised, and how political choices are coherently justified.[114] Even though it happened in a completely different legal context, distant in time, the Mexican story helps us to never stop interrogating who decides the question of intervention in civil wars, and with what justifications.

[113] Ibid., 10.
[114] Ibid.

PART IV

Investment

11

1917

Property, Revolution and Rejection in International Law

KATE MILES*

It is well appreciated that legal systems are imbued with patterns. Given their constructed nature, use of precedent, application of principles and multitude of law-making instruments, it is unsurprising that links, repetition, practices and relationships are identified within and across legal systems; and international law is no different in that respect. As a field, it has developed at various points in line with a range of patterns as it responds to particular propositions, assertions, circumstances, events or challenges. And as it has fractured and subdivided into specialist areas, that process has been replicated, each sector of international law producing its own distinct reiterations. Clearly not the sole pattern – but certainly an especially potent one – is the centrality of property and commerce.[1] When the history of international law is examined, a repeated process of right-construction can be observed and we can see that mechanisms and artificial constructs have repeatedly been developed to place property and commerce at the centre of international law. Concepts, treaties, arbitrations, even the use of language as a mechanism were all new devices, each responding to contemporary needs with a new construct: ostensibly a break or change of direction but always actually preserving core, central principles, supporting a private-rights focus in rules for international application, creating overall a continuity of approach.

The very notion of revolution would seem to be the antithesis of such a framework; revolution itself being an event of marked upheaval, one that ruptures social, political, legal and economic spheres. What revolution represents is a struggle. The question that arises then is: how that struggle is given form or expression within international law; how the event of

* Fellow and Lecturer in Law, Gonville and Caius College, Cambridge.

1 See the discussion in Martti Koskenniemi, 'Expanding the Histories of International Law' (2016) 56 *American Journal of Legal History* 104.

revolution is accounted for within the law. And for this chapter, it is also a consideration of the intersect of revolution with those patterns of centrality of property and commerce; how international law responds to that inevitable intersect. Where there is revolution, international rules on property are inevitably implicated.

Given the enormity of revolution in substance, it is significant that, on one level, international law has had little difficulty encompassing the concept of revolution. It found the capacity with relative ease to conceptualise ways in which to move from one legal order to another within a state so as to maintain the international legal order undisrupted. However, not so for property – with respect to property, international law is not tolerant of revolution. So, although revolution itself could be legitimised within international law, the interference with foreign-owned property as a result of revolution could not. In fact, there has, for some time, been a consistent rejection of challenges posed to the international rules on protection of foreign-owned property.[2]

This is the context in which I examine the October Revolution and the Mexican Constitution – as legal events within, and challenges to, the international legal order. I argue that these events have a place within that history of repeated processes of right-construction for property and commerce within international law. It is, however, one seeking to disrupt those processes, of seeking to do something substantively different in international law. I explore how, at every point, where those alternative perceptions could have shaped the rules of international law on the protection of property, those attempts to bring a different vision into the law were rejected.

Accordingly, a key theme running through my chapter is that of rejection – multi-layered stories of rejection. On the one hand, there was rejection in 1917 in Russia and in Mexico of the notion of private property and rejection by those states of the asserted rules on property in international law. And then, on the other hand, there was rejection of those attempts to reconceptualise property and international law by those in a position to do so: primarily European and North American states

[2] I have explored the history of challenges to those rules in detail elsewhere. See Kate Miles, *The Origins of International Investment Law: Empire, Environment and the Safeguarding of Capital* (Cambridge University Press, 2013). See also Kate Miles, 'History and International Law: Method and Mechanism – Empire and "Usual" Rupture' in Stephan W Schill, Christian J Tams and Rainer Hofmann (eds), *International Investment Law and History* (Edward Elgar, 2018) 136.

and legal communities. There was a rejection of the profoundly different rules that these events represented and, instead, a return to the continuous search for, and construction of, mechanisms in international law to maintain the Western position with respect to foreign-owned property.

Ultimately, this chapter is a meditation on the very nature of revolution and the way in which international law conceptualises an event of such magnitude. It explores how we choose to construct legal spaces out of such events, how international law interrogates the layers of revolution – an event that reaches into every aspect of a state's being – and how international law responds to the immense struggle that revolution represents.

11.1 Revolution and International Law

Conceptually, revolution can be understood through a variety of lenses. At a base level, it has been characterised as an event of 'particularly rapid and extensive political change, generally with the involvement of a large portion of the population, and generally involving a change in leadership'.[3] This approach often entails discerning additional defining elements of revolution, such as both the loss of legitimacy of incumbent authorities and the use of revolution as an instrument of political legitimacy restoration.[4] However, Taylor also discusses the displacing of descriptive accounts of revolution through the infusing of the concept with ideals and a form of romanticism, exploring the way in which the term evolved into representing progressive notions of human experience.[5] Overlaying the factual occurrence of a revolutionary event with a narrative of mysticism produces what Taylor calls a 'transcendental

[3] Owen Taylor, 'Reclaiming Revolution' (2011) 22 *Finnish Yearbook of International Law* 259, 263. See also the discussion in Jack A Goldstone, 'Theories of Revolution: The Third Generation' (1980) 32 *World Politics* 425. See also for a discussion on the concept of revolution, Fred Halliday, '"The Sixth Great Power": On the Study of Revolution and International Relations' (1990) 16 *Review of International Studies* 207.

[4] Nimer Sultany, *Law and Revolution: Legitimacy and Constitutionalism after the Arab Spring* (Oxford University Press, 2017) 97. See also the discussion in Matthew Noah Smith, 'Rethinking Sovereignty, Rethinking Revolution' (2008) 36 *Philosophy & Public Affairs* 405, 407–8: 'Revolution involves the destruction of the governing institution and its replacement with some other set of institutions' .... 'revolution [is] ... (i) profound and thoroughgoing substitution of one governing sociopolitical institution with another (ii) achieved through means (revolutionary activities) that involve the spectacular rejection of the authority of both the target institution and its rules'.

[5] Taylor, n 3, 263–4.

process' conceptualisation of revolution[6] and what Nesiah terms the traditions of 'nostalgia' and 'utopia' that look respectively to past 'revolutionary passions' and future 'alternative political imaginaries'.[7] The concept has also been firmly situated within socialist theories of revolution.[8] In these respects, revolution is inextricably linked with ideas rather than solely with actions.[9] On one view, this can be seen to mirror the progress narrative that also sits within international law, constructing legitimacy through flawed notions of 'progress', 'virtuous' ideals and transformative effect.[10] However, a reflection on the explicit modes of interaction between revolution and international law reveals a more directly conflicted relationship. International law is concerned with maintaining stability. It inherently forms a site of contestation when called upon to rationalise revolution, an event designed to disrupt the incumbent forms of stability. That tension was illustrated in the response from legal communities in Western states to the potentially disruptive impact of the revolutionary events of 1917 on asserted international property rules. The next section of this chapter examines those attempts to use international law to continue a process of right-construction in the Western mould, which involved both the rebuffing of objections to asserted property-protection rules and the containment of the property-related implications of revolution.

11.2 The October Revolution, the Mexican Constitution and Foreign-Owned Property

Inarguably, the October Revolution and the 1917 Mexican Constitution had innumerable implications for the international legal order at that

[6] Ibid., 264.

[7] Anne Orford et al., 'Roundtable: Law, Force and Revolution' (2006) 100 *American Society of International Law Proceedings* 261, 264.

[8] Ibid. See Miéville's discussions throughout. See Taylor n 3, 270; Goldstone, n 3. See, for example, G I Tunkin, *Theory of International Law* (Harvard University Press, 1974). See generally, David Bakhurst, *Consciousness and Revolution in Soviet Philosophy: From the Bolsheviks to Evald Ilyenkov* (Cambridge University Press, 1991); Prabhat Patnaik, 'Marxist Theory and the October Revolution' (2017) 6 *Agrarian South: Journal of Political Economy* 175.

[9] Taylor, n 3, 263.

[10] See, for a discussion on the progress narrative of international law, Tilmann Altwicker and Oliver Diggelmann, 'How Is Progress Constructed in International Legal Scholarship?' (2014) 25 *European Journal of International Law* 425.

time.[11] However, it is in the specific context of the property transfers that occurred following these events that I consider the relationship between, and treatment of, revolution and the international rules on the protection of foreign-owned property. In particular, this chapter not only examines those property reassignments as attempts to bring a different vision into international law, one that took account of perspectives of nations other than those in Western Europe and North America, but also as events that constituted 'stories of rejection' – in this sense, the rejection of the very notion of private property.

The entrenching of dominant Western perspectives over centuries through repeated practices and processes of both imperialism and non-colonial international engagement has been articulated by Lauren Benton and Antony Anghie.[12] Despite the uneven implementation of international legal authority during the emergence of modern international law frameworks from the sixteenth and seventeenth centuries onwards, an enduring pattern has been the placing of property, commerce and private rights at its centre.[13] That process itself is not the subject of this chapter, but those deeply ingrained notions, reflected as far back as the lectures of Vitoria,[14] go some way to explaining the recurring rejection of attempts to reshape international rules on the protection of foreign-owned property. I have suggested elsewhere that those rules are the most visibly explicit manifestation of that history of centrality of property and commerce in international law.[15] In other words, the expression of the historical economic and political rationale for significant components of modern international law was represented in those rules, as well as by the

[11] See, for example, the discussion in Anne Peters, 'The "Great October Socialist Revolution": What Remains in and for International Law?' (2017) *Max Planck Institute for Comparative Public Law & International Law (MPIL) Research Paper Series*, No 2017-09.

[12] See, generally, Lauren Benton, *A Search for Sovereignty: Law and Geography in European Empires, 1400–1900* (Cambridge University Press, 2010); Antony Anghie, 'The Evolution of International Law: Colonial and Postcolonial Realities' (2006) 27 *Third World Quarterly* 739.

[13] Koskenniemi, 'Expanding the Histories of International Law', n 1; Miles, 'History and International Law', n 2; Martti Koskenniemi, 'Empire and International Law: The Real Spanish Contribution' (2011) 61 *University of Toronto Law Journal* 1; Martti Koskenniemi, 'Histories of International Law: Significance and Problems for a Critical View' (2013) 27 *Temple International and Comparative Law Journal* 215.

[14] See, for example, Francisco de Vitoria, 'On the American Indians' (lecture delivered in 1539) in *Vitoria: Political Writings* (Anthony Pagden and Jeremy Lawrence, trans and eds, Cambridge University Press, 1991) 231.

[15] Miles, 'History and International Law', n 2.

relationships embodied in those rules. Consequently, a challenge to those rules was a challenge not only to those specific property-protection doctrines but, in fact, to the system of international law itself and, indeed, a challenge to the social, economic and political assumptions lying at the core of those doctrines. For these reasons, the property takings that followed the October Revolution and those that relied upon Article 27 of the Mexican Constitution were a significant challenge to the international legal order.

The term 'expropriation' was used by Western states and their legal communities to describe the property transfers that occurred in the Soviet Union and Mexico following their revolutionary events. It was not a neutral term and, in 1917, its criteria and consequences in international law remained in dispute. By the mid-nineteenth century, capital-exporting states were asserting the existence of rules protecting foreign-owned property through the law on diplomatic protection of aliens.[16] This included declaring an international minimum standard of treatment for aliens, a breach of which was said to enliven a right of intervention by an aggrieved foreigner's home state.[17] According to this framing of the doctrine, the taking of foreign-owned property by a state, or 'expropriation', was permitted under international law if: (a) it was carried out for a public purpose; (b) it was not arbitrary or discriminatory and (c) compensation was paid.[18]

Although this was a period of right-construction, these purported rules were treated by capital-exporting states as established rules of public international law. They also came to be applied in arbitrations and by courts in line with the capital-exporting state position in both the nineteenth and early twentieth centuries.[19] They were described as settled

[16] Edwin M Borchard, *The Diplomatic Protection of Citizens Abroad* (Banks Law Publishing Company, 1919) 25–9, 39–42; John Westlake, *International Law* (Cambridge University Press, 2nd ed, 1910) 327–34; Clyde Eagleton, *The Responsibility of States in International Law* (Banks Law Publishing Company, 1928) 3, 6, 22.

[17] Borchard, *Diplomatic Protection*, n 16, 25–9, 39.

[18] Ibid., 439–56; B A Wortley, *Expropriation in Public International Law* (Cambridge University Press, 1959) 33–5.

[19] See, for example, the arbitral award in the *Delagoa Bay Railroad Arbitration*: John Bassett Moore, *A History and Digest of the International Arbitrations to Which the United States Has Been a Party* (Government Printing Office, 1898) vol II, 1865; see also Jackson H Ralston, *Venezuelan Arbitrations of 1903* (Government Printing Office, 1904); recognising an international minimum standard of treatment, see on the recognition of foreigners' vested rights and reparations for the seizure of foreigners' property, respectively, *Case concerning Certain German Interests in Polish Upper Silesia (Germany v Poland)* (1926) PCIJ Ser A, No 7 and *Case concerning the Factory at Chorzów (Claim for Indemnity) (Germany v Poland)* (1928) PCIJ Ser A, No 17.

rules in treatises[20] and in diplomatic correspondence.[21] And they were used as a premise for political interference and military incursions into host states.[22] However, the existence of the asserted rules was contested by capital-importing states throughout this period. One form of response was the development of the Calvo Doctrine.[23]

The Calvo Doctrine was a direct challenge to the process of right-construction surrounding the international minimum standard and its realisation through the doctrine of diplomatic protection. It sought to confine the regulation of foreign-owned property to domestic courts. Its central principles were that: (a) the doctrine of state sovereignty precludes a state from intervening in the domestic affairs of another; (b) aliens should be afforded no more than the same treatment as nationals and (c) aliens must limit themselves to filing claims in the local judicial system.[24]

The response from European and North American states and legal communities was to reject the proposed rules embodied in the Calvo Doctrine.[25] The volume of repetition and vehemence of that rejection

20 See, for example, Borchard, *Diplomatic Protection*, n 16.

21 See, for example, the views expressed in diplomatic correspondence concerning the *Britain (Finlay) v Greece* dispute, Viscount Palmerston to Sir Edmund Lyons, British Envoy at Athens, 7 August 1846, Great Britain, Foreign Office (1849–50) 39 *British and Foreign State Papers* 431–2. See also the correspondence between Secretary of State Bayard and Mr Connery (1 November 1887) *Foreign Relations of the United States,* 1885–9, Grover Cleveland, 1887 vol, 751, 753.

22 M Sornarajah, *The International Law on Foreign Investment* (Cambridge University Press, 4th ed, 2017) 46–9; Miriam Hood, *Gunboat Diplomacy 1895–1905: Great Power Pressure in Venezuela* (Allen & Unwin, 1975) 189–92; Charles Lipson, *Standing Guard: Protecting Foreign Capital in the Nineteenth and Twentieth Centuries* (University of California Press, 1985) 14–15, 40, 53–4, 187.

23 One of the most prominent advocates of this position was the Argentinian lawyer and legal scholar, Carlos Calvo, after whom the doctrine is named. He completed a six-volume treatise, *Le Droit International Théorique et Pratique*, first published in 1868, and then, five editions later, in its final form in 1896: M Charles Calvo, *Le Droit International Théorique et Pratique* (Arthur Rousseau, 5th ed, 1896)

24 Ibid. Donald Shea, *The Calvo Clause: A Problem of Inter-American and International Law and Diplomacy* (University of Minnesota Press, 1955).

25 See, for example, the correspondence between Secretary of State Bayard and Connery (1 November 1887) *Foreign Relations of the United States,* 1885–9, Grover Cleveland, 1887 vol, 751, 753:

> If a Government could set up its own municipal laws as the final test of its international rights and obligations, then the rules of international law would be but the shadow of a name and would afford no protection either to states or to individuals. It has been constantly maintained and also admitted by the Government of the United States, that a Government

were key components in the process of Western right-construction around the protection of foreign-owned property. It was not a settled area of international law, but it was treated as such by capital-exporting states, with significant implications for the substance of the rules applied to takings of foreign-owned property. In that sense, there was a constant state of contestation surrounding the law, but one in which the challenges of capital-importing states were ignored by Western states, legal commentators and arbitrators. As a result, the asserted nineteenth-century, capital-exporting state position was maintained and applied as representing the international rules on protection of foreign-owned property. Against that background, it can be seen that the land reforms of 1917 were part of a wider story of non-acceptance of the capital-exporting states' framing of international rules on foreign-owned property protection and an ongoing, parallel process of alternative rule-construction by capital-importing states.

For both the Soviet Union and Mexico, the argument ran that agrarian reform for social purposes did not amount to expropriation, but rather that a new category called 'nationalisation', which did not require compensation, had been created; that where there was a widespread programme of land reform with social objectives, the very character of the taking of property had changed to such a degree that the provision of compensation to the foreign investor would not be required.[26] From the

> cannot appeal to its municipal regulations as an answer to demands for the fulfilment of international duties.

See also Institute of International Law, *Regulations Respecting the Responsibility of States by Reason of Damages Suffered by Aliens in Case of Riot, Insurrection or Civil War: Recommendation* (Session of Neuchatel, 10 September 1900):

> The Institute of International Law recommends that states should refrain from inserting in treaties clauses of reciprocal irresponsibility. It thinks that such clauses are wrong in excusing states from the performance of their duty to protect their nationals abroad and their duty to protect foreigners within their own territory.

26 See the statements made in various Soviet Decrees issued with the express aim of dismantling capitalism on a global scale through, among other means, the non-honouring of treaties and international loans: for example, Articles 2 and 3 of *The Declaration of the Rights of the Toiling and Exploited People,* adopted by the 3rd All-Russian Congress of Soviets, January 1918, incorporated into the Constitution of the RSFSR, adopted by the 5th Congress 10 July 1918, Coll of Enact, RSFSR (1918) no 51, Article 582. See also, for example, the following statements:

> If the Soviet government has refused to assume the obligations of former governments, or the satisfaction of claims of persons on account of

host state perspective, these measures were necessary, core, structural reforms made internally to address deep-seated socio-economic inequalities. Foreign investors and their states, however, strongly objected, stating that 'nationalisation' did not constitute a separate category of taking or a social justice exemption. States protested officially, reiterating that international rules on the treatment of foreigners were clear and that compensation was required in the circumstances.[27] This difference in approach was not merely a matter of divergence in interpretation; it amounted to a fundamental collision of ideology and the construction of international law.

> measures of internal order, such as nationalisation of enterprises, municipalisation of houses, requisition or confiscation of property, this is not because it is incapable of adhering to its obligations, or disinclined to do so, but because of matters of principle and political necessity.... The revolution of 1917 entirely destroyed the old economic, social and political relations, and replaced the old society by a new one ... neither the systematic activities of the Soviet Government itself, such as the nationalisation of industrial equipment, nor the requisition of property belonging to foreigners, imposes upon the Soviet Government the obligation to compensate persons suffering loss.

'Memorandum of the Russian Delegation to Genoa Conference, 20 April 1922', reproduced in RSFSR, *The Soviet Union and Peace: The Most Important of the Documents Issued by the Government of the USSR Concerning Peace and Disarmament from 1917 to 1929: With an Introduction by Henri Barbusse* (Martin Lawrence, 1929) 89–90. See also the discussion in Josef L Kunz, 'The Mexican Expropriations' (1940) 17 *New York University Law Quarterly* 327; Alexander N Sack, 'Diplomatic Claims against the Soviets (1918–1938)' (1938) 15 *New York University Law Quarterly Review* 507; Isi Foighel, 'Nationalization: A Study in the Protection of Alien Property in International Law' (1956) 26 *Nordic Journal of International Law* 89.

27 See, for example, the declaration delivered to the People's Commissariat of Foreign Affairs in Petrograd in the name of twenty states, 13 February 1918, which provided:

> In order to avoid any misunderstanding in the future, the representatives of all the foreign powers in Petrograd declare that they consider the decrees on repudiation of the debts of the state of Russia, on confiscation of property and other analogous measures as invalid in so far as their nationals are concerned; and the said representatives reserve the right to claim from the Russian Government at an opportune time damages for all loss which these decrees may cause their nationals.

The United States Ambassador in Russia (Francis) to the Secretary of State, Telegram (12 February 1918) *Foreign Relations of the United States*, 1913–21, 1918, Russia, vol III, 'Loans to Russia: Soviet Decrees', 33. See Sack, n 26. See also the discussion in Kunz, n 26, 335–42. See also, for example, the arguments put forward in Edwin Borchard, 'The "Minimum Standard" of the Treatment of Aliens' (1940) 38 *Michigan Law Review* 445.

11.2.1 Property Takings Following the October Revolution

The dissolution of private ownership of land was a priority for the new Soviet authorities. In the first wave of confiscations, large land holdings were taken without compensation through the October 1917 Decree on Land.[28] This approach was extended in 1918 to all land, the principle subsequently forming the basis for Article 6 of the 1936 Constitution of the Soviet Union:[29]

> The land, mineral deposits, waters, forests, mills, factories, mines, railways, water and air transport systems, banks, means of communication, large state-organised agricultural enterprises (state farms, machine and tractor stations and the like) as well as municipal enterprises and the principal dwelling house properties in the cities and industrial localities, are state property, that is, the possession of the whole people.

A series of decrees annulling public debt and incrementally transferring ownership of banks and industry to the state also followed in late 1917 and the first half of 1918.[30] The orders encompassed all targeted loans, property and businesses whether owned locally or by foreign entities, so this was not a case of discrimination against foreign investors. They did amount, however, to substantial takings of foreign-owned property and debt, framed as 'expropriation' by investors and their home states but as 'nationalisation not requiring compensation' by the Soviet Union.[31]

In its rejection of the notion of private property, it is clear that the October Revolution constituted a fundamental reconceptualisation of the nature of property. This was a form of collectivism in ownership and an assertion of a right to property seizure without the need to provide

[28] Decree of 26 October 1917, Sob Uzak RSFSR, 1917, I, no 1, Article 3. See also the discussion in John N Hazard, 'Soviet Property Law' (1945) 30 *Cornell Law Quarterly* 466, 468.

[29] *Constitution (Fundamental Law) of the Union of Soviet Socialist Republics*, adopted at the Extraordinary Eighth Congress of Soviets of the USSR, 5 December 1936.

[30] See, for example, Decree of 21 January 1918, Coll of Enactm, RSFSR (1918) no 27, Article 353; Decree of 10 February 1918, Sbo Dek 25 okt 1917–25 okt 1918, 1918, 875; Decree of 14 December 1917, Sob Uzak RSFSR (1917) no 5, no 10; Decree of 28 June 1918, Sob Uzak RSFSR (1918) I, no 47, Article 559.

[31] See, for example, Articles 2 and 3 of *The Declaration of the Rights of the Toiling and Exploited People*, n 26, 2. See also the declaration delivered to the People's Commissariat of Foreign Affairs in Petrograd in the name of twenty states, 13 February 1918: The United States Ambassador in Russia (Francis) to the Secretary of State, Telegram (12 February 1918) *Foreign Relations of the United States*, 1913–21, 1918, Russia, vol III, 'Loans to Russia: Soviet Decrees', 33.

compensation on the basis of necessary social and economic reform. The nineteenth-century rules applied by capital-exporting states were not equipped to deal with such a dramatically different approach to property and its taking. Rather, those rules on expropriation had been developed with isolated incidents in mind, not a deliberate, systematic, wholesale abolition of the notion of private property.[32] For capital-exporting states, the question in 1917 was whether the still-contested principles on expropriation could also be extended to general, widespread land reforms that applied to both nationals and foreigners.[33] In some respects, then, the immediate response of investors and their states to the impacts of the October Revolution was somewhat muted. However, official protests and strident statements soon began to reassert that the international rules were clear and required the provision of compensation. Rather than adapting to incorporate the view expressed by the Soviet Union, investor states professed that their nineteenth-century rules were not only reaffirmed but that their application was expanded to encompass the land reform actions of the Soviet Union. For example, the declaration delivered to the People's Commissariat of Foreign Affairs in Petrograd in the name of twenty states, 13 February 1918, stated that:[34]

> In order to avoid any misunderstanding in the future, the representatives of all the foreign powers in Petrograd declare that they consider the decrees on repudiation of the debts of the state of Russia, on confiscation of property and other analogous measures as invalid in so far as their nationals are concerned; and the said representatives reserve the right to claim from the Russian Government at an opportune time damages for all loss which these decrees may cause their nationals.

The Memorandum delivered by a coalition delegation to the Soviet Union at the 1922 Genoa Conference also stated:[35]

[32] See the discussion in Kunz, n 26, 338. See also Nicholas R Doman, 'Postwar Nationalization of Foreign Property in Europe' (1948) 48 *Columbia Law Review* 1125, 1125–6; Seymour J Rubin, 'Nationalization and Compensation: A Comparative Approach' (1950) 17 *University of Chicago Law Review* 458, 459.

[33] See, for example, the discussion between Fachiri and Fischer Williams: A P Fachiri, 'Expropriation and International Law' (1925) 6 *British Yearbook of International Law* 159; J Fischer Williams, 'International Law and the Property of Aliens' (1928) 9 *British Yearbook of International Law* 1.

[34] See the declaration of 13 February 1918, cited at n 27.

[35] 'Memorandum handed to the Russian Delegation on the 15th April, 1922, after preliminary conversations between British, French, Italian and Belgian Delegations' reproduced in *Papers Relating to International Economic Conference, Genoa, April–May 1922* (H M Stationery Office, 1922) 25.

> that there can be no allowance made to the Soviet Government against:
>
> (a) Either the debts and financial obligations due to foreign nationals, or
> (b) The right of such nationals with regard to the return of their property and compensation for damage or loss in respect thereof.

Such responses were an unequivocal rejection of the proposed social policy exemption to compensation rules in the international law on foreign-owned property and a rejection of the idea that 'nationalisation' was a separate category of taking to expropriation. This continued to be the view put forward by investors, their states and their legal communities not only at the time of the Soviet property transfers but at other points in the twentieth century, in particular, in response to the land and oil nationalisations in Mexico and later to nationalisations in various states during decolonisation.[36] Kunz exemplified this conventional position in his 1940 assertions that the pre-World War I rules on expropriation had been reaffirmed by those home state responses:[37]

> It has been reaffirmed and upheld by the practice of states against Soviet Russia, against the Eastern European agrarian reforms, at the League of Nations by the majority of states, in all the many post-war negotiations of the United States with Mexico.
>
> As a rule of international law cannot be changed or abolished by the action of one or a few governments, a study of the problem reveals that the rule of international law, forbidding the expropriation without just compensation of the private property of aliens, continues to be the positive international law. This rule, it is true, has been attacked, and may be, from a sociological point of view, in a state of transition. But the jurist has to state what the law at a given moment is. And as the actions of certain states have not been recognized, have been protested against, and certainly have failed, up to now, to win the consent of the majority of states, the pre-war rule has legally lost nothing of its validity and is, and would be today, the law governing the decision of international courts.

In practice, however, the reality was somewhat less clear-cut than such statements might suggest. While the official position of affected states

[36] See, for example, Kunz, n 26, 2; see also International Law Association, 'Report of the Protection of Private Property Committee' (1926) 34 *International Law Association Reports of Conferences* 227, 233–49; Harvard Research in International Law, 'Responsibility of States' (1929) *American Journal of International Law Supplement XXIII* 133, Article 2; see the discussion on decolonisation in Antony Anghie, *Imperialism, Sovereignty and the Making of International Law* (Cambridge University Press, 2004) 10–11, 211–20, 235–44.

[37] Kunz, n 26, 339–42.

was that international law was unchanged and that compensation for the expropriations was required, during the 1920s, as potentially lucrative investment opportunities opened up in the Soviet Union, Western companies and their states individually entered into negotiations to secure new contracts, loan agreements and commercial treaties, even though compensation for the earlier property takings had not been received.[38] In this way, a situation emerged in which capital-exporting states were loudly professing their traditional rules, but their conduct was inconsistent with those same principles. The framing of these actions was also significant. In his influential analysis of the Mexican and Soviet land reforms, Kunz described the official responses of investor states in repudiating the Soviet property takings as state practice for the purposes of affirming the pre-World War I rules on expropriation.[39] However, neither the tacit acceptance by investor home states of the non-payment of compensation, nor the actions of the Soviet Union in the original taking of the property for a socio-economic land reform programme were considered by Kunz to constitute 'law-creating' actions. The significance of this position is more than the evident hypocrisy and signalling of the role and identity of 'gate-keeping' in international law-making; it is also that the continued assertions of the solidity of the nineteenth-century rules masked an opportunity to modify those rules to encompass views other than those of Western states, and to bring in notions of socio-economic justice and compensation exemptions or reductions for takings made as part of widespread reform programmes for the public good.

Attempts to advance more representative rules continued. Soviet scholars developed and cultivated the idea of a 'Soviet international law' or 'socialist international law'.[40] The concept was neither accepted

[38] See the discussion in Alexander N Sack, 'Diplomatic Claims against the Soviets (1918–1938)' (1939) 16 *New York University Law Quarterly Review* 253. See the discussion on American business interests in the Soviet Union during the 1920s and 1930s in J H Wilson, 'American Business and the Recognition of the Soviet Union' (1971) 52 *Social Science Quarterly* 349.

[39] Kunz, n 26, 339–42.

[40] See the discussion in Peters, n 11; Lauri Mälksoo, *Russian Approaches to International Law* (Oxford University Press, 2015) 4–6; Ignaz Seidl-Hohenveldern, 'Communist Theories on Confiscation and Expropriation: Critical Comments' (1958) 7 *The American Journal of Comparative Law* 541, 545. See also the discussion in Veronika Bílková, 'Sovereignty, Property and the Russian Revolution' (2017) 19 *Journal of the History of International Law* 147. See, for example, G I Tunkin, *Theory of International Law* (William E Butler trans, Harvard University Press, 1974).

by Western states as a separate variant on international law, nor was it directly absorbed as a shaping factor into mainstream international law. However, Peters suggests that it did, in fact, impact on international law in very specific ways, triggering new developments as reactions against the ideas embodied in socialist international law.[41] As an illustration, Leiter also argues that socialist pressure has, indeed, left an imprint on international law in this form, in generating the need to counteract its impact. In particular, Leiter argues that the renaming of 'foreign-owned property' to that of 'international investment', with its inherent suggestion of a social good for the recipient state, was one such manifestation, as in 'investment' equates to 'development', which equates to 'social good'.[42] In this way, it was not so much that socialist international law was taken into account and adopted but more that its key tenets were rejected so as to neutralise its influence.

11.2.2 Article 27 of the Mexican Constitution

Article 27 of the 1917 Mexican Constitution also proved to be a challenge to the international rules on property protection.[43] Much as with the October Revolution, the Mexican Revolution and its resulting Constitution provided a channel for widespread national agrarian reform. As Baitenmann discusses, land reform activities were ongoing from the start of the military phase of the revolution in 1910 but often at the administrative, perhaps less readily visible, level than the later larger-scale redistributions. In particular, she points to the decentralised and local nature of the collective land rights negotiations initiated by villages even during the unsettled period of armed hostilities.[44] The mechanism through which the land reforms were ultimately effected on a national scale was Article 27 of the new 1917 Constitution, which rendered all

41 Peters, n 11, 2.

42 Andrea Leiter, 'The Silent Impact of the 1917 Revolutions on International Investment Law: And What It Tells Us about Reforming the System' (2017) 6(10) *ESIL Reflection*.

43 *Constitucion Politica de los Estados Unidos Mexicanos,* Article 27 (*Mexican Constitution*). For an English translation of the Constitution, see 'Constitution of the Republic of Mexico: Signed 31 January 1917' (1917–18) 111 *British & Foreign State Papers* 778. For a comparison of wording between the 1857 and 1917 Constitutions, see H N Branch and L S Rowe, 'The Mexican Constitution of 1917 Compared with Constitution of 1857' (1917) 71 *Annals of the American Academy of Political and Social Science* 1 (*Mexican Constitution*).

44 Helga Baitenmann, 'Popular Participation in State Formation: Land Reform in Revolutionary Mexico' (2011) 43 *Journal of Latin American Studies* 1, 3, 6–9.

land, water resources and mineral rights the property of the nation, as well as vesting in the state rights of redistribution of property. Extensive tracts of land could be expropriated from large landholders and title reissued to agrarian communities.[45] Ownership in land and the holding of concessions was restricted to Mexican nationals or those non-nationals who agreed to be treated as Mexican in respect of their property and renounce any recourse to the international rules on protection of foreign-owned property. Where Article 27 differed from the Soviet Decree on Land was in its reference to compensation being payable – which in this respect appeared to conform with Western assertions of the rules of international law on expropriation. The article provided expressly that: 'Private property shall not be expropriated except for reasons of public use and subject to payment of indemnity'. It was noteworthy that the specific term 'expropriation' was used, the original Spanish being 'las expropiaciones'.[46] That sense of conformity was, however, tempered by the conditions attaching to indemnity, such as valuation processes and the issuing of bonds, and provisions that were, in effect, Calvo Clauses, together with the fact that this constituted a large-scale programme of national land reform, not isolated instances of expropriation.[47]

Diplomatic correspondence between Mexico and the United States of America ensued, tying the recognition of the Mexican government to the settling of claims by affected US citizens.[48] In the course of the diplomatic exchanges during this period, Mexico affirmed that it would indemnify American citizens in accordance with the rules of international law.[49] General and Special Claims Commissions to hear individual claims were established.[50] However, rather than a resolution of the

[45] *Mexican Constitution,* Article 27. See the discussion in James J Kelly, 'Article 27 and Mexican Land Reform: The Legacy of Zapata's Dream' (1994) 25 *Columbia Human Rights Law Review* 541, 550–1.

[46] *Mexican Constitution,* Article 27.

[47] Ibid.

[48] See, for example, correspondence between Mr Roberto Pesqueira, Agent of the Mexican Government, and Mr Bainbridge Colby, Secretary of State of the United States, and later Mr Charles E Hughes, Secretary of State of the United States, in 'Notes and Official Statements regarding the Recognition of Mexico' (1923) 9 *International Conciliation* 409.

[49] Ibid.

[50] *General Claims Convention*, United Mexican States–United States of America, 4 US Treaty Series 4441 (signed and entered into force 8 September 1923); *Special Claims Convention for the Settlement of Claims of American Citizens Arising from Revolutionary Acts in Mexico from November 20, 1910, to May 31, 1920*, United Mexican States–United

matter, this was a hiatus in what would continue to be an exceptionally complex set of circumstances. In fact, by 1938, those claims made in the early 1920s were still unpaid and Mexico maintained its view that general international law did not require compensation for takings pursuant to a programme of agrarian reform.[51] A series of later land takings and the oil expropriations of the 1930s, also based on Article 27 of the Constitution, would prove to be particularly problematic for the United States and the established international legal order. Renewed implementation of the agrarian reforms, the suspension of compensation payments, governmental attempts to improve conditions for Mexican workers in the oil industry and the 1938 Decree taking oil operations into state ownership triggered a new round of discord and diplomatic exchanges.[52]

In essence, the entrenched nature of the dispute came from what the oil expropriations represented to each of the governments and companies involved: the Mexican government, aware that the benefits of Mexican oil production had largely stayed with the foreign-owned oil companies and had not produced deep-seated local value, sought to reorient its natural resources' management to support Mexican socio-economic development; the oil companies, having strongly resisted previous attempts to regulate their operations more closely, wanted not just compensation for their investments to date but continued control over the oil facilities and damages for their future lost profits; and the United States, supporting its oil company nationals, wanted to maintain the protection of private property in international law to the fullest extent and to prevent the

States of America, 4 US Treaty Series 4445 (signed and entered into force 10 September 1923).

51 See the exchanges in the Note handed to the Mexican Ambassador at Washington, Dr Francisco Castillo Najera by the Honourable Cordell Hull, Secretary of State, 21 July 1938, in 'Correspondence between the United States and Mexico regarding Mexico's Expropriation of Agrarian Properties Owned by American Citizens' (1938) 19 *International Conciliation* 521, 523; and the Note from the Mexican Minister for Foreign Affairs, Señor Eduardo Hay to the American Ambassador at Mexico City, Mr Josephus Daniels, 3 August 1938, in 'Correspondence between the United States and Mexico regarding Mexico's Expropriation of Agrarian Properties Owned by American Citizens' (1938) 19 *International Conciliation* 521, 526.

52 Decreto Expropriatorio, 18 March 1938, *Diario Oficial*, 19 March 1938. For an English translation, see 'Mexican Decree expropriating on behalf of the Nation the Property of certain Oil Companies: Mexico, March 18, 1938' (1938) 142 *British & Foreign State Papers* 726. See also the discussion in Kunz, n 26, 346–8. See also the discussion in L H Woolsey, 'The Expropriation of Oil Properties by Mexico' (1938) 32 *American Journal of International Law* 519, 525–6. See also B A Wortley, 'The Mexican Oil Dispute: 1938–1946' (1957) 43 *Transactions of the Grotius Society* 15.

notion of 'nationalisation' becoming embedded within those rules as an independent category of taking that did not require compensation.[53]

The following extract from its notes to the Mexican government is illustrative of the United States' framing of the issue, rejecting the pursuit of public welfare policies as a justification for property takings affecting its citizens:[54]

> the Mexican Government both in its official correspondence and in its public pronouncements has adverted to the fact that it is earnestly endeavoring to carry forward a program for the social betterment of the masses of its people. The purposes of this program, however desirable they may be, are entirely unrelated to and apart from the real issue under discussion between our two Governments. The issue is not whether Mexico should pursue social and economic policies designed to improve the standard of living of its people. The issue is whether in pursuing them the property of American nationals may be taken by the Mexican Government without making prompt payment of just compensation to the owner in accordance with the universally recognized rules of law and equity.

In response, Mexico reiterated its position that under international law takings as a component of widespread socio-economic reform did not attract the need for immediate compensation:[55]

> My Government maintains, on the contrary, that there is in international law no rule universally accepted in theory nor carried out in practice, which makes obligatory the payment of immediate compensation nor even of deferred compensation, for expropriations of a general and impersonal character like those which Mexico has carried out for the purpose of redistribution of the land. ... the agrarian reform is not only one of the aspects of a program of social betterment attempted by a government or a political group for the purpose of trying out new doctrines, but also constitutes the fulfilling of the most important of the

[53] See the discussion in Clayton R Koppes, 'The Good Neighbor Policy and the Nationalization of Mexican Oil: A Reinterpretation' (1982) 69 *Journal of American History* 62, 64–7.

[54] Note handed to the Mexican Ambassador at Washington, Dr Francisco Castillo Najera, by the Honourable Cordell Hull, Secretary of State, 21 July 1938, in 'Correspondence between the United States and Mexico regarding Mexico's Expropriation of Agrarian Properties Owned by American Citizens' (1938) 19 *International Conciliation* 521.

[55] Note from the Mexican Minister for Foreign Affairs, Señor Eduardo Hay to the American Ambassador at Mexico City, Mr Josephus Daniels, 3 August 1938, in 'Correspondence between the United States and Mexico regarding Mexico's Expropriation of Agrarian Properties Owned by American Citizens' (1938) 19 *International Conciliation* 521, 526, 527.

> demands of the Mexican people who, in the revolutionary struggle, for the purpose of obtaining it, sacrificed the very lives of their sons. The political, social, and economic stability, and the peace of Mexico, depend on the land being placed anew in the hands of the country people who work it; a transformation of the country, that is to say, the future of the nation, could not be halted by the impossibility of paying immediately the value of the properties belonging to a small number of foreigners who seek only a lucrative end. On the one hand, there are weighed the claims of justice and the improvement of a whole people, and on the other hand, the purely pecuniary interests of some individuals. The position of Mexico in this unequal dilemma could not be other than the one she has assumed, and this is not stated as an excuse for her actions but as a true justification thereof.

Furthermore, in his note of 3 August 1938, Hay expressly invoked justifications that had formed the basis for the Calvo Doctrine in the nineteenth century, arguing that when Mexico had suspended all compensation payments in 1930, it would be inequitable to treat affected alien property holders differently from Mexican nationals.[56] In so doing, Mexico was continuing to assert its long-standing rejection of the minimum standard of treatment for the protection of alien property. In this respect, part of the significance of the 1917 Constitution, and the land reforms that accompanied it, was that they built on those earlier assertions of alternative international rules, rejected the property-protection principles relied upon by the United States and other capital-exporting states and continued to attempt to remould the rules to take better account of Mexico's social needs.

The Mexican position was clearly an arguable one, yet it was consistently rejected in official statements by the United States.[57] Ultimately, however, settlements were eventually reached when the US government adopted a different line from the oil company position on future access and loss of profits, and compromises were made on amounts to be paid and deferred payment schedules.[58] In other words, the actual outcomes

[56] Ibid., 529.

[57] See the United States correspondence generally in 'Correspondence between the United States and Mexico regarding Mexico's Expropriation of Agrarian Properties Owned by American Citizens' (1938) 19 *International Conciliation* 521.

[58] 'Compensation for Petroleum Properties Expropriated in Mexico: Agreement in Mexico', 17 April 1942, *Department of State Bulletin*, vol VI, no. 147 (18 April 1942) 351 ('Cooke–Zevada Agreement') in which Mexico agreed to pay the oil companies US$23,995,991 million; the original sum claimed had been US$450 million. See the discussion in Koppes, n 53, 72–4.

did not reflect the way in which the United States presented the law on expropriation at the time but rather pointed to the more ambiguous reality on the ground: that although the rules were continuously professed by capital-exporting states to be unaffected by Mexico's actions, in practice, they were accepting settlements and resolutions to the disputes that did not correspond with those rules in a straightforward manner. It is also clear that Mexico was seeking a more radical outcome than it was able to achieve. Its actions and correspondence indicated a desire to shed not only inequitable forms of domestic land tenure and reassert local control over its oil resources but also to disrupt the international application of disputed rules that facilitated the maintenance of systemic inequities such as these. The American response rejected the opportunity that this presented to carve out a new social justice exception within rules on protection of foreign-owned property, maintaining instead the traditionally enforced rules on compensation for expropriation. And it is that rejection that reverberated so significantly into the shaping of international investment law in the second half of the twentieth century.

11.3 Concluding Remarks

Reflecting on the impact of the events of 1917 on the assertion and application of international rules on the protection of foreign-owned property and on any lasting resonance of the challenge that these revolutionary events posed for those rules, it is, in my view, a dispiriting, if unsurprising, outcome given the historical patterns of right-construction around the protection of property and commerce in international law. The events of 1917 did not lead to a reconceptualisation of the nineteenth-century, capital-exporting state manifestation of those rules; they did not lead to a reconfiguration of rules to set international investment law on a new path; a new category of taking known as 'nationalisation' to permit affordable socio-economic reform through an adjustment to compensation requirements did not emerge; revolution itself did not lead to revolution in the foreign-owned property protection regimes of international law. In fact, quite to the contrary, capital-exporting state assertions of those rules would subsequently become embedded within the substantive protections in the bilateral investment treaties that came to dominate the field from 1959 onwards.[59]

[59] The first bilateral investment treaty was signed in 1959: Treaty between the Federal Republic of Germany and Pakistan for the Promotion and Protection of Investments (signed 25 November 1959, entered into force 28 April 1962) (1963) 457 UNTS 23.

In considering why that reconstituting of the rules did not occur, it seemed to me that this tied in with key questions excavated throughout this volume – questions about the very nature of revolution and the way in which international law conceptualises and responds to an event of such enormity. It implicates how we choose to construct legal spaces following revolutionary change, how international law understands the layers of revolution and how international law responds to the deep national struggle that revolution represents. I was struck by how that struggle is not given form or expression within international law, and how muted the response is, effectively neutralising the rupture of revolution under the guise of acceptance. That same desire for stability and continuity underlies the non-acceptance of challenges to international rules on foreign-owned property. In this sense, the response of international law to both revolution and to the attempt to reconfigure the international rules on protection of property was consistent in seeking to avoid cataclysmic ruptures, maintaining an unrippled surface of law and international responsibility.

As discussed elsewhere, there is an historical pattern of privileging commercial interests, particularly those of foreign-owned property-holders, within international law.[60] In my view, the events of 1917 and the rejection by the international community of their objectives relating to the law on foreign-owned property have a place within that history of repeated processes of right-construction for property and commerce within international law. These events were attempting to disrupt those processes and bring a different perspective into the substance of the rules on protection of alien property. They were met with visceral rejection. And, in the twenty-first century, there remains no capacity within international investment law to allow for 'nationalisation' conceptualised as a separate category of taking, one carried out as part of widespread socio-economic reform to which an adjusted or erased level of compensation attaches. In this respect, the neutralising of revolution, the events of 1917 and their challenges to asserted rules on foreign-owned property protection was successful, leaving that particular international regime with a less representative, less equitable and less imaginative framework than might otherwise have been possible.

[60] Koskenniemi, 'Expanding the Histories of International Law', n 1; Miles, *The Origins of International Investment Law*, n 2.

12

1917 and Its Implications for the Law of Expropriation

DARIA DAVITTI*

12.1 Introduction

In this chapter I examine three specific legal interventions which flowed from the revolutionary events of 1917 in relation to the law of expropriation. These legal interventions, and the doctrines and principles that they engendered, still hold significance in investor-state arbitration as they are systematically referred to in legal reasoning presented by counsel and continue to shape and influence the decisions of international arbitration tribunals. In light of the analysis carried out in this chapter, it is possible to articulate two main arguments. The first argument relates to the claim, often put forward by international investment law proponents,[1] that international investment law and investment treaty arbitration are crucial to the depoliticisation of disputes between investors and host states. According to this view, the international investment law system is capable of 'avoiding espousal of investors' interests by their home states', mainly by directly excluding recourse to diplomatic protection to solve conflicts arising between host states and foreign investors.[2] Depoliticisation, within this view, is understood as the transfer of such conflicts 'from the political arena of diplomatic protection to a judicial forum with *objective, previously agreed standards* and a pre-formulated

* University of Nottingham, School of Law and Lund University, Faculty of Law.

1 This view was initially articulated, inter alia, in the World Bank report by I F I Shihata, 'Towards a Greater Depoliticization of Investment Disputes: The Roles of ICSID and MIGA' (World Bank, 1992). Since then, this claim that international investment law effectively depoliticises investment disputes continues to be presented as one of the main reasons for the inherent worth of the system, despite the systemic faults it presents. See, for example, Ursula Kriebaum, 'Evaluating Social Benefits and Costs of Investment Treaties: Depoliticization of Investment Disputes' (2018) 33 *ICSID Review – Foreign Investment Law Journal* 14.

2 E T Odumosu, 'The Law and Politics of Engaging Resistance in Investment Dispute Settlement' (2007) 26 *Penn State International Law Review* 251, 271.

dispute settlement process'.[3] This view also acknowledges, however, that the disputes decided upon by international investment tribunals indeed remain political in nature for both host and home states.[4] In this chapter, I seek to demonstrate that international investment law, rather than depoliticising investor-state disputes, merely creates an artificial separation between law and politics by transferring such disputes to purportedly neutral and independent legal fora, ideally placed to offer market responses to inherently political controversies.[5] Thus, I argue, it is perhaps more appropriate to understand international investment law, and its ongoing attempts at depoliticisation, as a set of processes put in place to 'remove or displace the potential for choice, collective agency, and deliberation around a particular political issue'.[6]

A study of the revolutionary events of 1917 and an examination of the legal interventions that followed them to 'control' the very meaning of property and, in turn, of the law of expropriation help shed some light on such 'depoliticisation' claims put forward in support of international investment law. I focus, specifically, on three legal events: the decision on the expropriation of the factory at Chorzów (1927),[7] the *Lena Goldfields* arbitration (1930)[8] and the United States' pronouncement of the Hull formula (1938) as a standard of compensation.[9] These events illuminate the way in which some of the conflicting interpretations that

[3] Kriebaum, n 1, 15 (emphasis added).

[4] Ibid.

[5] Nicolás M Perrone and David Schneiderman, 'International Economic Law's Wreckage: Depoliticization, Inequality, Precarity' in Emilios Christodoulidis, Ruth Dukes and Marco Goldoni, *Research Handbook in Critical Legal Theory* (Edward Elgar, 2019).

[6] Paul Fawcett et al., 'Anti-Politics, Depoliticization, and Governance' in Paul Fawcett et al., *Anti-Politics, Depoliticization, and Governance* (Oxford University Press, 2017) 3, 5 as quoted in Perrone and Schneiderman, n 5, 5.

[7] *Case concerning the Factory at Chorzów (Germany v Poland) (Indemnities)* [1927] PCIJ (ser A) No 12.

[8] As noted by Veeder, the original award is filed in the Moscow archives and includes seven pages (from paras 1–4, 26 and 27) that are missing from the English version published in the London *Times* on 3 September 1930. The latter version was reproduced in Arthur Nussbaum, 'Arbitration between the Lena Goldfields Ltd and the Soviet Government' (1950) 36 *Cornell Law Review* 31. See V V Veeder, 'The *Lena Goldfields* Arbitration: The Historical Roots of Three Ideas' (1998) 47 *International and Comparative Law Quarterly* 747.

[9] The Hull formula was reproduced in 'Chapter XI – Aliens' (1942) 3 *Digest of International Law* 549, 658–9, and it reads as follows: 'The Government of the United States merely adverts to a self-evident fact when it notes that the applicable precedents and recognized authorities on international law support its declaration that, under every rule of law and equity, no government is entitled to expropriate private property, for whatever purpose, without provision for prompt, adequate, and effective payment therefor'.

were at the heart of legal, political and economic tensions at the time of these events are still present today when international investment tribunals are called to ascertain whether an indirect expropriation has occurred and, ultimately, whether and how compensation to the foreign investor should be paid. As I attempt to demonstrate in this chapter, a closer look at these three legal events also enables us to call into question the presumed 'neutrality' of investment treaty arbitration. An examination of the way in which the standard of compensation and the doctrine of unjust enrichment came into being reveals their specific contextualisation, in turn showing that the way in which these standards are understood and invoked in international investment arbitration is not entirely obvious.

As discussed below, these three legal events were all linked to intensely contested moments and controversial policy decisions. They were de facto legal interventions linked to the revolutionary events that characterised 1917 and the years that followed. Based on my first claim that international investment law does not 'depoliticise' investor-state disputes,[10] my second main argument is that, because of the revolutionary contexts in which they arose, the doctrines derived from these three events cannot be too easily applied to disputes arising in contemporary investor-state arbitration. When we consider more carefully the political-economic circumstances that engendered the *Chorzów* standard of compensation, the doctrine of unjust enrichment, and the Hull formula, it becomes apparent that their routine invocation in investment treaty arbitration may indeed be inappropriate. The aim of this chapter, therefore, is to bring evidence in support of these two claims by examining the political-economic context that characterised these three legal events.

This chapter examines the way in which the law of expropriation was influenced by two key historic events in 1917: the approval of the Political Constitution of the United Mexican States (5 February 1917)[11] with its

[10] See also Jonathan Bonnitcha, Lauge N Skovgaard Poulsen and Michael Waibel, *The Political Economy of the Investment Treaty Regime* (Oxford University Press, 2017) in which the authors describe the ongoing controversies that continue to characterise international investment law and 'the economics and politics of both foreign investment and investment treaties': at 260; Lauge N Skovgaard Poulsen, *Bounded Rationality and Economic Diplomacy: The Politics of Investment Treaties in Developing Countries* (Cambridge University Press, 2015).

[11] A scanned copy of the 1917 Constitution, from the *Diario Oficial Número 20*, can be found on the website of the Library of Congress at www.loc.gov/exhibits/mexican-revolution-and-the-united-states/constitution-of-1917.html.

Article 27, according to which 'ownership of all lands and waters within the boundaries of the national territory [were] vested originally in the Nation';[12] and the abolition of private property by the Bolshevik Decree on Land (8 November 1917, OS 26 October) following the October Revolution.[13] These two events formed the basis of significant land nationalisation and redistribution programmes, which in turn exacerbated Western concerns about expropriation without compensation.

In the years that followed, the law of expropriation experienced profound developments, mainly aimed at containing the effect of these revolutionary events and at preventing their future reoccurrence. Attempts to assert an obligation to compensate for the 'taking' of foreign property in fact accelerated after (and because of) these revolutions,[14] although political considerations, as discussed in this chapter, were not the only factors that influenced the formulation of legal standards of compensation: economic considerations also played a significant part in such formulations.

The study of these revolutionary historic phases is useful in order to understand and make visible the political and economic reasoning that underpinned certain legal doctrines that are still deployed in contemporary international investment tribunals, especially in cases related to indirect expropriation. The three legal interventions analysed in this chapter were all aimed at asserting an obligation in international law to compensate for the expropriation of alien property, and all three are often portrayed as establishing 'clear and unequivocal' standards of compensation. As such, these standards are systematically invoked in investor-state arbitration in relation to expropriation, and also

[12] More specifically, Article 27 also established that 'the Nation shall at all times have the right to impose on private property such limitations as the public interest may demand, as well as the *right to regulate the utilization of natural resources* which are susceptible of appropriation, in order to conserve them and to *ensure a more equitable distribution of public wealth*' (emphasis added). Paragraph iv of Article 27 also established that 'in the case of petroleum, and solid, liquid, or gaseous hydrocarbons no concessions or contracts will be granted or continue, and the Nation shall carry out the exploitation of these products, in accordance with the provisions indicated in the respective regulatory law'. See Lorenzo Meyer, *Mexico and the United States in the Oil Controversy, 1917–1942* (University of Texas Press, 1972) 54–5: 'Basic to the change proposed was the return of the rights to the subsoil – in other words, the oil – to the nation, and this was precisely the purpose behind paragraph iv of Article 27'.

[13] V I Lenin, *Collected Works* (Progress Publishers, 1977) vol 26, 258.

[14] See Charles Lipson, *Standing Guard: Protecting Foreign Capital in the Nineteenth and Twentieth Centuries* (University of California Press, 1985), especially chapters 3 and 4.

increasingly in relation to non-expropriation standards of protection such as fair and equitable treatment.[15] As I discuss in this chapter, however, these interventions should be carefully contextualised and understood within the historically contingent settings that engendered them. As such, their importance in establishing 'clear' standards of compensation is largely overestimated, not least because these standards remain highly contested. They continue to reflect long-standing controversies between capital-exporting and capital-importing countries,[16] controversies which in part mirror the political tensions over the meaning of property at the heart of the revolutionary events of 1917.

12.2 The Chorzów Factory Case (1927)

International investment tribunals often refer to *Factory at Chorzów* (*Chorzów Factory*) as the case establishing the standard of payment of compensation for unlawful expropriation. According to what is known as the *Chorzów* standard, foreign investors suffering unlawful expropriation are entitled to either restitution or, alternatively, restitutionary damages beyond the fair market value of the property (fair market value being the standard of compensation for lawful expropriation). The Permanent Court of International Justice (PCIJ) held in *Chorzów Factory* that, in the context of unlawful dispossession,

> reparation must, as far as possible, wipe out all the consequences of the illegal act and re-establish the situation which would, in all probability, have existed if that act had not been committed. Restitution in kind, or, if this is not possible, payment of a sum corresponding to the value which a restitution in kind would bear; the award, if need be, of damages for loss sustained which would not be covered by restitution in kind or payment in place of it – such are the principles which would serve to determine the amount of compensation due for an act contrary to international law.[17]

Foreign investors seeking to recover heightened damages in investor-state arbitration thus rely on the *Chorzów* standard to argue that

[15] See L Paradell, 'The BIT Experience of the Fair and Equitable Treatment Standard' in Federico Ortino et al. (eds), *Investment Treaty Law: Current Issues II* (British Institute of International and Comparative Law, 2007) 117, 137.

[16] M Sornarajah, *Resistance and Change in the International Law of Foreign Investment* (Oxford University Press, 2015), especially chapter 2.

[17] *Chorzów Factory (Germany v Poland) (Indemnities)* [1927] PCIJ (ser A) No 12, 47.

'compensation must be calculated not at the time of the wrongful act, but at the time of the award to reflect the possible rise of the value of the affected property after the wrongful act'.[18]

Yet, a closer examination of the *Chorzów Factory* case indicates that this automatic application of heightened damages to unlawful expropriation cannot be so easily justified. The case, brought by Germany against Poland before the PCIJ in 1926, related to the unlawful taking of a factory in Chorzów, within the context of the conflict between the two states over Upper Silesia soon after the end of World War I. Historically, Upper Silesia was a Polish territory but became part of Germany in the late eighteenth century. The strategic and political importance of the region was linked to its rich mineral deposits, of crucial importance for powering the coal, steel and chemical industries concentrated in the so-called industrial triangle, where Chorzów and its many factories were also located. The continued functioning of the 'industrial triangle' and, therefore, control over Chorzów were crucial for Germany, not only to ensure its economic recovery after World War I but also for it to be able to pay reparations.[19] The dispute over Upper Silesia was also of critical geopolitical significance. While France supported Poland in its efforts to see a weakened Germany, Great Britain was concerned that Germany would be unable to pay its reparations and, more gravely, that it would be unable to resist the rise of Bolshevism.[20] This latter concern, more specifically, was related to fears over the 1917 split in the German Social Democratic Party (SPD) that saw the Spartakusbund (the Spartacist League), led by Rosa Luxemburg, Karl Liebknecht and Franz Mehring, distance itself from the centrist orientation of the SPD and set up the Independent Social Democratic Party (USPD). These developments were closely linked to the German Revolution of November 1918 (*Novemberrevolution*), during which the divide between the SPD and the Spartakusbund grew deeper. The SPD took power in coalition with the USPD, while the Spartakusbund published its own manifesto to declare

[18] Ronald E M Goodman and Yuri Parkhomenko, 'Does the *Chorzów Factory* Standard Apply in Investment Arbitration? A Contextual Reappraisal' (2017) 32 *ICSID Review* 304, 305.

[19] Ibid., 305. As explained by Goodman and Parkhomenko, Germany's reparation amounted to a total sum of 269 billion gold marks, equivalent to approximately GBP 23.6 billion as at 2005, which Germany paid off on 3 October 2010.

[20] Ibid., 306.

full solidarity with the 'proletarians of all countries' and openly espouse a socialist platform.[21] In December 1918 the Spartacists contributed to the formation of the German Communist Party (KPD). In January 1919, in an attempt to empower the proletariat and overthrow the government, the Spartacist Uprising saw the seizure of public buildings in Berlin. The revolt, however, was violently quelled by a group of paramilitaries enlisted by the government, the Freikorps, who arrested the demonstrators and executed many of them on the spot, including Luxemburg and Liebknecht on the night of 15–16 January 1919.[22] The elections for the new Weimar National Assembly were held on 19 January 1919 and the Weimar Constitution, setting up the Weimar Republic, was adopted in August of the same year. Due to these revolutionary events in Germany, Britain was concerned that another communist revolutionary state could emerge in Europe. With the support of US President Woodrow Wilson, Great Britain proposed a plebiscite in Upper Silesia (eventually endorsed by the text of the Treaty of Versailles) for its inhabitants 'to indicate by a vote whether they wish[ed] to be attached to Germany or to Poland'.[23]

Before the plebiscite took place on 20 March 1921, there were two violent Polish uprisings in August 1919 and August 1920. The first one, on 15 August 1919, was triggered by the murder of ten civilians by German border guards to end a labour dispute at the Mysłowice coal mine.[24] As a result, Polish miners called a general strike across Silesia demanding the institution of more ethnically mixed police and local government. Armed insurgents took over several small towns in the region before the uprising was quelled by the Weimar Republic Provisional National Army. This first uprising was followed by retaliatory executions and hangings of approximately 2,500 Polish Silesians.

[21] See 'The Call, 30 January 1919 – Manifesto of the German Spartacists' www.marxists.org/historyinternational/social-democracy/call/1919/30.htm. See also Georg Adler, Peter Hudis and Annelies Laschitza (eds), *The Letters of Rosa Luxemburg* (Verso, 2013); 'Our Programme and the Political Situation, Letter by Rosa Luxemburg on 31 December 1918' www.rosalux.de/stiftung/historisches-zentrum/rosa-luxemburg/100-tage-dokumente/englisch/artikel-rl/by-henry-holland/our-program-and-the-political-situation/.

[22] Klaus Gietinger, *The Murder of Rosa Luxemburg* (Verso, 2019).

[23] *Treaty of Peace between the Allied and Associated Powers and Germany*, signed 28 June 1919, 225 ConTS 188 (entered into force 10 January 1920) art 88 (*Treaty of Versailles*) cited in ibid.

[24] Henryk Zieliński, 'The Social and Political Background to the Silesian Uprisings' (1972) 26 *Acta Poloniae Historica* 73. See also Barbara Dotts Paul, *The Polish-German Borderlands: An Annotated Bibliography* (Greenwood Press, 1994) 39–44.

Following the failure of Allied diplomatic intervention, a second uprising took place on 19 August 1920, with strikes and seizures of industrial cities by the insurgents across the region. The uprising was brought to an end by the armed and diplomatic intervention of the Allies, forcing the two parties to negotiate a ceasefire. As a result a new police force for the area (50 per cent German and 50 per cent Polish) was established, as well as a more ethnically balanced local administration. Discontent, however, continued to rise and these two initial uprisings were followed by a third one in May 1921, after the results of the plebiscite, when the International Plebiscite Commission issued conflicting recommendations, with France supporting Poland's claims and Great Britain and Italy assigning the 'industrial triangle' to Germany. The uprising in May 1921 reached a critical level when the Polish Silesians controlled most of Upper Silesia, and the Principal Allied and Associated Powers, considering that the conflict threatened to disturb international peace and security within the meaning of Article 11(2) of the Covenant of the League of Nations, requested the urgent intervention of the Council of the League of Nations to resolve the German-Polish dispute in Upper Silesia.[25] The Council's recommendation was to divide the industrial region, while ensuring 'the continuity of the economic and social existence of Upper Silesia', and to require both Germany and Poland 'to recognize and respect, in the territory which shall be allotted to them, rights of all kinds – in particular, concessions and privileges acquired at the date of the partition by individuals, companies or other legal entities'.[26]

According to the recommendation, Poland also had to wait for a period of fifteen years before exercising its rights under Articles 92 and 297 of the Treaty of Versailles, enabling it to liquidate and expropriate German property in the area under its control, which crucially included Chorzów.[27] Despite both countries' discontent, a dictated agreement was

[25] Goodman and Parkhomenko, n 18, 307.

[26] 'Recommendation of the Council of the League forwarded to the Supreme Council of the Principal Allied Powers on October 12th, 1921' (December 1921) *League of Nations Official Journal* 1230, as referenced in ibid., at 308.

[27] According to Articles 6 and 24 of the Geneva Convention 1922, Poland would regain these rights for a limited period of two years. The only exception to the fifteen years' moratorium on liquidation and expropriation was obtaining the specific permission to the Upper Silesian Mixed Commission, without which any expropriatory measure of German property by Poland would be a prohibited measure. See Goodman and Parkhomenko, n 18, 309.

signed and ratified by the end of May 1922, and the Geneva Convention on Upper Silesia thus entered into force on 15 June 1922.[28] The fifteen-year moratorium on liquidation and expropriation, however, was immediately challenged by Poland, which liquidated one of the largest nitrate factories in Europe in Chorzów. A series of PCIJ decisions arose from the claims brought by Germany against Poland, the most relevant of which established that Poland had breached the Geneva Convention on Upper Silesia.[29] In the *Chorzów Factory* case, as I mentioned earlier in this chapter, the PCIJ dealt with the nature, amount and method of compensation, thus formulating the well-known principle of full reparation.[30]

For the specific purposes of our discussion, it is important to understand the exceptional nature of the decision in *Chorzów Factory*: the principle of full reparation established in the case needs to be understood within the context of the politically sensitive interests protected by the Geneva Convention on Upper Silesia, of the threat to international peace and security that the tensions in the region caused and of the gravity of the conduct by Poland. This specific historical context of the *Chorzów Factory* case, however, is systematically overlooked by international investment tribunals, which rely on the *Chorzów* standard to grant *heightened* compensation to foreign investors. In the *Enron v Argentina* award, for instance, the tribunal found that, because the relevant international investment treaty did not specify the damages to which the investor was entitled, 'absent an agreed form of restitution by means of renegotiations of contracts or otherwise, the appropriate standard of reparation under international law is compensation for the losses suffered by the affected party, as was established by the Permanent Court of International Justice in the Chorzów Case'.[31] Despite the fact that this decision related to a breach of a standard of treatment different from expropriation,[32] the tribunal did not explain the applicability of the *Chorzów* standard of reparation, and merely stated that numerous other investment arbitration tribunals had applied it when deciding damages for breach of fair and equitable treatment.[33] Directly referring to the *SD*

[28] Ibid.

[29] *Case Concerning Certain German Interests in Polish Upper Silesia (Germany v Poland) (Merits)* [1926] PCIJ (ser A) No 7.

[30] *Chorzów Factory (Germany v Poland) (Indemnities)* [1927] PCIJ (ser A) No 12.

[31] *Enron Corporation v Argentine Republic (Award)*, ICSID Case No ARB/01/3 (22 May 2007) [359] ('*Enron v Argentina*').

[32] Ibid.

[33] Ibid [360].

Myers v Canada award, the *Enron v Argentina* tribunal interpreted the silence of the treaties as an intention of the drafters 'to leave it open to tribunals to determine a measure of compensation appropriate to the specific circumstances of the case'.[34] It also found that the approach to compensation taken 'should reflect the general principle of international law that compensation should undo the material harm inflicted by a breach of an international obligation'.[35]

In the *ADC v Hungary* award, decided in 2006, the tribunal went further and determined that in situations in which the value of the investment had risen 'very considerably' after the date of the expropriation, the *Chorzów* standard of reparation 'require[d] that the date of valuation should be the date of the Award and not the date of expropriation, since this is what is necessary to put the Claimants in the same position as if the expropriation had not been committed'.[36] While some arbitrators have openly challenged this application of the *Chorzów* standard to support an ex-post valuation at the date of the award,[37] various tribunals have followed the approach in *ADC v Hungary*.[38] For the purposes of our discussion, it is important to remember that the Geneva Convention on Upper Silesia was drafted to respond to the conduct by Poland and the escalated tensions in the region, both perceived at the time as a threat to international peace and security. The interests protected by the Geneva Convention on Upper Silesia, therefore, were very different from the interests of foreign investors generally

[34] *SD Myers Inc v Canada (Partial Award)* UNCITRAL (*ad hoc*) (13 November 2000) [309] ('*SD Myers v Canada*), as quoted in ibid., [360].

[35] *Enron v Argentina (Award)*, ICSID Case No ARB/01/3 (22 May 2007) [360], quoting *SD Myers v Canada* [315].

[36] *ADC Affiliate Limited and ADC & ADMC Management Limited v Republic of Hungary (Award)*, ICSID Case No ARB/03/16 (2 October 2006) [497].

[37] For a detailed consideration of the *Chorzów* standard favouring an *ex-ante* valuation at the date of expropriation, see the dissenting opinion in *Quiborax SA, Non/Metallic Minerals SA and Allan Fosk Kaplún v. Plurinational State of Bolivia (Partially Dissenting Opinion by Professor Brigitte Stern)* ICSID Case No ARB/06/2 (7 September 2015).

[38] See for instance *Von Pezold v Republic of Zimbabwe (Award)* ICSID Case No ARB/10/15 (28 July 2015) [763]–[764]; *El Paso Energy Intl Co v Argentine Republic (Award)*, ICSID Case No ARB/03/15 (31 October 2011) [703]–[704]; *Siemens AG v Argentine Republic (Award)*, ICSID Case No ARB/02/8 (6 February 2007) [355]. For a more detailed discussion of the *Chorzów* standard by a tribunal that still supported ex-post valuation at the date of the award, see *ConocoPhillips Petrozuata BV, ConocoPhillips Hamaca BV and ConocoPhillips Gulf of Paria BV v Bolivarian Republic of Venezuela (Award)*, ICSID Case No ARB/27/30 (8 March 2019) [207]–[229].

protected in international investment agreements (mainly financial and property interests). Because of this substantive difference, the heightened *Chorzów* standard of compensation 'may not be lightly transposed into the context of investment arbitration'.[39] In fact, the PCIJ in its reasoning made a distinction between two types of wrongful conduct: one related to expropriation occurring when the state has the right to expropriate – which would not trigger compensation – and one related to property that cannot be expropriated even against compensation. Different levels of illegality would, therefore, trigger different levels of damages.[40]

Thus, when a state fails to pay compensation for expropriated property, reparations should not exceed the value of the property at the moment of the expropriation, since heightened compensation as per the *Chorzów* standard should only be applicable in case of grave conduct in interstate matters, in circumstances analogous to the facts of the *Chorzów Factory* case itself.[41] A state's treatment of a foreign investor, in the vast majority of circumstances, would not entail wrongful conduct similar to that of Poland in the *Chorzów Factory* case, which was deemed by the PCIJ to threaten international peace and security.

Crucially for our discussion, reliance on heightened damages à la *Chorzów* in investor-state arbitration is not limited to claims for expropriation.[42] As mentioned earlier in the chapter, the *Chorzów* standard is increasingly invoked for breaches of non-expropriation standards of

39 Goodman and Parkhomenko, n 18, 322.

40 Ibid., where the authors state that 'while failure to pay compensation may still be a wrongful act, it is not inherently unlawful compared to illegality of a higher magnitude. It is based on the distinction between different levels of illegality, that the Court also distinguished between different levels of damages'. See *Chorzów Factory (Germany v Poland) (Indemnities)* [1927] PCIJ (ser A) No 12, 47: 'It follows that the compensation due to the German Government is not necessarily limited to the value of the undertaking at the moment of dispossession, plus interest to the day of payment. This limitation would only be admissible if the Polish Government had had the right to expropriate, and if the wrongful act consisted merely in not having paid to the two Companies the just price of what was expropriated'.

41 See James Crawford, 'Similarity of Issues in Disputes Arising under the Same or Similarly Drafted Investment Treaties' in Emmanuel Gaillard and Yas Banifatemi (eds), *Precedent in International Arbitration* (International Arbitration Institute, 2008) 97, 99–100: 'The Permanent Court in *Chorzów Factory* itself distinguished between the principles of quantification of damages applicable in inter-state matters and those applicable in cases between States and private parties; of course *Chorzów* fell in the first category not the second'.

42 Diane A Desierto, 'The Outer Limits of Adequate Reparations for Breaches of Non-expropriation Investment Treaty Provisions: Choice and Proportionality in *Chorzów*' (2017) 55 *Columbia Journal of Transnational Law* 395.

protection, in particular, of the fair and equitable treatment standard, and heightened damages are often awarded through the application of the principle of proportionality, although often without an explanation of how proportionality would lead to the applicability of the *Chorzów* standard.[43] Proportionality, understood as an international legal principle 'inherent to the concept of reparations under the international law of responsibility' should explicitly guide the decision-making of investment tribunals to ensure that reparations are not punitive in nature and that the causal link between the state's wrongful conduct and the damage incurred is clearly established.[44] Flowing from the above, it transpires that the automatic application of the *Chorzów* standard to reparations for breaches of standards of investment protection (including non-expropriation standards) cannot be easily justified, especially in the absence of careful reasoning on how the principle of proportionality is deployed in the decision-making process.[45]

12.3 The Lena Goldfields Arbitration (1930)

The *Lena Goldfields* arbitration was the first time that a transnational contract was internationalised. Veeder has referred to this internationalisation as 'a gigantic first step for international commercial arbitration, almost equivalent to the caveman's discovery of fire'.[46] Since this arbitration is discussed at length in Chapter 13 of this volume,[47] I will limit the discussion in this chapter to one specific aspect of *Lena Goldfields*, that is the tribunal's reliance on 'general principles' of

[43] See *Avena and Other Mexican Nationals (Mexico v United States) (Judgment)* [2004] ICJ Rep 12, 59 [119], 59–60 [121]–[122], as discussed in Desierto, n 42, 402.

[44] Desierto, n 42, 413–14.

[45] See, for example, *Khan Resources Incorporated v Government of Mongolia (Award on the Merits)*, PCA Case No 2011-09 (2 March 2015) [368]–[382]; *Mobil Investments Canada Inc. and Murphy Oil Corporation v Canada (Decision on Liability and Principles of Quantum (redacted))*, ICSID Case No ARB(AF)/07/4 (22 May 2012) [414]–[430]; *Unglaube v Republic of Costa Rica (Award)*, ICSID Case No ARB/08/1 (16 May 2012) [307]–[308]; *Bernardus Henricus Funnekotter v Republic of Zimbabwe (Award)*, ICSID Case No ARB/05/6 (22 April 2009) [108]–[112]; *LG&E Energy Corporation v Argentine Republic (Award)*, ICSID Case No ARB/02/1 (25 July 2007) [31]–[32]; *Siemens AG v Argentine Republic (Award)*, ICSID Case No ARB/02/8 (17 January 2007) [349]–[353]. For a more detailed discussion of the inapplicability of the *Chorzów* standard in investor-state arbitration, see section III of Desierto, n 42.

[46] This should be: Veeder, 'The Lena Goldfields Arbitration', n 8, 772.

[47] Andrea Leiter, Chapter 13 in this volume.

international law rather than on Soviet law as the law governing the concession agreement in question. The decision is often presented as a milestone in the development of international arbitration, as it broke new ground in clearly establishing the principle of unjust enrichment in international law.[48] It is on the basis of the unjust enrichment arising from the expropriation of Lena Goldfields' assets that the two arbitrators in the case awarded GBP 13 million in damages against the Soviet Union. They did so by referring to and applying 'general principles' of international law, and this is, in turn, why *Lena Goldfields* is recalled as the first case in which a contract was internationalised. According to some international investment law commentators, the case was 'historically noteworthy' not only because of its legal innovation but also because it was perceived as opposing the revolutionary sentiments which underpinned the Soviet decision to withdraw their arbitrator and to refuse to recognise the proceedings as valid.[49] A closer examination of the decision, however, would seem to indicate that the withdrawal of the Soviet arbitrator was technically and legally correct, while the invocation of 'general principles' of international law would appear rather questionable based on the standards prevailing at the time.

The contract between Lena Goldfields and the Soviet government was entered into in 1925 and concerned a concession to extract precious minerals and carry out extraction-related activities in the Lena–Vitim area.[50] Following the adoption of the Five-Year Plan in 1929, which inter alia sought to radically transform and collectivise the use of land, various parts of the Lena Goldfields' concession were withdrawn. During the night of 15 December 1929, various company sites were simultaneously raided, company documents seized and managers arrested on charges of counter-revolutionary activities and espionage.[51] In February 1930, Lena informed the government by telegram that the 'undue difficulties and interferences' encountered had made it impossible for it to continue

[48] See, for example, Sergei N Lebedev and Natalia G Doronina, 'Arbitrating Russian Concession Contracts: The Lena Goldfields Case' in Ulf Franke, Annette Magnusson and Joel Dahlquist (eds), *Arbitrating for Peace: How Arbitration Made a Difference* (Wolters Kluwer, 2016).

[49] T G Nelson, '"History Ain't Changed": Why Investor-State Arbitration Will Survive the "New Revolution"' in Michael Waibel et al. (eds), *The Backlash against International Investment Arbitration: Perceptions and Reality* (Kluwer Law International, 2010) 555, 557.

[50] Veeder, n 8, 758–9.

[51] Ibid.

performance of the concession agreement and that the company therefore sought the initiation of arbitration proceedings. The mandates of the Soviet arbitrator and counsel for the government, however, were withdrawn by the government and they did not attend the tribunal session convened in May 1930. The Soviet government claimed that the telegram sent by Lena represented a termination of the concession agreement in advance of its expiration date, following which the tribunal had 'lost its reason for existence'.[52] Under Article 86 of the concession agreement, in fact, termination of the concession 'before its time' could only occur by a decision of the arbitration court itself. The Soviet government also argued, seemingly with reason, that under the contract recourse to arbitration related to the 'interpretation or execution' of the contract, rather than to its 'suspension or annulment'[53] and that 'the arbitrators as a matter of law did not have the capacity to determine the extent of their own competence'.[54] The tribunal ignored the objections of the Soviet government and held that 'the jurisdiction of the court remain[ed] unaffected' because the concession was to be considered as still operative.[55] A settlement was eventually agreed in 1934 for a sum of GBP 3 million over twenty years, but payments were suspended in May 1940 following the start of World War II and the signing of the Treaty of Non-Aggression between Germany and the USSR.[56]

A key aspect of the *Lena Goldfields* arbitration, as briefly mentioned earlier in the chapter, is that the tribunal based its decision on the application of general principles of international law, and more specifically on the recognition of the applicability of the general principle of unjust enrichment. In doing so, rather than recognising a mere breach of the concession contract to grant damages, the tribunal relied on 'a right of action for what in French law is called *Enrichissement sans cause*'.[57] As the tribunal explained, this right of action 'arises where the defendant has in his possession money or money's worth of the plaintiff's to which he has no just right'.[58] The argument on unjust enrichment had been put

[52] As quoted from the arbitration award in Francis M Ssekandi, 'Contracts between a State and a Foreign Private Company: Reflections on the Effectiveness of the Arbitration Process' (1966) 2 *East African Law Journal* 281, 285.
[53] Ibid., 286.
[54] Ibid.
[55] Ibid.
[56] Veeder, n 46, 788.
[57] See text of the award as reproduced in Nussbaum, n 8, 51.
[58] Ibid.

forward by counsel for Lena Goldfields, who requested 'restitution to the company of the full present value of the company's properties, by which in the result the [Soviet] Government had become "unjustly enriched"'.[59] This request was accepted by the tribunal without further elaboration, and by simply accepting that the principle existed because, as put forward by Lena Goldfields' counsel, it existed in Russian national law, the German Civil Code (especially Article 812), Scottish law and in the English right of action 'for money had and received' on 'total failure of consideration', as confirmed by the House of Lords in the 1924 case of *Cantiere San Rocco SA v Clyde Shipbuilding Company*.[60] This reliance on unjust enrichment rather than on the relevant domestic law applicable to the concession contract was strongly criticised at the time.[61] The tribunal failed to consider the basis for finding a general principle of international law but merely endorsed the authorities put forward by Lena's counsel without analysing them. In doing so it relied on the circular argument that a duty to pay compensation arose from the fact that otherwise an unjustified enrichment would occur, thus contributing 'nothing but a great deal of confusion' to the discussion.[62] The tribunal had all the tools to rely on a breach of the concession contract, and in fact it explicitly referred to the terms of the special agreement contained in Schedule 3, 'whereby Lena guaranteed the Government against claims by the old companies mentioned in that schedule, which were expropriated in 1918–19, when the Government nationalized private mineral properties, or by their shareholders'.[63]

Thus, while the appropriateness of this reliance on unjust enrichment is not questioned by modern-day investment arbitrators who invoke *Lena Goldfields* as the leading case on unjust enrichment, the normativity of unjust enrichment was considered questionable in the 1970s, when scholars still observed that there was no consensus that the concept had developed into a general principle, or even a 'precept capable of guiding an international decision-maker'.[64] In 1974, for instance, Christoph

[59] Ibid.

[60] Ibid.

[61] Veeder, n 8, 766. As noted by Veeder at 767, the tribunal failed to 'justify the leap in logic from interpretation, performance and domestic matters governed by Soviet law to unjust enrichment governed by general principles of law'. See also Nussbaum, 'Arbitration Between the Lena Goldfields Ltd and the Soviet Government', n 8, 36.

[62] Christoph H Schreuer, 'Unjustified Enrichment in International Law' (1974) 22 *American Journal of Comparative Law* 281, 289.

[63] Text of the award as reproduced in annex in Nussbaum, n 8, 52.

[64] Schreuer, n 62.

Schreuer, who is widely recognised as one of the founding fathers of international investment law, argued that restitution for unjust enrichment, as awarded in *Lena Goldfields*, was 'hardly more than a decision-technique to be applied once the basic policy decisions have been made, and not a normative principle or general rule from which specific "correct" decisions can be logically derived'.[65] We should therefore be cautious about claims that the *Lena Goldfields* arbitration established the general principle of unjust enrichment, especially in the absence of further reasoning and elaborations by investment tribunals when they rely on general principles of international law. Such elaborations are necessary, as well as highly desirable, to identify the ways in which the tribunals come to their determinations and to clearly understand which elements of the case make relevant general principle applicable or, indeed, which legal precedents and developments testify to the existence of such principle.

12.4 The Hull Formula (26 March 1938)

The last legal event discussed in this chapter is the pronunciation of the Hull formula, which was transcribed by US Secretary of State Cornell Hull in his 1938 diplomatic memos in response to the Mexican nationalisations of 1917. The formula, which encapsulates the concept that compensation for expropriation should be 'prompt, adequate and effective', reads as follows:

> The Government of the United States merely adverts to a self-evident fact when it notes that the applicable precedents and recognized authorities on international law support its declaration that, under every rule of law and equity, no government is entitled to expropriate private property, for whatever purpose, without provision for prompt, adequate and effective payment therefor.[66]

My argument is that this widely known formula needs to be understood in the complex context of the oil expropriation of 1938 following the Mexican Revolution. What is key to our understanding of such context is that the oil fields and the mines operated by foreign investors were not expropriated during the period of 1910–20, when Mexico was basically

[65] Ibid., 301. See also Wolfgang Friedmann, *The Changing Structure of International Law* (Stevens & Sons, 1964) 206.

[66] As reproduced in 'Chapter XI – Aliens' (1942) 3 *Digest of International Law* 549, 658–9.

too big to invade but the United States continued to control the situation and protect foreign investors generally without resorting to the use of force.[67] The revolutionary factions knew that they would not be able to use the refineries, the mines and the smelters and that the sector relied heavily on the US market.[68] The situation, however, was very different in 1938, under President Cárdenas. Due to domestic opposition to foreign intervention and interference to protect oil investments abroad, by the late 1930s the US government had adopted a different approach to the protection of foreign investments.[69] Oil companies had also changed their approach to Mexican oil fields, which by the late 1930s were not as productive as they used to be. The interest of the oil companies was in sending a message that strike action would not be successful to militant workforces and governments in other Latin American countries (in particular Venezuela) in which they had more lucrative interests.[70] Oil companies and the US administration also never thought that Mexico would nationalise the oil industry.[71]

Yet, if we look at what prompted Cárdenas' decision to nationalise, we can see that what is often portrayed as an ideological struggle over the inherent meaning of property, and over the insistence or refusal to grant compensation for property expropriation, had at its roots deeper economic interests and political manoeuvrings. The latter undoubtedly resulted in struggles (also of a legal nature) over the issue of compensation for expropriation, but I would argue that these struggles only represented the tip of the iceberg and were mainly secondary to the economic interests at play. Essentially, Cárdenas' main interest was not in achieving a symbolic political victory but in keeping the oil-dependent

[67] Noel Maurer, *The Empire Trap: The Rise and Fall of US Intervention to Protect American Property Overseas, 1893–2013* (Princeton University Press, 2013) 137–47.

[68] Ibid.

[69] As noted by Maurer, oil production in Mexico and Venezuela was in direct competition with, and significantly cheaper than, domestic oil production from Texas, California, Oklahoma and other smaller oil fields throughout the United States. During the Depression the US administration felt the pressure of protectionist demands against the 'Big Four' oil companies that domestic smaller producers felt were receiving too much support by the low tariffs on imported oil. Therefore, new tax measures and voluntary quotas were introduced during the 1930s, although they did not really affect the big oil companies operating in Latin America (as they exported very little crude oil to the United States and had it refined in Mexico and mostly exported to Europe). See ibid., 269–70.

[70] Ibid., 289–91.

[71] Ibid., 276.

Mexican economy and tax revenue going. The oil expropriations thus appeared to be the easiest option to ensure that the oil fields and refineries remained open.[72] What is often presented as one of Cárdenas' most revolutionary actions was, in fact, not his primary political consideration. Interestingly, the oil expropriations also marked the beginning of his political decline. As explained in the remainder of this section, the expropriations irreversibly broke the already strained relationship between Cárdenas and the unions and, most importantly, between him and the cause of Mexican organised workers, his oldest allies. This weakening was in turn exploited by forces that began to mobilise against him, in preparation for a conservative return to power in Mexico.[73]

As mentioned above, by March 1938 the Roosevelt administration had little interest in protecting oil companies operating in Mexico and in the rest of Latin America. Nevertheless, after the expropriation took place, Roosevelt came under pressure by the oil lobby, which attempted - not too successfully – to mobilise public opinion by portraying the expropriation as an assault on American interests and as a series of 'terrorist' incidents aimed at Americans.[74] Most importantly, the economic dimension of the expropriation profoundly influenced Cárdenas' decisions during the labour dispute and after the expropriation. This economic dimension needs to be further analysed and understood in order to contextualise the US response and the related proclamation of the Hull formula. By the end of the 1930s, the Mexican oil industry was no longer as lucrative as it used to be and the oil unions were increasingly militant in pursuing job security, rather than merely wage increases. While the oil companies and the unions were thus on a collision course,[75] Cárdenas' aim was to ensure the oil industry remained open and to keep the Mexican economy going, because of the country's high dependence on oil tax revenues. Cárdenas' decision to nationalise, therefore, although presented and celebrated as a national triumph against the capitalist oppressors and as a 'responsibility' that the nation would face with collective sacrifice,[76] had the specific purpose of breaking the strike and

[72] Ibid., 278.

[73] Alan Knight, 'The Politics of the Expropriations' in Jonathan C Brown and Alan Knight (eds), *The Mexican Petroleum Industry in the Twentieth Century* (University of Texas Press, 1992) 90, 117.

[74] Maurer, *The Empire Trap*, n 67, 279.

[75] Ibid., 278.

[76] Knight, n 73, 110.

ensuring the continuation of oil production. The decision can be best understood as a culmination of many years of labour disputes, including various violent strikes that affected the Mexican oil refineries from 1915 to 1924 and into the 1930s. The response to the strikes often saw the oil companies and the Mexican government united in trying to mediate with the unions and stop the strikes.[77]

The final wave of strikes occurred in 1934–5, but given the low productivity of the Mexican fields the companies threatened to close their facilities and refused to reach a compromise with the oil unions, which by then had united into the Sindacato de Trabajadores Petroleros de la Republica Mexicana (STPRM). The dispute escalated throughout 1936 when the STPRM demanded an increase in wages, paid holidays, health insurance and severance pay, as well as control over hiring and firing decisions – demands that were rejected by the oil companies. Cárdenas intervened and, in an attempt to encourage a compromise, appointed a commission to look into the oil companies' finances. The commission, however, found that the oil companies could indeed afford to meet the demands of the workers.[78] This outcome triggered a series of strikes without union authorisation; the strikes were condemned by Cárdenas, who ordered the workers to return to work. The strikes were suspended only when a compromise was reached on lost wages and other benefits.[79] In the meantime, in December 1937, the Federal Labour Court (Junta Federal de Conciliación y Arbitraje) published its decision on the union demands, agreeing with the union with regard to the USD 7.3 million requested but allowing the companies to reduce their personnel, based on certain criteria of seniority and assured contributions.[80] Needless to say, the companies appealed the decision, but this appeal was immediately denied by the Federal Labour Board, and upheld by the

[77] See for example, Maurer, *The Empire Trap*, n 67, 147, where the author explains why the oil industry was not expropriated in 1914, when all revolutionary factions 'understood that if they seized the oil fields they would enter an unwinnable conflict with the United States'. At 271, the author also details how a successful strike action against the oil company Mexican Eagle in 1924, which achieved 'an eight-hour workday and the first collective bargaining agreement in the history of the Mexican industry', was followed by 'a more determined response from the companies, *with the support of the Mexican government*' (emphasis added).

[78] Ibid., 273.

[79] Ibid.

[80] The demands of the Mexican oil workers' union were based on wage increases, overtime, holidays, vacations, saving funds, medical services, housing benefits and other services and benefits that had not been provided to the workers. See ibid., 274, table 7.4.

Supreme Court in March 1938.[81] The situation then deteriorated when, following the rejected appeal the companies refused to comply with the decision, the Federal Labour Board suspended all contracts and the workers began to seize control of the pipelines and shut down the oil facilities. At this point Cárdenas, fearing the collapse of the most important sector of the Mexican economy, reached the decision to expropriate the oil companies on 18 March 1938, placing them under the control of the state-owned Petróleos de México ('Pemex'). Following nationalisation of the industry, he ordered the workers to suspend all strikes.[82]

Seen from the perspective of the economic dimension of the expropriation: 'Nationalization was the easiest way to ensure that the industry would remain open – the political benefit was merely icing on the cake'.[83] The nationalisation of the Mexican oil fields, therefore, although considered by many as bringing to life the promises of Article 27 of the Mexican Constitution, was far from the revolutionary victory that many historians have depicted as 'dealing a blow to imperialism, marking a fresh revolutionary conquest'.[84] Similarly, the Hull formula, which was seen as the leading strategy deployed by the US administration to defend the inherent meaning of private property following Cárdenas' nationalisation of the oil industry, was in fact only a mere tool in a series of US responses to the oil expropriations. In the aftermath of the nationalisation, US oil companies tried to push the US government into protecting their property. A private memorandum of 28 March 1938 from US Secretary of State Cordell Hull to the Mexican government, in which he demanded 'fair, assured and effective compensation' was leaked to the press in an attempt to tie the hands of the US administration,[85] which was instead trying to keep the negotiations fairly confidential and low-key. Cárdenas, on the other hand, had already promised compensation to the oil companies and ruled out the possibility of any further strike action in the now nationalised oil fields, thus breaking any link that might have remained between his government and the revolutionary cause of the striking workers.[86] In light of the above, claims like the one by Katzarov that the nationalisations of property that followed the Russian and

[81] Ibid., 274–5.
[82] Ibid., 275.
[83] Ibid.
[84] Knight, n 73, 103.
[85] Maurer, *The Empire Trap*, n 67, 279.
[86] Knight, n 73, 105.

Mexican revolutions were underpinned by 'the same ideological motives, namely the desire to implement the long maturing principles of the transformation of property' might not fully reflect the political and economic interests that were clearly at stake when the Mexican oil expropriations occurred.[87] As demonstrated in this chapter, it is essential to have a more nuanced understanding of the events that prompted specific legal interventions. Although the oil expropriation accelerated the shift to a more conservative transition post-Cárdenas,[88] his prestige and popularity reached their peak. The Hull formula, on the other hand, is often presented as a demonstration of US power opposing the oil expropriations,[89] but given the various factors that influenced the settlement with the oil industry, this might not entirely be the case. Consequently, the insistence in modern day investment arbitration on the primacy of this formula as the 'traditional' standard of compensation whenever an expropriation takes place, based on the strong political basis for its pronouncement, should also be questioned.[90]

An analysis of decisions made outside of investor-state arbitration, especially by the International Court of Justice and by the Iran–US claims tribunal,[91] on the matter of expropriation of aliens' property also indicates that the standard of compensation set in the Hull formula does not find firm support in international law, except perhaps in circumstances where there was a prior finding of illegality in the expropriation of

87 Konstantin Katzarov, *The Theory of Nationalisation* (Martinus Nijhoff, 1964) 34.

88 Knight, n 73, 116–17.

89 Paul Peters, 'Recent Developments in Expropriation Clauses of Asian Investment Treaties' (1995) 5 *Asian Yearbook of International Law* 45, 71–3; Rajesh Babu, 'Changing Trajectories of Investment Protection in India: An Analysis of Compensation for Expropriation' (2014) 6 *Trade Law and Development* 359, 378. See also Noel Maurer, 'The Empire Struck Back: Sanctions and Compensation in the Mexican Oil Expropriation of 1938' (2011) 71 *Journal of Economic History* 590, 606.

90 Much has been written in international investment law textbooks on the primary legal status of the Hull formula in relation to the Calvo Doctrine, developed by Carlos Calvo in 1868, demanding that foreign investors should bring their claims to local courts and tribunals, rather than resorting to international arbitration. See Brice Clagett, 'Just Compensation in International Law: The Issues Before the Iran-United States Claims Tribunal' in Richard Lillich (ed), *The Valuation of Nationalized Property in International Law* (University Press of Virginia, 1987) vol 4, 31. See also Clayton Koppes, 'The Good Neighbor Policy and the Nationalization of Mexican Oil: A Reinterpretation' (1982) 69 *Journal of American History* 62, 66–8. For a historical analysis of the Calvo Doctrine, see Juan Pablo Scarfi, *The Hidden History of International Law in the Americas: Empire and Legal Networks* (Oxford University Press, 2017) 69–70.

91 Samuel K B Asante, 'International Law and Foreign Investment: A Reappraisal' (1988) 37 *International and Comparative Law Quarterly* 588, 602–4.

property.[92] Post–World War II state practice also seems to indicate a trend to adopt ad hoc negotiated arrangements for compensation, such as lump-sum agreements guided by non-judicial considerations, rather than 'prompt, adequate and effective' compensation à la Hull. According to Asante, however, the tendency among international investment law scholars and commentators is to look primarily at international investment agreements as evidence of state practice, ignoring decisions from other courts and tribunals, in order to celebrate so-called traditional principles.[93]

12.5 Conclusion

In this chapter I focused on three key legal interventions that were developed during the 1920s and 1930s in the aftermath of the revolutionary events of 1917 and are still invoked in legal debates surrounding the law of expropriation. As explained throughout the chapter, these legal interventions, and the doctrines and principles that they engendered, still hold significance in investor-state arbitration, as they are systematically referred to in legal reasoning presented by counsel and in awards issued by arbitrators. As such, they continue to shape and influence the legal decisions of international arbitration tribunals. The historical analysis presented in this chapter, however, helps us illuminate the way in which investor-state disputes remain ultimately profoundly political, and show that investor-state arbitration is used to shift these disputes to another – equally political and equally charged – locale, despite claims of investment tribunals' neutrality. Doctrines and principles that are systematically invoked in investor-state arbitration and presented as 'traditional' standards have, as evidenced in this chapter, a very specific pedigree, making their transferability to modern investor-state arbitration difficult, and all too often inappropriate. Rarely do the claims presented in investor-state arbitration threaten international peace and security, for instance, or the standards invoked appear uncontestably appropriate in the context of the facts examined by the tribunals.

Most importantly, opinions on the principle of compensation for expropriation remain deeply divided. While it is indeed generally recognised that there is a duty to pay compensation for expropriation, the fundamental question as to whether such a duty is a *condition* of the

[92] Ibid.
[93] Ibid., 607–8.

legality of an expropriation remains unanswered and highly controversial. In other words, is a failure to pay compensation (and/or to pay compensation according to certain 'traditional' standards) an element that can render the expropriation illegal as such, or is something more required? These questions continue to characterise the debate surrounding the protection of foreign investment, ultimately bringing into question the legitimacy of investor-state arbitration and of international investment law. With this chapter I set out to contribute to this debate, challenging the transferability of so-called traditional doctrines and principles to investor-state arbitration, given their particular historical context and their political-economic specificity.

The first of the two main arguments advanced in this chapter, therefore, is that international investment law does not depoliticise investor-state disputes, despite various claims to the contrary. The analysis of the decision on the expropriation of the factory at Chorzów (1927), of the *Lena Goldfields* arbitration (1930) and of the US pronouncement of the Hull formula (1938) as a standard of compensation indicates that existing claims that investor-state arbitration effectively avoids political interference by the home states cannot be substantiated. As stated at the beginning of this chapter, and as demonstrated throughout its analysis, the depoliticisation that takes place in international investment law is better understood as a set of processes aimed at 'remov[ing] or displac [ing] the potential for choice, collective agency, and deliberation around a particular political issue'.[94] The three legal interventions analysed in this chapter were all related to highly politicised decisions, linked to the revolutionary events that characterised 1917 and the years that followed. Thus, because international investment law does not depoliticise investor-state disputes but merely transfers them to a preferred decision-making setting, I have also argued that the systematic invocation in investor-state arbitration of the Chorzów standard of compensation, of the doctrine of unjust enrichment and of the Hull formula needs to be challenged. The study of the legal interventions that followed the revolutionary events of 1917 enables us to make visible the political and economic reasoning that underpinned these legal doctrines and that are still deployed in contemporary international investment tribunals, when arbitrators are called to ascertain whether an expropriation has occurred and to determine the way in which such compensation should

[94] Fawcett et al., n 6, 5.

be paid. The three 'traditional' standards discussed in this chapter are aimed at asserting in international law an obligation to compensate (and to compensate in a certain specific way) for the expropriation of alien property, and all three are often considered as being unequivocal and uncontroversial by investment tribunals. As evidenced in this contribution, however, these standards remain highly contested and should, therefore, be understood within the historically contingent settings that engendered them. They continue to reflect contrasting political and economic conceptualisations of power, intervention and international law – tensions from the revolutionary events of 1917 that continue to reverberate.

13

Contestations over Legal Authority

The Lena Goldfields Arbitration 1930

ANDREA LEITER*

The Russian Delegation must call attention to the fact that the trial of disputes of this kind [arbitration over nationalisations] will inevitably end in opposing to one another two forms of property, whose antagonism assumes today for the first time in history, a real and practical character. In such circumstances there can be no question of an impartial super-arbiter.

Soviet delegate Georgy Chicherin at the Genoa Conference 1922[1]

13.1 Introduction

The socialist revolution in Russia introduced large-scale nationalisations and land reforms in order to empower the peasantry and the proletariat with a vision of establishing the 'first worker's state'.[2] A key instrument in this undertaking was the nationalisation of private property, a transformation that was legal in nature. Indeed, as Scott Newton put it: 'the elimination of private ownership of the means of production remains a breathtaking and unexampled demonstration of the puissance of law'.[3]

When Soviet Russia was losing the support of its population over famine and hardship in the transition from a war economy to the proclaimed socialist state in the early 1920s, Lenin introduced the New Economic Policy. This invited European capital for the purpose of restoring large-scale industry as quickly as possible.[4] Concession agreements granting foreign companies the right to operate certain businesses in return for a share in the profits for the state were one of the

* Assistant Professor at the Amsterdam Center for International Law.

1 Jane Degras (ed), *Soviet Documents on Foreign Policy 1917–1924* (Oxford University Press, 1951) vol 3, 316.

2 Scott Newton, *Law and the Making of the Soviet World* (Routledge, 2014) 33.

3 Ibid., 12.

4 V I Lenin, *Lenin: Collected Works* (Progress Publishers, 1965) vol 32, 407.

cornerstones of this initiative. Against the criticism that these measures meant a return to capitalism, Lenin held that this was 'state capitalism': a 'capitalism under the control and surveillance of the state'.[5] These concession agreements and the disputes resulting from them became emblematic of the debate over the extent of authority the state should have over economic relations. Where socialist visions advanced state planning, liberal visions defaulted to market mechanisms. The main argument of this chapter is that these two default positions were not mediated through legal proceedings but resulted in a contestation over the site of legal authority. Where the socialist state asserted domestic legal authority, foreign companies and governments invoked the international legal order. Consequently, legal authority and the definition of lawfulness emerge as one of the main sites of contestation to the revolutionary changes in the international arena.

The story of the concession for the exploration of goldmines in Siberia, concluded between the British company Lena Goldfields and the Union of Soviet Socialist Republics (Soviet Union) in 1925, serves as a window into this contestation. The resulting arbitration from 1930, the so-called Lena Goldfields Arbitration,[6] is the only international arbitration in which the Soviet Union ever participated. It allows me to explore the role of arbitral proceedings in contested visions of state and market. In order to be functional on its own terms, the arbitration proceeding had to claim to occupy a meta-position that could do justice to the situation regardless of the underlying assumptions of the actors. It presumed a certain degree of shared expectations that were necessary for the functioning of the proceedings and the acceptance of its findings. By reverse-engineering the events of the arbitration, I try to undo the perceived consensus and uncover the modes of assertion of authority and the points of disagreement.

[5] Ibid., 296–7.

[6] *Lena Goldfields v Soviet Government (Award)* (2 September 1930), English version, as reproduced in Arthur Nussbaum 'Arbitration between the Lena Goldfields Ltd and the Soviet Government' (1950) 36 *Cornell Law Quarterly* 31. The English version is excerpted, but there is a complete German version, *Schiedsgerichtssache zwischen Lena Goldfields Co Ltd und der Regierung der UdSSR, Schiedsspruch vom 2 September 1930*, which can be found at Translex.org with the Document ID 261300: www.trans-lex.org/261300. See also 'The Lena Goldfields Arbitration' (1929–30) 5 *Annual Digest of Public International Law Cases* 3, 426 (cases nos 1 and 258).The arbitration is exceptionally well documented, since the arbitration hearings were open to the public and consequently almost entirely reproduced in *The Economist* and *The Times*.

The chapter will proceed in two parts. The first part contextualises the arbitration in its historic setting. The second part analyses the role of legal forms as attempts at mediating the contesting perspectives and techniques of assertion of authority deployed within the arbitration. Ultimately, it is precisely not the mediation of interest that brings the proceedings to a conclusion but the location of legal authority outside the nation state and thus outside the authority of Soviet law. In particular, I trace this process through the introduction of the legal form Kompetenz-Kompetenz, as well as the invocation of general principles of law as contained in Article 38 of the Statute of the Permanent Court of Justice as substantive law.

13.2 Concession Agreements as Compromise

13.2.1 Private Property and Debt

One way of understanding the political and economic stakes of the concession granted to Lena Goldfields is to look at the period that lies between the nationalisation of the gold mines in 1920 and the signing of the concession agreement in 1925. During this period, the Soviet government, Western governments and private enterprises were considering various strategies for reorganising economic ties.[7] The point of disagreement lay precisely in the question of the limits of state authority. Western governments insisted that the new Soviet government had to accept two rights claims. The first concerned Soviet acceptance of the public debt, including of the tsarist regime.[8] Shortly after its coming to power on 3 February 1918, the new Soviet government had issued a decree annulling all state debts incurred by the tsarist and provisional governments.[9] The Allies renounced the decree as one 'shaking the very foundations of the law of nations'[10] and thereby appealed to an established body of law preceding the Soviet state as the basis for the obligation. The second condition was aimed at returning private property confiscated after the

[7] A detailed account of the complicated relationships between the government and corporate actors can be found in Thomas S Martin, 'The Urquhart Concession and Anglo–Soviet Relations, 1921–1922' (1972) 20 *Jahrbücher für Geschichte Osteuropas* 551.

[8] The overall foreign debt was considered to amount to 13.832 million roubles: James Bunyan and H H Fisher, *The Bolshevik Revolution, 1917–1918: Documents and Materials* (Stanford University Press, 1934) 603.

[9] Stephen White, *The Origins of Detente: The Genoa Conference and Soviet–Western Relations, 1921–1922* (Cambridge University Press, 2002) 26.

[10] Bunyan and Fisher, n 8, 604.

revolution, a position communicated in a joint note by the Allied powers to the Soviet foreign ministry on 15 February 1918.[11] The protesting diplomats declared that their governments considered the decrees confiscating private property to be 'non-existent' and that they 'reserve[d] the right to demand firmly that compensation be rendered for all damage and all losses which the operation of these decrees may cause to foreign states in general and to their subjects living in Russia in particular'.[12] The Soviet government refused to accept either of these conditions. This refusal needs to be understood as part of the attempt to reinvent the relationship between workers, the state and the economy. The Soviet government did not perceive itself as a successor taking over an existing state machinery but rather the inventor of 'the first worker's state'.[13] As such, it saw itself as an exception in the landscape of European states and consequently could not be bound by any set of pre-established norms.

Despite some differences between the Allied powers,[14] there was a general understanding that the problems with the Soviet government should be resolved in an international setting to prevent the weakening of the joint economic and political strength of the Allies.[15] Given that neither the Soviet Union nor the United States were members of the League of Nations, British Prime Minister Lloyd George suggested a meeting outside the auspices of the League. The Genoa and Hague Conferences of 1922 were the result of this effort. Falling back on the above-mentioned preconditions, in a preparatory meeting for the Genoa Conference in Cannes on 6 January 1922, the Allied powers drafted the so-called Cannes Resolutions.[16] The articles reflected the tension between the unconditional commitment to sovereign equality and the request of the acceptance of sovereign debts and private claims of restitution as an

[11] White, n 9, 26.

[12] Bunyan and Fisher, n 8, 604.

[13] Newton, n 2, 33.

[14] Even though France and Britain held the largest amounts of Russian foreign debt in 1922, 43 per cent and 33 per cent respectively, three-quarters of British debt was held by the government, whereas in the French case, this same amount was owed to private individuals. This difference allowed the British government more political space to manoeuvre negotiations and led to disagreements between the French and British governments: White, n 9, 27.

[15] Carole Fink, *The Genoa Conference: European Diplomacy, 1921–1922* (Syracuse University Press, 1993) 27*ff*.

[16] Supreme Council of the Allied Powers, *Resolutions Adopted by the Supreme Council at Cannes, January 1922, as the Basis of the Genoa Conference* (His Majesty's Stationery Office, 1922). The full text reads as follows:

international legal obligation. The first article stipulated that 'nations can claim no right to dictate to each other regarding the principles on which they are to regulate their system of ownership, internal economy and government'. Notably, the stipulation referred to 'internal' economy, already anticipating the limitation of the clause in the following paragraphs. Even though there was an acknowledgment of the freedom to choose a system of property, any system had to ensure that the 'property [of foreign investors] and their rights will be respected'. Thus, sovereign decision-making was limited by an imposed international legal order defining what it means to respect property and rights. The third paragraph in the Cannes Resolutions explicitly demanded the recognition of public debt and compensation for nationalisations. More importantly, an 'impartial' juridical system was supposed to protect the sanctity of contract. Impartial in this context meant that the state's prerogative to define rights and obligations stemming from contracts was limited by an outside understanding. The last stipulation encapsulates the bargain the Allied powers intended to strike. They were willing to offer de jure recognition of the Soviet government if the Soviets were willing to accept the Cannes Resolutions.

1. Nations can claim no right to dictate to each other regarding the principles on which they are to regulate their system of ownership, internal economy and government. It is for every nation itself to choose the system which it prefers in this respect.
2. Before, however, foreign capital can be made available to assist a country, foreign investors must be assured that their property and their rights will be respected and the fruits of their enterprise secured to them.
3. The sense of security cannot be re-established, unless the Governments of countries desiring foreign credit freely undertake –
   (a) That they will recognise all public debts which have been or will be undertaken or guaranteed by the State, by municipalities, or by other public bodies, as well as the obligation to restore or compensate all foreign interests for loss or damage caused to them when property has been confiscated or withheld.
   (b) That they will establish a legal and juridical system which sanctions and enforces commercial and other contracts with impartiality.
4. An adequate means of exchange must be available, and, generally there must be financial and currency conditions which offer sufficient security for trade.
5. All nations should undertake to refrain from propaganda subversive of order and the established political system in other countries than their own.
6. All countries should join an undertaking to refrain from aggression against their neighbours.

If, in order to secure the conditions necessary for the development of the trade in Russia the Russian Government demands official recognition, the Allied Powers will be prepared to accord such recognition only if the Russian Government accepts the foregoing stipulations.

Recognition was important for the Soviets in order to acquire the foreign capital necessary to foster its damaged economy. Furthermore, it was a precondition for participating in the various peace conferences convened after World War I, in which the new world order was negotiated. The catch attached to the recognition was the acceptance of a limitation of sovereign decision-making in the economic sphere. This last condition sat uncomfortably with the Soviet delegation's own non-negotiable principles. The chief Soviet delegate to the Genoa Conference, Georgy Chicherin, summarised those principles as respect for Soviet sovereignty, unconditional acceptance of the social achievements of the revolution and exclusive Soviet control over the economic system.[17] In Chicherin's terms, the question was how a temporary collaboration between two different systems of property could be designed.[18] The Soviet delegation argued that even if it were to accept the Allied claims on compensation, it would make counterclaims on behalf of its own population due to damages incurred during the foreign intervention and the civil war.[19] The respective expectations were hard to square and the crucial line of contestation concerned the quest for authority over the economic sphere. The Genoa Conference was held between 10 April and 19 May 1922 but ultimately failed to produce an agreement due to these and other tensions and left the question of the reconstruction of trade relations without a formal solution.[20]

What is important to note is that the Allied governments represented their stipulations as 'conditions upon which every *civilised* Government conducted its affairs'.[21] The term 'civilised' is a marker of racialised hierarchy in international law, but as Tzouvala argues, it is also a concept with a 'materialist transformative dimension' that played a significant role in the 'diffusion of capitalist relations of production'.[22] A fundamental part of the premise was an institutional transformation inscribing guarantees for property and commerce, particularly in conformity with international law.[23] Tzouvala's insistence on the

[17] White, n 9, 120.

[18] Ibid., 134.

[19] Ibid., 137.

[20] For a detailed account of the various complications and causes for the failure of the Genoa Conference, see generally White, n 9.

[21] Ibid., 64 (emphasis added).

[22] Konstantina Tzouvala, 'Letters of Blood and Fire: A Socio-Economic History of International Law' (PhD dissertation, Durham University, 2016) 37.

[23] Ibid., 44.

institutional rather than cultural aspect of the standard bears much explanatory value for the Soviet Revolution that, by its own claim, was directed at a transformation of the capitalist relations of production. The Allied insistence on sanctity of contract and repayment of debts as an expression of 'civilised' relations or as the 'foundations of the law of nations' shows the close connection between the international legal order and liberal economics. The creation of a legal framework regulating concession agreements became one of the most important means of implementing an international legal order shielding parts of the economy from sovereign decision-making.

13.2.2 Concessions for the Private Sector

One of the most important parts of Lenin's proclaimed New Economic Policy, officially adopted at the tenth Congress of the All-Russian Communist Party in May 1921, was the decree on concession agreements.[24] The decision received great criticism of various kinds, but Lenin insisted that 'we cannot seriously entertain the idea of an immediate improvement of the economic situation, unless we operate a policy of concessions'.[25] The goal of the decree was to attract foreign capital into the resource sector to enable large-scale production based on the latest technology in a short amount of time.[26] The concession policy was criticised for re-establishing capitalist modes of production by reintroducing rights titles. Scott Newton observes: 'As a trained lawyer, he [Lenin] recognised that the restoration of private trade would demand the restoration of private right: it was a banal syllogism'.[27] Lenin's argument in defence of the policy revolved around two fundamental ideas. The first was the structure of ownership and the second was a general functionalist understanding of law. For Lenin the concession was 'something in the nature of a contract of lease'[28] whereby 'the capitalist becomes, for a specified period, the lessee of a certain part of state property under a contract, but he does not become the owner. The state remains the owner'.[29] Thus, the construction of the concession contract was

[24] Lenin, n 4, 399–437.
[25] Ibid., 301.
[26] Ibid., 345–6.
[27] Newton, n 2, 75.
[28] Lenin, n 4, 345–6.
[29] Ibid., 368.

embedded in the conventional logic of civil law, but state capitalism meant that ownership could be held only by the state. The contours of this ownership, however, were determined by the theoretical position that law is supposed to further socialist purposes. This instrumentalisation can also be seen in the temporal horizon of the validity of the legal regime: 'Far from being imagined as timeless and perfected [the Soviet civil state] was created mortal, destined in the fullness of time to be superseded'.[30] Thus, the Soviet conception of the subordination of the role of law to the achievement of a classless society was embedded in state socialism from the very beginning. This understanding also extended to concessionary policy. Lenin argued that it was one of the attractive features of concession agreements, that 'the annulment of an agreement means a sudden rupture of the practical relations of economic alliance, or economic coexistence, with the capitalist'.[31] State capitalism was only a stage on the path to socialism, and concession agreements were a tool that could and should be left behind when the time was ripe.[32] As we will see in the following, this understanding is at odds with the liberal conception of timeless validity of the sanctity of contract and acquired rights. Before moving to the analysis of the difference between these approaches, I will lay out the general setting in which concession agreements were negotiated and, in particular, how the Lena Goldfields concession came into being.

13.2.3 *The Lena Agreement*

Against the background of the failure of the international solution and Lenin's promulgation of state capitalism, private initiatives were of increased importance and the negotiation of concession agreements with the Soviet government became an attractive option.[33] An important and influential organisation in this regard was the Association of British Creditors of Russia, counting in its ranks thirteen members of Parliament, forty company directors and a wide range of industrial representatives.[34] The president of this organisation from 1921 onwards was Leslie Urquhart, chairman of a mining and metallurgy company in

30 Newton, n 2, 75.
31 Lenin, n 4, 348.
32 Ibid.
33 Martin, n 7, 552.
34 Ibid., 553.

Russia which was nationalised after the revolution. Urquhart's tactics for regaining his economic assets can be seen as a blueprint for the dealings of the Lena Goldfields Company. As early as 9 September 1922, Urquhart signed a concession agreement with the Soviet Commissar of Foreign Trade that was intended to recover the companies' losses from nationalisation.[35] The Urquhart concession was never ratified by the Soviet Council of People's Commissars, apparently mainly because of objections from Lenin.[36] Despite that failure, the idea of recovery of assets through concession agreements as proposed by Urquhart was in the background of Lena's concession agreement. The concessionary policy saw the Soviets grant sixteen concessions to foreign companies between 1924 and 1928 – seven in mining, four in metallurgy and five in machine building. Payments to the Soviet state increased in the same period from 6.8 million to 16 million roubles, and concessions became an integral part of Soviet industry.[37]

The story of the Lena Goldfields concession begins before the revolution and was an attempt at recovering lost assets through the Soviet concessionary policy. Lena Goldfields was a British company incorporated in London in 1908 in order to purchase 75 per cent of the shares of the Russian Lenskoie Company, established in 1855. Lenskoie was by far the largest gold-mining company in the Russian Empire and controlled an area of approximately 46,000 acres in Eastern Siberia.[38] In tsarist Russia, it was not possible for a foreign company to acquire property but only to hold shares in operating companies.[39] Consequently, the

[35] Ibid., 552. The story of the economic, political and personal relationship of these two men allows for a deep and nuanced understanding of the complicated negotiations that were held on several fronts.

[36] Ibid., 556*ff.*

[37] Monica von Schulze, 'Die Lage der Arbeiter und der Klassenkampf in Kapitalistischen Betrieben der Sowjetunion in der Periode der Neuen Ökonomischen Politik' (1997) 18 *Jahrbuch für Wirtschaftsgeschichte/Economic History Yearbook* 9. The author refers to Statističeskij Spravočnik SSSR 1927 as the source of these numbers, which I am unable to verify.

[38] 'Lena Goldfields, Limited – Report of the Statutory Meeting held on 4 November 1908', *The Economist* (7 November 1908). *The Economist* printed reports of the annual general meetings of the company from the first one in 1909 until its ninth ordinary general meeting in 1919.

[39] 'The Lena Gold Mines and Anglo-Russian Companies', *The Economist* (18 May 1912) 1054. 1912 was also the year of the infamous Lena Massacre in which workers protested against the poor working conditions in the mine and were brutally suppressed by the military, with a death toll of over 200. This brutal event has little to do with the later arbitration, but it is worthwhile mentioning that the British shareholders refused any responsibility given that they were only shareholders and even went as far to denounce

nationalisation of the gold mines in 1920 affected the property of the Russian company Lenskoie, but the economic loss was greatest for Lena Goldfields since it held 75 per cent of the shares in Lenskoie.[40] Indeed, the concession agreement granted to Lena Goldfields was the company's attempt to broker a favourable deal in relation to losses incurred by the earlier nationalisation of its subsidiary Lenskoie without making an actual claim for compensation. The proposition followed Urquhart's earlier attempt at receiving an extensively generous concession in lieu of official compensation. The key figure in the negotiation of Lena's agreement was Alexander Malozemoff, the former general manager of Lenskoie, who was in charge of the company at the time of the nationalisation in 1920. It was Malozemoff who reinitiated the mining enterprise that he then led as company director from 1925 to 1930.[41] Upon ratification of the concession agreement, Lena waived all its claims against the Soviet government and indemnified the government against claims from its Russian subsidiaries by acquiring all the shares of these companies.[42]

In light of this backstory, the Lena concession was a pragmatic solution to the incompatible positions that led to the failure of the Genoa Conference. It enabled the resumption of gold mining with the best technology available, while providing enough assurance to the private sector to invest capital in the Soviet Union. Instead of acknowledging a duty to compensate for nationalisation, the Soviet government offered a profitable concession agreement, conditional upon a waiver of all compensation claims resulting from nationalisation. That the concession agreement was considered profitable enough to satisfy the company is evidenced by a statement from the chairman of the Lena company, Herbert Guedella, at the twelfth general meeting on 15 January 1926:

> We have been criticised, but the criticism acknowledges that our case is not strictly analogous with others for not seeking compensation. After due

any harmful conditions in the mines: 'Lena Goldfields, Limited. The Strike – Report of the Annual General Meeting held on 3 December 1912', *The Economist* (7 December 1912) 1183.

40 Plato Malozemoff, son of the then general manager, Alexander Malozemoff, offers a comprehensive account of the battle for the takeover between the Bolsheviks and the White Army during the civil war: Plato Malozemoff, *A Life in Mining: Siberia to Chairman of Newmont Mining Corporation, 1909–1985: Oral History Transcript* (Regional Oral History Office, Bancroft Library, University of California, 1990) 28*ff*.

41 Ibid., 54*ff*.

42 V V Veeder, 'The Lena Goldfields Arbitration: The Historical Roots of Three Ideas' (1998) 47 *International and Comparative Law Quarterly* 747, 757.

> consideration we came to the conclusion that recognition of the present state of circumstances was to the best benefit of our shareholders. Additional properties have been included in the concession, so that, on a whole, we are entitled to consider that a fair bargain has been made.[43]

The actual agreement is an eighty-three-page document[44] covering all sorts of interests and contingencies and was negotiated over the course of two years.[45] The concession gave Lena the right to operate the former Lenskoie gold mines for a period of thirty years. In addition, the company acquired the rights to develop and work three additional mining sites – Sissert, Revda and Altai – for iron, copper, zinc, lead, silver and gold, as a going concern for a period of fifty years.[46] The drafter of the agreement can be assumed to be Dr Vladimir Robertovich Idelson, a Russian émigré in Britain escaping arrest after the Soviet revolution by fleeing to London in 1920.[47] He was also the lawyer Lena appointed as counsel in the arbitration in 1930 and played an important role in shaping the legal arguments that paved the way for the internationalisation of concession agreements.

13.3 The Arbitral Proceedings: Escaping Domestic Law

After five years of operation, Lena Goldfields sent a notice of arbitration to the Soviet government on 7 March 1930, claiming that it was impossible to commence its work.[48] An accurate account of the events leading

43 'Lena Goldfields, Limited. Resumption of Active Operations – Report of the 12th Ordinary General Meeting Held on 12 January 1926', *The Economist* (16 January 1926) 116.

44 The entirety of the concession agreement has not yet been discovered and thus this research is based on excerpts reprinted in *Materialien zur Frage der Zustaendigkeit des Schiedsgerichts in Sachen 'Lena Goldfields' – Union dSSR* (Hauptkonzessionskommittee des Rates der Volkskommissare der UdSSR, 1930) 37*ff* (containing Articles 75, 76, 80, 82, 83, 85, 86, 89, 90). References to the concession agreement are made in the award: see n 6. Finally, excerpts of the protocols of shareholder meetings of Lena reprinted in *The Economist* and in *The Times* offer an account of the contents of the concession agreement.

45 'Lena Goldfields. Negotiations with the Soviet Government. Concession for Working the Properties. Mr Guedella's Speech – On the Occasion of the Extraordinary General Meeting held on 30 July 1925', *The Times* (31 July 1925) 19.

46 'Lena Goldfields, Limited. Statement of the Board of Directors (16 May 1925)', *The Economist* (16 May 1925) 987.

47 Veeder notes this similarity in the wording of the Lena concession agreement and the Anglo–Iranian concession agreement of 1933 in Veeder, n 42, 769.

48 *Materialien zur Frage der Zustaendigkeit des Schiedsgerichts in Sachen 'Lena Goldfields' – Union dSSR*, n 44, 14.

up to the arbitration is difficult, particularly because the accounts by the company diverge strongly from the accounts of the government. Thus, instead of trying to recount the facts, to give some sense of the conflict I will rely on the claims made in the arbitration and the material provided by the parties. There were three major claims that informed the proceedings. Lena's claims against the government can be summarised in two major allegations. Lena contended, first, that the Soviet government had created conditions such that the performance of the contract became nearly impossible, and second, that Lena was consequently entitled to compensation.[49] The Soviet Union launched a counterclaim alleging non-performance of the contract on the part of Lena.

The establishment of the tribunal could be seen as an agreement or at least an attempt at an agreement about a fundamental conception of law. After all, the submission of both parties to a common authority indicates the acceptance of this authority by both sides. Recalling, however, the difference in the legal understanding between the functionalist Soviet view and the timeless liberal view, such agreement appears unlikely. Indeed, before the tribunal met for its first session, the Soviet Union withdrew its arbitrator and the arbitration proceeded as a truncated tribunal with only two arbitrators. Chicherin's statement from the Genoa Conference is prescient: 'the trial of disputes of this kind [arbitration over nationalisations] will inevitably end in opposing to one another two forms of property, whose antagonism assumes today for the first time in history, a real and practical character. In such circumstances there can be no question of an impartial super-arbiter'.[50] One issue was the contours of a property right held by the state under Soviet law. The purpose of the revolution was precisely a break with capitalist modes of production and thus liberal models of ownership. What then could serve as common ground for the interpretation of rights and obligations from a concession agreement? In the end, the remaining arbitrators, together with Lena's counsel Idelson, constructed an interpretation of both the events and the legal regime appropriate to govern them that hinged on the successful establishment of legal authority outside the nation state and in disregard of the Soviet revolution and of Soviet law. The conflict was not resolved by a ruling on substance but by establishing the right to define law outside and above the revolutionary realm.

[49] *Lena Goldfields v Soviet Government (Award)* (2 September 1930) 8.
[50] Degras, n 1, 316.

13.3.1 *The Establishment of the Tribunal and the Construction of Facts*

The composition of the tribunal is an important part of this story because it meant the installation of the 'super-arbiter', the authority to be accepted by both parties. The selection followed the formal appointment procedure as laid out in the concession agreement, and each side chose their nominee. The arbitrator on Lena's behalf was Sir Leslie Scott, while the Soviet government appointed Dr S B Chlenov.[51] Lena then made two suggestions for the head of the tribunal, but both were rejected.[52] In turn, Lena rejected the proposal made by the Soviets, a scientist by the name of Albert Einstein.[53] As a consequence, according to Article 90 of the concession agreement, the Soviet Union had to nominate six individuals from either the Freiberg University of Mining and Technology or the Royal High Technical School of Stockholm and submit a respective list to Lena. Lena chose the German professor of geology Otto Stutzer, and he became the head of the tribunal. Before Stutzer's appointment, but after the submission of the list, the Soviet government discovered that Stutzer had an unfavourable disposition towards the government.[54] After Lena appointed him, the Soviet government decided to withdraw their arbitrator. In the proceedings, the Soviets relied on a jurisdictional objection to the tribunal as such, rather than on the person of the arbitrator, so that Stutzer was never officially discussed.

Despite the Soviet withdrawal, the tribunal commenced the proceedings with the remaining two arbitrators as was provided for in Article 90(f) of the concession agreement. The absence of the Soviet arbitrator led to the establishment of the facts of the arbitration based solely on the evidence provided by Lena. Furthermore, the arbitration relied on 'procedural flexibility' regarding the rules of evidence.[55] The tribunal found that, since the Soviet government refused to cooperate, the tribunal was unable to attain from it the necessary evidence to ascertain the 'truth

[51] Both men had been working for their respective governments in prominent positions and were lawyers by discipline.

[52] 'Telegram to Lena 17 March 1930' in *Materialien zur Frage der Zuständigkeit des Schiedsgerichts in Sachen 'Lena Goldfields' – Union dSSR*, n 44, 23.

[53] Most likely, the rejection was simply a reaction to the earlier rejections by the Soviets: 'Telegram to Lena 21 March 1930' in *Materialien zur Frage der Zuständigkeit des Schiedsgerichts in Sachen 'Lena Goldfields' – Union dSSR*, n 44, 23.

[54] Kamenev wrote to the chairman of the Council of the People's Commissar that Stutzer had written a report 'in which he spoke in sharply negative terms about the situation in the USSR and our Five-Year-Plan': Kamenev quoted in Veeder, n 42, 775.

[55] Ibid., 753.

upon the issues before it'.[56] The jurisdictional objection was dismissed and the Soviet government's refusal to participate in the proceedings was considered a breach of contract and its duty to cooperate. The tribunal held that even though 'the Government has thus refused its assistance to the Court, it still remains bound by its obligations under the Concession Agreement', particularly by the arbitration clause and by the duty to 'present to the Court ... all the information necessary respecting the matter in dispute'.[57] As a consequence of this finding, it decided to allow 'second-best' evidence, as a substitute for documents and witnesses that were unavailable.[58] This second-best evidence rule meant that the tribunal did not require the adduction of primary evidence,[59] but instead relied on written and oral statements to reproduce the content of documents confiscated by the Soviet government.[60] Based on the evidence produced in the proceedings, the tribunal accepted the claimants' allegations of raids, arrests and show trials against Lena employees, as well as the withdrawal of construction material and resources necessary for the workings of the mines. The main witness for Lena was the former managing director Alexander Malozemoff, who was a known opponent of the revolution and socialism.[61] The tribunal's main position was that the introduction of the first Five-Year-Plan was a 'complete reversal' of the concessionary policy and rendered Lena's undertakings 'radically incongruous'.[62] Therefore, 'however obedient it [Lena] might be to the laws of the U.S.S.R., or however purely commercial and non-political it might be in its behaviour, as the Court finds that Lena in fact was', Lena came to be regarded as 'a capitalist outcast'.[63] The tribunal found that 'Lena in general duly carried out its obligations under the Concession Agreement, save in so far as it was directly or indirectly prevented by the Government or by subordinate authorities'.[64] It found that the breakdown of the commercial undertaking was exclusively caused by actions of the Soviet government required by the installation of the Five-Year-Plan.

56 *Lena Goldfields v Soviet Government (Award)* (2 September 1930) [15].
57 Ibid.
58 Ibid.
59 Ibid.
60 Veeder, n 42, 753.
61 Malozemoff's attitude is expressed in an interview his son gave about his experience of the revolution and the nationalisation of the Lena golf fields: Malozemoff, n 40, 27*ff*.
62 *Lena Goldfields v Soviet Government (Award)* (2 September 1930) [19].
63 Ibid.
64 Ibid. [20].

The tribunal awarded the company 13 million pounds sterling, comprising approximately 3.5 million in investments (according to the company's own calculations) and 9.5 million in lost profits.[65]

Two documents were published by the Soviet Union in 1930 that offered a counter-narrative to these facts. The first was an official publication by the Soviet Union's Main Concession Committee titled 'Documents concerning the Competence of the Arbitration Court set up in connection with the Questions outstanding between the Lena Goldfields Company Limited and the USSR' containing part of the correspondence between the government and the Lena Company between 1928 and 1930.[66] The correspondence was followed by opinions by two Soviet professors discussing the legal validity of the Soviet jurisdictional objection to the tribunal.[67] With regard to the economic situation, a document with the title 'The Financial and Economic Results of the Working of the Lena Goldfields Company Limited'[68] was published by Dr S A Bernstein under the instructions of the Politburo.[69] In Bernstein's account, the undertaking started failing in early 1928 when the company was unable to acquire the necessary capital to finance the expenditures agreed upon in the concession agreement.[70] According to his report, Lena failed to mine the amount of gold it had promised, as well as to develop the mining equipment as outlined.[71] He further alleged that from 1929 onwards the company was unable to pay appropriate royalties to the government and wages to the workers.[72] Bernstein concluded with a calculation of the overall indebtedness of the company both in the Soviet Union (15 million roubles) as well as abroad (1,666,000 pounds sterling) against the approximate value of its assets (17–18 million roubles) and found that the assets barely covered the debt incurred towards the Soviet government.[73] As a result, even if a tribunal

[65] Ibid. [26].

[66] The German version was used for this study: *Materialien zur Frage der Zustaendigkeit des Schiedsgerichts in Sachen 'Lena Goldfields' – Union dSSR*, n 44.

[67] Ibid., 45*ff*.

[68] S A Bernstein, *The Financial and Economic Results of the Working of the Lena Goldfields Company* (Blackfriars Press, 1930).

[69] Veeder, n 42, 755.

[70] Bernstein, n 68, 10.

[71] Ibid., 20.

[72] Ibid., 24.

[73] Ibid., 34–5.

were to find in Lena's favour, its losses could not be higher than 2 or 3 million roubles.

These two accounts show that there was substantial disagreement on the facts underlying the dispute. Bernstein's report was sent to the tribunal during the proceedings[74] but was not mentioned in the award. Instead, the tribunal based its decision on Lena's account of events. As a result, the tribunal held that it was 'satisfied that even if the Government case had been put and proved before it, whatever claims for damages could have been substantiated are amply covered by the very generous allowances in favour of the Government which the Court has made in the assessment of the amount due to Lena'.[75] If taken at face value, the numeric difference in the calculated damages would be 2–3 million roubles according to the Soviets, and 13 million pounds sterling according to the tribunal. It remains open to speculation how things could have developed had the Soviet government participated in the proceedings, and whether the tribunal would have established a different factual basis. Regardless of these speculations, what remains at the centre of the claim is that a change in policy in the Soviet Union was taken to have led to a breach of the concession agreement. Indeed, the tribunal held that the introduction of the Five-Year-Plan 'necessarily meant, when measured in terms of contractual obligation, the breach by the Government of many of the fundamental provisions, express and implied, of the Concession Agreement'.[76] At the heart of the dispute was a question of the relationship between the new Soviet law and the concession agreement and how this relationship was defined in legal terms. This in turn depended on who decides and according to what law. As we will see in the following, the problem was not framed in terms of competing property systems but in terms of jurisdiction, which carried with it implicit understandings of property rights.

13.3.2 *Jurisdictional Objection and Kompetenz-Kompetenz*

When the Soviets had agreed to the arbitral proceedings in March 1930, Lena was still operating the concession. However, at the end of April it withdrew all personnel and power of attorney of its representatives and declined further responsibility for the operations of the company in the

[74] Veeder, n 42, 756.

[75] *Lena Goldfields v Soviet Government (Award)* (2 September 1930) [20].

[76] Ibid. [19].

Soviet Union.[77] The Soviets based their jurisdictional objection on these events, which they called unilateral termination of the concession agreement. The Soviet argument went like this: the arbitral tribunal was established to decide the performance of the concession agreement and possible claims of damages resulting from a violation of the agreement.[78] The crucial legal argument for the Soviets was that the tribunal had never been asked to decide on the termination of the agreement.[79] Given that Lena Goldfields had unilaterally terminated the agreement after the tribunal was established, the tribunal had lost its subject matter: namely, the performance of the contract. The topic the tribunal would thus have to consider, according to the Soviets, was the termination of the concession agreement.[80] The Soviets argued that this was outside the original jurisdictional scope of the tribunal, since it was not part of the compromis establishing the tribunal. With this jurisdictional objection, the Soviets withdrew from the arbitration and suggested the establishment of a new arbitral tribunal with the jurisdictional scope to decide upon the damage claims and property relations that come with termination.[81]

In response to the Soviet objection, the tribunal followed the understanding and argument presented by the British counsel Idelson.[82] This position has been reproduced in almost all accounts of the Lena Goldfields Arbitration ever since.[83] Arthur Nussbaum, an American legal scholar who commented on the arbitration in 1950, described the argument as follows: 'an arbitration agreement loses its force if one of the parties (as alleged was done by Lena) rescinds the underlying contract'.[84] Thus, it was claimed that the Soviet Union had withdrawn its arbitrator on the basis that the concession agreement had ceased to exist through

[77] 'Telegram from Lena 29 April 1930' and 'Telegram from Lena 1 May 1930' in *Materialien zur Frage der Zustaendigkeit des Schiedsgerichts in Sachen 'Lena Goldfields' – Union dSSR*, n 44, 30–1.

[78] See notice of arbitration in 'Telegram from Lena 12 February 1930' in *Materialien zur Frage der Zustaendigkeit des Schiedsgerichts in Sachen 'Lena Goldfields' – Union dSSR* n 44, 21.

[79] Veeder, n 42, 782*ff*.

[80] 'Telegram from Lena 6 May 1930' in *Materialien zur Frage der Zustaendigkeit des Schiedsgerichts in Sachen 'Lena Goldfields' – Union dSSR*, n 44, 27–8.

[81] 'Telegram to Lena 5 May 1930' in *Materialien zur Frage der Zustaendigkeit des Schiedsgerichts in Sachen 'Lena Goldfields' – Union dSSR*, n 44, 31–2.

[82] *Lena Goldfields v Soviet Government (Award)* (2 September 1930) [9]–[11].

[83] An exception is the article by V V Veeder, in which he points out the misunderstanding but does not further inquire into its reasons and meaning: Veeder, n 42, 775–7.

[84] Nussbaum, n 6, 38.

the unilateral announcement of termination by Lena Goldfields.[85] The argument supposedly went as follows: since the concession agreement had ceased to exist, the basis for the establishment of the tribunal, namely Article 90 of the concession agreement, also ceased to exist and consequently the tribunal was without foundation. The Soviet argument was however not aiming at the dissolution of the agreement and therefore the dissolution of the arbitration clause Article 90 but instead at the jurisdictional scope agreed upon in the compromise. This misunderstanding had little significance for the arbitration at stake, but it has become the basis of a whole body of literature arguing for the survival of the arbitration clause independent of the agreement, a principle which has come to be known as 'separability'.[86] However, as Veeder expresses it: 'Thus, with regret, it must be concluded that the Lena case flies false colours on the doctrine of separability for which it is often cited'.[87]

What is of significance is that the jurisdictional objection raises the question of who can decide upon the jurisdiction of the tribunal. Or to put it differently: who has the competence to decide the question of whether or not the tribunal exceeded its powers? At the time of the arbitration, it was common in civil and commercial arbitration to refer a question of competence to the national courts, with the resulting possibility that the original decision rendered by the tribunal could be annulled.[88] In his commentary on the Lena Goldfields Arbitration in 1950 Nussbaum held that 'generally, in civil or commercial arbitration a dissenting party may turn to the ordinary law courts for a re-examination of the question of competence; the court, if it approves of the dissent, will then annul the arbitral proceedings and the award for excess of power'.[89]

85 'Telegram from Lena 29 April 1930' and 'Telegram from Lena 1 May 1930' in *Materialien zur Frage der Zustaendigkeit des Schiedsgerichts in Sachen 'Lena Goldfields' – Union dSSR*, n 44, 30–1.

86 Separability or severability of the arbitration clause means that an arbitration clause contained in a contract does not have to follow the contract. If a contract ceases to exist, the arbitration clause can be treated separately and can still serve as the basis for an arbitration. See, for example, Lawrence Atsegbua, 'International Arbitration of Oil Investment Disputes: The Severability Doctrine and Applicable Law Issues Revisited' (1993) 5 *African Journal for International and Comparative Law* 634.

87 Veeder, n 42, 785.

88 Nussbaum, n 6, 40–1. The application of domestic law to procedural questions was an international standard as expressed in the Geneva Protocol on Arbitration Clauses of 1923: *Protocol on Arbitration Clauses*, opened for signature 24 September 1923, 27 LNTS 157 (entered into force 28 July 1924).

89 Nussbaum, n 6, 40–1.

The *lex arbitri*, and thus the applicable procedural law in the Lena Goldfields Arbitration, was the British Arbitration Act of 1889 prescribing recourse to domestic courts for allegations of excess of power.[90] A Soviet court would have had to decide whether there was an excess of power in the Lena case and whether the tribunal would have to be reconstituted. According to British law at the time, an award lacking the signature of an arbitrator would have to be considered a nullity.[91] Instead of following this tradition, the tribunal resorted to an idea stemming from public international law, namely that of Kompetenz-Kompetenz, meaning the authority of the tribunal to decide upon its own jurisdiction.[92] The tribunal held that 'the jurisdiction of the Court remained unaffected' by the Soviet jurisdictional objection and that it 'accordingly dealt with the preliminary questions of procedure'.[93]

Within the field of public international law, the notion of Kompetenz-Kompetenz had its predecessors in state-to-state arbitration, most famously in the Alabama Arbitration between Great Britain and the United States in 1872.[94] The Hague Convention for the Pacific Settlement of International Disputes contained the principle in its Article 81,[95] and it was then enshrined in Article 36(4) of the Statute of the Permanent Court of Justice stipulating that 'in the event of a dispute as to whether the Court has jurisdiction the matter shall be settled by the decision of the Court'.[96] Even though the principle was widely accepted in international law at the time of the Lena Goldfields Arbitration,[97] the particular jurisdictional objection of 'excess of power' remained unsettled.[98] While some authors held that the court's competence should be unlimited, others argued that an excess of power would lead to the nullity of the

[90] W Outram Crewe (ed), *The Law of Arbitration; Being the Arbitration Act, 1889, with Notes of Statutes, Rules of Court, Forms and Cases, and an Index (1890)* (William Clowes and Sons, 2nd ed, 1898) ss 1, 4.

[91] Veeder, n 42, 753.

[92] Phillip Landolt, 'The Inconvenience of Principle: Separability and Kompetenz-Kompetenz' (2013) 30 *Journal of International Arbitration* 511, 513.

[93] *Lena Goldfields v Soviet Government (Award)* (2 September 1930) [11].

[94] Ibrahim F I Shihata, 'The Power of the International Court to Determine Its own Jurisdiction – Compétence de la compétence' (SJD dissertation, Harvard Law School, 1964) 28.

[95] Hersch Lauterpacht, *Private Law Sources and Analogies of International Law* (Longman, Green & Co, 1927) 209.

[96] For a detailed drafting history, see Shihata, n 94, 52*ff*.

[97] Shabtai Rosenne, *The Law and Practice of the International Court 1920–2005* (Brill, 4th ed, 2006) vol 2, 814.

[98] Shihata, n 94, 116*ff*.

decision.[99] Despite this debate, the majority of scholars in the 1960s found that a jurisdictional objection by one party should not alleviate the other party's duty to comply with the decision.[100] This is mainly due to the fact that the question rarely constituted a practical problem.[101]

The application of the principle of Kompetenz-Kompetenz in the Lena Goldfields Arbitration was highly inventive. First, it deviated from the established practice in commercial arbitration of referring the matter to a national court, in this case a Soviet court, and instead relied on a principle established in international law. Second, the objection based on the argument of an excess of power was also unresolved in the realm of public international law. Thus, even though the tribunal did not justify its decision and simply asserted that 'the jurisdiction of the Court remained unaffected',[102] this assertion allowed the tribunal to escape the Soviet courts and establish itself as autonomous proceeding in the international sphere. In this example we can see the highly political nature of questions of jurisdiction. As Rosenne puts it: 'The question whether and to what extent the Court has jurisdiction is frequently of political importance no less than the decision on the merits, if not more'.[103] The escape from Soviet law on the grounds of jurisdiction allowed the tribunal to uphold its liberal understanding of law.

13.3.3 General Principles as Applicable Law

As we saw, the application of rules of public international law to concession agreements in the 1930s was unconventional and inventive on both the procedural as well as the substantive level. Indeed, the Lena Goldfields Arbitration was hardly considered a matter of international law at the time of its conclusion. Hersch Lauterpacht only reluctantly included it in the *Annual Digest* of 1930.[104] He only did so because the award referenced '*general principles of law recognized by civilised nations*' as contained in Article 38 of the Statute of the Permanent Court of International Justice, and he considered that it stood 'half-way between international and municipal arbitrations'.[105] The Lena award is one of

[99] Ibid., 120.
[100] Ibid., 125.
[101] Ibid., 123.
[102] *Lena Goldfields v Soviet Government (Award)* (2 September 1930) [11].
[103] Rosenne, n 97, 803.
[104] 'The Lena Goldfields Arbitration' (1929–30) 5 *Annual Digest of Public International Law Cases* 3, 426 (cases nos 1 and 258).
[105] Ibid., 428, case no 258.

the first in a line of awards and concession agreements referencing general principles as applicable law.[106] Following Idelson's submission, the tribunal found that even though 'in regard to performances of the contract by both parties inside the U.S.S.R. Russian law was "the proper law of the contract" . . . for other purposes the general principles of law such as those recognized by Article 38 of the Statute of the Permanent Court of International Justice' were applicable.[107] The tribunal went on to hold that 'many terms of the contract contemplated the application of international rather than merely national principles of law'.[108]

The principle in question was that of unjust enrichment or, as it was called in the award, 'enrichissement sans cause', which 'arises where the defendant has in his possession money or money's worth of the plaintiffs to which he has no just right'.[109] Unjust enrichment was established as the principal basis for Lena's claims for compensation. The arbitrators characterised it as a principle stemming from French law that could also be found in Scottish law as well as in other continental legal traditions, including Soviet law.[110] The tribunal further held that 'on ordinary legal principles this constitutes a right of action for damages, but the Court prefers to base its award on the principle of "unjust enrichment", although in its opinion the money result is the same'.[111] As mentioned before, based on its construction of the principle of unjust enrichment, the tribunal awarded a total of 13 million pounds sterling to the company, consisting of 3.5 million for investments made up to the present and 9.5 million for lost profits.[112]

The tribunal's argument had two important implications. First, the tribunal held that the general principle was actually also part of Soviet law and thus the reference to general principles was somewhat an expression of domestic law. Second, it declared that the outcome was identical in monetary terms to applying domestic law. Both of these implications, however, are doubtful. If the applicable law in the case is Soviet law, then that would have meant the application of the Five-Year-Plan. The Five-Year-Plan was the core of Soviet law. As Newton puts it: 'The Plan in this sense did not merely

[106] See further Andrea Leiter, 'The Sheikh of Abu Dhabi Arbitration' (2019) [unpublished manuscript].
[107] *Lena Goldfields v Soviet Government (Award)* (2 September 1930) [22].
[108] Ibid.
[109] Ibid. [23].
[110] Ibid.
[111] Ibid. [25].
[112] Ibid. [26].

fill the interstices of the legal space of economic permission, but acted as a kind of general background condition on the exercise of other rights'.[113] Even though the concession agreement contained the explicit guarantee that the contractual relationship should not be altered unilaterally by decree or administrative act, it also stipulated that it would be subject to all existing and future legislation if not explicitly specified otherwise.[114] Thus, the relationship between the Five-Year-Plan and the concession agreement would have to be interpreted in accordance with Soviet law. However, as stated above, the tribunal started from the premise that the Plan's implementation 'necessarily meant, when measured in terms of contractual obligation, the breach by the Government of many of the fundamental provisions, express and implied, of the Concession Agreement'.[115] Such a breach of legal obligations could only be established if the obligations could be argued to arise from outside the national legal sphere. This constituted a fundamental departure from the established rule at the time that 'any contract which is not a contract between States in their capacity as subjects of international law is based on the municipal law of some country'.[116] Furthermore, even if the application of Soviet law would have led to a duty of compensation on behalf of the Soviet state, it is by no means obvious how it would have been calculated. Since the principle of unjust enrichment was vague and lacked clear content,[117] the inclusion of future profits was an assertion by the tribunal, rather than an application of a legal principle. We can recall from Bernstein's report that the Soviet government made its own calculation in which it restricted the claim to investments made up to the present.[118] Thus, the reliance on general principles as contained in Article 38 was a means to ascertain the protection of Lena's assets by dislocating Soviet law as applicable law.

13.4 Conclusion

This brings us back to the argument I raised above: namely, that upholding a liberal version of property rights was attained through allocating jurisdiction

[113] Newton, n 2, 154.
[114] *Lena Goldfields v Soviet Government (Award)* (2 September 1930) [18(i)].
[115] Ibid. [19].
[116] *Case Concerning Various Serbian Loans Issued in France (France v Kingdom of the Serbs, Croats and Slovenes) (Judgment)* [1929] PCIJ (Ser A) No. 20, 41.
[117] Christoph H Schreuer, 'Unjustified Enrichment in International Law' (1974) 22 *American Journal of Comparative Law* 281.
[118] See above at 329.

outside the national sphere. The assertion of the principle of Kompetenz-Kompetenz allowed the tribunal to escape review by a national court, and the introduction of general principles enabled the dislocation of Soviet law as applicable law. That the tribunal operated with a liberal understanding of property rights becomes more evident when considering how its legal value is explained. As O'Connell put it: 'The juridical justification for the obligation to pay compensation is to be found in the concept of unjust enrichment, which lies at the basis of the doctrine of acquired rights'.[119] Acquired rights were the stronghold against attempts of redistribution in precisely the manner in which the Soviets were reorganising economic relations.[120] In consequence, the legal obligation to respect acquired rights and pay compensation, including for lost profits, was introduced as a 'general principle of law as recognized by civilised nations' superseding domestic law from the outside. In this construction we again encounter the qualifier 'civilised', not just as racialised cultural marker but as a marker of political and economic organising. It was in the very notion of 'civilised' as the expansion of a capitalist mode of production that the principle of unjust enrichment was introduced for the protection of assets and the dogma of sanctity of contract.

Thus, as much as the Soviet Revolution was indeed revolutionary and produced a 'revolution in the forms of ownership',[121] on the international level law was mobilised by Western states as an instrument of continuation of economic relations. As Lauterpacht put it, 'from the point of view of municipal law a new revolutionary system of government is a totally new legal creation separated from its legal predecessor by the abyss of the revolutionary phenomenon'. But when it comes to the international sphere, 'the Law of Nations cannot strip itself of a function which is common to all law, namely, the protection of established rights and the continuity of law'.[122] In his vision, there can be no plurality of laws, and the function of law is universally understood to be in service of protecting established rights. The revolutionary proposition would not reach the international sphere but be contained to the internal affairs of the nation state.

119 Daniel P O'Connell, *International Law* (Stevens, 2nd ed, 1970) vol 2, 780.

120 On the necessary separation of the economic and political sphere and the role of acquired rights, see Alfred Verdross, 'Règles internationales concernant le traitement des étrangers' (1931) 37 *Recueil des cours* 323.

121 Newton, n 2, 74.

122 'Succession of States with Respect to Private Law Obligations' in Hersch Lauterpacht, *International Law: Being the Collected Papers of Hersch Lauterpacht* (Elihu Lauterpacht ed, Cambridge University Press, 1970) vol 3, 126.

Today, Kompetenz-Kompetenz has become an established feature in international investment arbitration[123] and the doctrine has been 'widely celebrated in arbitral lore as among the foremost achievements for [its] rendering arbitration efficacious and independent of the state'.[124] The significance of the invocation of general principles, although not fully appreciated in scholarship,[125] laid the groundwork for the body of substantive laws we have come to call 'international investment law'. This chapter has shown that the Lena Goldfields Arbitration was one of the first iterations of the establishment of an autonomous sphere of economic law, located outside the nation state, and operating under liberal economic assumptions such as the sanctity of contract and the protection of private property. Viewed in this light, international investment law emerges as an international legal regime aimed at containing the potential of redistribution, as proclaimed by the Soviet revolution, through an assertion of international legal principles.

[123] It is expressed in Article 41(1) of the ICSID Convention. See Christoph H Schreuer et al. (eds), *The ICSID Convention: A Commentary on the Convention on the Settlement of Investment Disputes between States and Nationals of Other States* (Cambridge University Press, 2009) 517. It is also part of the UNCITRAL Arbitration Rules in Article 23.

[124] Landolt, n 92, 512.

[125] In his article on unjust enrichment, Christoph Schreuer commented on the Lena Goldfields Arbitration and stated that the references to general principles, 'far from being decisive for the outcome of the award, were merely used to add an appearance of broad general justice': Schreuer, n 117, 289.

14

The Mexican Revolution

Alien Protection and International Economic Order

KATHRYN GREENMAN*

> The underlying problem was essentially an economic one and involved the question how a presumably necessary economic and social reform could be brought about in the national sphere without unduly upsetting the international economic system as embodied in the existing body of international law.
>
> —F S Dunn (1933)[1]

14.1 Introduction

The Mexican Revolution is commonly perceived to have been the first social revolution. The revolutionary Mexican Constitution of 1917, at the time perhaps the most radical the world had seen, is well known, as is the subsequent oil nationalisation of the 1930s that it facilitated. Another significant, albeit less immediately striking, consequence of the revolutionary events that took place in Mexico between 1910 and 1920 was that a large number of claims were made against the Mexican state in respect of injuries caused to foreign nationals as a result of the revolution. Such claims found their basis in a (hotly contested) body of international legal rules that had emerged during the second half of the nineteenth century and first decades of the twentieth concerning alien protection: that is, concerning the rights of states to protect their nationals overseas and the duties of states when it came to the treatment of foreign nationals in their territory.[2] The law of alien protection was also known as, or

* Lecturer at the Faculty of Law, University of Technology Sydney.

[1] Frederick Sherwood Dunn, *The Diplomatic Protection of Americans in Mexico* (Columbia University Press, 1933) 331. Dunn was writing specifically about Article 27 of the revolutionary Mexican Constitution of 1917 (on which more below). Here I propose that his understanding of Article 27 can be extended to the revolution more generally.

[2] See, for example, Edwin M Borchard, *The Diplomatic Protection of Citizens Abroad, or, The Law of International Claims* (Banks Law, 1915); Frederick Sherwood Dunn, *The*

incorporated, state responsibility for injuries to aliens and diplomatic protection. Subsequently, six mixed claims commissions – with the United States, France, Germany, Spain, Britain and Italy – were set up to adjudicate Mexico's international responsibility for claims that had arisen in respect of loss or damage caused by 'revolutionary acts' between 20 November 1910 and 31 May 1920.[3] Loss or damage here encompassed personal injury, property loss or damage and breach of contract.[4] Claims could be brought by 'corporations, companies, associations, partnerships or individuals'.[5] In addition, there was a second US commission, the 'general commission' (in contrast to the 'special commission', as the other US commission was known), which also had jurisdiction over certain other 'revolutionary damage' claims.[6]

The first aim of this chapter is to look at how the Mexican commissions came to be established. In doing so, I seek to explore the role played by the international law of alien protection in mediating the threat posed to the international economic order by revolution in Mexico. The origins of these questions of economic order can be traced back to the period of capitalist expansion in Mexico under Porfirio Díaz (Mexican president 1876–80, 1884–1911), to which the revolution was a response and a challenge. This period marked the integration of Mexico into the North Atlantic economy and the entrenchment of foreign capital in Mexico. When the revolution disrupted this economic transformation – both

Protection of Nationals: A Study in the Application of International Law (Johns Hopkins Press, 1932).

3 See, for example, Article 1 of the *Convention of 10 September 1923*, Mexico–United States, establishing the US-Mexican special commission ('*US Special Convention*'). All the conventions setting up the Mexican claims commissions are reprinted in the annexes to A H Feller, *The Mexican Claims Commissions, 1923–1934: A Study in the Law and Procedure of International Tribunals* (Macmillan Co, 1935).

4 Although the conventions only referred to 'losses or damages suffered by persons or by their properties', it had been established by practice of earlier commissions that this included jurisdiction over contract claims and the Mexican commissions followed this line. See Feller, n 3, 172*ff*.

5 See, for example, Article 1 of the *US Special Convention*.

6 Article 1 of the *Convention of 8 September 1923*, Mexico–United States, setting up the US-Mexican general claims commission excluded claims 'arising from acts incident to the recent revolutions'. The general commission nevertheless considered revolutionary damage claims arising after 31 May 1920 (such as those relating to the 1923 uprising of Adolfo de la Huerta) and claims that arose between 20 November 1910 and 31 May 1920 from administrative acts rather than from acts of government or revolutionary forces. Regarding the latter category see, for example, *George W Hopkins (USA) v United Mexican States*, 4 RIAA 41 (31 March 1926) (*Hopkins*).

practically and ideologically – the question of alien protection was one important means through which the contest over the shape of Mexico's economic and political relations with the North Atlantic system played out.

For claimant states, the enforcement of alien protection claims was part of a wider practice of political interference and forcible intervention in Mexico to protect the property, investments and lives of their nationals during the years of the revolution. International arbitration, despite its association with the peace movement,[7] was a part of – rather than a replacement for – such practices. This is not to say, however, that the mixed claims commissions as eventually agreed were simply imposed upon a passive Mexico. Successive Mexican administrations resisted the international adjudication of alien protection claims arising out of the revolution. At times, however, this was impossible or not strategic. Offering international arbitration could serve as a useful bargaining chip to secure foreign recognition or to avoid more violent types of intervention. In such instances, Mexican governments at least sought to reserve Mexico's position under international law. Apart from the US general commission, all of the commissions had equitable rather than legal jurisdiction. First, this enabled Mexico to maintain that payments were being made ex gratia rather than in accordance with an international legal obligation. This was done to avoid setting precedents that would support expansive international responsibility for revolutionary damage going forwards.,[8] Second, it allowed Mexico to argue for more restrictive responsibility than would have been provided for under international law in particular cases before the commissions.

The second aim of this chapter is to reflect on the place of the Mexican commissions within a much longer narrative about international law and its prioritisation of the protection of foreign investment against

[7] See, for example, Martti Koskenniemi, 'The Ideology of International Adjudication and the 1907 Hague Conference' in Yves Daudet (ed), *Topicality of the 1907 Hague Conference, the Second Peace Conference* (Martinus Nijhoff, 2008) 127; Christian J Tams, 'World Peace through International Adjudication?' in Heinz-Gerhard Justenhoven and Mary Ellen O'Connell (eds), *Peace through Law: Reflections on Pacem in Terris from Philosophy, Law, Theology, and Political Science* (Nomos, 2016) 215.

[8] Nevertheless, despite their equitable jurisdiction, the decisions of these commissions have been held to have precedential weight, being cited, for example, by the International Law Commission. See, for example, 'Draft Articles on Responsibility of States for Internationally Wrongful Acts' (2001) 2(2) *Yearbook of the International Law Commission* 1, 51.

revolution in the decolonised world. At stake in this struggle over whether alien protection claims were subject to domestic or international, legal or equitable jurisdiction was the space for radical economic and political change at the domestic level and the postcolonial state's right to require foreign capital to bear the risk of revolutionary violence. The international law of alien protection gave foreign nationals, who were often commercial actors, internationally enforceable rights to property, contractual and personal protection – in effect, mandating trade and investment liberalisation. The international enforcement of alien protection claims took the regulation of foreign capital out of the scope of national authority. In practice, the result was that to a significant extent the state guaranteed foreign capital against the costs of revolution.

The outcome of this struggle was somewhat ambiguous since Mexico defended its interests relatively successfully, particularly compared to previous similar occasions, for example, Venezuela in 1902–3.[9] The commissions were not directly imposed by force; apart from one, they had equitable jurisdiction; many of their decisions were sympathetic to the Mexican position; and on several occasions, Mexico successfully negotiated subsequent restrictions on the commissions' jurisdictions. Although Mexico might not have been able to resist the internationalisation of the alien protection issue and insist on dealing with the claims domestically, it did to a certain extent succeed in resisting its 'legalisation'. At the same time as the commissions were sitting, the League of Nations was trying to codify state responsibility for injuries to aliens. These efforts were, however, unsuccessful. A group of largely Latin American and former Austro-Hungarian states voted together to reject rules which they believed were biased against them.[10] However, in the long run, internationalisation of alien protection – now foreign investment protection – has prevailed. Today, international investment law provides a high standard of protection to foreign investors in times of revolution and civil war, based on the nineteenth- and early twentieth-century alien protection arbitrations but in fact much stricter than the standard they applied.

[9] See, for example, W L Penfield, 'The Anglo-German Intervention in Venezuela' (1903) 177(560) *North American Review* 86; Amos S Hershey, 'The Venezuelan Affair in the Light of International Law' (1903) 42 *American Law Register* 249.

[10] For recent accounts, see Arnulf Becker Lorca, *Mestizo International Law: A Global Intellectual History 1842–1933* (Cambridge University Press, 2014) 305ff; Tzvika Alan Nissel, '*A History of State Responsibility: The Struggle for International Standards* (1870–1960)' (PhD dissertation, University of Helsinki, 2016) 289*ff*.

14.2 The Economic Transformation of Mexico 1876–1910: Capitalist Expansion and Foreign Trade and Investment

One place to begin the story of the Mexican commissions is with the rise to power of Porfirio Díaz in 1876. His rule, known as the 'Porfiriato', lasted thirty-five years. It was a period of apparent stability but also of rapid capitalist development and increasingly brutal authoritarianism.[11] Thus, in contrast to the first half-century of Mexican independence,[12] it was also a period during which the issue of alien protection took a back seat.[13] The economic transformation of Mexico during the Porfiriato was dramatic. Foreign investment increased from 110 million to 3.4 billion pesos, with the United States as the largest foreign investor.[14] Nearly a quarter of Mexico's total territory was enclosed,[15] with foreign interests acquiring enormous landholdings.[16] There was expansion in commercial agriculture and mining. In 1884, a new mining code was adopted, providing for private ownership of the subsoil. This was a departure from the legal position that had subsisted since the colonial era, whereby

[11] See Friedrich Katz, 'Mexico: Restored Republic and Porfiriato 1867–1910' in Leslie Bethell (ed), *The Cambridge History of Latin America* (Cambridge University Press, 1984–1995) vol 5, 23–4.

[12] This period saw several foreign interventions and mixed claims commissions as a result of the alien protection claims arising from the frequent regime changes and uprisings of the early decades of Mexican independence. See John Bassett Moore, *History and Digest of the International Arbitrations to Which the United States Has Been a Party* (Government Printing Office, 1898) vol 2, 1209–359.

[13] See, for example, Dunn, *Protection of Americans in Mexico*, n 1, 307. The United States did delay recognition of Diaz's government for two years, however, one of the issues being injuries to US citizens in Mexico and unpaid claims from the 1868 Mexico–United States commission, and there was some diplomatic correspondence about alien protection issues during the Porfiriato. On the controversies surrounding Diaz's recognition, see Dunn, *Protection of Americans in Mexico*, n 1, 166; J Fred Rippy, *The United States and Mexico* (Knopf, 1926) 296–310; Katz, 'Mexico: Restored Republic', n 11, 1, 21–3. On the diplomatic correspondence during the Porfiriato, see Dunn, *Protection of Americans in Mexico*, n 1, 189–98, 229–73, 286–305.

[14] The United States had 38 per cent, while 62 per cent came from Europe (of which 90 per cent was British or French). See Adolfo Gilly, *The Mexican Revolution* (The New Press, revised ed, 2005) 26. For another account of Mexico's economic transformation during the Porfiriato and the role played by foreign interests, see John Mason Hart, *Revolutionary Mexico: The Coming and Process of the Mexican Revolution* (University of California Press, 1987) 129–62.

[15] Gilly, n 14, 4.

[16] The Richard Construction Company of Los Angeles, for example, held 547,000 hectares in northern Mexico, and one of US newspaper tycoon William Randolph Hearst's estates in Chihuahua amounted to 350,000 hectares. See Stuart Easterling, *The Mexican Revolution: A Short History 1910–1920* (Haymarket Books, 2013) 18.

this vested in the nation.[17] By 1917, 90 per cent of Mexico's oil was foreign owned.[18] Exports increased by six times,[19] facilitated by the increase in railway tracks from approximately 600 kilometres in 1876 to nearly 20,000 in 1910. The railway, described as the 'very symbol of capitalist expansion in Mexico', was built by foreign companies, which enjoyed extraordinary privileges.[20] At the same time, Mexico's deepening integration into the North Atlantic economy left it vulnerable to that system's volatilities. The devastating recession of 1908 was one result.[21]

One way of accounting for the revolution is as a rejection of the economic transformation that Mexico underwent under Porfirio Díaz and its devastating social consequences and impact on local economies.[22] Since the growth of foreign trade and investment was a decisive part of this transformation, revolution threatened it in terms of both the practical disruption it caused and its ideology. Although this threat was real, it did not always materialise,[23] at least not evenly across regions and sectors. For example, the threat of *social* revolution was more genuine and manifested to a greater extent in the south.[24] Despite the revolutionary upheavals, there was huge expansion in oil production during the revolutionary period,[25] and overall trade with the United States expanded.[26] To a certain extent, revolutionaries left foreign interests

[17] Katz, 'Mexico: Restored Republic', n 11, 26.

[18] W Dirk Raat and Michael M Brescia, *Mexico and the United States: Ambivalent Vistas* (University of Georgia Press, 4th ed, 2010) 126.

[19] Gilly, n 14, 24–5.

[20] Ibid., 20–1; Stuart Easterling, 'Mexico's Revolution: 1910–1920' (pt 2) (2011) 75 *International Socialist Review*.

[21] On the economic crisis that preceded the revolution, see Hart, n 14, 163*ff*.

[22] There were of course other causes of the revolution as well, such as the authoritarianism, corruption and abuse of power of the Porfirio Díaz regime. For more nuanced accounts of the revolution's causes, see Alan Knight, *The Mexican Revolution* (Cambridge University Press, 1986); Friedrich Katz, *The Secret War in Mexico: Europe, the United States, and the Mexican Revolution* (University of Chicago Press, 1981); Gilly, n 14. For a consideration of the causes of the revolution in a global context, see Hart, n 14, 187–234.

[23] See John Womack, 'The Mexican Revolution, 1910–1920' in Leslie Bethell (ed), *The Cambridge History of Latin America* (Cambridge University Press, 1986) vol 5, 79, 81: 'On the whole, business adjusted and continued. Over the long run it increased'.

[24] Ibid., 89.

[25] Ibid., 86 (table 1). Haber et al argue that oil was the most immune sector while banking was more vulnerable and railways particularly badly affected. See Stephen Haber, Armando Razo and Noel Maurer, *The Politics of Property Rights: Political Instability, Credible Commitments, and Economic Growth in Mexico, 1876–1929* (Cambridge University Press, 2003) 14, 93–4, 138, 190–1.

[26] Raat and Brescia, n 18, 136.

alone because they did not want to provoke foreign intervention and because they wanted to tax their exports.[27]

The perception of a threat to foreign trade and investment was particularly intense after the adoption of the new revolutionary Constitution in February 1917, even if the radical potential of this document was not really fulfilled until the 1930s. Its Article 27 returned ownership of the subsoil to the nation and provided for land reform and the breaking up of large estates, although in the end only around 180,000 hectares of land were redistributed by the Carranza government (1917–20),[28] less than half the amount held by the biggest US landowners.[29] Article 27 also gave the state the right to limit private property, regulate the utilisation of natural resources and revise 'all contracts and concessions made by former Governments since the year 1876, which have resulted in the monopolization of lands, waters, and natural resources of the Nation, by a single person or company'.

During the revolutionary period, the issue of international claims thus returned, as the gains made by foreign capital during the Porfiriato were threatened by the forces of the revolution. As Abraham Feller, author of the leading book on the Mexican commissions published in 1935, explained:

> The thirty-five years of the Diaz regime represented a period of tranquillity in Mexico under a government which exhibited marked hospitality to foreign capital. From time to time claims of American citizens were presented but these were either disposed of through diplomatic channels or permitted to stagnate in Foreign Office files. No . . . attempt was made to conclude a claims convention until the Diaz regime was brought to an end by the Madero revolt in 1910 . . . The stake of foreign nationals, particularly of those of the United States, had increased to such an extent [during the Porfiriato] that a period of political instability [1910–1920]

[27] US mining companies were relatively safe since a US company, ASARCO (American Smelting and Refining Company), also controlled all the important ore-refining capacity, something in which Mexico lacked local expertise, and because the powerful mining lobby with its strong connections to the US State Department could quickly bring about a boycott of Mexican exports, meaning that any confiscation of the mines or their products would be fruitless for the revolutionaries. As for oil, the revolutionaries knew that if they seized the oil fields, the United States would intervene with force and thus it was not worth risking the fields' destruction. See Noel Maurer, *The Empire Trap: The Rise and Fall of US Intervention to Protect American Property Overseas, 1893–2013* (Princeton University Press, 2013) 142–7.

[28] Womack, 'The Mexican Revolution', n 23, 122 (table 4).

[29] See n 16.

> reacted with increased force on their interests. It was inevitable that the subject of claims which had become dormant during the Diaz regime should be revived.[30]

It is to the revolutionary period that I now turn to explore this revival of alien protection claims and the wider context of foreign intervention and Mexican resistance in which it occurred.

14.3 The Revolutionary Period 1910–1920: Claims, Intervention and Arbitration

The United States insistently intervened, both directly and indirectly, in Mexico during the decade of the revolution.[31] This intervention took the forms of unofficial behind-the-scenes shenanigans, military operations and even (local) occupation. The United States also manipulated the flow of funds and arms into Mexico. It sometimes bent neutrality laws for the revolutionaries and sometimes strictly applied them, depending on its interests; arms embargoes were lifted and raised, applied selectively or not at all, subject to the desired outcome.[32] The United States went so far as to draw up contingency plans to invade the entirety of Mexico on a number of occasions during the revolutionary period, but it was not clear that there was the military capacity or political appetite for what would have been an enormous undertaking.[33]

While the United States unsurprisingly looms large in the story of intervention in revolutionary Mexico, it was not just a case of 'simple antagonism from the US government' but also 'complicated Euro-

[30] Feller, n 3, 7, 15. See also Dunn, *Protection of Americans in Mexico*, n 1, 8.

[31] For the authoritative account of foreign intervention by both US and European governments and business interests, in the Mexican Revolution, see Katz, *The Secret War*, n 22. See also on US intervention particularly, P Edward Haley, *Revolution and Intervention: The Diplomacy of Taft and Wilson in Mexico, 1910–1917* (MIT Press, 1970); Berta Ulloa, *La Revolución Intervenida: Relaciones Diplomáticas entre México y los Estados Unidos, 1910–1914* (Colegio de Mexico, 1971).

[32] For example, during Madero's government only arms destined for rebels were embargoed, while upon Huerta's rise to power a blanket embargo was put in place. This was then lifted in favour of the Constitutionalists to try and break the stalemate that had arisen in early 1914, although US authorities had already been allowing arms for the rebels to 'slip through'. The blanket embargo had favoured Huerta because he was able to buy arms from Germany and Japan, while the Constitutionalists were landlocked. See Haley, n 31, 103, 125–8; 'The Secretary of State to Ambassador W H Page' (29 January 1914) in *Foreign Relations of the United States* (*FRUS*, 1913–21, 1913 vol, 445.

[33] Maurer, *The Empire Trap*, n 27, 140–2.

American imperialist rivalries', especially during World War I.[34] Nor was it only a question of states; foreign business interests were also influential actors here,[35] even if their interests did not always align with each other or with those of their governments.[36] Moreover, Mexico was not just a passive subject of intervention. As Friedrich Katz put it in his classic work on foreign intervention in the Mexican Revolution, 'not only can local rifts be exploited for global ends, but global rifts can be exploited for local ends'.[37] Since the days of the Porfiriato, Mexican leaders had sought to play different foreign states and business interests off against each other, for both personal and national gain. Díaz had courted German, French and British interests as a counterweight to US power in Mexico, a policy continued by subsequent administrations.[38] It is in this context of intervention, and resistance to intervention, that I will explore the story of the struggle over the internationalisation of alien protection claims. In this section, I follow the efforts of foreign states to enforce their alien protection claims, as well as the attempts by different Mexican administrations to resolve such claims domestically and/or outside judicial processes. In doing so, I seek to draw out the role played by international law in mediating the impact of revolution on economic order.

In 1911, Díaz was ousted by the revolutionary movement led by liberal democrat Francisco Madero that had begun a year earlier. Soon after, Madero set up a domestic commission – the Consultative Claims Commission – in response to pressure from a number of states to

34 Womack, 'The Mexican Revolution', n 23, 81; Raat and Brescia, n 18, 127. For example, during World War I, Germany sought to stop Mexican oil reaching the Allies and encouraged war between Mexico and the United States so as to divert US troops from Europe. With the infamous Zimmerman telegraph, Germany proposed an alliance with Mexico, offering the Mexicans, in return for their support, the northern territories they lost in to the United States in 1848 as spoils of war after Germany defeated the Allies. For more detail, see Katz, *The Secret War*, n 22, 350–67.

35 On the ways in which foreign investors in Mexico protected their interests, see Haber et al., n 25, 10.

36 See, for example, Katz, *The Secret War*, n 22, 158–67.

37 Ibid., x–xi.

38 Ibid., 22–7; Raat and Brescia, n 18, 127. For example, during World War I, Carranza, despite declaring Mexico's neutrality, continued to pursue German loans and permit the operation of German spies in Mexico. He sought to use Germany as a counterbalance to US influence in Mexico without going so far as a public alliance with Germany, which would have aggravated the United States. For more detail on Carranza's foreign policy during World War I, see Katz, *The Secret War*, n 22, 512–24.

adjudicate the alien protection claims arising out of his revolution.[39] Claimant states were wary of domestic adjudication but did not initially object,[40] although the United States did reserve its rights to bring claims internationally.[41] The Consultative Claims Commission's activities, however, proved unsatisfactory to the claimant states. Its work progressed sluggishly and US Ambassador Henry Lane Wilson, a virulent critic of Madero's government,[42] accused the commission of 'playing for time'.[43]

By 15 September 1912, Wilson's patience had run out. He wrote a vaguely threatening letter to Mexican Foreign Minister Pedro Lascuraín, excoriating Madero's regime for failing to protect US citizens and submitting a series of claims, including a number of 'general claims arising out of revolutions', for diplomatic consideration.[44] Lascuraín denied US and German claims for revolutionary damage, citing two principles of international law: first, that 'when a government finds itself temporarily unable to repress within its territory all the punishable acts resulting from insurrection or civil war it is not responsible for the damages which foreigners may suffer in person or property'; and second, that 'states are exonerated from the payment of damages suffered by foreigners during times of disturbance within the territory of such States; for there is no reason, either in justice or in equity, to differentiate such damages from those suffered by the nationals of the country'.[45]

[39] Feller, n 3, 16, 201. The French-Mexican commission in the *Pinson* case also carried out a detailed analysis of Mexico's domestic claims laws. See *Georges Pinson (France) v United Mexican States*, 5 RIAA 327 (19 October 1928) 433–45, 454–9 (*Pinson*).

[40] See 'The American Ambassador to the Secretary of State' (6 July 1911) in *FRUS*, 1909–13, 1912 vol, 934.

[41] 'Note Transmitting Claims' (October 1911) in *FRUS*, 1909–13, 1912 vol, 945–6.

[42] Wilson referred to the 'anti-American spirit' of the Madero government, which he argued, 'shows a decided preference for European markets in all lines but is harassing and discriminating against American interests': 'The American Ambassador to the Secretary of State' (22 August 1912) in *FRUS*, 1909–13, 1912 vol, 826–7.

[43] 'The American Ambassador to the Secretary of State' (16 January 1912) in *FRUS*, 1909–13, 1912 vol, 953.

[44] 'The American Ambassador to the Minister for Foreign Affairs' (15 September 1912) in *FRUS*, 1909–13, 1912 vol, 842–6.

[45] 'The Minister for Foreign Affairs to the American Chargé d'Affaires' (23 November 1912), and 'The Minister for Foreign Affairs to the German Minister to Mexico' (2 December 1912) in *FRUS*, 1909–13, 1912 vol, 982–4. These principles are commonly associated with the thought of Carlos Calvo. See, for example, Carlos Calvo, 'De la non-responsabilité des États à raison des pertes et dommages éprouvés par des étrangers en temps de troubles intérieurs ou de guerres civiles' (1869) 1 (1st series) *Revue de droit international et de législation comparée* 417.

These principles were at the heart of the contestation of alien protection between Latin-American and US international lawyers during the late nineteenth and early twentieth centuries. While there was a generally accepted principle of non-responsibility on the basis of lack of control, US lawyers argued this was subject to an extensive exception in the case of negligence. This effectively created a two-tier system, while providing at least a veneer of universality. Under such an approach, it was always possible to explain away the different distribution of responsibility between the newly decolonised Latin American states and the imperial powers as a result of diligence on the part of the latter and lack of diligence on the part of the former, even if they should both experience civil war, rebellion and disorder. Equal treatment was the classic principle associated with the Latin American position on alien protection. US international lawyers also accepted this principle but made it subject to an *international* standard of protection, so that equality with nationals was only a defence where the state had been judged to have provided a baseline of adequate protection.[46]

Madero's government not only faced growing criticism from the US government and US business for discriminating against US companies and nationals and failing to protect US lives and property.[47] It also faced internal opposition from the Zapatistas in the south,[48] and from the military: generals Pascual Orozco, Bernardo Reyes and Felix Díaz (Porfirio's nephew) all led attempted coups against Madero.[49] When it came to claims, Lascuraín distinguished those arising from Madero's revolution, for which Mexico accepted a certain – albeit voluntary – responsibility via the Consultative Claims Commission, and those arising from the more recent uprisings, for which it did not.[50] Lascuraín made it clear that from Mexico's point of view the assumption of responsibility for Madero's revolution was not obligated by international law.[51] This

46 I have written about this elsewhere in Kathryn Greenman, 'Aliens in Latin America: Intervention, Arbitration and State Responsibility for Rebels' (2018) 31 *Leiden Journal of International Law* 617.

47 See Katz, *The Secret War*, n 22, 93.

48 For more on the Zapatista movement, see John Womack, *Zapata and the Mexican Revolution* (Knopf, 1969); Arturo Warman, *'We Come to Object': The Peasants of Morelos and the National State* (Stephen K Ault trans, Johns Hopkins University Press, 1980).

49 See Katz, *The Secret War*, n 22, 42–6.

50 'The Mexican Minister for Foreign Affairs to the British Minister to Mexico' (9 November 1912) in *FRUS*, 1909–13, 1912 vol, 986.

51 'The Mexican Minister for Foreign Affairs to the American Ambassador' (20 January 1913) in *FRUS*, 1909–13, 1913 vol, 939.

refusal to recognise an international legal obligation to pay claims was an ongoing strategy for the Mexican authorities. Given the contested nature of the rules of alien protection, they did not want to create practice damaging to the Latin American position, especially since intervention and national authority over foreign capital were at stake.

In December 1912, Henry Lane Wilson proposed international arbitration to Madero's government,[52] to no effect, and in January 1913, he wrote to the Secretary of State proposing to send an ultimatum to Madero. The proposed ultimatum is instructive in the way that it frames revolution as a matter of international responsibility to the extent that it harms foreign capital and economic interests, as well as lives, and understands international law as the basis for economic order and the creation and maintenance of the conditions for business within the domestic state:

> During all of this long period a state of anarchy, intermittent, sporadic, and rising and falling as the tides, has prevailed through a large part of the territory supposedly under the control of the Mexican Government, and for the administration of which it is responsible not only to its own citizens, but, under accepted principles of international law, to the nations of the world, which, upon the invitation of Mexico, have sent their nationals and their capital hither, relying upon the ability of this Government to afford to both the usual safeguards guaranteed by civilized states ... Government and the law have ceased to be respected, and general and local administrations are helpless and impotent to deal with a situation of constantly increasing gravity and which has become a menace not only to the material interests of foreigners who have invested their money in Mexico and contributed to the development of the material resources of the Republic, but it has also placed in jeopardy and in numerous cases actually sacrificed the lives of foreigners who must necessarily rely upon the Government for protection.[53]

The ultimatum was, however, never sent,[54] since less than one month later, Madero was overthrown. Victoriano Huerta, one of Madero's own generals, betrayed the president and, with the involvement of the US

[52] 'Memorandum of an Interview between the American Ambassador and the Mexican Minister for Foreign Affairs in New York City, December 21, 1912' in *FRUS*, 1913–21, 1915 vol, 985.

[53] 'The American Ambassador to, the Secretary of State' (18 January 1913) in *FRUS*, 1913–21, 1913 vol, 887–8.

[54] See ibid., 893, noting that there was apparently no further reference to the draft memorandum in the correspondence.

embassy,[55] took power in a counter-revolutionary coup.[56] Ambassador Wilson urged recognition of Huerta's government, citing its 'decided pro-American proclivities'.[57] Writing to the Secretary of State the week after the coup, he argued that 'the prospects for settlement of all of our existing complaints against Mexico in a prompt and just way are excellent. If this Government cannot be maintained, chaos must inevitably result and the demands and necessity for intervention could hardly be resisted'.[58]

Despite the role played by the US embassy in Huerta's rise to power, Woodrow Wilson, inaugurated as president a few weeks after the coup, refused to recognise the Huerta government. This was not only – if at all – due to Wilson's squeamishness about Huerta being a murderous dictator,[59] but also because Huerta was perceived to favour British (oil) interests.[60] The US embassy circulated a note to its counterparts in Mexico City in November 1915, setting out the threat that Huerta's coup posed to economic order:

> Usurpations like that of General Huerta menace the peace and development of America as nothing else could. They not only render the development of ordered self-government impossible; they also tend to set law entirely aside, to put the lives and fortunes of citizens and foreigners alike in constant jeopardy, to invalidate contracts and concessions in any way the usurper may devise for his own profit and to impair both the national credit and all the foundations of business, domestic or foreign.[61]

When Huerta dissolved parliament and declared himself president in the elections of October 1913, after promising not to run, Wilson was from then on committed to toppling him.[62] In 1914, Wilson found a pretext to

[55] Although the extent to which Wilson had official approval for his activities is unclear. See Haley, n 31, 53–73. Ambassador Wilson was dismissed by Woodrow Wilson in July 1913.
[56] For a full account, see Hart, n 14, 260–1.
[57] 'The American Ambassador to the Secretary of State' (26 February 1913) in *FRUS*, 1913–21, 1913 vol, 742.
[58] Ibid.
[59] As Katz, *The Secret War*, n 22, 156, notes, the 'driving forces and motivations behind Wilson's Mexico policy remain to this day one of the most disputed questions in American history'.
[60] Ibid., 162–5; Womack, 'The Mexican Revolution', n 23, 93. Opposing Huerta also enabled Wilson to fulfil one of his campaign promises – to defend the middle classes against big business. See Katz, *The Secret War*, n 22, 156.
[61] 'The Secretary of State to Chargé O'Shaughnessy' (24 November 1913) in *FRUS*, 1913–21, 1914 vol, 443–4.
[62] Katz, *The Secret War*, n 22, 167–71.

invade and occupy the port city of Veracruz, after the Mexican authorities refused to apologise for briefly detaining some US sailors who had come ashore from vessels that were patrolling the gulf-coast area near the Tampico oil fields to protect US oil installations there.[63] At the same time, it had emerged that a German steamer, carrying arms destined for Huerta's forces, was headed for Veracruz.[64] Veracruz was Mexico's main port and politically and economically crucial to Huerta's regime. Without its customs revenues and military supplies during the six-month occupation, Huerta struggled to maintain himself in power against the Constitutionalist revolt, the liberal resistance against Huerta being led from Mexico's north by Venustiano Carranza.[65]

Once Huerta took power, foreign states, led by the United States, began insisting on an international commission to resolve alien protection claims.[66] The United States informed Huerta that recognition of his government was dependent on a number of conditions, including, most importantly, agreement that all US revolutionary damage claims would be settled internationally.[67] In September 1913, still seeking foreign recognition, Huerta made a presidential address in which he publicly promised that he would set up a committee in accordance with the rules of international law to resolve claims.[68] However, in private, the foreign minister's sub-secretary had already met with representatives of Spain, France, Britain, Italy, Belgium, Germany and Austria-Hungary to offer a domestic commission, based not on international law but 'for the purpose of inspiring good will and with a desire for closer relations'. None of

[63] For a detailed account of the occupation, see Lester D Langley, *The Banana Wars: United States Intervention in the Caribbean, 1898–1934* (University Press of Kentucky, 1985) 87–114.

[64] For more on the *Ypiranga*, see Michael C Meyer, 'The Arms of the *Ypiranga*' (1970) 50 *Hispanic American Historical Review* 543; Thomas Baecker, 'The Arms of the *Ypiranga*: The German Side' (1973) 30 *The Americas* 1. In an eventful career, the *Ypiranga* had also taken Porfirio Diaz into exile in 1911 and was one of the ships in contact with the *Titanic* while she was sinking.

[65] Womack, 'The Mexican Revolution', n 23, 103.

[66] 'The American Ambassador to the Secretary of State' (31 March 1913) in *FRUS*, 1913–21, 1913 vol, 946: 'The opinion was unanimous at an informal meeting of the Diplomatic Corps today that an international claims commission ought to be insisted on'.

[67] 'The Secretary of State to the American Ambassador' (21 February 1913) in *FRUS*, 1913–21, 1913 vol, 728–9. See also 'The Secretary of State to the American Ambassador' (11 March 1913) in *FRUS*, 1913–21, 1913 vol, 943.

[68] 'The American Chargé d'Affaires to the Secretary of State' (15 September 1913) in *FRUS*, 1913–21, 1913 vol, 831.

the foreign representatives present would commit.[69] France later formally refused.[70]

At around the same time, Carranza, seeking US support, issued a decree providing for the creation of a national and an international commission should his revolution succeed.[71] Once Huerta was forced to flee in July 1914, the United States did not, however, support Carranza. Instead, they initially supported his ally,[72] popular regional leader Pancho Villa,[73] who controlled the strongest military force and Mexico's most important mining zones and had publicly proclaimed his friendliness towards the United States.[74] Villa – and fellow Constitutionalist ally Emiliano Zapata – split with Carranza in October 1914 over disagreements about, above all, land reform. Mexico suffered a period of outright civil war until Carranza eventually prevailed, taking decisive control in May 1915. Once he had established his government, Carranza publicly announced that foreigners would be indemnified for revolutionary damage.[75] The United States recognised Carranza's regime as the de facto government of Mexico later that year,[76] less than two weeks after Carranza confidentially promised to the Secretary of State that he would 'recognize and satisfy indemnities for damages caused by the revolution, which shall be settled in due time and in terms of justice'.[77]

Despite radical proclamations to the contrary,[78] in practice Carranza was economically relatively conservative, particularly in terms of land

[69] 'Minutes of a Meeting relative to the Creation of a Commission for the Settlement of Claims Growing out of the Disturbances in Mexico' (22 July 1913) in *FRUS*, 1913–21, 1913 vol, 951–4.

[70] 'The American Chargé d'Affaires to the Secretary of State' (10 December 1913) in *FRUS*, 1913–21, 1913 vol, 956. Apparently Russia did too, even though there is no mention of the Russian representative being present at the 22 July 1913 meeting.

[71] This was the Decree of Monclova of 10 May 1913. The full text is reprinted in *FRUS*, 1913–21, 1913 vol, 955.

[72] For a detailed account of changing US relations with Villa and Carranza in 1914 and 1915, see Arthur S Link, *Wilson: The Struggle for Neutrality 1914-1915* (Princeton University Press, 1960) 232–66, 456–94.

[73] For a (very) detailed history of Villa and his movement, see Friedrich Katz, *The Life and Times of Pancho Villa* (Stanford University Press, 1998).

[74] Womack, 'The Mexican Revolution', n 23, 110; Maurer, n 27, 143.

[75] 'Manifesto to the Nation' (11 July 1915) in *FRUS*, 1913–21, 1914 vol, 706.

[76] 'The Secretary of State to Mr Parker, Representing American Interests in Mexico' (19 October 1915) in *FRUS*, 1913–21, 1915 vol, 771.

[77] 'The Confidential Agent of the Constitutionalist Government of Mexico to the Secretary of State' (7 October 1915) in *FRUS*, 1913–21, 1915 vol, 763–4.

[78] Such as the agrarian law he proclaimed in January 1915. See Katz, *The Secret War*, n 22, 271.

redistribution.[79] Nevertheless, the Carrancistas believed in limiting the power of foreign companies and acting against foreign capital, be it in the form of higher taxation, greater state control or even, for the most radical wing, total expropriation.[80] In 1915, the Carranza government promulgated a decree requiring foreign oil companies to obtain licences for their operations.[81] This kept US companies and the State Department wary of Carranza's intentions.

In 1916, cross-border violence irreparably damaged relations between Carranza and the United States. Seeking this very outcome, Villa had led a raid into New Mexico. In retaliation, the United States sent an expedition of 5,000 men to Mexico in pursuit of Villa,[82] nearly leading to war between the two countries. With President Wilson concerned that such a war would play into German hands, a commission was set up to negotiate the withdrawal of US troops.[83] The US commissioners – who had strong links to the US oil industry – demanded as a condition for US withdrawal that the Mexican government agree to the United States' right to intervene again should Mexico fail to provide such protection to lives and property of US citizens 'adequate to enable [them] … (to operate) industries in which they might be interested'.[84] Carranza called the US commissioners' bluff and refused to agree, insisting that Mexico would not negotiate until US troops withdrew. Wilson backed down,[85] but Carranza had lost access to US arms and credit, weakening his domestic control.[86]

Harking back to his earlier promises regarding claims, in November 1917 the Carranza government promulgated a decree for a domestic commission to 'handle claims for damages to persons or property, resulting from the revolutionary movements in the Republic from 1910 to 1917'.[87] The United States objected to a number of features of

[79] In fact, Carranza returned confiscated haciendas to their original owners. See ibid., 256–8.
[80] Ibid., 256.
[81] Womack, 'The Mexican Revolution', n 23, 113.
[82] Two relatively recent (and more journalistic-style) accounts of this expedition are Eileen Welsome, *The General and the Jaguar: Pershing's Hunt for Pancho Villa* (Little, Brown & Co, 2006); James W Hurst, *Pancho Villa and Black Jack Pershing: The Punitive Expedition in Mexico* (Praeger, 2008).
[83] Katz, *The Secret War*, n 22, 310–11.
[84] Ibid., 311–12.
[85] Ibid., 312–13.
[86] Ibid., 315.
[87] See 'Decree of November 24, 1917, Creating a Commission to Pass upon Claims for Damages to Persons and Property Growing out of the Mexican Revolutions' in *FRUS*, 1913–21, 1918 vol, 793–6.

the new law.[88] First of all, the commission's jurisdiction was limited to claims for damage caused by revolutionary forces that succeeded in forming a legitimate government or had been recognised by such a government. The United States wanted the commission to cover claims for damage caused by 'outlaws and bandits' and 'unsuccessful revolutionists' where the Mexican government had been negligent in failing to prevent the harm, which, the US ambassador argued, 'should under the generally accepted rules of international law be repaired at the hands of the Mexican Government'.[89] This was a key dispute; Mexican governments consistently rejected responsibility in international law for unsuccessful revolutionary forces. Although the new law provided for appeal to an international mixed commission – with one Mexican commissioner, one commissioner from the claimant state, and an umpire – the United Staes objected to the fact that if the two national commissioners could not agree on the appointment of the umpire, this task would revert to the Mexican authorities.[90] Their final objection was that companies incorporated in Mexico were defined as Mexican and not as aliens for the purpose of making claims, even if their shareholders were entirely foreign.[91]

At this time, all the diplomats in Mexico City were writing to one another to ask each other their government's position regarding the new law. The mood was cautious, even suspicious; nobody wanted to commit to recognising the commission.[92] The United States always gave the same answer: that they were waiting for more information from the Mexican authorities regarding their objections but hoping to accept the commission if possible.[93] It took the Mexican foreign ministry eight months to respond to the United States' request for further information.[94] Such

[88] 'The Acting Secretary of State to the Ambassador in Mexico (Fletcher)' (8 March 1918) in *FRUS*, 1913–21, 1918 vol, 801–5.

[89] Ibid., 802.

[90] Ibid., 804.

[91] 'The Acting Secretary of State to the Ambassador in Mexico (Fletcher)' (8 March 1918) in *FRUS*, 1913–21, 1918 vol, 803. Other states had similar concerns. See, for example, 'The French Ambassador (Jusserand) to the Secretary of State' (8 February 1918) in *FRUS*, 1913–21, 1918 vol, 800; 'The Ambassador in Italy (Page) to the Acting Secretary of State' (7 April 1919) in *FRUS*, 1913–21, 1919 vol II, 633–44; 'The Ambassador in Mexico (Fletcher) to the Secretary of State' (15 November 1918) in *FRUS*, 1913–21, 1918 vol, 813.

[92] See, for example, *FRUS*, 1913–21, 1918 vol, 806–8; *FRUS*, 1913–21, 1919 vol II, 632–5.

[93] See, for example, 'The Secretary of State to the British Ambassador (Reading)' (19 March 1918) in *FRUS*, 1913–21, 1918 vol, 806.

[94] 'The Mexican Acting Secretary of State for Foreign Affairs (Pérez) to the American Ambassador (Fletcher)' (29 November 1918) in *FRUS*, 1913–21, 1918 vol, 815.

delay – whatever its reason – seemed to damage irrevocably the credibility of the Mexican government in the eyes of the claimant states, if they had ever really had faith in Carranza's administration. The British ambassador wrote to the US Secretary of State in March 1919 that 'the Mexican Government appears to have framed this decree, hoping that foreign governments may commit themselves to accepting it in which event that Government may arrange it should remain a dead letter and a bar to any diplomatic action'.[95] Subsequently, the US ambassador was instructed to inform the Mexican foreign ministry that:

> because of the delay which has occurred in effective dealing by the Mexican Government with the claims of foreigners, there has arisen in this country a feeling that the Government of Mexico is not earnestly endeavouring to bring about a satisfactory adjustment of the matter. In view of this feeling, which my Government is bound to say seems not to be without some justification, it, as at present advised, finds itself unable to recommend to American citizens that they submit their claims to the Commission and Board of Arbitration provided for in the Decrees mentioned, and must point out the desirability of the establishment of an arbitral tribunal of undoubted international standing to deal with such claims.[96]

Things were certainly proceeding slowly on the Mexican side. In April 1919, the commission had considered forty-two foreign claims, but Congress was yet to authorise any awards.[97] Mexico did later allay some – albeit not all – of the concerns about the commission. A new decree in August 1919[98] extended its jurisdiction to cover claims based on damages caused by 'outlaws or rebels' in the event of negligence or fault on the part of the Mexican authorities,[99] and removed the article regarding foreign-owned corporations, although the Mexican executive retained the right to choose the umpire in case of disagreement.[100]

[95] 'The Ambassador in Great Britain (Davis) to the Acting Secretary of State' (28 March 1919) in *FRUS*, 1913–21, 1919 vol II, 633.

[96] 'The Secretary of State to the Chargé in Mexico (Summerlin)' (25 July 1919) in *FRUS*, 1913–21, 1919 vol II, 637–8.

[97] 'The Chargé in Mexico (Summerlin) to the Acting Secretary of State' (26 April 1919) in *FRUS*, 1913–21, 1919 vol II, 635.

[98] 'Executive Decree of August 30, 1919, Establishing a Claims Commission' in *FRUS*, 1913–21, 1919 vol II, 640–4.

[99] Ibid., 641. In 1924 the commission's jurisdiction was further extended to include claims arising from losses caused by Villa and Zapata's forces (after their split with Carranza) in the event of negligence. See Feller, n 3, 17–18, 202.

[100] 'Executive Decree of August 30, 1919, Establishing a Claims Commission', n 98, 643.

However, the fate of the commission was overtaken by events when, in May 1920, Carranza was deposed by his popular general, Álvaro Obregón. In 1921, the Obregón government, seeking foreign recognition, sent circular telegrams to all the countries that had revolutionary damage claims against Mexico, inviting them to participate in negotiations for the establishment of international mixed commissions to resolve such claims.[101] This was a significant move: the first time a Mexican government had offered international adjudication, although the circular made it clear that any indemnities paid would be ex gratia.[102] While the Mexican government had conceded internationalisation to try and gain recognition, it still sought to protect its legal position, particularly in respect of its non-responsibility for unsuccessful revolutionary forces.[103]

During the negotiations with the United States, Mexico succeeded in resisting demands that recognition of the Obregón government be made conditional upon a commercial treaty – containing provisions for claims settlement – that would guarantee US oil and agricultural interests acquired prior to the 1917 Constitution.[104] This question of the retroactivity of the provisions concerning ownership of the subsoil, land reform and the regulation of concession agreements under Article 27 of the 1917 Constitution took over the negotiations,[105] and prevented claims conventions being agreed for two years.[106] They were finally agreed at the Bucareli Conference in 1923, which US commissioner Charles Beecher Warren opened with the following statement reinforcing the US vision of international law as the basis for economic order and the guarantor of the conditions for doing business across borders:

> The Government of the United States, [and] the people of the United States, seek no special advantages in Mexico, no rights which it and they are not willing to share with others. We have no intention or desire of interfering with the sovereignty of Mexico. We are convinced, however, that certain principles are essential as the basis of economic cooperation

101 Feller, n 3, 19–20.
102 Ibid.
103 Ibid., 21.
104 Ibid., 20–3.
105 For example, at the Bucareli Conference of 1923 where the claims conventions were agreed, all the substantive meetings were about the oil and agrarian questions. See United States–Mexican Commission, *Proceedings of the United States–Mexican Commission: Convened in Mexico City, May 14, 1923* (Government Printing Office, 1925).
106 Feller, n 3, 20.

> between nations. The principles of justice recognized by international law must prevail between nations in order that trade and commerce may flow with a feeling of certainty between different peoples. We are certain that there must be a belief on both sides of the border that business can be conducted with safety and security . . . There can be no compromise with the fundamental principles essential to international business.[107]

Mexican negotiators were successful in getting claims that had arisen in respect of loss or damage caused by 'revolutionary acts' between 20 November 1910 and 31 May 1920 carved out into a separate 'special' claims convention under which they would be settled in accordance with 'justice and equity' rather than international law, and indemnities paid ex gratia.[108] The jurisdiction of the special claims commission was essentially the same as that of the 1917 domestic commission (as amended).[109] All other US claims would be decided by a 'general' commission, which would be mutual, 'in accordance with the principles of international law, justice and equity'.[110] The US special convention was the model for the conventions which were agreed with France, Germany, Britain, Italy and Spain between 1923 and 1927.[111]

14.4 Assessing the Mexican Commissions and the Legacy of Alien Protection

The outcome of the struggle over the internationalisation of revolutionary damage claims during the Mexican revolution was somewhat ambiguous. Essentially, in return for recognition, the Obregón government offered full indemnity while managing to reserve its position under

[107] United States–Mexican Commission, n 105, 3–4.

[108] Feller, n 3, 23. For the text of the special claims convention, see Feller, n 3, 385–93.

[109] Under Article 3 of the *US Special Convention*, the US special commission had authority to decide claims arising out of acts: '1) by forces of a Government de jure or de facto; 2) by revolutionary forces as a result of the triumph of whose cause governments de facto or de jure have been established, or by revolutionary forces opposed to them; 3) by forces arising from the disjunction of the forces mentioned in the next preceding paragraph up to the time when the government de jure established itself as a result of a particular revolution; 4) by federal forces that were disbanded; and 5) by mutinies or mobs, or insurrectionary forces other than those referred to under subdivisions 2, 3 and 4 above, or by bandits, provided in any case it be established that the appropriate authorities omitted to take reasonable measures to suppress insurrectionists, mobs or bandits, or treated them with lenity or were in fault in other particulars'.

[110] Some revolutionary damage claims did make it into the general commission: see n 6.

[111] Feller, n 3, 24.

international law.[112] Mexico was unable to resist the internationalisation of the alien protection issue and deal with the claims domestically. However, it did succeed in limiting the 'legalisation' of alien protection claims. Mexico wanted to avoid setting a precedent that would support expansive international responsibility for revolutionary damage by keeping revolutionary damage claims under equitable rather than legal jurisdiction. This was significant given that once legal responsibility was established its enforcement could be used as a pretext for intervention. In this respect, the Mexican commissions were part of a broader regional and historical pattern of arbitrations associated with foreign intervention. They were the last of a series of nearly forty mixed claims commissions that addressed the issue of state responsibility for 'revolutionary damage' during the nineteenth century and the early decades of the twentieth.[113] While the Mexican commissions were not imposed directly by force, this cannot be said of some of their most notable predecessors. In 1902, Britain, France and Italy had blockaded Venezuela over unpaid debts, including revolutionary damage claims arising out of the revolutions and civil wars that had disrupted a period of capitalist expansion under Venezuela's own 'moderniser', Antonio Guzmán Blanco.[114] Due to the blockade, Venezuela was forced into international arbitration on unfavourable terms,[115] the resulting commissions described at the time as 'the most notable instance of international arbitration in the history of the world'.[116] Unpaid revolutionary damage claims were also used to justify the US invasion of Mexico in 1846, in which Mexico lost over half its territory, and the 1862 intervention in Mexico by Britain, France and

112 See ibid., 22; G Godfrey Phillips, 'The Anglo-Mexican Special Claims Commission' (1933) 49 *Law Quarterly Review* 226, 227.

113 As there is no comprehensive collection of international arbitral awards, in coming up with this figure I have been dependent on cross-checking secondary sources such as Moore, n 12; W Evans Darby, *International Tribunals* (Peace Society, 4th ed, 1904); Jackson H Ralston, *The Law and Procedure of International Tribunals* (Stanford University Press, 1926); Haig Silvanie, 'Responsibility of States for Acts of Insurgent Governments' (1939) 33 *American Journal of International Law* 78; A M Stuyt, *Survey of International Arbitrations, 1794–1938* (Martinus Nijhoff, 1939).

114 For a historical account of the blockade see, for example, Nancy Mitchell, 'The Height of the German Challenge: The Venezuela Blockade 1902–1903' (1996) 20 *Diplomatic History* 185.

115 See Jackson H Ralston, *Venezuelan Arbitrations of 1903* (Government Printing Office, 1904).

116 *Kummerow, Otto Redler and Co, Fulda, Fischbach, and Friedericy Cases* 10 RIAA 369 (1903) 392.

Spain that led to the French occupation and the imposition of Emperor Maximiliano.[117]

Their equitable jurisdiction also enabled Mexico to argue before the commissions for more restricted responsibility for revolutionary damage than would have been provided for under international law and to challenge rules contested by Latin American diplomats and international lawyers. While the claimant states argued that Mexico was responsible for the acts of all the revolutionary forces and governments between 1910 and 1920, Mexico denied responsibility for the Huerta regime, Orozco's forces and the Zapatistas and Villistas once they broke with Carranza. The commissions were often sympathetic to Mexico's arguments. For example, the German and Italian commissions agreed with Mexico that there was no responsibility for Huerta's government. Their presiding commissioner argued that:

> It does not appear to me to be just or equitable to hold responsible for the acts of a spurious administration created with all the vices condemned by public law, the very people who repudiated it on the battlefield [that is, the Constitutionalists] and which, through its legitimate representatives, has refused to recognise the validity of the acts of Victoriano Huerta and his satellites. A commission of equity cannot, by its decision, legitimise the system of military uprisings which has so greatly retarded progress in a majority of American countries. Nor can it condone the violation of political morality as a means of assuming representative power in a republic. On the contrary it should condemn such acts as violative of the high principles upon which our civilisation is based.[118]

In *Naomi Russell*[119] and the *Santa Isabel Claims*[120] Mexico was held not to be responsible by the US special commission for the acts of the forces of Orozco and Villa respectively. There were few successful claims for negligence in failing to protect foreign interests against harm done by revolutionary forces.[121] In various cases, for example the relatively well-

[117] See Moore, n 12.

[118] *Adolfo Stoll (Germany) v United Mexican States* (1931–2) 6 *Annual Digest of Public International Law Cases* 215. For references to other cases similarly decided by the German and Italian commissioners, see Feller, n 3, 161, at nn 12–14.

[119] *Naomi Russell, In Her Own Right and as Administratrix and Guardian (USA) v United Mexican States*, 4 RIAA 805 (24 April 1931).

[120] *Cornelia J Pringle et al (Santa Isabel Claims) (USA) v United Mexican States*, 4 RIAA 783 (26 April 1926).

[121] For successful negligence claims, see *Edith Henry (Great Britain) v United Mexican States*, 5 RIAA 268 (3 August 1931); *John Gill (Great Britain) v United Mexican States*, 5 RIAA 157 (19 May 1931); *William McNeill (Great Britain) v United Mexican States*,

known *Home Insurance Co* and *Solis*,[122] responsibility was denied by the commissions on the basis either that the Mexican authorities had done as much as they could in the circumstances or for lack of evidence.[123] In *Mexican Union Railway*, the British commission enforced a very broad Calvo clause against the claimant, meaning that the company was considered Mexican and thus unable to bring an alien protection claim for revolutionary damage caused to its railway concession.[124] Of course, there were also cases that went against Mexico and that confirmed controversial aspects of the alien protection doctrine,[125] but overall Mexico probably had the best of it. Moreover, the British, French and Spanish claims conventions were later revised in Mexico's favour so as explicitly to exclude claims arising out of acts of Huerta's government or forces and claims arising out of acts of unsuccessful revolutionaries without negligence, since these issues had proved so controversial.[126]

At the same time as the Mexican commissions were sitting, the parallel efforts taking place to codify state responsibility for injuries to aliens through the League of Nations failed, blocked by a group of largely Latin

5 RIAA 164 (19 May 1931) 168; *William E Bowerman and Messrs Burberry's (Ltd) (Great Britain) v United Mexican States*, 5 RIAA 104 (15 February 1930); *Santa Gertrudis Jute Mill Company (Ltd) (Great Britain) v United Mexican States*, 5 RIAA 108 (15 February 1930).

122 *The Home Insurance Co (USA) v United Mexican States*, 4 RIAA 48 (31 March 1926); *G L Solis (USA) v United Mexican States*, 4 RIAA 358 (3 October 1928). *Home Insurance Co* was cited in *Asian Agricultural Products Ltd (AAPL) v Republic of Sri Lanka (Final Award)* (1991) 6(2) *ICSID Review* 526 (Case No ARB/87/3) ('*AAPL v Sri Lanka*') (on which more below), while *Solis* was cited in the ILC's 'Draft Articles', n 8, 50.

123 See also, for example, *James F Bartlett (Great Britain) v United Mexican States*, 5 RIAA 151 (13 May 1931); *Christina Patton (Great Britain) v United Mexican States*, 5 RIAA 224 (8 July 1931); *George Creswell Delamain (Great Britain) v United Mexican* States, 5 RIAA 229 (10 July 1931); *AH Francis (Great Britain) v United Mexican States*, 5 RIAA 99 (15 February 1930); *Annie Bella Graham Kidd (Great Britain) v United Mexican States*, 5 RIAA 142 (23 April 1931); *Alfred Hammond Bromly (Great Britain) v United Mexican States*, 5 RIAA 238 (22 July 1931); *Bond Coleman (United States) v United Mexican States*, 4 RIAA 364 (3 October 1928).

124 *Mexican Union Railway (Ltd) (Great Britain) v United Mexican States*, 5 RIAA 115 (February 1930). See also *The Interoceanic Railway of Mexico (Acapulco to Veracruz) (Ltd), and the Mexican Eastern Railway Company (Ltd), and the Mexican Southern Railway (Ltd) (Great Britain) v United Mexican States*, 5 RIAA 178 (24 March 1931); *Veracruz (Mexico) Railways (Ltd) (Great Britain) v United Mexican States*, 5 RIAA 221 (7 July 1931). These cases significantly extended the application of the rule established by the US general commission in the influential case *North American Dredging Company of Texas (USA) v United Mexican States*, 4 RIAA 26 (31 March 1926).

125 See, for example, *Pinson*, n 39; *Hopkins*, n 6.

126 The full text of the revised conventions can be found in the appendices to Feller, n 3.

American and former Austro-Hungarian states, which voted together to reject rules which they believed were biased against them.[127] Taking this failure together with Mexico's relative success in resisting claims and the fact that the Mexican commissions were the last big mixed claims commissions to consider state responsibility for revolutionary damage might suggest that alien protection was on the wane. However, such a decline as this was, was only temporary; in the long term, alien protection has survived and, indeed, thrived. Today in investment arbitration,[128] tribunals rely on alien protection cases from nineteenth-century and early twentieth-century mixed claims commissions, including the Mexican commissions, in order to continue to hold postcolonial states to a high standard of protection of investments in times of revolution and civil war. In the long run, internationalisation of alien protection – now foreign investment protection – has been consolidated.

While *AAPL v Sri Lanka* is mainly (in)famous for its expansive approach to jurisdiction,[129] its facts concerned the destruction of the claimant's prawn farm during the Sri Lankan civil war.[130] Despite the fact that neither side managed to adduce evidence as to how or by whom – whether by government forces or by the rebels – the farm was destroyed, and the tribunal concluded that Sri Lanka's responsibility was established, applying a standard of protection drawn from alien protection cases, including *Home Insurance Co.*[131] It held that the government had failed to take 'important precautionary measures' to get the suspected rebels out of the farm peacefully; 'this would have been essential to minimize the risks of killings and destruction when planning to

[127] See n 10.

[128] For accounts of what happened in between, see Antony Anghie, *Imperialism, Sovereignty and the Making of International Law* (Cambridge University Press, 2004) 196–244; James Thuo Gathii, 'War's Legacy in International Investment Law' (2009) 11 *International Community Law Review* 353; Sundhya Pahuja, *Decolonising International Law: Development, Economic Growth and the Politics of Universality* (Cambridge University Press, 2011) 95–171; Kate Miles, *The Origins of International Investment Law: Empire, Environment and the Safeguarding of Capital* (Cambridge University Press, 2013).

[129] *AAPL v Sri Lanka* was the first case in which an ICSID tribunal was found to have jurisdiction on the basis of the investor-state dispute settlement provision in the investment treaty rather than on the basis of the investment contract: *AAPL v Sri Lanka*, n 122. This subsequently became standard practice, leading to an explosion in the caseload of ICSID after 1990. See M Sornarajah, *Resistance and Change in the International Law on Foreign Investment* (Cambridge University Press, 2015) 2.

[130] *AAPL v Sri Lanka*, n 122, [3].

[131] Ibid. [72]–[75].

undertake a vast military counterinsurgency operation in that area for regaining lost control'.[132] The claimant was awarded $460,000 plus interest.[133] While in *Home Insurance Co* the commission was relatively deferential to national authority, here the tribunal is much stricter. One commentator has suggested that the result of the decision in *AAPL v Sri Lanka* was 'effectively to apply the standard [of strict liability] through the back door . . . render[ing] the government of Sri Lanka an all-weather insurer or guarantor of foreign investors operating in its territory'.[134]

More recently, in a 2017 ICSID award *Ampal American Israel Corporation v Egypt*, the defendant state was held responsible for failing to exercise due diligence in preventing attacks on an oil pipeline in the context of the Egyptian revolution of 2011.[135] According to the tribunal, following the overthrow of President Mubarak, the Sinai region where the pipeline was located became lawless and 'armed militant groups took advantage of the political instability, security deterioration and general lawlessness . . . to perpetrate the attacks'.[136] Although it found that 'the adequacy of the State's response should be assessed in the light of the scale of the disorder and the extent of its resources',[137] in practice the tribunal made no such assessment. Despite acknowledging the difficult circumstances faced by the Egyptian authorities in Sinai, the tribunal simply found that Egypt had failed to take any concrete steps to protect the claimant's investment.[138]

14.5 Conclusion

Thus, despite the fact that alien protection seemed to be on the wane in 1930, this victory for the newer or smaller and formerly colonised states

[132] Ibid. [85].
[133] Ibid., 572.
[134] John Baloro, 'Aspects of the Law on the Responsibility of a Host State for Injuries to Foreign Investment during Internal Armed Conflicts: The ICSID Award in *Asian Agricultural Products Limited (AAPL) v Republic of Sri Lanka*' (1992–1993) 18 *South African Yearbook of International Law* 105, 125–6.
[135] *Ampal-American Israel Corporation v Arab Republic of Egypt (Decision on Liability and Heads of Loss)* (ICSID Case No ARB/12/11, 21 February 2017).
[136] Ibid. [284].
[137] Ibid. [244].
[138] Ibid. [283]–[291]. Cf *Pantechniki S A Contractors & Engineers (Greece) v Republic of Albania (Award)* (ICSID Case No ARB/07/21, 30 July 2009), a case arising out of the Albanian civil war of 1997, in which Albania was held not responsible, with sole arbitrator Jan Paulsson arguing for 'an element of proportionality in applying the international standard': at [77].

was only a temporary one. I have argued that what we find today in international investment law is a high standard of protection owed to foreign investors in times of revolution and civil war, based on the nineteenth- and early twentieth- century alien protection arbitrations but in fact much stricter than the standard they applied. In the long run, internationalisation of alien protection – now foreign investment protection – has prevailed. The result is that international law allocates the costs of revolution to the state, guaranteeing foreign capital against losses in revolution and civil war, and thus serves to insulate an economic order based on trade and investment liberalisation against revolution. That is not to say, however, that resistance to the internationalisation of revolutionary damage claims has not left its mark. It fundamentally shaped the trajectory of the project of state responsibility, the split between primary and secondary rules serving the purpose of severing it from its controversial origins in alien protection.[139] It also finds its resonances in contemporary resistance to investor-state dispute resolution and attempts to protect or restore domestic regulatory space against the rights of foreign investors.[140]

[139] See Nissel, n 10.

[140] For an overview, see Kate Miles, 'Investor–State Dispute Settlement: Conflict, Convergence, and Future Directions' (2016) 7 *European Yearbook of International Economic Law* 273.

PART V

Rights

15

'Animated by the European Spirit'

European Human Rights as Counterrevolutionary Legality

ANNA SAUNDERS*

> The advantage of a European Tribunal of the Rights of Man is obvious. Besides constituting a precious safeguard for individuals, it recognizes them as subjects of supranational law, the strait gate through which the liberation from statist totalitarianism can pass. At the outset, moreover, it affords the gathering of the debris of civilization and the beginning of the reconstruction of a common thought, the basis of a common order. Since there is no more Christianity, it is necessary to create something else.
>
> —Louis Salleron[1]

15.1 Introduction

The struggle within tsarist Russia culminating in the revolution of 1917 was a legal and political event of global significance. The establishment of the Soviet state and its deployment in service of a programme of socialist transformation represented a foundational challenge to prevailing forms

* LLM candidate and Frank Knox Memorial Fellow, Harvard Law School. I am grateful to Anne Orford for her guidance and supervision of the paper on which this chapter is based; to Kathryn Greenman and Ntina Tzouvala, as well as Luís Bogliolo and Fabia Veçoso for thoughtful comments on the ideas contained in this chapter; and to Jessica Whyte, Julia Dehm, and Ben Golder, and the participants in the 'Redistributive Human Rights?' workshop at UNSW Law which a version of this chapter was presented. Unless indicated otherwise, all translations are the author's. This chapter is based on a paper submitted in partial fulfilment of the requirements of the Melbourne Law School JD.

1 French academic and right-wing intellectual. The quote in translation is from Marco Duranti, *The Conservative Human Rights Revolution: European Identity, Transnational Politics, and the Origins of the European Convention* (Oxford University Press, 2017), citing Louis Salleron, 'Pour un Tribunal européen des droits de l'homme' (1947) 5 *Terre d'Europe* 26, 31.

of political organisation.[2] Rhetorically, if not always in practice, the socialist Soviet state condemned the capitalist economic system and its political encasing, liberalism, as well as the violent imperialism which it saw as an inevitable expression of that system.[3] In seeking both to consolidate and internationalise its own state form,[4] through communist politics as well as through force both at home and abroad, the revolutionary state challenged liberal conceptions of civil and political freedoms and attracted condemnation in turn.

In response to this challenge to both political and propertied freedoms, European international lawyers and later, European states, sought new answers to the question of how to internationalise the protection of the liberal-capitalist model as *the* way of understanding the state form. During both the interwar period as well as in the years following the Second World War, human rights and their predecessors emerged in part as a means of responding to that question. How could political freedoms, integral to the ethos and appeal of the liberal state, be encoded into law without also making those freedoms available in service of a different and revolutionary politics?

This chapter will argue that early European conceptualisations of international instruments for the protection of rights, while seeming open in principle, were counterrevolutionary in origin and in design. The first part of this chapter will examine the earliest European example of a legal instrument for the protection of rights, the Declaration of the International Rights of Man, and the thought of its progenitor, André Mandelstam, in the interwar period. It will then argue that aspects of this early conceptualisation, which responded to the internationalisation of the Soviet state, carried through in important ways to the postwar period, and were incorporated in Article 17 of the European Convention. In its final form, that article states: 'Nothing in this Convention may be interpreted as implying for any State, group or person any right to engage in any activity or perform any act aimed at the destruction of any of the rights and freedoms set forth herein or at their limitation to a greater

[2] See generally Sheila Fitzpatrick, *The Russian Revolution* (Oxford University Press, 4th ed, 2017).

[3] See Vladimir Ilyich Lenin, *Imperialism: The Highest Stage of Capitalism* (International Publishers, first published 1917, 2013 ed).

[4] On Soviet internationalism and internationality, see Scott Newton, Chapter 6 in this volume.

extent than is provided for in the Convention'.[5] The imprecision of Article 17, and its predecessors, reflected the drafters' appreciation of both the necessities of diplomatic accommodation and of the benefits of ambiguity. As applied by the European Commission of Human Rights (the Commission), and later, the European Court of Human Rights (the Court), that article would eventually act to limit the range of possible claims to rights guarantees — both communist and otherwise — on the basis of the politics advanced by the claimant.[6] In other words, it put forward a theory of rights as legally bounded, rather than politically accessible, and able to conserve their intended political orientation through being tied to and interpreted by particular institutions. That article has played an unassuming but important role in shaping European politics both during the early Cold War as well as in more recent history.[7]

In writing the European history of rights as a response to revolution, this chapter also speaks to contemporary debates in human rights scholarship. Prominent scholars have spoken of a growing divide in scholarship on rights between emissaries of the 'human rights movement' wishing to keep the faith with human rights as a vehicle for achieving a just world, and critical scholars pointing to the dangers that such a faith poses for conceptions of justice that seek to go beyond the limits of liberal ideals.[8] However, as Ben Golder has demonstrated, the claims that critique effects a disillusionment with rights are overstated: much critical theoretical scholarship, while acknowledging that rights are not the panacea they were once dreamed to be, nevertheless makes a 'redemptive

[5] *Convention for the Protection of Human Rights and Fundamental Freedoms*, opened for signature 4 November 1950, 213 UNTS 221 (entered into force 3 September 1953) Article 17 (*European Convention*).

[6] See Paolo Lobba, 'Holocaust Denial before the European Court of Human Rights: Evolution of an Exceptional Regime' (2015) 26 *European Journal of International Law* 237.

[7] For examples of the recent scholarly interest in Article 17 as a means of combating anti-semitic historical revisionism and fascism, see Lobba, n 6; Frederick Cowell, 'Anti-Totalitarian Memory: Explaining the Presence of 'Rights Abuse' Clauses in International Human Rights Law' (2018) 6 *Birkbeck Law Review* 35. Much of the recent jurisprudence under Article 17 has also related to the inadmissibility of rights claims from pan-Islamist groups, although less has been written about this. See, for example, *Kasymakhunov and Saybatalov v Russia* (European Court of Human Rights, First Section, Application Nos 26261/05 and 26377/06, 14 March 2013).

[8] See, for example, Philip Alston, suggesting that much critical work is 'unenlightening dead-end scholarship', of little use in combatting the 'populist challenge' to human rights: Philip Alston, 'The Populist Challenge to Human Rights' (2017) 9 *Journal of Human Rights Practice* 1, 13.

return' to rights as an imperfect vehicle for progressive politics.[9] The same might be said of recent work highlighting the contingency of neoliberal expressions of rights, and articulating the historical advancement, or present political urgency, of alternative visions of economic and social equality through the language and form of rights.[10]

In part, these continued engagements with rights as a resource for, and locus of, struggle evidences a persistent belief in rights as 'continually open-ended': valuable tools that might be reinterpreted and repurposed in service of a progressive agenda, despite having borne witness to substantial increases in inequality over the last several decades.[11] That this belief has not been wholly unsettled by the substantial body of scholarship showing rights also to be part of a conservative project at home and an imperial project abroad demonstrates the persistence of rights as an object of study and as a site of resistance, even for many critical international lawyers and legal scholars.[12] In contrast to these

[9] Ben Golder, 'Beyond Redemption? Problematising the Critique of Human Rights in Contemporary International Legal Thought' (2014) 2 *London Review of International Law* 77.

[10] For an exposition of the place of rights in the Third World challenge to the structure of the international economic order in the 1970s, see Julia Dehm, 'Highlighting Inequalities in the Histories of Human Rights: Contestations over Justice, Needs and Rights in the 1970s' (2018) 31 *Leiden Journal of International Law* 871. For an argument that 'the classic rights of liberalism … can also serve as important tools to allow subordinate groups to challenge the extant social order', if successfully reformulated through radical struggle, see Paul O'Connell, 'On the Human Rights Question' (2018) 40 Human Rights *Quarterly* 962, 985. See also Susan Marks, 'Four Human Rights Myths' in David Kinley, Wojciecj Sadurski and Kevin Walton (eds), *Human Rights: Old Problems, New Possibilities* (Edward Elgar, 2013) 217, 235 (on 'refocus[ing] the gaze of the human rights movement'); Ratna Kapur, *Gender, Alterity and Human Rights: Freedom in a Fishbowl* (Edward Elgar, 2018) 23 (exploring 'the potential for human rights to be aligned with, though not necessarily commensurable with, a non-liberal paradigm of freedom').

[11] See the theory of rights advanced in Pamela Slotte and Miia Halme-Tuomisaari, 'Revisiting the Origins of Human Rights: Introduction' in Pamela Slotte and Miia Halme-Tuomisaari (eds), *Revisiting the Origins of Human Rights* (Cambridge University Press, 2015) 1, 1. Cf. Robert Knox's argument that while progressive actors can usefully deploy law to make political interventions and challenge the prevailing order, it is essential that they avoid any attendant reification of legalism. Knox proposes instead a position of 'principled opportunism': Robert Knox, 'Strategy and Tactics' (2012) 21 *Finnish Yearbook of International Law* 193.

[12] That body of scholarship includes Duranti, n 1; A W B Simpson, *Human Rights and the End of Empire: Britain and the Genesis of the European Convention* (Oxford University Press, 2001); Samuel Moyn, *Christian Human Rights* (University of Pennsylvania Press, 2015); Anne Orford, *Reading Humanitarian Intervention: Human Rights and the Use of Force in International Law* (Cambridge University Press, 2003); David Kennedy, *The*

engagements, a second set of responses to this unsettling of rights has involved attempts to disengage critical scholarship from rights, in recognition that 'the investment in making human rights mean something different takes place at the imaginative cost of creating new forms and new political vehicles and affiliations for the realisation of that universality, or justice or freedom however conceived'.[13] This chapter's first contribution, in the ways outlined above, will be to add to the growing third way of responding to this unsettling that suggests that, far from being a 'powerless companion' that merely detracts attention or removes oxygen from different forms of struggle, rights instruments and rights-thinking have actively – and effectively – worked to sustain liberal forms of political and economic organisation against other utopian forms of politics.[14]

A further contribution of this chapter will be to suggest, following Golder's work, that this persistent belief in, and engagement with, rights is no accident. Rather, it shows us something important about the credo of human rights, and the way they present themselves to the world. Golder has suggested that the promises that rights make of being open to radical struggle remain 'unactualised textual possibilities, traces and memories, which solicit a certain faith in the human rights form – as endlessly capable of transcending its present instantiations'.[15] This chapter takes up his challenge to 'provide an account of the process by which

Dark Sides of Virtue: Reassessing International Humanitarianism (Princeton University Press, 2004).

[13] Golder, n 9, 114. See, for example, Samuel Moyn, 'A Powerless Companion: Human Rights in the Age of Neoliberalism' (2015) 77 *Law and Contemporary Problems* 147; Martti Koskenniemi, *The Politics of International Law* (Hart, 2011) 133. See also Linarelli, Salomon and Sornarajah's argument that 'even though capitalism looms large in the fabric of international human rights law, human rights law has the potential for being progressive'. In this account, the problem is only that rights 'operate almost fully *within* ... global capitalist orthodoxy', not that they sustain it in a political, intellectual or material sense: John Linarelli, Margot E Salomon and Muthucumaraswamy Sornarajah, *The Misery of International Law: Confrontations with Injustice in the Global Economy* (Oxford University Press, 2018) 267.

[14] Anne Orford, 'Beyond Harmonization: Trade, Human Rights and the Economy of Sacrifice' (2005) 18 *Leiden Journal of International Law* 179; Jessica Whyte, 'Is Revolution Desirable? Michel Foucault on Revolution, Neoliberalism and Rights' in Ben Golder (ed), *Re-reading Foucault: On Law, Power and Rights* (Routledge, 2013); Jessica Whyte, 'Human Rights and the Collateral Damage of Neoliberalism' (2017) 20 *Theory & Event* 137; Umut Özsu, 'Neoliberalism and Human Rights: The Brandt Commission and the Struggle for a New World' (2018) 81 *Law and Contemporary Problems* 101.

[15] Golder, n 9, 96.

that possibility is sustained and yet never quite made real'. In doing so, it treats European human rights both as a legal order with a particular history, and as a means of illustrating the distance between the political promise of human rights and the ways those rights are brought into being through law.

15.2 André Mandelstam and Rights after Revolution

The Declaration of the International Rights of Man is now acknowledged, particularly by histories that seek to show the importance of rights to the European regional imaginary, as an important philosophical and juridical precursor to the postwar rights instruments.[16] Its drafting and adoption by the Institut de Droit International, in its 1929 session, was intellectually and politically driven by Russian émigré and international lawyer André Mandelstam.[17] The Declaration is generally remembered as having accomplished the leap from a patchwork of minority protection treaties to a generalised instrument for the international protection of rights.[18]

In this context, Mandelstam's contribution, in particular, is often positioned as a response to the Armenian genocide, to the persecution of Russian Jewry prior to 1917 or to Bolshevik revolutionary violence.[19] A reading of Mandelstam's later work, however, suggests that the politics of this contribution can also be understood as a response to the anti-imperial politics of the Soviet state, as much as to its violent acts.[20] Much

[16] See, for example, Duranti, n 2, 67–71; J H Burgers, 'The Road to San Francisco: The Revival of the Human Rights Idea in the Twentieth Century' (1992) 14 *Human Rights Quarterly* 447; Helmut Aust, 'From Diplomat to Academic Activist: André Mandelstam and the History of Human Rights' (2015) 25 *European Journal of International Law* 1105. The text of the Declaration is reproduced as an annex to Aust's article in the *European Journal*.

[17] Aust, n 16, 1107.

[18] Simpson, n 12, 151.

[19] See Dzovinar Kévonian, 'André Mandelstam and the Internationalization of Human Rights (1869–1949)' in Pamela Slotte and Miia Halme-Tuomisaari (eds), *Revisiting the Origins of Human Rights* (Cambridge University Press, 2015) 239, 241; Mark Toufayan, 'Empathy, Humanity and the Armenian Question in the Internationalist Legal Imagination' (2011) 24 *Revue Québécoise de Droit International* 171; Aust, n 16; Burgers, n 16.

[20] Mandelstam himself stated of his proposal for the commission that led to the Declaration that it was 'only natural that a Russian should have taken this initiative': André Mandelstam, *Les droits internationaux de l'homme* (Éditions internationaux, 1931) 7. In this context, it is notable that the Bolshevik Revolution prevented Mandelstam from

of Mandelstam's 1931 masterwork, *Les droits internationaux de l'homme*, can be read as an international lawyer's response to the revolutionary challenge to the standard of civilisation, then an essential characteristic of the international legal order.[21] What he perceived as the failure of the international community to respond adequately propelled him both to draft the Declaration and to propose mechanisms for guarding it against abuse. Although Mandelstam is sometimes pictured as a thinker without disciples, this chapter suggests that aspects of his thought persisted in important ways into the postwar period.[22] This reading of his work positions the emergence of human rights in Europe as a response to revolution, with a complicated lineage in the politics and practices of intervention.[23]

Up until the Declaration of the International Rights of Man, the development of the international legal regime for the protection of rights had been facilitated almost entirely by the major powers. Before the First World War, what was then hailed as the 'progressive recognition of the rights of man' in the international sphere had largely taken the form of great power intervention in other European or peripheral states.[24] These interventions had entailed the use of armed force by 'civilised' great power states against 'uncivilised' ones.[25] The significance of these interventions, for Mandelstam, was their stated justification of protecting the freedoms, of conscience, or of religion, of inhabitants of states subject to

taking up a prominent position in the Ministry of Foreign Affairs and made him an exile in Paris: Aust, n 16, 1108. For his criticism of the Bolsheviks, see André Mandelstam, *La protection internationale des droits de l'homme* (1931) 38 *Recueil des cours* 125, 216.

21 Mandelstam, *Droits internationaux*, n 20. Mandelstam described the work as the culmination of his extensive previous scholarly efforts: at 10.

22 See Burgers, n 16, 264.

23 On intervention as a response to revolution, see also Chapter 10 by Fabia Veçoso and Chapter 9 by Juan Pablo Scarfi in this volume.

24 Mandelstam, *Droits internationaux*, n 20, 30. Mandelstam dates the origins of this practice back to the Anglo-Spanish War and Cromwell's intervention in favour of the Protestant Vaudois.

25 On guarantees of rights as a key determinant of 'civilised' status, see Gerrit Gong, The Standard of 'Civilization' in International *Society* (Oxford University Press, 1984) ch 1. For an argument that the standard of civilisation functioned to promote the economic (and social) transformation of the non-Western world along capitalist lines, see Ntina Tzouvala, 'Civilisation' in Jean d'Aspremont and Sahib Singh (eds), *Concepts for International Law: Contributions to Disciplinary Thought* (Edward Elgar, 2018) 83. For a discussion of selected interventions during this period, as well as the notable counterexample of great power non-intervention in the Ottoman massacre of Armenian populations in 1915–16, see Simpson, n 12, 94–5.

intervention and the fact that they were often followed by a peace treaty making formal provision for such.[26] The development of the right to life of the national community itself, recognised by the Congress of Vienna in its final Act, was a significant further step in what Mandelstam saw as a trajectory toward a recognisable, if inconsistent, practice of intervention by 'humanity' in favour of the rights of man.[27] However, Mandelstam perceived this practice to suffer from two ongoing flaws – its regional character, limited to particular areas of Eastern Europe and the former Ottoman Empire in which the major powers had shown themselves willing to intervene, and the fact that its legal realisation was through a state's 'obligation . . . to the Great Powers' in the form of treaties, rather than any right attaching to the individual under international law.[28]

Of these interventions, those against the Ottoman Empire were for Mandelstam the best and most systematised example of a practice of the limitation of sovereignty in favour of the 'higher rights of man'.[29] Contrary to their recent condemnation by Ottoman negotiators – on the basis that these supposedly humanitarian interventions were in fact a pretext for war and territorial acquisition, and the result of deliberate great power provocation of Christian minority uprisings[30] – Mandelstam argued that the collective nature of certain of these interventions, and the lack of alignment of the interests of the powers intervening,

[26] Citing the treaties of Oliva (1660, Sweden–Poland–Prussia), Nimègue and Ryswick (1678, 1697, France–Holland) as well as the Polish treaties of cession of 1673 and 1793: Mandelstam, *Droits internationaux*, n 20, 29–30. But see Lingelbach, writing in 1900, who had argued of the ongoing practice of 'humanitarian intervention' that 'nearly all cases nominally undertaken on the plea of religion are at bottom political in character' and that 'moral and religious causes for intervention are usually joined with commercial reasons . . . humanitarian reasons of themselves are rarely sufficient to bring about intervention': W E Lingelbach, 'The Doctrine and Practice of Intervention in Europe' (1900) 16 *Annals of the American Academy of Political and Social Science* 1, 17–21.

[27] A trajectory untroubled by the interventions based on the principle of legitimacy, or the maintenance of governments threatened by revolution that Mandelstam argued were declining in frequency: *Droits internationaux*, n 20, 35.

[28] Ibid., 39.

[29] Ibid., 36.

[30] For example, by Ismet Pasha, the chief Turkish negotiator at Mudanya and Lausanne, and later the second president of the Republic of Turkey: George Nathaniel of Curzon and Simeon Eben Baldwin, *Lausanne Conference on Near Eastern Affairs 1922–1923: Records of Proceedings and Draft Terms of Peace* (His Majesty's Stationery Office, 1923) 192–204. On how Western interventions contributed to the solidification of a Turkish ethno-nationalism, see Umut Özsu, *Formalizing Displacement: International Law and Population Transfers* (Oxford University Press, 2015) 80.

demonstrated their truly humanitarian character.[31] Not only that, but the procedural practice that had developed of proposing reforms that 'could only have consolidated the strength and cohesion of the Ottoman State', and intervening after these reforms remained 'obstinately inexecuted' was proof of the objective and disinterested nature of this militaristic regime of rights protection.[32] The creation of the League of Nations, an institution tasked among other things with the supervision of postwar treaties imposing minority protection obligations on newly formed states, he argued, offered further evidence of the collectivisation and depoliticisation of international practices recognising rights.[33]

It was to this gradual generalisation of the international protection of rights that Mandelstam argued the Bolshevik Revolution of 1917 represented an existential challenge. Relinquishing Russia's role as a indisputably 'civilised' great power on the European stage, the Soviet state chose to 'repudiate[] the concept of European civilization altogether, along with imperialist distinctions between civilized and uncivilized'.[34] Consonantly with the articulation of a Soviet anti-imperialist philosophy, the Bolsheviks also renounced the unequal treaties of the tsarist regime.[35] Rather than managing to suppress this brazenly anti-imperial internationalism, Western states eventually reached a political and legal accommodation with the Soviet state. The Cannes Resolutions, proffered by the Allies to the Soviet state at Genoa in 1922, put in place a legal arrangement of coexistence that recognised the right of each nation to choose its own 'system of ownership, internal economy and government' in exchange for the security of foreign capital and public debt.[36] This

[31] Mandelstam, *Droits internationaux*, n 20, 36–7.

[32] Ibid., 36–9.

[33] Ibid., 48. On the rejected proposal of Lord Robert Cecil that the League Covenant include, in Mandelstam's words, a right of intervention into states that 'threatened world peace with a politics of religious intolerance', see also Mandelstam, *Protection internationale*, n 20, 134–5. See Simpson, n 12, 107–45 for an overview of how minority protection, from the sixteenth through to the twentieth century, transformed from a relatively exceptional practice of securing favourable religious and commercial exemptions for Christian populations to a standard set of treaty conditions imposed on newly created European states, overseen through the institution of the League.

[34] Duranti, n 2, 57.

[35] G I Tunkin, *Theory of International Law* (George Allen and Unwin, 1974) 11. For a detailed exploration of the concept of imperialism in Soviet international legal thought, see Chapter 2 by Robert Knox and Ntina Tzouvala in this volume.

[36] Mandelstam, *Droits internationaux*, n 20, 73. See generally Carole Fink, *The Genoa Conference: European Diplomacy, 1921–1922* (University of North Carolina Press, 1984); Stephen White, *The Origins of Détente: The Genoa Conference and Soviet–*

commitment was realised, to a certain extent, through the subsequent Allied recognition of, and entry into diplomatic and legal relations with, the Soviet State without attaching conditions regarding the Soviet protection of the rights of its population.[37] Western states such as France and Britain professed to be interested 'neither in the internal affairs of Russia nor in the form of its government': a commitment to political and military non-intervention that was borne out by insistence on mutual agreement to refrain from anti-Soviet or anti-Western propaganda.[38] This commitment also reflected the extent to which non-intervention in 'matters of domestic jurisdiction' continued to feature as a prominent concern of states during the interwar period.[39] It seemed to Mandelstam, then, that outside of the minority rights treaties, the idea of intervention as a means for the protection of religious or political freedoms had had its day.[40]

Mandelstam's response to the challenge posed by the revolution was to propose an overhaul of the basis on which intervention in the internal political arrangements of a state could lawfully occur. Both the revolution and what followed it, he argued, ,had demonstrated that international law's division between 'civilised' and 'uncivilised' nations, rendering the latter vulnerable to interventions in the name of humanity, was no longer useful.[41] The moral stature of these interventions and the 'salutary effect' they had depended, for Mandelstam, not on the geopolitical dominance of the major powers. Rather, it hinged on a perceived 'gap ... between the *political ideals and governmental practices* of the intervening powers and the methods of the governments undergoing intervention'.[42] After 1917, when an atheistic and revolutionary state once characterised as

Western Relations, 1921–1922 (Cambridge University Press, 1985). The full text of the resolutions is reproduced in Fink at 40.

37 Mandelstam, *Droits internationaux*, n 20, 68–9 (United Kingdom, 1924), 70–1 (France, 1924), 71 (Italy, 1925), 71 (Japan, 1925).

38 See ibid., 69 (United Kingdom), 70 (France), 72 (US). Although Britain, France and the United States did insist on recognition and maintenance of existing Russian debts and compensation for nationalisation of enterprises: at 68, 70–2.

39 One closely related to theoretical debates over whether the individual was or was not a proper 'subject' of international law: Simpson, n 12, 92–3. See also J L Brierly, 'Matters of Domestic Jurisdiction' (1925) 6 *British Yearbook of International Law* 8.

40 For a similarly mournful analysis of great power neutrality in relation to the Mexican revolution, see Mandelstam, *Droits internationaux*, n 20, 77–9.

41 According with the growing cautiousness among Western jurists of the period about an explicit articulation of the standard of civilisation in international law: Duranti, n 2.

42 Mandelstam, *Droits internationaux*, n 20, 98 (emphasis added).

'civilised' openly flouted international treaties, no such 'gap' could be assumed to exist. 'Any state, however "large" or "major" it be . . . [was] not assured against the *temporary passage of power* into hands entirely disrespectful of international law and the laws of humanity'.[43] The solution to this quandary was therefore to embrace a new concept of juridical equality, under which rights obligations would attach to all nations, whether 'civilised' or not.[44] In other words, the existing obligations to protect rights under the minority treaties, which so far had been limited to particular states created after the First World War, should be generalised to all states.[45] Despite the unevenness of the rights afforded to minorities, on the one hand, and to inhabitants and nationals of these states, on the other, Mandelstam argued that these treaties had taken the key first steps of both recognising the rights of the individual, and of limiting the power of the state to act in contravention of those rights.[46] Portraying the universalisation of these rights as a natural next step following the creation of this 'common juridical basis for humanity'[47] was for Mandelstam a means of achieving through codified legal standards what was no longer certain to be achieved through intervention.

At the same time, Mandelstam warned that the universalisation of the minority rights provisions through an international declaration would render them open to political redeployment towards other ends. In language prevalent at the time, he termed this the danger of 'abuse' by 'propagandistic' elements within the state.[48] It was this concern to prevent open-endedness that led Mandelstam to take the rather contorted position of arguing both *for* the subjecthood of the individual as a rights-bearer in international law, and *against* the right of individual petition to

[43] Ibid., 99 (emphasis in original).

[44] 'Before international law, States are equal, in the sense that they can all invoke its protection and they all must submit to its empire': ibid., 97, citing Politis, *Les nouvelles tendances du droit international* (Hachette, 1927) 30.

[45] Ibid., 45–57. The generalisation of minority rights into a human rights regime was first suggested in André Mandelstam, *La protection des minorités* (1923) 1 *Recueil des cours* 513. This proposal, after being rejected by the League of Nations in 1925, was abandoned by the Institut de Droit International in favour of an international convention, and it remained unclear how the eventual Declaration was to be implemented: Kévonian, n 19, 257–8.

[46] The latter being evidence too of movement towards an international constitution: Mandelstam, *Droits internationaux,* n 20, 50–1.

[47] Ibid., 151: 'un *fond juridique commun de l'Humanité*'.

[48] Ibid., 105. See, generally, Vernon Van Dyke, 'The Responsibility of States for International Propaganda' (1940) 34 *American Journal of International Law* 58.

a court. Opposing fellow jurists' proposals in favour of direct access to an international forum, he emphasised the damage that would follow if the Permanent Court of Arbitration or the League of Nations were forced to examine claims 'brought on purely political grounds' and in doing so 'serving … the propaganda goals pursued by the applicants'.[49] The possibility of abuse was not, for Mandelstam, an indication that a generalised regime of rights protection should be abandoned altogether: 'the experience of our time demonstrates that abuses are much less to be worried about than what results from the recognition of a State with an unlimited power over the life and liberty of its subjects'.[50] If a right of individual petition was to be realised, however, the way to do this would be an international organisation with a means of deciding which claims merited examination. This organisation would be tasked with excluding 'all manifestations of intrigue and chicanery' while simultaneously assuring 'the rapid and impartial examination of all claims of a serious character'.[51] A procedural mechanism of this kind would seemingly allow the declaration to retain its political potency, while effectively preventing its subversion in the service of a radical agenda.

Rereading Mandelstam's work shows us that scholarly articulations of universal rights, and the emergence of European instruments for their protection, were informed in significant measure by his political opposition to the Soviet state. What was needed in the post-revolutionary period was, for him, 'a Declaration of the rights of man, an intervention of peaceful humanity, opposed to the intervention of the military inhumanity of the Soviets, a rule of law, as opposed to the rule of violence'.[52] Framing rights as universal obligations that could be imposed on all states, no matter how great, was both a direct response to the revolution and a way of reframing its politics. Since liberal states had proven themselves no longer willing to be sufficiently concerned, diplomatically or militarily, with forms of internal governance, it was time for international lawyers to enter the fray. At the same time, Mandelstam's proposal to attach legal and procedural safeguards against *abus de droit*

[49] Mandelstam, *Droits internationaux*, n 20, 105–6. The other danger was that pitting the state against its subjects ran the risk of 'poisoning the relations between the State and its nationals'. Confining the rights to foreign nationals, as had been the practice, was no longer possible as it would hardly be accepted by national publics: at 106.

[50] Ibid., 138.

[51] Ibid., 106.

[52] Ibid., 90.

(or 'abuse of rights')[53] to these universal guarantees was an attempt to ensure that rights maintained their liberal political orientation – one which would be replicated when rights came next to be rearticulated in the context of heightened Cold War rivalries.

15.3 Article 17, Human Rights and the Constitution of Europe

15.3.1 Postwar Europe: Contexts and Categories

The counterrevolutionary politics of human rights took on a new meaning and urgency in the context of postwar Europe.[54] During the 1930s, opposition to both fascism and communism was articulated in the language of 'freedom and democracy' but not that of human rights. It was not until the end of the Second World War and the beginning of the next (Cold) war that human rights began to be thought of as a means for juridifying the boundaries of political possibility. By this time, minority protection had largely become an anachronism, consigned to the dustbin of the interwar period.[55] Soviet internationalism, however, was in full flight by 1945, with both a number of new Eastern European states incorporated within the expanding Union and increased Soviet support for communist parties and movements within Western European states.[56] During this period, the possibility that European colonies and the 'peripheral states' of Europe – in particular, Greece and Turkey – might organise along communist lines was of particular concern to the West.[57] The European Convention is best understood in the context of broader moves towards European regionalism, not only as a postwar condemnation of fascism but also as 'an ideological response to the threat

[53] On the doctrine of *abus de droit* in public international law see generally Georg Schwarzenberger, 'Uses and Abuses of the "Abuse of Rights" in International Law' (1956) 42 *Transactions of the Grotius Society* 147.

[54] See generally Duranti, n 2; Mikael Rads Madsen, 'From Cold War Instrument to Supreme European Court: The European Court of Human Rights at the Crossroads of International and National Law and Politics' (2007) 32 *Law & Social Inquiry* 137.

[55] Simpson, n 12, 333.

[56] See Scott Newton, Chapter 6 in this volume. As Newton notes, the lack of active support to communist actors in Greece and Yugoslavia were exceptions to the general rule of communist internationalism.

[57] On the centrality of the Balkans to the development of techniques of contemporary international law, see Ntina Tzouvala, '"These Ancient Arenas of Racial Struggles": International Law and the Balkans, 1878–1949' (2018) 29 *European Journal of International Law* 1149. On concerns regarding the European colonies, see Simpson, n 12, 293.

posed by Russian Communism', as well as by other kinds of progressive politics that had grown in influence since the First World War.[58] As Simpson states, 'the purpose of such a charter was not to restore freedom to the West, where, currently, it was fully enjoyed. The object was conservative: to protect what already existed'.[59] More recently, Marco Duranti has demonstrated that the cause of European human rights (and of European unity more broadly) represented a rallying point for conservatives of various stripes who opposed both communist revolution as well as more influential socialist or Christian democrat forms of political life.[60]

One such means of protection would be through erecting a barrier to external influences by having rights act as a 'ticket of entry' to the Council of Europe. This meant preventing states who did not already provide such guarantees of rights, through signing up to the Convention, from joining the group of European nations.[61] Another such means was the placing of international controls, in the form of rights guarantees, on the nature and limits of the state's ability to govern – thereby preserving the internal shape of the European compact. Unlike the Universal Declaration of Human Rights, which was the product of compromise between liberal and socialist states, the European Convention emphasised (liberal) civil and political freedoms above all. The drafters 'saw future salvation in restoring the primacy of the individual against the over powerful state, in establishing civil and political freedom, and in restoring and safeguarding democracy'.[62] This view came to be encapsulated in the Convention over the protests of a small minority, who felt that the provision of economic welfare, not political freedom, was the best defence against totalitarian advances, and that this should be incorporated into the human rights project.[63] Accordingly, the Convention contained no real 'economic and social' rights except those essential to liberal internationalism: the freedom to trade, as well as, eventually, the right to own property, which was unsuccessfully proposed in the initial drafting but later codified in the first protocol to the Convention.[64] At the same time, however, a straightforwardly liberal philosophy of human rights

[58] Ibid., 224; Madsen, n 54.
[59] Describing Churchill's opening speech at the Congress of Europe in 1948: Simpson, n 12, 605–7. See also at 671 on the 'defensive' character of the convention.
[60] See Duranti, n 2, especially chs 5 and 6.
[61] Simpson, n 12, 605.
[62] Ibid., 157.
[63] Ibid., 675.
[64] Ibid., 157.

provided little answer to the question of how to respond to the threat of communist politics within European member states.[65]

Early proposals for European regional institutions can be seen as clumsy attempts to navigate a quandary produced by international law's emphasis on and renewed commitment to non-intervention in the first half of the twentieth century. Wartime invocations of human rights, as part of the broader framework of the Allied war aims, show an awareness of the dangers of circumscribing the principle of non-intervention, even as they invoked the denial of those rights in wartime enemy states as justification for interference in the internal arrangements of states.[66] Perhaps for this reason, wartime iterations of European regionalism were largely presented as a need to prevent a resurgence of German aggression, rather than as a question of human rights.[67] This tactic had the added benefit of masking what at least some Western European states viewed as regionalism's underlying purposes: namely, preventing Germany's internal organisation along communist lines, as well as presenting a united European front against the Soviet Union.[68] Some of these early proposals had a strongly interventionist and militaristic flavour: for example, a report produced by the British proposed the establishment of an Emergency Council, with a 'mixed armed force ... to assure conditions in which free elections could be held' where member states had been found by a European Court to have insufficiently protected the civil and political rights of the electorate.[69] It was resistance at home to these types of proposals, as well as a wish to avoid being tarred with the brush of anti-Soviet conservatism, that coaxed regional proposals towards the language and logic of human rights.[70]

At the same time, any human rights convention needed to signal its opposition to non-liberal forms of government. The 'plastic' concept of totalitarianism, with its even-handed hostility towards communist and

65 For example, the popular support for communism within Yugoslavia.

66 For example, Lord Halifax's statement from 1939 that 'in general it is no business of one nation to interfere with the internal administration of another .... But when the challenge in the sphere of international relations is sharpened, as today in Germany, by the denial to men and women of elementary human rights, that challenge is at once extended to something instinctive and profound in the universal conscience of mankind. We are, therefore, fighting to maintain the rule of law and the quality of mercy in dealings between man and man and in the great society of civilised states': Simpson, n 12, 159.

67 Ibid., 234, 554.

68 Ibid.

69 Duranti, n 2, 120.

70 Ibid., 118–21.

fascist ideologies, provided something of a solution to this fix.[71] Originating in interwar Italian political discourse, it had been deployed both by anti-fascists seeking to describe the expansion of the state under Benito Mussolini, and, subsequently, by Mussolini himself in his fascist writings.[72] Internationally, however, the term had come to prominence during the middle of the twentieth century largely as a means through which liberal thinkers might both understand and classify the common ills of the Nazi and Soviet states. In this sense, it came to offer an alternative to the more explicit anti-fascism of the 1930s that preceded it.[73]

One place in which the language of totalitarianism found expression was through the political and economic thought of Friedrich Hayek, who in his *The Road to Serfdom* had associated sustained social and economic planning with a system of state control that would inevitably result in the decline of individual freedom.[74] The concept was also evident in the framing of the Truman Doctrine, which promised economic and military support to Greece in its civil war against communist partisans, and to Turkey in its resistance to Soviet claims to territory and the Dardanelles.[75] By the end of the 1940s, it had come to figure in European intellectual and political debates.[76] The fact that totalitarianism was able to encompass both communist and fascist politics, while avoiding the explicit condemnation of either, made it a serviceable if somewhat uncomfortable concept on which to ground limits to liberal rights protections for Europe.

15.3.2 Drafting Article 17

The article itself was first introduced by Pierre-Henri Teitgen, rapporteur of the Committee on Legal and Administrative Questions, anti-

[71] Enzo Traverso, 'Totalitarianism between History and Theory' (2017) 55 *History and Theory* 97, 97. It had the added benefit of painting European conservatism in a favourable light, thereby deflecting criticism of said conservatives' 'lack of anti-Nazi zeal' during World War II: Abbott Gleason, *Totalitarianism: The Inner History of the Cold War* (Oxford University Press, 1995) 11.

[72] Traverso, n 71, 99.

[73] Samuel Moyn, 'Modernity and the Spectre of Totalitarianism' in Peter E Gordon and Warren Breckman (eds), *The Cambridge History of Modern European Thought* (Cambridge University Press, 2019) 417, 420–1.

[74] See Friedrich Hayek, *The Road to Serfdom* (Routledge, first published 1944, 2001 ed) 37–41. On the influence of Hayek on the founders of the European human rights order, see Duranti, n 2, 221–4, 365.

[75] Harry S Truman, 'Address before a Joint Session of Congress' (12 March 1947).

[76] Silvio Pons, *The Global Revolution: A History of International Communism, 1917–1991* (Allan Cameron trans., Oxford University Press, 2014) 201.

communist and former member of the French Resistance.[77] As mentioned, it would come to be interpreted as limiting the possible rights claims that could be considered or upheld under the Convention.[78] The article did not operate, at least in the Commission or the Court's account, as a positive requirement on states to condemn particular political movements which fell afoul of the article. Instead, it created an opaquely-worded exception to the otherwise wide limitations on the authority of signatories to the Convention, particularly where political freedoms are concerned. Its effect would be to enable, where states desired it, the exclusion of particular politics from the new European regional order – and in inquiring into the nature and terms of this proposed exclusion, the drafting history is illuminating.

For Teitgen, the purpose of the Assembly's meeting was both to 'work [] out proposals which will enable Europe to fulfil its promise'[79] and to reaffirm the need to protect that promise against the dangers European leaders felt it faced. Although the Second World War had done much to make those evident – in Teitgen's eyes, Europe 'needed war, and ... enemy occupation to make [it] realise afresh the value of [its] humanism' – he saw the drafting as a means of refocusing attention on the threats to European freedom, rather than merely the values it espoused.[80] These threats were, for Teitgen, threefold. The first, and most briefly referred to, was the 'eternal reason of state': the possibility of abuse of parliamentary power against individual freedoms, which Teitgen acknowledged plagued even the most democratic of parliaments.[81] The second was the lingering remnants of fascism that although much weakened following the end of the war, 'have left their mark ... Racialism did not die out with Hitler'.[82] He warned that 'a certain brand of anti-Communism, which claims to fight Communism not with democratic methods but with dictatorial methods, sometimes puts in jeopardy the very principles of democracy'.[83]

77 Madsen, n 54, 141.

78 See n 5.

79 Council of Europe, *Collected Edition of the Travaux Préparatoires of the European Convention on Human Rights* (Martinus Nijhoff, 1975–1985) vol 1, 38 (*European Convention Travaux*).

80 Ibid., 40.

81 Ibid.

82 Ibid.

83 Ibid.

In his view, the gravest threats to European democracy, however, were the dangers produced as a result of 'economic liberalism, free enterprise, freedom of competition, of profit and money'.[84] This was not because the liberal-capitalist system of the early twentieth century was inherently unjust, but because it had created conditions which inadvertently enhanced the appeal of the communist message:

> Freedom, because it implies liberalism, harsh competition and sometimes, the crushing of the weak by the strong, does not and cannot provide social justice; you should therefore choose equality. And some poor creatures have yielded to this temptation. So they agreed to renounce their freedom in exchange for a little more bread . . ..[85]

Against this threat, national processes of law-making would not be enough: the appeal of socialist and communist politics, and the danger of revolution from within could 'only be solved by means of a collective effort'.[86] In this respect, Teitgen's views were at odds with those of other socialist politicians present who argued that the 'prelude to real totalitarianism' was the failure of the state to provide for its population.[87] The European Convention in general, and Article 17 in particular, was for him a means of 'repelling this abominable temptation':[88] not by providing a marked improvement in economic equality or the conditions of the working poor but by enabling juridical constraints on European government, and thereby protecting European liberal ideals from domestic contest.

15.3.2.1 Textual Inspirations: Universal Declaration of Human Rights and the Soviet Contribution

Much of the textual inspiration for Article 17 appears to have been drawn from a functionally equivalent article in the Universal Declaration of Human Rights.[89] Although the Universal Declaration is remembered for transcending the liberal-communist divide, in both rejecting fascism and

[84] Ibid.
[85] Ibid., vol 1, 42.
[86] Ibid., vol 1, 44.
[87] Ibid., vol 1, 146 (Mr Norton, Ireland).
[88] Ibid., vol 1, 42.
[89] Adopted two years earlier by the General Assembly, Article 30 reads 'Nothing in this Declaration may be interpreted as implying for any State, group or person any right to engage in any activity or to perform any act aimed at the destruction of any of the rights and freedoms set forth herein': *International Bill of Human Rights*, GA Res 217(III), UN GAOR, 3rd session, 183rd plenary meeting, UN Doc A/RES/217(III) (10 December 1948) pt A, 'A Universal Declaration on Human Rights'.

endowing political and socio-economic rights equally with universal status, Article 30 is best understood as the product of a compromise between anti-fascism and anti-communism.[90] The concept was first introduced by Charles Malik, the Lebanese representative and *rapporteur* of the drafting commission.[91] Malik argued that 'a provision of that nature was an essential protection' for the rights of man that the Universal Declaration sought to guarantee, whose 'object was to prevent any persons from engaging in any subversive activities which might be in any direct or indirect manner damaging' to those rights.[92] The oblique nature of the article's wording enabled its inclusion with a relative lack of debate and opposition from the states present – both liberal and communist.[93] However, it also meant that the politics of the 'regulative' article, and exactly what kinds of acts it would serve to condemn, were far from clear.[94]

During the drafting process, the Soviet delegation had been eager to make the anti-fascist politics of the Universal Declaration explicit.[95] It

[90] Cf. Morsink, who describes the article as a straightforward expression of anti-fascist and anti-Nazist sentiment in the wake of the Holocaust: Johannes Morsink, *The Universal Declaration of Human Rights: Origins, Drafting and Intent* (University of Pennsylvania Press, 2000) 87–8.

[91] Described by Simpson as the 'most remarkable member' of the Commission and one of its principal intellectual forces: Simpson, n 12, 367, 377. On Malik's opposition to social and economic rights, see Jessica Whyte, Chapter 16 in this volume.

[92] *The Universal Declaration of Human Rights: The Travaux Préparatoires* (William A Schabas, ed, Cambridge University Press, 2013) vol 2, 1308 ('*Universal Declaration Travaux*'). While initially the article had only applied to 'persons', it was later amended by two proposals from Australia and France condemning any attempt by both 'States' and 'groups', respectively, to destroy the rights and freedoms set out in the Universal Declaration: vol 2 1308 (Australia); vol 3, 2780 (France). Malik would later characterise Article 30 as a 'regulative' article preventing abuse of the Universal Declaration: Charles Habib Malik, *Human Rights in the United Nations* (United Nations Department of Public Information, 1952) 7.

[93] Although initially only included by a vote of eight, with seven abstentions, the debate surrounding the article was very limited relative to the other articles of the Universal Declaration. Belgium went so far as to later state that 'the fact that there were so few amendments to it proved that article 28 [later, Article 30] . . . had great merits [and it] was essential to include that article in the declaration': *Universal Declaration Travaux*, n 92, vol 3, 2781. Later proposals to omit the provision seem to have been based on a general feeling that the Universal Declaration had become bloated and overlong rather than any particular objection to it: vol 2 at 1624.

[94] Uruguay stated that it was abstaining because a translation had not been provided and because it found the text of the provision to be 'obscure': ibid., vol 2, 1308.

[95] See Simpson, n 12, 438. The Soviets had also attempted to insert a specific reference to Nazism in the Genocide Convention: at 335. On the Soviet contribution to the drafting of the Declaration, see also Chapter 16 in this volume.

did so largely through proposing an amendment excluding both fascism and aggression, or the incitement of war, from the scope of the article providing for freedom of speech – one the Soviet Union considered to be essential in view of the rise of fascist aggression and expansionism that had led to the Second World War.[96] Here, the Soviet delegates proffered their own definition of fascism that, in referring to the 'bloody dictatorship of the most reactionary section of capitalism and monopolies', avoided any possible condemnation of states organised along communist lines.[97] Many states disagreed outright with both the inclusion of the language of fascism and of the Soviet conceptualisation of the term,[98] arguing that the term 'fascist' was often used to describe persons who were not deserving of the epithet, and that there could be no agreement on the meaning of fascism.[99] In place of the Soviet Union's definition, which highlighted the inclination of the capitalist and imperialist state toward aggression, France proposed substituting one that emphasised the importance of liberal freedoms.[100] Others opposed the amendment on the basis that the definition of fascism was too vague, and open to misuse.[101] Against these concerns, the protestations of the Soviet Union that 'countries which had suffered occupation by the Axis forces had no need for a legalistic definition to tell them the nature of the horrors of fascism' were unsuccessful.[102] In this respect, Cold War divisions and

[96] *Universal Declaration Travaux*, n 92, vol 3, 2520. The amendment stated: 'The use of freedom of speech and of the Press for the purposes of propagating Fascism and aggression or of inciting war between nations shall not be tolerated': *Report of the Third Session of the Commission on Human Rights*, UN SCOR, UN Doc E/800 (28 June 1948) 28. It had the support of the Soviet satellite states and republics: *Universal Declaration Travaux*, n 92, vol 3, 2518 (UkSSR), 2513 (BSSR), 2510 (Czechoslovakia), 2519 (Poland), 2520 (Yugoslavia).

[97] *Universal Declaration Travaux*, n 92, vol 3, 2520.

[98] Upsetting the delicate consensus that, as the Soviet Union pointed out, had been the basis of the Yalta and Moscow declarations and the wartime alliance. The Soviets also attempted to incorporate other aspects of the wartime consensus into the Universal Declaration, such as an insistence on non-intervention and self-determination: Simpson, n 12, 417, 444–5, 455.

[99] Since 'for some, the term fascist applied to the majority of regimes excluding the so-called popular democracies, while for others, it extended to communist dictatorships': *Universal Declaration Travaux*, n 92, vol 3, 2524 (Greece). See also at 2509 (United Kingdom), 2515 (France).

[100] Ibid., vol 3, 2525.

[101] Ibid., vol 3, 2513 (Belgium), 2523 (Haiti).

[102] Ibid., vol 3, 2520. See also at 2519 (Poland).

anti-communist sentiment had already begun to supersede the anti-fascist alliances of the Second World War.

In this debate, Article 30 came both to act as a compromise between these divergent views. It satisfied the concerns of Latin-American states, such as Chile and Cuba, that had objected to the specifically anti-fascist focus of the Soviet amendment.[103] Representatives of liberal states such as Canada, on the other hand, stated that Article 30 went some way to circumscribing the concept of freedom of expression, denying it to individuals who wished to destroy the liberal 'free institutions' that they viewed the Universal Declaration as intended to protect, and without which they argued that 'human rights would be a fiction'.[104] The Soviet delegation, for its part, cited its concern that a failure to condemn fascism and take steps to prevent its resurgence 'might lead the fascists to hope that their enemies of yesterday would, tomorrow, provide them with arms for a new war'.[105] In the end, it was willing to accept the text of Article 30, once modified to limit the rights of groups as well as individuals and states, as at least some barrier to this threat. Precisely because of its ambiguity, the article was thus perceived as having the potential to be repurposed in the service of anti-communism and anti-fascist agendas alike.

15.3.2.2 Drafting the Convention, Guarding the Peripheries

One critical difference between the drafting of the Universal Declaration, and the later repurposing of this part of its text in the Convention, was the relationship of the Convention to institutions for its interpretation. The proposed Commission, to which individuals would have the right of petition, would be the gateway through which claims had to pass in order to be considered in full before the European Court.[106] Early proposals published by the European Movement's Juridical Committee (chaired by

[103] Given that 'in addition to fascism there existed Nazism and other political theories equally dangerous to human dignity': ibid., vol 3, 2523 (Cuba); see also vol 3, 2524 (Chile).

[104] Ibid., vol 3, 3061.

[105] Ibid., vol 3, 2785 (Soviet Union).

[106] According to Simpson, the idea of a Commission that could act as a screening mechanism for rights claims was first put forward by the US Commission for the Building of the Peace: Simpson, n 12, 195. Sohn has elsewhere detailed the route by which he brought the 1929 Declaration of the International Rights of Man and the work of André Mandelstam to the attention of the American Law Institute in the 1940s: Louis Sohn, 'How American International Lawyers Prepared for the San Francisco Bill of Rights' (1995) 89 *American Journal of International Law* 540, 546–7.

Teitgen) had emphasised the immediate need 'to establish juridical mechanisms for enforcement ... [reflecting] the fears of the period, whereby a communist takeover of western Europe was viewed as a serious possibility'.[107] However, states differed on the usefulness of the right of individual petition in a Cold War climate: the British felt it was inadvisable given the propensity of Convention rights to be exploited, while the French argued that such a right was essential to shore up against any eventuality of communist rule.[108] As one British representative put it, 'people will appear before the Commission, not to get its judgment but simply for the political propaganda that is involved in the processes of appearing before it'.[109] In this context, the establishment of a rights jurisprudence anchored in the text of the Convention, as well as institutional procedures that could minimise the political ramifications of the invocation of rights by non-liberal politics, would be key.

During the drafting of the Convention itself, opinion divided on the best textual method of ensuring this exclusion of certain politics from the European space. In the same session where Article 17 was first introduced, a vote to omit that paragraph passed unanimously. The British delegate agreed that the delegates did 'not desire by sentimentality in drafting to give evilly disposed persons the opportunity to create a totalitarian Government'[110] but saw a possible solution in a limitation clause that prevented rights from infringing 'the legal rights of others or public order, including the safety of the community'.[111] Teitgen's own statements responding to the Turkish representative's concern that 'some party ... of either nazi, fascist or communist tendency, were to take advantage of the declarations of human rights ... [and] like a wolf in sheep's clothing, were to attempt to wipe out and abolish democracy',[112] show that he himself was sympathetic to this view.[113] For some of the French and British delegates, at least, the state's ability under the general limitations clause to 'define, limit and restrain such freedoms when public order and security are threatened' was entirely sufficient to contain such 'revolutionary intrigues'.[114]

[107] Simpson, n 12, 658.
[108] Ibid., 708.
[109] *European Convention Travaux*, n 79, vol 2, 192 (Nally).
[110] Ibid., vol 1, 118.
[111] Ibid.
[112] Ibid., vol 2, 28.
[113] Ibid., vol 2, 32.
[114] Ibid.

Italy's delegation, having recently experienced fascist rule, considered that more robust and interventionist techniques were needed. Following the removal of Article 17 from the list of amendments, the Italian delegate submitted a proposal to encourage 'uniformity in legislation' for the protection of the rights required for a functioning democracy.[115] The purpose of such a provision was to prevent totalitarianism from making an 'attempt to put itself in power by pseudo-legitimate means'.[116] The delegate used the Italian experience, under which a fascist regime had been able to make use of the Italian constitutional framework to 'acquire a character, an appearance, of legality', to highlight the dangers of relying on the limitation clause alone to protect states being 'menaced by a totalitarian movement enjoying the protection of the law'.[117] This was a concern, he admitted, for all the democratic regimes of the Council of Europe but was particularly salient for the 'internal regimes' of those who would in the future likely be invited to join that Council, who 'must be and must stay democratic'.[118] By this reference – 'I speak in general terms, but I think that my allusion is only too obvious' – the Italian delegate seemed to be suggesting that since 'peripheral' states, like Greece and Turkey, but also those states in close proximity to the Soviet Union, might wish to join, some means of political control needed to be imposed in order to ensure the persistence of a particular vision of Europe.[119] A proposal introducing the limitation into the constitution of every member state would serve the purpose, therefore, of both enabling states that wished to – and requiring those who did not – to modify their 'free institutions' so as to protect against totalitarianism, without answering to charges of violating human rights.[120] Although the proposal was roundly opposed for the inevitable delays its implementation would cause,[121] the delegate's speech had clearly struck a chord, and others began to express

[115] Ibid., vol 2, 134.
[116] Ibid., vol 2, 136.
[117] Ibid., vol 2, 136–40.
[118] Ibid., vol 2, 136, 142.
[119] Ibid., vol 2, 136.
[120] *European Convention Travaux*, n 79, vol 2, 140.
[121] See Teitgen's comments at ibid. The Italian delegate's amendment mirrored Lebanon's failed proposal during the drafting of the Universal Declaration to add a paragraph to Article 30 stating that 'no law in any country may, so far as it relates to such rights and freedoms, be repugnant to the purposes and principles of the United Nations': *Universal Declaration Travaux*, n 92, vol 3, 2781–3.

doubts about mere guarantees of freedoms as a serviceable means of repelling either fascist or communist threats.[122]

The most vocal advocates of some form of juridical insurance on liberal institutions, however, were the Greek and Turkish delegates themselves. For the Greek government, reconciling the ongoing suppression of communism with the protection of human rights was far more than a theoretical concern.[123] According to the Greek delegate, 'Human freedom, just because it is sacred, must not become an armoury in which the enemies of freedom can find weapons which they can later use unhindered to destroy this freedom'.[124] He described the experience of the recent communist revolution-turned-coup in Czechoslovakia in this respect as a cautionary tale. The Greek experience, on the other hand, he framed as one in which having been 'able to defend herself, to anticipate danger, and to exercise the duties as well as the rights of free men, she succeeded in surviving'.[125] A system of rights that failed to make such exceptions, the Greek delegate argued, would be tantamount to the provision of aid to Communist partisans.[126] Here Article 17, through labelling certain political doctrines as a 'permanent threat to the peace and prosperity of humanity',[127] and the resultant emphasis on the 'duties' that Greece argued should accompany any declaration of rights,[128] can be seen to have played a double role: buttressing Greece's justification for welcoming the military intervention of stronger powers, such as Britain

[122] UK delegate McNally that same day voted against the draft Convention as it stood, voicing concerns that the Convention was turning out to be 'an extremely expensive and difficult machine to operate, which, when it does operate, will be just as much at the service of democracy's enemies as of its friends': *European Convention Travaux*, n 79, vol 2, 256.

[123] Propped up at the time by American military aid in a brutal anti-communist civil war which was nearing its end. See generally Amikam Nachmani, 'Civil War and Foreign Intervention in Greece: 1946–49' (1990) 25 *Journal of Contemporary History* 489.

[124] *European Convention Travaux*, n 79, vol 1, 108.

[125] Ibid., vol 1, 110.

[126] See ibid., vol 6, 14: 'In the Greek interior, the enemy is beginning to reorganise his system of partisan activities .... To apply the rules of human rights and individual freedoms without any restrictions in exceptional cases would mean encouraging the preparations taking place within Greece for a renewal of the armed attack with the help of forces which had fled beyond the frontiers'.

[127] Ibid., vol 1, 58.

[128] 'When stating our rights, let us also state our duties; when proclaiming our freedom, let us also proclaim our will to defend and to safeguard it. When inscribing the European Charter of mankind on granite, let us not be one-sided: let us write a true gospel, which shall include equally sacred obligations': ibid., vol 1, 110.

and the United States, in the beginnings of the European Cold War, as well as sanctioning the repression of communist politics by the Greek state itself. In this sense, the Greek delegate's urgings that 'the Council of Europe must be the active instrument for the defence of human rights; it must forge an adequate political weapon and watch very closely over its use' take on a rather literal, rather than merely metaphorical, cast.[129]

The Turkish representative, for his part, expressed concern that 'a small minority urged on by an unprecedented imperialism' would undermine Turkish national independence.[130] For him, Article 17 was a means not for preserving a 'European' politics that already existed but instead for inviting the intervention of European powers through juridical rather than forcible means. 'What we want', he said, 'is to have some supreme control; some lofty supervision animated by the European spirit. I am fully in agreement with the theory according to which ... a Europe conscious of its greatness and of its fidelity to human rights should intervene' in neighbouring states whose political systems were perceived as in danger.[131] This supervision, which Article 17 was to enable, made no distinction as to whether or not the character of the political system was endangered by popular (even democratic) demand from within or forcible intervention from without. Ultimately, the Turkish representative's requests that 'clauses ... be embodied in the Convention to ensure the protection of democratic institutions, without which the defence of human rights will be a mere illusion'[132] resulted in Article 17's reintroduction, and inclusion in the final Convention, in essentially its original form.[133]

The debate over Article 17's inclusion and its relationship to individual rights shows that the Convention has always been at least as concerned with restrictions on the governmental form as with ordinary conceptions of 'human rights' proper. As Teitgen would put it:

[129] Ibid., vol 1, 158.

[130] Ibid., vol 6, 342. On the use of Article 17 to justify the amendment of the Turkish constitution in 1961 and subsequent restrictions on political freedom and the dissolution of leftist political parties, see Yasemin Özdek and Emine Karacaoğlu, 'Turkey' in Robert Blackburn and Jörg Polakiewicz (eds), *Fundamental Rights in Europe: The European Convention on Human Rights and Its Member States, 1950–2000* (Oxford University Press, 2001) 879, 886, 893–4, 910–11.

[131] *European Convention Travaux*, n 79, vol 2, 30.

[132] Ibid., vol 6, 344.

[133] Including only the additional clause at the end of the Article, which clarified its relationship to the limitations clauses. See ibid., vol 3, 206, 266.

> We are less concerned to set up a European juridical authority capable of righting isolated wrongs, isolated illegal acts committed in our countries, than to prevent, from the outset, the setting up in one or other of these countries of a regime of the Fascist or Nazi type. That is the essential element of our purpose . . . And so it is, that intervention by the European Court must be possible immediately after a totalitarian dictatorship has been set up.[134]

This intervention was no longer a militarised practice, as it had been before Mandelstam's time, but a largely juridical one. However, in operating to conserve liberal government, the 'intervention' that Article 17 was thought to enable contributed to an essentially similar purpose: to internationalise decisions about the political life of the state.[135] Through being framed in the language of a rights-centred internationalism, Article 17 also avoided openly stating the opposition of its drafters to a radical or redistributive politics. As it exists, the Convention represents a compromise with more extreme proposals to constitutionalise limitations on permissible forms of politics. However, rereading the drafting reveals the judgement of its creators that, for states who wished it, the same result might be achieved less visibly through other means.

15.4 Afterlives: The European Commission and the Borders of Europe

Thus far, this chapter has argued that Article 17 was an aspect of a broader postwar scheme for European integration, aimed at enabling the conservation of national political and constitutional orders. Both before and following the article's drafting, Europe would witness the proliferation of anti-communist politics justified and underpinned by concepts of 'militant democracy'. This new postwar liberalism, in which Article 17 played an important role, would aim to strengthen both the coherence of new European alliances and the frontiers of European political and economic organisation. In this part, the chapter will examine the first case in which the European Commission of Human Rights invoked the article, the appeal of the West German Communist Party against its

[134] Ibid., vol 5, 294, in relation to the debate over the guarantee of democratic institutions that would later be enacted as Article 3 of Protocol 1 to the Convention.

[135] See, for example, the discussion of a 'critical period of transition' in which the Court could have an influence: Simpson, n 12, 662. Czechoslovakia had recently gone through such a transition in the form of a democratic election of the Communist Party followed by a Moscow-backed coup.

constitutional ban, *Kommunistiche Partei Deutschlands v Germany* (*KPD v Germany*). Although the article went on to assume new lives in later cases and contexts, its first application is illustrative of the politics in which it was formed, and provides us with a means of considering the broader question this chapter aims to address: namely, how rights might act as a jurisprudential limit to politics.[136]

15.4.1 The Case

In the postwar context, it is perhaps unsurprising that the first reported case in which Article 17 found its expression was brought by the German Communist Party (KPD) against the West German state. If states such as Greece and Turkey are today sometimes referred to as the 'peripheries' of Europe, in the postwar era West Germany was seen as another such crucial frontier. In this context, the facts giving rise to the case itself, appealing the ban of the KPD by the West German Constitutional Court, was part of a long line of anti-communist measures originating under the Adenauer government.[137]

However, it was only in 1956, three years after the Convention entered into force in West Germany, that the Constitutional Court banned the KPD outright. The ban itself had a complicated international politics. In part, it reflected postwar anxieties about Soviet militarism, communist incursion and the Stalinist sympathies of the KPD. According to Major, however, it was also the product of US efforts to foster anti-communism in West Germany, and thereby ensure the safety of a European-American economic and military alliance.[138] During the early 1950s, the West German government had pursued a programme of remilitarisation, citing the needs of the war in Korea and culminating in the joining of NATO in May 1955; and a major plank of KPD policy since 1949 had been to oppose this rearmament.[139] The blanket ban on the party led the

[136] For these other lives, see n 7.

[137] These had included removing communists from the public service, disentitling communists to compensation for Nazi persecution and instigating a series of political prosecutions for 'endangering the state': Patrick Major, *The Death of the KPD: Communism and Anti-Communism in West Germany* (Clarendon Press, 1997) 279–83.

[138] Ibid., 265.

[139] Also opposed by the German Democratic Socialist Party (*Sozialdemokratische Partei Deutschlands* or SPD) and others from the early 1950s, by which time the marginalisation of the KPD, as well as its links to the East German government, had rendered it too politically unpopular to be included in this coalition: Major, n 137, 142–8.

KPD to bring a case to the Commission, citing violations of human rights protections for freedom of thought and conscience, freedom of expression and freedom of assembly and association.[140]

Against this backdrop, the ban of the KPD can be seen as part of a broader process of the postwar strengthening of the West German state, justified by reference to the German concept of 'militant democracy'.[141] Originating in the thought of legal scholar Karl Loewenstein, the concept is generally thought of as a liberal one and in recent years has undergone something of a revival in contemporary legal scholarship.[142] However, its legal instantiation in postwar West Germany was somewhat more complex than the liberal defence against both radical right and radical left as which it is often presented. As Major notes, the trials of KPD officials prior to the outright ban borrowed heavily from Nazi jurisprudence and were implemented by a state judiciary and bureaucracy still somewhat populated by former officials of the Reich.[143] When the ban itself was brought as an action by the Adenauer government in the Constitutional Court of Germany, the party's continued existence was ruled unlawful on the basis of provisions of the Basic Law declaring that parties which 'by reason of their aims or the behaviour of their adherents, seek to undermine or abolish the free democratic basic order or to endanger the existence of the Federal Republic of Germany shall be unconstitutional'.[144] More specifically, the judgment held that there was no need that there be an actual danger of the party achieving its revolutionary

[140] Articles 9, 10 and 11. This followed the ban of the national socialist party in 1952 – which was not challenged before the Commission.

[141] A phrase attributed to Karl Loewenstein, 'Militant Democracy and Fundamental Rights' (1937) 31 *American Political Science Review* 417, who argued that liberal democracy would be required, in the years ahead, to betray its commitments to individual freedoms if it were to survive the fascist threat (and noting that 'the Communist partner's devotion to constitutional government and to the principles of private property [were] justly mistrusted': at 429). See, on Loewenstein's contribution to the development of human rights charters in the 1940s, Udi Greenberg, 'Militant Democracy and Human Rights' (2015) 42 *New German Critique* 169.

[142] See, for example, Angela K Bourne and Fernando Casal Bértoa, 'Mapping "Militant Democracy": Variation in Party Ban Practices in European Democracies (1945–2015)' (2017) 13 *European Constitutional Law Review* 221; Carlo Invernizzi Accetti and Ian Zuckerman, 'What's Wrong with Militant Democracy?' (2017) 65 *Political Studies* 182.

[143] Even relying in one instance on a prior conviction under the Nazi regime to demonstrate a defendant's criminality: Major, n 137, 279–82.

[144] *German Communist Party v Germany (Admissibility)* (European Commission on Human Rights, App no 250/57, 20 July 1957) (*KPD v Germany*); Basic Law (Germany) Article 21(2).

goals; what was important was 'political action according to a fixed plan' to promote those goals.[145] In the result, the party was dissolved and prevented from reforming, and its funds were appropriated by the West German state.[146]

The appeal to the Commission, brought by the KPD itself, as well as two members of its Steering Committee, Walter Fisch and Max Reimann, was rejected as inadmissible and never heard in full.[147] Meeting in private almost a year after the claim, the Commission relied on Article 17 to dismiss the case.[148] This 'fundamental provision', the Commission ruled, was 'designed to safeguard the rights listed therein by protecting the free operation of democratic institutions', citing Italy's statement that the European regional order required preventing 'totalitarian currents from exploiting, in their own interests, the principles enunciated by the Convention'.[149] This same motivation, it said, had guided the German Bundestag during the final years of occupation in designing Article 21 of the Basic Law, on which the Constitutional Court's decision was based.[150] The central question that the Commission set itself to decide was whether the applicants had 'committed acts or engaged in any activity aimed at destroying the rights or freedoms set forth in the Convention or at securing more comprehensive limitations of those rights or freedoms than are provided for in the said Convention'.[151]

The Commission ruled that the KPD's actions were incompatible with the Convention and therefore it could not rely on the protections for freedom of expression, thought or association that would otherwise have been available. The basis for doing so was previous statements by the party, setting out the aim of establishing 'a socialist-communist system

[145] Donald P Kommers and Russell A Miller, *The Constitutional Jurisprudence of the Federal Republic of Germany* (Duke University Press, 3rd ed, 2012) 291. Kommers and Miller record that the action against the German national socialist party was brought in the same year as the action against the KPD. However, the Court took a further four years to decide the latter, due to judicial concerns that the action was unwarranted at the time: at 290.

[146] *KPD v Germany*, n 144, 3.

[147] Since then, Article 17 has operated both as a bar to admissibility and as an additional limitation on the extent of the rights in the Convention. More recent jurisprudence has tended towards the latter, particularly given the assumption of the Commission's functions by the Court in 1998.

[148] *KPD v Germany*, n 144, 3. Twelve members of the Commission, including Commission president C H M Waldock, met to dismiss the case.

[149] Ibid., 4.

[150] Ibid.

[151] Ibid., 4.

by means of a proletarian revolution and the dictatorship of the proletariat'.[152] This phrase referred to Marx's theory of a transitional stage of the state form between capitalism and communism, and had been used to describe and justify Bolshevik rule in the name of workers following the 1917 revolution.[153] The Commission ruled that 'recourse to a dictatorship for the establishment of a régime is *incompatible* with the Convention', as it would destroy the rights that it sought to protect.[154] As it had been before the Constitutional Court, the party's protest that it had not been current policy to advocate for a dictatorship of the proletariat was unsuccessful:[155] the Commission's ruling stated somewhat obliquely that even if that were true, and the party had confined itself to 'constitutional means' of politics, 'this would in no sense imply that the Party had renounced its traditional objectives'.[156]

In relying on the limits imposed by Article 17, the Commission avoided an examination of whether the same result could have been reached by the limitation clauses attaching to each of the articles on which the applicant sought to rely. Instead, the language it used to frame the issue at hand – whether the applicants were engaged in 'securing more comprehensive limitations of those rights or freedoms than are provided for' – directs attention to whether the party's political statements outline an alternative mode of government, one which is inimical to the rights included in the Convention.[157] This enabled the Commission's decision to be, controversially, based on statements of aim or intent rather than any actual endangerment of those rights. In

152 Ibid., 4.

153 Fitzpatrick, n 2, 70, 89.

154 *KPD v Germany*, n 144, 4 (emphasis added). This was a distinct basis for inadmissibility from that provided by the 'abuse of rights' provisions in Article 29 of the Convention: see Michel Hottelier, 'La requête abusive au sens de l'article 27, 2e de la Convention Européene des Droits de l'Homme' (1991) *Revue Trimestrielle des Droits de l'Homme* 301.

155 In 1956, the same year as the ban, Krushchev had delivered a speech calling for a renewed Soviet foreign policy of 'peaceful co-existence': Pons, n 76, 210. Major suggests, however, that the KPD's policy shift was influenced by the ongoing litigation: Major, n 137, 226.

156 *KPD v Germany*, n 144, 4. On the ruling of the Constitutional Court, see Major, n 137, 291.

157 *KPD v Germany*, n 144, 4. The Constitutional Court had held that it was sufficient that the party intend an 'impairing' or 'endangering' of the basic democratic order, and whether or not it was in a position to carry this out was irrelevant: Carl J Schneider, 'Political Parties and the German Basic Law of 1949' (1957) 10 *Western Political Quarterly* 527, 538.

so deciding, the Commission implicitly positioned the KPD and its members as a challenge to liberal forms of authority, rather than a subject of that authority, and located them within a historical trajectory of liberal-communist rivalry that reached back to the revolutionary challenge of 1917. The ruling also established a practice of declaring claims falling foul of the article inadmissible, as opposed to meriting full examination – a practice that recalls Mandelstam's injunction to protect against 'manifestations of intrigue and chicanery'.

15.4.2 *Beyond or Before the Law: Liberalism and the Preservation of Form*

Reading the Commission's decision, together with early theories of rights, as a response to revolution shows that Article 17 was an expression of the political and juridical limits of postwar liberalism. In the early stages of the Cold War, the nascent West German government was not inclined towards the accommodation of alternative forms of politics; nor was the Commission, as its European supervisor, willing to protect them. However, it also makes visible one possible operation of Article 17 and its relationship to the history of the revolution of 1917. This part will suggest that the Commission's resort to notions of incompatibility in preference to fuller adjudication illustrates the anti-formalism latent in the Convention, and will explore the implications of this for the politics of engagements with rights today.

What is meant here by anti-formalism is an approach to law in which law acts as a mechanism for realising purposes, rather than as a set of rules for dividing, allocating or restraining power.[158] Within a realist or pragmatic tradition, anti-formalism is a move which abandons the idea of law as a rule-oriented technique, with corresponding conventions of argumentation and adjudication, in favour of the pull of the desired object or end. As Koskenniemi has written: 'Anti-formalism is always a call for transformation: to overrule existing law either because it does not really exist at all, or if it does, it should not'.[159] In this sense, the

[158] Martti Koskenniemi, 'What Is International Law For' in Malcom Evans (ed), *International Law* (Oxford University Press, 5th ed, 2018) 28, 35. See also the discussion of 'deformalisation' in Koskenniemi's 'The Fate of Public International Law: Between Technique and Politics' (2007) 70 *Modern Law Review* 1.

[159] Koskenniemi, 'What Is International Law For', n 158, 38. Compare with the vision of formalism outlined in Martti Koskenniemi, 'Formalism, Fragmentation, Freedom: Kantian Themes in Today's International Law' (2007) 4 *No Foundations* 7.

Commission's decision to abandon the 'rule' of the limitation clause in favour of the regulative ideal embodied in Article 17 can be understood as a particular kind of anti-formalist move: not one which reinterprets a given rule in favour of a normative end but one which calls for abandoning the formal exercise of balancing rights with state prerogatives. In doing so, the decision draws on an extra-legal imaginary of the limits of the Convention's politics, one which can be gestured to, but never fully represented through, legal text. It also draws on a particular kind of legal thinking: one which looks directly to the kinds of institutional (or perhaps constitutional) justifications for the Commission that Teitgen outlined, rather than also relying on the factual inquiries and interpretative results habitually involved in the adjudication of substantive rights. Instead of identifying interests to be balanced against regulatory ends, it asks the adjudicator to imagine the needs of the system as a whole, and identify those that pose a danger to it.[160]

Here, the idea of Europe as frontier acts as fertile ground for reinscribing the boundaries of the Convention. As I have shown, the provenance of the legal thinking on which the Commission's reasoning draws stems from the revolutionary history of 1917, and liberal responses to it. That history, which enables the Commission to render the outcome of the decision intelligible, is here re-enacted through the jurisprudential gesture and rhetorical device of the 'dictatorship of the proletariat', rather than an analysis of the past actions or the present political significance of the applicants. Schlag has described this type of legal theorising, which works primarily with desired belief rather than available fact, as a kind of 'magical thinking' akin to the theologian's proof of divine existence:

> The key aspect of 'magical thinking' is the creation of metaphysical entities that make certain worldly events come out the way one desires. To engage in magical thinking, one simply posits a thought that will make things come out the way one desires and one then affirms that the thought is or refers to something that is ontologically real and ontologically effective. In magical thinking, epistemic necessities are transformed into ontological actualities.[161]

[160] On the 'move from law to regulation', see also Koskenniemi, 'Formalism, Fragmentation, Freedom', n 159, 13.

[161] Pierre Schlag, 'Law as the Continuation of God by Other Means' (1997) 85 *California Law Review* 427, 437. Here Schlag is referring to the thinking of legal theorists, and not judges or practitioners, but I am adapting his thought to describe the Commission's reasoning.

This 'magical thinking' is not immediately apparent, either to the lawyer or to the observer, precisely because it works to produce something *resembling* formalised legal argumentation. For Schlag, however, behind that screen of argumentation lies the 'sublimated' desire of the legal thinker.[162]

Recognising that the legal form of the Convention operates on one level to repress and on another to realise the desire to reconcile liberal freedoms with political enmities, then, illustrates the dangers of the 'redemptive return' to rights as open-ended concepts. In Schlag's account, it is precisely this 'slippage from the epistemic to the ontological' that allows for the continued belief in law as a formalist set of rules that is both responsive to argument and open to reinterpretation.[163] In other words, Schlag helps us to see here that it is law's *appearance* of being a field for argument and a terrain of struggle, despite its material constraints and sublimated desires, that 'enables the widely shared faith in the otherwise odd belief that social institutions and practices are responsive to reason'.[164] Viewed from this angle, the critical aspects of the Commission's decision are not only its denial of the claim but the fact of the appeal to the Commission itself. Given the political consensus evident during the drafting of the Convention, this appeal has a dual resonance today: both as a challenge to the vision of rights that the drafters had articulated but also as an expression of faith in the possibility or availability of rights despite their legal circumscription.

Examining the KPD's appeal to the Commission, and the ruling in response, shows us that human rights do not always function as a principled restraint on state power.[165] Rather, the implementation of Article 17, and its sympathies with ideas of 'militant democracy', demonstrates that the Convention works equally as a mechanism for imagining a particular kind of European politics and for authorising its constituent parts, states and institutions alike, to take measures in order to maintain it. Paradoxically, then, what is described here as the anti-formalist dimensions of an appeal to history work to preserve another type of legal form – the form of a liberal Europe. At the same time, the privacy of the proceedings and the brevity of their rejection prevented the

[162] Ibid., 438.
[163] Ibid., 440.
[164] Ibid.
[165] Cf. Simpson, n 12, 12.

claim from using the 'spectacle and publicity of law' to advance a politics in parallel, consigning what lay off the record to the historical past.[166]

15.5 Conclusion

This chapter has sought to illustrate the legacies of the Russian Revolution of 1917 for European forms of human rights and for the European regional order. International instruments for the protection of rights emerged in part as a response to the revolutionary Soviet state and its disruption of the civilised/uncivilised binary on which the lawfulness of military intervention was premised. In the interwar period, Western jurists turned to rights as a possible means of performing that task, while also suggesting new theories and procedural mechanisms in order to protect rights from being claimed for a revolutionary agenda. In the postwar period, and given the decreasing defensibility of intervention through force in order to erect or maintain liberal methods of government, rights figured more prominently in the set of tools for establishing or preserving a liberal politics for European states – displacing other, more interventionist proposals, as well as appeals to the welfare state. Article 17 was central to this endeavour, and the circumstances of its first use show that the revolutionary Soviet state loomed large in the workings of rights, as well as in the theories of their inception.

Situating rights in longer histories of intervention by Western states in European peripheries shows the continuity of purpose, and procedural devices for achieving that purpose, adopted by different actors across different locations. It also demonstrates the awareness of these actors that rights might be capable of being put in service of a different politics, and a quiet circumscription of the ways in which this could effectively be achieved. The history of Article 17, and of human rights as defenders of a liberal and capitalist Europe, stands therefore as a partial explanation for rights' persistent appeal to those seeking a radical utopia, and a cautionary tale for those who would now seek their redemption.

[166] Knox, n 11, 225.

16

Human Rights, Revolution and the 'Good Society'

The Soviet Union and the Universal Declaration of Human Rights

JESSICA WHYTE*

16.1 Introduction

It has often been suggested that the human rights politics of the late 1970s intended 'not to open the gates of paradise, but to bolt the gates of hell'.[1] This conception of human rights as protections against 'the worst' was bound up with a reassessment of revolutionary politics as, at best, hubristic folly, and, at worst, totalitarian. As Soviet dissidents embraced the language of human rights to campaign against the Soviet state, a new NGO-led human rights politics came to express a realist rejection of revolutionary utopias.[2] This human rights politics renounced the revolutionary aspirations of the communist left, while marginalising even the social-democratic ideals that had informed the Universal Declaration of Human Rights' social and economic rights. Epitomising this divorce of human rights from more expansive visions of social and economic justice, Michael Ignatieff suggested in 2001 that the 'elemental priority of all human rights activism' should be to mitigate suffering by preventing torture, beatings, killings, rape and assault. Ignatieff argued for prioritising the civil and political rights of a 'capitalist rights tradition' against what he framed as a 'Communist rights tradition – which put

* University of New South Wales. I would like to thank Lars Lih for very helpful feedback on an earlier draft, and all the editors for their astute editorial guidance.

1 André Glucksmann argued this of the founder of Médecins sans Frontières, Bernard Kouchner, who he celebrated for founding 'the duty of international meddling' in the name of human rights. Andre Glucksmann, 'The 2004 *Time* 100: Bernard Kouchner', *Time Magazine* (26 April 2014).

2 Robert Horvath, '"The Solzhenitsyn Effect": East European Dissidents and the Demise of the Revolutionary Privilege' (2007) 29 *Human Rights Quarterly* 879.

primacy on economic and social rights'.[3] Arguing that this latter tradition risked sliding into tyranny, Ignatieff portrayed human rights minimalism as 'the most we can hope for'.[4]

Ignatieff's insistence on foreclosing larger emancipatory visions was soon criticised from the left. Wendy Brown notably insisted that his endorsement of a 'capitalist rights tradition' overstepped the bounds of his purported minimalism by advocating a whole social and economic system.[5] Brown contended that human rights campaigns presuppose visions of a good polity – even, or especially, when they portray themselves as animated by apolitical, moral concern for human suffering.[6] From such a perspective, the foreclosure of egalitarian social transformation has made the recent politics of human rights particularly compatible with a neoliberal insistence that there is no alternative to liberal individualism and austerity.

If human rights campaigns carry specific visions of social and political life, this raises the question of how the rise of an NGO-driven politics of human rights relates to other social and political visions. One particularly influential answer is that of the historian Samuel Moyn, for whom human rights came to prominence only because grander and more expansive utopias – notably communism and anti-colonial nationalism – failed.[7] Moyn's thesis has been criticised, including by those who argue that alternate utopias flourished into the 1970s.[8] Nonetheless, the claim that human rights emerged as 'a minimalist, hardy utopia that could

[3] Michael Ignatieff, *Human Rights as Politics and Idolatry* (Princeton University Press, 2001) 19.

[4] Ibid., 173.

[5] Wendy Brown, '"The Most We Can Hope For . . .": Human Rights and the Politics of Fatalism' (2004) 103 *South Atlantic Quarterly* 451, 453. See also Joshua Cohen, 'Minimalism about Human Rights: The Most We Can Hope For?' (2004) 12 *Journal of Political Philosophy* 190.

[6] This position challenges what Susan Marks calls 'the myth of no politics'. Susan Marks, 'Four Human Rights Myths' in David Kinley, Wojciech Sadurski and Kevin Walton (eds), *Human Rights: Old Problems, New Possibilities* (Edward Elgar, 2013) 217.

[7] Samuel Moyn, *The Last Utopia: Human Rights in History* (Harvard University Press, 2010).

[8] Antony Anghie, 'Whose Utopia? Human Rights, Development, and the Third World' (2013) 22(1) *Qui Parle* 63; Seyla Benhabib, 'Moving beyond False Binarisms: On Samuel Moyn's *The Last Utopia*' (2013) 22(1) *Qui Parle* 81; Jason Frank, 'Human Rights Regimes and *The Last Utopia*' (2013) 22(1) *Qui Parle* 49; Pheng Cheah, 'Human Rights and the Material Making of Humanity: A Response to Samuel Moyn's *The Last Utopia*' (2013) 22 (1) *Qui Parle* 55; Joseph Slaughter, 'Hijacking Human Rights: Neoliberalism, the New Historiography, and the End of the Third World' (2018) 40 *Human Rights Quarterly* 735.

survive in a harsh climate' gave voice to a sense that something had been lost as human rights supplanted other oppositional projects to become a dominant language with which power is both contested and legitimised.[9] In the wake of the global financial crisis, as public attention shifted towards the economic inequality resulting from decades of austerity, mainstream human rights NGOs were increasingly criticised, even by their strongest supporters, for having neglected the economic transformations and rising inequality that accompanied their rise.[10] Human rights may have become the 'common standard for humanity' that the Universal Declaration contended they should be, but, for many critics, a world of human rights turned out to be a disappointing utopia.

Although they generally proceeded without acknowledging their precursors, these debates about the relation between human rights and a good social order are not new. In this chapter, I return to the drafting of the Universal Declaration and trace a spirited conflict about whether or not a society that guaranteed human rights would be, by definition, *good*. My focus is on the (partly successful) efforts of the Soviet Bloc delegates to strip the new human rights bill of a proposed right to a *good* social and international order. By 1947, as the drafting began, Russia's own revolutionary days were long in the past. Nonetheless, Soviet diplomats continued to argue that a good society would be achieved by workers' revolutions, not rights declarations. Even if all the rights in the declaration were granted, the Soviet Bloc delegate Alexei Pavlov argued, late in the drafting, 'there was still no ground to conclude that the resulting social and international order would necessarily be good'.[11] As long as the world was 'divided into exploiters and exploited, as long as there was private ownership of the means of production', he argued, 'the social order could not possibly be a good one'.[12] In what follows, I argue that this position left open a space for political struggles and hopes that pointed beyond the newly enshrined human rights, even as the Soviet Union betrayed such hopes at home.

[9] Moyn, *The Last Utopia*, n 7, 121.

[10] Philip Alston, *Extreme Inequality as the Antithesis of Human Rights* (27 August 2015) Open Global Rights, www.openglobalrights.org/extreme-inequality-as-the-antithesis-of-human-rights; Philip Alston, *Report of the Special Rapporteur on Extreme Poverty and Human Rights*, UN Doc A/HRC/29/31 (27 May 2015).

[11] William A Schabas (ed), *The Universal Declaration of Human Rights: The Travaux Préparatoires* (Cambridge University Press, 2013) vol 3, 2750 (Pavlov).

[12] Ibid.

This debate about the good society requires us to reconsider the standard story according to which the nascent Cold War saw the Eastern Bloc push for social and economic rights, while the Western Bloc sought civil and political rights.[13] No doubt, the October Revolution gave significant impetus to the codification of social and economic rights internationally. It prompted the 1919 establishment of the International Labour Organization that enshrined labour rights in order to secure class compromise and ward off revolution, and the extensive list of social and economic rights in the 1936 Soviet Constitution generated demands for such rights elsewhere.[14] Many historians and scholars of human rights have therefore taken for granted that the social and economic rights in the Universal Declaration are there largely as a consequence of Soviet Bloc efforts.[15] On the contrary, I argue that while Soviet delegates voted in favour of social and economic rights, and even helped to concretise them in some cases, they did not lead the campaign to include them in the document, nor did they believe their inclusion was particularly significant.[16] Rather, they were contemptuous of the belief that declaring

[13] Even careful readers of the Soviet Bloc position on social and economic rights and law have advanced this dichotomy. Mark B Smith, for instance, argued that the Universal Declaration's drafters were split between those who 'claimed that civil and political rights were the cornerstone of human rights, and those, led by the Soviet delegation, who argued that social and economic rights made all other rights possible': Mark B Smith, 'Social Rights in the Soviet Dictatorship: The Constitutional Right to Welfare from Stalin to Brezhnev' (2012) 3 *Humanity* 385, 395.

John Quigley contends that, at the UN, 'the USSR pressed for inclusion of economic and social rights as human rights', yet he skips from Soviet advocacy for international economic cooperation during the negotiation of the UN Charter to the drafting of the human rights covenants, passing over the Universal Declaration: John B Quigley, *Soviet Legal Innovation and the Law of the Western World* (Cambridge University Press, 2007) 103. Benjamin Nathans argues that, despite the fact the Soviets abstained when the final Universal Declaration was put to the General Assembly, 'the Soviet position profoundly shaped the final document, ensuring that economic, social, and national rights entered and remained part of the emerging ensemble of international norms': Benjamin Nathans, 'The Disenchantment of Socialism: Soviet Dissidents, Human Rights, and the New Global Morality' in Jan Eckel and Samuel Moyn (eds), *The Breakthrough: Human Rights in the 1970s* (University of Pennsylvania Press, 2014) 33, 35.

[14] Quigley, n 13; Bill Bowring, 'Forbidden Relations? The UK's Discourse of Human Rights and the Struggle for Social Justice' (2002) 1 *Law, Social Justice & Global Development.*

[15] An exception is Johannes Morsink, who recognises that the Latin American delegates were the real advocates of these rights: Johannes Morsink, *The Universal Declaration of Human Rights: Origins, Drafting, and Intent* (University of Pennsylvania Press, 1999).

[16] I discuss the Soviet contribution to social and economic rights in more detail in Jessica Whyte, *The Morals of the Market: Human Rights and the Rise of Neoliberalism* (Verso, 2019).

economic rights would heal class antagonisms or overcome poverty and economic inequality, and deeply sceptical about the realisation of such rights under capitalism.

Far from believing that a human rights declaration could instantiate a society of economic equality and justice, I argue that the Soviets shared the view that the most we can hope for from human rights is that they bolt the gates of hell. Facing the devastation of the Second World War and wary of the threat of the postwar resurgence of fascism, Soviet Bloc delegates argued that the first principle of the Universal Declaration should be the 'destruction of discrimination and inequality'.[17] Racial discrimination, from Jim Crow in the United States to South Africa's racial laws to colonial rule, was the key target of Soviet criticism. It was in this realm of *formal* equality, not social and economic rights, that the primary Soviet contribution to international human rights lay. Yet, in refusing to accept that a society of human rights would necessarily be a 'good society' the Soviet Bloc delegates also held open a gap between formal equality and a communist horizon. In the Soviet Union itself, communism was becoming a distant prospect, pushed into a far-off future. But in the United Nations, the Soviet Bloc delegates insisted that history had not ended and human rights, for that reason, could not be the last utopia.

16.2 'Everyone Has the Right to a Good Social and International Order'

During June of 1948, the Commission on Human Rights (the Commission), which wrote the Universal Declaration, explicitly considered the conditions under which the rights they were enumerating could be realised. The distributional struggles of the previous decades made it difficult to ignore the extent to which rights to education, healthcare or social security required both material resources and political will. The French delegate René Cassin's argument that social and economic rights required more resources than the older civil and political rights has since been challenged – both on the practical grounds that an effective justice system and political enfranchisement require material resources and state action, and on conceptual grounds, by those, notably Étienne Balibar, who have contested the very split between liberty and

[17] Schabas, n 11, vol 1, 777–9 (Koretsky).

equality that underpinned the discourse of 'old' and 'new' rights.[18] However, in the immediate wake of the Second World War, the difference struck most delegates as obvious. Cassin looked back on the recent establishment of national welfare states and argued that delegates should not ignore the 'practical difference' that economic and social rights 'required material assistance to be furnished by the state'.[19] The Czech delegate agreed that, while a 'purely legal and formal instrument' would be sufficient for the implementation of civil and political rights, 'to render the right to social security effective it had to have a proper basis – an economic basis without which there could be no social security properly so-called'.[20]

The Commission's debates about the social conditions under which rights could be realised were crystallised by two draft articles: the first, proposed by Cassin, sought to give special attention to the social and economic preconditions for social and economic rights, which belonged, Cassin's draft article stated, to 'everyone as a member of society'.[21] The second, proposed by the Lebanese delegate Charles Malik, endorsed unanimously by the drafting committee and sharply criticised by the Soviets, stated that 'everyone has the right to a good social and international order in which the rights and freedoms set out in this Declaration can be fully realized'.[22] Malik was an Orthodox Christian who advocated a natural law conception of the person and a society structured to shield the conscience from the pressure of organised groups.[23] Malik initially opposed social and economic rights altogether, on the basis that the state action required for their realisation would 'mean the destruction of free institutions in a free world'.[24] He worried

18 Philip Alston, United Nations Special Rapporteur on Extreme Poverty and Human Rights, *Statement on Visit to the USA* (15 December 2017) United Nations Human Rights Office of the High Commissioner, www.ohchr.org/EN/NewsEvents/Pages/DisplayNews.aspx?NewsID=22533&LangID=E; '"Rights of Man" and "Rights of the Citizen"' in Étienne Balibar, *Masses, Classes, Ideas: Studies on Philosophy and Politics before and after Marx* (James Swenson trans., Routledge, 1994) 39.

19 Schabas, n 11, vol 2, 1882 (Cassin).

20 Ibid., vol 3, 2588 (Nosek).

21 Ibid., vol 2, 1827. Cassin's original draft article read: 'Everyone as a member of society has the economic, social and cultural rights enumerated below, whose fulfilment should be made possible in every State separately or by international collaboration'.

22 Ibid., vol 2, 1826.

23 Charles Malik, 'Human Rights and Religious Liberty' (1949) 1 *Ecumenical Review* 404, 408; Alexandre Lefebvre, *Human Rights and the Care of the Self* (Duke University Press, 2018) 161.

24 Morsink, n 15, 224, quoting Malik.

that Cassin's draft article privileged social and economic rights over civil and political rights, and pointed out that the draft declaration contained 'no statement to the effect that society must be so organized as to guarantee those rights and freedoms [civil and political rights] to the individual'.[25]

Malik described the attempt to formulate a list of basic rights as 'a faint echo, on the international plane, of a spiritual reaction against the modern dissolution of the human soul'.[26] In numerous speeches and articles of the period, he, like the personalist philosopher Jacques Maritain, depicted this dissolution as intimately bound to the rise of socialism and communism and the 'blind fatalism of Marx'.[27] In a 1960 speech at Saint Louis University, Malik warned that the 'communist tide has been rising for 43 years' (that is, since the Russian Revolution of 1917).[28] It was to hold back this tide that he insisted on including a right to a *good* social and international order in the Universal Declaration. Malik's statement that 'everyone has the right to a *good* social and international order in which the rights and freedoms set out in the Declaration can be fully realised' was ultimately adopted by the Drafting Sub-Committee.

Malik was not the first to propose something like a human right to a good international order.[29] In his 1941 'Four Freedoms' speech, US President Franklin D Roosevelt had argued that the freedoms he sought – freedoms of speech and worship and the less-traditional freedoms from want and fear – would constitute 'the moral order': an order of freedom and 'the supremacy of human rights everywhere'. Human rights and freedoms, according to such a position, formed the basis for a distinctive conception of the good society capable of competing with schemes for world domination and 'foreign revolutions'.[30] 'Freedom from want' was a response to the social dislocation of the Great Depression and a vindication of working-class struggles, but it was also an attempt to suppress revolutionary politics and win domestic workers away from communism. In this respect, Roosevelt's shadow hung long over the drafting of the Universal Declaration.

25 Schabas, n 11, vol 2, 1883 (Malik).
26 Malik, 'Human Rights and Religious Liberty', n 23, 404.
27 Charles Malik, 'Call to Action in the Near East', *Foreign Affairs* (1 July 1956).
28 Edward Teller and Charles Habib Malik, *To Meet the Communist Challenge* (St Louis University, 1960).
29 Schabas, n 11, vol 2, 1936 (Malik).
30 Roosevelt cited in ibid., vol 1, 'Introductory Essay: The Drafting and Significance of the Universal Declaration of Human Rights' lxxi, lxxiv.

Looking back in 2013, the former French diplomat Stéphane Frédéric Hessel argued that it was this insistence on founding a new world on the basis of a particular set of values that distinguished the United Nations and its human rights process from anything preceding it. Hessel, who was then the 'last surviving witness to the drafting process' told an interviewer: 'It is ambitious and daring to say: "It is us, who today will describe the values, according to which the world of tomorrow will have to live!"'[31] However ambitious they may have been, many delegates were nonetheless wary of Malik's desire to 'define the standard of an *ideal* society in which the individual could develop and in which his rights could be guaranteed'.[32] The meaning of the good was 'extremely debatable', Pavlov contended, and 'discussion of the ideal social order could not bring any positive results'.[33]

16.3 A Right to Have Rights?

In attempting to remove the word 'good', Pavlov acknowledged that, were it deleted, 'the proposed article would become merely tautological: everyone would have a right to the realization of his rights'.[34] Yet, it was precisely the 'right to have rights' that was at stake in the debate over the two so-called covering articles. The question of the form of political organisation that would make these rights more than mere phrases was the same one that the German-Jewish political theorist Hannah Arendt made the starting point for her own account of the 'right to have rights'. There has been much recent discussion of Arendt's contention, in her essay 'The Decline of the Nation-State and the End of the Rights of Man', that mass population expulsions since the First World War revealed that those who had no other status than their mere humanity were deprived even of the 'rights of man'.[35] From this experience, Arendt concluded that the 'right to have rights' meant 'to live in a framework where one is

[31] As a junior diplomat, Hessel worked in New York managing the office of Henri Laugier, Assistant Secretary-General for the Department of Social Affairs, which was tasked with developing the UN's human rights position: Thomas M Krapf, 'The Last Witness to the Drafting Process of the Universal Declaration of Human Rights: Interview with Stéphane Frédéric Hessel' (2013) 35 *Human Rights Quarterly* 753, 760.

[32] Schabas, n 11, vol 2, 1809 (Malik) (emphasis added).

[33] Ibid., vol 2, 1884 (Pavlov).

[34] Ibid.

[35] See in particular the collection Stephanie DeGooyer et al., *The Right to Have Rights* (Verso, 2018).

judged by one's actions and opinions'.[36] Yet it is little noted that her account of the right to have rights was initially formulated in the 1949 essay, '"The Rights of Man": What Are They?' in which she explicitly criticised what she called the 'Bill of Rights of the United Nations' for its conspicuous 'lack of reality'.[37]

The question of human rights had become deeply confused, Arendt argued there, because despite recent evidence that rights materialise only within a political community, human rights continued to be viewed within the naturalistic categories of the eighteenth century. Challenging defenders of 'the Bill of Rights of the United Nations', who argued that enumerating existing civil rights would prompt countries to legislate them, she contended that this would be more valid 'if the Bill of Rights did not claim to be the legal expression of the Rights of Man'.[38] Arendt criticised the drafters for framing those rights currently granted by one or another state in the language of eighteenth-century natural law. This anachronism, she contended, 'invariably leads to philosophically absurd and politically unrealistic claims such as that each man is born with the inalienable right to unemployment insurance or an old age pension'.[39] To Arendt, it was all too obvious that claims about natural rights valid outside a political community were indeed 'nonsense upon stilts', as Jeremy Bentham had argued, and she endorsed the 'pragmatic soundness' of Edmund Burke's criticism of the 'abstraction' of the inalienable rights proclaimed by French revolutionaries and his preference for the 'rights of an Englishman'.[40] Belief in natural rights, Arendt contended, detracted from the work of finding mutual agreement among the 'comity of nations' on 'the one right without which no other can materialize – the right to belong to a political community'.[41]

Arendt was not the only major political thinker of the twentieth century to scoff at the lack of reality of the Universal Declaration, and especially of its social and economic rights. In a scathing 1966 critique, the Austrian neoliberal thinker Friedrich Hayek argued that the

[36] Hannah Arendt, *The Origins of Totalitarianism* (Harcourt Brace and Co, 1973) 296.

[37] Hannah Arendt, '"The Rights of Man": What Are They?' (1949) 3 *Modern Review* 24, 37.

[38] Ibid., 38.

[39] Ibid.

[40] Ibid., 31. Arendt also appears to endorse the racialised political imaginary animating Burke's critique when she writes that survivors and inmates of the concentration and internment camps distrusted natural rights and preferred national rights because they realised that the former 'were granted even to savages': at 32.

[41] Arendt, 'The Rights of Man', n 37, 37.

'conception of a "universal right" assures to the peasant, to the Eskimo, and presumably to the Abominable Snowman, "periodic holidays with pay" shows the absurdity of the whole thing'.[42] For Hayek, the whole declaration was an incoherent attempt 'to fuse the rights of the Western liberal tradition with an altogether different conception derived from the Marxist Russian Revolution' and expressed in the document's social and economic rights.[43] Although the difficulties of producing a human rights declaration acceptable to both sides of the nascent Cold War were real enough, in one respect, the Soviets were much closer to Hayek than he realised: they too were deeply sceptical about the impact that such a declaration would have on the reality of poverty and inequality.

Declaring social and economic rights without establishing the conditions for their realisation was largely futile, the Soviet Bloc delegates believed. Speaking to the UN General Assembly, the Soviet legal theorist, prosecutor and United Nations delegate Andrei Vyshinsky argued that, while the final document had some positive qualities, it also had 'serious defects, among which might be counted its ultra-legal form and the absence of provisions for the implementation of the principles laid down'.[44] Vyshinsky, and the Soviet Bloc delegation he closely supervised, would have agreed with both Arendt and Hayek about the absurdity of declaring that one is born with a right to paid holidays and an old-age pension.[45] Referring to Article 23, which declared a right to social security, Vyshinsky told the General Assembly that 'the article certainly contained fine ideas expressed in high-sounding phrases, but the experience of the last hundred and fifty years had shown that the realization of an ideal came into daily conflict with existing facts'.[46]

For the Soviet delegates, questions of rights could not be divorced from questions of social organisation. In a capitalist country, the delegate of the Ukrainian Soviet Socialist Republic argued, there would always be a 'flagrant contradiction' between what was said in the declaration and

[42] F A Hayek, 'Justice and Individual Rights: Appendix to Chapter Nine' in *Law, Legislation and Liberty: A New Statement of the Liberal Principles of Justice and Political Economy* (Routledge, 1998) vol 2, 101, 105.

[43] Ibid., 103. This essay was first published in 1966 in the Norwegian journal *Farmand* (Oslo, 1966).

[44] Schabas, n 11, vol 3, 3024 (Vyshinsky).

[45] Vyshinsky oversaw the drafting and communicated directly with Stalin about the draft text: Anton Weiss-Wendt, *The Soviet Union and the Gutting of the UN Genocide Convention* (University of Wisconsin Press, 2017) 119.

[46] Schabas, n 11, vol 3, 3024 (Vyshinsky).

reality. The declaration of a right to rest, for instance, 'had a hollow ring in a society in which a small group always rested, while the overwhelming majority worked all the time'.[47] Without drastically altering a system based on private enterprise and profit, the Soviet Bloc delegates argued, declarations of social and economic rights would be hypocritical testaments to the 'hiatus between reality and theory' that the main Soviet legal textbook of the period, edited by Vyshinsky, described as endemic to the rights declarations of 'bourgeois law'.[48] In language similar to Arendt's, the Polish delegate criticised the absence of measures for implementation in the final declaration: 'The right to work, to rest, the right to leisure of the working classes . . . should be more than a statement in a declaration of principle'; he argued, 'those rights should be based on reality'.[49] Summarising the Soviet Bloc position, Vyshinsky concluded that 'human rights meant nothing unless they were guaranteed and protected by the State; otherwise they became a mere abstraction, an empty illusion easily created but just as easily dispelled'.[50] The primary Soviet Bloc contribution to social and economic rights was the argument that, without state investment and economic transformation, these rights would remain scraps of paper.

The Soviet Bloc delegates had their own vision of a good society, which Pavlov argued could only mean 'a socialistic society in which there was real equality'.[51] In a good society, they contended, the interests of the individual coincided with the interests of the collective – something Pavlov contended (spuriously) had been 'proved in practice' since the Russian Revolution.[52] These delegates framed their vision of the good society as a society of economic equality without class division or

[47] Ibid., vol 3, 3035 (Manuilsky). This contradiction also existed in the USSR. A decade earlier, just after the adoption of the Stalin Constitution, a group of school cleaners wrote to the leading Soviet official Viacheslav Molotov: 'The constitution of the Union says that every citizen of the USSR has the right to rest. We, the cleaners, don't see any of this rest, because most of us are working all hours in order to feed ourselves and our children': Smith, n 13, 393.

[48] Andrei Y Vyshinsky, *The Law of the Soviet State* (Macmillan Company, 1948).

[49] Schabas, n 11, vol 3, 3068 (Katz-Suchy).

[50] Ibid., vol 3, 3082 (Vyshinsky). Here, they echoed Stalin, who told Roy Howard in a 1936 interview that freedom would obtain 'in reality and not merely on paper' only where 'there is no unemployment and beggary, where man does not tremble for fear that tomorrow he will lose his work, his dwelling and his bread': cited in Vyshinsky, n 48, 43.

[51] Schabas, n 11, vol 2, 2750 (Pavlov).

[52] Ibid.

exploitation, and they contrasted this with what Pavlov called the 'formalised concept of equality' that was generally accepted by the drafters. 'As long as society was divided into exploiters and the exploited', he argued, 'as long as there was private ownership of the means of production, the social order could not possibly be a good one'.[53] Pavlov made clear that he was not asking delegates to endorse the Soviet Union's social model. What he did ask was that, 'since two conflicting views were involved, there should be no moral evaluation in the declaration of either order and that the final verdict would be left to history'.[54] Here, the contention that history was not finished motivated a refusal to sanction the present as 'good'. Yet it also evacuated the terrain of moral judgment to the agency of 'history' – something that would prove fateful within the Soviet Union, as we shall see.

Pavlov's insistence that formal equality was insufficient for a good society would seem to support the standard story according to which the Soviets disparaged civil and political rights in favour of an emphasis on social and economic rights to further economic equality. Certainly, Soviet Bloc delegates criticised the Universal Declaration on grounds taken straight from Karl Marx's critique of the abstraction of bourgeois rights declarations. The Czech delegate argued that Marx's criticisms of the 1789 'Declaration of the Rights of Man and Citizen' in 'On the Jewish Question' 'retained all their relevance today' and he in turn criticised the Universal Declaration for similarly treating man as an 'isolated monad' whose right to freedom amounted only to a right to private property.[55] However, by 1948, Soviet officials were faced with the task of reconciling Marx's critique of rights with the model of rights that had been constructed in the Soviet Union in the period leading up to the promulgation of the 1936 Soviet Constitution. The 'Stalin Constitution' provided 'paper guarantees of a number of fundamental rights', including rights to work and to rest, along with rights to freedom of speech, press and assembly.[56] These constitutional protections have been described as 'an analogue of socialist realism', which presented an accessible representation of an idealised reality that did not exist in the present.[57] In attempting to

[53] Ibid.

[54] Ibid.

[55] Schabas, n 11, vol 3, 2092 (Hoffmeister).

[56] Bill Bowring, 'Russia and Human Rights: Incompatible Opposites?' (2009) 1 *Göttingen Journal of International Law* 257, 263.

[57] Smith, n 13, 388.

mediate the distance between this present and a communist future, Soviet legal theorists of the period turned to Marx's account of 'bourgeois right' in his 'Critique of the Gotha Programme'.

16.4 Equality and the Critique of the Gotha Programme

Although the Soviet Union of 1947 to 1948 was an oppressive and dictatorial system that departed markedly from the allusions to Communism in Marx's writings, the Soviet Bloc delegates at the United Nations still sought to ground their arguments by referring to Marx's authority. Marx's 1875 'Marginal Notes on the Programme of the German Workers' Party' (later titled 'The Critique of the Gotha Programme') played a particularly significant role in Soviet legal argumentation during the Stalin period and exerted a marked influence on the Soviet Bloc approach to human rights. Marx's text came to provide what Nicolas Guilhot calls the 'canonical description of the general form of the transition' to communism.[58] It also offered one of the most explicit accounts of the latter by a thinker who was far more comfortable critiquing capitalism than drawing the outlines of a future communist society. In attempting to mediate between the capitalist present,. the socialist transition and the communist future, the Gotha Critique became an object of significant contestation as it was used to legitimise the Stalinist state's approach to social equality, distributive justice and rights. Before turning to that legitimising strategy, and its influence on the Soviet Bloc approach to the Universal Declaration, it is worth examining the text in some detail.

The Gotha Critique disparaged the draft programme of the United Workers' Party of Germany, which Marx and Engels believed had capitulated to their rival, Ferdinand Lassalle. The substantive dispute prefigured that between revolutionary socialists and reformist social democrats in the mid-twentieth century, with Marx criticising the Gotha Programme for its expressions of faith in 'state aid' as a solution to the 'social question'.[59] As Otto von Bismarck's government introduced social insurance and welfare measures to pacify social conflict and

[58] Nicolas Guilhot, '"The Transition to the Human World of Democracy": Notes for a History of the Concept of Transition, from Early Marxism to 1989' (2002) 5 *European Journal of Social Theory* 219, 224.

[59] 'Critique of the Gotha Program' in *Karl Marx, Friedrich Engels: Collected Works* (Lawrence and Wishart, 2010) vol 24, 81.

'anesthetise radicalised and increasingly organised workers', Marx argued that the Gotha programme was tainted by 'the Lassalle sect's servile belief in the state'.[60] Singling out its call for workers' cooperatives supported by 'state aid', Marx snidely commented that his opponents imagined 'that with state loans one can build a new society just as well as a new railway!'[61] In a letter, Engels wrote that 'all the palaver about the state ought to be dropped'.[62] For both Engels and Marx, Bismarck's despotic and pacifying welfare state was a barrier to revolutionary transformation, not a means to it.

Although similar arguments informed Soviet scepticism about social and economic rights in the twentieth century, by then, the most influential aspect of Marx's Gotha Critique was not its rejection of the early welfare state but its account of the transition from the lower to the higher stage of communism. Marx devoted much of his scorn to the draft Gotha programme's claim that the emancipation of labour demands a 'fair distribution' of the proceeds of labour.[63] Criticising the vagueness of the notion of fairness in terms that prefigured later Soviet arguments about the 'good', Marx asked: 'Do not the bourgeois assert that present day distribution is "fair?"'[64] Marx disputed the existence of a universal and ahistorical standard of fairness that could be applied to any society, whatever its level of development and social organisation. In contrast, he laid out two historically specific principles of distribution that would achieve programmatic status by the mid-twentieth century. A post-revolutionary society emerging from capitalism would still operate on the principle that governs commodity exchange, the exchange of equivalents, he argued; distribution would be based on work, and each individual would receive from society what she contributed in the form of labour. It would only be in the 'higher phase of communist society' that this principle of distribution would be replaced by another principle: 'From each according to his abilities, to each according to his needs!'[65]

[60] Patricia Owens traces the imperial context of this first welfare state, arguing that Bismarck sought to replace class conflict with national identification: Patricia Owens, *Economy of Force: Counterinsurgency and the Historical Rise of the Social* (Cambridge University Press, 2015) 26. This capitulation to nationalism was the other key point of Marx's criticisms: ibid.

[61] Marx, 'Critique of the Gotha Program' in Marx and Engels: Collected Works, n 59, vol 24, 93.

[62] Friedrich Engels, 'Letter to August Bebel' in *Marx and Engels: Collected Works*, n 59, vol 24, 71.

[63] Marx, 'Critique of the Gotha Program' in Marx and Engels: Collected Works, n 59, vol 24, 84.

[64] Ibid., 84.

[65] Ibid., 87.

In his history of social and economic rights, Samuel Moyn has construed Marx's Gotha Critique as an argument for prioritising basic needs over egalitarianism. There 'is *no evidence* – for all his association with the currency of egalitarian justice since', Moyn writes, 'that [Marx] envisioned material fairness in a communist state'.[66] Moyn claims that Marx rejected distributional equality because he believed that people have vastly different needs and should be rewarded for their work. Yet, far from upholding differences in working capacity as an argument against equality, Marx criticised distribution according to work *from the perspective of equality*. Distribution according to work entrenches inequality, Marx argued, by tacitly recognising the differences between individuals, who may be more or less capable of work, as their natural privileges. It is therefore a principle of 'bourgeois right', and, like all rights, is a right of inequality – an 'unequal right for unequal labour'.[67]

For Marx, all right was unequal because, in measuring individuals by an equal standard, it abstracted from the differences between them. It was in this sense that, as a much younger man, he had argued that the individual in bourgeois society leads a double life – a celestial life in the state (as an equal citizen) and a terrestrial life in civil society (as an unequal, egoistic individual).[68] Rather than arguing against equality, Marx criticised the abstract equality of citizenship for leaving untouched – indeed for *masking* – the inequalities of civil society. Although Marx believed that such inequalities would inevitably persist as 'defects' in a society just emerging from capitalism, he gestured towards a society in which the division of labour had been transcended, enabling individuals to develop freely as the 'springs of common wealth flow more abundantly'.[69] Such a society, he argued, would enable the crossing of the 'narrow horizon of bourgeois right' and the distribution of resources according to needs.[70] Far from this focus on needs constituting a rejection of equality, equality remained Marx's animating horizon and the standpoint from which he criticised the inequality enshrined by equal right. In contrast to the formal equality satirised by Anatole France that prohibits both rich and poor from sleeping under the bridges, Marx

[66] Moyn, *Not Enough*, n 13, 28 (emphasis in original).
[67] Marx, 'Critique of the Gotha Program' in Marx and Engels: Collected Works, n 59, vol 24, 86.
[68] 'On the Jewish Question' in Karl Marx, *Early Writings* (Penguin, revised ed, 2000).
[69] Marx, 'Critique of the Gotha Program' in Marx and Engels: Collected Works, n 59, vol 24, 87.
[70] Ibid., 87.

believed that real equality must begin from the premise that people have different needs. Consequently, 'right, instead of being equal, would have to be unequal'.[71]

The Gotha Critique reveals Marx at his most utopian, drawing on the utopian socialism of Gracchus Babeuf, Charles Fourier and the Comte de Saint Simon to imagine a society beyond capitalism and right. Two distinctive utopias animate Marx's text, one of them oriented to equality and the other to the flourishing of human capacities. Before Marx held a reworded version of it up as the principle of socialism, the slogan 'Each according to his capacity, to each capacity according to its works' appeared on the masthead of the Saint Simonian newspaper *The Globe,* where it distilled a utopian vision oriented to the development of individual talents.[72] Although Marx and Engels were sympathetic to this vision of flowering human capacities supposedly enabled by the boundless expansion of science and the exploitation of nature, they rejected the Saint Simonian principle of hierarchy and embraced the idea of distribution according to needs, which was originally formulated precisely as a rejection of this hierarchical principle.[73]

In contrast to his sympathy for these utopias of human flourishing, Marx poured scorn on the asceticism of the egalitarian utopianism that animated the 1796 'Conspiracy of the Equals', launched by the followers of Babeuf. The Babeufist exhortation to 'let all the arts perish, if need be, as long as real equality remains' seemed to exemplify the 'universal asceticism and social levelling in its crudest form' that Marx and Engels rejected in *The Communist Manifesto.*[74] Frank E Manuel has argued that

[71] Ibid., 87.

[72] Frank E Manuel, 'In Memoriam: "Critique of the Gotha Program", 1875–1975' (1976) 105(1) *Daedalus* 59, 65.

[73] Ibid., 71. Marx's *communist* principle, 'from each according to his capacities, to each according to his needs', was initially used by the French socialist Louis Blanc in the early 1840s to criticise this Saint-Simonian principle. 'A hierarchy of capacities is necessary and fruitful', Blanc wrote, 'recompense in accordance with capacities is more than just disastrous – it is impious': Louis Blanc, *Organisation du travail* (9th ed, 1850) 72–4, cited in ibid., 71.

The slogan also appeared on the title page of Étienne Cabet's Fourierist 1840 utopian novel *Voyage en Icarie*. Although Marx wrote soon after of the need to begin with the reality of the religion and politics of the present, 'not to oppose them with any ready-made system such as the *Voyage en Icarie*', he nonetheless had recourse to this utopian imaginary when, much later, he outlined his own good society: Karl Marx, 'Letter from Marx to Arnold Ruge' (September 1843) *Marxists Internet Archive*, www.marxists.org/archive/marx/works/1843/letters/43_09-alt.htm.

[74] Ian Birchall, *Spectre of Babeuf* (Haymarket Books, 2016).

the 'loathing for instant egalitarianism' was a constant of Marx's thought, and it is true that Marx was dismissive of egalitarian utopias that looked backwards towards a pre-industrial condition.[75] Yet, the Babeufists were less ascetic than these later communists assumed and their critique of the 'beautiful and sterile legal fiction' of the French Revolution's Declaration of the Rights of Man and Citizen in the name of 'real equality' prefigures Marx's own.[76] 'We need not only that equality of rights written into the Declaration of the Rights of Man and Citizen', the 1796 Babeufist 'Manifesto of the Equals' stated; 'we want it in our midst, under the roofs of our houses'.[77] The Babeufist's proposal to guarantee every citizen 'healthy, comfortable and decently-furnished accommodation', wool or cotton work clothing, laundry, lighting and heating in the home, medical assistance, and food (including meat, poultry, eggs, wine and seasonings) sufficient for 'a moderate and frugal sufficiency' would hardly have seemed ascetic to many workers and peasants in the late eighteenth century.[78] Nonetheless, the equality sought by Marx and Engels was premised on the abundance that would supposedly follow the development of the forces of production – an 'equality in the rich satisfaction of material and intellectual needs in a dynamic economy, not returns equal in their paltriness', as Manuel puts it.[79] Only in the midst of such abundance, Marx argued, would it become possible to transcend the horizon of bourgeois right and distribute on the basis of needs.

16.5 Soviet Legal Theory and the 'Famous Instructions of Marx and Engels'

Marx was notoriously vague about the transition to communism, but this was to become the central problem for Marxists in the wake of the October Revolution. The main Soviet law textbook of the Stalin period, edited and closely supervised by Vyshinsky, begins with a chapter on 'The October Socialist Revolution and the State'. The Revolution, it contends, 'followed the great historical instructions of Marx and Engels', and destroyed the bourgeois state, replacing it with a proletarian

[75] Manuel, n 72, 62.
[76] Sylvain Marechal, 'The Manifesto of the Equals' (2004) *Marxists Internet Archive* [*La Conspiration pour L'égalité*, first published 1957], www.marxists.org/history/france/revolution/conspiracy-equals/1796/manifesto.htm.
[77] Birchall, n 74.
[78] Ibid. In Moyn's terms, this egalitarianism was also a vision of sufficient provision.
[79] Manuel, n 72, 74.

state.[80] Vyshinsky's textbook is replete with expressions of fidelity to the October Revolution and the writings of Marx and Engels, especially the Gotha critique, which it presents as the definitive statement of the 'Marx–Engels–Lenin–Stalin doctrine' on 'the two phases of communism and their distinguishing characteristics'.[81] With the rise of Stalin and the ascendancy of 'socialism in one country', the very meaning of transition changed, as did the official interpretation of Marx's Gotha Critique. For Lenin, the October Revolution was itself a transition that held open a space that could remain open only on the basis of a victorious revolution in Europe. The preface to the official Progress Press edition of Marx's Gotha Critique laid out the new position, according to which Marx 'stressed that a relatively long period would inevitably be required to carry out the immense creative work of the revolutionary remoulding of society'.[82] Similarly, Vyshinsky's textbook attributes to Marx the view that the transition 'occupies an entire period of history' – a period in which, far from withering away, law and the state become increasingly significant.[83]

Having defined law as 'the will of the dominant class, elevated into a statute', Vyshinsky could argue that in a *proletariat* dictatorship law spells out the rules and obligations that serve the interest of the ruling class of 'toilers'.[84] Vyshinsky's ascendancy marked the defeat of the idea of the withering of law, and of its key proponent Evgeny Pashukanis, for whom communism entailed 'the gradual disappearance of the juridic element in human relationships'.[85] From Marx's Gotha Critique, Pashukanis developed the idea of an 'innermost connection' between the commodity form (the exchange of equivalents) and the legal form. He drew the implication that legal relationships would persist only as long as the commodity form did. Communism, understood as a society of (planned) distribution according to needs, would therefore require not a new form of law but the liberation from the legal form. As late as 1929, Pashukanis could still argue that 'the problem of the withering away of

80 Vyshinsky, n 48, 6. The reference to the 'famous instructions of Marx and Engels' in the subheading appears at 16.
81 Ibid., 205.
82 Marx, 'Critique of the Gotha Program', n 59, 95.
83 Vyshinsky, n 48, 38.
84 Ibid., 13.
85 Evgeny Bronislavovich Pashukanis, *Pashukanis: Selected Writings on Marxism and Law* (Piers Beirne and Robert Sharlet ed, and Peter B Maggs trans, Academic Press, 1980) 46.

law is the cornerstone by which we measure the degree of proximity of a jurist to Marxism'.[86] Yet, by then, his anti-legalism was already coming into conflict with the demands of rapid industrialisation, forced collectivisation and the state coercion needed to secure labour productivity, and no amount of 'self-criticism' could save him from the Stalinist purges.[87] Pashukanis' murder saw the rise of Vyshinsky as the Soviet Union's most important legal theorist and a new valorisation of the role of law in the building of communism and the struggle against counter-revolution.

Before he became Stalin's feared prosecutor during the great purges, Vyshinsky's most significant experiences of the law were as a defendant. Having been arrested for revolutionary activities by the tsarist regime (spending a year in prison alongside Stalin), he was arrested again for counter-revolutionary activities by the Bolsheviks in the immediate wake of the October Revolution.[88] These experiences seem only to have enhanced his commitment to law, and, in power, he set himself against what he depicted as the 'fantastic and sickly sentimentality' of 'pseudo-Marxists' who believe that once the proletariat seizes power, 'the Kingdom of universal freedom had come'.[89] In turning to Marx's Gotha critique, Vyshinsky sought not a critique of bourgeois right and the inequality it sanctioned but a justification for the perpetuation of both law and inequality. In it, he found confirmation that, in the 'transitional period':

> there is as yet no 'equality', no 'equal rights' (no equal right of each to an equal product of labour). This law is still unequal law inasmuch as it starts by applying an equal and identical gauge to dissimilar persons, dissimilar in their needs and in their positions.[90]

Challenging the anti-legalist position of 'the wrecker Pashukanis', Vyshinsky argued that law would wither away only in the higher stage

[86] Ibid., 286.

[87] Piers Beirne and Robert Sharlet, 'Toward a General Theory of Law and Marxism: E B Pashukanis' in Piers Beirne (ed), *Revolution in Law: Contributions to the Legal Development of Soviet Legal Theory, 1917–38* (Routledge, 2015) 17, 19.

[88] During the later purges, an old Bolshevik, the former chief of the Military Department of the Moscow Party Committee Ter-Vaganyan, responded to Vyshinsky's charges by retorting, 'I had you arrested during the Civil War for genuine counter-revolution!': Robert Sharlet and Piers Beirne, 'In Search of Vyshinsky: The Paradox of Law and Terror', in Piers Beirne (ed), *Revolution in Law: Contributions to the Legal Development of Soviet Legal Theory, 1917–38* (Routledge, 2015) 136, 140.

[89] Vyshinsky, n 48, 39.

[90] Ibid., 52.

of communism; in the meantime, justice would be determined by the 'socialist' principle of distribution according to labour, with its correlate: 'he who does not work must not eat'.[91] Vyshinsky acknowledged the injustice of such distribution but argued that this was mitigated by a socialist state that provided sanatoria, rest houses, free (general and higher) training, pensions and relief for those unable to work, and thereby laid those material foundations for social and economic rights that he would later argue were missing from the Universal Declaration of Human Rights.

By the time Vyshinsky's textbook was published in 1938, the Stalinist state was embracing the inequality of 'bourgeois right' and waging a concerted campaign against what Stalin termed the 'infantile equalitarian exercises of the "Left" blockheads'.[92] In the Stalin years, 'universal welfare' lost out to 'break-neck industrialisation' and the expansion of the security state.[93] Peter Petroff, who returned to Russia from the United Kingdom in 1918 and was briefly vice-commissar for foreign affairs, reflected later that the early system of 'equal payment for all' – which saw everyone from the commissar for foreign affairs to the messenger paid 500 roubles per month – was soon dispensed with.[94] As early as 1918, Lenin argued it was essential to test and apply 'payment by the job, to apply much that is scientific and progressive in the system of Taylor'.[95] It was not until 1931, however, that Stalin launched a complete struggle against what Vyshinsky referred to as 'petty-bourgeois wage leveling'.[96] 'With the advent of Stalinism', Petroff writes, 'the gospel of inequality began to be preached'.[97] Not only wages but also pensions now became highly unequal, and Marx's remarks about payment according to work were used to legitimise Stakhanovism and 'shock working', the increasing use of piecework, and the abolition of *maximum* wages for party officials.[98] At the 17th party congress in 1934, Stalin told delegates that,

91 Ibid.

92 Josef Stalin, 'Report to the Seventeenth Party Congress on the Work of the Central Committee of the CPSU(B)' (26 January 1934) *Marxists Internet Archive*, www.marxists.org/reference/archive/stalin/works/1934/01/26.htm.

93 Smith, n 13, 392.

94 Peter Petroff, 'The Soviet Wages System' (February 1938) *Marxists Internet Archive*, www.marxists.org/archive/petroff/1938/soviet-wages.htm.

95 V I Lenin, 'The Immediate Tasks of the Soviet Government' (March–April 1918) *Marxists Internet Archive*, www.marxists.org/archive/lenin/works/1918/mar/x03.htm.

96 Vyshinsky, n 48, 208.

97 Petroff, n 94.

98 Stakhanovism, named after the coal miner Aleksei Grigorievich Stakhanov, was an attempt to increase labour productivity through a system of incentives and competition

by equality, Marx never meant equalisation of daily life and personal requirements. 'Every Leninist knows, if he is a real Leninist, that equalisation in the sphere of requirements and personal everyday life is a reactionary petty-bourgeois absurdity, worthy of some primitive society of ascetics, but not of a socialist society organised along Marxist lines', he argued.[99] Different people have different tastes and needs, Stalin contended, and therefore cannot be moulded on a single model. 'It is time to understand', he told the party, 'that Marxism is an enemy of equality'.[100]

16.6 What Were Human Rights For, for the Soviets?

Despite this anti-equality campaign, Soviet Bloc delegates at the United Nations continued to criticise the Universal Declaration from the perspective of 'real equality'. Their key goal, however, was not to secure social and economic rights but to enshrine *formal equality* and non-discrimination. There was more than early Cold War Realpolitik in the Soviet championing of non-discrimination. In the racial segregation and white supremacy that persisted in the colonies, the United States and South Africa, the Soviet delegates saw disturbing parallels to European fascism. They depicted the attempt to enshrine provisions against racial discrimination in the Universal Declaration as the continuation of the struggle against fascism – a struggle in the course of which the Soviet Union had 'sacrificed millions of lives, the best of its blood' the Polish delegate reminded his fellow diplomats.[101] Early in the drafting, the Soviet representative Vladimir Koretsky (a future judge at the International Court of Justice) argued that the key rationale of the new bill of rights was to 'prevent the rebirth of fascist systems and fascist ideology'.[102] Far from seeing human rights as proletarian weapons against the ruling class, Koretsky proposed that the declaration should mimic the universalism of the Ten Commandments. Paraphrasing Paul's

between workers. Vyshinsky's textbook explained that the 'principle of socialism: "From each according to his capacity, to each according to his toil" is, in the USSR, the dominant principle of organizing labour and distributing its products': Vyshinsky, n 48, 207.

99 Stalin, n 92.

100 Ibid. Moyn's account of Marx's attitude to equality appears to accept this Stalinist characterisation of Marx's writings.

101 Schabas, n 11, vol 3, 3067 (Katz-Suchy).

102 Ibid., vol 1, 778 (Koretsky).

'Letter to the Romans', he argued that it should be 'acceptable both to rich and poor, to the famous and those who were not famous, to Gentile and to Jew, to black and white, to everyone regardless of race or nationality'.[103]

Recent revisionist historians of human rights have challenged the received wisdom that the Universal Declaration was primarily a response to the Holocaust. Far from emerging from 'the shocked conscience of an international community confronted with the knowledge of the radical evil that the Nazi regime had perpetrated against European Jewry', Marco Duranti has argued that the drafting records provide 'only the most tenuous of evidence' to support the view that the drafters even invoked the Holocaust.[104] For Moyn too, if the Universal Declaration was a response to the experience of the past, 'it was essentially a reaction to depression and dictatorship, not atrocity and genocide'.[105] To date, this revisionist historiography has not specifically attended to the Soviet role in the drafting. Yet, it was the Soviet Bloc delegates who repeatedly insisted that the primary purpose of an international bill of rights was to forestall the resurgence of fascism. In doing so, they foregrounded Nazi racial ideology and depicted the prevention of racial hatred and discrimination (not social welfare) as the key role of human rights. Far from focusing on economic rights at the expense of political ones, from the earliest drafting meetings the Soviet delegation argued that 'respect for human rights would only be assured by condemning fascism, by combating its remnants and by creating conditions of such a nature that no fascist regime could spring up again in any part of the world'.[106]

It would be anachronistic to suggest that the Soviet Bloc delegates viewed human rights as a response to the 'Holocaust', in contemporary terms, and there is little evidence to suggest that they believed the genocide of European Jewry was 'qualitatively distinct from the totality of horrors perpetrated by the Nazi regime', in Duranti's words.[107] However, they were unique in their stress that the human rights document was a response to the rise of Nazism, and were also unique in

[103] Ibid., vol 1, 779 (Koretsky).

[104] Marco Duranti, 'The Holocaust, the Legacy of 1789 and the Birth of International Human Rights Law: Revisiting the Foundation Myth' (2012) 14 *Journal of Genocide Research* 163.

[105] Samuel Moyn, 'The Universal Declaration of Human Rights of 1948 in the History of Cosmopolitanism' (2014) 40 *Critical Inquiry* 375.

[106] Schabas, n 11, vol 3, 3065 (Katz-Suchy).

[107] Duranti, n 104, 168.

making the only specific reference to anti-Semitism during the drafting, the only reference to a Nazi ghetto and the sole reference to the extermination camps.[108] Pavlov's response to the draft declaration provided a stark account of the position articulated by the Soviet Bloc delegates throughout; 'after the frightful experience of the past', he argued:

> when Fascism not only trampled on human rights and freedoms and spread inequality and oppression by dividing people into 'higher' and 'lower' races, but actually destroyed millions of innocent people in the Maidaneks, Oświęcims [Auschwitz-Birkenau] and other death camps in the countries ruled by them and in the occupied territories and subjugated whole peoples to the horrors of terror, slavery and ruin, – after all this we cannot and will not forget the Fascist danger and look on complacently while people who deem themselves democratic are preparing to set the Fascist beast at liberty.[109]

Throughout the drafting, racial discrimination and the status of the colonies 'topped the Soviet priority list'.[110] They criticised those who spoke of equality while maintaining racial discrimination, domestically and in the colonies (and refusing to consider married women as legal persons), and campaigned to remove references to 'civilised nations' from the document, while fighting trenchantly for an explicit acknowledgement that its rights would apply in the colonies.[111] They also campaigned, unsuccessfully, for bans on fascist propaganda and racist hate speech, and criticised the final declaration for lacking a prohibition on 'war-mongering and fascist ideas'.[112] This was particularly important, Pavlov argued, given the rise of 'a new racial theory, which alleged the superiority of the Anglo-Saxon race'.[113]

The same teleological vision that saw communism pushed into a distant future also motivated this Soviet Bloc emphasis on holding back

[108] Schabas, n 11, vol 3, 3065 (Katz-Suchy). The delegate of the Byelorussian Soviet Republic pointed to the Minsk ghetto, 'where Byelorussian Jews and those of Western European countries had been subjected to torture': at vol 2, 1725 (Stepanenko); and Pavlov argued that in the constitution of the USSR, 'anti-Semitism and racial and religious hatred was considered as a crime' and called for the same in the Universal Declaration: at vol 2, 1856. Of course, as the Soviet delegates stressed in other contexts, constitutional provisions without enforcement remained scraps of paper.

[109] Ibid., vol 2, 1519–20.

[110] Weiss-Wendt, n 45, 119.

[111] I discuss this in detail in Whyte, n 16.

[112] Schabas, n 11, vol 3, 3024 (Vyshinsky).

[113] Ibid., vol 2, 1856.

the worst. Fascism was a historical regression, the Soviets believed, and it presented the proletariat with the task of fighting for the civil rights of the revolutionary tradition. Vyshinsky's textbook depicted the bourgeoisie as anxious to turn back the clock, not only on the Russian Revolution but also on the French Revolution, by restoring the rightlessness of feudalism. The Soviet response mimicked the approach of early Bolsheviks, who organised under the conditions of absolutism and stressed that political freedom was an indispensable condition for an independent working-class movement.[114] Soon after the Bolsheviks came to power, as Lars T. Lih notes, 'the goal of political freedom, almost the *raison d'être* of Old Bolshevism, was forgotten if not actively scorned'.[115] Yet, faced with the reality of fascism, Soviet delegates in international forums placed renewed emphasis on political freedoms and non-discrimination. 'Under capitalism, the proletariat is extremely interested in bourgeois-democratic "freedoms" and "civil rights"', Vyshinsky contended, because they make it possible to organise. 'Fascism', on the contrary, 'drags this society backwards from bourgeois democracy to the feudal state of lawlessness and to medievalism, perpetuating the slavery of the toiling class and dooming it to extinction and to eternal bondage'.[116]

16.7 Conclusion: Human Rights – The Most We Can Hope For?

Even as the Soviet Bloc delegates portrayed cross-class alliances as necessary to forestall the evils of fascism, they also sought to hold open the gap between preventing evil and realising the good. 'Good', Pavlov argued, was an evaluation that the 'new democracies, in the name of millions of workers and indigenous inhabitants of colonies, in the name

[114] Stalin's position in 1905 was representative of this Old Bolshevik concern with political freedom. A future provisional revolutionary government 'must introduce freedom of speech, of the press, of assembly, and so forth', along with the freedom to strike, he argued: cited in Lars T Lih, 'Lenin and Bolshevism' in S A Smith (ed), *The Oxford Handbook of the History of Communism* (Oxford University Press, 2014) 53, 60.

[115] Ibid., 69. 'One of the most important political facts about the late nineteenth and early twentieth centuries was that the most orthodox and militant advocates of revolutionary Marxism were staunch fighters for political freedom', Lih writes. 'One of the most important political facts about the rest of the twentieth century was that the most orthodox and militant advocates of revolutionary Marxism were devoted to regimes that crushed political freedom to an unprecedented degree': at 68.

[116] Vyshinsky, n 48, 12.

of posterity itself, felt bound to reject'.[117] History had not ended, they insisted, so human rights could not be the last utopia. The Universal Declaration, which did not countenance even the right to self-determination of peoples let alone the end of capitalism, did not demarcate the bounds in which a good society could be imagined.[118] The refusal to sanction even an order of fully realised human rights as 'good' was informed by scepticism about the realisation of rights under capitalism. Yet, it also reflected the weak echo of Marx's belief in a world beyond the inequalities of bourgeois right. This echo brought the utopian traditions on which Marx drew in formulating his Gotha critique into confrontation with the attempt to narrow the horizons of human possibility within a liberal juridical frame. By 1948, the Soviet Union was certainly not a utopia. Yet, as Perry Anderson notes, in the wake of the Russian Revolution, the 'deep longing for another human order which had found expression in the utopias of the nineteenth century was now fastened to the – often scarcely less imaginary – socialism in the Soviet Union'.[119] Even as it engaged in a brutal process of primitive accumulation and enforced a highly coercive labour discipline, this 'imaginary socialism' was still capable of inspiring new social and political imaginaries, and great heroism, sacrifice and solidarity in the struggle to realise them.

This was particularly so in the context of decolonisation. Long after what the Algerian lawyer and diplomat Mohammed Bedjaoui called the 'strong wind of the Bolshevik Revolution in October 1917' had died down in St Petersburg, it continued to blow in what was then called the 'Third World'.[120] Anticolonialists continued the struggle against racial discrimination while also taking up Marx's critique of equal (bourgeois) right to challenge the 'phantom sovereignties' that masked the perpetuation of domination under the cover of formal equality.[121]

117 Schabas, n 11, vol 3, 2750 (Pavlov).

118 On unsuccessful Soviet attempts to enshrine the right to self-determination in the Universal Declaration, see Bill Bowring, 'The Soviets and the Right to Self-Determination of the Colonized: Contradictions of Soviet Diplomacy and Foreign Policy in the Era of Decolonization' in Jochen von Bernstorff and Philipp Dann (eds), *The Battle for International Law: South–North Perspectives on the Decolonization Era* (Oxford University Press, 2019); Whyte, n 16.

119 Perry Anderson, *Arguments within English Marxism* (Verso, 1980) 171.

120 Mohammed Bedjaoui, *Towards a New International Economic Order* (Holmes & Meier, 1979) 58.

121 Ibid., 81.

Decolonisation, Bedjaoui argued, was 'a structural revolution on a world scale' that was to the international order what the French and Russian revolutions were to the internal orders of France and Russia.[122] After winning independence from colonial rule, there was a need for another decisive struggle, he argued, which goes beyond the limitations of equal right to erode the privileges of the former colonial powers through economic decolonisation. For this, Bedjaoui noted, anticolonialists had to go further than the Soviet Union, which he contended had contested the rules of international law but accepted the international legal order without 'radical upheaval'.[123] The task facing anticolonial revolutionaries was more akin to that facing the Russian revolutionaries: how to break with the rule of wealth.

While the possibility of such a break had motivated the Soviet Bloc attempts to expunge the word 'good' from the Universal Declaration, their success in doing so was premised on winning the support of those for whom a social and international order that guaranteed human rights was, by definition, 'good'. Malik had attempted to win support for his position by telling his fellow delegates that his reference to 'a "good social and international order" did not imply any particular system, whether capitalist or socialist'.[124] The Canadian delegate, Ralph Maybank, speaking on behalf of the United Kingdom, Norway and Peru, similarly considered the word 'good' to be redundant. Avoiding the question of the 'right to have rights' that had motivated the covering articles to begin with, Maybank contended that an order that realised these rights would, for that very reason, be 'good', whether this occurred under 'capitalism, communism, feudalism, or any other system'.[125] Manifesting precisely the lack of reality Arendt disparaged, these delegates simply ignored the question of whether equality before the law could be achieved under feudalism, the right to private property under communism or the universal right to holidays with pay under capitalism. Ironically, it was the refusal to countenance a gap between a society of human rights and a good society that ultimately led to the erasure of the 'good' from the Universal Declaration. Eleanor Roosevelt, for once at odds with Malik, lined up with Pavlov in supporting the deletion of the word 'good', although for the opposite reason: 'Any order which permitted individuals

[122] Ibid., 88.
[123] Ibid., 141.
[124] Schabas, n 11, vol 3, 2751 (Malik).
[125] Ibid., vol 3, 2752 (Maybank).

to achieve the rights and freedoms set out in the declaration would obviously be a good one', she argued.[126] From such a perspective, the word 'good' was tautological – human rights were the only vision of the good one could ever need – 'the most we can hope for' in Ignatieff's phrase.

What point is there in returning to the debates sparked by the October Revolution and retrieving the alternate visions of the good society that still animated the drafting of the Universal Declaration? What can these debates offer us, in the wake of the collapse of the Soviet Union and after many of 'the anticolonial utopias have gradually withered into postcolonial nightmares?'[127] As human rights advocates turn their attention to global poverty and inequality and call for greater emphasis on social and economic rights, even while dismissing revolutions as violent folly, it is worth remembering the revolutionary struggles that helped to spark such rights. As Leon Trotsky remarked in the mid-1920s, in response to British Fabian socialists who desired working-class welfare while denouncing revolution, 'even children's picture-books teach us that if you want to have acorns you must not dig up the oak tree'.[128] More importantly, the Soviet refusal to sanction their world as 'good' offers us a way to think critically about our own present. Such critical thought, as David Scott suggests, should be less a teleology of a new utopian future than a 'refusal to be seduced and immobilised by the facile normalization of the present'.[129] That means that we keep asking, even in times of danger, whether there is more we can hope for.

[126] Ibid., vol 3, 2752 (Roosevelt). The amendment to delete the word 'good' was ultimately adopted by thirty-four votes to two, with two abstentions: at vol 3, 2753.

[127] David Scott, *Conscripts of Modernity: The Tragedy of Colonial Enlightenment* (Duke University Press, 2005) 2.

[128] Leon Trotsky, 'The Fabian "Theory" of Socialism' (1925) *Marxists Internet Archive*, www.marxists.org/archive/trotsky/britain/wibg/ch04.htm.

[129] Scott, n 127, 2.

INDEX

For EU product safety concerns, contact us at Calle de José Abascal, 56–1°,
28003 Madrid, Spain or eugpsr@cambridge.org.

www.ingramcontent.com/pod-product-compliance
Lightning Source LLC
LaVergne TN
LVHW011659200926
848484LV00004B/995
* 9 7 8 1 1 0 8 4 9 5 0 3 5 *